DISCARD

THE STATES OF MEXICO

THE STATES OF MEXICO

A Reference Guide to History and Culture

Peter Standish

GREENWOOD PRESS
Westport, Connecticut • London

Library of Congress Cataloging-in-Publication Data

Standish, Peter.
   The states of Mexico : a reference guide to history and culture / Peter Standish.
     p. cm.
   Includes bibliographical references and index.
   ISBN 978-0-313-34223-3 (alk. paper)
    1. Mexico—History, Local—Handbooks, manuals, etc. 2. Mexican
states—Handbooks, manuals, etc. I. Title.
   F1228.9.S73   2009
   972—dc22   2008040911

British Library Cataloguing in Publication Data is available.

Library of Congress Catalog Card Number: 2008040911
ISBN: 978-0-313-34223-3

First published in 2009

Greenwood Press, 88 Post Road West, Westport, CT 06881
An imprint of Greenwood Publishing Group, Inc.
www.greenwood.com

Printed in the United States of America

The paper used in this book complies with the
Permanent Paper Standard issued by the National
Information Standards Organization (Z39.48-1984).

10 9 8 7 6 5 4 3 2 1

The publisher has done its best to make sure the instructions and/or recipes in this book are
correct. However, users should apply judgment and experience when preparing recipes, especially parents and teachers working with young people. The publisher accepts no responsibility for the outcome of any recipe included in this volume.

Cartography for maps on chapter opening pages by Bookcomp, Inc.

Contents

Preface

The official name of the country that is commonly called Mexico is Los Estados Unidos Mexicanos. Mexico is a federal republic consisting of thirty-one states, plus the Distrito Federal, which includes much of Mexico City and has a status somewhat similar to that of Washington, D.C. *The States of Mexico* offers narrative information on each Mexican state and the federal district. The aim is to encourage a deeper appreciation of Mexico's rich history and culture by providing a solid, authoritative overview of the states, with key information for students, researchers, and travelers.

The thirty-two political entities are presented in alphabetical order. The following topics are described for each:

State Characteristics

The first section discusses geography, demography, flora and fauna, and climate. Major administrative divisions and towns are identified. (Population figures throughout this book are based on data published by Mexico's Instituto Nacional de Estadística. In 2005, when the last census was taken, Mexico's total population was given as 103,263,388.) Available space prohibits the inclusion of details relating to health and education, though each entry does contain an indication of the level of provision of higher education, which may suggest the extent of the educational infrastructure. Information about the state's newspapers is also given.

Cultural Groups and Languages

The next section deals with ethnic and cultural diversity—in particular, the presence of indigenous peoples in each state. In some states, the indigenous peoples are highly integrated into the mainstream culture and their traditional practices have become hybridized with Hispanic ones. However, there are also places where indigenous peoples preserve their customs and languages in relative isolation. Over sixty different indigenous languages are still spoken in Mexico, some of them by small numbers of people, others by tens of thousands. The principal indigenous languages currently in use are Maya, Zapotec, and Náhuatl. The search for work has led to increased migration by indigenous-language speakers from places like Oaxaca, and this has been changing the distribution of such people in recent decades. The concentration of indigenous-language speakers varies a great deal from state to state, from minimal numbers in some northern and central states to as much as a third of the population in the states of Chiapas, Oaxaca, and Yucatán.

History

The third section describes the historical evolution of the area (and to some extent its politics) from pre-Hispanic times to the present. In most states, the main focus is on the era of republican development, from the beginnings of independence in the early nineteenth century until the Revolution of the early twentieth. Twentieth-century politics in Mexico were dominated by one party, the Partido Revolucionario Institucional. (There is also a brief overview of the general history of the country in the introduction to this book.)

Economy

The following section focuses primarily, if not exclusively, on the economy in modern times. Colonial Mexico developed agriculture and became a major provider of raw materials, particularly precious metals. Industrialization made significant strides in the late nineteenth century, when foreign companies were encouraged to invest in the country. The Revolution in the early twentieth century led to the nationalization of some industries and the redistribution of some of the land that had hitherto been in the hands of a few rich families or of foreign concerns. Further industrialization took place in the second half of the twentieth century, a time when tourism increased dramatically in importance. However, it is still the case that the country's wealth is concentrated in the hands of a minority, and there are huge disparities between those people and the majority of Mexicans.

Arts

Creative cultural manifestations, whether popular or elevated, are discussed in the fifth section. Included are such things as handicrafts (which are often a source of regional pride), music, literature, and painting. Emphasis is placed on individuals who have had an impact beyond the confines of the state in question; for example, José Guadalupe Posada, an engraver and caricaturist, was born in Aguascalientes; the writer Rosario Castellanos was a native of Chiapas; and the composer Silvestre Revueltas came from Durango. Those aspects of the culture that are social rather than creative and artistic are generally covered under the next section.

Social Customs

This section includes festivities and celebrations, popular entertainments, and other common social activities. Since many such events, such as Carnival, the Day of the Dead, and various saints' days are shared all over Mexico, the entries emphasize the peculiarities of each state. Festive and traditional dress is also described.

Noteworthy Places

The penultimate section deals with important buildings and landmarks, whether man-made or natural. Items range from the archaeological sites of the great Indian civilizations (such as those at Uxmal and Chichen-Itzá, in Yucatán), through colonial architecture (for example, the churches and monasteries of the State of Puebla), the homes of famous people (such as Frida Kahlo's house in Coyoacán, now a museum), and historical sites such as the place where Miguel Hidalgo issued the first public demand for independence from Spain, to natural beauties such as canyons and waterfalls.

Cuisine

After a brief general characterization of the local cuisine, the last section gives some sample recipes.

Under the various sections, some names of important individuals are highlighted in boldface print. Such people are often natives whose impact has been felt outside the state in question. In reference to this, one cannot overemphasize the centripetal attraction that Mexico City has exerted on people of all walks of life—especially on creative artists and intellectuals. With few exceptions, writers, painters, musicians, and the like have felt drawn to the capital city, because it is the focus of artistic activity and in many respects the only place with the infrastructure to support it. Thus a person may have been born and raised at least partially outside the capital but have gravitated toward it once mature; many such people have lived in Mexico City for the rest of their lives.

There are, in addition, photographs, a chronology, a glossary, a selective bibliography of works in English, and a general index.

Acknowledgments

My overtures to the various states requesting information met with a predictable range of responses, from complete silence through wordy but empty promises, to real support in varying degrees and forms. Baja California Sur, Coahuila, Durango, Guerrero, Guanajuato, Nayarit and Tlaxcala all supplied some information, and Sinaloa was exceptionally generous with it. I was warmly received during my visits to several places and would particularly like to acknowledge the help given by Milena Kaprivitza, Eduardo Fregoso, Esther Hernández and Fernanda Casas. In North Carolina, two students spent brief periods gathering together information: Sarah Biehn and Teodora Stoica. Greenwood's Wendi Schnaufer was patient and firm with my eccentric British inclinations and guided the project to an orderly conclusion.

Introduction

Historical Overview

Before the Conquest

Anthropologists and historians generally agree that the Americas were populated by migrants who crossed the Bering Strait from Asia, perhaps 50,000 years ago. They made their way south, spreading across the plains of the north and down into South America. Many of these were nomadic peoples, hunters and gatherers. In the area that was to become Mexico, the first to settle and develop a significant civilization were the Olmecs, who occupied certain parts of the Gulf Coast and whose civilization is sometimes referred to as the mother of those that came later. The Olmec civilization and another at Monte Albán, near Oaxaca, together with the early Maya civilization at Tikal in modern-day Guatemala, are the mainstays of what anthropologists call the Early or Formative Period of Indian civilizations, a period that runs from approximately 1500 BC to AD 300.

A later era, the Classical Period (300–900), saw the rise of a civilization centered on the city of Teotihuacán, in the central valley of Mexico, together with further developments at Monte Albán and in Maya lands. At the end of the Classical Period, for reasons that are not yet fully understood, the Maya peoples moved quite abruptly to the north, into the Yucatán Peninsula, where they established the cities of Chichen-Itzá and Uxmal. Meanwhile, another culture, that of the Toltecs, extended its own influence from their capital Tula in the central valley. In time, Toltec dominance gave way to migrants from the north. These migrants were speakers of the Nahua language, and from among them emerged the Aztec civilization, the most powerful civilization the invading Spaniards would encounter in the early sixteenth century.

The Aztecs had come to the central valley on a pilgrimage in search of a promised land, which according to legend they would be able to identify when they saw an eagle perched on a cactus and holding a snake in its mouth—hence the image at the center of the modern Mexican flag. The place the Aztecs found in the valley of Mexico and transformed into the center of their empire was a shallow lake, about seven feet deep on average, which they called Texcoco. The Aztecs proceeded to reclaim parts of it for building and for cultivation: they made *chinampas*—reclaimed land—by placing stakes or reeds in the water in such a way as to fence off areas with basket-like structures, which they then filled with soil. In this way, they created land for what was to become a great city—one that in the early 1500s, when the Spaniards first saw it, was more populous than any in Europe, and was indeed one of the world's largest, with perhaps 250,000 inhabitants. This was the city of Tenochtitlán, the Aztec capital, founded in 1325. The sight of it left the Spaniards awestruck: they were impressed by its scale, its structures, its orderliness, and its cleanliness.

By the time the conquistadores arrived, Tenochtitlán was the center of a highly developed culture and a well-organized society; it was the political capital of an empire that the Aztecs had built by waging war on other Indian peoples, bringing them into an uneasy federation where they paid tribute with taxes and human lives. Though renowned for their bloody human sacrifices, the Aztecs were a sophisticated and moral people; they would wage wars (called *guerras floridas*—"flower wars") whose specific aim was to take live captives for subsequent sacrifice to their gods, because the Aztecs believed that only by making sacrifices could the gods be appeased and the universe protected. Thus the sacrifices, though indeed horrific, were not gratuitous acts of cruelty; instead, they were something the Aztecs thought was essential in order to preserve the continuity of life, a matter of obligation.

The Colonial Period

Spanish expeditions from the Caribbean islands had already touched the Yucatán Peninsula some years before the real invasion took place. In 1511, a wrecked ship had left some Spanish survivors stranded on the coast. These people lived among the Mayas and learned the language, and their knowledge ultimately proved helpful to the Spaniards who later came to conquer the lands, in 1519. Hernán Cortés, the leader of that expedition of conquest, came from Cuba, despite opposition from the island's governor. He arrived with only a few hundred men and some horses. Shortly after reaching the Mexican mainland, he acquired a partner in Malintzin—more commonly known these days as Malinche—an Indian princess who was given to Cortés by a local chieftain. She became his mistress and interpreter. Malinche has become a key historical figure in the Mexican psyche: on the one hand, her role in facilitating the Spanish conquest has made her a symbol of treachery, but on the other, she has also acquired a symbolic importance as mother of the first of a new, characteristically Mexican race, the *mestizos*.

Force alone could not account for the Spanish conquest, for they were vastly outnumbered. But they had several extraordinarily helpful factors on their side. Firstly, the Aztecs were expecting the return from the sea of a benign god, Quetzalcóatl, who had been banished in an earlier era; secondly, they believed that he would do so having assumed a physical appearance that happened to be like that of Cortés. On a less speculative level, the Aztecs had no acquaintance with firearms or with horses. And on a yet more practical level, disaffection among other Indian peoples subjugated by the Aztecs made it easy for Cortés to forge alliances with them, benefit from their knowledge, and dramatically reinforce his numbers. In 1521, Cortés laid siege to Tenochtitlán. The Aztec emperor, Moctezuma, was killed, the people were slaughtered or died from smallpox (a European disease, brought in unknowingly by the invaders, and one to which the Indians had no resistance). Eventually the city was obliterated; on its site, the Spaniards built Mexico City.

That act—the imposition of one structure upon another—was highly symbolic. Systematically, the Spaniards of the colonial period placed their own structures (especially churches) on top of Indian ones, as they attempted to imposed their own cultural practices on the Indians. In a further symbolic gesture, the conquered lands were dubbed "New Spain." Viceroys, representatives of the Spanish Crown, came to rule these lands; native-born Spaniards were put into administrative positions; and religious orders were entrusted with the conversion of the natives to the "true faith" of Catholicism. Political and ecclesiastical power went hand in hand. By 1527, Mexico had its first bishop.

In many cases, the clergy who dealt with the Indians saw them as pagan and viewed their practices as idolatrous, with the result that many Indian artifacts and documents were destroyed. An important aspect of the management of the Indian population was the *encomienda* system, which by royal decree put groups, or even whole communities, under the control of Spaniards, for whom the Indians would work, with the fruits of their toil going to their masters or the Crown. Although in principle the people in charge of the Indians were also responsible for their well-being, there were naturally many abuses. The most famous of the people who raised their voices against such abuse was Fray Bartolomé de Las Casas, a man who spoke from experience, having once had an encomienda himself. Las Casas wrote *Brevísima relación de la destrucción de las Indias* (A Most Brief Account of the Destruction of the Indies), which came to the attention of the king and led to some attempts at reform.

There were other friars who, as they went about the process of indoctrinating the natives, recognized the importance of preserving some aspects of native culture. Chief among these was Bernardino de Sahagún. Sahagún, a teacher at the Colegio de Santa Cruz de Tlatelolco, which had been founded in 1536 for the purpose of indoctrinating the Indian nobility, the intermediaries through whom the Spaniards sought to communicate their message to ordinary Indian folk. Very unusually, Father Sahagún used sophisticated interviewing techniques to gather information, rather as would a modern anthropologist: he sent people out to conduct the interviews and then produced a digest of the results. Sahagún compiled Náhuatl and Spanish versions of his four-volume *Historia general de las cosas de Nueva España* (General History of Things in New Spain), but died thinking that his work was unrecognized. In fact, the authorities were suspicious of his activities, and the work was not published until some two hundred years later. Yet history has vindicated him: Sahagún's efforts have provided the most valuable account available of the Aztec civilization.

In the long run, much of the Indian culture as it was prior to the invasion has, of course, been lost, or transformed by contact with other cultures and by time. But vestiges remain, and these are essential to that particularly hybrid identity that characterizes modern Mexico. Indian elements are as inbred in the national culture as is Indian blood in most Mexican people.

The Indian population suffered a disastrous decline in the early colonial period. The mestizo population grew. A class or caste system developed based on breeding—on *limpeza de sangre*, "purity of blood." At the top of the social scale were the true Spaniards, the immigrants who had been born in Spain itself; these were known as the *peninsulares* or, more disparagingly, the *gachupines*. They enjoyed the greatest privileges and held the important positions. Next in the hierarchy came the *criollos*, those who had been born in the New World but were of Spanish parentage. The mestizos (part European, part Indian) were next, and they were soon the most numerous group. The Indians were at the bottom of the scale—save for the African slaves, but the latter were not many by comparison with those in other colonial territories. Power was thus firmly in the hands of the Spaniards, particularly the political administrators and the secular clergy. It is no surprise, then, that once independence was sought and a republic established, two of the principal aims were to replace the peninsulares who were in the top jobs and to curtail the political influence of the Catholic Church. However, the administrative structures that existed were colonial, and the peninsulares were the people with the experience and expertise in administration; once those people were ousted, there was a vacuum—which helps explain some of the ups and downs of Mexican political life during the nineteenth century.

In the early nineteenth century, the thinking of Enlightenment reformers and the examples of the French Revolution, and particularly of the United States as a successful rebel against a colonial power inspired thoughts of independence in Mexico. The first open sign of this movement was spearheaded by a priest in the small town of Dolores, near Guanajuato. Father Miguel Hidalgo had been banished to this backwater after having had brushes with the colonial authorities, and together with other malcontents he had been planning a rebellion. At midnight on September 15, 1810, he rang his church bell and called openly for independence, a call that came to be known as the *Grito de Dolores*, the "cry from Dolores." His "army" then engaged in a massacre in Guanajuato, but after some further violence, Hidalgo and his supporters were defeated and he was executed. Another priest stepped into the leadership breach, only to meet a similar fate at the hands of forces loyal to Spain.

But in the drift toward independence, there was another major factor to be considered: there was significant unrest in Spain itself, which during the early 1800s suffered a number of unsettling changes. Early in the century, Napoleon had invaded the country, put his brother on the throne, and driven the king into exile. A rebel government in Spain opposed to Napoleon drafted a new and liberal constitution, which was eventually adopted once Napoleon had gone and the king had returned. Still, the political situation thereafter was by no means stable, anticlericalism was strong, and the future of Spain remained unclear. In Spanish America, many criollos, already resentful of the privileges of the peninsulares, were thinking that it was time to break away.

Mexico, the Republic

Throughout the colonial period, people had informally said "México" when referring to what was officially Nueva España (New Spain), a territory that extended from modern-day Panamá to Oregon. With independence, México would become the official name of the new republic, although that republic's boundaries would take some time to define; today's borders were not established until well into the nineteenth century.

The country was to go through more than fifty rulers over the course of the sixty-odd years following its achievement of independence: it was not a time of stability or continuity. Mexico would be invaded by France and find itself at war with the United States. On the domestic political front, the nineteenth century was to be one of a constant struggle between centralized power in Mexico City on the one hand and a federal system on the other; the country would be treated to a whole gamut of regimes, ranging from the democratic to the dictatorial.

The movement toward independence had begun with the Grito de Dolores, Father Hidalgo's call to arms. In late 1820, the last of the viceroys of New Spain, Juan Ruiz de Apodaca, put Agustín de Iturbide, a criollo army officer who had distinguished himself by his zeal in crushing the rebellions of Hidalgo and José María Morelos y Pavón, in charge of what was intended to be the decisive blow against the insurgents. Iturbide was a conservative and religious man who generally supported the established system but, like many criollos, he resented the superior status of the peninsulares.

By the time Iturbide went to Oaxaca to take on Vicente Guerrero's rebel army, Napoleon had withdrawn from Spain and Fernando VII had been restored to the throne—only to be ousted by a military coup that led to the introduction of the liberal constitution just as Iturbide was taking on Guerrero's rebels. Iturbide saw the situation in Spain as a threat to the status quo but also as an opportunity for the criollos to assert themselves and seize power. Hence the strange situation of a new drive for independence predicated on preserving most of the colonial order: the breakaway was fundamentally a conservative affair. Iturbide first clashed with Guerrero's forces, then made a compromise with them. While in the town of Iguala, he came up with a plan that was based on three "guarantees": that a newly independent Mexico would be a monarchy ruled by a transplanted European monarch, perhaps Ferdinand himself; that the Church would keep its privileges; and that criollos and peninsulares would henceforth be equals.

Seeing that the rebels and the army that had once been loyal to Spain were now coming together behind the Plan de Iguala and that defeat was inevitable, the viceroy stepped down. Iturbide had taken care to put a clause into his plan providing that if no suitable European monarch could be found, a criollo might take his place, and thus it was that he managed to insinuate himself into the position of ruler of the newly independent Mexico. His grand and pompous coronation as emperor in 1822 was bizarrely Napoleonic in style. Ironically, Mexico would be subjected to real Napoleonic imperial ambitions a few decades later, and much of its nineteenth century would be characterized by a schizophrenic relationship with France, a country perceived variously as savior, as imperial invader, and as provider of cultural models that were slavishly to be imitated.

At first, Iturbide's empire comprised Mexico and the territories that later became the countries of Central America. That empire, however, was short-lived. There were economic problems, and in 1822, there was also a major uprising in Veracruz, the country's major port, led by Antonio López de Santa Anna, who then joined forces with other like-minded people against Iturbide. By 1823, the latter had abdicated and the Central American Federation had broken away (later to break up into several countries). Following the establishment of a provisional government in Mexico, there were elections to a Constituent Congress, which convened in November of that same year. At that time, there were nineteen states and four territories.

Mexico's first republican constitution dates from 1824. It was influenced by the liberal Spanish 1812 Constitution of Cádiz, which had in turn been strongly influenced by the ideals of the French Revolution. In an effort to guard against the excesses of power suffered previously, the Constitution of 1824 required the president to share power with Congress and the judiciary. In principle, there was to be a strong federal structure, with the president elected by the nineteen states to serve a four-year term. The 1824 Constitution provided for a tripartite division of powers at the federal level and a bicameral legislature; however, the chief executive was still allowed overriding authority, and this was a provision that would be widely abused during the nineteenth century, effectively undermining federalism.

In the 1850s, a reform movement led to the promulgation of a series of laws restricting the privileges of certain people, including the clergy. These laws were duly incorporated into a reformed constitution, the Constitution of 1857. In addition to introducing new civil provisions, such as allowing civil marriage, the reform laws represented a real attack on long-standing privileges, and so met with considerable opposition. Church and State had been as close as peas in a pod during the colonial era (and indeed, they could be said to have been just as close in pre-Hispanic times, too). But now, under the reform laws, the Church could not, for example, own real property apart from the churches themselves, and it was obliged to give the sacraments to all people, regardless of whether they could pay. In addition to curtailing ecclesiastical and military privileges, the Constitution of 1857 reasserted the claims of federalism and the need to elect the president, at the same time giving certain guarantees of personal liberty. There followed much strife between vested conservative interests and the reformers. In 1861, Benito Juárez, champion of the reformist cause, was elected president, but his power was soon usurped by intervention from France.

The costly fighting between liberals and conservatives, coupled with the arbitrary rule of some regional *caciques* (strongmen), had left Mexico weak and hugely in debt, especially to European rivals of Spain. In these circumstances, and with the support of other European creditors, Napoleon III of France decided to take control: he installed an Austrian archduke, Maximilian, as emperor of Mexico. Although Juárez eventually returned to power, the country was by then in ruin. In 1872, Juárez died, after which the reform movement collapsed and the country fell under the rule of the dictatorial Porfirio Díaz, who maneuvered in such a way as to remain in power for the next three decades. And so the 1857 Constitution lost force, rule by edict took over, and the old privileges were once again enjoyed by the Church and private landowners.

Faced with the prospect of the aging Díaz returning to power yet again in 1910, the opposition was galvanized into action and the Revolution was the result. Any ideological cohesion there was at the start of it, however, was soon lost as the country fell prey to violent rivalries. The Revolution was not one driven by a clear and shared political agenda, but a chaotic affair in which regional leaders jockeyed for position, making alliances with and betraying one another. After the Revolution's chaos came the Constitution of 1917, which, though amended over a hundred times since then, has been continuously in force (though not necessarily acted upon) to the present day.

The 1917 Constitution reflects both the influence of the U.S. Constitution and the Mexican experience of dictatorship and revolution. At the time of its promulgation, it was the most radical constitution in the Western Hemisphere—one that gave detailed prescriptions regarding state control, national development, and civil rights. Furthering the revolutionary goals required (ironically, rather as had the authoritarian regimes of the past) a strong executive and a strong central government. Although the 1917 Constitution allows for shared power between the executive, legislative, and judicial branches, and although it provides for a federal system, the powers of the executive are clearly dominant and the federal government can and does intervene in the affairs of the various states. There are many paradoxes: for example, whereas the president is all powerful, he may not be reelected for a second term; the national Congress is weak, but there is guaranteed membership in it for opposition parties; state governors have considerable local autonomy, providing they stay loyal to the president; there is universal suffrage, but in practice there has not been much choice open to voters. The prime reason for this lack of choice is the monopoly of political power that was enjoyed by the Partido Revolucionario Institucional (PRI), a party whose very name speaks of the contradiction between change and stasis. The PRI was broadly based and very adept at protecting its own interests until the late twentieth century, when serious internal divisions became apparent. It was not until 2000 that it finally lost the presidency.

The States and Their Powers

Most Mexican states came into being during the first half of the nineteenth century. When the first republican constitution was promulgated, in 1824, the following nineteen were named: Chiapas, Chihuahua, Coahuila y Texas, Durango, Guanaxuato (*sic*), México, Michoacán, Nuevo León, Oaxaca, Puebla, Querétaro, San Luis Potosí, Sonora y Sinaloa, Tabasco, Tamaulipas, Veracruz, Jalisco, Yucatán, and Zacatecas. In addition, some areas were designated as "territories": these were Alta California, Baja California, Colima, and Santa Fe de Nuevo México. In most cases, these states and territories were based on administrative divisions that had already been in existence under the Spaniards. Many of the states named in the 1824 constitution have survived into present times, albeit with some territorial adjustments along the way. Zacatecas, for example, shed part of its territory that became the State of Aguascalientes. In mid-century, Texas broke away and joined the United States. Several border states—Chihuahua is an example—suffered massive losses of territory as a result of the war with the United States, while Alta California and Santa Fe de Nuevo México disappeared altogether from the Mexican map at that time. By the time of President Comonfort's reformist 1857 constitution, there were twenty-four states and one territory (which consisted of the whole of the Baja California peninsula). The 1917 constitution enshrined all the states that are now in existence, save that Baja California Sur and Quintana Roo were designated as territories; both of these became fully-fledged states only in 1974.

The very strong executive at the national level is mirrored at the state, and even the local, level. The states are equal, and all of them are represented in both houses of the National Congress. The National Congress is empowered to create new states. Whereas existing states are free to agree among themselves as to where their mutual boundaries lie, failing that, the National Congress or the Supreme Court can step in to resolve disputes.

Each state is obliged to have a representative, elected government on republican lines; so, too, are the municipalities (*municipios*), the units of local government. State governments consist of an elected president and a chamber of deputies. States must accept as valid each other's public acts, official documents, and legal proceedings. They may grant their own professional licenses and may acquire real estate for public purposes, including the possible expropriation of land.

A great many powers are reserved by the National Congress; for example, unless the Congress gives consent, the states may not levy import or export duties, nor may they maintain permanent armies or make war, except when attacked. The central government is obliged by the constitution to protect the states and may send troops at the request of a state governor. The Congress also has authority to decide that a governor should be replaced, in which case the president makes a nomination, which is subject to approval by a two-thirds majority vote in Congress. Prior to the Revolution, governorships often fell into the hands of caciques; with the PRI in power, over the next seventy-odd years, the national president would negotiate with local interests to identify a candidate loyal to the party.

Modern Mexico

With the exception of Guadalajara and a few areas in the central valley—Aguascalientes, the State of Mexico, and the Distrito Federal—the further north one looks, the greater the prosperity. However, generalizations regarding matters economic in Mexico mask huge disparities between individuals. Thus, for example, income in the border states may on average be relatively high, but that does not mean that there are not many cases of extreme hardship. Nationally, despite a growing middle class, a minority of people live a life of great prosperity and are able to send their children to private schools or abroad to be educated, while the vast majority of people have great difficulty in making ends meet. The relative economic prosperity of the northern states is matched by other indicators of well-being: the provision of public education and health care is better there, for example. At the other extreme, in the state of Oaxaca, more than half of all dwellings are without running water and most of the population is below the official poverty line. It is in rural areas that the level of poverty is most acute.

Among the poorest people are the Indians. The indigenous peoples of Mesoamerica suffered huge losses due to fighting, disease, and harsh work conditions during the colonial era and were further exploited by rich landowners during the nineteenth century. In the present day, it is difficult adequately to identify them and describe their situation. Being Indian is not simply a matter of who one's parents were; it also relates to how people regard each other and themselves. Are traditional Indian customs characteristic of the person's lifestyle? How does the person dress? Does the person speak Spanish? Is the person poor? These are the sorts of measures by which people are identified as Indian. Paradoxically, being Indian usually carries a stigma in the eyes of the majority, and yet that majority has some Indian blood and is generally proud of Mexico's distinctive indigenous heritage.

The hope of a better life brings a great many people into the major urban centers, where about a third of the national population now lives. It has been estimated that Mexico City alone receives a thousand new immigrants every day, and the infrastructure of that city clearly cannot cope with such an influx. There is generally high unemployment, even for skilled and educated workers; those who are neither have to turn to informal activities such as street vending or engage in illegal activities.

For decades, another promise of a better life—across the northern border—has led Mexicans to migrate to the United States. There was once a guest worker program (the *bracero* program) that allowed them to cross into the United States and work there legally on a temporary basis; once that was withdrawn, the immigrants became illegal, ever more subject to being taken advantage of by middlemen, and ever more desperate. With increased controls over the traditional crossing points, they have tried to cross the Rio Grande, some perishing in the attempt, and they have faced the rigors of the Arizona desert, where many have also died. The United States devotes ever-increasing resources to stopping them, building walls and arming itself with the latest technology for the purpose, yet the U.S. economy depends to some significant degree on their cheap labor. In addition, the *remesas* (the earnings sent back home by the migrants) now constitute a significant part of the Mexican economy.

Mexico has huge problems, many of them with very deep historical roots. It suffers from the degradation of its land, from pollution, from economic inequalities, and from widespread corruption among those in positions of power. There are signs of hope for the future: for example, slowly, a new and more healthy political ethos is in the making and the media are becoming more independent of the powers that be. But negative signs are also easy to identify, perhaps the most important of these being the ever-increasing power of those associated with the drug trade.

Chronology

c. 50,000 BC	First people arrive in the Americas, presumably from Asia.
c. 12,000 BC	Age of the earliest human remains found in Mexican territory.
c. 9000 BC	First domestication of maize (corn).
1500 BC–AD 300	Preclassical Period. Early civilizations of note in Mesoamerica are the Olmecs, with ceremonial sites at La Venta, Tres Zapotes, and San Lorenzo; ancient cultures at Monte Albán, Copilco, and Cuicuilco; and the Mayas at Tikal.
300–900	Classical Period of Mesoamerican civilizations features the rise of the Teotihuacán culture in the central valley, Zapotec development at Monte Albán, and Mayan civilization at Uxmal, Palenque, and Bonampak.
900–1519	Postclassical Period. The Mayas move to Yucatán and establish Chichen-Itzá, the Toltecs extend their influence from Tula throughout central valley before declining, and Nahua tribes from the north migrate into the central valley, leading to the rise of the Aztec (Mexica) Empire.
1325	Aztec capital of Tenochtitlán is founded on an island in Lake Texcoco.
1511	Spanish expedition ship wrecks on the Yucatán coast. Spaniards Jerónimo de Aguilar and Gonzalo Guerrero survive among the Mayas.
1519	Spanish conquistador Hernán Cortés and his men arrive in Yucatán. He encounters Aguilar and Doña Marina/La Malinche in Tabasco and employs them as translators.
1521	Having made an alliance with the Tlaxcalans, Cortés lays siege to Tenochtitlán and defeats the Aztecs.
1522	Cortés is named captain-general and governor of New Spain.
1524	Twelve Franciscan priests arrive to undertake Christian conversion of the native population.
1527	Mexico's first bishop, Fray Juan de Zumárraga, arrives.

1531	Virgen de Guadalupe appears before Indian Juan Diego at Tepeyac, near Mexico City.
1536	Colegio de Santa Cruz de Tlatelolco is founded for the education of the Indian nobility, with Fray Bernardino de Sahagún as a faculty member.
1537	First printing press in Mexico (and the New World) begins operation.
1542	Fray Bartolomé de Las Casas's *Brevísima relación de la destrucción de las Indias* is published, calling attention to the abuse of Indians by Spaniards.
1553	Royal and Pontifical University, the first university in the New World, is founded.
c. 1570	Diego de Landa writes *Relación de las cosas de Yucatán*, an account of Mayan culture.
1571	Holy Office of the Spanish Inquisition is formally established in Mexico.
1572	First Jesuit missionaries arrive.
1577	Sahagún completes his four-volume *Historia general de las cosas de Nueva España*, but the manuscripts are lost and not rediscovered for some two centuries.
1692	Ordinary people riot in Mexico City and burn government buildings.
1712	Indian uprising in Chiapas.
1767	Jesuits are expelled by royal decree from Mexico and other Spanish territories.
1810	In the early morning hours of September 16, Father Miguel Hidalgo's *Grito de Dolores* launches the movement for independence from Spain.
1811	José María Morelos takes up leadership of the independence struggle.
1821	Independence from Spain is achieved, and Agustín de Iturbide leads his victorious troops into Mexico City.
1822	Iturbide is crowned emperor of newly independent Mexico and rules for eleven months.
1823	Central American Federation of territories declares independence from Mexico.
1824	New constitution establishes a federal republic. Iturbide is executed. Guadalupe Victoria is elected the first president of the republic.
1830	Antonio López de Santa Anna assumes the presidency for the first time; he would subsequently assume and abandon the presidency several times between 1830 and 1855.
1833	Valentín Gómez Farías leads efforts to secularize education.
1836	Santa Anna is defeated at San Jacinto, and Texas declares its independence from Mexico.
1838	Interest grows in Yucatán about the possibility of secession.
1846–47	Mexican-American War. U.S. troops invade Mexico City, and the Mexican government flees to Querétaro.
1848	Mexico cedes more than half of its territory to the United States under the Treaty of Guadalupe Hidalgo.

1848–51	Violent "Caste Wars" are waged in Yucatán.
1854	Liberals, many exiled in New Orleans, proclaim the Plan de Ayutla and launch a revolt.
1855	Santa Anna abandons Mexico.
1857	Liberal constitution is promulgated.
1858–61	Civil war is fought between liberals and conservatives, with two different governments claiming legitimacy. Benito Juárez is installed as president of the liberal government in Veracruz and promulgates his "Reform Laws."
1862	French troops, allied with the Mexican conservatives, disembark in Veracruz. On May 5, Mexican liberal forces defeat the French troops at Puebla.
1864	Maximilian of Hapsburg, an Austrian prince, is installed by Napoleon and arrives as head of Mexico's "Second Empire."
1867	Liberal forces defeat troops loyal to Maximilian, and the "Restored Republic" is ushered in. Juárez is elected president.
1872	Death of Juárez.
1877–1911	During the "Porfiriato," a period of stability and infrastructural modernization is established under the authoritarian rule of Porfirio Díaz.
1910	Mexican Revolution, in its political phase, is launched by Francisco I. Madero, seeking the ouster of Díaz and the institution of free elections. Rebels Pancho Villa and Emiliano Zapata fight in the north and the south, respectively.
1911	Díaz flees into exile, and Madero is elected president.
1913	Madero is assassinated in a coup led by Victoriano Huerta. Villa, Zapata, Venustiano Carranza, Alvaro Obregón, and others return to arms.
1914	Huerta flees Mexico City and triumphant revolutionary factions march in. At the Convención de Aguascalientes, the various revolutionary leaders attempt to reconcile their differences but fail.
1915	Revolutionary factions led by northern landholders Carranza, Obregón, and Plutarco Elías Calles gain ascendancy over the more "popular" revolutionaries Villa and Zapata.
1917	Carranza and the Constitutional Congress promulgate a new "revolutionary" constitution. Carranza is elected president.
1920	Factions from Sonora led by Obregón and Calles launch a rebellion. Carranza flees and is assassinated.
1920–24	Presidency of Obregón.
1924–28	Presidency of Calles.
1926–29	Cristero Rebellion.
1928	Obregón is reelected president but assassinated before taking office.
1929	Calles forms the Partido Revolucionario de la Nación (PRN) and establishes the populist "machine" politics of the government party.
1930s	Migration into the metropolitan area of Mexico City (DF) begins to increase.

1934–40	Socialist presidency of Lázaro Cárdenas puts many of the ideals of the Revolution into practice.
1938	Cárdenas seizes foreign company holdings in Mexico and nationalizes the oil industry. He changes the name of the official party to Partido de la Revolución Mexicana (PRM) and restructures it.
1939	Partido de Acción Nacional (PAN), the conservative opposition party, is founded.
1942	United States and Mexico inaugurate the *bracero* program, allowing U.S. employers to take on Mexican agricultural workers legally.
1943	National health, disability, and pension systems are established under the Instituto Mexicano del Seguro Social.
1946	Miguel Alemán is elected as the first civilian president in the postrevolutionary period. Mexico's ruling party adopts the name Partido Revolucionario Institucional (PRI; Institutional Revolutionary Party).
1953	Women win the right to vote and to hold elective office.
1964–65	Bracero program is suspended. Mexico starts border industrialization.
1968	Series of student and worker protests culminates when government forces open fire on demonstrators in the Tlatelolco district of Mexico City on October 2; hundreds die.
1970s	Political refugees from Chile and Argentina flood into Mexico.
1975	Changes in the Civil Code are enacted protecting women's rights and birth control.
1976	The peso suffers a 50 percent devaluation against the dollar.
1981	Fall in oil prices triggers economic hardships.
1982	The peso again undergoes drastic devaluations. President José López Portillo nationalizes the banking industry.
1985	Major earthquake in Mexico City rallies the populace and new civic groups against government corruption.
1987	Cuauhtémoc Cárdenas and Porfirio Muñoz Ledo, two leading politicians, publicly renounce their PRI membership.
1988	PRI presidential candidate Carlos Salinas de Gortari defeats candidate Cárdenas. Massive protests against apparent fraud in the state and federal elections ensue, especially in Chihuahua and on the U.S. border.
1989–93	Salinas government undertakes new neoliberal economic reforms, selling off state-owned enterprises.
1989	The social democratic opposition Partido de la Revolución Democrática (PRD) is founded, with Cárdenas as its leading figure.
1993	North American Free Trade Agreement (NAFTA; Tratado de Libre Comercio [TLC] in Spanish) is signed.
1994	Ejército Zapatista de Liberación Nacional (EZLN), under the leadership of Comandante Marcos, launches an armed rebellion in Chiapas. Rash of political assassinations besets PRI.
1995	President Ernesto Zedillo confronts another economic crisis and announces another 50 percent devaluation of the peso.

1996	Zedillo advances real electoral reform, with the creation of an autonomous Federal Elections Institute.
2000	Election of PAN presidential candidate Vicente Fox ends the seventy-one-year dominance of the PRI.
2006	PAN presidential candidate Felipe Calderón wins by a narrow margin.
2008–09	He attempts to deal with the drug trade as violence increases.

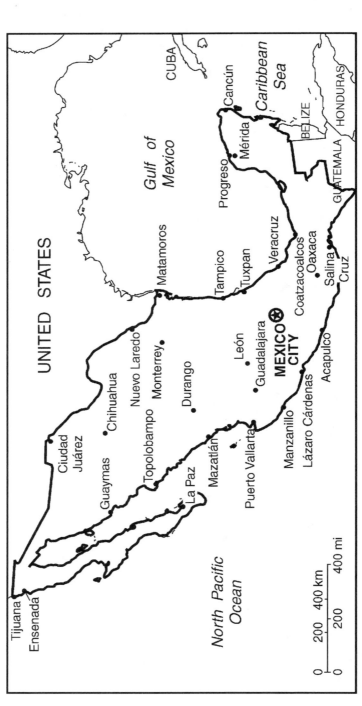

Mexico. Cartography by Bookcomp, Inc.

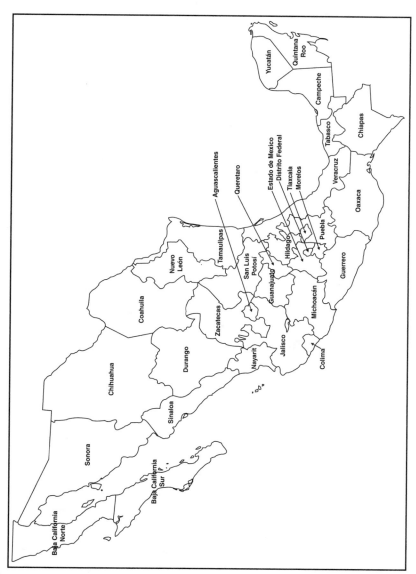

States of Mexico. Cartography by Bookcomp, Inc.

THE STATES OF MEXICO

Aguascalientes

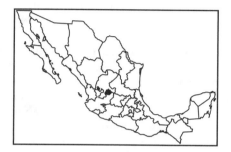

State Characteristics

Located more or less in the center of Mexico, and one of the country's smallest states, Aguascalientes owes its name to the fact that it has many hot springs. The state of Zacatecas lies to its north, that of Jalisco to the south. The inhabitants of Aguascalientes are popularly known as *hidrocálidos*, though the more learned term is *aguascalentenses*. Aguascalientes occupies 5,585 square kilometers (2,178 square miles), which puts it at number 27 in the national ranking by area; it covers only 0.3 percent of Mexico. Most of the approximately 1,065,000 inhabitants are concentrated in and around the state capital, which is also called Aguascalientes and is located some 500 kilometers (310 miles) northwest of Mexico City. The state comprises eleven municipalities. It is represented by seven people in the National Congress. The population of Aguascalientes is 95.6 percent Catholic. Aguascalientes has seven institutions of higher education. Five newspapers are published in the state, all in the capital city; they are *El Sol del Centro*, *El Heraldo*, *Hidrocálido*, *Aguas*, and *Página 24*.

The highest elevations are to be found in the ranges known as the Sierra Fría (3,050 meters/10,065 feet above sea level), the Sierra del Laurel (2,760 m/9,108 ft.), and the Sierra de Asientos (2,650 m/8,745 ft.) and in the mountains or hills known as Cerro del Mirador (2,700 m/8,910 ft.), Cerro de la Calavera (2,660 m/8,778 ft.), Cerro de San Juan (2,530 m/8,349 ft.), Cerro de Juan el Grande (2,500 m/8,250 ft.), Cerro del Picacho (2,420 m/7,986 ft.), and Cerro de los Gallos (2,340 m/7,722 ft.). The lowlands themselves are roughly a thousand meters (3,300 feet) above sea level. There are few rivers; the most important are the Aguascalientes (or San Pedro) and the Calvillo, to the west. Underground waters are more significant, providing the hot springs that are at the origin of the state's name.

A small area south of Calvillo (Sierra del Laurel), lying in the southwest of the state and representing about 15 percent of its total area, has a temperate climate. The rest of the state is semiarid, a land of scrub and desert, with limited rainfall. In such semiarid areas, the rate of evaporation exceeds the rate of precipitation; total annual rainfall in most of Aguascalientes runs between 500 and 600 millimeters (20–24 inches) and most of that falls in June. The average annual temperature is 18°C (65°F) and the range is from a maximum of 22°C (72°F) to a minimum of 13°C (55°F). The frequency of frosts is quite variable, from as few as ten days a year to as many as eighty, mostly occurring between November and February. Usually, the Sierra Fría is the only part of the state to see snowfall.

Oak, pine, and cedar trees can be found in the mountainous areas (parts of which are protected), together with wildlife such as deer, boars, lynx, and pumas. In lower areas, on the *mesa*, there are mesquite, palms, and various types of cacti, but much of the land is quite dry and barren. Fauna in the lower areas includes wolves, coyotes, hares, and quail. In the municipality of Calvillo, where the climate is less dry, plants of the *Bursera*, *Ipomoea*, and *Acacia* genera are common. The state's vegetation has suffered from overgrazing. There are 250 species of wildlife, of which 19 are endangered, including the royal eagle, which is close to extinction. Fourteen animal species and seventeen bird species are routinely hunted, including hares, coyotes, wild turkeys, quail, ducks, and geese.

Cultural Groups and Languages

According to the 2005 census, there were only 2,713 people in the state—just 0.3 percent of the total population—who spoke indigenous languages. This makes Aguascalientes one of the most "Hispanic" states in the country, with one of the smallest proportions of indigenous-language speakers of any state in Mexico. The main languages spoken are Náhuatl and Mazahua.

History

In the sixteenth century, more than two and a half centuries before statehood, the area that is now Aguascalientes was already being occupied by Spanish settlers. From the start, they came under attack from Indian inhabitants of the region; these were the Chichimecs, predominantly nomadic peoples who lived by hunting and gathering. Their attacks encouraged the Spaniards to establish fortified townships to provide safe havens for residents and travelers. Santa María de los Lagos was the first of these townships, established in 1563, and settlers from it, keen to escape the constraints of

Rural railroad.

local authority and venture into new lands, went on in October 1575 to found the settlement that eventually became the town of Aguascalientes. Almost abandoned at some points following Indian attacks, in 1584 this community consisted of sixteen soldiers, a leader, and two other settlers. Initially the place was called Villa de Nuestra Señora de la Ascensión de las Aguas Calientes, but it appears that that name was soon forgotten and replaced by Virgen de la Asunción (Virgin of the Assumption). In 1602, Bishop Alonso de la Mota y Escobar, while passing through the town, dubbed her its patroness, and to this day an annual pilgrimage is held in her honor.

According to one report, by 1620 there were still only between fifteen and twenty Spaniards in the town. However, in the sixteenth century, Aguascalientes became a mining area in its own right (there were mines at Tepezalá and Asientos de los Ibarra), and it rose in significance, especially because it was a point of confluence of trade routes to and from silver mines in Zacatecas to the north. As noted, the annual rainfall is generally low and seasonal, making it difficult to grow crops, although underground water sources have been used to alleviate the shortfall. There was enough in colonial times for some food production, but the area was very well suited to raising livestock, and thus it developed as a supplier to the mining communities to the north. In fact, many miners also became cattle ranchers (*hacendados*).

Following the troubled years of early settlement, the late sixteenth and seventeenth centuries were times of greater peace and prosperity for

Aguascalientes, the Indians having been brought under control, if not exterminated. Gaspar de la Fuente is credited with bringing about improvements in town planning in the Aguascalientes of the seventeenth century, a time when it gradually grew in size and in political and commercial importance, particularly as the halfway point between Zacatecas and Guadalajara on the *ruta de la plata*, the silver trade route.

The achievement of statehood for Aguascalientes, like most things that involve the Mexico of the nineteenth century, has a complicated history. The Audiencia de la Nueva Galicia, whose headquarters were in Guadalajara, had been the colonial administrative authority with jurisdiction over the lands of the future Aguascalientes, along with other lands. The audiencia was reorganized by Spain in 1786 and thereafter administered in two subdivisions, the *intendencias* of Guadalajara and Zacatecas, with Aguascalientes coming under the former. However, after years of wrangling between the two intendencias, in 1803 Madrid decided to transfer control of Aguascalientes to Zacatecas, despite the fact that Aguascalientes itself preferred an association with Guadalajara, with which it had strong historical ties and which it had found comfortably distant and noninterventionist in the past. Nonetheless, the relationship with Zacatecas proved to be a cordial and beneficial one.

In the early nineteenth century, when Mexico began to break away from Spain, Pedro Parga was a prominent aguascalentense who joined Miguel Hidalgo (the father of Mexican independence) and others in the campaign for independence. Following the fall of Guadalajara to rebel forces in 1821, Nueva Galicia lost its authority. Mexico was soon independent, and by 1824 Aguascalientes had officially been declared a city. Soon after that, Mexico set up its republican institutions, with Zacatecas as one of its states, one of the largest and richest. Among politicians who were born in Aguascalientes—a number of whom have risen to national prominence— **José María Bocanegra** (1787–1862) is probably the most intriguing case. He was a member of the first Constituent Congress of the newly independent Mexico, early in the nineteenth century. Bocanegra was even named president of the country, but he occupied that lofty position for less than a week before he was ousted, in December 1829.

In 1835, Aguascalientes became a territory in its own right. President Antonio López de Santa Anna had decided to march to Zacatecas, which had been a bastion of liberal opposition, and to impose his authority by putting an end to the Zacatecas militia, which was under the governor's control. On his way to do so, Santa Anna spent a couple of days in Aguascalientes, where he was given a royal welcome. This came as something of a surprise, since technically Aguascalientes was one of the areas that had taken up arms against his centralist control from Mexico City. Having been duly flattered and having listened to endless criticisms of the Zacatecas government, Santa Anna went away leaving the impression that, once back in Mexico City, he would take action on the matter. He then liquidated the

Zacatecas militia (a matter of a couple of hours) and returned to the capital.

The federal constitution now underwent reform as Santa Anna strengthened his control. Extraordinary sessions of the government were called, during which the state legislatures were dissolved and the governors made answerable to the president. In the process, Aguascalientes became independent of Zacatecas. When the federal structure was reestablished at the time of the U.S. invasion, in late 1846, Aguascalientes was formally constituted as a state. Yet less than six months later, the charter was changed for unexplained reasons, and somehow the name of Aguascalientes had disappeared from the list of states. The aguascalentenses were outraged, but the country had bigger things to attend to: there was unrest in the regions, especially Yucatán, and Mexico was on the verge of losing half its territory to the United States.

Aguascalientes again came under the control of Zacatecas, and there was much resentment because of it. Then, in December 1853, with Santa Anna once again in power, Aguascalientes was separated off from Zacatecas for the second time. A few years later, when the federal structure was reinstated in 1856, the granting of statehood to Aguascalientes was more or less automatic. Perhaps by that time legislators were simply tired of the "Aguascalientes question."

During the Mexican Revolution, Aguascalientes was one of the staunchest supporters of Venustiano Carranza, so it is not surprising that once in power he chose it as the place to convene a conference of rival revolutionary leaders with the aim of thrashing out possible structures of postrevolutionary government. After the Revolution, the state was firmly in the hands of the Partido Revolucionario Institucional (PRI) until 1998, when it elected its first governor from the conservative Partido de Acción Nacional (PAN).

Economy

Geographical location is a major contributor to the importance of the city of Aguascalientes. Largely modern and having undergone extensive industrial development, though still with a colonial center, Aguascalientes lies strategically between the three most populous cities in the country (Mexico City, Guadalajara, and Monterrey). Tourism has been on the increase; as well as being well connected to other areas, Aguascalientes as a city claims a reputation for cleanliness, safety, and a friendly, relaxed style. Aguascalientes also hosts Mexico's most important fair, the Feria de San Marcos, which takes place every April and brings in millions of visitors. The mountains to the southwest attract recreational visitors for camping, picnics, hiking, and hunting. There is the added attraction of the hot springs.

The land in general supports seasonal wheat crops and the cultivation of peppers, corn, and some fruit. Cattle ranching is important. Some livestock range freely, whether on large farms or smallholdings, and some are reared intensively; cattle, goats, sheep, and poultry are all raised. A once-important wine industry has declined somewhat since the mid-twentieth century, but Aguascalientes is still known for its wine production, much of which is now destined for the production of brandy or use as communion wine.

The capital city has developed a great deal in recent decades and is now home to some major industrial concerns, many of them foreign. The textile industry is among the most important of these. As compared with other states, Aguascalientes now ranks fifth in terms of prosperity, thanks largely to the industrial developments around its capital.

Arts

Craftwork in this state includes embroidery and needlework. Aguascalientes makes *charro* costumes, hats, jewelry, glasswork, and ceramics, and perhaps more especially marquetry and onyx ornaments. Earthenware skulls are made in some lowland areas. Weaving and embroidery are traditions in the mountainous areas of the state.

The *deshilado* sewing tradition has its local roots in the capital city; the technique involves drawing out threads and tying them. This practice was brought over from Spain during the earliest days of colonization, but can be traced back to Venice and Flanders, with a dose of Arabic influence added. It is thought that during the nineteenth century there were additional oriental and French influences brought to bear. Somehow, deshilado caught on particularly among the women of Aguascalientes, and they became famous for their skills in it. The development of sewing skills in the town of Aguascalientes was tied to its place in the railway network; women in the stations, often the wives of the railway workers, would sell their handiwork to travelers who were passing through. Later the art spread to other communities, such as Jaltiche de Arriba and La Labor, as well as Calvillo. This is a traditional form of handiwork, learned by apprenticeship rather than in classes; such skills are disappearing as it becomes less common for new generations of women to appreciate and acquire them.

As in many parts of Mexico, *corridos* and *sones* are popular musical forms, and as in many northerly states, there are dances based on German and eastern European traditions, such as the polka, the mazurka, and the waltz.

Hidrocálidos (natives of the state) who have won national or international recognition in the arts have been quite numerous. **José Guadalupe Posada** (1852–1913) is one of the best-known figures in Mexican art. He was an engraver who worked in Mexico City, making cuts in wood, copper, or zinc that, initially at least, were reproduced in cheap papers designed to please ordinary people by expressing piety and good humor; later, his images became more satirical and political in nature. Some of Posada's early illustrations are a little like French political cartoons of the mid-nineteenth century, but he became more expressionistic in style and famous for his use of skulls (*calaveras*) to represent human foibles and satirize public figures. Posada was admired by, and influential upon, muralists such as Diego Rivera. Aguascalientes holds a Fiesta de las Calaveras (Skull Festival) and has a museum that bears Posada's name.

Jesús F. Contreras (1866–1902) was one of Mexico's most prominent nineteenth-century sculptors; having trained at Bellas Artes in Mexico City, at an early stage in his career he helped make that city's famous monument to Cuauhtémoc, the martyred Aztec leader. There are now no less than twenty bronzes by Contreras on the Paseo de la Reforma, Mexico City's most famous artery, and one of them is of his uncle, who was a governor of the state. Despite a short life and the loss of an arm, Contreras was a prolific sculptor.

Understandably, **Manuel M. Ponce** (1882–1948) is claimed as a native son, though in fact he was born in Zacatecas and spent his first few weeks there before moving to Aguascalientes. A towering figure in Mexican music, Ponce was a composer and musicologist. He did much to track down traditional forms of Mexican music and to arrange them or describe them for posterity. In 1913, for example, he published *La música y la canción mexicana* (Mexican Music and Song) together with some arrangements of traditional tunes. His recognition of regional forms of music led to a canonization of some of them. As a composer, Ponce began in a nationalistic, folksy style, but later became more impressionistic, and he produced some of Mexico's first symphonic works, including *Concierto del sur* (1941). In 1933 he became director of Mexico's National Conservatory of Music.

Saturnino Herrán (1887–1931) was perhaps the first Mexican painter to use art as a way of expressing social concerns. His sympathetic portrayals of indigenous subjects and scenes from popular life are in a stylized form of realism, and his works are notable for the predominance of warm colors, especially gold tones. During his lifetime, he was best known as a magazine illustrator. Herrán was commissioned to do the reproductions of the Teotihuacán frescoes that can be seen in Mexico City's Anthropological Museum, and his most famous original work, *Nuestros dioses* (Our Gods, 1918), represents an Aztec sacrificial rite. He was a close friend of both Ponce and the famous poet Ramón López Velarde. All three worked in Mexico City, and they shared similar attitudes, including a discomfort with the European pretensions of the times of President Porfirio Díaz.

Ramón López Velarde (1888–1921), like Ponce, was born in Zacatecas, though he spent a full ten years there before moving to Aguascalientes. One of the foundational figures of modern Mexican poetry, López Velarde began his literary career with a regular column in an Aguascalientes journal called *El Observador*. After working for a while as a lawyer and teacher, he turned more fully to literature, publishing his first book of poetry, *La sangre devota*, a sentimental and provincial work, in 1916. López Velarde reacted against the rarified style of the *modernista* poets of the late nineteenth century, cultivating instead a return to simpler values. But his poetry could also be thoroughly modern and ironic, bringing sophistication and originality to the treatment of Mexican reality. An important mature work of his is *El son del corazón* (1932).

Gabriel Fernández Ledesma (1900–1983) is often listed as one of several second-ranking figures in the Muralist movement, the sort of painter whose work was overshadowed by that of Rivera, José Clemente Orozco, and David Alfaro Siqueiros. But Fernández Ledesma's art is not to be undervalued, and in any case he was not only a painter: he also worked as an engraver, lithographer, photographer, set-designer, puppeteer, and writer on popular art.

Antonio Acevedo Escobedo (1909–1985) was a writer, critic, and journalist who after working for José Vasconcelos on *La antorcha* went on to become a frequent contributor to the country's major newspapers, a member of the Academia Mexicana de la Lengua, and the director of the Department of Literature at the Instituto Nacional de Bellas Artes in Mexico City. He also wrote books with a regional flavor, such as *Los días de Aguascalientes* (1952).

Another important writer-journalist was **Anita Brenner** (1905–1974). She was born and died in Aguascalientes, though she spent a good part of her life in the United States, which was her father's native land. With the outbreak of the Mexican Revolution in 1910, the family moved from Aguascalientes to El Paso, Texas. Later, she earned a doctorate from Columbia University and for a time worked as a reporter for the *New York Times*, covering the Spanish Civil War. Brenner's life consisted of a constant to-and-fro between the United States and Mexico. She wrote about Mexican history, notably in *El viento que barrió México* (The Wind That Swept through Mexico, 1943), a book she coauthored with George R. Leighton. *El viento* is an account of the Mexican Revolution and the years thereafter, incorporating a large number of photographs from the famous Casasola Archive, together with others by photographers such as Tina Modotti. Brenner also translated several of the most important novels of the Revolution, including Mariano Azuela's *Los de abajo*, Gregorio López y Fuentes's *El indio*, and Mauricio Magdaleno's *El resplandor*. In general, she did much to help publicize Mexican culture north of the border; for example, she was one of the first people to introduce the United States to the work of Orozco and Rivera.

In more recent times, **Jaime Humberto Hermosillo** (1942–) has acquired a reputation for being one of the country's most successful and respected movie directors, with films such as *María de mi corazón* and *Doña Herlinda y su hijo*. At a less elevated level, **Yadhira Carrillo** (1974–) went from being Miss Aguascalientes to being one of the country's best-known soap opera stars.

Social Customs

The most important event in the social calendar is the Feria Nacional de San Marcos, a tradition over 175 years old. The fair begins in mid-April and lasts for three weeks, drawing visitors from all over the country and abroad, and such is its importance that it is sometimes called the Feria de México. Its origins date back to early-seventeenth-century initiatives designed to expand agricultural and livestock markets by drawing interest from other parts of the country. The fair was first held in November 1828, and it has had its own designated precinct since 1842. The timing was later changed so that it would coincide with the Feast of San Marcos in April. Bullfights have always been a major component of the fair. Over the years, they have been joined by *charreadas* (Mexican-style rodeos), cockfights, agricultural and trade shows, exhibitions, displays of local arts and crafts (such as embroidery), dances and music, and literary awards, not to mention the crowning of a Reina de la Feria (Queen of the Fair) and a corresponding ball. There is even a chicken dish, *pollo de San Marcos*, that is said to have come into being because of the fair. Calvillo also has a regional fair, held in early December.

On August 15, the Feast of the Assumption coincides with the grape festival in Aguascalientes. During the day, there are *matachines* (mummers) who dance in front of the cathedral, and in the evening there is a colorful procession. Around the time of the Feast of the Ascension in May, Calvillo celebrates Nuestro Señor del Salitre, with similar activities, and on July 25, the day of Spain's patron saint Santiago, Jesús María celebrates a festivity known as Chicahuales, during which the locals enact battles between Moors and Christians. Other festivities of note are San Isidro Labrador (May 15), Nuestra Señora del Refugio (July 4), and the Romería por Nuestra Señora de la Asunción (August 1–15). As elsewhere in Mexico, Todos los Santos (the Feast of All Saints, November 1–2) is widely celebrated. The run-up to Christmas begins with *pastorelas* (tableaux and pageants) in mid-December.

The dress that Aguascalientes has consciously adopted as "typical" is for women and is based on styles that were predominant in the early twentieth century. The high-necked blouse has long sleeves that are ample at shoulder level but closely fitted at the wrist; it is gathered at the waist. The skirt is full, with a broad, gathered, decorated band at the bottom of it. The whole outfit makes a show of traditional skills in embroidery and deshilado, highlighted against a plain background. Such dress can incorporate representations of local motifs and activities, such as the San Marcos fair.

Noteworthy Places

The Museo José Guadalupe Posada, located in Aguascalientes itself, beside the Templo del Señor del Encino, is a museum that has four main areas: the principal gallery has original works by Posada, a second area is devoted to works by his colleague Manuel Manilla, a third presents other artists who followed in a similar vein, and the fourth is a library of some 5,000 books, with many theatrical and poetic works among them. On Sundays, the central patio of the building serves as a venue for cultural events in collaboration with the Instituto Cultural de Aguascalientes. There is also a museum of the city of Aguascalientes, a bullfighting museum, the Museo Manuel M. Ponce, the Pabellón de Hidalgo, and the Museo de la Insurgencia.

There are archaeological sites at Monte de Huma, where remains of buildings have been found, and at Jalpa and Metabasco, where there is evidence of early human settlement.

Cuisine

Birria, a stew that can be found, with variations, in a number of states, is popular in its local incarnation. In an area that rears livestock, meat is a key ingredient in many dishes. Typical dishes include *tacos dorados, tamales, gorditas, pacholas, condonches, pollo de San Marcos, enchiladas rojas con longaniza*, and desserts such as *jamoncillos* and *charamuscas*. There is considerable use of the fruits that are grown locally, especially guavas, from which, in addition to jellies and jams, they make *copitas de leche con guayaba, guayabetes*, and *rollos de guayaba con cajeta y nuez*; these are associated in particular with Calvillo and the temperate zone. Many drinks are fruit based, some of them alcoholic. Common drinks are *dulce uvate, aguamiel, pulque*, and *calanche*.

Pacholas

Ingredients:

> ³/₄ lb. finely ground beef
> 1 *ancho* chile
> ¹/₂ tsp ground cumin
> ¹/₂ clove of garlic
> 2 tbsp olive oil
> Salt to taste

Fry the pepper, taking care not to burn it. Leave to cool, then cut the pepper open, remove the stalk, and clean out the inside. Cut into strips and leave to soak in a bowl of salt water for several hours or overnight. Then drain off the water and grind the pepper with the garlic and cumin. Add the meat and mix together. Shape thin patties from the mixture and fry in olive oil immediately before serving. This goes well with a salad.

Pozole Verde de Elote

Ingredients:

> 12 young *elotes* (corncobs)
> 1 lettuce
> ¹/₂ lb. green tomatoes
> 10 *serrano* chiles
> 5 *poblano* chiles
> 1 medium onion

2 chicken breasts
1 lb. lean pork
Chicken broth (sufficient to make a thick soup)
5 avocados
Cilantro to taste

Cut the corn from the cobs and put to boil with the meat. Once cooked, remove the meat and chop it up. Clean out the peppers, and chop these finely (or put them in a food processor,) together with all other ingredients except the avocados. Fry the mixture briefly; add the corn, broth, and meat; heat and serve with slices of avocado. Serves a large group of people.

Chile Aguascalientes

This dish is similar to, though simpler than, the *chiles en nogada* for which Puebla is famous. Ingredients:

Dry red ancho chiles
Ground pork
Ground beef
Onion
Garlic
Raisins
Guavas
Walnuts
Sugar
Salt
Ground black pepper
Viznaga (leaf of the Mexican lime cactus)
Milk
Cream

Soak the chiles in water with a little sugar, then drain them and clean out the insides. Soak a roll or piece of bread in milk. Fry the onion, chopped garlic, and pork, then add the beef. Remove the seeds from the guava, and then chop the fruit finely, together with the viznaga, nuts, and raisins. Add to the ingredients in the frying pan. Season with salt and pepper. Drain and break up the bread, adding it to the mixture to thicken it. Once cool, stuff the chiles with the mixture. Puree the remaining nuts with a little milk and cream to serve as a sauce. May be eaten warm or cold.

Chiles Morrones Rellenos (Stuffed Peppers)

Ingredients:

6 red bell peppers
$1/2$ lb. ground beef
$1/2$ lb. ground pork
4 oz. finely chopped mushrooms

3 medium potatoes
$^1/_2$ cup diced tomatoes
Oil
Garlic
Onion
Salt and pepper

Roast the chiles, peel and clean them, and rub a little salt on them. Fry garlic, onion, and meat, together with finely diced potatoes, mushrooms, and tomatoes. Season with salt and pepper and allow to simmer, covered, over a low flame, until the mixture has thickened a good deal. Then stuff the peppers with the mixture.

Pai de Guayaba

Ingredients:

For the pastry:
1 packet Galletas María (English Rich Tea Biscuits are closest substitute)
1 stick butter
$^1/_2$ cup chopped walnuts
$^1/_2$ cup coconut

For the filling:
1.5 packets gelatin
1 cup guava juice
1 can guava (drained)
1 can condensed milk

Preheat oven to 350°F. Grind up the cookies, adding the walnuts and coconut. Knead in the butter to make a paste and use it to line a baking dish. Bake for eight or nine minutes. Heat the guava juice and dissolve the gelatin in it, then allow it to begin to set. Blend the guava with the condensed milk, then add to the gelatin mixture before placing in the piecrust and allowing to set.

Baja California

State Characteristics

In its entirety, the Baja California peninsula has a length of 1,200 kilometers (744 miles) and a surface area (excluding its neighboring islands) of 143,600 square kilometers (56,004 square miles). It is one of the longest peninsulas in the world.

However, the *state* of Baja California, the most northwesterly in the country, occupies only the northern half of the peninsula. To its south lies the state of Baja California Sur. Sometimes, in order to make the distinction clear, Baja California is informally referred to as "Baja California Norte" (before statehood, it was officially the Territorio de Baja California Norte). The name California is believed to have come from an early sixteenth century novel of chivalry by Garcí Ordóñez de Montalvo, published in Spain and entitled *Las sergas de Esplandián*, in which the hero comes across an island called California, close to paradise.

The state's capital city is Mexicali. Baja California shares a border with the United States and is bounded on the east by the Colorado River and the Mar de Cortés (Sea of Cortez, better known in the United States as the Gulf of California). The distance along the border with California, from the Pacific Ocean and the city of Tijuana at the western end eastward to the Colorado River, is 233.4 kilometers (approximately 145 miles), and there is an additional 28.5 kilometers (18 miles) of border shared with Arizona. The state of Baja California has 720 kilometers (446 miles) of Pacific coastline and 560 kilometers (347 miles) on the Gulf of California side.

Tijuana River with Tijuana in the background. (AP Photo)

The state's total surface area, including islands, runs to 69,921 square kilo-meters (27,269 square miles); it is thus the twelfth largest state in Mexico in terms of area. The state is divided into five administrative *municipios*: Ensenada, Mexicali, Tecate, Tijuana, and Playas de Rosarito.

For a long time, Mexicans thought of this as a remote place, but Baja California has grown dramatically in recent decades with an influx of both Mexicans and foreigners. There has been major growth in the border region, in particular in the towns of Mexicali and Tijuana, in addition to which, cer-tain parts of the coast have been developed for tourist and residential use. There were concerns, in the light of nineteenth-century territorial losses to the United States, that the peninsula ought to be populated and developed by Mexicans, but the fact is that the population of Baja California in the early twentieth century grew slowly; by 1910, the territory (as it then was) had some 10,000 inhabitants, and ten years later about twice that number. Growth was slowed by the Revolution. It was after about 1940 that more rapid growth became evident, partly because of the development of parts of the region for agriculture. By 1970, the population had risen to 870,000, and by the end of the century it was approaching 2.5 million. The increases in the native Mexican and nonnative populations were at comparable rates, each category representing about half the population. The 2005 government census gives a total state population of 2,844,469 and reports that, among those over five years of age, 1.4 percent speak an indigenous language. Cath-olics comprise 81.4 percent of the total population; 7.9 percent are Protes-tant or evangelical. Currently, more than 50 percent of the total population is in the municipio of Tijuana; Mexicali has 28.2 percent, Ensenada 14.5

percent, Tecate 3.1 percent, and Playas de Rosarito 3 percent. CONEPO, a government agency concerned with population questions, predicts a rise in Baja California's population to about 4 million inhabitants by 2010. Ten people represent the state in the National Congress.

Baja California has thirteen establishments devoted to higher education. Nine newspapers are published in the state, mostly shared by Tijuana, Ensenada, and Mexicali (e.g., *El Sol*, *El Heraldo*, *El Mexicano*, *La Voz de la Frontera*), though one is published in Cabo San Lucas (*La Tribuna*).

Cachanilla is a pungent local plant that was used by the original inhabitants of Baja California to make huts and similarly (though mixed with mud) by the early *mestizo* settlers of the region. That term came into popular use as a way of referring to the inhabitants of Mexicali and its valley, and it has since been generalized as the common term for people from all over Baja California.

Mountain ranges run most of the length of this dry and rugged peninsula. The highest peak (of granite, metamorphic, and volcanic rock) is at 3,096 meters (10,217 feet), in the Sierra de San Pedro Mártir. The other main mountain range is known as the Sierra de Juárez and is of granite. Otherwise, the land consists of the Colorado River basin, desert coastal plains to the east and west, flatlands to the south, and about thirty-five islands, mostly on the gulf side.

The climate is broadly of two types: the northwest enjoys a Mediterranean climate, with moderate to warm temperatures for most of the year and winter rains; this is where most of the population is concentrated. Eastern regions are more harsh and arid. The mountain ranges, which have their own climatic characteristics, separate the two. Rainfall is least along the coast of the Gulf of California, at an average of 40 millimeters (1.6 inches) a year.

There are no significant rivers apart from the Colorado, close to which most of the state's agriculture is carried out, fed by the river. On the mainland, there is little surface water, just a few trickles in the north and a few intermittent springs that serve as oases in the central and southern areas.

There are two basic flora regions. The first is to the northwest, running from the border with the United States down to about the level of El Rosario and inland to the mountain ranges. This region, with its Mediterranean-style climate (mild and fairly damp winters, hot and dry summers), boasts 4,452 native plant species. In mountainous areas, one finds conifers and varieties of oak. However, most of the peninsula is desert. The part of it that falls within the state of Baja California is notable for the frequency of agave and dudleya, *Franseria chenopodifilia*, yucca, *Idria columnaris* (popularly known as the *cirio*), and *Pachycormus discolor* (better known as the *árbol elefante*—the elephant tree). Other common plants are *sahuero*, *viznaga*, cholla, and jojoba. It is said to be the most fertile desert in the world, with about a hundred plant varieties that are not found anywhere else. As for wildlife, there are rattlesnakes, chameleons, ducks, quail, eagles, falcons, diverse small rodents, foxes, pumas, coyotes, deer, and wild sheep. The Isla Rasa y Guadalupe, the Valle de los Cirios, and the Parque Morelos (in Tijuana) are ecologically protected areas.

Cultural Groups and Languages

Indigenous-language speakers make up 1.4 percent of the population of this state, a proportion that no doubt is going to decline. Although the Indian element in Baja's population is less strong than in many states, there are some communities of note, including those of the Cucupá Indians in the Colorado River basin, and of the Cochimí and Kiliguua in the central mountains, the Pay-Pay in the northern mountains, and the Kumiai in the northwestern coastal area and the mountains.

History

The process of migration from Asia—via Alaska, across the plains of North America, and down through Mexico—which accounts for the early populations of the Americas, is believed to have brought three main nomadic tribes to Baja California, perhaps 14,000 years ago. These were the Pericués, the Guaycuras, and the Cochimíes. The latter occupied the more northerly parts, the Guaycuras the middle of the peninsula, and the Pericués its southern part.

Until the late nineteenth century, the history of the state of Baja California is a peninsular one, a history inextricably linked with that of its neighbor to the south. From conquest to independence from Spain, that history is fundamentally one of the missions. The exploration of the Californias was fueled by the typical factors behind Spanish colonization of the Americas. The Spaniards dreamed of exotic lands, cities of gold, and strange beings; they were looking for trade routes to the Orient, and were intent on converting the natives to Christianity. The very name of California speaks of a Quixotic quest.

Following the Conquest of Mexico, Hernán Cortés sent expeditions to explore the Pacific, known at the time as the Mar del Sur (Southern Sea). As part of the second of these expeditions, in 1534 Fortún Jiménez de Bertadoño made his way to an island which he dubbed Santa Cruz (Holy Cross), in the bay of La Paz; he and others were killed by Indians, but men who returned from that second expedition told enticing tales of pearls, and so a year later Cortés himself headed a third expedition. In the course of this, Cortés landed at what is now La Paz itself (the present-day capital of Baja California Sur), though he gave it the name Puerto y Bahía de la Santa Cruz. While he was not the first European to set foot on Baja California, Cortés is generally credited with the foundation of the state, and the date of his arrival is still celebrated as such in Baja California Sur.

The intention had been to settle it, but faced with such an inhospitable, uncultivable terrain, the expedition turned back, leaving Francisco de Ulloa behind in command of thirty men, with twelve horses and sufficient provisions for a further ten months; however, even these people were called back by the viceroy before a year had passed. The fourth and last expedition sent by Cortés was in 1539, and again Ulloa was in command; this time, however, the aim was not to settle so much as to explore. And so the process continued in ensuing years, officially and unofficially, mapping the lands and searching for pearls. The Viceroyalty of New Spain was responsible not only for American territories but also for the Philippines, and the Californian coastal ports were to become important stopping points on the route from Acapulco to Manila.

Settlement really began in the late seventeenth century. In 1697, the viceroy authorized two Jesuits, **Juan María de Salvatierra** (1648–1717) and **Eusebio Francisco Kino** (1644–1711), who was also a geographer, to gather the necessary military support and set up missions in California. They were told to do so, however, only if they found private funds to support the project and no cost fell upon either the Society of Jesus or the viceroy as representative of the Crown: Spain had more pressing concerns to attend to and did not wish to commit financial resources to the development of an area that seemed to promise little in return. With the help of Father Juan de Ugarte, Salvatierra raised the money (it became known as the "Fondo Piadoso," the Pious Fund) to finance the establishment of the Californian missions. Salvatierra set out to found the first of them, which he called Nuestra Señora de Loreto, and which for a long time thereafter would effectively be the capital of California. Instructed to do so by King Philip V, Salvatierra also wrote a history of the territory.

The Spaniards' goal was to "reduce" the scattered Indians—to wean them away from their lifestyle and put them in settlements where they would cultivate the land, in the European style; two harvests were anticipated, one of the fruits of newly established agricultural practices and the other of Indian souls. Future efforts were concentrated on finding suitable sites for the missions, the prime prerequisite being a reliable natural supply of water. The early part of the eighteenth century saw the establishment of Santa Rosalía Mulegé, San Juan Malibat, San José de Comondú, and, a little later, La Purísima Concepción Cadegomó; the hybrid names of these missions reflect the imposition of Catholicism on the Indians. Salvatierra's efforts to deal with the Indians to the south (the Guaycuras and the Pericués) were slower to bear fruit, the mission of La Paz being founded in 1720. Beginning in 1734, there was a significant Pericué rebellion that cost a large number of Spanish lives and hindered progress in the development of the missions, but more were established in the ensuing years. By the time Charles III's royal decree expelling the Jesuits from Spanish America was made known in 1767, there were fourteen active missions in the Californias; the Jesuits in them gathered at Loreto, and by 1768 they had gone.

Their work was now entrusted to the Franciscan order, under Father Junípero Serra. However, the Franciscans enjoyed less independence with regard to the administration of the missions than had the Jesuits, for there was now to be a regional and military governor, representing New Spain, and the cultivable lands were to be managed by soldiers. The only mission set up by the Franciscans in what is now Baja California was San Fernando Velicatá (1769), a staging post on the way to Alta California, where Serra had already established the Mission of San Diego. Pressures in favor of civilian settlement and administration of the Californias increased, and there was a decline in the Indian population in some missions, due primarily to smallpox and measles. It was proving logistically difficult for the Franciscans to handle missions scattered over so vast a territory, and so it was that the order voluntarily relinquished responsibility for Baja California and the Dominicans took their place, founding their first mission, Rosario Viñadacó, in 1774. Among those that were established in the following years, San Vicente Ferrer (founded in 1780) deserves a mention, since it became the base from which late-eighteenth- and early-nineteenth-century explorations were launched.

In 1804, political control was divided: the colony of California was split into two divisions, Alta (Upper) and Baja (Lower), the dividing line between the two being the Arroyo del Rosario, which separated the Franciscan missions of the north from the Dominican ones of the south. Due to the fact that supplies from the south could not be relied upon, a lively contraband trade developed during this period, with English, Russian, and U.S. ships taking part. Pressures to secularize the missions continued, but in the border area the change was slow to happen, and since the Church had control of the best land in that area, settlers headed for Alta California, which was quicker to change and more fertile. Nineteenth-century attempts to reduce Church privileges had mixed success, but eventually the missions became secular townships.

The movement in favor of independence from Spain (beginning around 1810) had not greatly affected the remote Californias; they remained under Spanish control until 1822 and then, once a republic had been established, they fell in line behind Agustín de Iturbide's independent empire and were designated as territories. In 1846, with the country at war with the United States, Alta California was invaded and Monterrey, San Francisco, and San Diego were lost. The Treaty of Guadalupe Hidalgo in 1848 brought peace with the United States, but Mexico had to cede (Alta) California and other lands to its opponent. In 1853, William Walker took La Paz and other areas in Baja California, but he was defeated in Sonora and withdrew to the north.

Baja California had a more prominent role at the time of the 1910 Revolution. Within the territory, Alejandro Allison, **Ignacio Bañuelos Cabezud** (d. 1959), and Manuel José Quijada were active in support of Francisco Madero as an alternative to the longtime authoritarian president, Porfirio Díaz. Bañuelos founded a daily newspaper called *Eco de California* and came to be regarded as the doyen of journalists in the territory. North of the border, the Flores Magón brothers, prominent advocates of change who had been publishing their own opposition newspaper in exile and also supported Madero for president, issued a call to arms in 1910 that led to a confrontation with the authorities of Baja California and, for a while, the occupation of Tijuana and Ensenada.

In the early days of the Revolution, with Victoriano Huerta in power, Mexicali was made the capital of Baja California in a move designed to reinforce frontier security. The division by Mexico of the whole peninsula into two separate territories (Baja California and Baja California Sur), each of a similar size, was confirmed by Congress in 1930. In the first half of the century, successive committees were formed with the aim of enhancing Baja California's status. In 1951, President Miguel Alemán declared that, because of population and economic growth, the territory was eligible to become a state, and his decree to that effect was approved by the National Congress before the year was out. The governor of the territory was appointed provisionally to the post of state governor; following this, elections were held of the first deputies, with the Partido Revolucionario Institucional (PRI) sweeping the board. Braulio Maldonado Sánchez took office in 1953 as the first fully fledged governor of a newly constituted state of Baja California. It is worth noting that the 1953 elections were the first in Mexico in which women were allowed to vote.

Like other states that border the United States, modern Baja California has in many ways been governed by the effects of its proximity to and dealings with its neighbor to the north, including being plagued with problems associated with trafficking in human beings and drugs and with corruption among its politicians and law officers. At the border crossing of Tijuana alone, some 45,000 vehicles pass every day, while there is a constant flow of illegal entrants to the United States and an extensive network of *coyotes* to help and exploit them.

Political corruption associated with the drug traffic propelled Baja California into the national limelight in the late twentieth century. A governor of the state had maneuvered to gain control of the one newspaper, *ABC*, that had dared to be openly critical of him and his associates. Deprived of their mouthpiece, the newspaper's editors, Héctor Félix Miranda and **Jesús Blancornelas** (1936–2006) responded by launching a critical weekly called *Zeta*, a judiciously chosen title since it also happened to be the name of a hit squad working for the drug barons. In 1985, *Zeta* published an article under the headline "Mafia Invades Baja California." Miranda's subsequent murder was investigated, and its roots were traced to agents of the PRI, though no charges were brought against any instigator of the assassination. About ten years later, Blancornelas became the target; he was badly injured and his bodyguard was killed after a contract on Blancornelas's life had been put out by the Arellano brothers of the Tijuana cartel. In 2004, another investigative journalist associated with *Zeta* and engaged at that time in a further probe into the earlier attacks was also gunned down by a contract killer. These events sent shock waves nationally, and there were demands for federal investigations and protection, the state authorities being assumed to be corrupt. As an illustration of the extent of police corruption, it is striking that in October 2006 the federal government announced that every single member of the Tijuana police force was under investigation for suspected corruption.

Ever since the Revolution, Baja California's political representatives to the National Congress had invariably been members of the PRI, but in 1989 Ernesto Ruffo Appel of the conservative Partido de Acción Nacional (PAN) became the first governor of Baja California who was not a member of the ruling party—indeed the first postrevolutionary governor in the whole country not from the PRI. Since that time, the PAN has been dominant in Baja California, but the state's problems have by no means gone away.

Economy

Population growth was boosted in the first half of the twentieth century by the opening up of more territory for agricultural use (for example, the cultivation of cotton in the Mexicali valley), by the introduction of an irrigation system drawing on the Colorado River and by improved rail links. For the most part, agricultural production is now focused on wheat, barley, grapes, olives, and cotton.

Juan de Ugarte (1660-1730), who had been instrumental in raising funds in support of the first missions, was a Jesuit born in Honduras; he is remembered for his efforts to expand education and also for having encouraged the cultivation of wheat and vines in early colonial days. Baja California, probably thanks to its remoteness, escaped a royal ruling during colonial times that vines and olive trees should no longer be cultivated. Shortly after the Conquest, Spain had brought both to the New World, and they had prospered to such a degree that Spanish producers at home protested to the Crown about the increasing competition. Nowadays, L. A. Cetto is one of the best wine producers in Mexico. Tecate beer, now widely exported, was founded by Alberto Aldrete (1891-1959), at one time the state governor.

Foods, drinks, and tobacco, together with textiles, wood products, and paper, are significant for the economy of Baja California. A predictably wide range of fish and shellfish is the basis of a major seafood industry, and meat production is also important. The state also has a wide variety of mineral resources, including iron, copper, gold, silver, magnesium, tungsten, and sulfur, together with a large supply of natural resources for use in the construction industry.

Indian communities have traditionally made use of the medicinal properties of several native plants, also using them for food and for weaving. There is potential for commercial use in the wide variety of plant life found in Baja California: 211 species found in the state have been identified as exploitable, 47 of them for human consumption, 29 for medicinal purposes, 10 for forage, and others for industrial use.

What transformed the economic base and brought many people to the state, beginning in the middle of the twentieth century, was the *maquiladoras*—assembly plants for consumer products of all kinds whose components have generally been made elsewhere, including in the countries to which the assembled final product is destined. Low labor costs keep down the prices of products that feed U.S. consumerism. The maquiladoras arose in the wake of the U.S. *bracero* program that once allowed Mexican guest workers to take jobs across the border on a temporary basis; when that program was ended, in the mid-1960s, the industrial development of border areas took off. The maquiladoras have been controversial, attracting criticism for their treatment of workers, especially women, but their products have been enthusiastically embraced by people in the United States and elsewhere. The maquiladora industry has recently faced increased competition from low-cost labor in Asian countries, especially China.

In border areas, there is also a lively trade in artifacts of all kinds, ranging from traditional products such as baskets and straw hats to spin-offs from U.S. television series such as *The Simpsons* and pirated copies of movies. Furthermore, there is a constant traffic in humans and drugs across the border. Since this and many other parts of Mexican economic activity are informal, even illegal, there are no reliable statistics on such areas of the economy. The principal formal economic activities are described below by municipality.

In Mexicali, metal goods such as parts for building, trailers and truck boxes, doors and metallic curtains, boilers, nails and staples, vehicle parts, and agricultural equipment are an important economic segment, along with repairs of metal products, for instance for rail systems. Cotton-based products of all kinds, such as textiles, threads, and cotton wool, plus printed and dyed cotton garments, are another major industry. Agriculturally related activities include vegetable and fruit packing, drying of fruits, and the production of canned foods. There is also aquaculture of shellfish and fish.

Tijuana is the main area for the maquiladoras, which assemble, *inter alia*, goods for the medical profession, tools, car parts, and consumer electronics and appliances. Furniture, structural metals, and electronic components are also produced.

Tomatoes and potatoes figure prominently in agricultural production in Ensenada, along with food packing, preparation of frozen and canned foods for export, and wine production. There is aquaculture, as in Mexicali, together with the cultivation of algae. Smoked and dried fish are also prepared.

Tecate is another area of maquiladoras, assembling or producing much the same items as Tijuana, although with more plastics.

The contribution of tourism to the Baja California economy is significant, thanks to the natural attractions of the state, not least its many beaches. Ensenada is one of the most important tourist areas. Some 85 percent of Baja's tourists come from the United States.

Although there are huge disparities between individuals, the average level of prosperity in the state is high by comparison to the rest of Mexico, as is the case in the northern states in general.

Arts

Baja California is more of a recreational state than one distinguished by its range of cultural activities. However, some border writers have emerged in recent decades, among them **Luis Humberto Crosthwaite** (1962–), one of the most important to come to prominence in the 1980s. He has written novels and stories and also collaborated in theater adaptations. Similarly, **Rosina Conde** (1954–) is a successful woman writer who has worked in those same genres, as well as in poetry; she is also a jazz singer.

Baja California, like other border states, is particularly associated with *norteño* music, a style that shows signs of the influence of musical traditions (the use of the accordion, for example, and of genres such as the waltz and the polka) from the time when the southwestern United States belonged to Mexico and immigrants came from places like Germany and Czechoslovakia. The key element in the repertoire of modern norteño bands is the *corrido*, a narrative ballad genre whose content may be resolutely Mexican (after all, corridos often tell of the exploits of Revolutionary leaders) but whose formal origins can be traced back to medieval Spain. A border subgenre of the corrido has developed in recent years: the *narcocorrido*, in which the Revolutionary leaders are replaced by drug dealers. A related subgenre in film has developed: the *narcofilm*. Indigenous songs, such as they are, may be unaccompanied, or accompanied by the *sonaja*, a type of rattle.

Local crafts are not especially varied or numerous, but there are Indian artifacts made with shells and snails, and there is a tradition of basketry.

A book festival, the Feria del Libro Nezahualcóyotl, is held every November and Video Fest in the same month.

Social Customs

The first Sunday in July is the time for Tecate's *romería*, originally a religious pilgrimage to a shrine but now more of an excuse for general merry-making, processions, and dancing. Expo-Tecate also takes place in July. On December 12, groups converge on Tecate from the surrounding valleys to celebrate the Feast of the Virgin of Guadalupe, Mexico's patroness. There are shows of cowboy skills, dancing, and fireworks.

On September 16, Tijuana has a large-scale celebration of the anniversary of the call for independence from Spain. Mexicali holds its Fiestas del Sol in September, a Wheat Festival, and a beach festival in July. Rosarito has an International Fish Festival in June.

Many events take place in Ensenada: car races, the sighting of gray whales (between December and March), an Expo-Fiesta in October, and a cycle race in April and again in September. Ensenada is also noted for its Carnival celebrations, which attract many people from across the border.

A number of local wine festivals are held in late summer. In March, there is a Taco, Tamal, and Sope Festival. Sporting events include the June Baja 500, a 500-mile tour of the state in which not only cars take part, and the April Newport Beach Regatta, in which typically more than 600 boats sail from Newport Beach, California, to Ensenada.

This young state with such a diverse population does not have an easily identifiable traditional form of dress. In an attempt to remedy this, in 1955 a competition was organized to design one. The winning design was the "Flor de Pitahaya," named after a typical desert plant. For women, this means wearing a white blouse with an oval neck and the image of the *pitahaya* embroidered on it, a red skirt with a fringe around the bottom and embroidered images of cacti. The embroidery is usually in green, pink, or yellow. A headdress suggests the sprouting plant. On festive occasions men wear cotton pants, checked shirts, boots with spurs, and palm hats.

Noteworthy Places

There are archaeological sites at Montevideo and Catarina. Rock paintings exist at the Cañón de Guadalupe in the Sierra de Juárez: stylized representations in red and black of anthropomorphic and geometrical shapes. Significant cave paintings have been found at Vallecitos.

The old missions include Ensenada's Misión de Nuestra Señora de Guadalupe del Norte and Misión de Santo Tomás de Aquino, El Sauzal's Misión de San Francisco de Borja, Colonia Guerrero's Misión de Santo Domingo, San Vicente's Misión de San Vicente Ferrer, San Pedro Mártir's Misión de San Pedro Mártir, and Tijuana's Misión de San Miguel de la Frontera.

Natural attractions include lagoons such as the Chica, the Juárez, the Hardy, and the Salada. Ensenada's dramatic La Bufadora is a cave carved out by the sea. The Parque Nacional Constitución 1857 in Tecate, near Ojos Negros, is set at about 1,500 meters (5,000 feet) and has a natural lake. The Playa Estero, in Ensenada, is one of the main beaches. Many places attract divers and recreational fishermen.

Mexicali has the most important museum (the Museo de la Universidad Autónoma de Baja California); it covers the geology, peoples, and history of the state. Tijuana has an important Centro Cultural. Mexicali's former government palace is of some architectural interest, but dates back only to 1918. Important from a historical standpoint is Real del Castillo in Ensenada, the first capital of the Partido Norte de Baja California. Ensenada has a few civic buildings dating from the nineteenth century: the prison (a former barracks), the Cantina Hussong, and the Customs House. Tecate has an imposing train station.

Cuisine

With so long a coastline, on two flanks, the range of seafood is incomparable; seafood is the basis of a great deal of Baja cuisine. Among the more interesting dishes are *sopa de aleta de tiburón* (shark fin soup) and *abulón en salsa de ostión* (abalone in oyster sauce). There is a traditional "poor man's menu"—a basic fisherman's meal that has now become fashionable among tourists; it consists of shellfish soup, rice, beans, and tortillas. Among regional drinks, *damiana* is an infusion of pre-Hispanic origin, made with local herbs said to have medicinal properties; it may be combined with red wine to make *jeque. Licor de nanche* is a fruit-based alcoholic drink.

Perhaps diversity is the key ingredient in the food of Baja California, given that there have been significant foreign influences upon its cuisine, such as the Russian in the valley of Guadalupe and the Asian (Chinese, for the most part) in Mexicali. In general, it can be said that there are three types of cuisine in Baja: food that shows the historical influences of Spanish missionaries and native Indians; food of the sort that is more widely offered across Mexico; and food of a cosmopolitan kind that shows how far Baja has become an international melting pot. It is said that the Caesar salad was devised in Baja California, in 1925, by one César Cardini.

Sopa de Aleta de Tiburón

Ingredients:

> $1/4$ shark's fin
> 2 pieces crabmeat
> 2 pieces chicken
> Chicken broth
> Cornmeal
> Ginger
> Whites of two eggs
> Salt and pepper

Boil the meat and fish in the broth, seasoning with a little chopped ginger, salt, and pepper. Soak the cornmeal in water, drain, and once the fin is soft, add the cornmeal to the pot so that the soup thickens. Add the egg whites just before serving.

Tortas de Camarón con Nopales (Shrimp and Cactus Fritters)

Ingredients:

> 8 chiles (*mirasol* variety, or similar)
> 4 eggs
> 1 lb. fresh, cleaned shrimp, finely chopped or pureed

$^1/_2$ cup canned nopales
1 clove of garlic
Oil
Flour or cornstarch
Salt

Clean out the chiles, then boil, drain, and blend them together with the garlic and a little salt. Add a little flour to thicken the mixture, and set it aside. In a separate bowl, beat the eggs well and add the shrimp to them. Add the nopales. Heat the oil in a frying pan and then pour in the egg and shrimp mixture, bit by bit, making round, flat shapes; allow these to begin to turn golden, turn over to brown the other side, and then remove them and set them on a platter. Pour the mixture from the blender into the frying pan, bring gently to a boil, then remove from heat. Serve with the tortas on top.

Baja California Sur

State Characteristics

If California can be described as the northern big brother of Mexico's state of Baja California, then perhaps the latter can be called the big brother of the state of Baja California Sur. Baja California (that is, the state comprising the northern half of the peninsula, and for that reason sometimes called Baja California Norte) is much more heavily populated, has a more diverse and vibrant economy, and has been a state for longer than Baja California Sur. The two states have equal shares of the 1,200-kilometer-long (744-mile) peninsular landmass. The Pacific Ocean lies to the west, the Mar de Cortés (otherwise known as the Gulf of California) to the east. Baja California Sur is more remote than Baja California and is known above all for its natural features and as a playground for nature lovers and prosperous Americans.

It was in 1888, under President Porfirio Díaz, that this long peninsula was divided into separate territories of equal area, the dividing line being drawn from just north of the town of Guerrero Negro on the western coast to somewhat south of San Francisquito on the eastern one. Baja California Sur was not upgraded from territory to state until 1974. For all its size (approximately 72,000 square kilometers, about 28,000 square miles, or 3.7 percent of Mexico's total area), its total population by 2005 stood at only 512,170, which was the lowest number for any Mexican state. As for religion, 89 percent of the total population in 2005 was Catholic and 4 percent was Protestant or evangelical.

The capital of the state is La Paz, a city of about 150,000 people. Baja California Sur is administered in five municipalities: Mulegé, Loreto,

Isla Espiritu Santo, an uninhabited 23,380-acre island in the Gulf of California.
(AP Photo/Marco Ugarte)

Comondú, La Paz, and Los Cabos. Six people represent the state in the
National Congress. Baja California Sur has a total of nine newspapers, all
but one published in La Paz; they include *El Sudcaliforniano*, *Diario Peninsular*, *La Extra*, *BCS*, *El Periódico*, and *Tribuna de La Paz*. San José del
Cabo has *Tribuna de Los Cabos*. The university in La Paz is called the Universidad Autónoma, and that city also has an Instituto Tecnológico.

The land consists of coastal plains and mountainous areas. The mountain
range known as the Sierra de la Giganta (average height: 600 meters/2,000
feet) is volcanic in origin, runs parallel with the coast, and has gentle
slopes on its western side and precipitous drops down to the Gulf of California. The plains on the western side (Santa Clara, Berrendo, La Magdalena, Hiray) are on average 40 kilometers (25 miles) wide and are made of
sedimentary rock and limestone. The beaches on the eastern coast are narrow. The highest elevation is 2,080 meters (6,864 feet), in the Sierra La Laguna. There are some islands on the Pacific side (the main ones are
Natividad, Magdalena, and Santa Margarita) and many more on the gulf
side. The peninsula has a central desert, another known as the Vizcaíno Desert, and more plains at Los Cabos in the south.

Only occasionally, in the rainy season, do the streams of Baja California
Sur become rivers and flow with any strength, most of them into the Pacific; examples are the San Benito, the San Miguel, and the longer San Ignacio. The climate is for the most part dry and desertlike, with summer
maxima of 40°C (104°F) and winter minima of 0°C (32°F). Only in the Los

Cabos region is the climate semihumid. On the plains and in the desert areas, thistles, mesquite, and cacti are prevalent; in the hills, there are pines and oaks. Terrestrial fauna include deer, wild sheep, and mountain cats, and there is a variety of migratory birds; the rich sea life includes gray whales, seals, and dolphins. There are a number of conservation areas, for example, at Bahía Sebastían Vizcaíno, Laguna San Ignacio, Sierra La Laguna, Ojo de Liebre, and the islands of the Gulf of California.

Cultural Groups and Languages

The indigenous peoples who inhabited this part of the peninsula were the Pericués in its southern part, the Guaycuras in the middle, and the Cochimíes in the north. These people were hunters, gatherers, and fishers and left no significant structures. Their provenance is not very clear. It has been estimated that there were some 40,000 of them prior to the arrival of the Spaniards, but in the present day only a handful of Cochimí people survive around the border between the two peninsular states. The languages of these peoples have practically disappeared. According to the 2005 census, 7,095 people, 1.6 percent of the population over five years of age, spoke an indigenous language. However, these were overwhelmingly speakers of Náhuatl, Zapotec, and Mixtec, languages brought in by much later immigrants from other parts of the country.

History

The history of Baja California Sur, at least until well into the nineteenth century, is a history shared with the northern half of the peninsula—essentially a history of the Catholic missions.

Prior to the arrival of the Spaniards, the Pericués, the Guaycuras, and the Cochimíes were the three principal groups that had become established in the peninsula; the Cochimíes were in the more northerly parts of it, the Guaycuras in the middle, and the Pericués in the south. The exploration of the Californias by Spain was fueled by the typical factors behind that country's colonization of the Americas. The Spaniards dreamed of exotic lands, cities of gold, and strange beings. Spain wanted to find new trade routes to the Orient, and many individuals were greedy for wealth; it was also intent on converting the natives to Christianity. The very name of California speaks of a Quixotic quest: the name comes from an early sixteenth-century novel of chivalry by Garcí Ordóñez de Montalvo, published in Spain and entitled *Las sergas de Esplandián*, in which the hero comes across an island called California, close to paradise.

Following the Conquest of Mexico, the conquistador Hernán Cortés sent expeditions to explore the Pacific, known at the time as the Mar del Sur (Southern Sea). As part of the second of these expeditions, **Fortún Jiménez de Bertadoño** (?–?) made his way to an island which he dubbed

Santa Cruz (Holy Cross), in the bay of La Paz; he and others were killed by Indians, but men who returned from that second expedition told enticing tales of pearls, and so a year later Cortés himself headed a third expedition, in the course of which he landed at what is now La Paz itself (the present-day capital of the state), though he gave it the name Puerto y Bahía de la Santa Cruz. While he was not the first European to set foot on Baja California, Cortés is generally credited with the foundation of the state, and the date of his arrival is still celebrated as such in Baja California Sur.

Although Cortés's intention in 1535 had been to settle the land, faced with such an inhospitable, uncultivable terrain, his expedition turned back, leaving Francisco de Ulloa behind in command of thirty men, with twelve horses and sufficient provisions for a further ten months; however, even these people were called back by the viceroy before a year had passed. The last expedition sent by Cortés was in 1539, and again Ulloa was in command; this time, however, the aim was not to settle so much as to explore. And so the process continued in ensuing years, officially and unofficially, mapping the lands and searching for riches.

The Viceroyalty of New Spain was responsible not only for American territories but also for the Philippines, and the Californian coastal ports were to become important stopping points on the route from Acapulco to Manila. Settlement really began in the late seventeenth century. In 1697, the viceroy authorized two Jesuits, **Juan María de Salvatierra** (1648–1717) and **Eusebio Francisco Kino** (1644–1711), who was also a geographer, to gather the necessary military support and set up missions in California. They were told they could do these things if they found private funds to support them and no cost would fall upon either the Society of Jesus or the viceroy, the representative of the Crown: Spain had more pressing concerns to attend to, and it did not wish to commit financial resources to the development of an area that seemed to promise little in return. With the help of Father **Juan de Ugarte** (1662–1730), Salvatierra raised the money (it became known as the "Fondo Piadoso," the Pious Fund) to finance the establishment of the Californian missions. Salvatierra set out to found the first of them, which he called Nuestra Señora de Loreto, and which for a long time thereafter would effectively be the capital of California. On the instructions of King Philip V, Salvatierra also wrote a history of the territory.

The Spaniards' goal was to "reduce" the scattered Indians—to wean them away from their lifestyle and put them in settlements where they would cultivate the land, in the European style; two harvests were anticipated, one of the fruits of newly established agricultural practices and the other of Indian souls. Future efforts were concentrated on finding suitable sites for the missions, the prime prerequisite being a reliable natural supply of water. The early part of the eighteenth century saw the establishment of Santa Rosalía Mulegé, San Juan Malibat, San José de Comondú, and, a little later, La Purísima Concepción Cadegomó; the hybrid names of these missions reflect the imposition of Catholicism on the Indians. Salvatierra's attempts at dealing with the Indians to the south (the Guaycuras and the Pericués) were slower to bear fruit, the mission of La Paz being founded in 1720. Beginning in 1734, there was a significant Pericué rebellion that cost a substantial number of Spanish lives and hindered progress in the development of the missions, but in the longer term more were established. By the time Charles III's royal decree expelling the Jesuits from Spanish America was made known in 1767, there were fourteen active missions in the Californias; the Jesuits in them gathered at Loreto, and by 1768 they had gone.

Their work was now entrusted to the Franciscan order, under Father Junípero Serra. However, the Franciscans enjoyed less independence with regard to the administration of the missions than had the Jesuits, for there was now to be a regional and military governor, representing New Spain, and the cultivable lands were to be managed by soldiers. The only mission set up by the Franciscans in what is now Baja California was San Fernando Velicatá (1769), a staging post on the way to Alta California, where Serra had already established the Mission of San Diego. Pressures in favor of civilian settlement and administration of the Californias increased, and there was a decline in the Indian population in some missions, due primarily to smallpox and measles. It was proving logistically difficult for the Franciscans to handle missions scattered over so vast a territory. So it was that the Franciscans voluntarily relinquished responsibility for Baja California and the Dominicans took their place, founding their first mission, Rosario Viñadacó, in 1774. Among those that were established in the following years, San Vicente Ferrer (founded in 1780) deserves a mention, since it became the base from which late-eighteenth- and early-nineteenth-century explorations were launched.

In 1804, political control was divided: the colony of California was split into two divisions, Alta (Upper) and Baja (Lower), the dividing line between the two being the Arroyo del Rosario, which separated the Franciscan missions of the north from the Dominican ones of the south. Due to the fact that supplies from the south could not be relied upon, a lively contraband trade developed during this period, with English, Russian, and U.S. ships taking part. Pressures to secularize the missions continued, but in the border area the change was slow to happen, and since the Church had control of the best land in that area, settlers headed for Alta California, which was quicker to change and more fertile. Nineteenth-century efforts in Mexico to reduce Church privileges met with mixed success, but eventually the missions became secular townships.

The movement in favor of independence from Spain (beginning around 1810) did not greatly affect the two Californias; due perhaps to their remoteness, they remained under Spanish control until 1822 and then fell in line as part of Iturbide's independent empire and were designated as territories. Loreto was destroyed by fire in 1830, and at that time La Paz was made the new capital. In 1846, with the country at war with the United States, Alta California was invaded and Monterrey, San Francisco, and San Diego were lost. Following the Treaty of Guadalupe Hidalgo in 1848, there was peace with the United States, but Mexico had to cede (Alta) California and other lands to its opponent. A few years later, in 1853, William Walker took La Paz and other areas in Baja California but he was defeated in Sonora and withdrew to the north.

During Mexico's national War of Reform (1858–1860) liberal forces took La Paz, and conservatives opposed to the reform movement appealed to France for help, emphasizing their support for Maximilian, the Austrian prince sent to rule Mexico by France. But republican forces then reasserted their control over the peninsula, and it continued in opposition to Maximilian's government until the end of French Intervention.

Under Porfirio Díaz, concessions to foreign companies put large amounts of land under foreign control but also encouraged industrial expansion and increased communications. One company that availed itself of these opportunities was a French mining concern that set up operations under the name of El Boleo in the region that is now known as Santa Rosalía; another was a U.S. company called El Progreso, at El Triunfo. It was Díaz who divided the peninsula that had previously been known simply as Baja California into two separate territories.

Alejandro Allison, Ignacio Bañuelos (d. 1959), and Manuel José Quijada were active in the increasing opposition to the longtime authoritarian president, Díaz. Bañuelos founded a daily newspaper called *Eco de California* and came to be regarded as the doyen of journalists in the territory. Soon the Revolution would begin. North of the border, the Flores Magón brothers, who were prominent advocates of change who had been publishing their own opposition newspaper from exile in the United States, issued a call to arms in 1910 that led to a confrontation with the authorities of Baja California and, for a while, the occupation of Tijuana and Ensenada. Their preferred candidate for president was Francisco Madero.

In 1911, Madero was indeed elected president of Mexico, only to be deposed two years later in a coup by Victoriano Huerta. In opposition to Huerta, an action committee gathered in La Paz; led by Félix Ortega, troops defeated federal forces and returned victorious to La Paz in 1914. In 1915, Carranza made Urbano Angulo the chief political officer of Baja California.

The construction of a transpeninsular highway began in the 1930s, and at that time areas such as Los Planes, the Valle de Santo Domingo, and the Valle de Vizcaíno were settled and developed. Educational opportunities began to improve, as did local services (e.g., the water supply) and sea routes to other parts of the country. As previously noted, the state of Baja California Sur was created in 1974, more than twenty years after its northern sibling. La Paz, Comondú, and Mulegé were the first three municipalities to be established in Baja California Sur, the other two being created in the early 1980s.

Economy

Nowadays, the most profitable crops are wheat, cotton, and chickpeas, which together account for some 70 percent of agricultural production.

Desert.

Other crops include grapes, citrus fruit, sugarcane, and tomatoes. The natural water supply has been overextended by agricultural activity. The rearing of animals is widespread but not intensive, being again very limited by the water supply and the poor quality of pastureland. Naturally, there is a long and strong fishing tradition; fishing became very significant for the state's economy from about the 1940s, encouraged by the federal government and by the organization of fishermen into cooperatives, operating particularly in the northwestern Pacific coastal areas and exploiting upmarket species such as abalone, lobster, and tuna. Fish farming (of oysters, shrimp, and clams, in particular) has become significant more recently. There are about 220,000 hectares (543,400 acres) of protected waters.

In general, the economy has relied heavily on the use of the state's natural resources, exporting some of these for industrial use elsewhere. Forestry has been limited by climate, and wood products have played only a relatively minor part in the economy, but the same cannot be said of minerals. However, distances and difficulties with the transportation of materials, combined with the low level of local demand from the small local population, have not encouraged industrial growth in Baja California Sur. Many goods are imported, and not only from other parts of Mexico, and this has led to attempts to restrict imports to essential items. Tourism, on the other hand, is very important and growing. There are three main tourist areas: the northern area runs from Guerrero Negro to Ciudad Constitución, the central one from La Paz to Todos Santos, and the southern one from Los Barriles to Cabo San Lucas, at the tip of the peninsula.

Arts

There are local traditions of leatherwork, basket weaving, and decorative objects made with seashells. More practically, fishing nets are also produced.

During the second half of the nineteenth century, the popular music of the northern states was influenced by the arrival of immigrants from Germany and Eastern Europe. Prior to that time, the standard instruments used in popular festivities had been the guitar and the violin. To these were added the accordion and a large, twelve-string derivative of the guitar called the *bajo sexto*. Similarly, new dance forms such as the polka became popular. Simple narrative ballads known as *corridos* were given a boost by the Revolution, which provided colorful people such as Pancho Villa to sing about and their popularity soon extended over much of the country.

One consequence of the fusion of new musical instruments and genres with more traditional ones was the new, northern style known as *norteño*. The related *banda*, as its name indicates, is brass based. It usually involves woodwind and percussion also, and a signature instrument is the *tambora*, a type of bass drum that provides the insistent rhythmic drive. Another common instrument is the *redova*. The ensembles are relatively large, perhaps of fifteen people. The repertoire for norteño and banda ensembles is both instrumental and vocal, and usually ranges over *canciones rancheras*, corridos, *cumbias*, waltzes, polkas, and *boleros*. Electronic music has also been entering the mixture. Among popular traditional dances of the kind performed at festivities are the *conejo*, *apasionado*, *chaverán*, *yuca*, *cuera*, *calabazas*, and *tupé*.

In so young and sparsely populated a state, with only one town of any real size, it is not easy to identify notable cultural figures apart from those associated with the state's historical development. Cultural activities derive primarily from the importance of the environment, especially the sea, and the role of tourism. For example, there are many visual artists, foreigners who have taken up residence or spend long periods in the state. In the field of education, **Rosaura Zapata** (1876–1963) was a schoolteacher who organized the first kindergarten in Mexico and went on to help found the National Association for Preschool Education, while **Jesús Castro Agúndez** (1906–1984), also a teacher, wrote about the state and did much to foment education locally.

Social Customs

Carnival is a major event for La Paz, with folk dancing, allegorical floats, music of all kinds, masked balls, and fireworks. Residents decorate the local boats suggestively and hold various competitions. The Fiestas de la Pitahaya take place in July, and the Fiestas de la Fundación de la Ciudad de La Paz are in May. Other events include the Fiestas Santorales, the Feria del Libro, Expo-Comondú, the Cabo San Lucas Fishing Festival, and in October, the Fiesta de la Fundación de Loreto. Among the many religious celebrations is March 19 in San José del Cabo, which brings the Festival del Día del Señor San José, the town's patron saint, with the usual mixture of processions, dancing, cockfights, and merrymaking.

In the absence of any particular traditional dress, an official competition organized in 1955 led to the choice of the "Flor de Pitahaya" design of dress for festive occasions, as in the state of Baja California. The *pitahaya* is a common desert plant. For the woman the costume consists of a white blouse with an oval neck, with the image of the *pitahaya* embroidered on it, a red skirt with a fringe around the hem and embroidered images of cactuses. The embroidery is usually in green, pink, or yellow. The shape of the headdress suggests the sprouting plant. At festivities, men wear cotton pants, checked shirts, boots with spurs, and palm hats.

Noteworthy Places

Evidence of early settlement, such as utensils, trinkets, rock paintings, and arrowheads, has been found at Comondú, Las Palmas, and Concheros. There are spectacular rock paintings, perhaps 10,000 years old, over an area of about 12 square kilometers (5 square miles) in the canyons of the Sierra de San Francisco. Now designated by UNESCO as a World Heritage site, this area and its riches were first documented by Jesuit missionaries during the eighteenth century, after which they were largely ignored for some two hundred years. The paintings were in Cochimí territory, yet these Indians did not claim to have made them, attributing them instead to a race of giants from the north; whatever their origin, they provide ample evidence of prehistoric occupation by hunters and gatherers. In the 1960s, the U.S. mystery writer Erle Stanley Gardner was instrumental in publicizing the paintings' existence, having first sighted them from a helicopter. Thereafter they became increasingly visited, and anything portable was plundered from them. Remote and difficult to access, they became a source of income for local ranchers, who still serve as guides to them. The paintings represent a variety of animals (for example, pumas, deer, mountain lions, snakes, and sharks) in dynamic silhouettes, often being hunted, while human figures are portrayed face-on and in stylized fashion. Some of the paintings are over 4 meters (13 feet) high. Visitors have remarked on their scale, comparing them to murals, and also on the vividness of their colors, and yet those characteristics are in jeopardy: not only has the number of visitors increased, but erosion—the very natural processes that created these places—is threatening the paintings. Nowadays, the federal and state governments are collaborating with local interests to manage the number of visitors and implement conservation strategies.

The most important of the surviving mission buildings are those of Loreto, San José del Cabo, and San Javier, the last of these being the most impressive. The cathedral at La Paz is also noteworthy. La Paz and Loreto both have archaeological museums, and one in Mulegé is housed in a former prison. The Palacio Municipal in La Paz, neoclassical in style, dates from 1899. Among religious buildings, the capital boasts the Jesuit Misión de Nuestra Señora de la Paz, set on a hill overlooking the sea; its original 1720 structure, however, was destroyed by a hurricane and it was rebuilt in 1861 by the Dominicans. A dramatically original church was designed in 1887 and transported from Belgium to Mexico in 1895 by Gustav Eiffel, the man who designed the famous tower in Paris. This church, the Templo de Santa Barbara, in Mulegé, is built of steel sections about 30 meters (100 feet) long, and has the shape of a whale's tail.

There are countless beaches and natural attractions; much of the land is unspoiled. Bahía Concepción is an example of a major tourist area.

Cuisine

Seafood is the cornerstone of the state cuisine; some varieties used in the peninsula are not found in the cooking of other parts of the republic. There is much use of clams, and many types of fish are put in tacos. Shrimp may be deep-fried or put in tamales. At a more refined level, there are lobster and smoked marlin. Oregano and *damiana* are common herbal seasonings. Examples of typical savory food are *almejas empanizadas* (breaded clams) and *machaca* (salt beef flavored with herbs and sometimes served with egg). Flour tortillas are widely used. Sweets often involve the use of dates and papayas. *Guayabate, mangate,* and *pitahayate* are typical of the San Bartolo region; these are like jellies. In areas where sugarcane is grown, they make *panocha de gajo, alfeñique,* and *piloncillo.* Santa Rosalía is famous for its breads and pastries. Drinks include wine and others made from fruits and herbs.

Tacos de Baja California Sur

Ingredients:

$1/4$ cabbage, finely chopped
2 grated carrots
Black pepper
Mayonnaise
3 small white onions, two finely chopped, the other cut into thin slices
3 medium tomatoes, peeled and chopped
3 *serrano* chiles, cleaned and diced
$1/2$ cup chopped cilantro
Juice of 3 limes
Salt

2 lb. fresh fish fillet
Flour
A little finely chopped garlic
2 cups milk
1 egg
Tortillas

First prepare the salad, mixing together the cabbage, carrots, mayonnaise, and some black pepper. Set it aside and then make the sauce by mixing the chopped onion, tomatoes, chiles, and cilantro together and seasoning with salt and a third of the lime juice. Set aside. Then mix together the finely sliced onion, the juice of two of the limes, and some salt and pepper and let them stand for about 15 minutes. Sprinkle flour on the fish. Beat some flour into the egg, together with the milk and the garlic. Coat the fish in the beaten mixture and fry until golden, then drain on paper towels. Serve everything with folded warm tortillas. Serves six.

Sopa Fría de Melón y Papas

Ingredients:

1 cantaloupe
1 and $1/2$ cups potato (peeled, boiled, and diced)
1 cup half-and-half, or a mixture of cream and milk
$1/2$ cup dry sherry or white wine
Salt and pepper to taste
1 lime
Mint leaves or ground nutmeg, as preferred

This is a chilled soup. First wash the melon, then halve it so that each half can serve as a bowl. Scoop out the flesh and blend it with the diced potatoes and the half-and-half. Add the wine or sherry, season with a little salt and pepper and stir, then leave the mixture in the refrigerator for at least an hour. Once it is thoroughly chilled, add a generous squeeze of lime. Serve the soup in the melon halves, garnishing each serving with a thin slice of lime and a sprinkle of nutmeg or chopped mint leaves.

Campeche

State Characteristics

On the coast of the Gulf of Mexico, moving southwest along the Yucatán Peninsula, lies the state of Campeche. Southwest of it lies Tabasco, while Quintana Roo lies to its east. To the south, Campeche shares a border with Guatemala. The name of the state is of Mayan origin. The Mayas dominated the region, known to them as *Ah Kim Pech* ("The Place of the Snakes and Ticks"), prior to the advent of the Spaniards in the early sixteenth century. Consequently there are many Mayan ruins.

The city of Campeche (population 211,671, according to the official 2005 figures) is the state's capital. The Spaniards first occupied the area in 1517, and they formally founded the city of Campeche in 1540, using it thereafter as a base for explorations and attacks on the Mayan people during the early colonial period. In later years, Campeche became a haunt for pirates.

The second largest city is now Ciudad del Carmen (population 154,197), another port. There are eleven *municipios* in the state; from north to south and west to east, they are Calkiní, Hecelchakán, Tenabo, Campeche, Hopelchén, Champotón, Carmen, Escárcega, Calakmul, Palizada, and Candelaria.

The state covers 56,860 square kilometers (22,175 square miles), which amounts to 2.6 percent of Mexico's total area. In 2005, the total state population was 754,730, one of the lowest populations of all states, and also at a very low population density. The people of Campeche have six elected representatives in the National Congress. The average age of the 2005 population was in the mid-twenties; it has been estimated that the population of the state of Campeche will exceed a million by 2010. As has occurred in other southern states with significant indigenous populations, Catholicism has been losing ground to Protestant sects, particularly evangelicals. About 70 percent of Campeche is Catholic, according to the 2005 survey. The state has five newspapers: *Tribuna, El Sur, Novedades, Crónica*, and *Expreso*. There are two universities.

Much of the state consists of hot, humid, and unhealthy lowlands. Rainfall can be heavy in some areas, predominantly in the summer and early autumn. In drier seasons, winds from the east and southeast are noticeable, but for the most part the prevailing breezes are from the northeast. There are occasional hurricanes. Averages for rainfall vary, from 900 millimeters (35 inches) a year in the northern regions, close to Yucatán, up to 2000 millimeters (79 inches) in the southwest, where the land supports more abundant vegetation. The driest municipios are Calkiní, Hecelchakán, Tenabo, Campeche, and the northern part of Hopelchén. The rest of Hopelchén is more humid, as are Champotón, and most of Escárcega and Carmen; the remaining areas are even more tropical. About two-thirds of the state is forested. There are four ecosystems: forest, savannah, coastal, and marine.

The highest elevations are close to the borders with Guatemala and Quintana Roo; in the Zoh Laguna area stand hills called the Cerro Champerico, Cerro de los Chinos, Cerro el Ramonal, Cerro el Doce, and Cerro el Gavilán, all of which are more than 200 meters (650 feet) high; the highest is Champerico, at 390 meters (1,287 feet). These hills are separated by extensive flat areas, like a low-lying *meseta*. The mean temperature for the state at large is 26°C (79°F), with average maxima of 36°C (97°F) and minima of 17°C (63°F).

There are 404 kilometers (250 miles) of coastline, with some notable cliffs and bays. Rivers are most numerous in the southern and southwestern areas; in the north, the limestone table allows rapid drainage of surface water, but there are large natural wells, called *cenotes*. The most important of the southern river basins is that of the Grijalva-Usumacinta system, followed by the Candelaria, the Chumpún, and the Mamantel. Some rivers meander a great deal and are inclined to divide or change course. Another feature is the Laguna de Términos and its group of lagoons, which are of relatively recent formation, having been caused by sedimentary barriers left by rivers. Near Campeche City, there are some lakes that appear only during the rainy season, known locally as *aguadas*.

Trees naturally vary with altitude and climate, from the evergreens of higher elevations, such as cedar, down to *caoba* (mahogany), *palo de tinte* (dyewood), logwood (sometimes called *campeche*), and many others at lower elevations. Palms and mangroves grow on the coast. There is a wide range of medicinal and aromatic plants, and there are numerous fruit trees, including *guanábana* and *saramuyo* (varieties of custard apple), *zapote* (which goes by many names in Latin America and by "naseberry," among others, in English), *mamey* (somewhat like an apricot), *capulín* (a type of cherry), and *nance* (a fruit long consumed by Indian peoples in southern Mexico and Central America: *Byrsonima crassifolia*). Vegetables include yucca and *chaya* (tree spinach). Orchids are plentiful, both wild and cultivated.

Fauna has suffered in Campeche, as in other places where unbridled deforestation has taken place and more and more land has been given over to grazing. Nonetheless, some two-thirds of the state has forest. Another attack on wildlife has come in the form of overhunting; species such as deer and some of the big cats have been much affected. One response to the pressure on animals was the creation of the Calakmul Biosphere Reserve. The richness of fauna and flora is still impressive. In the coastal region, in addition to the usual aquatic birds—gulls, ducks, herons, pelicans—one finds lizards, manatees, turtles, and snakes. Coastal waters are home to clams, shrimp, octopuses, sharks, and many other fish. In the mountains to the north and east of the state, there are deer, armadillos, rodents, snakes, and birds such as partridge and quail. The tropical jungle regions of the central and southern parts of the state are home to monkeys, big cats, wild boars, pheasants, cockatoos and parrots, many snakes, and not a few insects. In the southwest, where there are a number of rivers, the freshwater environment supports species such as the *pejelagarto* (gar), *mojarra* (bream), *bobo* (beardfish), and alligator and several types of turtle. Where salt and freshwater mix, the variety of wildlife is especially great: bass, pompano, snapper, dogfish, and all sorts of shellfish, together with dolphins, nutrias, manatees, pelicans, and storks, to name a few.

Campeche was much changed by the discovery, in the 1970s, of oil reserves in the Gulf; this suddenly made the state truly important as a contributor to the national economy. Prior to that, the state's economy had relied mainly on forestry and agriculture.

Cultural Groups and Languages

The number of speakers of Indian languages, according to the 2005 census, was 89,084 (13.3 percent of Campeche's total population). Most of the people above the age of five who speak indigenous languages were speakers of Mayan (69,249 people) or Chol (9,119). While the Indian language element in Campeche is strong by comparison with many Mexican states, it falls well below the level of neighboring Yucatán, where Indian-language speakers exceed a third of the total state population.

Something like 95 percent of the speakers of Indian languages in Campeche are thought to speak Spanish also. The number of immigrant Indians from Guatemala was significant in the last decades of the twentieth century, due to political troubles in that country; in 1984 alone, it is estimated that 13,000 came into Campeche. However, some of these immigrants later returned to Guatemala following an improvement in the situation there. (For a fuller illustration of this phenomenon in a comparable border state, and of the difficulties of classification, see the chapter on Chiapas.) The arrival of people of African origin from the islands of the Caribbean, whether as escapees or as imported workers, added a new element to the racial mix in most states bordering the Gulf. Such has been the intermingling of races since then that the black contribution to the population is not very apparent in modern Campeche; it is less noticeable, for example, than in Veracruz.

History

The early history of Campeche cannot be separated from that of the Yucatán Peninsula as a whole. The second Mayan empire (roughly from AD 300 to 900), which led to the establishment of many important cities in the peninsula, had fallen under the influence of the Toltecs, and the Liga de Mayapán (League of Mayapán) had disintegrated into a number of fiefdoms by the time the Spaniards arrived.

Francisco Hernández de Córdoba discovered the small settlement of Ah Kim Pech in March 1517. In 1518, another Spanish expedition passed through, led by Juan de Grijalva. Previous Spanish expeditions had touched on the coast of the Yucatán Peninsula, leaving two men shipwrecked, Jerónimo de Aguilar and Gonzalo Guerrero, who had become integrated into Mayan civilization. Guerrero married the daughter of a tribal chief, and their son was the first officially recorded *mestizo*, though he was not destined to be the most famous and the most symbolic one—that honor was to be accorded to the son of Hernán Cortés and his Indian interpreter and mistress Malintzin (Malinche). Aguilar encountered and helped Cortés when the latter headed the expedition to conquer Mexico in 1519. Cortés went on to found Veracruz and thence to invade the Aztec capital, Tenochtitlán.

The task of bringing Yucatán under Spanish control was left to Francisco de Montejo, who, beginning in 1527, met with such resistance from the natives that he fled, to return three years later and fail once again. However, his third attempt, in 1537, was successful, and he proceeded to found the cities of Campeche and Mérida (in 1540 and 1542, respectively). Montejo also introduced the cultivation of sugarcane into Campeche.

Determined to bring the natives to the Catholic faith, the Franciscans established more than thirty convents in the area. But the Indians were rebellious. Their revolts during the colonial period consolidated Yucatán's reputation as a fierce and indomitable region, something of a thorn in the side of colonial Spain. A remarkable early figure who has entered Campeche's mythology was **José Jacinto Uc de los Santos Canek** (d. 1761), a Mayan in the service of the friars in Campeche. From them, Canek acquired a good education, but this did nothing to reduce his loathing of the invaders. Once expelled from the religious order, he began to appear at local festivities and celebrations, where he would use his historical knowledge and bilingual skills to drum up support for violent rebellion. In 1761, Canek was taken prisoner by the Spaniards and sentenced to death.

He was hung, drawn, and quartered, after which his body was burned in Mérida's main square. He thus became a symbolic figure for Mayan resistance over the centuries.

Apart from Indian rebellions, the Spaniards had to face the fact that since Campeche was a strategic port through which much trade passed in colonial times, it was of interest to other countries. Campeche was repeatedly attacked by rival countries and by pirates and corsairs such as Sir Francis Drake, Henry Morgan, Laurent Graff, and Diego el Mulato. The now famous fortifications around the city demonstrate Spain's need to protect Campeche not only against other European nations and pirates but also against Indians.

Yucatán did not participate in the independence movement of 1810, since by that time the Spanish authorities had the region under their control. However, in 1821, under the Plan of Iguala, Yucatán did become part of the newly independent Mexico, and Campeche became one of the peninsula's five major seats of government. **Pedro Sáinz de Baranda y Borreyro** (1787–1845) was a local son, born in Campeche in 1787, who distinguished himself during the war of independence. He had made his name initially in the navy, starting at eleven years of age as a cabin boy, had been wounded while fighting on behalf of Spain at Trafalgar, and had risen to high rank, holding a number of commands. Sáinz de Baranda was elected a member of the monarchic congress in 1820 and then as a substitute deputy to the republic's first national congress. With Spain still trying to reaffirm its control of Mexico and occupying the Fortress of San Juan de Ulúa, Sáinz de Baranda organized a naval blockade that forced the Spaniards to surrender, and in doing so he effectively put an end to Spanish power in Mexico.

The state of Yucatán was formally established under the 1824 Constitution. In 1857, civil war divided Campeche from Yucatán, and Campeche became a region in its own right, with the city of Campeche as its capital. As was the case almost everywhere in Mexico, the nineteenth century was turbulent, with many changes of ruler, much rivalry between federalists and centrists, and trouble with the French and the United States. Beginning in 1847, Yucatán saw the so-called Caste Wars, an indigenous rebellion that destroyed many towns and, somewhat ironically, encouraged the governor, Manuel Barbachano, to seek help from Mexico City and so reinforce ties with the center.

In the mid-nineteenth century, the drive toward complete independence on the part of Yucatán itself was strong, but Campeche was more inclined to remain part of the Mexican republic. There were many who wished Campeche were independent of Yucatán, among them Barbachano. Their separatist movement was quite violent, and at one point in the early 1860s they even occupied Mérida, the capital of Yucatán. The Mexican Congress voted to make Campeche a state in 1863, while Benito Juárez was president of the country. Two years later, the railroad would make its first run through the peninsula, from Mérida to Campeche.

The invasion of Mexico by French troops in 1864 complicated things further. Yucatán sided with the invaders, and Campeche had to decide whether to do the same. The French attacked and eventually overpowered the city of Campeche. Carlota, Emperor Maximilian's wife, visited the city during their short period in power, but prorepublican forces fought back against Maximilian and the French. The conclusion of the French Intervention did not bring peace or stability to Campeche, however: from 1876 to 1910, the state had no fewer than twenty-five different governors.

During the *porfiriato* (1830–1915), Campeche lost Quintana Roo, which had been part of its territory. With the Mexican Revolution imminent, Porfirio Díaz's main rival for the presidency, Francisco Madero, came to Campeche, and soon a supporter of Madero was elected governor of the state. Following the assassination of Madero and some of his supporters, the state rose up in arms (against Victoriano Huerta, then in power in Mexico City), only to be defeated. By 1914, Campeche had a military governor appointed by Venustiano Carranza. This was Joaquín Mucel Acereto, who took steps to give greater powers to the municipios and free *hacienda* laborers from servitude. Another postrevolutionary governor who took positive steps was Angel Castillo Lanz (in office 1923–1931); he introduced legislation to protect historic buildings and places of natural beauty, and he made improvements in educational provision.

Finally, in the late 1930s, President Lázaro Cárdenas separated Campeche from Quintana Roo once and for all. The latter, however, would not achieve the full status of a state until 1974; there was opposition in Campeche to that idea, but the opposition was quelled with promises of industrial and economic development.

Campeche has become one of the most important states for the Mexican economy since the discovery of oil fields off its coast. In 1971, Rudescindo Cantarell, a fisherman, reported that he had seen a 7-kilometer-long (4-mile) oil slick off of the coast near Ciudad del Carmen. A few years later, drilling began (the first rig was called "Chac" in honor of the ancient rain god), and the first platforms were in place by 1979. There has been some local unrest and resistance to the changes that flowed from this discovery; for example, in the mid-1970s there were signs of burgeoning guerrilla activity in the region. But the Mexican government has kept tight control: the strategic and economic importance of Campeche is now such that the central government intervenes in state politics and exerts its powers to a degree that is not usual.

Economy

The colonial system of *encomiendas*, which had granted settlers rights to land and the fruits of Indian labor, effectively enslaving the Indians, led to the development of huge haciendas that were under the control of a small elite and on which the *peones* (laborers), even after independence from Spain, also worked under disadvantageous conditions. By the beginning of the twentieth century, 147 such estates, covering a fifth of the state, were in the hands of just fourteen landowners. Eighty percent of the population was illiterate and only a quarter of eligible children were attending school, which at the time made Campeche number 20 in the national rankings by state.

After the porfiriato, foreign investments slumped, but the key areas of the economy remained under foreign, mostly U.S., control. During the first half of the twentieth century, the economy was based on agriculture and forestry, with some commercial fishing on the coast. Corn, sugarcane, and sisal were the main agricultural products. *Chicle* (latex for chewing gum), began to be exported in 1890, and the first cooperative for its production was set up in 1937, but after about ten years, production trailed off as synthetic substitutes took over. The most lucrative woods were those from which dyes or oils could be extracted, or those that could be used to make furniture, but deforestation at home and political conflict abroad, affecting the main markets, made these activities lose profitability. Sugarcane came to serve only the regional market, whereas sisal production did increase, though not significantly enough to have a major effect on the economy.

The situation, at least as far as the coast was concerned, was transformed after the discovery of the oil reserves in the 1970s. Among other things, the discovery of oil promoted the ugly development of Ciudad del Carmen, a place of overindulged foreigners living in luxurious conditions and served by poor and resentful locals who sometimes wax nostalgic about the days before the oil was found. Oil production figures for 2004 give an idea of the scale and importance of Campeche's production: approximately 850,000 barrels of crude oil, or about 84 percent of national production. Mexico is now a major world producer.

Something like two-thirds of Campeche is still covered with forest. Among the many woods that are highly prized are *ciricote* (*Cordia dodecandra*), *guayacán* (*Guialum sanctum*), and *dzalam* (*Lysiloma bohamensis*). Apart from dyes, oils are extracted from several trees, such as the coconut palm and the *higuerilla* (*Ricinus communis*). Another of the many varieties of palm, the *palma de huano* or *guano*, is used for roofing. Cotton, sisal, and pita fiber are used for textiles and in industry. Within the agricultural sector, one also finds rice, corn, sugarcane, peanuts, chiles, *jamaica* (a hibiscus plant from which a popular infusion is made), beans, tomatoes, squashes, avocados, citrus and many other fruits, and honey (of which Campeche is the nation's third most important producer). About a quarter of the land is used to raise livestock, and only about 3 percent for agriculture. Less than half of the land devoted to raising animals is natural pastureland; the rest has been adapted for that purpose.

Manufacturing has undergone considerable diversification and increase since the onset of the North American Free Trade Agreement in 1992.

Arts

Campeche City's Casa de las Artesanías exemplifies the craftwork produced in the state, including embroidery, textiles, hammocks, articles carved from wood or bull's horns, hats and baskets woven from natural fibers such as palm, jewelry and decorative objects made from shells and coral, and wooden furniture.

Guitars, harps, pipes, drums, maracas, and violins are all commonly used in the state's popular music tradition. The repertoire includes forms that are Spanish in origin: *jaranas*, *sones*, and *seguidillas*, with some rhythmic influence from the Caribbean. The jarana, for example, is a couple dance requiring complicated foot stamping, some of which is specific to particular regions. There is a $6/8$ version (whose origin is Andalusian) with some syncopation and a characteristic emphasis on the second triplet. The $3/4$ version is more like a waltz and has its Spanish roots in Aragón; though for a long time this was only a dance, rhymed words have been sung to it also. The *habanera* is of Caribbean origins and became popular in the nineteenth century. The *danza del cochino* or *cabeza de cochino* is an example of a ritual dance. It involves a complex sort of maypole routine, with paper streamers and an altar on which a pig's head sits with a loaf in its mouth; a child, armed with corn, calls to the pig and directs the proceedings.

In the arts, **Joaquín Clausell** (1866–1935), Mexico's leading Impressionist painter, is the most famous person to have emerged from Campeche. After beginning his education locally, Clausell went on to earn a degree in law in Mexico City. There he became a journalist and wrote for prominent newspapers such as *El Monitor Republicano* and *El Universal* and helped found *El Demócrata*. Like many other intellectuals of his time, he was involved in the opposition to Porfirio Díaz and was imprisoned because of it. In serial form, *El Demócrata* published his novel *Tomóchic*, which was based on a real-life massacre of some rebellious Indians by Díaz's army. This publication led to Clausell and others being incarcerated once more, as also to the closure of the paper. Clausell escaped to the United States and then went to Paris, where he was inspired by the work of Camille Pisarro. In 1906, the Mexican artist Gerardo Murillo (otherwise known as Dr. Atl) included Clausell in an important exhibition of up-and-coming painters, saying that in his art he displayed the same qualities as in his public life: clarity and integrity. Clausell was self-taught. His paintings are characterized by limited palettes, sharp color contrasts, and simplicity; nature is often their subject.

Juan de la Cabada (1899–1986) was a creative writer and a folklorist who achieved some national recognition and was instrumental in promoting the study of Mayan musical traditions. Also important for music and the documentation of local history was **Francisco Alvares Suárez** (1834–1916).

Social Customs

The Purification of the Virgin (February 2) is widely celebrated in the Catholic world, but at that time of year, a township called Hool, in the municipality of Campotón, becomes a special place of pilgrimage for many people. They come to the town church to kiss the raiment of the effigy of the Virgin, which is then taken in a procession to a nearby lake before being returned to her place in the church. Symbolically, the fertility of nature is also being celebrated. Another important religious celebration takes place in July in Ciudad del Carmen, in honor of the Virgen del Carmen. In Campeche, the feast of San Román, in September, has an interesting

Man holds a skull as he cleans the bones of a loved one in the cemetery in Campeche. As part of the local tradition, residents clean and polish the bones of dead loved ones at the end of October in time for the upcoming Day of the Dead celebrations on November 1. (AP Photo/Israel Leal)

history. After the area had been destroyed in early colonial times by a plague of lobsters, which was interpreted as divine retribution, it was decided that a chapel should be built in the hope of warding off any such disasters in future. The choice of a saint to be so revered was made by drawing lots, and a black effigy of Christ was brought over from Europe: thus the celebration becomes the Fiesta del Cristo Negro de San Román. Other fiestas are the "Mini Christmas Eve" (Purísima Concepción) on December 8 in Campeche and Champotón and, around Easter, the Fiesta del Señor de la Salud in Hecelchakán and the Fiesta de Chuiná. Hopelchén holds a Feria de la Miel y del Maíz (Honey and Corn Festival) at about that time.

Campeche is noisy with street vendors touting their wares, rather as was the case in the Europe of the Middle Ages. One unusual but explicable custom is that in the capital it is the men, not the women, who go to market; this custom dates from the time when it was not safe for women to venture out, even during the day.

The traditional women's dress is a mixture of Mayan and Spanish styles and is associated with the custom of "coming out" four times a year, at Carnival time and for the feasts of San Juan, San Román, and La Purísima Concepción. It was the custom of wealthy patronesses to give humbler women complete outfits. Within the walled precinct of Campeche, at least, such outfits consisted of *huipiles*—blouses with dark, boxed embroidery across the neckline, often with floral motifs (onions and squashes)—and from the waist down to the ankles a gathered taffeta skirt with a white petticoat, in the Spanish tradition. The *mantillas* and *pañoletas* of Spain gave way to the use of *rebozos* (shawls). The shoes are flat soled and of patent leather, with white stitching and turned up at the toes in the Moorish style.

Noteworthy Places

The city of Campeche was formally founded in 1540 by Francisco de Montejo, who gave the settlement the name of San Francisco de Campeche. It is a model of city planning that now offers fine examples of architecture from the sixteenth century on. In 1999, the city was designated a World Heritage site by UNESCO. More than a thousand buildings of historical value have been identified.

Campeche is probably best known for its forts and walls, outstanding examples of military architecture of the sixteenth and seventeenth centuries.

The Iglesia del Jesús, in the heart of the city of Campeche, began as a simple chapel with a palm roof and grew into one of the finest examples of sixteenth- and seventeenth-century architecture. In 1685, it was sacked by pirates, its altars were destroyed, and most of its treasures lost, but it still has impressive *retablos*. It is an austere building in the Franciscan tradition, somewhat like a small fortress.

Campeche's cathedral, on the main square, began as a small church, the Iglesia de la Purísima Concepción, in the sixteenth century and was built to mark the foundation of the city; it was extended and remodeled in the eighteenth century. Its façade is flanked by two distinctive towers, and its interior is laid out in a cruciform pattern.

The building referred to as Sáinz de la Barrada's birthplace was at one time or another a prison, a law court, a warehouse, and a royal residence; like other public buildings of the early colonial era, it is also on the main square.

The nineteenth-century mansion known as the birthplace of **Justo Sierra** (1848–1912) was also the place where the Empress Carlota stayed during her visit to Campeche in 1865. Justo Sierra Méndez was a lawyer, writer, and journalist who occupied several important administrative and diplomatic positions at the national and international levels. He was a member of Mexico's Supreme Court, secretary for education and the arts, and ambassador to Spain. In 1948, his complete works were published by the Universidad Autónoma de México.

"Los Portales de San Francisco" is the local name for the Plazuela de San Francisco, an eighteenth-century square that appears to have been built for commerce. The popular name derives from its two long corridors with porticos.

Other places of note in the city include the Arab-influenced Mansión Carvajal; the former Jesuit college that became the Instituto Campechano, then (much modified) the Universidad de Campeche, the Universidad del Sudeste, and finally the Universidad Autónoma de Campeche; and the Alameda Francisco de Paula Toro, Campeche's first public park, dating from the early nineteenth century. Much of the historic center of Campeche has been restored, and parts of the bulwark's house museums.

The principal archaeological sites are Edzná, Dzibilnocac, Hochob, Becán, Chicanná, X'puhil, Hormiguero, Río Bec, and Calakmul. These exemplify six distinctive architectural styles. The Calakmul site lies within the protected area of the Biosphere Reserve, which was established in 1989 and covers about 7,300 hectares (18,000 acres), almost 13 percent of the state. The archaeological site itself covers 113 square kilometers (44 square miles) and is thought to have some 6,000 structures, many of them largely hidden by jungle. It appears that Calakmul was the largest Mayan city of its time.

Cuisine

The cuisine of Campeche is a rich mixture of Mayan, Spanish, and other foreign influences that came via the ports. There is much use of a wide range of fish and shellfish, and local shrimp have a national reputation for quality. *Achiote* (annatto) and the hot *habanero* peppers are common condiments in savory foods, and almonds and vanilla in sweets. As in many places, *tamales* are ubiquitous, usually filled with chicken or pork. Inevitably, Campeche has its own version of the intoxicating liquor *mezcal*, called *ron mezcal*, which is sugar based. There are many fruit drinks, and some made from corn. A good number of households follow the tradition of preparing specific dishes on specific days of the week, for example a stew on Mondays, beef on Thursdays, and, of course, fish on Fridays; for Saturday evenings, the standard dish is *chocolomo* (a meat and mushroom casserole).

Jaibas en Chipachole

Ingredients:

Tomatoes
10 cloves
3 cloves of garlic
1 cinnamon stick
2 dried *chipotle* chiles
Oil
Salt
Pepper
12 whole crabs (cleaned)
5 pints water
About 3 oz. cornmeal (for thickening)
Sprig of *epazote*
Tomato paste

Roast the tomatoes and garlic. Boil and deseed the chiles. Then puree these items in a blender together with some black pepper, the cloves, and the cinnamon. Use a deep pan to fry this mixture in a little oil, then add the crabs and the water. Bring to a boil and add the cornmeal. Reduce heat, season the mixture with salt, add the epazote and the tomato paste, cover, and leave to simmer for about an hour.

Dulce de Papaya (Papaya in Syrup)

Ingredients:

2 lb. papayas
Juice of 1 lime
1 lb. sugar
1 fig leaf
2 tsp limewater (*cal*)

Peel the papaya, reserving the peel. Deseed and cut up the papaya into small pieces, then put them to soak in the limewater for an hour. Boil some water (enough water to submerge the pieces of fruit) in a suitable pot (avoiding tin and lacquered pottery). Drain the papaya and wash off the limewater. Put the papaya in the boiling water, cover, and boil until the fruit is soft. Lift out the fruit and put it in cold water. Drain. Prick the fruit with a fork and squeeze it gently to express excess liquid. Heat 2 cups of this water and add the sugar; once the sugar is dissolved and the mixture is boiling, add the lime juice. Lower the heat and reduce the mixture to the desired thickness. Then add the pieces of papaya and turn the heat up again for a short while before reducing to a simmer. Use the fig leaf as decoration, putting it in the syrup.

Pibipollo

Traditionally, a *pib* is an improvised underground oven. After a hole has been dug out, firewood is laid in it and covered with a layer of stones upon which the food to be cooked is placed. *Pibipollo* (or *muk'bipollos*) is a dish that is traditionally served at the time of Hanal-Pixán, the Day of the Dead. It consists of a huge cornmeal *tamal*, about 20 inches wide and 3 or 4 inches thick, filled with chicken, pork, tomatoes, baby onions, and sometimes beans and flavored with annatto, epazote, and hot chile. The whole tamale is carefully wrapped in banana leaves, tied up with strands of *majagua* (a type of hibiscus), placed in the pib, covered with guava branches, enclosed, and left to cook for several hours, during which time people visit the graves of the dead and socialize with friends and relatives.

Ingredients:

    3 young chickens
    2 lb. pork loin
    20 large, ripe tomatoes
    10 small onions
    Cabbage leaves, lightly cooked
    Epazote
    Banana leaves
    4 lb. cornmeal
    1 lb. lard
    Recado (see Yucatán chapter)
    Salt

Spread recado on the meat. Brown the meat in some of the lard, and then add enough water to cover it. Bring to a boil. Mix some broth from the pot and a little salt into the cornmeal to form a thick paste. Line a large baking dish with banana leaves. Use some of the remaining lard to grease hands before placing a ball of the cornmeal in the middle of the pan and working it out toward the sides. Lay rest of ingredients in the pan, keeping back about six of the tomatoes. Pierce these tomatoes and put them on top of the rest of the pieces of meat, sprinkling with epazote leaves and then adding more broth. Habanero chiles can be added if a truly spicy dish is preferred. Cover with pieces of cabbage leaf. Take a large banana leaf, put a ball of the cornmeal *masa* in it, and press it out to make a large, thick tortilla, big enough to cover all the food. Then fold over the banana leaves that line the pan, so that they cover the whole dish. Cover with foil and bake in the oven at about 300°F, taking care not to burn.

Chiapas

State Characteristics

Tucked away in the southeast, at the bottom of the curve of the Isthmus of Tehuantepec and bordering on Guatemala, is the Estado Libre y Soberano de Chiapas. Clockwise around this state's borders, starting at the Pacific Ocean, are the neighboring states of Oaxaca, Veracruz, and Tabasco.

Chiapas ranks eighth in terms of surface area: its 73,724 square kilometers (28,752 square miles) represent 3.8 percent of Mexico's total area. In terms of population, it ranks seventh: according to figures from the 2005 census, it had 4,255,790 people and a population density of 58 per square kilometer (150 per square mile). Sixteen people represent the state in the National Congress.

The capital of the state is Tuxtla Gutiérrez. There are well over a hundred municipalities; for practical purposes, these can be grouped into nine regions: Centro, Altos, Fronteriza, Frailesca, Norte, Selva, Sierra, Soconusco, and Istmo-Costa. The major towns are Tuxtla Gutiérrez (population 490,445, according to the 2005 census) and Tapachula (189,991), and both are of some industrial importance. San Cristóbal de Las Casas (142,364), Comitán (83,571), Chiapa de Corzo (37,627), and Palenque (37,301) are all of greater archaeological or architectural interest.

Chiapas is one of the richest Mexican states in terms of natural resources, and yet it also has some of the country's poorest people. It has consistently had Mexico's highest levels of malnutrition and infant mortality. Most of Mexico considers itself Catholic, but in southern regions, evangelical Christian sects have made inroads; in Chiapas, about 20 percent of the people are Protestants, while in most parts of Mexico, the figure is below 10 percent. In the late twentieth century, Chiapas occupied the international news because of its Zapatista guerrilla movement. Given the political situation in recent years, the administrative divisions of the state and their relationship with central powers have been somewhat volatile.

Chiapas has four institutions of higher education, including a campus of the Tecnológico de Monterrey, one of the largest systems in the country. The state has a great many newspapers, of which ten are published in Tuxtla Gutiérrez (including *Diario de Chiapas*, *Cuarto Poder*, *La República*, and *El Heraldo*), six in Tapachula (including *Chiapas Hoy*, *El Observador*, and *La Voz del Sureste*), *Voz Maya* in Palenque, *Diario Las Casas* in San Cristóbal, and *El Mundo* in Comitán.

Chiapas has much higher rainfall levels than most parts of the country. The range of climates runs from pleasantly cool in mountainous areas and pleasantly warm in others to tropical in jungle areas and on the coast. In many areas, frosts are almost unknown. Chiapas's highest peak is the Tacaná Volcano, at 4,080 meters (13,464 feet). Unlike most of Mexico, Chiapas can boast a number of important rivers, such as the Grijalva, the Usumacinta, and the Lacanja. Its major lagoons are La Joya, Buenavista, and the Bahía del Suchiate. There are many other lagoons along the 287 kilometers (178 miles) of mostly sandy, low-lying coast. The physical geography of the state can be broken into five regions: the coastal plains, the northern sierra, the central *meseta* (plateau), the central lowlands, and the Sierra Madre. There are eight ecosystems.

A small sample of the huge variety of flora includes *cuajiote*, pine, and oak at the higher elevations; *cazahuate*, ash, laurel, and royal poinciana on the meseta; and mangroves, mesquite, and *palo fierro* in coastal areas. The tropical areas harbor a huge variety of evergreen plants, flowers, and wildlife, some of which are at risk of extinction. Among the fauna are the *tlacuache* (a variety of opossum), the *sarahuato* (black howler monkey), porcupines, and deer in the sierras; the *tepecuintle* (a rodent somewhat like a large guinea pig), wild boars, monkeys, lizards, jaguars, and deer on the meseta; and crocodiles, turtles, and aquatic birds near the coast.

Cultural Groups and Languages

In general, the cultures of Chiapas spring from three sources: the Indian peoples, the Spanish invasion, and the Afro-Caribbean. The same can be said of some other parts of Mexico, but in Chiapas, the Indian element is exceptionally rich. The state has long been recognized for its ethnic characteristics and rich archaeological heritage.

Like neighboring Guatemala, modern Chiapas has a high proportion of Indians; over a quarter of its population speaks indigenous languages, particularly dialects of Maya. While official recognition in the constitution is given to only nine Indian groupings, there are in fact twelve in the state (of sixty-two known to exist in the whole of Mexico). The principal Indian groups are the Tzeltal, Tzotzil, Chol, Tojol-abal, Zoque, Chuj, Kanjobal, Mam, Jacalteco, Mochó, Cakchiquel, and Lacandón. If "Indians" is understood to mean people who speak indigenous languages, then the Indians of Chiapas now represent approximately 13.5 percent of Mexico's total Indian population, the second highest proportion of all states. Many more people live in Indian communities and have Indian customs, while not routinely speaking an Indian language. Indians can be found in four-fifths of the state. Migration to the larger towns has been changing and extending their distribution, but they are most concentrated in six of the regions of the state: Norte, Sierra, Centro, Selva, Altos, and Fronteriza.

The human geography of Chiapas is very complex. There are peoples of the Mixe-zoque group whose roots can be traced back to the Olmecs and who preserve some of their old cultural practices. There are rather more people whose roots are Mayan, and these groups preserve much of what is traditional in their culture; such peoples include the Tzotziles, Tzeltales, Tojolabales, Choles, Mames, Mochos, and Lacandones. While many Indians live in relative isolation and follow traditional Indian cultural practices, many also straddle cultures, making concessions to the *ladino* culture when they come to town to trade. In some Indian communities, the cultural practices are hybridized with Spanish ones. Moreover, anomalous modern "Western" elements, such as electronic communication devices, have infiltrated Indian communities. For practical purposes, being "Indian" is not only a matter of speaking an Indian language but also of one's lifestyle, of whether one has traditional Indian cultural habits. People are viewed or see themselves as Indian if they are not integrated into ladino culture.

Official criteria used in government surveys for identifying people as Indian have shifted over the years. By the time of the 2005 census, when language was the sole criterion, 26 percent of the total state population was identified as Indian. In 32 of the 118 *municipios* of Chiapas, 50 percent or more of the population were speakers of an Indian language; in 21 of these, the figure was over 90 percent. The majority of these people—about a quarter of the state's population—did not speak Spanish. A total of 362,658 people age five or older spoke Tzeltal, and 320,921 Tzotzil; together they accounted for just over 70 percent of speakers of Indian languages in Chiapas. Other major languages were Chol (161,794 speakers), Zoque (43,936), and Tojolabal (42,798).

Nowadays the Tzotzil people can be found living everywhere in Chiapas, but they are most numerous in Los Altos region. It used to be the case that they inhabited parts of the central highland region of Chiapas, to the northwest and southwest of San Cristóbal de Las Casas. The Tzotzil live in organized communities, each of which has its own social identity, its own dialect, and its own customs and rituals. For their livelihood, they have depended primarily on growing corn, beans, and squash, but the economic picture in Chiapas has been changing and its diversity increasing, and as a result the Tzotzil have expanded into the urban areas of the north. Use of their language is most audible in twenty of Chiapas's municipios. Under Spanish rule, the Tzeltal people were much affected by the *encomienda* system, obliged to work in the mines, mills, and *haciendas*. Like the communities of the Tzotzil, those of the Tzeltal have separate identities, dialects, and customs. The Tzeltales are largely engaged in agriculture.

The Choles, whose lives focus on cultivation of and reverence for corn, sometimes call themselves the *milperos*, the people who work in the *milpa* (cornfield). They are related to Indian groups in Guatemala and Tabasco, and it is in areas contiguous with that latter state that they are most numerous. The fundamental economic activity of the Choles is again agriculture: apart from corn, they cultivate beans, sugarcane, rice, coffee, and fruit. The Zoques live primarily in fifty-seven of the most northerly municipios. Tradition holds that the Tojolabales migrated north from Guatemala, as did the Choles. In 1980, fifty Tojolabal Indians who had occupied a farm near Comitán were massacred by the army. The Kanjobal speakers of Chiapas, numbering 5,259 according to the 2005 census, live for the most part along the border with Guatemala; more speakers of that language live in Guatemala itself. Probably many of the Kanjobales were born in Guatemala and later moved to Chiapas, and they still have strong cultural ties with Guatemala. The Mame language (5,446 speakers) is one of the oldest varieties of Mayan. The Mames primarily inhabit Guatemala; in Chiapas, they are found in Fronteriza, Sierra, and Soconusco.

Complex changes have affected the cultural picture. There has been a movement of peoples as a result of the Zapatista rebellion—an influx of other indigenous peoples from outside the state, and a movement of traditional inhabitants to nontraditional areas within it. Some of the immigrants are refugees from political and religious conflicts, some driven by a need to find cultivable land. Most of the growth in the indigenous population has occurred in the Selva, the western central zone, and the area along the Oaxaca border. Besides this, indigenous society is becoming more stratified both economically and socially; indigenous elites are moving to urban centers that were once the province only of *criollos* and *mestizos*. It is a little as though places such as San Cristóbal were slowly being repossessed by the Indians. Finally, significant numbers of Indians, especially Kanjobales, Chujes, and Mames, sought refuge in Chiapas from a troubled Guatemala during the late twentieth century, though many went back once that conflict subsided.

History

The area that is now Chiapas had been populated by many Indian groups for thousands of years even before the Aztecs arrived; for example, the Olmecs had been there around 1000 BC, but most significantly so had the Mayas, from about AD 600. It was in 1486 that the Aztec empire took over Nandiumé, a major settlement made by Indians who had previously come up from the south. The Aztecs renamed this settlement Teochiapan. The

Tzotzil Indian village leader, dressed in a traditional costume, walks past a line of
military police guarding the site of peace talks between the Zapatista rebels and
the Mexican government in San Andres Larrainzar, in the southern Mexican state of
Chiapas, April 1996. To the right are some of the 300 Indians who arrived to
provide security and support for their rebel leaders. (AP Photo/Scott Sady)

name of Chiapas is thus thought to come from the Náhuatl language of the
Aztecs and to refer to lands that lie beside the water, where sage grows.

Less than forty years after the Aztecs took Nandiumé, the Spaniards van-
quished the Aztec capital of Tenochtitlán (now Mexico City) and then
turned their attention to gaining control of other areas. The first contact
between Spaniards and the people of Chiapas came in 1522, just a year after the fall of the Aztec capital; Hernán Cortés dispatched tax collectors to
the area. Soon after, in 1523, Luis Marín, one of Cortés's officers, arrived in
Chiapas to take control. Marín pacified some of the indigenous groups, but
others, such as the highland Tzotzil, offered fierce resistance, and in the
end the Spaniards had to send a new military expedition, under Diego de
Mazariegos. Faced with the inevitability of defeat and the prospect of capture and slavery, some indigenous warriors chose to die instead; at the Battle of Tepetchia, many jumped to their deaths in the Sumidero Canyon.

By 1528, Chiapas was firmly under Spanish control. On May 1 of that
year, Mazariegos founded Villa Real de Chiapa (Chiapa de los Indios), the
town that later became Chiapa de Corzo. He then went on to find an area
with a more attractive climate in which to found the town that for a long

time would be the capital: Villa Real de Chiapa de los Españoles. By 1530, Chiapas had its own cathedral. Chiapa de los Españoles was then renamed San Cristóbal de Las Casas, in recognition of Fray Bartolomé de Las Casas, who had once been bishop of Chiapas and had distinguished himself in the early colonial era by arguing for Indian rights.

One major strategy employed by the Spaniards was to introduce the *encomienda* system, a way of keeping the Indians under control and benefiting from their labors. It was this system that was the focus of Las Casas's complaints. An encomienda was a grant of land and Indian labor made to settlers by the Spanish Crown; both the Crown and those receiving such grants benefited from the fruits of Indian labor on land that had belonged to the Indians before being expropriated by the Spaniards. The system left the natives poorly fed and cared for and deeply resentful of their masters. As a result, there was a revolt by the Tzeltal communities in Los Altos in 1712; they were soon joined by other Indian peoples, but it took only a year for Spain to regain control.

By 1814, some 130,000 people lived in Chiapas, according to a census conducted at that time. They comprised 105,352 Indians, 21,477 mestizos, and 3,409 Spaniards or criollos. A number of Spanish and mestizo ranchers had come to Chiapas in the late eighteenth century, forming an elite group whose increasing land ownership and economic power steadily undermined the traditional Indian communities. This process did not stop when Mexico became independent of Spain. Chiapas was fertile ground for the encomienda system and for the large haciendas that followed. From Spain's point of view, Chiapas had some strategic importance, but it was also remote and lacked the mineral deposits that made other parts of the country so attractive.

As a political entity, Chiapas only began to take shape well into colonial times: late in the eighteenth century, it was made an administrative division of the huge Capitanía General de Guatemala, which in turn answered directly to the viceroy of Nueva España. At that time, Chiapas included all its present-day regions save Fronteriza and Soconusco. Later, when Mexico became independent and Agustín de Iturbide came to power, the Capitanía General de Guatemala (which covered most of what is now Central America) joined his empire for a while, later to break away and form the Central American Federation. As for the *chiapanecos* (as the inhabitants of Chiapas are called), they were divided as to which way to go: whether to be part of Mexico or not. After a period of some instability and conflict with Mexico, and despite considerable opposition in some quarters, a plebiscite was held, revealing that about 56 percent of voters favored continuing as part of Mexico. So it was that Chiapas became a state under the 1824 Constitution. Two years later, the state had its own constitution.

It was in the early 1840s that the last two regions, Fronteriza and Soconusco, joined the others and the state acquired its present-day dimensions. Tuxtla Gutiérrez, which owes part of its name to an homage to a major figure in journalism in Chiapas who became a liberal governor of the state, **Joaquín Miguel Gutiérrez** (1796–1838), became the capital in 1892. By 1900, Chiapas officially had about 360,000 inhabitants. The railroad came in 1906, regular postal and passenger carriage service by road a year later. The year 1911 saw an armed movement in favor of restoring power to San Cristóbal, but it failed, as did an Indian rebellion a year later. This was by no means the first Indian rebellion. Thirty years before, for example, the Mexican government had feared that a rebellion by the Tzotzil people in the Chiapas highlands might lead to the sort of major caste war that it had to deal with in Yucatán.

Geographical remoteness, a lack of organization among its many Indian groups, and the deep-rooted feudal power of landowners are factors that have truly colored the history of Chiapas and exacerbated its inequalities. For example, during the Revolution, the landowners closed ranks in an effort to protect their interests. On their behalf, a mestizo force that became known as the Mapache Army repelled the advances of Venustiano Carranza; in the course of the fighting, they set fire to the state capitol building and destroyed the state archives. For a short while, two opposing state governments coexisted. But at the end of the Revolution, an agreement was made with the landowners. The latter kept their privileges, and therefore postrevolutionary changes had little effect in Chiapas.

In later years, Chiapas developed far more slowly than most of the country, both economically and socially. One small indicator of this slow development is the fact that by 1935 Chiapas had just 83 buses, 198 trucks, 200 private cars, 29 motorcycles, and 298 bicycles. In the 1940s, there were a number of important developments. The first Indian Congress was held, and late in the decade the press brought the world's attention to the newly discovered Mayan ruins. The Pan-American Highway linked Chiapas with Central America. Some advances were made in the provision of education and health services. Industrial developments were taking place, and foreign companies such as Ford and Coca-Cola were setting up operations in Chiapas.

However, the Indians remained marginalized or ignored; wealth remained in the hands of a privileged elite, whether individual or corporate. And so it continued until the combination of poverty and lack of respect for Indian communities provoked the uprising that brought Chiapas not only to national but to the world's attention in the late twentieth century. In 1994, coinciding with the introduction of the North American Free Trade Agreement, indigenous rebels of the Zapatista National Liberation Army (EZLN) rose up in protest against the government, capturing a number of people and taking over several towns, in particular San Cristóbal de Las Casas.

The rebel movement took its name in memory of the southern Indian leader of the days of the Mexican Revolution, Emiliano Zapata, the most idealistic of the revolutionary leaders. The spokesman for the new rebel movement, and by far its most prominent representative nationally and internationally, was the savvy and mysterious **Subcomandante Marcos**, a young man who kept his anonymity by wearing a balaclava, though it was evident from his pale skin and his manner of speaking that he was neither an Indian nor from Chiapas. The rebel movement was seeking autonomy for Indian communities in Chiapas and greater democracy and economic equality for Mexicans at large. Neoliberal economic policies followed by the government in recent years, in particular, had had a devastating effect on communities that history had already left impoverished.

The immediate government response to the rebellion was to send in the Mexican Army, but protests grew nationally and a major confrontation was avoided. The differences between the two sides seemed to be irreconcilable. From the government's point of view, it would have been better if the issues had been only regional, but the Zapatistas had wider ambitions. Various proposals were taken back to Chiapas and roundly rejected.

Rather than engage in a war they would no doubt lose, and with presidential elections approaching, the rebels then held a congress at Lacandón to discuss a common strategy. However, while they were united in their hatred of the ruling party (the Partido Revolucionario Institucional or PRI), otherwise there was little agreement among them. After the election of President Ernesto Zedillo, the PRI candidate, the Zapatistas retreated from the national scene but continued to take over land and evict landowners, creating autonomous municipalities that began to threaten to encroach on the oil fields of the northeastern part of the state. The army tightened its cordon, but the rebels broke through, only to go into hiding thereafter. The army then renewed its offensive, but the cries of support in Mexico City were no longer for peace but for solidarity with the rebels, and once again the army had to back off. Moreover, investments were flooding out of Mexico and the peso had suffered another devaluation. Late in 1995, peace talks began at San Andrés Larrainzar, leading to what became known as the San Andrés Accords; these dealt with indigenous peoples' rights and the protection of their cultures. Though seen as a great victory by the Zapatistas, the fact was that government did not follow through on the provisions of these accords.

The creation of the FZLN (Frente Zapatista de Liberación Nacional) in 1996 was an attempt by the Zapatistas to set up a political forum outside Chiapas, but they themselves had little role in it, and it became torn by the ideological divisions of the Mexico City left. The Zapatistas, meanwhile, turned to national publicity initiatives, aimed at keeping their struggle and the continued militarization of eastern Chiapas in the public eye. One of the worst episodes of violence in Chiapas was the Acteal massacre in 1997, in which a paramilitary group gunned down forty-five Zapatista sympathizers, including women and children. It is thought that such paramilitary groups were tolerated and even trained by the army, and that the PRI would claim the need to curtail paramilitary activities as a pretext for sending in more regulars.

Despite years of intermittent negotiations, during which the PRI lost the presidency, no lasting peace treaty has been signed. The enigmatic

Subcomandante Marcos has had his voice heard, not least through his writings for the national daily *La Jornada*. He has also had his moments of controversial behavior. The Zapatistas still enjoy widespread support outside the state and abroad, though some question their motives.

The election of Vicente Fox to the presidency in July 2000, the first non-PRI president for seventy years, renewed hopes for peace. In 2001, the Zapatistas staged a two-week march that ended in Mexico City; there they demanded that Congress approve a bill of rights based on the San Andrés Accords. This was indeed done, though not in quite the form anticipated. The rebels nevertheless proceeded to create thirty-two autonomous municipalities in Chiapas, thus partially implementing the agreement without government support but with some funding from international organizations. The Zapatistas continue to campaign peacefully nationwide, for example, with a "zapatour" for propaganda purposes, through all Mexico's states. But tensions remain, and Chiapas is still in some sense a frontier territory, a little beyond the rule of national law. The time of Fox and his proposals is now gone. It still remains to be seen whether things in Chiapas will change significantly for the better.

Economy

Given the state's recent history, it is appropriate to begin discussion of the modern economy by noting the changing and increasing production of Indian artifacts and the lively trade in them with tourists. In Chiapas, in addition to traditional products, residents are making and selling Zapatista spin-offs, such as Subcomandante Marcos effigies (dolls that come primarily from San Juan Chamula, which has a long tradition of doll making). Supporters of the Zapatistas have even alleged that this trade is encouraged by the Mexican government as a means of defusing and trivializing the tensions. There is no doubt that since travel restrictions have eased, tourists, journalists, and students have flocked in, and this in turn has stimulated interest in the economy even among foreign corporations that had been wary of Chiapas. Now, below the surface of friendly new dealings with the outside world, lurk secrecy and suspicion of authority.

Curiosity about the Zapatistas apart, tourism is a major contributor to the economy, engendered by the greenness of Chiapas and its many natural attractions, such as the Lacandón jungle, the Agua Azul waterfalls, and the Sumidero Canyon, not to mention immense cultural and archaeological offerings.

For a long time, though, the economic backbone of this fertile state has been agriculture. Chiapas is one of Mexico's major producers of coffee; in 1995, coffee accounted for almost 75 percent of state exports, but there has since been greater diversification of exports. The state also produces corn, cotton, cacao, bananas, tropical fruits such as tamarinds and mangoes, beans, rice, and tobacco, among many other things. Livestock production—pigs, cattle, and poultry—is particularly important in Frailesca, whereas sugarcane is significant on the meseta and in Soconusco. There are rich supplies of wood; cedar, oak, pine, and mahogany are the most widely exploited. The coast and its lagoons provide extensive fishing stocks, including shrimp, bream, bass, catfish, and mullet, as well as turtles.

Sulfur and limestone production are important. Industrially, sugar, milk, and tobacco products should be mentioned, together with chemicals and rubber-based products; Tuxtla Gutiérrez and Tapachula are the main industrial cities. Chiapas generates no less than 30 percent of Mexico's hydroelectric energy and produces almost a quarter of Mexico's oil. There are also deposits of amber, used to make jewelry.

Arts

One of Tuxtla Gutiérrez's main parks is the Parque Jardín de la Marimba, a modern park named in acknowledgment of the role of the marimba in the state's popular music. The instrument is much in evidence in public parks in the southern states of Mexico and is Guatemala's national instrument. Its roots are in the Far East, and it is believed to have come to the Americas in early colonial times, via Africa. It acquired a second keyboard and chromatic capabilities in 1896, an invention by the Chiapas musician Corazón de Jesús Borraz. Another distinctive *chiapaneco* instrument is the reed flute.

Pottery, ironwork, articles made with shellac, candles, basketry, and textiles (especially in the Mayan tradition) are some of the main craft traditions in Chiapas.

In the mainstream Hispanic culture, there have been a number of distinguished figures. **Matías de Córdoba** (1768–1828) was a priest, humanist, creative writer, and journalist. He is credited with introducing the first printing press into Chiapas, founding one of its newspapers, and fostering the study of the state's economy and geography. In 1821, in Comitán, he proclaimed Mexico independent. Revealingly, among his works was one entitled "On the Appropriateness of All Indians Dressing and Using Footwear in the Spanish Style." **Blanca Lydia Trejo** (1906–1970) represented her country in Barcelona during the Spanish Civil War and was also a noted children's writer. The Centro Cultural de Chiapas bears the name of **Jaime Sabines** (1926–1999), one of the state's most distinguished cultural figures and a man who became widely known throughout Mexico as a popular poet. Sabines studied medicine before turning to literature and producing accessible, heartfelt, and spontaneous poems that enjoy a broad appeal, occupying a place on Mexico's cultural stage that is a little similar to Pablo Neruda's on Chile's. Sabines was also active in politics; at one time, he was a state representative to the National Congress.

Another major literary figure of the same generation was **Rosario Castellanos** (1925–1974). The daughter of rich landowners, she spent her formative years in the care of an Indian nanny, an experience that informs much of her writing, especially the novel *Balún Canán* (1957); in general, her books provide plenty of evidence of her sympathy with the plight of the Indians. Given her upbringing, it is perfectly understandable that she should have felt that way, and yet improving the lot of the Indians had meant the loss of some of her own family's property after the Revolution, during the redistribution of land that took place under President Lázaro Cárdenas. For a time, Castellanos directed an Indian theater program in Tuxtla Gutiérrez, under the auspices of the Instituto Nacional Indigenista, and she also worked for the institute in San Cristóbal. But she was no mere provincial. Castellanos was a highly educated woman who studied in Mexico City and in Madrid and worked in the Universidad Autónoma in Mexico City as a teacher and press officer. For a while, she wrote editorials for the national daily *Excelsior*. This modern and cosmopolitan side of her is reflected in the other major issue that occupied her pen: the position of women and their struggle to find a suitable role and be accepted in a male-dominated society—topics she treats in quite a modern way in essays, stories, poems, and plays. She can be called an early feminist; that said, she also wrote scathingly about facile manifestations of feminism. Castellanos died fairly young, in an accident while serving as her country's ambassador to Israel.

Social Customs

The regional chiapaneco women's dress is known worldwide. It includes a flounced skirt with profuse floral hand-embroidery in silk, and nowadays, not only the skirts are decorated in this way. In many cases, the textile techniques employed have survived from pre-Hispanic times, and the embroidered designs on the clothing are symbolic.

The traditional dress of San Juan Chamula will serve as the first of several illustrations of traditional clothing worn in the state. Given its cool climate, much of the clothing in San Juan Chamula comes from sheep's wool. The association of the patron saint, John the Baptist, with lambs fosters a sense that the animal is sacred. For the *fiestas patronales* (the festivities in his honor), most men wear black, long-sleeved, buttonless coats called *chujes*, which open at the neck and are tied with suede belts; however, the town worthies wear white, buckled chujes. The women wear the traditional Mayan *huipiles*, simple shifts that are embroidered across the yoke in red, yellow, and green—colors representing Saints Peter, John, and Sebastian. On their heads, they wear the ancient *mochibal*, a type of shawl that is secured at the front by red pom-poms. They also wear a double skirt with a red sash that is of pre-Hispanic origin, combined with a European-style satin blouse in blue or white, with embroidered strips on the sleeves and neck.

In Tenejapa, where the climate is more humid and temperate, the women wear huipiles of cotton, richly decorated with embroidery in red, yellow, and ocher tones that come from natural dyes. The predominant motif is the rhombus, which symbolizes the universe. Male dress consists of cotton breeches with geometric designs embroidered along the seams,

Market stall.

mostly in red or black. They also don a showy, dyed, sewn hat with a rounded crown and a wide rim from which colored tassels hang; the hat is held around the chin by a woven woolen strap that has matching pompoms. This outfit is accompanied by a rosary of glass beads and medallions with a central metal cross, the whole symbolizing prestige and authority.

Magdalenas, a small Tzotzil community 25 kilometers (15 miles) northeast of San Cristóbal de Las Casas, has huipiles that are real works of art, with elaborate and profuse geometric designs that are reminiscent of oriental rugs. These are made from naturally dyed wool or cotton and are eight to ten months in the making. Such clothing has a ritual significance, hence the lavish work; for the women of Magdalenas, it is an honor to make such a huipil for religious or civic use. The production process involves much ceremony, including invoking the Virgin's blessing of the materials involved and praying that the tips of the seamstress's fingers rise to the challenge.

An ancient tradition found only in Zinacantán is the plumed huipil that is used in marriage ceremonies. This is of *teotihuacano* origin—in other words, from central Mexico. This type of huipil has white chicken feathers attached, the chicken being preferred because it does not fly, walks on two legs like humans, and depends on them for sustenance; it is thought that the bride might behave similarly. The feathers are generally sewn into seams, making three or four lines interspersed with embroidery. The garment comes down to the ankles and is worn over a blue cotton under-skirt; a large white shawl modestly covers much of the face and body.

For the Fiesta Grande de Chiapa de Corzo (Feria de Chiapa) in January, people disguise themselves as Spanish men and women in memory of mem-bers of the household of Doña María de Angulo, who went from house to house in colonial times, giving children gifts of fruit and money. The *para-chico* masks (those for the men) are carved from cedar wood and painted to emphasize facial features such as broad foreheads, long straight noses, blue eyes, rosy cheeks, beards, and curly hair—in short, the features that fit the stereotypical Indian view of the European. The festivities last about ten days. First there is a big meal (the *comida grande*; see below) in honor of the Señor de Esquipulas, and a couple of days later another in honor of San Antonio Abad. The next day, the meal is dedicated to the memory of past patrons of the parachicos and is held in a mansion with an effigy of San Sebastián. Two days after that, people dress up for the parachico festivities. A little later, there is a mock naval battle and there are fireworks on the Grijalva River. There is a procession with allegorical floats, led by the parachi-cos. Doña María de Angulo is represented by a pretty young girl, who passes out sweets and coins to the onlookers. The festivities end with another procession in which the parachicos take their leave, first visiting the Church of Santo Domingo Guzmán and promising to return the next year.

The December Feria de Chiapas in Tuxtla Gutiérrez is also a major event but is quite different and more like those found in other parts of Mexico. It includes an agricultural and livestock show, arts and crafts, and industrial displays. A beauty queen is chosen, and there are dancing, concerts of pop and *ranchera* music, horse races, processions, cockfights, auctions, stalls selling food and trinkets, as well as sideshows and rides.

For Carnival, in San Juan Chamula, men put on headdresses made from monkey skin, with ribbons, and black jackets with red decorations on them, together with leather chaps, to dance the *bolonchón*. Barefoot Indi-ans race across burning coals in front of the church.

After Lent, many people go to bathe in the sulfurous waters of a beautiful spot called Baños de Uninajab, near Comitán. Some build huts from palm fronds so that families may stay for the series of nine bathings thought to help with rheumatism and other ailments. Drinking the waters at their source is believed to cure infirmities, put flesh on the skinny, get rid of pim-ples, and impart fertility to women. At around this time of the year, the *tenocté* is flowering, a sign in the popular imagination that young girls will elope with their suitors. Another Comitán tradition has to do with birth-days: colored paper curtains, perforated with geometric or floral figures, are placed in the early morning at the door of the person whose birthday it is.

Here, as in many parts of Mexico, Holy Week brings the custom of the *Quema de Judas*, in which an effigy of Judas is put on show in a public place where people can mock and insult it; on the Saturday, it is ceremoni-ously burned or made to spin around and explode. Quite frequently, this ceremony has political overtones, and effigies of prominent people or representing aspects of Mexican society are used.

Noteworthy Places

There are many places of archaeological interest in Chiapas, which boasts some of the finest Mayan ruins known. The most famous and most visited is Palenque, 190 kilometers (118 miles) northeast of San Cristóbal de Las Casas and a similar distance southeast of the Tabasco town of Villahermosa. Palenque reached its zenith as a political center between 600 and 800, though it had been inhabited long before that time. It was in 1785 that the first explorations took place, drawings were made, and a report was drawn up by the Spaniards. It transpired that the natural lay of the land had been modified by the Mayas to create flat terraces on which to construct imposing squares and palaces. In its heyday, the city occupied 125 square kilometers (49 square miles); it had a ball court, several squares, twisting corridors, galleries, and underground passageways linking its many temples and also serving as a form of defense. But in about 900, Palenque, like other major centers of what is commonly called the First Mayan Empire, was abandoned, and the focus of Mayan civilization then shifted to the Yucatán Peninsula. The reasons for this displacement are still a matter for debate; it has been suggested that supernatural signs, natural disasters, or wars might have been determining factors.

Palenque, along with Tikal (in Guatemala) and Copán (in Honduras), has some of the most impressive Mayan ruins of all. Among those who explored, inhabited, or otherwise exploited Palenque was the eccentric Count Waldeck, who in 1831 set up house with his mistress in what is now known as the Temple of the Count. The renowned amateur archaeologists John Lloyd Stephens and Frederick Catherwood are remembered for their work in Palenque in 1840. Serious excavations under the direction of Frans Blom began in 1932. In 1952, a Mexican archaeologist, Alberto Ruz, uncovered the tomb of the ruler K'inich Hanab Pakal, who is believed to have held sway during the time of the city's greatest glory; it lay beneath what is now called the Temple of the Inscriptions. This impressive temple is important not only because of its inscriptions (only some of which have been deciphered) but also because of its size and position. It is at the southern edge of the main square, set upon an eight-tiered pyramid and approached by a staircase that rises some 24 meters (80 feet). Pakal's tomb has stucco reliefs showing nine richly clad priests bearing the shield of the sun and the scepter of the rain god; on top of the sarcophagus itself is a stone sculpture representing the cycle of life and death, in accordance with the Maya worldview. Palenque is a huge site with many other significant buildings.

Bonampak is another major archaeological site, located in the Lacandón jungle, 182 kilometers (113 miles) southeast of Palenque. Bonampak's name signifies "painted walls," and indeed the place is famous for its mural portrayals of courtly life and warfare. Hidden in the jungle, it was uncovered only in 1946, since when images from it have graced the pages of many a book about the Mayas. Some work has been done to slow the deterioration of Bonampak's murals due to the effects of humidity. There are three rooms in particular with walls decorated in remarkable tones of yellow, red, green, and blue in the Templo de las Pinturas (Temple of the Paintings).

It appears that Bonampak prospered at the same time as Palenque, but that it came under the control of neighboring Yaxchilán. At the latter, some extraordinary temples have been excavated, as well, together with many stone carvings; Yaxchilán ("The Place of the Green Stones") is less accessible than the two sites previously mentioned and has been a place of pilgrimage for the Lacandón people. It was on the trade route between Palenque and Tikal. Other places of archaeological interest in Chiapas include Toniná, Chinkultic, and Izapa.

San Cristóbal de Las Casas is the busiest colonial town. Its cathedral dates from the sixteenth century, but has been much modified since that time. Among the artworks that it houses are some important altarpieces, particularly the baroque Retablo de los Reyes, dating from 1790; another altarpiece, the Retablo del Perdón, has paintings by one of Mexico's most noted colonial artists, Juan Correa. At the back of the cathedral can be found the Church of St. Nicholas, now the diocesan museum. It is interesting as an example of *mudéjar* architecture and an exception in the town because it has kept its original design and shape. A town museum is housed in a former Dominican convent, with important relics from the town's history, including textiles from pre-Hispanic times. The Museo Na-Bolom is an old neoclassical house whose name means "House of the Jaguar." This was once used as a seminary but was turned into a museum by Frans and Trudi Blom (he was a Danish archaeologist, she a Swiss activist), and it also houses the Bartolomé de Las Casas Library.

San Juan Chamula, about 10 kilometers (7 miles) north of San Cristóbal, is celebrated for its religious and cultural heritage. The Hollow Mountains were discovered in 1947; a single entrance leads to a 10-kilometer-long (6-mile) cave that descends 550 meters (1,800 feet); there are other such caves and grottoes near San Cristóbal. The town of Comitán still preserves many colonial buildings, and there are also ancient ruins nearby. About 65 kilometers (40 miles) away from Comitán are the Lagos de Montebello, an area of natural beauty that has been officially designated a park. There are fifty-six lakes, surrounded by mountains, and the colors of their waters vary because of different mineral deposits.

Tuxtla Gutiérrez, the state capital, houses a zoo, a botanical museum, and several others, such as the one devoted to anthropology. This last won architectural awards when it was completed in the early 1980s and is predictably rich in its representation of pre-Hispanic peoples and cultures. Lying close to Tuxtla Gutiérrez is Chiapa de Corzo, so hot and mosquito-ridden that, not long after founding it, the Spaniards moved on to the friendlier climate of San Cristóbal. Chiapa de Corzo is close to the dramatic Sumidero Canyon (though which flows the Río Grijalva); the canyon runs for 23 kilometers (14 miles) and is one of Chiapas's most important scenic spots. Chiapa de Corzo also has a famous monument in its municipal fountain; built in brick in the Arab-influenced mudéjar style and with a Renaissance-style cupola, it is said to represent the form of the Spanish crown. The Church of Santo Domingo is one of the best-preserved examples of sixteenth-century architecture in Chiapas. Chiapa de Corzo also has a Museo de la Laca (Shellac Museum), reflecting local craft activity.

Tapachula, in the southwest corner of the state, close to the coast and the Guatemalan border, is the capital of Soconusco, a beautiful region encompassing beaches, frontierlands, mountain forests, places of archaeological interest, and coffee plantations. Some buildings are in the art deco style. Tapachula is the state's second city, with over a quarter of a million inhabitants.

Cuisine

In addition to food from the Spanish tradition, there are many more unusual things consumed in Chiapas, including fruits, plants, insects, and other creatures. Among unusual meats served there are armadillo (often stewed; it is greasy and has a flavor like that of pork); *tlacuache*, a marsupial sometimes called the "Mexican opossum" (stewed or roasted); rattlesnake (similarly prepared, with bay leaf or *epazote*, a much-used Mexican herb; the flesh is said to resemble the taste of cod); freshwater snails (or *shuti*, boiled with herbs, with the addition of balls of cornmeal; this dish is typical of Tapachula); *rata de campo*, a field rodent that feeds on insects and plants (slow-roasted and seasoned with salt and lime); and the chicken turtle (*tortuga pollo* or *pochitoque*; stewed with black beans or rice and shellfish). Edible insects include the *nucú*, also known as the *tzitzim*, *quiss*, or *chicatana*, which is found at dusk at the start of the rainy season (roasted and served with salt, lime, and chile); Another is the *nuti* or *mazán*, a ground insect that appears after rains beneath stones close to rivers (normally fried and then condimented in similar ways); *zats*, the larvae of a nocturnal butterfly found in the highlands near San Cristóbal (boiled, drained, and then fried in pork fat, eaten with green chiles and tortillas); and the *chapulín* (boiled for a minimum of 12 hours before being browned on a *comal*, rather as is done with *zats*).

There is a wide variety of *tamales* and other corn-based dishes. Corn is not simply a Mexican dietary staple but is fundamental to the Indian worldview: according to the Mayan creation myth, the gods made three attempts to create mankind, eventually succeeding in doing so with corn. A corn-based drink that is typical of Chiapas is *pozol*; white corn is first boiled in diluted slaked lime, then drained and ground before water is added and the drink is seasoned with salt and chile. The pre-Hispanic *pochotl*—named after a Toltec prince who was a great propagandist for the properties of corn—is a similar potion containing cocoa. Though the corn-and-cocoa variety of pozol was drunk at room temperature and unsweetened in pre-Hispanic times, early in the twentieth century it became popular in the main towns of Chiapas to add sugar and ice to it. Pozol can also be found in a bitter variety that is taken with chile and salt. *Tascalate* is another drink that is similar to the sweet variety of pozol; it comes colored with annatto.

Temperante is a drink that also has a red dye; it is flavored with cinnamon and honey and is typical of Comitán. San Cristóbal makes a sweet ginger beer called *cervecita dulce*. Many nonalcoholic drinks are made from fruit. Among alcoholic beverages, there is *comiteco*, a relative of Oaxaca's *mezcal* and Jalisco's *tequila*, made by distilling *pulque* (a product of the *maguey* cactus, which was of divine significance in pre-Hispanic times). A sugarcane-based variety of comiteco is commonly used to make *encurtidos*; this is a way of preserving fruit by placing them in an earthenware vessel, covering them with the liquor, and allowing each to absorb the flavor of the other. The flavored liquor so produced has its own name: *mistela*. Another alcoholic drink is made from *chilacayote*, a type of gourd. *Chicha*, also known as *guarapo* and *tibique*, is a highly intoxicating fermented drink made from sugarcane, as is the drink that rejoices in the name of *posh*. The *coyol* is a palm tree from which yet another highly alcoholic drink comes: *taberna de coyol*.

The coyol is also known as the *colconave*. It grows in semitropical areas, and its edible part can be eaten fresh, served with pineapple vinegar and olive oil, fried, or made into a sweet delicacy. *Dulce de oreja de mico* is another sweet delicacy, made from papaya and often eaten with pozol. Other pastries, cookies, and desserts include *chimbos, suspiros, turuletes, pan de salvadillo con temperante*, and *maíz de guineo*.

Comida grande is a phrase that refers to the main meal that is de rigueur at times of major festivities. The key dish is *pepita con tasajo*, which consists of strips of salt-cured beef in a sauce made of ground pumpkin seeds and spices.

Pijijiapán is a place known for its milk products, as San Cristóbal is known for its bread.

Chipa Correntino

Ingredients:

1 lb. cassava flour
1 egg
3 oz. butter, chopped or softened
1/2 tsp salt
1 cup shredded red cheese (*queso cascara*)
1 cup shredded white cheese
Milk

Put the flour and salt together in a bowl. Add the butter and work into the flour until granular. Add the shredded cheese and the egg and mix, adding a little milk during the process. It is important not to knead the mixture, only to bind the ingredients together, making a soft dough that does not stick to one's hands. Shape into balls and place on a greased baking sheet. Bake at 400°F until golden brown.

Albóndigas (Meatballs)

Ingredients:

2 lb. ground beef
2 *ancho* chiles
2 *cascabel* chiles
1 tsp marjoram
1 tomato
$^1/_2$ small onion
$^1/_2$ clove of garlic
Black pepper
A pinch of cumin
2 bay leaves
A pinch of finely ground coffee

Make small balls with the meat, and put them to boil briefly in water with a little salt and pepper and a bay leaf. Devein and clean the chiles, chop them up, and fry them in olive oil together with pieces of tomato, chopped onion, and garlic. Add the other bay leaf, the marjoram, and the cumin. (If allowed to burn it will become bitter.) Dilute this mixture with a little of the meat broth, add the coffee, then return it to the pan. Put the meatballs in the mixture and simmer.

Estofado de Pollo con Frutas (Chicken and Fruit Stew)

Ingredients:

1 chicken, cut into pieces
1 small onion, grated
2 cloves of garlic
$^1/_4$ tsp ground cinnamon
4 tbsp cider vinegar
1 oz. butter
2 tomatoes
1 ancho chile
$^1/_2$ lb. potatoes
$^1/_2$ lb. carrots
1 *chayote* (prickly pear), peeled
8 pitted prunes
2 oz. raisins

2 slices fresh, ripe pineapple
2 bay leaves
$^1/_4$ tsp dried thyme
1$^1/_2$ cups chicken broth
Salt and pepper

Prepare a paste with the onion, the garlic (squeezed through a press), the cinnamon, 2 tablespoons of the vinegar, and a little salt and pepper. Marinate the chicken pieces in this for at least half an hour. Peel and chop the tomatoes. Devein and deseed the chile, soak it in hot water, and make it into a paste. Cut the other vegetables into small pieces and parboil them. Cut the chayote, prunes, and pineapple into small pieces. Brown the meat in a large pot, then remove the meat and reserve. Sauté the tomatoes in the same pot until they begin to caramelize, then add the remaining ingredients, including the remainder of the vinegar. Put the chicken back in the pot, cover and cook over a low heat until the meat is tender. Cornmeal may be used to thicken the sauce, if necessary.

Chuletas de Cordero con Miel (Lamb Chops with Honey)

Ingredients:

4 lamb chops
Oil
Flour
Juice of $^1/_2$ lime
1 tsp honey
$^1/_2$ cup vegetable broth

Rub the chops with oil and sear them on both sides, then lower the heat and allow them to cook through. Set them aside, keeping them hot. Put a little flour in the pan to make a roux; when it begins to brown, add the lime juice, honey, and broth. Cook vigorously for two or three minutes, stirring frequently. Pour over the chops.

Chihuahua

State Characteristics

Chihuahua is one of the Mexican states that shares a border with the United States. The states of Sinaloa and Durango lie to the south of it, Coahuila to the east, and Sonora to the west. Census figures from 2005 give the total state population as 3,241,444, which is to say approximately 3 percent of the national total. Chihuahua has sixty-seven administrative municipalities and sends nine state representatives to the National Congress.

The state occupies a total area of 247,938 square kilometers (96,696 square miles), which is 12.5 percent of Mexico and makes Chihuahua the largest state in the country. Consequently, the population density has been low; however, industrialization and migration have been having a major effect on the nature and number of the inhabitants of this state. The most extreme example is Ciudad Juárez (commonly referred to simply as Juárez), on the U.S. border across from El Paso. Juárez, the largest town and the most populous *municipio* in Chihuahua, has a population of which some 75 percent were born elsewhere. Juárez is not the capital of Chihuahua; that honor goes to a city that shares the name of the state and is located in the middle of it. The city of Chihuahua has approximately 850,000 inhabitants, Juárez about twice as many. Other significant population centers include Hidalgo del Parral, a mining town dating from the early seventeenth century and located in the south; Cuauhtémoc, which lies west of the capital; and Delicias, southeast of Chihuahua City.

In general, Chihuahua's population is slightly more concentrated in urban areas than is the case for most of Mexico. According to the 2005 census, approximately 85 percent of the Chihuahuacans are Catholic and 10 percent Protestant. Chihuahua has five institutions of higher education. There are fifteen newspapers, most of them published in Ciudad Juárez, Hidalgo del Parral, and Chihuahua itself, including *Diario de Juárez*, *El Mexicano*, *Norte*, *El Diario de Chihuahua*, *El Heraldo*, *El Pueblo*, and *El Monitor*.

No less than five different explanations of Chihuahua's name have been suggested, most of them deriving from the Tarahumara language, which is still the dominant indigenous language in the state. However, it is an explanation that is attributed to Náhuatl roots that has become most widely accepted; according to it, the name refers to a dry and sandy place—a fairly accurate description of much of this state.

Western, central, and southern portions of Chihuahua are dominated by mountain ranges, with elevations frequently above 2,000 meters (7,000 feet). The dominant mountain system is the Sierra Madre Occidental (Western Sierra Madre). The highest elevations are to be found in the Tarahumara range. There are dramatic, deep canyons and ravines, such as the Tararécua, Cobre, and Urique. To the north and east lie plains that are part of the Mexican plateau, occasionally interrupted by minor mountain ranges.

In broad terms, Chihuahua has three geographical zones: the mountains, the *meseta*, and the desert. Northern and eastern parts of the state, representing well over half of its territory, are part of the Chihuahua Desert. Despite the limits implied by the name, this desert region runs from southern New Mexico though Chihuahua and southeastward, also covering large tracts of the states of Coahuila, Durango, Zacatecas, and San Luis Potosí. Within Chihuahua, in the southern part of the desert area, one finds the Bolsón de Mapimí and the Zona del Silencio (see below).

As for waterways, the Conchos River, a tributary of the Río Bravo, is joined by its tributaries, the San Pedro, Florido, and Chuviscar rivers, to run eastward toward the Gulf of Mexico, while the Bavispe, Papigochi, Mayo, Fuerte, Chinipas, Urique, and Verde Rivers all flow west toward the Mar de Cortés. In the interior, the Casas Grandes, Santa María, and Carmen Rivers feed into lagoons. Within the desert zone, only the Bravo and Conchos Rivers flow constantly, allowing modest agricultural activity.

The climate in the eastern part of the state is dry and fairly hot and has occasional rain, whereas the western parts are more extreme in their dryness and heat, except at the higher elevations of the Sierra Madre Occidental, where temperatures are milder and the climate somewhat more humid. The average annual temperature for the state as a whole is 20°C (68°F). Average rainfall runs from 220 to 1,020 millimeters (8.7 to 40.3 inches).

Lechuguilla (a variety of agave) is a characteristic plant of the Sonora and Chihuahua deserts that thrives in limestone. In addition to supporting insects and birds, it provides *ixtle*, a fiber that indigenous peoples have long used to make cords and mats. This plant is sometimes informally referred to as the "shin-dagger," due to its spikes than can readily pierce even leather clothing. While the leaves of the plant are poisonous to animals, its juice is used in making a sports drink and also distilled to make a clear liquor called *clandestino*. Also native to the plateau and the desert regions are the mesquite shrub, *guayule* (which gives a type of rubber), *gobernadora*, *hojasén*, and *ocotillo*. Trees in the mountains are mainly oaks, poplars, and conifers such as pines.

Wildlife is extremely rich and includes reptiles such as lizards and rattle-snakes, a number of small birds (e.g., quail and doves), shrews, rabbits, skunks, wild boars, prairie dogs, porcupines, wolves, deer, foxes, squirrels, raccoons, bears, and bats. The wolf, the bear, and the wild turkey are all threatened species. In the valleys, one can find parrots. In all, there are hundreds of bird species that are either native to or migrate to this state. There are also over eighty different species of reptile in Chihuahua.

Cultural Groups and Languages

According to the 2005 census, 93,709 people in Chihuahua spoke an indig-enous language, that is to say 3.4 percent of the population. About four-fifths of them also spoke Spanish. By far the most commonly spoken lan-guage was Tarahumara, with over 72,000 speakers; Tepehuano, the next most common, had less than a tenth as many.

After engaging in a number of uprisings against the Spaniards, the Tara-humaras took refuge in the most inaccessible area of mountains and ravines of the Sierra Madre Occidental, a part now known as the Sierra Tarahu-mara. There they still preserve many of their cultural traditions, living mostly in small and scattered groups, suspicious of outsiders thanks to their past experiences. There are even some places where they will not allow outsiders to go. The Tarahumaras elect their own supreme leader democratically. They were so named by the Spaniards, but are properly called the Rarámuris, a name that signifies "the light-footed" and alludes to their stamina when hunting deer. They are by far the most numerous indig-enous people in Chihuahua, now numbering perhaps 70,000. Traditionally, the Tarahumaras are seasonal nomads; they cultivate crops at higher eleva-tions during summer and come down to the valleys in winter. They grow corn, beans, and squash, and family groups will raise one or two sheep, goats, or cows. Their diet is largely a vegetarian one, and their medicines are plant based. *Peyote* (*jículi* in their language) is among the substances used to cure illnesses and ward off evil.

The Northern Tepehuanes—so called in order to distinguish them from those who live in the state of Durango—are the next most important indige-nous group, numbering four or five thousand. The Tepehuanes were the first to rise up against the Spaniards, before making an alliance with the Tarahumaras. Nowadays the Tepehuanes are found in the northern part of the Guadalupe *municipio*; their main communities are Baborigame and Nabogame. The supreme leader of the Tepehuanes appoints community leaders.

These and other indigenous peoples are slowly disappearing as the modern world encroaches, but some other smaller groups still survive in the mountain areas; for example, the Guarojíos number perhaps 1,500 and speak their own language (which is related to Tarahumara), but do not wear distinctive dress. The less numerous Pimas and Masculáis also maintain some distinctive cultural identity.

In 1921, during the presidency of Alvaro Obregón, a group of Mennonites from Canada was granted permission to settle in Chihuahua, with no strings attached. There they continue to live, marrying among themselves, speaking Low German, and hardly integrating at all with mainstream Mexican society. They live by farming and selling their products, especially cheeses, on a modest scale.

History

When the Spaniards first came to what is now Chihuahua, there were more than a hundred indigenous groups in the area, among them Apaches, Comanches, Tarahumaras, Tobosos, Pimas, Guarojíos, Tepehuanes, Opatas, Conchos, Julimes, Tapacolmes, Tubaris, Guazaparis, and Chínipas. Principal among the first Spanish explorers of the area was Alvar Núñez Cabeza de Vaca, an adventurer who came in search of the fabled Seven Cities of Gold, arriving in Chihuahua via Sinaloa. Cabeza de Vaca later wrote an account of

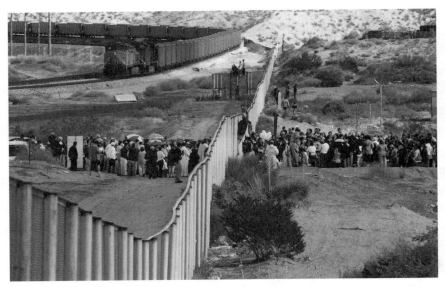

People partake in a Mass separated at the Mexico/U.S. border during Day of the Dead celebrations in Anapra. Since 1998, the Mass has been the culmination of a week-long trek along the border for missionaries and migrant-rights activists. (AP Photo/Eduardo Verdugo)

his own story, an extraordinary journey that began with a shipwreck in Florida and took him across the southern United States, living among indigenous cultures and even becoming a shaman before eventually he reencountered Spanish people. He and his fellow adventurers had heard fantasies about places with abundant gemstones, where the dishes were made of gold, for lack of other metals. For years, they wandered through the mountains in search of such riches.

In 1536, the Spanish viceroy dispatched Francisco Ibarra, the son of the man who had founded Zacatecas, to conquer the northern lands. Ibarra's first expedition brought him as far as the Río Conchos, and the second to Culiacán. Indian attacks forced the men back into the western mountains, but friendly Suma Indians encouraged them with more tales of cities of gold that lay beyond the Río Bravo to the north. The Spaniards made their way to Casas Grandes and Paquimé, a town of adobe. They struggled on, weathering more Indian attacks, having to eat their horses, and finally surviving on a diet of ants and plants, until they came to the plains of Sonora. Ibarra was subsequently appointed governor of Nueva Vizcaya, the name the Spaniards gave to these lands north of Zacatecas (the present-day states of Durango, Chihuahua, Sonora, and Sinaloa, as well as New Mexico and the Californias).

The Franciscans arrived before long to convert the natives. The town of Santa Barbara was founded, and soon silver was discovered in the hills near the River Conchos. To work the seven mines they had discovered, the Spaniards brought in Indians from other parts of Mexico—namely Tlaxcaltecas and Tarascos, people whose cultural influence is still in evidence. To the east, the town of San Bartolomé became the center of a productive agricultural and cattle-raising region.

Subsequent years saw many more expeditions, by no means all of which were successful. Spanish control of the lands was not firm during the sixteenth century, and there were continuing Indian attacks. But more mineral deposits were found, and during the seventeenth century, mining developed further. Nueva Vizcaya's first capital had been Villa de Guadiana (now Durango), but in 1635, in recognition of its importance as a mining center and its strategic position in the fight against the Indians, San José del Parral became the capital. In October 1709, a decree was issued authorizing the foundation of what was to become the town of Chihuahua, the new state capital; at the time of foundation, it was given the name San Francisco de Cuéllar, in honor of the Marquis of Cuéllar, the viceroy of the day, and also in recognition of the Franciscan Order.

Indian numbers were in decline. The missions founded by the Franciscans and Jesuits to convert and protect the Indians turned into places where they were exploited in feudal style, and others were made to work in harsh conditions in the mines. Rich landowners also settled in the fertile valleys, in places where there were rivers or underground sources of water. Frequently an imposing house would be set on a hill, along with a granary. Thick adobe walls ran around these huge properties, making them seem like fortresses; lookout towers and armed guards were required as precautions against Indian attacks. As in the case of the *haciendas*, the walls enclosed a spacious patio area, around which there were living and cooking quarters, stables, and sheds for carriages. Fountains and wells sometimes fed gardens, and proof of status was to be found in furnishings brought from Europe, which until the arrival of the train in Mexico had to be brought across country by mule. These ranches (*haciendas*) were almost societies in their own right, with *mestizo* laborers, Indians, and slaves living close to the principal residence, but in poorly built dwellings with no sanitation. Among these people, the mestizo cowboys did relatively well; they were paid, and they developed their own dress and culture.

Tensions arose between the miners and the owners of these haciendas, and during the colonial period the Spanish authorities tried several times to act as mediators. The miners and hacienda owners did close ranks, however, in support of the royalist cause—that is, against the movement toward independence from Spain, which took shape in the early nineteenth century. In fact, Chihuahua was the place to which several of the country's most prominent insurgent leaders were taken to be shot. Shortly after independence came, in 1821, Durango was separated off from Chihuahua and a new province was established; then, under the 1824 Constitution, Chihuahua became one of the new republic's states. Its first state constitution was ratified a year later.

In 1831, war was declared on the Apaches and Comanches, whose uprisings were having deleterious effects on the economy. The struggle against them would occupy the authorities for decades, until the Indians were all but exterminated. After Texas broke away from Mexico, there was a failed attempt to incorporate Chihuahua into the United States. However, with the Treaty of Guadalupe Hidalgo that marked the end of the confrontation with the United States in 1848, Mexico ceded a great deal of its territory, including part of Chihuahua. Later, Benito Juárez, the liberal president of Mexico, resisted French occupation of Chihuahua in the mid-1860s, helped by **Luis Terrazas** (1829–1923), then governor of the state. Terrazas was a soldier and a liberal politician who also represented Chihuahua in the National Congress. Among other things, he was instrumental in curtailing the powers of the clergy and nationalizing Church assets. Once an opponent of Porfirio Díaz, he later became reconciled with him and served again as state governor during the *porfiriato*. The Terrazas family was one of the richest and most influential in Chihuahua; in fact, its enrichment was to be a significant focus of resentment at the time of the Revolution.

As in many places, at the beginning of the twentieth century there was discontent with the regime of President Díaz. Once he had gone, President Francisco Madero approved the rise of Abraham González to the state governorship, but González was assassinated, as was Madero himself. There were also tensions between Chihuahua and neighboring Coahuila.

Chihuahua was mainstage during the Revolution (1910–1920), a major tramping ground for Pancho Villa, who gathered his famous Northern Division together there. Chihuahua was occupied by U.S. forces for almost a year. In 1913, Villa occupied Chihuahua and became provisional governor, but soon after, there was disagreement with Venustiano Carranza, the former governor of neighboring Coahuila and by then president of Mexico. Supporters of Villa refused to recognize the authority of President Carranza, and a great deal of confusion and instability followed. In 1915, Villa declared the hostilities at an end and gave in to Obregón, but then remained in control of Chihuahua. U.S. forces reached Parral and occupied Casas Grandes. Local armed bands were cropping up, and Villa was assassinated in Parral in 1923.

Thereafter, some attempts at land redistribution were made, and labor organizations began to take shape. After the Mexican Revolution, the state lay in the hands of the Partido Revolucionario Institucional (PRI), but Chihuahua has developed one of the strongest two-party rivalries in Mexico, with the Partido de Acción Nacional (PAN) very much in evidence. Chihuahua provided the PAN with its 1958 presidential candidate, Luis H. Álvarez. It was also among the first states to elect a governor who was not a member of the PRI, an event that occurred in 1992.

Economy

Chihuahua's economy ranks fifth in the country. Mining has been a major activity in the state of Chihuahua ever since the seventeenth century. Parral in particular became rich on its silver mines, a hundred of which have been exploited nearby. Other mining areas are around San Francisco del Oro, Villa Escobedo, and Santa Eulalia, which is close to the capital. There was even an occasion in 1780 when the order was given to pave the roads of a town with silver, in honor of an impending visit by a bishop. In colonial days, the products of the mines, enjoyed largely thanks to Indian labor, were shipped to Veracruz, and manufactured goods, livestock, and food were shipped back in return. Following independence, English, Canadian, and U.S. people came in to finance the mining operations.

The Potosí mine is particularly noted for its production of lead, zinc, and silver. The Compañía Fresnillo is important in Delicias, as is the Empresa Peñoles. The Naica mine has extensive underground operations that resemble the layout of a town. Also important is the Compañia Minera de México. There is even a food culture associated with mining.

As happened in other parts of Mexico, Chihuahua's economy grew under the rule of Díaz, despite continuing Indian uprisings and a good deal of political opposition to Mexico City's control. But, again as elsewhere in the country, that economic growth came at the expense of selling off some national assets and making concessions to foreigners; monopolies increased, as did the concentration of power and wealth into a few hands, whether foreign or

Mexican. Two-fifths of the state's land, including the best agricultural and livestock-raising areas, came under the control of only seventeen haciendas, and the men who ran these haciendas became powerful regional *caciques*.

The concentration of wealth in so few hands was one of the driving forces behind the Revolution, after which there were various moves to redistribute land in a more equitable manner. However, great inequalities remain here today, as elsewhere in Mexico.

Particularly in recent years, Chihuahua's economy has been much affected by its border position. The economy changed and developed quite radically during the second half of the twentieth century, particularly following the signing of the North American Free Trade Agreement in 1992.

Nowadays, agriculture is an important part of the economy, occupying approximately 10 percent of the state. Wheat, oats, and potatoes are the principal crops, but there is also some production of cotton, corn, sorghum, peanuts, soybeans, and alfalfa, all thanks to irrigation systems. The state is known for its apples, of which over thirty varieties are grown. Melons are also important. Pastureland covers about a quarter of Chihuahua. Mexicans value Chihuahua's beef, raised on its huge ranches; associated with this cattle raising comes a significant level of milk and cheese production. Sheep, goats, and pigs are also raised, but on a far more modest scale. Another major contributor to the economy is forestry; forests and woodlands cover about 30 percent of the land; several varieties of pine are used for industrial purposes, and oaks are used for fuel.

In addition to its mining industry, Chihuahua is the number-one state for manufacturing. It has the second most important *maquiladora* industry in the country. Maquiladoras, the assembly plants for goods to be shipped across the border to the United States, number more than 400. They are located mostly in and around Juárez, grouped in twenty-five industrial parks. About a quarter of all Mexican maquiladora workers are to be found in Chihuahua. Chihuahua is now second in the country in direct foreign investment. Petroleos Mexicanos (Pemex), the state oil company and the fifth largest such company in the world, has a pipeline that runs across the border into the U.S. close to Juárez.

It is generally the case that the further south one goes in Mexico, the poorer people become (barring one or two exceptions), and that generality is borne out in Chihuahua: Juárez, for all of its unevenness, is the ninth most prosperous town in Mexico. Overall, Chihuahua is the third most prosperous state. However, its majority urban population is a good deal more prosperous than its rural population.

Arts

Among crafts there is weaving with natural fibers, leatherwork, woodwork, and some nonindustrial production of textiles. Mountain areas are known for the production of toys and musical instruments.

During the second half of the nineteenth century, the popular music of the northern states was influenced by the arrival of immigrants from Germany and Eastern Europe. Prior to that time, the standard instruments used in popular festivities had been the guitar and the violin. To these were added the accordion and a large derivative of the guitar called the *bajo sexto*. New dance forms such as the polka and the mazurka became popular. The simple narrative ballads known as *corridos* were given a boost by the Revolution, which provided colorful people such as Pancho Villa to sing about; the corrido became popular over much of the country. One consequence of the fusion of new musical instruments and genres with more traditional ones was a new *norteño* style. The related *banda*, as its name indicates, is brass based. It usually involves woodwind and percussion also, and a signature instrument is the *tambora*, a type of bass drum that provides the insistent rhythmic drive. The ensembles are relatively large, perhaps of fifteen people. The repertoire for norteño and banda ensembles is both instrumental and vocal and usually ranges over *canciones rancheras*, corridos, *cumbias*, and *boleros*. Electronic music has been entering the mixture as well. "Indigenous" music is in fact a hybrid of ancient practices and imported ones from other cultures and times.

The mainstream Hispanic culture of Chihuahua has produced one or two figures of national or international standing. The actor **Anthony Quinn** (1915–2001) was born Antonio Quiñones in Chihuahua, but at the age of four his family moved to Los Angeles. He is best remembered for his roles in *Zorba the Greek* and *Lawrence of Arabia*. Chihuahua gave Mexico one of the most famous of its twentieth-century mural painters, **David Alfaro Siqueiros** (1896–1974). Siqueiros was the most politically active and the most doctrinaire of the three leading muralists (the others being José Clemente Orozco and Diego Rivera) in the postrevolutionary years. He also fought on the Republican side in the Spanish Civil War. Examples of his striking and dramatic works can be seen in many places, including the National Preparatory School, Palacio de Bellas Artes, and Poliforum Cultural in Mexico City. The Museo Nacional de Historia houses his *From Porfirio's Dictatorship to the Revolution*, and the Palacio de Congresos his *March of Humanity*. There are also works by Siqueiros in other countries, such as at the Plaza Art Center in Los Angeles and the Escuela Normal de Chillán, in Chile (where he was exiled for a time).

Martín Luis Guzmán Franco (1887–1976) was a soldier and a writer. He was active during the Revolution and for a while acted as Pancho Villa's secretary. He founded several newspapers and also wrote some novels that are important in Mexico's literary history: *El águila y la serpiente*, *La sombra del caudillo*, and *Memorias de Pancho Villa*. In addition, he held a high-ranking position at Mexico's largest university (the Universidad Nacional Autónoma, in Mexico City) and was director of the National Library. **Arturo Tolentino Hernández** (1888–1954) made a certain reputation as a raconteur and as a composer of popular music—corridos, mazurkas, and waltzes—of which the best-known example is "Ojos de juventud" (Young Eyes). **Porfirio Parra** (1854–1912) was a writer and journalist, a leading light among the positivists who dominated political and social thinking at the time of Porfirio Díaz.

Social Customs

Among the many Catholic-based fiestas that take place in Chihuahua is the Día de San Isidro Labrador, which is celebrated in Guadalupe de Bravos in May with dancing and merrymaking. The Feast of the Virgin of Guadalupe, Mexico's patroness, takes place everywhere in Mexico on December 12, and naturally it is especially important for Guadalupe de Bravos, an occasion for traditional indigenous dances and processions. In Jiménez in August, the Día de San Cristo de Burgos is cause for similar celebrations, coupled with a craft fair and entertainment. Santa Bárbara celebrates the Día de la Virgen de los Remedios in September, notable for its dance of the bowmen (*danza de los arqueros*), and the saint herself is honored on her day in December, with more traditional dancing. Other religious festivities are the feasts of San Francisco de Asís (October, celebrated in several places), Santa Rosa (September, in Camargo), Santa Rita (May, in Chihuahua), and San Antonio (June, in Cuauhtémoc). In July, Juárez hosts a trade fair.

Among the Tarahumara people, peyote is the focus of a festivity and a ritual dance. During the festivity in its honor, a special beef stew, seasoned with mountain herbs, is prepared. The *jículi* dance takes place around a fire and a cross; the priest chooses two women to grind peyote, whose thick, grayish juice is then drunk from a communal cup by the dancers. During Holy Week, they engage in a hybrid celebration, a dance ritual that represents good and evil making merry with *tesgüino*, a fermented, corn-based drink that is a sine qua non of Tarahumara rituals. The Tarahumaras also have traditional games, such as a race among men that involves dribbling a small wooden football (made of oak), and one for women that involves using a stick to throw a cloth hoop. These races over the hills can cover as much as 200 kilometers (120 miles) and last for several days. People bet sacks of corn, clothes, and animals on the outcome, and the conclusion of the races is celebrated with feasting and more tesgüino.

The customs of the Tepehuanes vary from one small community to another, but the women still wear distinctive dress (brightly colored scarves, blouses, and skirts). Their religious ceremonies include dances shared by the Tarahumaras, such as the *yúmare*. This is one of the most important dances, one which entails spending a night helping Father Sun and Mother Moon to produce rain. The dance itself involves movements in imitation of deer, from whom, according to tradition, people first learned the dance. The women make a circle around a bonfire and crouch down and touch the ground with their heads, chanting. Then they dance to the accompaniment of drums, tracing images of heavenly bodies with their feet.

Norteño cowboy dress—denim jeans, checked shirts, leather waistcoats, square-toed boots, and tall hats—has become emblematic of the northern Mexican macho man.

Noteworthy Places

Parral has many colonial buildings, such as the Palacio de Don Pedro de Alvarado, which was built on the orders of a millionaire mine owner. It is here that the revolutionary hero Pancho Villa was assassinated on July 20, 1923.

Ciudad Juárez was founded in 1659 by Spanish explorers and first called El Paso del Norte ("North Pass"), but it was renamed in honor of President Benito Juárez. At the end of the war with the United States, the city was divided, and the part on the northern side of the river became El Paso, Texas. Juárez has become one of Mexico's biggest cities—among the border towns, rivaled only by Tijuana. It is surrounded by makeshift dwellings with no services that house the thousands of migrants who have come to work in the maquiladoras or are waiting for their opportunity to cross over to the United States. Juárez is home to people from all over Mexico and is a place to which others from El Paso, across the border, come in search of sex, shopping, food, or entertainment such as rodeos. Naturally, it also has its prosperous areas. U.S. influence is everywhere, though less strong within Mexican homes than out on the street. Juárez is the busiest border town in the world, and it has all the usual problems one would expect in such a place, from exploitation of people wanting to cross the border to assassinations associated with the drug trade. It does have some historic and artistic interest: the sixteenth-century Church of Our Lady of Guadalupe on the Plaza de Armas (Main Square), the Museum of Art, and a historical museum that features Pancho Villa and the Revolution.

Interesting buildings elsewhere in the state include the church of San Felipe del Real de Chihuahua (late seventeenth century), Santa Rita, the cathedral (an important eighteenth-century example of the baroque style), San Francisco, and the Santuario de Guadalupe. Other examples of colonial religious architecture are Santa Ana (Aldama), Nuestra Señora del Rosario (Allende), several churches in Belisario Domínguez and Parral, the Misión de Nuestra Señora de Guadalupe (Juárez), and the Misión Jesuita (Creel). Notable civic buildings include the Palacio de Gobierno in Chihuahua, on a site where a colonial Jesuit college once stood; the present building, dating from the nineteenth century, has undergone several modifications. In its patio, there are murals detailing the history of the state and a plaque in recognition of the fact that Miguel Hidalgo, the man who sparked the movement for independence from Spain, was executed there.

The Hacienda de Encinillas, a three-hundred-year-old ranch, once belonged to the Terrazas family. At the close of the nineteenth century, the Hacienda del Torreón covered more than 70,000 hectares (173,000 acres). The Quinta Carolina, another property of the Terrazas family, comprised about 19,900 hectares (approximately 50,000 acres). The Hacienda El Sauz, first built in the seventeenth century, was extended during the porfiriato. The Casa de la Familia Touché is eclectic but basically European in style and dates from the same era. The tower that now houses the Banco Bancomer, in Chihuahua, is an example of the functional style in architecture that became fashionable in the 1960s.

There are archaeological museums in Delicias and Juárez. In addition to the art museum in Juárez, there is one in Chihuahua. Similarly, there are other museums of the Revolution in Chihuahua and Parral.

Paquimé (Casas Grandes) is the principal archaeological site. Here, pre-Columbian ceremonial structures bordered an area of private apartments approached by T-shaped doorways. There was a so-called Casa de la Noria (Waterwheel House), with around 340 private rooms, some on two floors, some underground, and the water itself 14 meters (45 feet) down. There was a steam room, a storeroom full of shells, and a place for raising parrots. In the Casa de las Guacamayas (House of the Macaws), the remains of ninety-five birds were found. The Casa de los Muertos (House of the Dead) comprised nineteen rooms and three courtyards; its name is due to the fact that the remains of humans and a large number of decapitated turkeys were found here. The Casa de las Pilastras takes its name from its adobe pilasters; it also has a number of courtyards and a ball court (one of a total of three ceremonial courts found at Paquimé). The Casa de los Cráneos is a place where six human skulls were found, hanging like trophies from the roof. There is also a defensive tower and an area that appears to have been used for cooking. One raised area, marked by crosses, is presumed to have been of astrological significance, another to have been used for ritual or religious purposes. The Montículo del Pájaro is another raised area, representing a decapitated bird, and the Montículo de la Serpiente is yet another, representing a snake; apparently these images allude to the god Quetzalcóatl, the Plumed Serpent. The place had aqueducts, a reservoir, and a drainage system.

Close to the former Hacienda de los Remedios, in the north, there are rock paintings of geometric and animal shapes, some also of human forms.

Basaseáchi National Park, in the heart of the Sierra Madre, is a major conservation area. Its waterfalls, plunging 246 meters (807 feet) deep into the Candemeña Ravine, are the highest in the country and among the highest in the world. Candemeña is in fact one of the series of seven ravines that are collectively called the Barranca del Cobre; they are the most impressive among the state's many dramatic and picturesque ravines, which also include the Barranca la Sinforosa in the Sierra Tarahumara and the Cañon del Pegüis. There is a notable series of fifteen caverns at Coyamé.

The Zona del Silencio (Zone of Silence), located in the area where Chihuahua meets Coahuila and Durango, lies in the part of the Chihuahua Desert that is known as the Bolsón de Mapimí. Here, electromagnetic factors render radio communication impossible. The flora and fauna are very unusual, and fossils point to the fact that many millions of years ago this was a sea. Since the discovery of these strange phenomena in the 1970s, popular myths have grown around this place.

Cuisine

The rigors of a climate that was too hot, too dry, or too cold led early inhabitants of Chihuahua to preserve food by drying it. That tradition provides the basis of much of Chihuahua's cuisine, which tends to be simple. *Caldo del oso* (bear broth), despite its name, is a spicy fish-based soup that uses dried chiles. *Chile con queso* is made with rings of *chilaca* chiles and melted cheese. *Cecina* is dehydrated meat in thin slices that is used in a number of soups and dishes, such as *machaca con huevo*. *Frijoles maneados* are fried beans, but not crushed ones, and they are usually accompanied by strips of cheese made with goat's or cow's milk. *Carne asada* (roast beef) is prepared with onions and potatoes.

A common snack is *empanadas de Santa Rita*, savory pastries that are filled with pork, almonds, and raisins, seasoned with herbs and spices, and sprinkled with sugar. *Gorditas de cuajada* are small corn tortillas ground up with fat, sugar, cinnamon, and egg and then grilled over orange leaves. *Jamoncillo de leche* is a kind of custard made with milk, cinnamon, and sugar and set in a wafer-lined dish. *Torrejas* are made with almonds, eggs, and sweet bread, drenched with honey and decorated with mint leaves.

Among local alcoholic drinks, the most distinctive is the fierce *maguey* cactus–based *sotol*, which is often combined with fruit juices. *Tehuino* is made from fermented corn. This is also the land of the *margarita*, which is said to have been devised in a Chihuahua bar in 1942.

Tacos de Discada

Ingredients:

2 lb. beef filet
3 oz. bacon
2 oz. *chorizo*
4 tomatoes, finely chopped
Salt and pepper
Garlic
2 large onions, chopped
5 *jalapeño* chiles (red bell pepper, if less spiciness is preferred)
2 bottles dark beer
Tequila
$^1/_2$ pint water
Corn tortillas

Fry the bacon until it has shed most of its fat. Season with black pepper, and then add the chorizo. Once the chorizo is cooked through, add the beef. When the beef is cooked, add the beer and a dash of tequila and leave to reduce. When the mixture is almost dry, add the remaining ingredients and cook through before serving on the folded tortillas.

Lengua Mechada

Ingredients:

1 beef tongue (or a combination of beef and calf)
$1/4$ lb. lean ham
2 oz. streaky bacon
$1/2$ lb. chopped tomatoes
1 small onion, finely chopped
4 cloves of garlic
$1/2$ cup vinegar
4 oz. red wine
Cloves
Cinnamon
Black pepper
Ground ginger
Oregano
Sage
Capers
Green olives
Oil
Butter
Salt

Boil the tongue in water until half done and skin it. Make cuts all over it and insert pieces of garlic and bacon, together with cloves, cinnamon, and pepper. Place it in a casserole dish, adding half the wine, the vinegar, and more cloves, cinnamon, and pepper to taste. Add the tomato, seasoned with ground ginger, sage, and salt. Put it in the oven at 400°F until it is thoroughly cooked. Fry any remaining garlic together with the ham, both finely chopped. Add a little of the meat broth to the frying pan, along with the rest of the wine and a pinch of oregano. Next, add the onion, capers, and olives. Season to taste. Combine both dishes and heat a little longer.

Pan Dulce

Ingredients:

3 oz. baker's yeast
$1/2$ cup lukewarm water
2 lb. whole meal flour
2 tsp cinnamon
1 pint sugar syrup (made by dissolving a pound of brown sugar in water)
1 tsp salt
2 tsp aniseeds

Dissolve the yeast in the warm water and then mix with the rest of the ingredients, making a smooth dough. Knead for about 15 minutes. Place the dough in a greased bowl and turn it over so that every part of it is coated. Cover with a cloth and leave to rise to twice the size (roughly for an hour). Make balls with pieces of the dough and put them on a baking tray, pressing each of them down to flatten them a little. Decorate with small strips of dough sprinkled with flour. Heat oven to 475°F and bake for about 45 minutes, until they sound hollow when tapped on the bottom.

Coahuila

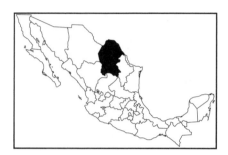

State Characteristics

Coahuila is in northern Mexico, on the border with Texas. To the east of Coahuila lies the state of Nuevo León, to the south Zacatecas and Durango, and to the west Durango and Chihuahua. Coahuila's border with the United States is 512 kilometers (317 miles) long. It is the third largest state in terms of land, occupying 7.7 percent of the whole of Mexico, and covering 151,571 square kilometers (59,112 square miles). However, the population, for such a large state, is modest: 2,495,200, the equivalent of 2.4 percent of the national population. The population density for Coahuila is thus 16 people per square kilometer (42 per square mile), as compared with a national average of 50.

Coahuila has thirty-eight municipalities and seven representatives in Mexico's National Congress. Ninety percent of the state population lives in urban areas (as compared with a national average of 76 percent). The capital of Coahuila is Saltillo, which has approximately three-quarters of a million inhabitants. Other major metropolitan areas are Monclova (pop. 300,000), a former state capital, and Piedras Negras (160,000). La Laguna, a region that lies where Coahuila, Chihuahua, Zacatecas, and Durango meet, is a major industrial area; 800,000 of the region's inhabitants live in Coahuila, 577,477 of those in the town of Torreón. Seven newspapers are published in Saltillo; of these the most important are *Palabra*, *El Diario de Coahuila*, *El Heraldo*, and *Vanguardia*. Torreón has four: *El Siglo de Torreón, La Opinión, Noticias de El Sol,* and *La Laguna.* In addition, Monclova publishes *La Prensa, La Voz de Coahuila,* and *El Tiempo*, and

Piedras Negras has *El Zócalo*, Múzquiz *El Factor*, and San Pedro *La Voz de San Pedro* and *El Diario de San Pedro*. Saltillo's Instituto Tecnológico dates from 1950, and the University of Coahuila from 1957.

The origin of the word *Coahuila* is not entirely clear, though the name is generally thought to derive from Náhuatl, a major indigenous language. It is known that when the Spaniards arrived, they encountered Indians who called themselves Coahuitlecos. The official full name of the state is Coahuila de Zaragoza, in recognition of Gen. **Ignacio Zaragoza** (1829–1862), who is remembered nationally for distinguishing himself against the French at the Battle of Puebla (commemorated annually on the Cinco de Mayo). Zaragoza was born in a territory that at the time was part of Coahuila, though later that was lost to Texas.

Coahuila is a state of deserts and mountains. The topographical backbone of the state is the Sierra Madre Oriental. There are six places where the mountains rise to altitudes in excess of 3,000 meters (10,000 feet), including the Cerro El Morro, Cerro San Rafael, Sierra Potrero de Abrego, and Cerro El Jabalí.

The climate is generally hot and dry, with few significant variations. Such rain as there is can be torrential; it falls mostly in the summer months, in some areas between May and October. Higher elevations are somewhat milder in climate. It is possible to distinguish three main climate zones in Coahuila: its western parts are very dry, comprising extensive desert flatlands and some mountainous areas; the central and southern parts are very to moderately dry, with some mountain areas that are somewhat milder and less dry; and the northeast portion of the state lies on the eastern side of the Sierra Madre and therefore has a warm and more humid climate, under maritime influence. At 233 millimeters (9.4 inches) per annum, rainfall is lowest in Cuatrociénegas, in the central region; it is highest in the extreme northeast, in Piedras Negras (564 millimeters/22.6 inches). The mean annual temperatures range from 15.5°C (60°F) in the coolest area (Carneros) to 22.5°C (73°F) in the hottest (Juárez). Summer maxima in many places are in excess of 30°C (86°F).

There are four hydrological regions: the Río Grande–Conchos region, the Mapimí, the Nazas-Aguanaval, and the Río Salado. Of these, the first is the most important; the Río Grande, which provides a natural frontier with the United States, runs for 740 kilometers (460 miles) along Coahuila territory. The Nazas and Aguanaval rivers have been truncated by dams that are located in the state of Durango. Despite the dry conditions and the low rainfall, there are a number of underground currents that sometimes surface and rivers that are fed by underground sources; examples can be found in the Cuatrociénegas Valley and the area known as Cinco Manantiales (Five Springs), in the north of the state. The waters of the Mapimí region are only apparent intermittently, depending on the rains; the main lagoons are El Guaje, El Rey, Viesca, and Mayrán. La Amistad and Venustiano Carranza are the names of two major man-made dams.

Vegetation in Coahuila is on the whole sparse. Low bushes, cacti, and scrub are predominant, especially *gobernadora*, *huizache*, *ocotillo*, *agave*, *maguey*, and *mezquite*. In the low-lying eastern region, there are rows of trees that are taller and more varied than is common in such a dry climate, because these trees line the course of streams or underground currents. Such trees, including walnuts and *sabinos*, have decreased in number, however, as many have been cut for wood or affected by bad land management. Similarly, fires (sometimes intentional) and unbridled deforestation have reduced the stock of oaks, pines, cedars, and poplars that grow at relatively high elevations, allowing other species such as cacti to take their place. There is a significant area of pasture on the northeastern side of the Sierra La Concordia mountains. In the warmer zone, the vegetation includes palms and subtropical plants.

There is a great diversity of wildlife in Coahuila. Mammals include bears, raccoon-like *cacomixtles*, prairie dogs, mountain cats, badgers, deer, bison, boars, armadillos, and miscellaneous rodents. Among reptiles and insects are snakes, lizards, turtles, and scorpions. There are various birds of prey, including the *zopilote* (a type of vulture), and also cardinals, quail, thrushes, blackbirds, woodpeckers, swallows, turkeys, doves, and owls; endangered species include the peregrine falcon, royal eagle, and dwarf parrot. Coahuila has four conservation areas designated for the protection of wildlife: Cuatro-ciénegas, Maderas del Carmen, Zapalinamé, and Los Novillos.

Cultural Groups and Languages

The 2005 census results asserted that only 0.3 percent of Coahuila's population over the age of five spoke an indigenous language, a percentage that was one of the lowest in the country. Of the 5,842 people involved, about 11 percent used Náhuatl and about 5 percent Mazahua. As many as two-thirds of the state's indigenous-language speakers were listed as speakers of "unspecified" languages.

Although Coahuila does not have strong indigenous cultural elements by comparison with many states, there is an interesting example of border culture provided by the Kikapúes (Kickapoos). These people originally inhabited a wooded region near the Great Lakes that is now part of Wisconsin, and culturally they are related to the Algonquin people. The Kickapoos' first contact with Europeans (the French) took place in the seventeenth century. Subsequently, colonialism drove them ever farther south, and eventually to Texas at a time when it was still part of Mexico. The Kickapoos were particularly resistant to Western customs and determined to preserve their own.

After the U.S. invasion of Mexico (1846–1848), the Kickapoos asked for permission to settle on the Mexican side, and this was granted on the condition that they would help fend off the attacks that were being made along the border by Apaches and Comanches. Along with Seminoles, the

Kickapoos made a further attempt at Mexican settlement in 1850, and eventually, in 1864, they put down roots on the banks of the Sabinas River, in El Nacimiento, part of the *municipio* of Múzquiz. At that time, they numbered about 200. The Coahuila state government granted them about 3,000 hectares (7,400 acres) of land. Under President Benito Juárez, territory was also granted to other Indians, but these lands were later abandoned.

For a long time, the Kickapoos were able to cross the U.S. border freely, in accordance with an agreement ratified in 1832 by a U.S. Army officer; in 1983, they became entitled to U.S. citizenship. In modern times, the Kickapoos can be said to be tricultural: many of them speak Algonquin but can also get by in Spanish and in English. They spend part of the year in each country and do not see themselves as formally belonging to either. The loss of their traditional culture has gathered speed since they were granted permission to operate a casino on the border, at Eagle Pass, Texas.

A similar story involves the Negros Mascogos, whose origins are in Florida and who were refugees from slavery. Some of the blacks were in fact bought as slaves; others were won as war booty by Seminoles. The two peoples learned to integrate peacefully and to cooperate with one another in an alliance against the slave traders who, after Florida had been annexed to the United States in 1821, launched the Seminole Wars. Apart from about five hundred who took refuge in the swamps, these people were driven out of Florida. In 1843, some of them, along with representatives of other Indian peoples, including the Kickapoos, sought a peace treaty with Coahuila; a year later, the Mexican federal government ratified the treaty and allowed the Indians to settle in Coahuila. Unlike the Kickapoos, however, the "Black Seminoles" were quick to assimilate to the host culture. Most of them are now Catholics. They do observe a Día de los Negros (Black People's Day), in memory of Abraham Lincoln's freeing of the slaves in 1863; however, racially they are now well integrated with other Mexican peoples.

History

Arrowheads found in Coahuila indicate that it was inhabited by hunters about 12,000 years ago, a time when the area was more verdant and fertile. A significant, though slow climate change forced people to adapt their hunting-and-gathering customs and their eating habits. It is believed that over the years more than two hundred groups of people in Coahuila came to have shared customs and traditions and to speak the Coahuitleco language. Other groups used Zapotec, Apache, Tobosco, and Cuachichil. Early peoples left rock paintings, vestiges of which can still be seen in the Zaragoza and Múzquiz municipalities. It is believed that when the Spaniards arrived in the sixteenth century, there were some 100,000 Indians in what is now the state of Coahuila.

The first explorations by Spain were carried out between 1550 and 1580; it was slow process due to both the harsh conditions and the

The governors of the Mexican border states of Sonora, Coahuila, Nuevo Leon and Tamaulipas, all of which border Texas, completed the first day of a two-day ride in 2004 from Hidalgo to the border city of Nuevo Laredo, to call attention to the preservation of Mexican tradition. (AP Photo/Raul Llamas)

resistance offered by the Indians, who constantly kept the Spanish settlements under attack. The first recorded settlement followed an expedition led by Francisco Cano in 1568, in the name of New Galicia. Later, in 1577, Alberto del Canto, representing New Vizcaya, founded La Villa de Santiago del Saltillo. Two hundred years later, politicians and soldiers were fighting over where to put the capital of the territory; Monclova and Saltillo were in the running, but the latter won the day, having the advantage of being the commercial and financial center, the place that was in contact with the authorities of New Spain.

In 1591, San Esteban de la Nueva Tlaxcala was founded, close to Saltillo; this reflected the fact that Indian families from Tlaxcala had been sent by the Spaniards to settle other lands, to aid the process of acculturation and evangelization, and it led to the implantation and adaptation of a number of Tlaxcalan customs. This settlement came under constant attack from other Indian peoples. Agriculture, cattle ranching, mining, and commerce increased during the sixteenth century, when Coahuila was administered by the Nuevo Reino de León, an entity that in addition covered the present-day states of Nuevo León, Tamaulipas, and Texas. But the arrangement had a number of problems.

When the movement toward independence from Spain began in the early nineteenth century, the local authorities and military detachments were keen to defend the royalist cause, but in 1811 Mariano Jiménez led a rebellion, occupying Saltillo and then turning his attention to Parras and Monclova. Rebel leaders now came to the province (as it then was), and Manuel Royuela, the king's treasurer, together with Bishop Marin de Porras, set an ambush for them. The rebel leaders Miguel Hidalgo, Juan de Aldama, and Ignacio Allende were taken prisoner, transported to Chihuahua, and shot. Another significant encounter occurred in Puerto Piñones, where Ignacio López Rayón defeated royalist troops. When the Constituent Congress for the newly independent Mexico was called together in 1823 to thrash out the details of Mexico's first republican constitution, a native of Coahuila, **Miguel Ramos Arizpe** (1775-1843), was one of the key architects of it; indeed, he has come to be known as the father of Mexican federalism.

In 1824, Coahuila and Texas were declared together to be a single new state, with Monclova as its capital. Texas broke away from Mexico in 1836. Ten years later, the United States invaded Mexico; some troops took the over the garrison at Río Grande (modern-day Guerrero) and advanced toward Monclova and Parras, while others took Saltillo. Forces sent by President Antonio López de Santa Anna to defend Mexican interests engaged and defeated the U.S. forces at La Angostura, close to Saltillo, only to withdraw for no apparent reason, with the result that neither side really gained.

Juan Antonio de la Fuente promulgated Coahuila's second constitution in 1852, asserting its sovereignty. However, just four years later, Santiago Vidaurri, the governor of the state of Nuevo León, annexed Coahuila. When Maximilian's imperialist forces took Mexico City in 1864, President Juárez was obliged to leave and set up a government in opposition elsewhere. He embarked on a journey that eventually took him north, and on arriving in Coahuila, he declared that it should be separate from Nuevo León; Juárez nominated Andrés Viesca as governor of Coahuila. In 1865, French troops occupied the state, but they were defeated by Mexican guerrilla tactics, under the leadership of Viesca, among others. Another distinguished Coahuila figure of the nineteenth century was **Melchor Múzquiz Arrieta** (1788-1844), a state representative for Coahuila, who was also twice governor of the state of México and eventually became president of the country.

During the long rule of Porfirio Díaz, the *porfiriato*, there were uprisings (in 1877 and 1878) led by Mariano Escobedo. Coahuila was quite prominent in the opposition movement against Porfirio, who had spent many manipulative years in the presidency and was seeking reelection for yet another term in 1910. That year, supporters of Díaz's chief opponent, **Francisco Madero** (1873-1913), proposed that **Venustiano Carranza** (1859-1920), a senator and an ally of Madero, should become governor of Coahuila. As events unfolded, Díaz kept control of the nation, and Madero was defeated and imprisoned. Carranza then organized an uprising in the north of the state against Díaz, while Rafael de Cepeda did the same in Saltillo. Madero soon was able to return to Coahuila and join the rebels.

In February 1911, a junta led by Cepeda took Saltillo from forces loyal to Díaz, while other rebels took control of the southeast of the state. Following further rebel victories, Carranza became provisional governor of the state, shortly after which he was elected to the post. Meanwhile, Madero became president of Mexico, but two years after his election in 1911, he was assassinated.

On March 26, 1913, following Madero's death, Carranza promulgated a political document known as the Plan de Guadalupe, so called because it was drawn up at a *hacienda* of that name; among other things, this plan denounced Madero's successor as president, Victoriano Huerta. A further sign of resistance to the central government was that on October 3, Pancho Villa, one of Carranza's rival revolutionary leaders, took Torreón, a former bastion of federal troops; Villa then advanced toward Saltillo. Nevertheless, by 1915, Carranza's forces had prevailed over most of Mexico. As president himself, Carranza supervised the creation of the 1917 national constitution, which, much amended, is still in force. Thus, in Madero and Carranza, Coahuila provided two of the leading political figures of early twentieth-century Mexico. Coahuila remained firmly in the control of the Partido Revolucionario Institucional (PRI) for the rest of the century.

Economy

Coahuila benefits from having huge coal deposits, which allow it to meet 100 percent of the country's industrial demand for coal. It also has significant deposits of lead, iron, silver, and, to a lesser degree, copper, zinc, gold, manganese, strontium, and antimony. This mining activity is concentrated in the municipios of Múzquiz, Nava, and San Juan de Sabinas. Nonmetallic reserves include barite and fluorite (in Acuña and Múzquiz); the state is a national leader in the production of both. There are also quantities of dolomite, phosphorus, sodium, and magnesium. Materials such as sand are provided for the construction industry. In the area known as the Gulf of Sabinas, major reserves of natural gas have been discovered.

For economic purposes, the state of Coahuila is best described as having five regions: the southeast, the Laguna region, the central region, the mining region, and the north. In the southeastern region, 45 percent of the economy depends on industry (manufacturing), 29 percent on commerce and services, and 8 percent on construction. In the Laguna region, agriculture is important, along with car parts manufacturing and textiles; industry and the commerce-and-services sector each account for approximately a third of the total economic activity. The Laguna region is Mexico's leading producer of milk. In the desert region, there is a major smelting industry (Altos Hornos de México y Teksid); industry accounts for half of this region's activity, and commerce and services for another 27 percent. The mining region has a growing *maquiladora* industry; in this region, mining accounts for 25 percent, industry for 21 percent, and commerce and services for 28 percent of the economy. Finally, the northern region is dominated by mining, energy, and maquiladoras; industry represents over 57 percent of economic activity, with commerce and services at almost 23 percent. Overall, Coahuila produces a third of Mexico's steel, particularly to supply the automobile manufacturing plants that have been set up in Mexico by U.S. companies such as Chrysler and General Motors.

Only 3 percent of Coahuila's land is given over to agriculture; pastureland accounts for a further 7.1 percent; woods cover 1.5 percent. While conditions in Coahuila do not generally favor agriculture, there is some production (principally in El Llano and El Guaje and to the east of the Sierra de Almagre mountains) of corn, wheat, beans, and squash for local consumption. The Laguna region has irrigation systems that permit the growing of cotton, alfalfa, safflower, oats, peppers, beans, tomatoes, melons, and grapes. In Coahuila, livestock rearing is quite important, and the livestock are generally fed natural vegetation; there are cattle, sheep, and goats.

As its name suggests (*parras* means "vines"), Parras de la Fuente is a place where wine is made. The vines are watered by underground streams. In fact, the very first winery in the Americas was established in this place in 1597; it now goes under the name of Casa Madero. Other wineries are Bodegas del Vesuvio (whose name betrays an Italian influence) and Hacienda del Perote. There is also wine production in the Valley of Cuatrociénegas.

The service sector is largely concentrated in Acuña, Monclova, Piedras Negras, Saltillo, and Torreón.

Manufacturing takes place especially in Frontera, Monclova, Saltillo, Torreón, and, in recent years, the northern areas of Acuña and Piedras Negras, where the maquiladora industry has developed. Ramos Arizpe is the place that saw the arrival of General Motors and Chrysler and then of other enterprises that supply and service these vehicle manufacturers; the result is that it has become one of Mexico's most important industrial areas.

The average Coahuilan worker earns about 90 percent of Mexico's national average wage, which is roughly a tenth of the average in the United States.

Arts

King among crafts in Coahuila—in Saltillo especially—is the making of *sarapes*. These are multicolored woolen wraps; the name comes from a Náhuatl word that means "blanket." However, the weaving of sarapes is not something that originated in Coahuila; once again it was the tlaxcaltecas who first introduced it. People in Saltillo also make wrought iron and wooden artifacts. Kickapoo women produce traditional protective footwear called *teguas*; they also make leather and laminated metal objects. Arteaga is known for its wood carvings, typically of animals.

Lechuguilla is a plant that grows in dry areas and is harvested for its silken *ixtle* fibers, which are used in decorative craftwork. It also gives its name to a dance in southern Coahuila, whose lively leaps are said to reflect the excitement of the harvesters. The dancers also make movements that simulate the cutting down or pruning of the cactus. This dance has some things in common with dancing in Tlaxcala (whence a number of immigrants were sent as "missionaries" by the Spaniards in the late sixteenth century). Another dance brought to Coahuila by people from Tlaxcala is the "dance of Ojo de Agua." On the second Sunday in September, it is the custom for people in Ojo de Agua to worship an image of the crucified Christ by making offerings and performing this dance. It is accompanied by violin and double-skin drum, sometimes by flute and tambourine, while the dancers themselves carry maracas. Both the *danza de la lechuguilla* and the dance of Ojo de Agua are also found in other areas to which the *tlaxcaltecas* migrated, such as Nuevo León, Zacatecas, and San Luis Potosí.

The Kickapoo people at El Nacimiento, on the flanks of the Sierra de Santa Rosa in the north of the state, are known for performing dances related to natural phenomena or to mark significant dates, such as the onset of a new year or the anniversary of their arrival in the area. Their dances include *la chueca, del hilo, del soldado, de oro, del estribo, del coyote, la cuarenta y nueve,* and *el baile de parejas.*

Harvest time in the municipality of General Cepeda traditionally involves dancing the *jarabe pateño.* The word *pateño* derives from the name of the Indians (the Patchos) who originally inhabited the area. The *jarabe,* however, is a dance with colonial roots. Similarly, the *contradanza de Arteaga* is based on a European genre, brought in by immigrants who came to cultivate vines. Initially, it was an aristocratic affair, but later it was popularized and modified into a genuine Mexican "country dance." As in other northerly states of Mexico, the nineteenth century saw more forms imported from Europe, largely from Germany and Eastern Europe. Examples are the polka, the waltz, and the *chotís.* These genres, too, were given a local popular character.

In the Laguna region, the traditional dances are *los panaderos* and *las cuadrillas,* which can last up to two hours, to the accompaniment of small ensembles, such as of string instruments, duos comprised of violin and accordion, or trios consisting of a clarinet, a harp, and a violin. The *canción cardenche* is also characteristic of the Laguna region. It is a polyphonic song form that is performed a capella, and its usual subject matter is love or historical events. The canción cardenche is full of double entendres; its melodies are handed down orally, and it is traditional to sing it after a day's work on the land.

No account of music in a border state is complete without reference to *norteño,* which is the dominant and generally most popular style of music. Norteño is characterized by an instrumental ensemble consisting of an accordion, the large guitar-like *bajo sexto,* and a bass, occasionally together with wind instruments such as flutes, clarinets, or saxophones.

During the second half of the nineteenth century, the popular music of the northern states was influenced by the arrival of immigrants from Germany and Eastern Europe. Prior to that time, the standard instruments used in popular festivities had been the guitar and the violin. New dance forms such as the polka and the mazurka became popular. The simple narrative ballads known as *corridos* were given a boost by the Revolution, which provided colorful people such as Pancho Villa to sing about; the corrido became popular over much of the country. One consequence of the fusion of new musical instruments and genres with more traditional ones was the new *norteño* style. The related *banda*, as its name indicates, is brass based. It usually involves woodwind and percussion also, and a signature instrument is the *tambora*, a type of bass drum that provides the insistent rhythmic drive. The ensembles are relatively large, perhaps of fifteen people. The repertoire for norteño and banda ensembles is both instrumental and vocal and usually ranges over *canciones rancheras*, corridos, *cumbias*, and *boleros*. Electronic music has been entering the mixture as well. "Indigenous" music is in fact a hybrid of ancient practices and imported ones from other cultures and times.

In literature, **Manuel Acuña** (1849-1873) was one of the leading poets of Mexican Romanticism; his most famous works were "Ante un cadáver" and "Nocturno a Rosario." Acuña committed suicide at the age of twenty-four. **Laura Esquivel** (1950-), the highly successful authoress of *Como agua para chocolate* (Like Water for Chocolate, 1991) was born in Piedras Negras.

The brothers **Andrés** and **Fernando Soler** (real names Andrés and Fernando García Pavía; 1899-1932 and 1900-1979, respectively) worked in theater and the movies. Andrés appeared in over a hundred movie roles and also became director of Mexico's IMCINE (National Film Institute), while Fernando made more of a reputation as a director. Another movie actor and director of the same generation was **Emilio ("El Indio") Fernández** (1904-1986), a key figure in the history of Mexican cinema. Fernández starred in several major films of the 1930s and '40s, such as *Soy puro mexicano* and *Flor silvestre*, before teaming up with cameraman Gabriel Figueroa and becoming a director. Together they went on to make many highly successful films, artistically influenced by the Russian director Sergei Eisenstein and politically influenced by the socialist agenda of the times. A key example is *María Candelaria*. Fernández later acted in films made by John Huston. The actor **Ricardo Montalbán** (1920-2009) was born in Torreón.

Another person from Coahuila was **Fermín Espinosa Saucedo** (1911-1978), popularly known as "Armillita"; he became one of Mexico's most legendary bullfighters.

Social Customs

In October, Ciudad Acuña and neighboring Del Rio, Texas, have parades that culminate with the two state governors embracing one another on the border bridge; this is the Fiesta de la Amistad y de la Buena Vecindad (The

Festival of Friendship and Good Neighborliness). Predictably, both Cuatro-ciénegas and Parras have wine festivals (in July and August, respectively), when the harvest is celebrated with dancing and spectacles. Parras also hosts a celebration of local products—milk products, nuts, preserves, and liqueurs—during which a competition is held to see who has produced the largest nut confection. In the same vein, Piedras Negras holds the Festival Internacional del Nacho, during which there is a competition for the biggest nacho (the nacho is said to take its name from its inventor, chef Ignacio "Nacho" Anaya). Both results are published in *Guinness World Records*.

A horse ride takes place along a 320-kilometer (190-mile) route from Ramos Arizpe to Sabinas to mark the anniversary of the foundation of the latter. After arriving in Sabinas, the horses continue their cavalcade about the town, leading to large-scale festivities. Similarly, a recent celebration of shared traditions brings thousands of people on horseback, led by the governors of Coahuila, Nuevo León, and Tamaulipas, to the town of Nuevo Laredo.

In September, Saltillo hosts an antiques fair (Muestra Internacional de Antigüedades) that has a national reputation. The Instituto Coahuilense de Cultura's Festival Internacional de la Artes in October brings in national and international figures in the performing and visual arts. Another note-worthy fiesta is that of San Isidro Labrador, the patron saint of Arteaga, in May. Matamoros also has a festival in honor of the same saint; during it, the *danza de la conquista* (dance of the Conquest) is performed, with a reenactment of the execution of Malinche. A ten-year-old boy plays the role of the Lady of the Conquest.

There is a March commemoration of the birth of Benito Juárez, also held in Matamoros, and in July a pilgrimage and noisy celebration in honor of the Virgen del Refugio, involving bright costumes and the performance of *mojigangas* and *matachines*. The latter are very much in evidence during the Festival del Sagrado Corazón (Festival of the Sacred Heart) at Villa Fran-cisco I. Madero, with all-day dancing in front of the church.

Noteworthy Places

Somewhat anachronistically, Parras de la Fuente has a Museum of Wine and Revolution. Ciudad Acuña hosts the Venustiano Carranza Museum. Ramos Arizpe is the location of the Hacienda de Santa María, where Hidalgo, the man who sparked the independence movement, celebrated his final Mass, and the Hacienda de Guadalupe, where Carranza drew up his famous plan of action, the Plan de Guadalupe. There is another Museum of the Revolu-tion in San Pedro, the place where Madero wrote his political tract *Presiden-tial Succession*. Sabinas has a Casa Villa where Pancho Villa surrendered.

Among important religious buildings are the Misión de San Bernardo at Guerrero (dating from 1702) and numerous churches: the Parroquia de Santiago Apóstol and the Iglesia de San Francisco (Monclova), the Iglesia Santa Rosa de Lima (Múzquiz), the Parroquia de Santa María (Parras), and the Catedral de Santiago, the Templo de San Esteban, the Iglesia de San Juan, and the Iglesia del Ojo de Agua (Saltillo).

A 580-ton statue of Jesus is set upon a hill near Torreón, in the Laguna region; this is known as the Cristo de las Noas, a name taken from a plant that once grew abundantly in the hills. At 21.8 meters (72 feet) in height, this statue is second only to Rio de Janeiro's Cristo do Corcovado. In addition to a church, in that same location there are replicas of holy places, such as Calvary and the Holy Sepulchre.

Notable civic buildings in Coahuila include the Colegio de San Ignacio de Loyola in Parras and the Palacio de Gobierno and the Ateneo in Saltillo.

Rincón Colorado, located in the municipio of General Cepeda, is a site where fossils of dinosaurs from the Mesozoic era have been found. In that same municipality, there is also an archaeological area called Narigua. Visitors are attracted by spas or sulfurous springs at places such as Abasolo, Allende, Villa Unión, and Muzquiz. There are caves and 30-meter (100-foot) waterfalls at San Buenaventura. The Parque Nacional de Boquillas del Carmen is a nature reserve with impressive canyons and wildlife. The Presa de la Amistad (Friendship Dam) at Acuña, a major example of Mexican and U.S. collaboration, is a recreational area to boot. Arteaga is sometimes called the Switzerland of Mexico due to its attractive mountain landscape. Cuatrociénegas ("Four Swamps") is another place of natural beauty and home to a wide variety of living creatures and plants. It also boasts a Carranza Museum, in the house where Carranza was born. Viesca is known for its impressive Dunas de Bilbao, fine desert sand dunes, as if in northern Africa.

Parras has some interesting colonial architecture, for example, at the Casa Madero winery. In Saltillo, the only bird museum in Latin America is housed in a fine nineteenth-century building. The Recinto de Juárez in Saltillo, literally the Juárez "Precinct," is in fact the house where Juárez lodged. Other impressive buildings in the capital are its Technological Institute, the Fernando Soler Theater, and the Casino. Monclova has the Coahuila-Texas Museum and a botanical garden, the Parque Xochitpilli. Saltillo, Torreón, and Múzquiz all have museums of some archaeological or artistic interest. Near Torreón is the mysterious Zona del Silencio (Silent Zone), a place often affected by falling meteorites, where radio communication is impossible and flora and fauna have undergone strange mutations.

Cuisine

Like other border states, Coahuila is a place for flour tortillas and charcoal-roasted meats, including goat. *Machaca* is made with dried meat, and Múzquiz is famous for it. Wine is produced here, and a strong alcoholic beverage, *sotol*, is distilled from a local plant known in English as desert spoon. For the sweet-toothed, there are confections of milk and nuts that have the appearance of soft cheeses, preserved fruits such as peach and quince, and jellies laden with pine nuts and almonds. There is also a cakelike product that has *pulque*, the fermented drink made from cactus, among its ingredients; it is called *pan de pulque* and is Tlaxcalan in origin.

Asado de Puerco

Ingredients:

> 2 lb. leg of pork, cut into small pieces
> 10 *ancho* chiles
> 5 tomatoes, chopped
> 1 small onion, chopped
> 1 cup orange juice
> 1 clove of garlic
> $1/2$ tsp cumin
> $1/2$ tsp oregano
> $1/2$ tsp black pepper
> Mixed herbs
> 1 slice of orange, including peel
> Oil
> Salt

Put the meat in a large pot and cover it with water. Boil it with the mixed herbs until the water has reduced a good deal, then remove the meat, fry it, and set it aside. Clean out the chiles and fry them with the onion, tomatoes, garlic, oregano, cumin, and black pepper, then puree. Return this to the pan and then add the meat, the orange, and the orange juice. Let cook for about 20 minutes before serving.

Arroz Huérfano

Ingredients:

> 1 cup rice
> 8 strips bacon
> $1/2$ red bell pepper, chopped
> $1/2$ onion, chopped
> 2 sticks celery, chopped
> Chicken broth
> $1/4$ cup chopped walnuts
> $1/4$ cup chopped almonds
> Garlic
> Pepper
> Salt
> Oil
> Butter

Cook and drain the rice. Cut the bacon into pieces and fry it, then add the red pepper, onion, and celery. Grease a pan with butter and put a layer of rice on the bottom. Spread the fried ingredients over it, then the nuts, and season with garlic, salt, and black pepper. Pour chicken broth over the dish and put it in the oven for 5 to 10 minutes at 350°F.

Colima

State Characteristics

Colima is one of Mexico's smallest states (twenty-ninth in the national ranking by area) and has the second smallest state population. It is located halfway down the Pacific coast, with Jalisco lying to its north and Michoacán to its east. The total surface area of the state, including a number of islands, is 5,455 square kilometers (2,106 square miles). Colima's name, which it shares with its capital city, has generally been held to derive from Náhuatl, the language of the Aztecs, but the precise meaning of it has been in dispute; some gloss it as "the land conquered by our ancestors [or gods]" and others as "the place where the waters change course."

Colima is a state with a 160-kilometer (100-mile) coastline that attracts swimmers, divers, recreational sailors, and fishermen, and it has many unspoiled places of natural beauty. In Mexico, this state has the reputation for being a good place to live; it also attracts significant numbers of tourists, most of whom are Mexican. A good part of Colima is agricultural.

The state comprises ten municipalities and has six representatives in the National Congress. The state population, according to the 2005 census, was 582,456. The highest municipal population density—in the capital Colima—is 193 people per square kilometer (almost 500 per square mile); that compares with an average density for the state as a whole of 99 (250). Despite being the state capital, Colima is not the most populous city; Manzanillo, a major port, is a little bigger, at about 150,000 residents. The next most populous and urban municipalities are Villa de Alvarez and Tecomán, with about 100,000 people each.

Ninety-three percent of the *colimenses* (i.e., the inhabitants of the state of Colima) identify themselves as Catholic, and just 3 percent as Protestant. Colima has three newspapers, *El Diario de Colima*, *Coliman*, and *El Mundo desde Colima*; Manzanillo has *El Correo de Manzanillo*. There are several institutions of higher education, including the University of Colima and a campus of the Tecnológico de Monterrey, one of Mexico's largest university systems.

There are two main geographical regions to Colima: the predominantly northern mountains and the coastal plains. The southern Sierra Madre, which comprises four subsystems, runs through the state and covers three-quarters of it, while other ranges cut across it—all of which makes for a complex pattern of mountains, valleys, and ravines. Faults in the region give rise to quite frequent earthquakes and have resulted in two volcanoes, one active and one dormant, that dominate the capital. The active one, the Volcán Colima, close to the Jalisco border and approaching 4,100 meters (13,500 feet) in height, erupts roughly once every ten years, which makes it the most active and volatile volcano in Mexico. The plains lie southwestward, toward the Pacific.

Colima's main rivers flow south into that ocean. They are the Marabasco-Cihuatlán and the Coahuayana, which mark the borders with Jalisco and Michoacán, and the Río Armería, which starts in Jalisco and runs more than 300 kilometers (almost 200 miles) south to Boca de Pascuales, in the municipality of Armería. The Cuyutlán Lagoon is a large body of water on the coast that is used for salt production. There are freshwater lagoons also, notably the Alcuzahue and the Amela (in Tecomán).

Temperatures in Colima vary according to elevation as much as according to season, and in general do not vary a great deal. Winter temperatures average 20°C to 28°C (68°F to 76°F), summer ones from 28°C to 34°C (82°F to 93°F). Average annual rainfall for the state as a whole is 983 millimeters (39.3 inches) and most of this falls in the summer months. The prevailing winds come from the west for most of the year, but from the south in winter.

As to flora, in the mountains one finds pines, oaks, and myrtles; in the valleys, species that provide forage and also fruit trees such as mango, papaya, tamarind, lime, and coconut; and on the coast, *guamuchil*, *guayacán*, mesquite, *chicalite*, *crucillo*, and mangrove. Colima's fauna includes squirrels, boars, deer, ocelots, and foxes in mountainous areas; *tapacaminos*, *torcazas*, *zanates*, *tlacuaches*, *tzentzontles*, rabbits, and coyotes in the valleys; and *aguajones*, *comudas*, *dorados*, sharks, and turtles on the coast. There are ecological reserves at Volcán de Fuego and El Jabalí.

Cultural Groups and Languages

Only 0.6 percent of the state population speaks an Indian language, which represents one of the lowest proportions in Mexico. Furthermore, by far the majority of Colima's Indian-language speakers also speak Spanish.

Colima was dominated by the Olmec culture, and later by the Nahuas, Toltecs, and Chichimecs, before the Tarasco Indians became dominant and the Spaniards arrived. Indian numbers declined during the colonial era from a figure of perhaps 150,000 to about a tenth of that by the mid-sixteenth century. Consequently, the Spaniards brought in some African slaves, possibly together with Indians from other territories, to reinforce a depleted labor force.

Today there are still vestiges of the Nahua or Otomí cultures in some areas, primarily in Comala, Juluapan, Pueblo Nuevo, Villa de Alvarez, and Las Pesadas. Colima—more specifically La Campana, which is on the outskirts of the capital city—is famous for its ancient ceramic plump figurines of dogs (known as *perros cebados*) that sometimes seem to be dancing; many of them have been found inside unusual burial shafts known as *tiros*. It has been suggested that perhaps these figures mark the transition of the soul to the next world. The fattened dogs may have been a source of food, or they may have been viewed as companions on life's journey. Most of the tombs consist of a shaft connected to a number of chambers housing the remains of the dead, together with funeral offerings. The shaft is typically blocked off from the chambers by a pot or stone. Archaeologists have speculated that such tombs represent the maternal womb, death being viewed as an entry into the womb of the earth and thus a completion of the life cycle.

History

It is now believed that the first human settlements in Colima date from 1500 BC, which makes them contemporaneous with the major Olmec settlements on the Gulf Coast, such as San Lorenzo. The *tumbas de tiro* (shaft tombs) and the burnished red pottery that are now regarded as characteristic of pre-Columbian Colima date from much later, around 500 BC, and are associated with a place called Comala. It appears that several peoples jockeyed for position prior to the time of conquest by Spain. Early in the sixteenth century, the Purépechas (or Tarascos) wrested control of the territory from the Tecos, only to be defeated by them thereafter. The Tecos proceeded to take control of Sayula, Zapotlán, and Amula, and so became the dominant group in the territory that is now Colima. The leader of the Tecos was Colimotl.

After they had defeated the Aztecs and destroyed their capital, Tenochtitlán, in 1521, the Spaniards set about exploring and conquering other territories. Their first incursion into Colima met with defeat, and so Hernán Cortés, the leader of the conquest, sent another expedition westward, this time under Gonzalo de Sandoval. Once the Tecos were subdued, Sandoval founded the Villa de San Sebastián (July, 1523); there, the Spaniards established the second town council in western Mexico. This town was later renamed Santiago de los Caballeros, and then Colima. However, rather as happened in the case of Veracruz, the first site chosen, close to the sea, proved to be too unhealthy for settlement, so the town was moved to its present location in 1527.

As the town of Colima grew, so did the importance of the coast. In 1533 Don Hernando de Grijalva discovered the Revillagigedo Archipelago. The port of Tzalahua became important strategically and as a place of commerce. Another port, then called Santiago de Buena Esperanza and now known as Manzanillo, played a vital part in the Spanish expeditions to explore the Californias and in trade with the Philippines. Consequently, it also became a target for pirates.

As far as legal matters were concerned, during the early colonial years Colima was subject to the Real Audiencia of New Spain, in Mexico City, but as a result of the administrative reforms introduced under the Bourbons, it later became answerable to the *intendencia* of Guadalajara. For religious matters, it began under the jurisdiction of the bishop of Valladolid, before being transferred to that of the bishop of Guadalajara in the late eighteenth century.

Early in the nineteenth century, there was disquiet among the Spanish settlers engendered by the news of Father Miguel Hidalgo's rebellion against Spain. In 1810, as that rebellion began, the authorities arrested some leaders of Indian communities who had gathered at the Cuartel de los Nahuales; while the authorities suspected that the Indians were themselves planning a revolt, the fact was that the Indians were equally alarmed by the activities of Hidalgo's army. It is probably significant that briefly, in 1792, Hidalgo had been a parish priest in Colima.

Soon after the independence movement began, Colima fell readily into rebel hands, encouraged by one of Hidalgo's former colleagues, Father **José Antonio Díaz** (d. 1820), who later joined the insurgent army. Although control of Colima was soon recovered by forces loyal to the Crown, it shifted several times between the two sides thereafter. By the end of the decade, Mexico's breakaway from Spain had become a reality, and by 1824 a new Mexican republic had come into being, with its own constitution. Colima was to cede northern parts of its territory before its present mainland borders were defined. In 1824, the National Congress deemed it a federal territory that was at last independent of its neighbors, Michoacán and Jalisco, although three years later, it found itself again subject to the control of Michoacán. During this period, the port of Manzanillo was opened up to international trade, albeit briefly.

The first local printing press came into operation only in 1826, publishing Colima's first newspaper, *El Observador de las Leyes*. The man behind it was **Ramón R. de la Vega** (1811–1896)—a soldier, politician, and teacher—who championed Colima's case for statehood, served for a while as governor, founded the state's Department of Education, its first textile factory, its first high school for boys, and its first teachers' college; he introduced the cultivation of coffee and of silkworms, promoted the development of telecommunications, built the Hospital Guadalupano, and even found time to write about Colima.

It was in 1828 that the town of Colima was elevated to the category of city. Nine years had to be spent under the control of Michoacán before

Colima regained its status as a federal territory. A further two years passed before international trade via Manzanillo could be resumed, and Colima had to wait until 1856 to be granted statehood. Barely a year after the installation of its first governor, Gen. Manuel Alvarez, the state found itself hosting President Benito Juárez and provisionally serving as seat of the national government.

In 1861, the Revillagigedo Archipelago was incorporated into Colima, and a prison was built there. The nineteenth century also saw the beginnings of industrialization, such as the establishment of textile factories—though they would only survive until the end of the century—and the arrival of telecommunications. The Teatro Hidalgo was built in 1871 (initially called the Teatro Santa Cruz), and the first state secondary school opened in 1874. In 1881, Colima became a bishopric, and in 1889 the railroad came. A major earthquake at the close of the century put a temporary damper on developments, but by 1908 Porfirio Díaz, the president whose motto was "Order and Progress," was triumphantly riding the train into Colima.

For this particular state, the revolutionary period was relatively peaceful, marked by squabbles rather than by bloody battles. As elsewhere in Mexico, the postrevolutionary period brought the organization of labor—for example, the creation of the Sociedad Cooperativa de Salineros de Colima (Salt Workers' Cooperative) and the Unión de Estibadores de Manzanillo (Dockworkers' Union). At the same time, the first *ejidos* were created, and church schools were secularized.

The publication of an anticlerical law, the Ley de Cultos, in 1926, unleashed a violent backlash known as the Cristero War, whose destructive effects in Colima were greater than those of any previous conflict. (It is no doubt significant that the Jaliscan author Juan Rulfo's outstanding novel *Pedro Páramo* [1955], is set in the aftermath of that war and in a place, which he calls Comala, ravaged by its effects).

Like many other states, Colima's politics became dominated by the Partido Revolucionario Institucional (PRI) and continued that way for the rest of the twentieth century. Toward the end of it, Colima supplied Mexico with a president, President **Miguel de la Madrid** (1934-).

Economy

In colonial times, the main industries were the production of salt and of a coconut-based liquor known as *vino de coco*. Agricultural activity concentrated initially on cacao, and later on coconut, sugarcane, and cotton, with some rice, vanilla, and indigo. There were also ranches raising cattle and mules. Following independence, a textile industry grew, but it had faded by the end of the nineteenth century; the cultivation of cotton, however, was boosted by the arrival of the railroad, which made shipments to Guadalajara easy. The 1940s saw the development of agriculture (especially citrus fruits) in the Tecomán Valley.

Today, 31 percent of the land is devoted to agriculture; there is very little pastureland indeed, less than 0.2 percent. Almost 10 percent of the state is covered with mountain woodlands, with oaks and pines supplying wood for industrial use. More than half the state (55 percent) is jungle, and this yields a number of useful trees and plants (*guácima* serves as forage, and *copal*, *papelillo amarillo*, and *tepemezquite* provide wood). In the wetter areas, there are mangroves and other varieties whose wood is also exploited.

The main economic activities are now service, tourism, agriculture, agro-industry, mining, and fishing. Apart from limes on a grand scale, Colima produces melons, mangoes, papayas, watermelons, coconuts, bananas, corn, sugarcane, chiles, tomatoes, and cucumbers. Honey and beeswax are also produced. Colima is home to a world leader in the production of pectin, the Danish company Danisco Cultor. Corn and rice are the principal crops sown. Nationally, Colima is number two in the production of coconuts. Palms of several varieties are cultivated on a major scale and put to use in landscaping or for making hats, mats, and the like. Most livestock breeding has to do with cattle, but there are also sheep and poultry. The agricultural sector generates a significant seasonal demand for labor, met by workers who migrate to Colima from the neighboring states of Michoacán and Jalisco.

The fishing industry was ranked seventeenth nationally in the mid-1980s but by the end of the century was in the top ten. In the five-year period from 1992 to 1997 alone, it grew by more than 150 percent. Major catches include tuna, squid, and sharks, but there are many other exploitable species, such as snapper and sea bass. Local aquaculture cultivates a number of freshwater species, as well as shrimp and oysters in the saltwater lagoons.

There are factories that make drinks, can fish, grind grains, preserve foods, make dairy products, build metal structures, produce cement (especially in Tecomán, where the Apasco Group operates), and produce lime and gypsum. Printing and publishing are important activities in this state, and it ranks second in the production of iron.

Colima has companies involved in technology and software development. Manzanillo is the country's main deep-sea port, and it handles more cargo than any other port on the Pacific coast of Mexico. The port is in private hands and includes its own railway, operated by FerroMex. Cargo is shipped to Mexico City, Guadalajara, and Aguascalientes and from those places back to Manzanillo and abroad to other countries in the Americas and the Far East. In Manzanillo, there is also a major plant owned by Pemex, Mexico's nationalized oil company.

Arts

Colima has a strong tradition of open air theater and dance. Dances that are commonly performed include the *conquista* (sometimes also called the *Virgen de Guadalupe*), the *capote*, and the *apache*. These are of colonial origin and are related to the traditional *moros y cristianos* and *matachines* dances. Dances with a more indigenous flavor are the *sonajera india* and the *morenos*. *Pastorelas* are an essential part of the open-air theater tradition. They consist of colloquies written originally during the sixteenth century, usually on religious topics; a common one is called "The Feast of the Magi."

The harp is a characteristic instrument in local *mariachi* ensembles, still in evidence in many popular celebrations. Drums, the *chirimía*, and other types of whistle or flute can also be heard accompanying dances.

Craftwork is produced with practical local uses in mind as much as for the tourist market. The *colimote* is a characteristic hat woven from palms; *huaraches* (sandals) are also woven. The city of Colima is known for tinwork and predictably also makes reproductions of perros cebados. Craft textilework is limited to the embroidering of Indian dresses, often using red thread on white cloth. Ixtlahuacán is known for its hammocks. Wooden furniture and other artifacts come primarily from the municipalities of Comala and Villa de Alvarez. In Suchitlán, which is in the municipality of Comala, masks and other ceremonial equipment are produced. The towns beside the hills of the Cerro Grande are great producers of baskets, while Santiago, in the Manzanillo municipality, makes articles from shells.

After a period of academicism, the painter **Alfonso Michel** (1897–1957) sought to apply cubist techniques to Mexican subjects. Other well-known painters from Colima were **Juan de Arrué** (1565–1637) and **Señorina Merced Zamora** (1866–1926). **Lucio Uribe** (1833–1892) was an architect. Musicians include **Arcadio Zúñiga y Tejada** (1858–1892), **José Levy Rheims** (1858–1931), **J. Jesús Alcaraz** (1898–1945), and **Luis Alcaraz** (1910–1963). **Alberto Isaac Ahumada** (1924–1998) was a caricaturist and filmmaker and is remembered for his movies *En este pueblo no hay ladrones* (1964), based on a short story by Gabriel García Márquez, and *El rincón de las vírgenes* (1972), which he based on two stories by Juan Rulfo.

Social Customs

A mixture of Spanish, indigenous, African, and Filipino influences is reflected in the culture and customs of Colima—a mixture that is often so thorough that the different roots are difficult to discern. From Spain came the predilection for bullfighting and other entertainments related to the countryside. From Africa a number of words came into Spanish, such as *guango* (baggy). The giant figures known as *mojigangos*, now particularly noticeable in Villa de Alvarez, are also of African origin. Customs associated with the coconut-producing areas are sometimes of Philippine provenance.

Some of the most interesting customs can be appreciated in regional celebrations. In January, Los Chayacates de Ixtlahuacán offers a mixture of indigenous and Christian traditions in the performance of a pastorela that represents the cycle of cultivation of maize (corn). Similarly, for the Feast of the Magi (Día de Reyes, January 6), Rancho de Villa and Coquimatlán have a celebration involving pastorelas and dancing of the *cuadrilla* (a genre that was originally French). In February, the Feast of La Candelaria is celebrated in several places, but above all in Tecomán, with a procession, a fair, and dances such as the *apache* and the *sonajera india*. Also in February, Villa de Alvarez has its cowboy show, the Fiestas Charro-Taurinas. Originally this was the time of celebration of Colima's patron saint, San Felipe de Jesús, its defender in times of earthquakes and hurricanes.

March is time for the Paspaques de Suchitlán, when the native Nahuas enact an agricultural ritual dating from pre-Hispanic days and focusing on the importance of corn in all its manifestations. Holy Week is important all over Mexico. In Colima it is marked by the building of altars and fires, in Cuauhtémoc and Tecomán by representations of the Passion of Christ, and in several places by the burning of effigies of Judas and readings from the New Testament. Other notable festivities are the Feast of Santa Cruz, held in May in Suchitlán and featuring the *morenos* dance; the Fiesta de San Miguel, in Tamala, involving the ceremonial handover of authority in the Cofradía de San Miguel (a guild), plus dances and a procession; and the October Fiesta de San Rafael in Cuauhtémoc, with dancing and a fair.

The city of Colima hosts an annual fair, the Feria Agrícola, Ganadera, Comercial e Industrial de Colima, which has been held since 1826. This is sometimes called the Feria de Todos los Santos (All Saints Fair), since its high spot is November 1. All regions of the state are represented, with agricultural, livestock, industrial, and craft displays, food stalls, rides, cultural events, and sporting competitions. The fair begins with a procession of allegorical floats and the crowning of the festival queen. As usual, there are cowboy shows, cockfights, choral groups, plays, and dances (both social and folkloric). The Universidad de Colima is represented by its Ballet Folklórico troupe. One popular spectacle is the dolphin show. All this takes place in late October and early November, over a period of two weeks.

A major open fishing contest, the Torneo Internacional de Pesca de Pez Vela (*pez vela* is a variety of marlin), has been held every year since 1954 in Manzanillo.

Noteworthy Places

Colima is not a state that is rich in colonial buildings. The capital's San Francisco de Almoloyán is a ruined Franciscan convent dating back to the sixteenth century. There are some *haciendas* that have been restored: the Hacienda del Carmen (municipality of Villa de Alvarez) is a nineteenth-century cattle ranch, and the Hacienda de San Antonio (Comala) is a nineteenth-century coffee plantation, with a chapel and an aqueduct. The former Hacienda de Nogueras, in Comala, has a seventeenth-century chapel, but the main building dates from the nineteenth; it is now the Alejandro Rangel Hidalgo Museum, covering the archaeology of the Comala area and samples of the art of Rangel, who is known for his woodwork. Comala is sometimes called "America's White Town" thanks to its architecture, which is characteristic of the area beside the volcano. The Mesón de Caxitlán, on the road from Colima to Tecomán, is the ruin of an eighteenth-century inn that sits on land that was once part of an Indian settlement called Caxitlán, which was the initial location of the town of Colima. Cuyutlán has a salt museum (Museo de la Sal).

Many of the most important buildings in the capital date from the late nineteenth or early twentieth century and are in the French neoclassical style that was fashionable in the Mexico of Porfirio Díaz. One such is the Palacio de Gobierno (Government Building), which houses murals by a local painter, Jorge Chávez Carrillo, that were added in 1953 to mark the bicentenary of Miguel Hidalgo, the progenitor of Mexico's independence movement. The four-wall sequence culminates with representations of national leaders (Benito Juárez, Venustiano Carranza, Emiliano Zapata, and Lázaro Cárdenas) and a fist-punching homage to the new, industrializing Mexico. Nor is the cathedral old, since its beginnings date back only to 1863 and it was completed only at the end of that century, not long after the Bishopric of Colima was established. Earthquake damage on at least three occasions made repairs to it necessary and led to modifications of the structure. The capital city's historical archive (Archivo Histórico Municipal de Colima) is housed in what was a typical large nineteenth-century house.

Colima's archaeological museum (Museo de Arqueología María Ahumada de Gómez) is one of the most important in western Mexico, due to the variety and number of its exhibits. These are arranged first to illustrate early stone carvings and petroglyphs and then seven successive cultural foci of pre-Columbian times: Capacha, Ortices, Comala, Colima, Armería, Periquillo, and El Chanal. There are valuable pottery figures of warriors, laborers, musicians, women, and children, plus ceremonial vases and urns representing animals, birds, and, of course, perros cebados.

A couple of kilometers north of the city of Colima lies El Chanal, an archaeological site with pyramids, a ball court, several squares, and staircases with hieroglyphs carved into the stone.

In pre-Hispanic times, La Campana, closer to Villa de Alvarez, was the most populous indigenous settlement in western Mexico. It comprises several temples, platforms, and pyramids with rounded edges; it is believed that at least one of these was a mausoleum. There is evidence of the influence of Teotihuacán during the Classical period of pre-Hispanic civilizations. Vestiges of Capacha pottery have been found here, dating from 1500 BC. Here are the tumbas de tiro, the shaft tombs housing burial chambers and effigies of well-fed dogs. There is a drainage system, a number of roads, an administrative center, and several religious monuments. Although the Spaniards discovered La Campana in 1524, in modern times it became open to the public only in 1995. Certain regional museums are also of archaeological and cultural interest, namely the Museo Comunitario de

Ixtlahuacán, the Museo Comunitario de Suchitlán, and the Museo de la Comunidad de Zacualpan.

The Parque Regional Metropolitano, in the capital, sports luxuriant vegetation, a zoo, and recreational facilities. One of many places of natural beauty elsewhere in the state is El Salto, close to the town of Peada, a picturesque waterfall formed by the Miniatlán River, with curious rock formations. Beaches are plentiful. Among the most famous are the tranquil Playa Las Hadas, the Playa La Audiencia, which is favored by divers and water sports enthusiasts, and the Playa La Perlita, which is popular among recreational sailors.

Cuisine

Colima's cuisine draws both on local seafood and the meat-eating traditions that are common in the interior; its culinary roots are as varied as are its cultural roots, benefiting from European, indigenous, Far Eastern, and African traditions. Examples include *tatemado*, a stew made with pork marinated in coconut vinegar and cooked with peppers, and *cuachala*, a corn-based dish with shredded chicken dating back to before the Spaniards. The influence of neighboring Jalisco can be seen in the popularity of dishes such as *birria*. A dry form of the corn-based stew called *pozole* is a traditional lunch dish. *Pepena* is an offal-based affair. A common way of preparing whole fish is to add green vegetables, wrap it in palm leaves, and bake it.

Comala, a place generally known for its dairy products, is famous for street snacks such as *sopitos*, small tortillas dressed with meat, cheese, and sauce. The *comal*, from which the town's name comes, is an ancient stone dish used for preparing tortillas. Villa de Alvarez is famous for its pastries. The coastal city of Manzanillo offers all sorts of seafood dishes, including the typical *ceviche de pescado ahumado*, made with marinated smoked fish. Colima itself has its own variant on ceviche, involving fresh fish chopped into small pieces and mixed with carrots. On the sweets front, the state makes full use of its variety of fruit; there are several varieties of *cocada* (candies or cookies made with coconut), *dulce de tamarindo*, candied bananas, and *alfajores de piña*.

The local nonalcoholic drinks are *tejuino*, *tuba*, and *bate*. Tejuino is made with crushed corn and served over ice, with salt and lime. Tuba derives from Philippine tradition and is made with coconut sap, which is collected by hanging coconut half-shells as if they were cups; it is drunk either straight or flavored with almonds, peanuts, or chopped fruit. Bate is made from a seed called *chan* and is served with corn honey. The local alcoholic drink is *ponche* (punch); the most traditional flavor thereof is pomegranate, but it can also be flavored with prunes, peanuts, guavas, or tamarinds. Ponche gets its punch from the local variety of *mezcal*, called *tuxca*.

Tatemado

Traditionally, this dish calls for a clay pot, but any covered cooking pot will do. The vinegar that is traditionally used is made from the coconut palm and is mild. Ingredients:

2$\frac{1}{2}$ lb. pork shoulder, cubed
1 cup vinegar
3 cloves of garlic, peeled and crushed
$\frac{1}{2}$ tsp cumin seeds, ground
Black pepper
Salt
2 bay leaves
2 sprigs thyme
1 cup water
6 chiles (three of the *guajillo* variety and three *ancho* or *pasilla*)
3 tbsp lard or oil

Preheat the oven to 300°F. Deseed the chiles and put them to soak in water until soft. Marinate the pork in a mixture of the vinegar, garlic, herbs, and spices. After a couple of hours, drain the pork, taking care to save the marinade. Put the marinade in with the chiles and blend. Now brown the pork in a heavy pot. Add the marinade and chile mixture, cover, and bake in the oven for an hour and a half, making sure that it does not dry out. Serve the meat with the juices along with marinated onions and refried beans.

Ceviche de Pescado Ahumado

Ingredients:

1 lb. smoked fish (e.g., tuna or mullet)
1 medium white onion
1 medium carrot
2 medium tomatoes
2 *jalapeño* chiles
2 tbsp fresh cilantro, chopped
Juice of 2 or 3 limes
Salt and pepper

Remove any bones from the fish and chop it up. Peel and finely chop the onion and tomatoes, shred the carrot, and deseed and finely chop the jalapeño pepper. Combine everything and let it sit for about an hour before serving.

Cocadas

Ingredients:

1 large coconut
Water
1 lb. sugar

3 egg yolks
1 tbsp butter
Ground cinnamon

Drain the coconut and save the milk. Grate the flesh. Add water to the coconut milk until there are 3 cups of liquid. Put this in a saucepan with the sugar and heat until it thickens. Remove from heat and stir in the beaten egg yolks and the grated coconut flesh. Return to the heat and stir constantly, until the mixture clarifies enough to see the bottom of the pan. Remove from the heat once again and stir in the butter. Spread the mixture on a baking sheet, sprinkle with cinnamon, and allow to cool.

Distrito Federal
(Mexico City)

State Characteristics

Mexico City occupies about two-thirds of a political entity called the Distrito Federal, which has a status that is comparable to that of any state. In the popular mind, the city *is* the Distrito Federal. Mexicans generally do not refer to the city by name but talk instead of the "D.F." or, more confusingly, of "México." But the truth is that the D.F. is an area that also has agriculture and forests, and that metropolitan Mexico City (whatever the official political border may indicate) is not only in the D.F. but also spills over into the state of México. In fact, the D.F. is almost completely surrounded by the state of México; only one other state, Morelos, shares a border with it, to the south. The adjective *chilangos* is often used, sometimes pejoratively, to refer to people from the D.F.

The D.F. as such came into being in the nineteenth century. When the republic was first established, in 1824, a state of México was created, with Mexico City as its capital; about five months later, the decision was made to make Mexico City (then still a city of modest size) part of a new and independent entity, the Distrito Federal. Officially, the D.F. now covers 1,490 square kilometers (approximately 581 square miles)—about ten times as much as its U.S. equivalent, the District of Columbia; this equates to 0.1 percent of the country. The D.F. is divided not into administrative municipalities, as are the states, but into *delegaciones* (delegations), of which there are sixteen. Thirty-four people represent the D.F. in the National Congress. The senior executive of the D.F. is its mayor, who used to be a presidential appointee but has been democratically elected since 1997; the election is timed to coincide with presidential elections. About two-thirds of the members of the legislative assembly of the D.F. represent specific electoral districts; the rest are there as a result of proportional representation.

To say how many people inhabit the D.F. it is not to say how many live in Mexico City and its sprawling suburbs—that is, the metropolitan area—into which it has been estimated that a thousand new people flow each day. The official total population of the D.F., according to the 2000 government census, was 8,605,239; according to the 2005 census, that figure had increased very modestly to 8,720,916. Based on the 2005 census, 90.5 percent of the inhabitants of the D.F. are Catholic, and 3.6 percent are Protestant or evangelical. The population density in 2000 was 5,799 per square kilometer (almost 15,000 per square mile). The relatively high densities in the two neighboring states reflect the geographic spread of the Mexico City Metropolitan Area, one of the world's most heavily populated conurbations, with something in the neighborhood of 20 million people.

Among its many institutions of higher education, Mexico City has the largest university in the Americas: the Universidad Nacional Autónoma de México (UNAM), founded in 1551 and now attended by about 270,000 students.

Mexico City is the cultural capital of the country and the location of its main print and electronic media. In many ways, it can claim to be those things for the whole of Spanish America as well. It is a magnet for refugees from other Hispanic countries and for people from the provinces in search of job opportunities and a better life; as a result, a great many of its present-day inhabitants were born elsewhere. The traditional concentration of power in this place, dating as far back as the time of the Aztecs, has caused a similar concentration of administrative agencies, industry, commerce, and finance; of course, the same can be said of most capital cities, but in Mexico the phenomenon is extremely pronounced.

Mexico City sits at about 2,100 meters (7,000 feet), in a wide valley surrounded by mountains. The D.F.'s highest point is at the Cerro La Cruz del Marqués in the south (Ajusco), which is just short of 4,000 meters (13,200 feet); there are several volcanoes that rise to 3,000 meters (10,000 feet) or more.

The climate is generally quite benign: cool or chilly nights and comfortably warm days, with very moderate rainfall. In the northwestern part of the D.F., the average annual temperature is 16.7°C (62°F) and the average annual rainfall is 584 millimeters (23 inches). In the mountains to the southwest and south, the figures are 11.4°C (53°F) and 1,129 millimeters (45 inches). Most rain falls during the summer months. The prevailing winds are from the north or northwest.

In flat parts of the D.F., most of the rivers have been canalized or made to run underground. A few surface rivers remain, such as the Tacubaya, the Remedios, and the Magdalena. There is only one natural lake, Xochimilco, which is partially fed by recycled water. The major dams are Ansaldo and Canutillo. Mexico City's water basin has been artificially linked to others, to guard against possible floods.

Because of the concentration of people, vehicular emissions, and industry, and because air is trapped in the Anáhuac Valley where the city sits, this has become one of the world's most polluted cities—one where the air is harmful to breathe about 80 percent of the time. Vehicles are registered to circulate either on odd or even days of the month, in an effort to control their numbers, and recent governments have been taking measures to improve air quality by controlling pollutants. Parts of the D.F. have been made into protected natural areas.

There are some agricultural areas in the southern part of the D.F., and some oaks, pines, and firs in the mountains; otherwise vegetation is to be found only in parks and gardens, and likewise the fauna. Wildlife found in nonurban areas includes coyotes, pumas, squirrels, foxes, rabbits, rattlesnakes, frogs, and birds such as falcons, eagles, hummingbirds, and ducks.

Cultural Groups and Languages

Although Mexico City was once the site of the Aztec capital, with many thousands of Indians, although thousands of indigenous people from other parts of the country have been migrating into it for decades, and although modern Mexico City still has identifiable *barrios* with distinctive social characteristics, it is frequently the case that its indigenous peoples have become integrated with the Hispanic majority. The 2005 census stated that 118,424 people (1.5 percent of the population) over the age of five spoke an indigenous language. The dominant language was that of the Aztecs, Náhuatl (with 30,371 speakers); the next most widely spoken, with figures ranging between 9,000 and 12,000, were Otomí, Mixtec, Zapotec, and Mazatec. Nine percent of those who said they were speakers of an indigenous language did not identify the language spoke.

History

In 1325, Mexica Indians who had made their way down from the north founded the city of Tenochtitlán, the capital of the Aztec Empire. They had been searching for a sign that, according to legend, would identify the place to settle: an eagle with a snake in its mouth, perched on a cactus. The sign was seen at Lake Texcoco, a body of water shallow enough to allow the Aztecs to reclaim land in it and build a sophisticated and orderly city with hundreds of thousands of inhabitants, accessed by boats or via a number of causeways. They made war with other peoples, took prisoners to sacrifice to their gods, and exacted tributes from the conquered, creating a loose federation. Some Indian peoples, such as the Tlaxcalans, resisted Aztec advances, however, and when the Spaniards came, they were to make alliances with them, ultimately helping to defeat the Aztecs.

The Spaniards, led by Hernán Cortés, arrived in Veracruz in 1519, and the Aztecs cautiously welcomed them. The Aztecs were overawed by these

Plaza de Santo Domingo.

men who had arrived on floating castles, had weapons that spouted fire, and rode on strange animals. Aztec legends had predicted the return of a benign god, Quetzalcóatl, who had previously been banished and had disappeared toward the east; moreover, it had been predicted that he would return in a new, bearded human form that happened to coincide with the appearance of Cortés. On hearing of the arrival of Cortés, Moctezuma, the Aztec emperor, sent emissaries to greet him. When the Spaniards reached Tenochtitlán, they were welcomed with great ceremony into a city that was larger, cleaner, and better organized than any in Europe at that time.

But things went wrong: Moctezuma virtually became a prisoner of the Spaniards, his people grew restive, and when Moctezuma was brought out in an attempt to calm them down, he was stoned to death (according to Spanish chroniclers of events; an Indian account of the incident says that Cortés stabbed Moctezuma in the back). In the ensuing riot, the Spaniards fought their way out of the city, laden with gold. Then, having carefully prepared for a definitive onslaught on the city, the Spaniards laid siege to it. Many of its inhabitants fell victim to smallpox, a disease to which they had no resistance, and one which had been inadvertently brought over from Europe. Finally, the Spaniards razed the city to the ground and built their own city on the ruins.

Cuitláhuac (1476–1520) was a chieftain who led the fight against the Spaniards on the *Noche Triste*, the night they were driven out of

Tenochtitlán after the killing of Moctezuma; he died of smallpox. **Cuauhtémoc** (1502–1525) also took part in that fight; he later became the leader of the Aztecs and was tortured by Cortés, but continued as lord of Tlatelolco and collaborated with the Spaniards, finally being assassinated.

Until the conquest of Mexico, the Spanish administrative hub in the New World had been Santo Domingo (now capital of the Dominican Republic); after the conquest of Mexico the city that had been set upon the site of Tenochtitlán took over that role. The initial layout of Mexico City was designed by one of Cortés's soldiers who had the relevant skills, and the work was coordinated by officials based in Coyoacán. The city was laid out on a grid pattern, as Tenochtitlán had been, even though such a rigidly practical layout as this was not characteristic of European cities. In 1524, the administrative seat was moved to Mexico Tenustitán, as they then called it; it was only in 1585 that the place was officially named La Ciudad de México (Mexico City). Beside an immense central square (the Zócalo), the Spaniards built a palace and a cathedral.

The year 1524 was also when the first Franciscan friars arrived, to begin the process of converting the natives to Christianity; three years later, Mexico had its first bishop, Juan de Zumárraga. In 1527, due to conflicts between the city authorities and Cortés, the crown decided to establish the Real Audiencia de México, a legal body with wide jurisdiction that would function like a government ministry, with a president and four legal officers under him, called *oidores*. This was followed by the establishment of the Viceroyalty of New Spain (Nueva España), which became the most powerful body in the New World; a viceroy (*virrey*) was appointed to govern this part of the world on the king's behalf. New Spain's geographical authority became immense, ranging over much of what is now the United States, Central America, the Hispanic Caribbean, and even the Philippines, to and from which New Spain shipped goods via the port of Acapulco. The first viceroy was Antonio de Mendoza.

The Colegio de Santa Cruz de Tlatelolco was established in 1536, for the education and indoctrination of the Indian nobility, whom the Spaniards saw as a means for converting their subjects and bringing them into the Catholic fold. By 1537, Mexico City had the first printing press in the New World, and by 1553 the first university. The Spanish Inquisition came to Mexico, to premises close to the Zócalo, in 1571. A year after that, the first Jesuit missionaries arrived. From Mexico City, the viceroy sent expeditions to conquer new lands, and from Mexico City came edicts, both viceregal and episcopal, designed to regulate the new lands and peoples. By the end of the century, Mexico City was a thriving and fashionable cultural center, with theaters and poetry contests, elegant and prosperous people at its heart, and impoverished Indians on its periphery.

At the time of the movement for independence from Spain, **Mariano Matamoros** (1770–1814), a priest, like Miguel Hidalgo and José María Morelos, joined the latter's forces and took part in several campaigns until he was captured and shot. **Leona Vicario** (1789–1842) also supported the insurgents, by sending them money and providing them with information about troop movements in the capital. She was the fiancée of one of the most prominent rebels of the time, Andrés Quintana Roo. Both had their possessions confiscated and were banished by loyalist authorities, but such had been their contribution to the struggle for independence that in 1822 the National Congress compensated them by giving them the Hacienda de Ocatepec and three houses besides.

In 1820, ten years after Hidalgo had uttered his call for independence, Mexico City finally fell to the insurgents. A year later, Agustín de Iturbide convened a Soberana Junta Provisional Gubernativa (Sovereign Committee of Provisional Government), which chose Iturbide himself to preside over the proceedings and later that day signed a declaration that established an independent Mexican Empire. A few months later, Iturbide was proclaimed emperor, but he was forced to abdicate after only a year. A congress was then convened to thrash out the basis for a republic and its foundational states and a constitution established in 1824. Mexico's first president was to be Gen. Guadalupe Victoria.

After a heated debate, it was agreed that the capital of the republic should be Mexico City, defined as the area within a radius of 8,380 meters (5.2 miles) from the main square. Since Mexico City was also the capital of one of the foundational states, the state of México, the state capital was moved to Texcoco a few years later (and thereafter to San Agustín de las Cuevas and to Toluca, the state's present capital). At the same time, the Distrito Federal was established. In subsequent years, there were reorganizations and redefinitions of the district, carried out against a political background of incessant struggles between centrists and federalists, conservatives and liberals. There was a revolving door for presidents, war with the United States, and an intervention by France that brought the creation of a second empire.

Late in the war with the United States, Mexico City was invaded by troops under the U.S. general Winfield Scott. The concluding battle, at the Chapultepec Castle, which at that time was a military barracks, has entered the national mythology of Mexico: a number of the cadets, who became known as the *Niños Héroes*, chose to sacrifice themselves rather than surrender to the invaders. The United States prevailed, and the result of that war, combined with the secession of Texas a few years earlier, was that Mexico lost almost half of its former territory.

Two decades later, a liberal government was in power, having inherited huge debts to European countries, especially France. With some support from Mexican conservatives, Napoleon III's France occupied the country and an Austrian, Maximilian of Hapsburg, was installed as emperor. The French intervention lasted for three years, during which the legitimate government of President Benito Juárez perambulated about the country. Napoleon then withdrew his troops, leaving Maximilian to rely on whatever support the Mexican conservatives would give him. He was defeated and killed, and the elected government was restored to power in Mexico City, whence it promulgated a new constitution and introduced reforms that sparked off a three-year civil war. The journalist and politician **Guillermo Prieto** (1818–1897) made a distinguished contribution to the liberal cause, fighting against the United States, jointly founding an important cultural institution (the Academia de Letrán), helping to draft the reform laws, and occupying a number of government posts. Prieto is said to have saved President Juárez from being shot in Guadalajara.

The period under Maximilian left a significant mark on the city: Chapultepec Castle was reconstructed, and a grand avenue somewhat in the style of the Champs-Elysées in Paris was built, cutting across diagonally to link the government palace with the castle. This new avenue was the Paseo de la Reforma. Later in the century, when Porfirio Díaz was president, the Paseo de la Reforma was further modified. It was lined with the residences of Mexico's elite and punctuated with statues of illustrious figures, most of them done by the country's leading sculptors. The *porfiriato*, Díaz's three-decade rule that covered the last twenty years of the nineteenth century and the first ten of the twentieth, brought more architectural changes to Mexico City, and ironically many were inspired by French models.

Díaz's regime was modernizing and in some ways progressive, but it brooked no opposition, sold off assets to foreigners, and exacerbated the gap between the rich and the poor. Opposition in exile gained strength, and eventually Francisco Madero succeeded Diaz as president, only to be ousted by a coup engineered by Victoriano Huerta with the help of the U.S. ambassador. But revolutionary leaders demanded constitutional government, and in 1917 a new national constitution was promulgated. This did not by any means signal an end to the fighting that had begun in 1910. Indeed, such were the tensions that the government of Venustiano Carranza functioned for a while with Veracruz as its base. Rivalries between the various revolutionary leaders led to continued changes of power, and then, in the late 1920s, there was another civil uprising in the form of the Cristero War, a rebellion by conservatives and clerics against postrevolutionary reforms that threatened their privileges once again. Among the leading local supporters of Madero was **Juan Sánchez Azcona** (1876–1938), who was vice president of the Partido Nacional Anti-reeleccionista, the party opposed to Díaz's reelection, represented the revolution as ambassador to several European countries and wrote for several newspapers. **Eduardo Hay** (1877–1941) was another supporter of Madero who went into government and diplomatic service.

The political party that emerged after the Revolution held power in most of Mexico for the whole of the twentieth century, though in the late 1940s, under President Miguel Alemán, it changed its name to reflect the belief that by then most of the revolutionary aims had been realized: it became the Partido Revolucionario Institucional (PRI; Institutional

Revolutionary Party). At that time, Mexico City had a population of about three million.

Two events stand out in the history of the Mexico City of the second half of the twentieth century. The first took place in 1968, when the city was about to host the Olympic Games. At the time, there was widespread dissatisfaction with the policies of the government of the day and an awareness that the PRI had degenerated into a corrupt monolith. These things, coupled with the example set by students in Paris in May of that year, led students to demonstrate on the eve of the Games in an attempt to embarrass the government when the world's attention was turned upon Mexico. They gathered in a square at Tlatelolco, a symbolic place that had once been an Aztec ceremonial site. It is sometimes known as the Plaza de las Tres Culturas, since its architecture reflects the cultures of the Aztecs, colonial Spain, and modern Mexico. Armed police shot at the students, who were unarmed, killing at least 350 of them; the event came to be known as the Tlatelolco Massacre, and it was something of a watershed for Mexico.

The second upheaval was a natural one: in 1985, the city was struck by an earthquake that measured 8.1 on the Richter scale. The official government estimate was that 5,000 people lost their lives, though others have suggested that the figure was four times as high. Between 50,000 and 90,000 people were left homeless. The response of the government was quite inadequate, and yet the event generated great solidarity among the people, who rallied around to help each other. There even emerged a figure called "Superbarrio" who, dressed like a popular wrestler known as "El Santo," acted as an intermediary between the people and the authorities.

Partly as a result of the government's inefficiencies in dealing with the earthquake, the inhabitants of the city began to seek greater autonomy. Another reason was that the people were starting to vote for opposition parties in elections; in 1988, for example, the majority vote went to the opposition candidate but the then president imposed a member of the PRI. In 1987, the D.F. was granted more autonomy, though it was not made into a fully fledged state as some had wished. Further steps increasing its autonomy followed, until in 1997 the people of the city could finally elect their head of government; the first person so elected was Cuauhtémoc Cárdenas, son of the most influential of postrevolutionary presidents, Lázaro Cárdenas, and an outspoken critic of the PRI. He resigned two years later in order to run for the presidency of the country, appointing a woman, Rosario Robles, to complete his term of office. Another opposition figure, Manuel López Obrador, was elected after her, and he too ran for the presidency.

It is not the PRI that dominates modern Mexico City but the PRD, the Party of Democratic Revolution; the conservative PAN (Partido de Acción Nacional/National Action Party) is also strong. Mexico City's status is still not quite that of a state, but it now comes close to it. The D.F. does not have a constitution of its own, but a Statute of Government; it administers its own finances, though its budget and its debts are capped by the National Congress.

Economy

Industrial activity in the Distrito Federal is far too extensive to describe here in any detail. In economic terms, the D.F. is Mexico's largest contributor in both the industrial and service sectors, but the smallest in agriculture. Most agriculture is concentrated in the south; 13 percent of the district is cultivated with oats for forage and corn, spinach, green beans, and *nopales* for human consumption. Another 5 percent is pastureland, and forests of pine, oak, eucalyptus, fir, and ash cover 19 percent of the district.

Overall, the D.F. accounts for approximately 20 percent of Mexico's gross domestic product (GDP). Mexico City has one of the world's largest urban economies. About a third of Mexicans countrywide live in poverty, but only about 15 percent of the inhabitants of Mexico City do; the city's per capita income is the highest in Latin America. In recent decades, manufacturing industries have spread out increasingly into the state of México, partly as a result of government incentives designed to combat pollution.

Arts

No other Latin American city can rival Mexico City in terms of cultural variety and tradition. The Aztecs valued the arts, music, dance, and poetry; Tenochtitlán—Mexico City has always been a place of performance. Moreover, Mexico City was an artistic powerhouse in the colonial era, known for its poetry, theater, music, and art.

Every imaginable type of music can be found in modern Mexico City, from organ-grinders to mariachis, jazz groups to rock bands, church choirs to symphony orchestras. Mexico City is the home of the National Conservatory, the National Symphony Orchestra, the famed Ballet Folklórico, and many other dance companies. It has a theater infrastructure that no other Latin American country can match; only a few cities in the world (such as London, New York, and Toronto) have more theaters.

Mexico has the most important cinema industry in the Hispanic world— one that has offered Spanish speakers an alternative to the dominance of Hollywood fare and produced a good number of films of real quality. The National Film Institute (IMCINE) is headquartered in Mexico City. The major international publishing conglomerates of the Hispanic world all have offices there, as well, and Mexico's own imprints figure prominently.

Given its political and cultural importance, Mexico City has attracted countless artists and intellectuals from all over the country and farther afield. Furthermore, it has become home to many creative people seeking a refuge from political pressures elsewhere; for example, many people from the southern cone of Latin America fled to Mexico during the dictatorships of the late twentieth century. Long before that, Mexico City had benefited from an influx of artists from Europe and the United States— the filmmaker Sergei Eisenstein, for example, and avant-garde figures such as the surrealist André Breton, the composer Aaron Copland, and the author D. H. Lawrence. Some of these people came because Mexico was fashionably "primitive." Others, such as Spaniards opposed to the dictator Francisco Franco, came because they could not stay in their own countries in the 1930s and 1940s. Many such foreigners put down deep roots in Mexico.

The list of distinguished artistic figures associated with Mexico City is very long, even if strictly limited to people born in the D.F. For example, **Carlos de Sigüenza y Góngora** (1645-1700) was an official astronomer, mathematician, cartographer, and writer who produced one of the key creative texts of his time, *Los infortunios de Alonso Ramírez*. **José Joaquín Fernández de Lizardi** (1776-1827) was a journalist, social critic, and writer, the founder of the influential newspaper *El Pensador Mexicano*, and a champion of independence. He also wrote what is generally regarded as Latin America's first novel: *El periquillo sarniento*.

Vicente Riva Palacio (1832-1896) fought against the U.S. and French invasions and served as a politician and diplomat, but is also remembered as a journalist and creative writer. **Angela Peralta** (1845-1883) acquired the nickname "The Mexican Nightingale." She was a soprano who sang grand opera internationally and also founded her own company. **Juan de Dios Peza** (1852-1910) was another politician and diplomat who doubled as a writer, especially of popular poetry; he was a professor at the National Conservatory of Music, as well.

Antonio Caso (1883-1946), a lawyer, writer, and philosopher, was one of a small group of leading thinkers in the first half of the twentieth century. He was a member of the Academy of the Language and cofounder of the influential Ateneo de la Juventud. **Alfonso Caso** (1896-1970) was an archaeologist, politician, and writer who occupied a number of high-level national positions, such as the directorships of the Museum of Anthropology, the National Indian Institute, and UNAM. He was also a vital force behind the excavations at Monte Albán, in Oaxaca.

Jaime Torres Bodet (1902-1974) became very influential in education during the time of José Vasconcelos. He also served as a government minister and diplomat and won the National Prize for Literature. **Salvador Novo** (1904-1974) was one of Mexico's leading modern dramatists, a cofounder of Teatro Ulises, and a writer in other genres besides. He, too, won the National Prize for Literature.

Carlos Monsiváis (1938-) has been one of the country's most acerbic journalists and cultural commentators. The painter **Frida Kahlo** (1907-1954) was born in Coyoacán, where there is now a museum in her name. The wife of muralist Diego Rivera, she was also active in the circle of intellectuals and artists that opposed the dictatorship in Spain.

Others on the long list of creative artists born in Mexico City include the poet, essayist, and Nobel laureate **Octavio Paz** (1914–1998); **Rodolfo Usigli** (1905–1979), probably Mexico's most famous dramatist; **Arturo Ripstein** (1943–) a leading film director; the actor **Mario Moreno**, alias "Cantinflas" (1911–1993); and **Carlos Chávez** (1899–1978), the most famous Mexican composer of classical music.

Social Customs

There are countless exhibitions, contests, and commercial events in the Distrito Federal. Every feast or saint's day has its celebrants in a district such as this. Some festivities are associated with particular communities; examples include Holy Week in Iztapalpa and Villa Milpa Alta; Santa Cruz and the Day of Builders, Engineers, and Architects in Santa Cruz Acalpixca, Xochiltepec, Xochimilco, and Villa Milpa Alta; the Feast of the Assumption in Tepepan, Xochimilco, and Milpa Alta (a major occasion also for the cathedral); the commemoration of the cry for independence, marked by a celebration and military processions in the Zócalo; and a similar commemoration of the start of the Revolution.

One festivity that has a very special meaning for Mexico in general and the D.F. in particular is December 12's Feast of the Virgin of Guadalupe. The story is that the Virgin Mary appeared to a Christian Indian laborer, Juan Diego, in 1531 at Tepeyac, addressing him in the Aztec language and telling him of her wish to have a shrine there. She gave Diego some roses to carry to the bishop, wrapped in a cloak made of maguey fibers, and when Diego opened the cloak in front of the bishop, the roses had miraculously been replaced by a *mestiza* image of the Virgin. The shrine was duly set up, and eventually a basilica to accommodate 20,000 people was constructed close by. Tepeyac, which was a sacred place even in Aztec times, has become a place of pilgrimage to rival Rome, receiving an average of ten million visitors a year. The dark-skinned Virgen de Guadalupe is seen as making Mexicans legitimate; Catholic authorities have deemed her the patron saint of the city, the country, and indeed of Latin America.

One Mexico City square, the Plaza Garibaldi, is famed for the mariachi bands and other regional ensembles that congregate in it. There are many places such as the Zócalo (officially the Plaza de la Constitución) where troupes perform indigenous music and dances, though the authenticity of these is in some doubt. Entertainers—for example, clowns—are commonplace in public squares and parks, which are also crowded with vendors of balloons and stalls selling drinks and snacks. Open-air markets are an Indian tradition that survives in the Zócalo and many other places.

The range of sporting activities is wide, but soccer is the most popular. Mexico City has twice hosted the World Cup; its Aztec Stadium has room for 126,000 fans. The D.F. has two first-division soccer teams: América and Cruz Azul. Baseball is also quite popular, as is Lucha Libre, Mexico's form of all-in wrestling.

Noteworthy Places

The center of Mexico City is the Zócalo, which has the long and imposing National Palace along one side. Construction of the palace was begun by Cortés, who set it on the site of Moctezuma's palace. For a long time, it was the palace of the viceroys. The present building dates from the late seventeenth century, except for one floor that was added in 1926. It is now a government building. Inside the palace are some of Diego Rivera's most famous murals, tracing the course of Mexican history. Others, by Rivera and the other leading muralists, can be seen in the Secretaría de Educación, not far away.

The other dominant building on the Zócalo is the massive and heavy cathedral, whose interior cracks show that there have been problems with subsidence and earthquakes. Work on building the cathedral was started in the late sixteenth century and continued intermittently for three hundred years thereafter; unsurprisingly, the overall effect is a mixture of the baroque and the neoclassical. There are fourteen domes and fourteen chapels in its cluttered interior. Beside the cathedral sits the Sagrario Chapel, which has paintings by Cristóbal de Villalpando. The Iglesia de San Francisco is an eighteenth-century church that sits on the site of Mexico City's first convent, which was built in 1524; what was intended as a Catholic church has served variously as a barracks, a circus, a theater, and a Methodist church. It is also the place where a mid-nineteenth-century conspiracy was hatched.

In 1978, telephone workers digging not far from the Zócalo came across a massive stone disk representing the Aztec goddess of the moon; they had unearthed the site of the Templo Mayor, the main Aztec temple. Archaeological excavations revealed the remains of several buried pyramids, a carved frieze of skulls, and about 3,000 artifacts that have since been housed in an adjacent museum.

Also in the historic center of Mexico City is the Plaza de Santo Domingo, with its church built of porous volcanic rock. It has a long gallery along one side of the square where people used to be burned at the stake by the Inquisition, whose headquarters are just opposite. Cuauhtémoc once had a palace there.

The Casa de los Azulejos (Tiled House) dates from the seventeenth century; it sports a tiled façade, iron grillwork, a mural by José Clemente Orozco, and a patio in the Moorish style. It is now occupied by Sanborn's, a department store. Banamex, one of the country's main banks, has taken over the baroque building that Emperor Iturbide made his residence. Under Mexico's second and much later emperor, Maximilian, the Paseo de la Reforma was built to link the palace with the Castillo de Chapultepec. This castle stands high in what were once the wooded hunting grounds of the Aztecs and the location of Nezahualcóyotl's palace. The castle was the site of a definitive battle between the Mexicas and the Spaniards. Later it became a cadet school famous for the cadets' self-sacrifice in the concluding battle of the war with the United States. Nowadays it is home to the valuable Museo de Historia (History Museum). Also in the expansive Bosque de Chapultepec (Chapultepec Forest) are two more major museums: The Museo Nacional de Antropología (Anthropological Museum), quite apart from its incomparable collection of Mesoamerican items, has a very attractive and simple design, the work of the Mexican architect Pedro Ramírez Vázquez; the Museo Rufino Tamayo de Arte Contemporáneo is the premier Mexican museum of modern art. The Bosque de Chapultepec also houses the presidential palace, called Los Pinos. The Bosque still has *ahuehuete* trees that survive from the time of the Aztecs, and it is still very beautiful in parts, even though busy roads cut through it and it has become the main recreational area of central Mexico City, with a zoo, an amusement park, and a children's museum.

The other main park in the central area is the Alameda Central, once a market area for the Aztecs. The Alameda is a more formal park and much more modest area in front of the Palacio de Bellas Artes. The palace itself was built during the *porfiriato* (in 1904) as an opera house; it is a ponderously impressive marble structure, the work of an Italian architect who also designed the surprisingly extravagant main post office. Bellas Artes has an art deco façade with pre-Hispanic motifs, and inside it has a Tiffany stained-glass representation of the major volcanoes, plus murals by Rivera, Orozco, David Alfaro Siqueiros, and Rufino Tamayo. There is also a concert hall where the Ballet Folklórico performs regularly.

During the nineteenth century, the Paseo de la Reforma was lined with the leafy residences of Mexico City's elite, but nowadays it has many office buildings and expensive hotels. The Torre Mayor, Latin America's tallest office building, is one of them. One of the most famous of the Paseo's many statues, built at the end of the porfiriato, is El Angel de la Independencia, a column with a victorious angel on top and a mausoleum beneath it, housing the remains of heroes of independence. One intriguing inclusion is an Anglo-Irishman, William Lamport, who became Guillén Lombardo de Guzmán. He was denounced by a neighbor, who discovered that he was planning to declare independence from Spain, make himself ruler, and free the slaves and the natives, whereupon the Inquisition judged Lamport a heretic, with predictable consequences. The Paseo leads through some of Mexico City's most exclusive and fashionable areas, such as Las Lomas, Polanco, and the trendy Zona Rosa.

The D.F. has more than 150 museums, with artistic and architectural interest in abundance. MUNAL (the National Museum of Art) has a collection that ranges from colonial times to the early twentieth century; other art museums include the Museo José Luis Cuevas, the Museo San Carlos, and the Museo Franz Meyer. The nation's premier art school, the Academia de San Carlos, became today's Escuela Nacional de Artes Plásticas. San Angel and Coyoacán, which were once separate towns but have become quiet suburbs as the city has grown, are the site of the Frida Kahlo Museum, the Ex-Convento del Carmen, the Museo de Arte Carrillo Gil, and the Casa

Municipal, which was once the residence of Cortés where Cuauhtémoc was held prisoner. Xochimilco has another museum, the Museo Dolores Olmedo, with works from the Rivera-Kahlo private collection, while the Museo del Anahuacalli was built by Rivera himself to house their important collection of pre-Hispanic artifacts. Other places of note include the library building of UNAM, famous for its mosaic façade (done by another of the muralists, Juan O'Gorman), and Tepeyac, with its shrine and basilicas dedicated to the Virgen de Guadalupe.

Xochimilco is the only place that still has part of the lake area settled by the Mexicas. There is a maze of islets and waterways—floating gardens— where people now spend their leisure time being paddled around and serenaded by mariachis. Xochimilco is also known for its flowers and its *tianguis* (open air markets). The Parque Nacional Desierto de los Leones takes its name not from lions but from a family named Leóna that once owned the land. This 2,000-hectare (5,000-acre) mountain park includes a ruined monastery.

Other archaeological sites apart from the Templo Mayor are Tlatelolco, Cuicuilco, the Cerro de la Estrella, Mixcoac, and Cuailama.

Cuisine

Mexico City offers a choice of food from all over the world, and its Mexican fare is very mixed, due to the influx of people from all over the

Nuns snacking in the Alameda.

country. If the local cuisine has a traditional identity, it is shared with nearby states such as Puebla and Hidalgo.

Romeritos con Tortas de Camarón

This recipe calls for using dry shrimp. An alternative is to begin with whole fresh shrimp, boil them whole for a short while, then clean and blend them with a very small amount of the water used to boil them. If necessary, the mixture can be thickened by adding beaten egg.

Ingredients:

$1^{1}/_2$ lb. waxy potatoes
1 lb. *romeritos* (a stringy, spinach-like plant whose botanical name is *Suaeda torreyana*)
2 *mulato* chiles
$^{1}/_2$ lb. dried shrimp
2 oz. chopped almonds
5 *nopal* cactus leaves, chopped
$^{1}/_2$ tsp sesame seeds
Stale French bread
Corn oil
Salt

Clean the romeritos, remove the main stalks, and chop them. Dice the potatoes and then boil them with a pinch of salt. When almost fully cooked, add the romeritos for five minutes, Then drain, reserving the water. Devein and deseed the chiles. Fry the cleaned chiles in a little corn oil, together with the chopped almonds and small pieces of the bread. Dry-roast the sesame seeds until they begin to pop. Grind the fried ingredients together with a little water and reduce the mixture to a thick paste. Now add the nopal leaves, the romerito-potato mixture, and the shrimp, and stir until a dough forms that can be shaped into patties and fried. Sprinkle with sesame seeds before serving.

Tacos al Pastor

These tacos are traditionally made with spit-roasted meat from which slices are cut as it cooks, as is common in the Middle East. Slices of pineapple placed on top of the meat while it is cooking allow it to absorb the fruit flavor. This recipe assumes that a spit is not available.

Ingredients:

1 lb. fresh lean pork or lamb, thinly sliced
5 *pasilla* chiles
5 *guajillo* chiles
(Jalapeños may be substituted for either *pasilla* or *guajillo* chiles)
2 cloves of garlic
Pinch of ground cumin

Pinch of oregano
1 onion
Vinegar
Pineapple juice
1 lime
Salt
Cilantro
Fresh pineapple
Corn tortillas

Make a marinade by deveining and cleaning out the chiles, chopping them up together with the garlic, putting them in a pan with some vinegar and/or pineapple juice, the cumin, a pinch of salt, and the oregano, and reducing all this to a thick sauce. Marinate the meat overnight in the sauce. Fry the strips of meat, turning them from time to time. When the meat is well cooked, put pieces of it in the tacos, top with chopped onion and cilantro leaves, squeeze a little lime juice over them, and add a piece of fresh pineapple.

Café de Olla

Ingredients:

5 cups water
$^1/_2$ cup *piloncillo* (dark brown sugar)
4 sticks cinnamon
1 cup freshly ground dark-roast coffee
Aniseeds (optional)

Heat the water, sugar, and cinnamon in a pan, stirring frequently until the sugar dissolves completely, then continue to simmer so that the volume reduces by about a quarter. Add the coffee and bring the mixture back to a boil, still stirring. When it reaches boiling, cover it and let it stand for 5 minutes before straining it. Some add a few aniseeds when serving.

Durango

State Characteristics

Durango is the fourth largest state in Mexico. It is located in the north-central part of the country and is roughly heart shaped. Chihuahua and Coahuila lie to its north, and Coahuila again to its east, along with Zacatecas; to the south are Zacatecas, Nayarit, and Sinaloa, and to the west, Sinaloa and Chihuahua. The land covers 123,181 square kilometers (48,040 square miles), 6.3 percent of the whole of Mexico's surface. The population in 2005 was 1,509,117, which represents about 1.5 percent of the national total and gives a low population density of about 12 people per square kilometer (31 per square mile). Ninety-five percent of Durango's towns and villages have fewer than 500 inhabitants, many of them fewer than 100. There are only six towns with more than 15,000 inhabitants, and only two of those have over 50,000. The capital city is Victoria de Durango, usually called simply "Durango," and a third of the total state population lives there. Emigration to the United States has been quite heavy in recent decades, but the state also has a high birth rate (the tenth highest in the world). Durango has thirty-nine administrative municipalities and five representatives in the National Congress. Ninety percent of the population identifies itself as Catholic, most of the rest as Protestant. *El Siglo de Durango* is the state's principal newspaper. There are many institutions of higher education in Durango.

On average, Durango is almost 2,000 meters (6,600 feet) above sea level. Its highest points, in the Sierra Madre, are the Cerro Gordo, Cerro Barajas,

Sierra El Epazote, Cerro Pánfilo, Cerro El Táscate, Cerro El Oso, and Cerro Los Altares, all of which exceed 3,000 meters (approximately 10,000 feet). The Sierra Madre Occidental is a complex mountain system, parts of which are designated by their own names; it covers about two-thirds of the state. It is not unusual to come across wide valleys and plains within the mountain system, for example, the Mesas del Salto and the Llanos de Otinapa, both lying 2,500 meters (8,250 feet) above sea level. There are other, lesser mountain ranges that run parallel with the Sierra Madre.

The western flanks of the Sierra Madre are characterized by deep ravines, with rivers that flow westward: the Sianori, the Jumaya, the Tamazula, and the Mezquital (although this last takes a rather tortuous route). Few rivers run inland: the Oro and Ramos rivers converge to feed dams and the Nazas basin, while the Aguanaval flows from south to north and then east, eventually providing irrigation waters for the Laguna Region. So does the Nazas, Durango's longest river and one of the most important in Mexico. The Río Florido starts in the state of Chihuahua, runs into Durango and out again, joins forces with the Río Conchos, and then heads for the Río Bravo and the Gulf of Mexico; it is the only river on the eastern side of Durango.

In the northwestern part of the state is a *meseta*, and in the northeastern part lie the canyons of the Chihuahua Desert. Mountains and plains run in a band across the middle from northeast to southeast. A great meseta and more canyons cover the western side and the areas bordering on Sinaloa and Nayarit. Durango shares the Zona del Silencio (Zone of Silence) and the Bolsón de Mapimí with neighboring states. The Zona del Silencio is a somewhat mysterious place about which legends abound; it takes its name from the fact that radio communication is impossible there, no doubt due to electromagnetic interference. In addition, the flora and fauna of this zone have unusual characteristics.

Averaged across the state, the maximum temperatures in summer are 35°C (95°F) and in winter 15°C (59°F); the lows are, respectively, 20°C (68°F) and 0°C (32°F). Were it not for the barrier provided by the Sierra Madre, the state would receive humid air from the Pacific and have a milder climate. As it is, one or two areas to the west of the mountains, such as the Quebradas area, do benefit from rains and have a maritime climate that is warm and quite humid. The mountains themselves tend to be cold, but they have significant snowfalls and heavy summer rains. The valleys and the meseta to the east of the Sierra Madre benefit from some seasonal Atlantic airflow; they have an agreeable climate, distinct seasons, and enough rain to support agriculture. Central parts, however, can suffer from extreme dryness and have marked changes of temperature, according to season. As a result of the contrasting climatic conditions, between January and April Durango has strong winds running from the southeast; these winds particularly affect the dry plains of the Bolsón. Average annual rainfall ranges from 273 millimeters (10.9 inches), in Ciudad Lerdo, to 890 millimeters (35.6 inches), in El Salto; the rains fall predominantly during the summer months. All this makes for four ecosystems: the semidesert, valley, mountain, and Quebradas systems.

The Sierra Madre has forests of pines, cedars, and oaks, with deciduous varieties in lower-lying areas on its western side; there are fruit trees on the eastern slopes. In the valleys, there is pasture or farmland, with much of the activity being fragmented and uncoordinated. Most agricultural activity is concentrated at the foot of the Sierra and on its eastern side. In the drier, more desertlike areas, the flora typically consists of cacti, such as *nopal* and *agave*, plus *gobernadora*, *candelilla*, and *ocotillo*. Mountain fauna includes white-tailed deer, wolves (an endangered species), various types of squirrels, owls, sparrows, wild turkeys (also endangered), and bears. The valleys support coyotes, foxes, deer, and crows, and in the driest areas, rattlesnakes, prairie dogs, and scorpions.

The Bolsón de Mapimí has a species of turtle that is unique to it and endangered. The Bolsón is home to 350 plant and 270 animal species, despite being one of the most arid areas. It consists of a closed basin, but was once a great lagoon fed by the Río Nazas and Río Aguanaval; in fact, the conquistadores were still able to witness it as such. Although it is one of the state's most prosperous and industrialized areas, parts of the Bolsón are a conservation area. Another conservation area is located at Michilia. There is also an ecological reserve for migratory birds at Lagunas de Santiaguillo, but illegal hunting has had a damaging effect on it.

Cultural Groups and Languages

Speakers of indigenous languages represent 2.1 percent of the state population; most of these people also speak Spanish. The most widely used indigenous language is Tepehuano, which accounts for about 80 percent of the indigenous-language speakers; Huichol comes next, with about 7 percent.

Among the non-Hispanic groups, the Tepehuanes (sometimes called the "Tepehuanes del Sur" to distinguish them from those who live in Chihuahua) are the most numerous; they are to be found in the municipalities of Mezquital, Pueblo Nuevo, and Canatlán. The Tepehuanes are known for the quality of their crafts and for a ritual called the *mitote*. They live primarily by agriculture, consuming their own produce, and they speak their own language. Their religious practices are a hybrid of their own traditions and Catholic ones.

The Huicholes, the second most numerous people, are in the southern part of the Mezquital municipality, close to Nayarit and Jalisco, where more of them live. Their cultural and religious practices have been less affected by foreign pressures. The Tarahumaras of the Guanaceví municipality are also quite self-sufficient and manage to preserve some of their traditions, despite outside influences. The smallest of the indigenous groups is that of the Mexicaneros, in San Pedro Xicoras and San Agustín de San Buenaventura, both in the Mezquital. These are speakers of Náhuatl, the language of the Aztecs, and their religion is largely pre-Hispanic.

A more surprising cultural contribution comes from the Mennonites, who have twenty-three settlements in the Guatimapé Valley and number about 15,000. These people are of Dutch or German descent; they live by agriculture on lands that were granted them during the presidency of Alvaro Obregón in the early twentieth century.

History

The first inhabitants of what is now Durango were, as in neighboring states, nomads who lived by hunting and gathering. Among the first to begin to practice agriculture were the Tepehuanes, whose society was the most organized. Other Indian peoples who lived here, most of them belli-cose, were the Acaxes, Apaches, Conchos, Julimes, Tapacolmes, and Tara-humaras. They were scattered over the dry and semidry regions and had little contact with one another. No ruins of ceremonial sites remain from precolonial days.

Durango, Chihuahua, Sonora, and Sinaloa together constituted a single region, called Nueva Vizcaya, for much of the colonial period. Coming north from Zacatecas, and with the support of the Spanish viceroy, Francisco de Ibarra took control of these lands between 1554 and 1567. Other explorers, including Nuño de Guzmán, Cabeza de Vaca, Gines Vázquez del Mercado, and Juan de Tapia, had been there before, but with less success. It was because some of these people were from Spain's Basque Country (Vizcaya) that they called the lands New Vizcaya. Durango, the capital city of the region, was called Villa de Guadiana when it was founded in 1563. Both of these names echo those of places in the Basque Country. Even the coat of arms is similar to that of a famous Basque town, Guernica.

By 1575, Durango had its first parish church, by 1595 its first hospital, by 1610 its first college, and by 1620 its first bishop. First the Franciscans and then the Jesuits came to set up missions: Nombre de Dios, Peñol, San Juan Bautista del Río, Analco, Indé, Topia, La Sauceda, Cuencamé, and El Mezquital were all Franciscan; Mapimí, Santiago Papasquiaro, Tepehuanes, Guanaceví, Santa Maria del Oro, Tamazula, Cerro Gordo, and San Juan de Bocas were Jesuit.

Nueva Vizcaya soon became one of the most prosperous provinces in the New World, due to both the discovery of precious minerals and the de-velopment of pastureland and horticulture, especially in the Guadiana Val-ley. Above all, there was growth in the mining industry, with the exploitation of rich deposits of silver, iron, gold, zinc, copper, and lead. A textile industry developed as well. Some of the products were consumed locally; others were shipped via Zacatecas to Mexico City, and thence to Spain. The transportation of goods increased substantially at the end of the nineteenth century, once it was no longer dependent on mules.

Throughout the colonial years, there were many uprisings by the Tepe-huanes and the Tarahumaras, and Durango was often a place where people

Mexican presidential candidate Andrés Manuel López Obrador, of the Democratic Revolution Party (PRD), right, shakes hands with a man dressed as northern Mexican hero Pancho Villa after a campaign rally in Durango, June 2006. (AP Photo/ Gregory Bull)

lived in fear, especially during the seventeenth and eighteenth centuries. More attacks came from Apaches and Comanches, and these lasted well into the nineteenth century. These Indians, unlike those farther south, were never organized and administered by the Spaniards under the *encomienda* system. The establishment of garrisons in northern Mexico gave some security to colonial settlers living in this remote region, but the progress of the province was slowed by the Indian attacks. Eventually, the Indians who survived the drive to eliminate them retreated to the hills of the Sierra Madre.

Over the colonial period, Nueva Vizcaya began to break up into smaller administrative provinces, first losing Sinaloa, then Coahuila, then Chihuahua, all of them territories that encompassed lands that were to be lost to the United States. Durango did not escape the struggle between the loyalists and the insurgents at the time of the breakaway from Spain, in the early nineteenth century. Many people were conscious of the fact that their prosperity and indeed their survival had been reliant on the support of the colonial authorities. The city of Durango fell successively into the hands of each side.

On the rebel side, **Guadalupe Victoria** (born Manuel Félix Fernández, 1786–1843) was a key political figure at this time. Having fought in support of José María Morelos and distinguished himself at the Battle of Oaxaca, Victoria made Veracruz his base of operations, signing the Plan de Iguala and opposing Emperor Agustín de Iturbide. He represented Durango at the new republic's first National Congress. As president of Mexico, Victoria took steps to centralize control of the national revenue and gathered together the naval force that finally drove the Spaniards from the fortress of San Juan Ulúa in 1825.

Once independence had become a matter of fact, it was clear that Durango had to be part of the new Mexico. Both Durango and Chihuahua were declared states at the time of the first National Congress, which convened in 1824. In 1858, at the time of the Reform Movement, liberals led by Esteban Coronado and José María Patoni took control of Durango, and ten years later, at the time of the French Intervention, it was taken by the French, with conservative backing. During the *porfiriato*, Durango also had its taste of local dictators, for example, Juan Manuel Flores, who was in power from 1884 to 1897, and Esteban Fernández, who held power from 1904 to 1911. But as elsewhere, the porfiriato brought some beneficial changes and economic developments; the railroad and the telegraph arrived, the now important towns of the Laguna Region were born, communications improved, and foreign investment increased.

By the beginning of the twentieth century, there were huge inequalities; for example, 5,400,000 hectares (133,338,000 acres) of land lay in the hands of the owners of just 145 *haciendas*. That was a major reason why Durango and neighboring Chihuahua became important locations for the Mexican Revolution. There were many who supported Francisco Madero, Porfirio Díaz's opponent. Most notoriously, Durango became the main stage of operations for **Pancho Villa**.

Francisco "Pancho" Villa (real name Doroteo Arango, born in Durango in 1878) recruited an army after the assassination of Madero and put it at Venustiano Carranza's service. Among other exploits, Villa took Torreón, Chihuahua, Ciudad Juárez, and Tierra Blanca and became provisional governor of Chihuahua. He was defeated by presidents Alvaro Obregón and Plutarco Elías Calles, but was successful in his incursions into U.S. territory. He published a manifesto calling for the expulsion of the United States from Mexican territories. In 1920, Villa signed the "Sabinas amnesty" that marked the end of the most violent period of the Revolution, which by then had gone on for ten years. He was assassinated in Hidalgo del Parral (Chihuahua) in 1923. He then became a mythical figure, the subject of popular song and poetry that tends to gloss over the violence of his record. Among the most significant moments of the Revolution were the siege of Durango in 1911 and its occupation and sacking by forces loyal to Villa in 1913.

Under the state governor Pastor Rouaix, a start was made on the process of land redistribution. That process was continued under Enrique Calderón, who carried out President Lázaro Cárdenas's orders to parcel out 100,000 hectares (247,000 acres) of land in the fertile Laguna Region.

In the middle of the twentieth century, there were improvements in educational provision—the establishment of a technological institute and a university, for example, the latter based in what had been an eighteenth-century Jesuit college. At about this time, the administrative divisions that are now in place were settled upon. Later years were marked by an exodus from the rural villages to the larger towns, or farther afield. The effect of this movement on the capital city of Durango has been particularly noticeable, not only in terms of numbers, but also in terms of architecture and lifestyle.

Economy

The economy of what is now the state of Durango was spurred on by the discovery of valuable mineral deposits during the early years of settlement by the Spaniards, and by the political importance of Durango itself as the administrative capital of the vast region of Nueva Vizcaya. Agriculture and industry developed, primarily in the Laguna Region. The advent of the railroad had a dramatic effect on transportation possibilities for Durango's products, which had hitherto been laboriously shipped by road, often by muleback, down to Mexico City or westward to the port of Mazatlán. The railroad not only eased the process and increased the volume of transportation along such traditional routes, but it also took them north, across the U.S. border via Ciudad Juárez. In the present day, Durango's two most important regions from an economic point of view are still the central one, where the capital is located, and the Laguna Region, where most of the major industrial concerns are to be found.

Wood is the basis for a number of processes: the production of construction materials such as lumber, doors, and particleboard, the manufacture of furniture, and the drying of oak, for example. Minerals are used by the smelting industry and for canning of foodstuffs. Durango is a supplier of materials to the automotive industry, such as engines, electric motors, radiators, and air conditioners. There is a growing electronics industry, especially since the advent of Philips Electronics to the eastern part of the state. The textile industry ranks second nationally in the production of denim, and fourth overall for clothing, much of it for prestige labels. Textiles are one of Durango's most important exports; hundreds of places are associated with the textile industry, and they employ tens of thousands of people, some in *maquiladoras*.

Agriculture occupies approximately 10 percent of the state land: crops include corn, beans, and apples for human consumption, alfalfa for cattle fodder, and sorghum for industrial use. Pastureland accounts for about 15 percent. Forests cover about half the state, with varieties of pines harvested for industrial use and oaks for fuel, and the more tropical areas yielding *guácima* (a medicinal plant) and *pitayo* (a cactus fruit sometimes called dragon fruit in English). Roughly 20 percent of Durango is dry scrubland: here the *gobernadora* and *hojasén* plants have medical applications, the *nopal tapón* cactus is used for forage, *lechuguilla* plants yield a useful fiber, and the *huizache chino* is used for fuel. There is some aquaculture (producing tilapia and carp), centered on the Guadiana Valley. Durango is Mexico's second most important producer of goat's milk and its sixth of cow's milk; it is its fourth most important producer of poultry.

Mining has been going on in Durango for four hundred years and was in fact the reason for the foundation of Durango itself in 1563. Nowadays, the state is the number-one producer of gold, second in silver, third in copper, and seventh in zinc. There are other exploitable minerals besides, such as strontium, onyx, and marble. Iron from the Cerro El Mercado is the most important aspect of the mining industry; the iron deposits there, which are 60 percent pure, have been exploited since the sixteenth century. The municipalities of Otáez and San Dimas are famed for their gold and silver, Cuencamé and Guanaceví for lead.

Arts

The popular musical tradition of the *mestizo* and *criollo* populations includes the polka, a genre that gained popularity at about the time of the Revolution and spread over the whole of northern Mexico. In some places, they still dance the *chotis* and the *cuadrilla*, both of which are also European in origin. One of the most popular of all song and dance forms is the *corrido*, a type of ballad that generally extols the exploits of revolutionary heroes or tells tales of love. There is even a "Corrido de Durango," composed by Miguel Angel Gallardo.

Durango has long been a favorite location for filmmakers, especially those making westerns. In fact, Pancho Villa was one of the first stars of cinema, an art that was coming into being at the time of his exploits. Aware of the propaganda value of this new medium, Villa had his battles filmed and was even prepared to reenact some if the conditions for filming were not good.

There are other famous sons and daughters of Durango with greater claims to distinction in the arts. **Francisco Zarco** (1829–1869) was a writer and above all a distinguished journalist. As a politician, he worked in foreign affairs, in government offices and as a member of Congress. As a journalist working in Mexico City, he is associated with a vigorous defense of freedom of expression. Intermittently, he was editor of *El Siglo XX*, which was published in Mexico City and was one of the most important and liberal newspapers of the nineteenth century. Zarco started many other publications, such as the satirical *Las Cosquillas* and the ideological *El Demócrata*. He was probably the most renowned journalist of the century.

Fanny Anitúa Yáñez (1887–1968) was one of quite a number of distinguished musicians—instrumentalists and singers—to emerge from Durango. She achieved a certain international reputation as an opera singer, performing at the National Theater in Rome, La Scala in Milan, and the Teatro Colón in Buenos Aires. She formed her own opera company in Mexico, called

Opera de Bonci, and was named honorary director of the National Conservatory by José Vasconcelos, the influential minister of education of the early twentieth century. Another distinguished musician was **Ricardo Castro** (1864-1907), a concert pianist, director of the National Conservatory, and a composer to boot.

Nellie Campobello (1909-1986) and her sister Gloria both became known for their work in the national School of Dance at the Instituto de Bellas Artes in Mexico City. Nellie was also a significant novelist and is especially remembered for *Cartucho* (1931) and *Las manos de mamá* (1937), books that present a personal view of life at the time of the Revolution. She died after having been kidnapped, apparently by robbers.

The Asúnsolo family provided **Ignacio Asúnsolo** (1890-1965), a soldier but more importantly a sculptor of some distinction and director of the Academia de San Carlos, Mexico's leading academy of art. Many of his sculptures were inspired by the Revolution. The actress Dolores Asúnsolo (1906-1983) is better known to the world as **Dolores del Río**, a name she acquired in Hollywood, where she made her reputation with the rise of sound cinema, and was marketed as "Spanish." She returned to Mexico to make films under Emilio Fernández and Gabriel Figueroa, and thereafter appeared opposite the actor Pedro Armendáriz in many films, an early example of which is *María Candelaria*. Del Río won a number of awards and decorations.

Similarly, the Revueltas family has provided its share of distinguished *duranguenses*. **Silvestre Revueltas** (1899-1940) was one of Mexico's leading composers and performers of music. After studying the violin and composition in Mexico and the United States, he formed a duo with Carlos Chávez, the doyen of Mexican classical music, and they performed a series of concerts of contemporary music. He worked as a violinist and conductor of orchestras in the southern United States and served as a professor at Mexico's National Conservatory. But he is most famous as a composer of music, a good deal of it for the cinema. Some people regard him as a better composer than Chávez. His brother **José Revueltas** (1914-1976) was a political activist, teacher, and writer. He took a courageous stand against the Mexican government at the time of the Tlatelolco Massacre, in 1968, and spent some time in prison as a reward. As a writer, he, too, was closely associated with cinema, producing screenplays. José Revueltas has acquired an almost legendary aura in Mexico, thanks to his dramatic life and his strong opinions. He was something of a literary iconoclast, and his works are very personal and unusual blends of the spiritual, the political, and the social. Apart from many essays, he wrote several novels, such as *El luto humano* (*Human Mourning*, 1943) and *Los días terrenales* (*Life on This Earth*, 1949). These two were not the only distinguished members of the Revueltas family; another brother, Fermín, acquired a reputation as a muralist, and a sister, Rosaura, was an actress.

In Durango itself, there is a School of Art, Sculpture, and Crafts attached to its Juárez University; the school has been particularly recognized for its glasswork and its decorative figures, such as flying fish and butterflies. Crafts include basketry in the Laguna Region, the valleys, and the mountains, together with wood carvings of decorative and utilitarian objects. Hats, leather goods, riding gear, and iron artifacts are also made. *Ixtle*, the fiber that comes from the lechuguilla variety of agave, along with such things as osier and mesquite roots and reeds, are used for making hats, baskets, mats, and decorative objects. There is some production of utilitarian clay pottery in the municipalities of Durango, Lerdo, Poanas, and Mezquital. Leather goods include bags and purses, belts, boots, and saddles. Some embroidered clothing is produced by Indian communities, along with simple domestic and farming implements and ceremonial artifacts. The Huicholes are noted for their hats, bags, wristbands, and wooden and clay artifacts, the Tepehuanes for their bows and arrows, baskets, hats, and textiles, the Tarahumaras for their clay pottery, arrows tipped with pieces of stone, flutes, and drums.

Social Customs

The mitote is the principal ritual of the Tepehuanes; it is a dance ceremony that lasts five days and is performed three times a year: in February to bring good health, in May to pray for rain, and in October to mark the harvest of the first corn. In their music, the Tepehuanes still employ the bow, a stringed instrument that is believed to be the only one that survives from pre-Hispanic times. Their dances are also accompanied by drums, rattles, whistles, and violins, and they are often similar to those of the Tarahumaras.

For the Indian communities, fiestas are usually associated with the cycle of the seasons and their religious calendar. Whether it is an Indian community or not, as elsewhere in Mexico, it is routine for places to celebrate the festivities of their patron saints; an example in Durango would be the fiesta of Santa Ana, in Nazas. There are many other Catholic celebrations: for example, Gómez Palacio celebrates the Fiesta de Santa Cruz. Civic celebrations in the nonindigenous communities, as well as many of the religious celebrations, are characterized by processions, music and dancing in the main square and its side streets, eating traditional food, wearing showy clothes, and setting off fireworks. Sometimes there are arts-and-crafts exhibitions and stalls and agricultural displays. Some festivities are associated with local produce; for example, Canatlán has an apple festival in mid-September, San Papasquiaro holds a Regional Fair in July, and during the same month Lerdo has a grape festival. Durango holds a National Fair starting in late June, and celebrating the foundation of the city is another occasion for organizing concerts and other artistic performances, art shows, and commercial events, attracting visitors from all over the country.

Nowadays the typical dress of the Tepehuanes is the result of adapting their old traditions to outside influences, but it remains striking, especially because of the bright, contrasting colors that women wear. The Huicholes, whether for daily or ceremonial use, wear a hand-embroidered blanket with tassels, leather *huaraches* (sandals) and necklaces, wristbands, and rings. The dress that has come to be considered typical for the mestizo population consists of a denim outfit, boots and a high hat for the men, and brightly colored skirts and blouses for the women, in the Spanish style, with little by way of adornment.

Noteworthy Places

There are quite a few museums in Durango, devoted to history, the arts, the Revolution, or cinema. For example, there is the Graphic Museum of the Revolution in Canatlán and the Regional Museum of History and Anthropology at Gómez Palacio. Durango boasts the Avocado Museum, dating from the second half of the nineteenth century and exemplifying the fashion for imitating French architectural styles; despite its name, this museum covers political, social, and natural history, along with exhibitions of art and craftworks.

A good example of a colonial civic building is Durango's Government Building (Palacio de Gobierno). The Teatro Ricardo Castro, named after the musician, is a theater dating from the very beginning of the twentieth century. Other interesting civic buildings are Durango's Casa de los Condes de Súchil and Tamazula's Casa del General Guadalupe Victoria.

There are many noteworthy haciendas, including the Hacienda La Sauceda in Canatlán, the Hacienda de Ferrería de Flores close to Durango, and the Hacienda Peñón Blanco; a number of them have interesting chapels, such as the one at the Hacienda Juana Guerrero, in Nombre de Dios.

Among Durango's religious buildings, the Parish Church of the Assumption, in the capital, was made its cathedral in 1623, but it suffered a fire and it was not until 1844 that the building was fully reconstructed. It contains some items of interest, such as the choir stalls and a canopy brought over from the Philippines (which in colonial days fell under the administrative control of New Spain, in other words, of Mexico). Also in Durango is the Church of Santa Ana. Other sites of interest include the Parish Church of San Antonio de Padua in Cuencamé, the Church of San Fermín in Pánuco, and the parish church at Canelas.

The curiosities of the area known as the Zona del Silencio have already been noted. Also among the natural attractions of Durango is the Balneario La Joya, which has waterfalls, sulfur springs, a canyon, and a subtropical microclimate. The Cascada Mexiquillo is a waterfall that runs through pine trees and over a riverbed that is red as the result of crystalline sediments. In the Sierra del Rosario, close to Mapimí, there is a half-kilometer (1,600-foot) sequence of underground caves. The Mapimí Biosphere is located about 160 kilometers (100 miles) northwest of Gómez Palacio. The Michilia Biosphere is close to the town of Súchil. At Carreras, there are curious, huge rock formations that were formed by centuries of erosion; local inhabitants use some of them as sanctuaries or as pens for their animals.

Cuisine

Meat and cheese are key components of Durango's cuisine, the first reflecting the cattle-ranching tradition and the second the cultural influence of the Mennonites. Corn, beans, walnuts, peaches, and apples are other common ingredients. One of the most typical dishes of the state capital is *caldillo durangueño*, a simple dish made with fresh meat and red chiles; others are roast venison, cow's head stew, stuffed chiles, and *gallinas borrachas* (literally "drunken hens"). Outside the capital, one finds such dishes as *quesadillas de asadero* (typical of Cuencamé) and *gorditas* (from Nombre de Dios). Fruit-based liquors are made from quince, pomegranate, and nuts, and there is a powerful local variety of *mezcal*, made from the agave cactus. Canatlán is known for its preserved fruits. Sweets, cakes, and creams are made with peaches, apples, almonds, and walnuts.

Gallina Borracha

Ingredients:

    1 chicken
    1/2 lb. uncooked ham, cut into strips
    1 large tomato
    1 cup dry sherry
    1 clove of garlic
    Sprig of parsley
    1 *chorizo* (sausage)
    1/2 cup chopped mixed almonds and raisins
    1/4 cup sugar
    A pinch each of cloves, cinnamon, nutmeg, and black pepper
    Oil

Clean and wash the chicken, then cut it into quarters. Crush the tomato and fry the chicken with it. Finely chop the garlic and parsley, then add to the chicken. Once the meat is thoroughly cooked, add the strips of ham and the chorizo. Cook a little longer, adding the sherry slowly, to make a thick sauce, then add the remaining ingredients. If necessary, the sauce can be further thickened by adding some fried breadcrumbs. Serve hot.

Venado Asado

Ingredients:

    1 leg of venison
    1 cup cream
    1/2 lb. butter
    1/2 lb. uncooked ham, in strips
    Salt and pepper

Preheat the oven to 475°F. Make sure the venison leg is clean and free of hair. Cut some gashes in it and stuff them with strips of ham. Brush melted butter over the leg, and sprinkle with salt and pepper. Place the meat in a buttered pan in the oven for a few minutes. Remove and brush with butter once again before returning it to the oven. Repeat this process periodically, adding a little warm water as necessary, to prevent the meat from drying out. Once cooked and brown all over, pour the cream over it and serve. If less rare meat is preferred, reduce the oven temperature to 300°F and cook for longer. The overall time needed depends on the size of the leg.

Enchiladas Almendradas

Ingredients:

1 cup corn oil
24 medium tortillas
$^1/_2$ cup peanuts, peeled
$^1/_2$ cup almonds, peeled
6 *ancho* chiles with the seeds removed
Sesame seeds
2 cups chicken broth
$^1/_2$ onion
1 clove of garlic
A small quantity of leftover bread, soaked in vinegar
Salt
1 chicken breast, cooked and diced
$^1/_4$ lb. *queso fresco* (ricotta cheese can be substituted)

Heat half the oil in a frying pan and briefly place the tortillas in it, taking care that they do not brown, but do separate. Then fry the nuts, chiles, and sesame seeds, taking care not to burn them. Grind up these ingredients together with a little of the broth. Add the onion, garlic, and bread, and drain. Heat the rest of the oil and add the drained mixture to it, together with a little salt. Simmer gently so that it becomes thick. Fill the tortillas with the chicken and the sauce. Sprinkle with cheese before serving.

Asado de Ternera con Pulque

Ingredients:

Oil or fat for cooking
4 cloves of garlic, peeled and crushed
4 lb. fillet of beef (or chicken)
3 carrots
Salt and pepper
Parsley, thyme, marjoram, and *toronjil* (Mexican hyssop) to taste
A glass of more of *pulque* (a fermented drink made from the agave cactus)

Heat some fat in a pot, add the garlic and the chunks of beef (or chicken), and brown. Season with salt and pepper and the herbs. Add a glass each of water and pulque. When half cooked (after about 20 minutes), add the carrots. Adjust the quantity of pulque added so that the dish does not dry out and a little liquid is still left at the end.

Guanajuato

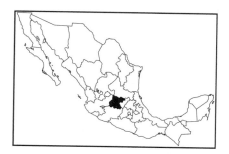

State Characteristics

Guanajuato is located in the southern part of the central plateau (*mesa*). This location makes it strategically important as an axis of communication by road and rail. Guanajuato is set inland, in the area known as El Bajío. Its neighboring states are San Luis Potosí to the north, Querétaro to the east, Michoacán to the south, and Jalisco the west. The name Guanajuato is thought to have come from the Purépecha Indian language and, like many such place names, to refer to physical characteristics: it means "The Place [or Hill] of the Frogs," reflecting the fact that some hills are frog-shaped.

Guanajuato is the twentieth largest state, occupying an area of 30,590 square kilometers (11,930 square miles), which amounts to 1.6 percent of Mexico's surface area. It has a population of approximately 4,600,000 people, about a fifth of whom live in the capital, Santa Fe de Guanajuato (usually referred to simply as "Guanajuato"). Some municipalities are far more heavily populated than others from which they draw migrant workers. Overall, the state has more women than men, and each year approximately seven in every thousand residents migrate to the United States. The population density for this state as a whole is still a good deal higher than it is for most Mexican states. The largest *municipios* in Guanajuato are Allende, Dolores Hidalgo, Pénjamo, San Felipe, and San Luis de la Paz. There are forty-six municipalities in all. Ninety-six percent of the inhabitants identify themselves as Catholic, and most of the rest are Protestant. In Congress, Guanajuato has twenty members in the national Chamber of Deputies and three in the Chamber of Senators.

A large number of newspapers are published in the state. Local editions of *El Sol*, a large national chain, appear in León, Irapuato, Celaya, and Salamanca. In addition, León has *El Heraldo* and *Periódico A.M.*, Irapuato has *El Heraldo* and *Guanajuato Hoy*, Celaya has *AM*, and Dolores Hidalgo has *El Regional Buen Día*. *Correo* is published in Guanajuato, the capital.

Well over a third of the state is covered by mountains, the principal ranges being the Sierra Gorda, Sierra de Guanajuato, Sierra de Comanja, and Sierra de la Codorniz. The highest places in the state are the Cerro Los Rosillos and the Sierra Los Agustinos, which both rise to over 3,000 meters (10,000 feet). There are many other places where the elevation is well in excess of 2,000 meters (6,600 feet), and even the state's flatlands are at an average height of over 1,700 meters (5,600 feet).

Guanajuato may be divided into three main regions. El Bajío is mostly flat, though with some hilly areas and extinct volcanoes (at Salamanca, Valle de Santiago, and Yuriria); this is the region that covers the southern part of the state, south of the Sierra de Guanajuato, and is primarily agricultural—indeed, it is one of the best areas in Mexico in terms of soil and climate conditions. The second region is that of the Sierra de Guanajuato itself, which is a complex of steep mountains and ravines, together with a few long and flat areas; cattle rearing is a main economic activity here. The third region is Los Llanos del Norte, the flatlands that lie north of the Sierra, which are drier and less fertile.

The main river system is the Lerma-Chapala-Santiago, which flows from east to west, toward the Pacific, forming the following basins: Río Lerma-Toluca, Río Lerma–Salamanca, Río Lerma–Chapala, Lago de Pátzcuaro-Cuitzeo-Yuriria, Río Lajas, and Río Verde Grande. All of these are located in the central and southern parts of the state, where most of the population and economic activity are concentrated. Another important river system is the Alto Río Pánuco, which runs from west to east, toward the Gulf of Mexico, through 17 percent of the state; it is located in the north and feeds the Río Tamuín and the Río Moctezuma. Guanajuato's main lakes are Cuitzeo, on the border with Michoacán, and Yuriria, which is rich in fish. Natural lakes have also formed in some of the volcanoes of the Valley of Santiago. There are a number of dams and reservoirs such as Ignacio Allende, La Purísima, Solís, La Gavia, El Conejo, and Santa Ifigenia.

A third of the state has a moderately hot climate with rain in the summer, a further 20 percent is similar but more moderate in temperature, and the remainder is dry or fairly dry. Average annual temperatures range from 16°C (61°F) in Villa Victoria to 20°C (68°F) in Irapuato. Average annual rainfall ranges from 598 millimeters (23.6 inches) in Celaya to 691 millimeters (27.2 inches) in Irapuato.

Fauna in the northern areas includes such birds as owls, eagles, vultures (*zopilotes*), thrushes, quail, pheasants, hummingbirds, crows, *zentzontles*, woodpeckers, magpies, and turkey buzzards. There are many insect varieties, including scorpions and dangerous spiders, as well as miscellaneous frogs, toads, snakes, and lizards. Rabbits, foxes, squirrels, deer, coyotes, armadillos, and mountain lions are among the mammals. In the waters, carp, bream, loach, and catfish predominate.

As for flora, the most common types are oak, mesquite, ash, the *nopal* and other cacti, ferns, and other plants or trees with native names such as *pirul, joconoxtle, tronadora, estafiate, zapote blanco, viznaga, garambullo, ahuehete, huizache, pepahuaje*, and *casahuate*. Cereals and pulses are grown in the northern region, primarily corn, chickpeas, beans, barley, and wheat. The central Bajío region was long thought of as the country's main supplier of grain. Much of it is irrigated, thanks to the Solís and Allende dams. In addition, it is blessed with a benign climate and adequate rainfall, which makes for the cultivation of a great variety of foodstuffs, from corn and barley to beans, lentils, alfalfa, sorghum, peanuts, tomatoes, green vegetables, herbs, and the inevitable chiles. The Bajío also has *jícama* (a vegetable that looks like a yam, but is more like a firm apple in texture and taste), cucumber, melons, and beetroot. Among the most common trees are pine, *oyamel*, casahuate, walnut, lime, avocado, *tronadora*, *pirul*, peach, mesquite, orange, eucalyptus, fig, and cedar. The Bajío's wildlife is much the same as in the northern region, but naturally with a greater predominance of the kinds that prefer flatter territory. The Solís dam supplies water to the most southerly part, which otherwise is moderately dry. This is an area of cattle raising, but agricultural production is otherwise similar to that of the Bajío region. The flora is much as in the Bajío region, too, but more abundant, since there are wooded hills.

Cultural Groups and Languages

Today as few as 0.2 percent of the inhabitants of Guanajuato speak indigenous languages, the lowest proportion for any of Mexico's states. The total number of indigenous-language speakers over five years of age, according to the 2005 census, was 10,347; approximately half of these were identified as speaking one of eight different languages or language groups. Most of the rest did not specify their language. It appears that the most widely spoken languages are Chichimeca, Jonaz, Náhuatl, Otomí, and Mazahua.

History

Around 800 BC, Coroneo was the site of the beginnings of Chupícuara-Tarasca culture, which would develop over a thousand years, producing ceramics and building civic and religious structures, until they abandoned the area, faced with invasions by the Chichimecs. Sedentary settlement in what became the state of Guanajuato is believed to have begun in a place called Chupícuaro, near Coroneo and the River Lerma. It is thought that the inhabitants of this place were quite numerous, although their dwellings did not survive the ravages of time to prove it. They cultivated corn, chiles, and tomatoes. Their principal legacy is their ceramic work, of coffee-colored clay decorated with pastel colors, or of a creamier-colored shiny clay, some of it brightly painted. The anthropomorphic pottery that survives suggests that these people wore such things as belts, sandals, jewelry, and headdresses. The men would color their hair white and the women red or black. There is also evidence of the use of simple wind and percussion instruments. The Chupícuara culture was much influenced by that of the Teotihuacanos, who had made advances in agriculture and weaponry and developed a powerful theocracy; once Chupícuara hegemony waned, there was immigration from other territories, and the Toltec and then the Chichimec cultures became dominant.

The Chichimecs were a conflictive and warlike people whose lifestyle was basically nomadic, though they would settle in winter. They wove mats and other utensils out of osier and cane, made polished stone artifacts (for example, from obsidian), and used tortoise shells as plates. They also made leather clothing. The Tarascos established settlements in Acámbar, Apaseo, Pénjamo, and Yuririhapúndaro prior to the arrival of the Spaniards.

In 1522, an expedition led by Cristóbal de Olid arrived in Yuririhapúndaro and Pénjamo, which by then were under Chichimec and Purépecha control. Here and in Michoacán, another Spanish explorer, Nuño Beltrán de Guzmán, was responsible for the killing of many Indians and for pillaging their communities, even after they had been organized under the *encomienda* system.

Colonization of the eastern part of what is now Guanajuato began in 1542, when permission was given to open cattle ranches there, in Apaseo and Chamácuaro. In 1555, Ángel de Villafaña founded the Villa de San Miguel el Grande, and two years after that the town of Santa Fe y Real de Minas de Quanaxhuato (later Guanajuato), with the aim of making the most of the area's silver deposits, discovered in 1548. In order to guard against Indian attacks, a number of towns were established: San Felipe in 1562, Celaya (and garrisons all along the route to Zacatecas) in 1571, and León in 1576. At last, thanks to the mediating skills of one Fray Gonzalo de Tapia, the Chichimecs were persuaded to cease hostilities and gather in a single town: in 1590, it was possible to mark a peace treaty between the Spaniards and the Chichimecs by founding Villa de San Luis de la Paz.

When the Jesuits were expelled from the New World in the mid eighteenth century there was a revolt in Guanajuato against the ruling; this revolt met with a firm response from the authorities and a fine was imposed on the city. For a while, it came under the jurisdiction of New Spain. Thanks to the rise in importance of mining during the eighteenth century, many notable civic and religious buildings were built in the city of Guanajuato, and in 1786 it became an *intendencia*, one the twelve administrative cities of New Spain. In 1792, Guanajuato acquired one of its most impressive buildings, an immense granary called the Alhóndiga de Granaditas; this was later to be the stage for a major moment in the state's history.

Guanajuato was very important at the beginning of the nineteenth century, the time of the independence movement from Spain, and was the scene of one of that movement's most dramatic events. The prime instigator of the independence movement was Father **Miguel Hidalgo y Costilla** (1753–1811), a freethinker whose brushes with the establishment had led to his being demoted and sent to serve as parish priest in one of Guanajuato's small towns, Dolores. Hidalgo had been a teacher at the Colegio de San Nicolás and had had a number of administrative posts. He had set up craft and literacy workshops and had encouraged the cultivation of bees, silkworms, and grapes. In Dolores, Hidalgo had been plotting with a group of like-minded people, and upon realizing that their plans were no longer secret, he took the initiative at midnight on September 16, 1810, and issued a public proclamation that became known as the *Grito de Dolores*. It was a demand for independence and a call to arms. Heeding the call, a motley group of poorly armed people formed a rebel army that took the city of Guanajuato, massacring many of its inhabitants. Other such exploits followed.

In Guadalajara, Hidalgo formed the first independent government and decreed the abolition of slavery. He also began a rebel publication called *El Pensador Mexicano* (The Mexican Thinker). Loyalist forces eventually contained the rebellion, and Hidalgo was captured, defrocked, and executed; he died apparently regretting the violence that his cry for independence had unleashed. But Hidalgo was by no means alone in wanting a free Mexico, nor was he the only rebel to lose his life for the cause. In time, military leaders would align themselves with Agustín de Iturbide's Plan de Iguala, and in July 1821, Mexico formally asserted its independence from Spain.

At the Constituent Congress held in 1824 to establish the federal republic, Guanajuato was declared to be one of the founding states, the Estado Libre y Soberano de Guanajuato. It lost that status for a while in midcentury, when the country was defending itself against the United States, despite the fact that Guanajuato sent a contingent of 6,000 men to fight against the U.S. troops. When the Treaty of Guadalupe was signed in 1848, marking the end of that war, there was a revolt against it, led by two generals, Mariano Paredes and Manuel Doblado, and a priest, Celedonio Dómeco Jarauta; they took the capital, then lost it, and the priest was shot.

After Ignacio Comonfort staged his coup and became president of Mexico, Guanajuato was one of the states that supported Benito Juárez. During his perambulations through the country, Juárez came to Guanajuato, at the time the most heavily populated state in Mexico, and for a while he established his provisional government there; after that he went via Guadalajara and Manzanillo to Veracruz, where he eventually based his government in opposition. After 1858 and over the course of the three years of the Reform War, control of the city of Guanajuato swung between liberals and conservatives on about twenty occasions. By 1863, it was in the hands of the conservatives; a year later, Guanajuato again lost its designation as a state, but by 1867 that status had been recovered.

As everywhere in the Mexico of the *porfiriato* in the late nineteenth century, foreign investment in Guanajuato grew, especially in the mining industry; Porfirio Díaz was a great promoter of foreign investment in Mexico. He was also a self-propagandist who lost no opportunity to be seen at favorable events, such as the opening of the sumptuous Teatro Juárez, which he personally inaugurated in 1903. He was not without his opponents. Ironically, one of his most articulate foes in Guanajuato was another Díaz, Francisco Díaz, the editor of a newspaper called *El Observador*, who was incarcerated because of his criticisms of Porfirio's regime.

The State of Guanajuato provided a lively stage for the Revolution. The effort began in November 1910 when Cándido Navarro took to arms and gained control of the town of La Aldea, near Silao; he went on to take others and eventually San Luis Potosí. The main local confrontation of the Revolution, however, took place between the forces of Alvaro Obregón and Pancho Villa at the Battle of Celaya. During the Cristero Rebellion, which occurred a little after the Revolution, places such as Pénjamo and León were active in opposition to the central government because it was curtailing the powers of the Church. Years later, León was once more the site of much bloodshed during a protest by the so-called Sinarquistas against election results in 1946. From about that time on, the rule of the Partido Revolucionario Institucional (PRI), and particularly its anticlerical stance, engendered increasing opposition in Guanajuato from the conservative Partido de Acción Nacional (PAN). In 1995 **Vicente Fox** (1942–) was elected the first non-PRI governor of the state. He went on to become Mexico's first non-PRI president since the Revolution, an office to which he was elected in 2000.

Economy

Guanajuato is centrally located. Ever since colonial times, it has had the benefit of access to both the Pacific and the Gulf of Mexico, while sitting conveniently between Mexico's three main cities (the capital, Guadalajara, and Monterrey). In addition, it is about as far from the Mexico's northern border as it is from its southern one.

Over 36 percent of the state is suitable for agricultural use, and about 40 percent of that portion is artificially irrigated. Cattle, pigs, sheep, goats and poultry are raised all over Guanajuato. There are 150,000 hectares (370,000 acres) of it that are wooded; half of that area is economically exploitable, but such exploitation as there has been has not been well controlled, however, so a number of species (notably pine, oak, and oyamel) have been severely depleted and soil erosion has increased. The main fruits that are cultivated in Guanajuato are peaches, strawberries, avocados, grapes, apples, quinces, prickly pears, guavas, and apricots. Of the agricultural land, over 60 percent is given over to the cultivation of chiles, corn, and beans for human consumption and alfalfa and sorghum for forage.

Mining has played a major economic role since early colonial days. In addition to silver, there are deposits of mercury, tin, copper, lead, and zinc. Nonmineral deposits include sulfur, fluorite, feldspar, lime, and kaolin.

There are now two thermoelectric plants, in Celaya and Salamanca. The oil refining and the petrochemical industries, also centered in Salamanca, are fed with crude oil by a pipeline from Veracruz. Natural gas comes in via a pipeline from Tabasco. Other pipelines go out from Salamanca to Guadalajara and Morelia. Irapuato and León are industrial zones also. In manufacturing, the three main areas of activity are leather goods, the food industry, and metal products. Overall, industry accounts for approximately 30 percent of the state's economy.

Following the passage of the North American Free Trade Agreement in 1992, the economy of Guanajuato grew quite rapidly, especially in the areas of trade, industry, and tourism. It has one of the lowest unemployment rates in Mexico and an export level about three times as high as the national average.

Arts

Within the Hispanic culture, and specifically within the field of the visual arts, Guanajuato has supplied many well-known personalities. **Francisco Eduardo Tresguerras** (1759–1833) was an architect, engraver, and painter. Another artist who trained locally was **Hermenegildo Bustos** (1834–1907); although he never thought of himself as a professional painter, Bustos has come to be highly regarded in Mexican art as a painter of portraits and still lifes.

By far Guanajuato's leading painter, however, was **Diego Rivera** (1886–1957), the most successful artist of the Muralist movement that dominated art in postrevolutionary Mexico. He and his fellow muralists were given government commissions and encouraged to spread the socialist word through art, in theory making it accessible to the masses. Rivera had trained in Europe and had absorbed some of the foreign techniques of the day. He exhibited widely abroad. No single Mexican artist is better known the world over. Some of his most famous murals in Mexico are at the Secretaría de Educación Pública in Mexico City. He also had several commissions in the United States, most notoriously one for John D. Rockefeller Jr. that was canceled when the financier realized that socialist images were being included. When Rivera died, he left Mexico his collection of pre-Hispanic artifacts, together with the rights to reproduce his and his wife's (Frida Kahlo's) works.

Among notable poets born in Guanajuato are **Agustín Lanuza** (1870–1936), **Efrén Hernández** (1903–1958), and **Efraín Huerta** (1914–1982); Hernández also wrote fiction. It was quite common, especially during the nineteenth century, for politicians to double as military men, teachers, and writers. Guanajuato was no exception, with many distinguished people of this sort, such as **Pedro García** (1790-1873), **Lucas Alamán y Escalada** (1792-1853), **José María Luis Mora** (1794-1850), **Santos Degollado** (1811-1861), **Manuel Doblado** (1818-1865), **Francisco Z. Mena** (1841-1908), **Praxedis G. Guerrero Hurtado** (1882-1910), and **Ignacio Ramírez** (1818-1879). Ramírez was one of the most significant: a politician, journalist, soldier, teacher, lawyer, and writer. As a politician, at one time or another he was chief officer for Tlaxcala, congressional representative for Sinaloa and for Mexico City, personal secretary to Comonfort, national secretary for justice and education (during which time he founded the National Library and took steps to improve provision of elementary education), secretary for economic development, and mayor of Mexico City. As an educator, he was associated with the groundbreaking Academia de Letrán and the Instituto Literario de Toluca. As a writer and journalist, be went by the pseudonym "El Nigromante"; he founded a number of newspapers and magazines and is particularly associated with the major nineteenth-century newspapers *El Renacimiento*, *El Siglo XIX*, and *El Monitor Republicano*. He also found time to write several books.

In the musical arena, **Juventino Rosas** (1868-1894) was a violinist, composer, and sometime accompanist of the famous soprano Angela Peralta; he composed many pieces that have become popular as waltzes and other dances, most famously "Sobre las Olas," which Hollywood turned into "The Loveliest Night of the Year." **María Grever** (1885-1951) was really María Asunción de la Portilla y Torres; she wrote more than 800 songs (the first at the age of four), mostly in the romantic *bolero* style, and spent much of her life in the United States, writing music for the cinema. **Jorge Negrete** (1911-1953) was one of the greatest idols of Mexican cinema during its golden years of the 1940s; he was particularly famous as a singer of *canciones rancheras*. **José Alfredo Jiménez** (1926-1973) was one of Mexico's most successful singer-songwriters of the twentieth century, who wrote over a thousand songs in traditionally popular Mexican styles.

The state of Guanajuato sponsors a dance company known as the Ballet Folklórico de Guanajuato, and its university has a symphony orchestra.

At festivities, the music and dancing draw on the colonial tradition (dances called *matachines* and *moros y cristianos*, for example), with some pre-Hispanic input, plus popular nineteenth-century forms such as the *corrido*. *Sones* and *jarabes* are common, accompanied by violin, guitar, and percussion.

In this state, there are artisans who work with tin, copper, wool, papier-mâché, and, of course, silver. Ceramics and leatherwork are also two major areas of craft activity. León is known for leatherwork, and Dolores Hidalgo for ceramics. Typical leather products are jackets, bags, and belts, and typical ceramics include eating and drinking vessels and vases, with yellow, green, and blue as the characteristic colors. Father Hidalgo was responsible for introducing majolica to the area, and it is also made in the state capital (though there it is usually light gray in color). Salamanca is known for its diminutive wax figures, examples of which can be seen in the Templo de San Agustín.

Social Customs

When they arrived, the Spaniards did not encounter a very unified or developed indigenous civilization. The modern culture of the state is heavily Hispanic, but infused with traditions brought from other places or inherited from its rather obscure and varied indigenous past.

For Acámbaro, July 4 means the Feast of the Virgen del Refugio, commemorated with a solemn procession, floats, musical bands, and folk dances. The most characteristic dances are the *danza de los moros y cristianos*, *danza de los franceses*, *danza de los viejitos*, *danza de los aztecas*, *danza de los chichimeas*, *danza del venado* (deer), and *danza de la calabaza* (gourd).

On the sixteenth of the month, Celaya celebrates the Virgen del Carmen, including the *danza de los sonajeros* and the *danza del plumero*. A month later, Celaya is busy with the Feast of the Assumption, which coincides with the Feria de la Cajeta (a creamy self-indulgence that comes in wooden boxes). Celaya is a place where the Mexican tradition of Las Posadas, which take place during the run-up to Christmas, has a very prominent role.

In early November, Guanajuato itself holds a Fiesta de las Iluminaciones, when the whole town is lit up and there is music, dancing, and fireworks. The Feast of Saint Sebastian in Guanajuato (in January) is one of Mexico's most engaging festivities, with a craft fair and much merrymaking. Another major celebration is in June, the time of the Festival de la Presa de la Olla. San Sebastián is also a major occasion for León, where, in addition to religious and popular celebrations, the town organizes an industrial and agricultural fair.

Naturally, September is a festive month for Dolores Hidalgo, since it marks the anniversary of Father Hidalgo's cry for independence. December 8 is the Feast of the Immaculate Conception, a time for Dolores Hidalgo to hold colorful religious events, dress up, and let its hair down. For the Feast of the Virgen de los Remedios in Comonfort, on September 1, the devout don traditional costumes and perform dances such as those of the sonajeros, apaches, and *compadres*, dedicating them to their patroness; on the last Sunday in November, there is a *reprise* and a craft and food fair. Other noteworthy occasions when similar activities take place are the days of Santiago Apóstol in Coroneo and in Nautla (in October), María Auxiliadora in Empalme Escobedo (in May), and San Miguel (in both May and September) in San Felipe; during the September celebrations, the Spanish conflict between the Moors and Christians is reenacted, with half the town "attacking" the other half and general hubbub until the infidels surrender and everyone can turn their attention to drinking and dancing.

San Miguel de Allende's main festivities are those of the Día del Señor de la Conquista (Day of the Lord of the Conquest), Good Friday, Palm Sunday, Corpus Christi, and especially the Feast of San Antonio. Two big occasions for Yuriria are the Día de la Preciosa Sangre de Cristo (Day of Christ's Precious Blood, in January) and Carnival, which entails religious and secular events, including processions, bullfights, and masked balls. During Holy Week in Santiago Maravatio, scenes from the scriptures are enacted, and on July 25 the town celebrates the Feast of Santiago.

Irapuato, where strawberries are grown, hosts a noisy Strawberry Fair (Feria de la Fresa) in April. Rather more grandly, ever since the 1970s the city of Guanajuato has been holding its Festival Internacional Cervantino (International Cervantes Festival). This has become a genuinely international affair, with a reputation for the quality of its operatic, dance, musical, and theatrical events, as also its more informal street entertainments. San Miguel de Allende organizes an annual Festival de Música de Cámara y de Jazz (Chamber Music and Jazz Festival). San Miguel is generally a haven for artists, both Mexican and foreign, and there are several galleries and workshops in the town. It also hosts a craft fair called the Feria de la Lana y del Latón (Wool and Tin Fair).

In Guanajuato, there is a style of women's dress that dates back to colonial mining days, when women would often help outside the mines by breaking up the rocks brought up by their men. Such women were called *galereñas*, and their characteristic garb has come to be considered the traditional way for *guanajuatense* women in general to dress. It comprises an A-line underskirt with a red flannel skirt over it, decorated with green triangles around the waist and along the hem, but otherwise plain. When the woman ventures out, she adds yet another layer of white poplin over the skirt, decorated so as to give a flowery effect. It has a tail to it, somewhat reminiscent of those on flamenco dresses. She also wears decorative stockings up to the knees and brogues on her feet. The blouse is white and square-necked, embroidered around the neckline and also at the edges of the short sleeves; over that, the galereña wears a tassled shawl and a brightly colored necklace, together with a lively kerchief and a straw hat, to guard against the sun's rays.

Noteworthy Places

Guanajuato is blessed with a rich heritage of colonial buildings. To begin with, the city of Guanajuato is one of the places that UNESCO has declared to be part of the world's cultural patrimony. It is set in a ravine and is full of neoclassical buildings, old cobbled streets, picturesque squares, and baroque churches. Through the middle of it runs a street that was once an underground river, and that has a number of arches and passageways. The main square is called the Plaza de la Paz. On it sit an impressive church, the Basílica Colegiata de Nuestra Señora de Guanajuato, the Palacio de

Main square at San Miguel de Allende.

Gobierno Municipal (Municipal Government Building), and the Casa del Conde Rul and Palacio Legislativo (law courts). Close to the square is a popular gathering place called the Jardín de la Unión. Other important churches in the capital are the Templo de San Cayetano and the Templo de San Diego de Alcalá. Many of the buildings referred to above reflect the prosperity of Guanajuato during the eighteenth century, which was due primarily to its mines. The imposing Teatro Juárez dates from the time of Porfirio Díaz.

The Monumento al Pípila, made out of stone in 1939, evinces the dominant ethos of postrevolutionary governments; it is a huge effigy of a miner (Juan José Martínez, alias "El Pípila") raising a torch in his hand, the message bolstered by an inscription that reads, "There are yet more granaries to burn down." The allusion is to a fire set by El Pípila at the Alhóndiga de Granaditas, a fine building that had been built between 1788 and 1809, after permission for its construction had been given by the viceroy, Miguel de la Grúa. For a while thereafter, it was popularly known as the "Corn Palace." Over one of its entrances, there is now a plaque that states that on September 28, 1810, the independentist army took control of the building. In another part of the building, there are corner plaques bearing the names of the insurgent leaders Hidalgo, Allende, and Jiménez; when these leaders were later shot, they were also decapitated, and their heads put on display at the corners of the building, in iron cages. In 1810, the miner El Pípila is said to have hidden himself behind a flagstone and set fire to one of the doors to the building, allowing access for Hidalgo's rebel troops. Much later, in 1864, while Emperor Maximilian was in power, the Alhóndiga became a prison. Since 1949, it has been put to use for civic ceremonies and cultural events. It also houses a museum covering, inter alia, pre-Hispanic artifacts, the paintings of local artist Hermenegildo Bustos, and things of historical interest from the independence and revolutionary periods.

Other notable places in the city of Guanajuato are the Hidalgo Market and the university, though the latter only dates from the mid-twentieth century. Close to the city are the Hacienda de San Gabriel, which includes a museum, and the Mineral de Valenciana, a witness to the riches that came from silver mining.

The town of San Miguel de Allende has become something of a mecca for U.S. and Canadian expatriates, who now account for about 10 percent of its resident population. The place draws artists and retirees with its fine old buildings, cobbled streets lined with brightly colored façades, favored location, and good cuisine. Among its buildings of interest are the Casa-Museo de Allende, the Casa del Conde de la Canal, and churches such as the Templo de la Concepción, the Oratorio de San Felipe Neri, the Parroquia de San Miguel Arcángel, and the Templo de San Francisco. The name of **Ignacio María de Allende** (1769–1811) was added to the town of San Miguel in recognition of his role in history as a military leader. Hidalgo appointed him officer-in-charge of the insurgent forces; like Hidalgo himself, Allende was eventually taken prisoner by loyalist troops and shot.

Twenty minutes from San Miguel along the road to Dolores Hidalgo lies the Santuario de Atotonilco, an eighteenth-century construction; this is the place where Father Hidalgo took up the flag of the Virgin of Guadalupe before leading his army to attack Guanajuato. The town of Dolores Hidalgo itself has its origins in the purchase of part of the land belonging to the Hacienda de la Erre, a cattle ranch. Hidalgo, the parish priest, established pottery, carpentry, and textile workshops here, and encouraged the development of agriculture, especially the growing of grapes. These activities help account for the peasants' loyalty to him at the time of his cry for national independence in 1810. Dolores Hidalgo is now officially "The Cradle of Mexican Independence" and naturally it has a Museo de la Independencia. As in other parts of Mexico, each year at midnight on September 16 the Grito de Dolores, Hidalgo's call for independence, is reiterated from the town hall. Dolores Hidalgo also has its share of fine colonial buildings, plus another museum in what was once Hidalgo's residence.

In Yuriria, there is a somber church (now a museum) that is like a fortress, as was quite often the case with early colonial convents; this is the Convento de San Agustín, which sits beside an artificial lake, the very first such piece of engineering of the colonial era, designed to help irrigate the region. Salamanca has a baroque gem in its Convento y Templo de San

Agustín, dating from the middle of the seventeenth century and housing exceptional altarpieces in the elaborate churrigueresque style. Celaya, once the home of the artist Francisco Eduardo Tresguerras, naturally displays his work, particularly in the Templo del Carmen. Apart from that, Celaya has the seventeenth-century Convento de San Francisco, the Templo de San Francisco, and the Claustro Agustino.

Acámbaro is a town that was founded in 1526, and it has many fine colonial buildings, such as the Iglesia del Hospital (sixteenth century) and the churches of Guadalupe and of San Francisco (eighteenth century). There is a sixteenth-century fountain that commemorates the first bullfight held in New Spain and also an arched stone bridge across the River Lerma. Salvatierra, in the Guatzindeo Valley, is another town with fine colonial structures, as many as three hundred of which have been classified as of historical value; these include convents, large private houses, and the Santuario Diocesano, an impressive church with work by the architect and sculptor Manuel Tolsà, as well as by Tresguerras. Salvatierra is one of Mexico's best examples of a colonial town.

Among the city of Guanajuato's museums are the Museo de Historia de la Alhóndiga de Granaditas (where the first battle for independence began), the Quijote Museum, Diego Rivera's House, and the Museo de las Momias (Museum of Mummies), a significant tourist attraction.

Rock paintings can be seen at San Andrés del Cubo. Plazuelas, located in the southwestern mountains, has an archaeological site with quite a few ruined buildings and a recreational area. The site was not revealed until 1998, and it is not yet entirely clear which culture or cultures were originally involved in building and using it. Less important sites are at Cañada de la Virgen, in San Miguel de Allende; at Peralta, in Abasolo; and at El Coporo, in Ocampo. The town of Acámbaro inherited a vast collection of Chupícuaro pottery, thousands of years old.

Cuisine

Typical of Guanajuato cuisine are dishes such as *patitas de puerco* (pigs' trotters), *pacholas guanajuatenses*, and *empanadas de carnitas* (meat pies made with a special dough containing mashed potatoes, filled with fried meat, and served with lettuce and radishes). There is *pan de Acámbaro* and *fiambre estilo San Miguel de Allende* (a mixture of cold meats plus fruit and vegetables in oil and vinegar), while *caldo michi* is a robust soup made with fish and vegetables. But the most famous typical dish is *enchiladas mineras*.

Among drinks, one finds *agua de betabel* (made with sugarcane, lime, apple, banana, orange, and lettuce and traditionally consumed during Holy Week) and, on the alcoholic front, *cebadina* (made with pineapple vinegar, tamarind water, and *jamaica*, an infusion from hibiscus leaves). There is also a drink called *agua de mezquite* and a local strawberry liqueur.

Desserts include several made with Irapuato's renowned strawberries, the cajetas that are typical of Celaya, and *charamuscas*, which are made with caramelized sugar and often have strange shapes, such as a representation of Don Quixote.

Enchiladas Mineras

Ingredients:

12 small tortillas
Pork fat (or oil)
For the filling:
15 *guajillo* chiles (deseeded)
1 clove of garlic
Pinch of cumin
$1/2$ tsp oregano
1 lb. grated cheese (*queso ranchero*)
1 onion, finely chopped
For the garnish:
Shredded lettuce
1 lb. potatoes, peeled, diced, and cooked
1 lb. carrots, cooked and diced
Slices of preserved jalapeño pepper

First prepare the filling by blending the ingredients. Dip the tortillas in the mixture and then fry them quickly in the fat or oil. Fry the potatoes and carrots. Fill the tortillas, put them on a serving dish, and garnish them with the fried vegetables, the shredded lettuce, a little of the cheese, and the slices of jalapeño.

Tumbagones

Ingredients:

3 green tomatoes
Pinch of *tequesquite* (a mineral salt used to leaven dough, preserve color, or soften foods such as beans—if unavailable, baking powder will do)
2 tsp dry sherry
10 egg yolks
$1/2$ lb. flour
1 egg white
Pork lard or butter
Powdered sugar

Boil the tomatoes in a little water, together with the tequesquite. Drain and reserve the water, allowing it to cool. Beat the egg yolks well, mix in the flour, and add the sherry and some of the reserved water until it forms a firm dough. Let it stand for a while before rolling it out into a thin layer. Cut strips from this, brush them with egg white, and fry them in hot fat. When brown, roll them in the sugar.

Cuete Encacahuatado

Ingredients:

2 lb. beef roast, in one piece
2 thick slices of bacon, cut into strips
1 thick slice of *jamón serrano* (similar to Italian prosciutto), cut into strips
1 thick slice of boiled ham, cut into strips
3 tbsp of corn oil
Salt and pepper
1 onion, peeled and cut in two
2 cloves of garlic
1 bay leaf
1 sprig of oregano
For the sauce:
2 tbsp of lard
$^1/_2$ onion, finely chopped
5 oz. roasted peanuts
1 slice of dry bread
3 tomatoes, roasted and peeled
2 cloves
4 peppercorns
1 small stick of cinnamon

Make cuts in the piece of meat and lace it with the bacon, jamón serrano, and ham. Brown it in the oil and season with salt and pepper. Boil the meat in enough water to cover it, with the peeled onion, garlic, bay leaf, and oregano, until it is thoroughly cooked. Remove and cut into slices when cool. Make the sauce by softening the onion in a little fat, then lightly frying the peanuts and adding the crumbled bread. Grind this mixture together with the tomatoes and other sauce ingredients, put it through a sieve, and then simmer it for a while in the rest of the fat. Before serving the meat, put it into the sauce and heat it thoroughly. Serve with mashed potatoes or rice and garnish with chopped parsley.

Guerrero

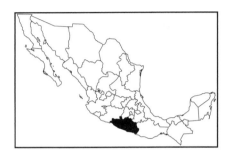

State Characteristics

The state of Guerrero bears the name of **Vicente Guerrero Saldaña** (1783–1831), who was one of the leading figures in Mexico's movement for independence from Spain and briefly president of Mexico. Guerrero State is in the southern part of the country, with the states of Michoacán, México, and Morelos lying to its north, Puebla and Oaxaca to its east, and the Pacific Ocean to its south. Its total area is the fourteenth largest in Mexico, at 64,586 square kilometers (26,150 square miles).

The full name of the capital city, which lies more or less in the middle of the state, is Chilpancingo de los Bravos; it is "Chilpancingo" for short. The only other cities whose population exceeds 50,000 are Acapulco and Iguala. The state population in 2005 was given as 3,115,202 and the density as 49 per square kilometer (121 per square mile), which was the sixteenth highest in the nation. For a long time, Guerrero had seventy-six municipalities, but a further five have been added in recent years, resulting in the current total of eighty-one. There are nine people representing the state in the National Congress. Approximately 90 percent of the population is Catholic.

Guerrero has a very large number of newspapers. No less than seven are published in Acapulco, including *El Sur*, *La Jornada*, and *El Observador*. Chilpancingo has as many, including *Ecos de Guerrero*, *Pueblo*, and *Diario de Guerrero*. In addition, Iguala has four papers, of which *Diario 21* and *El Guerrerense* are examples; Zihuantanejo has *El Diario*, *Despertar de la Costa*, and *La Voz*; and Arcelia and Marquelia each have one.

Traditionally, Guerrero has been seen as having six regions: Norte, the northern region that has the states of México, Morelos, and Puebla to the east of it; Tierra Caliente, to the north of which are the states of Michoacán and México; Montaña, which lies to the east, bordering on Puebla and Oaxaca; Centro, the central region that includes the capital; and two coastal regions, Costa Grande and Costa Chica. However, in addition, since 1983 Acapulco has been considered a region in its own right.

Guerrero is a mountainous state with a long, hot, and humid coastal plain. Between the main ranges, the Sierra Madre del Sur and the Sierra del Norte, lies a dry and hot region. The coastline runs from the mouth of the Río Balsas about 500 kilometers (310 miles) south to the munici-pality of Cuajinicuilapa. There are three hydrographic regions to Gue-rrero: those of the Río Balsas, the Costa Grande, and the Costa Chica—Río Verde. The Río Balsas, which is the biggest river in the state, has sev-eral dams. The Costa Grande is fed by short rivers: the Río Atoyac, Río Cayuquilla, Río San Luís, Río Ixtapa, and others that run into the Pacific. The rivers of the Costa Chica—Río Verde are bigger; the waters of the Río Omitlán and Río Azul feed into the Río Papagayo, and then into the Pacific.

In the Balsas Basin, temperatures can reach 45°C (113°F) and rainfall av-erage is quite modest, at 860 millimeters (34.4 inches) on average. Arati-changuio records a lower average rainfall of 685 millimeters (27.4 inches), but other areas of the state have average rainfall figures that are well in excess of 1,000 millimeters (40 inches). Most of the rain falls in the summer, and the determining factor is generally the wind and humid air that comes from the coast. The average temperatures range from 21.9°C (71.4°F) in Chilpancingo to 29.5°C (85.1°F) in Aratichanguio.

Approximately two-thirds of the state can be said to have a hot and tropi-cal climate. Consequently the flora and fauna are mostly those associated with warm and humid climates. Along the coast, there are mangroves, *amates*, and palms, and on the slopes grow such species as *chijol*, *huana-castle*, *parota*, *primavera*, *ramón*, mahogany, and red cedar. Beginning at altitudes of about 500 meters (1,600 feet), there are oaks, conifers, myrtles, and so forth. In the driest areas, mesquite, cacti, and *huizaches* (a type of acacia) are typical. Guerrero has quite a number of useful medicinal or culi-nary plants, too, such as annatto, aniseed, arnica, thyme, *chuachalote*, *estafiate*, *guarumba*, and many more with even more abstruse names. There are countless varieties of fruit trees.

Insects include wasps, bees, crickets, cochineal beetles, scorpions, ter-mites, and, inevitably, mosquitoes. Among Guerrero's reptiles are lizards, crocodiles, snakes, turtles, *tlicuates*, and iguanas. Common birds are eagles, owls, cardinals, hummingbirds, parrots, and, in coastal areas, cor-morants, herons, ducks, and pelicans. Squirrels, armadillos, badgers, *caco-miztles*, coyotes, jaguars, wild boars, pumas, bears, porcupines, and *tlacuaches* are among the many mammals. Freshwater fish include carp and catfish, while there is a plethora of seafood, notably snapper, bream, bass, swordfish, shark, shrimp, crab, lobster, squid, and octopus.

Cultural Groups and Languages

Quite a high proportion—14.2 percent of the state population, according to the 2005 census—speaks an indigenous language, and about 70,000 of those people speak no Spanish.

There are several indigenous peoples still represented in Guerrero: the Amuzgos, who also inhabit parts of the state of Oaxaca; the Chatinos; the Chochos or Chocholtecas; and the Triquis. The *municipios* that have the largest numbers of indigenous-language speakers are Chilapa de Álvarez, Malinaltepec, Tlapa de Comonfort, Metlatonoc, Zapotitlán Tablas, and Xochistlahuaca. The main languages that are still used are (in round figures) Náhuatl (40 percent), Mixteco (30 percent), Tlapaneco (20 percent), and Amuzgo (less than 10 percent). Many indigenous-language speakers live in relative isolation and still follow their traditional lifestyle. A number of Indian communities are known for their craftwork.

The culture and customs of Guerrero have grown from typical Mexican roots in the indigenous and Hispanic traditions, but with a significant African input, thanks to the numbers of slaves who were brought into the area. One finds evidence of the African contribution in the music, for example, and in the language, particularly in coastal areas. Slaves disembarked in Veracruz and were brought over to the Pacific coast, and it is therefore not surprising that there are cultural similarities with the state of Veracruz. In the Spanish of both states, one finds words that are clearly of African origin, and the speech characteristics of both places have something in common with those of the islands of the Caribbean.

History

Evidence of human remains found in a place called the Cueva Encantada indicates that there was a human presence in Guerrero 22,000 years ago. Further evidence from the northern mountains and central valleys points to human activity 15,000 years ago: arrowheads, axes, carved bones, and cave paintings have been found there. It is assumed that these were nomadic peoples who lived by hunting and gathering but eventually settled and began agricultural practices. Between 7000 and 5000 BC, the first villages were established beside rivers and lakes, and weaving and pottery began. One of the most revealing early settlements to have been found is at Puerto Marqués, close to Acapulco.

The precise identity of these early peoples has not been agreed upon. Some archaeologists believe they were Olmecs, while others assert that there was simply Olmec influence on other peoples, such as the Mezcala, who settled on the banks of the river of that name (also known as the Río

Balsas) and later spread to the Pacific coast and much further afield. The Mezcala culture developed distinctive characteristics, such as a predilection for jade, serpentine, and flint, with which they represented human bodies and faces, animals, and houses. Proof of the Olmec contribution is found in such things as the representation of the jaguar-man or were-jaguar, the grouping of villages, and the construction of ceremonial buildings. In time, the Mezcala culture also assimilated influences from Teotihuacán, visible in its ceramics, its stone sculptures, and its ceremonial use of ball courts.

Other peoples—Purépechas, Mixtecs, Mayas, and Zapotecs—came to the area that is now Guerrero, leading to a lively cultural exchange. In the eighth century, another people enriched the mixture: the Toltecs. They introduced metalwork, the use of resins and feathers for artwork, and *papel de amate*, a kind of paper made from the bark of a variety of fig tree. The Toltecs declined at the end of the twelfth century, and the dominant people then became the Chichimecs, who eventually became part of the Aztec Empire.

By the fourteenth century, a great many different peoples were occupying different parts of the territory, some of these peoples were more peaceful than others. Among the most important were the Purépechas, the Cuitlatecas, the Ocuitecas, and the Matlatzincas in the hot areas; the Chontales, Mazatlecos, and Tlahuicas in the northern sierra; the Coixcas and the Tepoztecos in the valleys; the Tlapanecos and Mixtecs in the mountains; and the Yopis, Mixtecs, Amuzgos, Tolimecas, Chubias, Pantecas, and Cuitlecas along the coast. Over the next century, the Mexicas (Aztecs) undertook a number of campaigns, eventually subduing all these peoples and taking control before the arrival of the Spaniards.

Among the distinguished sons of Guerrero was **Cuauhtémoc** (1502?–1525), heir of Moctezuma and last of the Aztec princes, who surrendered to Hernán Cortés rather than see more of his people die; he was tortured in an attempt by the conquistadores to find out the location of the imperial treasury and then killed. Once Tenochtitlán, the Aztec capital, had fallen to the Spaniards, they turned their attention toward the Pacific, largely for economic reasons. They were anxious to confirm the existence of the "Southern Sea" and to find more gold. They did not meet with a great deal of resistance, because the Indians either were too scattered and unable to form a cohesive force or had been too weakened by wars with the Aztecs. Some did resist, but others made alliances with the Spaniards, or simply withdrew and ceded their lands.

In 1521, Rodrigo de Castañeda took possession of the mining area of Taxco, while Gonzalo de Sandoval gained control of the Chontal area, the northern mountains, the Iguala Valley, and Coixcatlalpan. A year later, Sandoval was in control of part of the coast, where the Spaniards established the sixth town council in New Spain. Soon after, Juan Rodríguez de Villafuerte occupied Cihuatlán and most of the rest of the coast; he destroyed the Indian settlement at Zacatula and founded Villa de la Concepción on its site. On the orders of Cortés, boats were built there and an expedition set out to take Acapulco, which the Spaniards named Villa Fuerte. Isidro Moreno subdued a number of Indian communities in the mountains and on the northern reaches of the coast. Before the end of the decade, there were two significant Indian rebellions, which the Spaniards crushed.

As happened elsewhere, once control had been established, the individual conquistadores were rewarded with grants of land and Indian labor, known as *encomiendas*. Some seventy-six such grants were made, and Cortés was one of the prime beneficiaries; he was happy to be granted Tlapa, whose people, in his view, were more civilized and sophisticated than many other Indians. The task of evangelization was entrusted to the Augustinians in the central region and to the Franciscans in others. The decline in Indian numbers during the sixteenth century, due to disease and abusive treatment, made it necessary to import slaves to supplement the workforce.

By the middle of the sixteenth century, the first political divisions of New Spain had been decided upon; the Real Audiencia was set up as the body responsible for overseeing the new territories, which were divided into five provinces, each with its own institutions charged with keeping public order and regulating dealings between Spaniards and Indians. Much later, in 1786, a royal decree, the Real Ordenanza de Independencia, reorganized New Spain into twelve *intendencias*. Parts of what is now Guerrero came under the intendencias of México, Valladolid, and Puebla.

By the early nineteenth century, the people of the southern territories of New Spain were ready for change. The economic situation at the close of the eighteenth century had left many feeling very uncomfortable. There was unrest in the central region of Guerrero, where the Indians had been noisily asserting their right to the land. For their part, the *criollos* and *mestizos* were resentful of being sidelined by the more privileged *peninsulares*. The most important of several early plots to gain independence was hatched by José María Izazaga, in Valladolid in 1809. That plot was thwarted, but a year later Miguel Hidalgo made his famous declaration at Dolores, in Guanajuato, and the independence movement had become a palpable reality.

The response in Guerrero was almost immediate: the first local insurgents took up arms only two weeks after Hidalgo's cry. Hidalgo sent José María Morelos south to drum up support and secure the port of Acapulco; upon realizing that he would be unable to take it, Morelos put a cordon around it and set off to attend to the central valleys. After overcoming Chilapa, he decreed that a free province of Técpan was to be created; this province would encompass almost 40 percent of the territory that is now Guerrero, and so its establishment was seminal for the creation of the state later in the century. Naturally, the existence of this free province was never condoned by the authorities of New Spain.

After Morelos's death, Vicente Guerrero took up his torch, eventually facing a confrontation with the loyalist army under Agustín de Iturbide. Both men understood that neither could win, and so they compromised. The result was the Plan de Iguala, which laid down the basis for an independent Mexico and brought Iturbide to power as its first emperor. Iturbide ordered the creation of five military regions; one of these was the Capitanía General del Sur, and Vicente Guerrero was put in command of it. Guerrero set up his headquarters in Tixtla, which was to prove a significant choice in that it also affected how the borders of the state of Guerrero were eventually determined. However, after the fall of Iturbide and the creation of the republic, the territory was reorganized and assigned in parts to the new states of Michoacán, Oaxaca, Puebla, and especially México. An attempt was made in 1823 to have a state of Guerrero established, based on the territorial limits of the former capitanía general, but it met with no success. Guerrero himself, however, became Mexico's president for a while, later to be betrayed and shot. With the emergence of new political groupings, liberals on the one hand and conservatives on the other, the southern territories went into internal conflict.

Just as Guerrero championed the liberal cause until his death in 1831, **Nicolás Bravo** (1786–1854) championed the conservative. Keen to secure separate status for the region, in 1836 Bravo proposed the creation of a Departamento del Sur (Southern Region), but the central authorities were in a mood to increase the size of territorial divisions, not break them up further. In 1841 an alliance of forty-two towns tried to secure the establishment of a Departamento de Acapulco; President Antonio López de Santa Anna opposed that move, though he did accede to the creation of a new municipio, the municipality of Tecoanapa, thinking that such a step might undermine the drive toward greater recognition.

In 1847, after a period of great instability, Bravo and **Juan Álvarez** (1790–1867) once again tried to secure statehood, proposing to incorporate some areas that at the time belonged to the states of México, Puebla, and Michoacán, but on this occasion the U.S. invasion delayed a decision on their proposal. In October 1848, Puebla and México agreed to the proposed territorial concessions, but Michoacán continued to oppose them. It was an opposition that provoked protests in the affected area, the Tierra Caliente, where people declared that they wished to be part of the proposed new state; other similar protests followed, and eventually the president of the day, José Joaquín de Herrera, was obliged to mediate. On May 15, 1849, Herrera issued a decree creating the state of Guerrero. The birth of Guerrero as a state was thus difficult, and it came at a time when the country was suffering political and social convulsions.

In 1854, Álvarez, Ignacio Comonfort, and others proposed the Plan de Ayutla, which led to Comonfort becoming the new, liberal president of Mexico. There was a rebellion in the state against this new regime, and the rebellion was backed by the clergy. Later, the liberal Constitution of 1857 met with renewed fighting, and in the end Comonfort had to swing to the right. Juan Vicario was a prominent conservative leader and soldier who was bent on taking control of the state. Meanwhile, Álvarez, in the south, was moving to defend the constitution, while President Benito Juárez was doing the same nationally. Once the liberal forces triumphed and Juárez's government returned to Mexico City, the National Congress declared Álvarez a national hero, a "Benemérito de la Patria."

At the time of the French Intervention, the then governor of Guerrero, **Vicente Jiménez** (1818-1894), stepped down from his position in order to organize opposition to the foreigners. Meanwhile, Álvarez reorganized the southern army he had led previously, in order to defend the Tierra Caliente, the central valleys and the coastal areas, while he put his son **Diego Álvarez** (1812-1899) in charge of the defense of Acapulco. Fighting between Mexican and French forces was intense in Guerrero. Following the famous Battle of Puebla, Acapulco was bombarded, but after three days of fighting, the French were forced to retreat.

However, with the defeat of the republicans in Mexico City, conservatives who sympathized with the French, under Vicario, came back on the attack. They now faced forces led by Gen. Porfirio Díaz. Control swung back and forth for a while between the two factions, but once France withdrew its troops, leaving Maximilian with the backing of only the Mexican conservatives, the fate of the monarchy was sealed.

The reinstatement of Juárez's government did not bring stability to Guerrero, however; rivalries such as the one between the two generals, Jiménez and Diego Álvarez, clouded the political scene for years. The reelection of Juárez to the presidency in 1871 provoked a proclamation by Díaz in opposition to him, and supporters of Jiménez rallied behind that. After Juárez's untimely death, Sebastián Lerdo de Tejeda, the acting president, made peace with the rebels. During his second period as governor of Guerrero, in 1874, Diego Álvarez promulgated a new state constitution.

In the next national elections, Díaz stood against Lerdo, lost, and then called for an armed rebellion under the motto "No Reelection." Álvarez tried to defend constitutional order, and he did win several battles against the supporters of Díaz, but the latter eventually won the war and assumed the presidency of the country. He was to hold on to it for the next thirty years, and as discontent with his regime grew, the old motto of "No Reelection" that he had used against Lerdo would be turned against Díaz himself.

Guerrero had nine governors during the *porfiriato*; only three of them were from the state, but the important thing was that all were loyal to Díaz, whose authoritarian regime privileged the fortunate few, encouraging foreign investment and industrialization. During the last quarter of the nineteenth century, land was sold off, sometimes at risible prices, and at great cost to poor communities. Foreign mining and textile concerns arrived in the state, the first banks were set up, and the railroad came, linking Guerrero with Mexico City. Agriculture began to diversify, and raw materials left the area to be processed abroad. The peasants sometimes found themselves working as hired hands on what had been their own lands, and having to hand over half of the fruits of their labors to the landowners. One strategy employed by Díaz's puppet governors was to draft in Indians from other parts of the country, more or less as slave labor. In sum, all the industrial and technological advances benefited only a small elite of landowners and businessmen. José Martí, the distinguished Cuban intellectual, visited Chilpancingo and wrote that it was "misery's palace." In Guerrero, uprisings against the regime were frequent. The end of the century marked a crisis in the mining industry and the end of many construction projects; cotton production slumped as production by the northern states, closer to the U.S. market, increased. By the end of the century, many people were out of work.

In 1891, an opposition movement led by José Cuevas arose. Then, early in the twentieth century, an attempt was made to unseat the state governor via the ballot box; that attempt was crushed by Victoriano Huerta, who at the time was a colonel in the army. Other such oppositional initiatives followed. The most serious (and the first serious uprising against Díaz in the whole country) was in 1901, led by Anselmo Bello and Gabino Gardeño, who were demanding respect for the democratic process. On hearing of this, Díaz again dispatched Huerta, who brutally put an end to it all. Nevertheless, by 1910 there was support for an end to the porfiriato, among the poor and even among many more privileged people, who rallied in favor of Francisco Madero. In 1911, the last pro-porfirian forces surrendered at Acapulco.

Once victorious, though, Madero did not return all the lands to the people, as had been hoped, and so the Zapatistas refused to lay down their arms and kept control of some parts of the state. However, both sides later closed ranks to fight against Huerta, and by 1914 they had control of most of the state, naming their own governor, Jesús Salgado, who did much to restore democracy, expropriate mines and lands, and redistribute them to the peasants. Yet Venustiano Carranza did not accept this state of affairs. Conflict continued until the death of Emiliano Zapata in 1919, by which time the Zapatista movement was debilitated. After Alvaro Obregón came to power, the Zapatistas were granted recognition, and a wider program of reforms began under Governor Rodolfo Neri. Educational provision was strengthened, unions were established, and land was redistributed. But the struggles for power had by no means ended.

The history of Mexico is full of people who made their mark in an extraordinary combination of ways. One of many such people from Guerrero was **Adolfo Cienfuegos y Camus** (1889–1943). He began his working life as an unqualified primary school teacher, moved to Mexico City to become qualified but then turned to politics, organizing opposition to Huerta and subsequently joining Obregón's forces, in which he rose to the rank of colonel. Cienfuegos then went back to his studies to qualify as a teacher. However, no sooner had he qualified than he was appointed to a high government position under Obregón. Once Cienfuegos had finally returned to teaching, he rose to become a professor at the National University. He was also a member of the National Congress, and then Mexican ambassador to Cuba, Chile, and Guatemala.

Teófilo Olea Leyva (1893–1956) is another example. He became a member of a group of philosophers and social reformers known nationally as the Seven Wise Men. He was a member of the National Congress and subsequently had several important positions in the national administration, while he also taught law at the university in Mexico City. Olea became a member of the Supreme Court and in 1955 was honored by the National Academy of Jurisprudence for his publications on legal issues. He was also a regular contributor to the national daily *El Universal*.

After the Revolution and the Cristero War were over, and especially during the presidency of Lázaro Cárdenas, the redistribution of land acquired a new momentum; more of the large *latifundios* were broken up, sometimes violently. The oil industry was nationalized and the banking system developed. Local labor leaders were encouraged to stand up to employers and form cooperatives. One of the leaders was **María de la O.** (1882–1956), founder of the Fraternal Union of Working Women in 1937 and defender of the rights of poor people and of women.

In 1962, widespread opposition to the powers of the day led to the creation of the National Civil Revolutionary Association, headed by a teacher, Genaro Vázquez Rojas. In 1971, Acapulco saw the beginnings of a revolutionary movement, under Lucio Cabañas. A state gubernatorial candidate was kidnapped by guerrillas in 1974. Guerrero continues to be a state with a high level of rebel activity. Nonetheless, the PRI (Partido Revolucionario Institucional) has unquestionably dominated state politics since the Revolution. The state's governors have been prominent nationally, and conspicuously, presidential candidates have tended to court the favor of the governor of Guerrero.

Economy

For a long time, Guerrero was overwhelmingly an agricultural state. The tourist industry, which has become so very important for Guerrero, began to develop only in the early 1930s, but it soon attracted visitors both from Mexico and from abroad. The development of tourism was facilitated by the construction of a highway serving Acapulco. At about the same time, under President Cárdenas, government help was provided for improvements in agricultural efficiency and for diversification in the agricultural sector; the cultivation of coconut palms was encouraged on the coast, coffee in higher areas, and sesame in the Tierra Caliente. Exports of raw materials, such as olives and wood, increased as the infrastructure improved. The processing of these products and of minerals became the main occupation of industry, though on a quite modest scale. Craft production became quite important as well: for example, silver reproductions of pre-Hispanic artifacts. The generation of electricity began in the municipality of Quechultenango. Factories making soap and oils opened up in Acapulco, in the north, and in the Tierra Caliente. In Taxco, there was a bottling plant, and in Cocula sugarcane processing.

In many respects, however, present-day Guerrero still lags behind other states. Of the geographical regions, the mountain region is a marginalized and very poor one, whose inhabitants are largely Indians belonging to several different groups and speaking several languages. There is a high level of illiteracy among them, basic services are lacking, communications are poor, and so is security. Most of the roads are dirt, and some of them are inclined to become impassable during the rainy season. One problem is that there has been a lack of initiatives to exploit the region's natural resources and create jobs.

In the Costa Chica region, some communities that are distant from the coast are similarly poor, marginalized, and underdeveloped; once again, their inhabitants are mostly Indians of various groups and illiteracy is high. Other parts of the region fare a little better. The Costa Chica is home to much of the livestock industry, especially cattle, but there has been little investment to make for more balanced animal feed and genetically stronger animals. The potential of fishing and fish farming has not been exploited, either. Those municipalities of the Costa Chica region that are on the coast have fertile soil and are seeing the beginnings of agroindustrial development, but neither the infrastructure nor job security are good.

In the northern region, the picture is similarly dismal—a lack of basic services, poor communications, and high unemployment. However, parts of the region that are close to the neighboring states of Morelos and México have enjoyed more economic progress, largely due to the *maquiladora* industry and to tourism (especially Taxco).

The Costa Grande region has immense potential, thanks to its coastal resources, forests, and fertile fruit orchards, but economic development there has been slow. In this region, there is greater job security, thanks in part to tourism, but again there are problems of communication.

The Acapulco region has the highest population density and the greatest economic disparities between individuals. Once again, there has been a lack of economic and urban planning. However, Acapulco brings in more income and attracts more investment than any other part of the state.

About half of the municipalities in the central region have good roads and services, which have made for a certain amount of development in those places.

Finally, the Tierra Caliente region's economy depends on agriculture. The land is fertile and very well suited to fruit growing, but irrigation is lacking and production is dependent on the weather.

Nowadays, 16 percent of state land is used for agriculture, and 8 percent as pastureland for livestock; 35 percent is forested, and 39 percent is

tropical. For human consumption, the state grows rice, beans, corn, tomatoes, okra, chiles, chickpeas, sweet potatoes, safflower, coffee, sugarcane,
and *jamaica* (a hibiscus-like flower used to make an infusion that is popular all over the country). There are also peanuts, sesame seeds, and a whole
variety of fruits, including melons, papayas, mangoes, bananas, and citrus.
Corn serves as the staple locally, and little of it is exported from the state.
The rearing of animals has been important, though the pastureland itself is
generally of poor quality. There are the usual animals: cattle, pigs, goats,
and sheep, and both free-range and battery poultry. Sorghum is used for
forage.

Tourism is the single most important area of economic activity in
Guerrero—indeed, it is one of the most important tourist industries in the
country. The main tourist areas are Zihuatanejo, Taxco, Chilpancingo, and,
of course, Acapulco. Something like three-quarters of the economically
active population is occupied in the service sector, principally in tourism.
There are maquiladoras in the municipalities of Buena Vista de Cuellar and
Leonardo Bravo. Most fishing is coastal, and the catch is destined for local
consumption, although there is also some shrimp farming in the Chau-
tengo lagoon.

Arts

The characteristic features of the Tierra Caliente *son*, which is a very popular song and dance genre, are the contrastive use of $6/8$ and $3/4$ rhythms, together with syncopation; these features are attributed to the African
influence and are less common in the *sones* of neighboring states. The violin, the *sexto* (a guitar-like instrument), and a drum called the *tamborita*
make up the typical instrumental ensemble found in the Tierra Caliente.
The tamborita (also known as the *túa* or *changata*) is made of hollowed-
out wood and has two skins that are kept taut by a system of cords, in the
African style.

Among noted regional musicians was **Juan Reynoso** (1912–2006), a violinist popularly known as the Paganini of the Tierra Caliente. Another was
the one-handed **Angel Tavira** (1923–), whose music served as a consola-
tion and refuge through many times of regional insecurity and conflict.
Tavira's story became the focus of two films directed by Francisco Vargas,
the second of which, *The Violin*, brought the aged Tavira a prize for acting
at the Cannes Film Festival in 2006, despite the fact that he had had no experience as an actor beyond the two films mentioned.

The Tierra Caliente provides just one example of popular regional musical practices. In other parts of the state, the popular and traditional forms
vary. Wind bands and indigenous music are both common in the mountain
region. In the central and Costa regions, sones and *bolas* are performed
with harp, *vihuela* (another guitar-like instrument), and *jarana* (also a
strummed, string instrument, but smaller and of an unusual shape).

There are ritual dances found in many parts of Guerrero on social occasions and particularly at fiestas. The *danza de los tlacololeros*, for example, particularly associated with central areas, is based on the agricultural traditions of the *tlacololes*, the lands where corn is grown. Here the man in charge is the *tlacololero*, and in the dance, he uses a raucous instrument called the *chirrión*, which represents thunder and serves to drive away evil animals. There are about fifteen stock roles that have to be acted out as part of this dance.

Tecuanes is a name that comes from Náhuatl and means "something that eats." The corresponding dance of the tecuanes (also known as the *danza del tigre—*"tiger dance") represents the evildoings of the jaguar, which hunts and kills a deer and is itself hunted by some of the dancers. Some are wounded in the process and cured by the medicine man. In the end, the jaguar is killed and its skin is devoured by vultures. The participants in this dance wear calf-skin masks and beards made of horsehair, except for those who represent the vultures, who are clothed in black.

The *danza de los diablos* (devils) has its origins in the process of evangelization and is a good example of a hybrid. There are two main roles: Death and Lucifer, but there are also many parts for male and female devils and a few clowns, called *huesquistles*. The lead devil begins by pounding rhythmically on a donkey's cheek with a stone. In comes a she-devil, leading a line of devils and playing a tune on a guitar. Another devil beats time on a wooden box.

The *danza de los machos* is more modern but no less traditional. It represents a group of peasants who look after mules belonging to rich Spaniards. They carry wooden carvings of mule heads. There is only one woman dancer, who is dressed in the style of the early twentieth century (long skirt, decorative blouse, shawl, and a hat made from palm fronds) and who wears a mask that conveys the happy demeanor of a *mestiza*.

Other ritual dances include those of the *tlaminques*, apaches, *gachupines* (a pejorative name for the Spaniards), *chareo*, and *Santiagos*, as well as the Twelve Pairs of France.

Among many popular musicians in a more modern vein are Arturo Villela and Gerardo Reyes, singer-songwriters who have had national or international success. Mexico's oldest trio is from Guerrero: Los Cancioneros del Sur. There have also been several successful "tropical music" groups. Examples of folkdance troupes are the Ballet Folklórico Vicente Guerrero, based at Tixtla, and the Ballet Folklórico Citlalli, which is associated with the Universidad Autónoma de Guerrero.

In literature, **Juan Ruiz de Alarcón y Mendoza** (1580–1639) is the most distinguished figure to have emerged from Guerrero. He was a criollo, born in Taxco, and became the greatest Mexican dramatist of the early colonial era. But more than that, he became one of the leading playwrights in Spain during the Golden Age, when theater was one of its finest cultural assets. Alarcón studied to be a lawyer in Mexico City and then at the

University of Salamanca, the oldest and most prestigious university in Spain. From 1514 on he lived in Spain, and it was there that he died. Alarcón was a hunchback, and he suffered some cruel comments because of it, but prejudice against him was probably based above all on the fact that he had been born in the colonies. All this did not prevent Alarcón from becoming a huge success and going down in history as a major literary figure. Probably his most famous play is *La verdad sospechosa*. Taxco—Taxco de Alarcón, to give the town its full name—now holds a festival in his honor.

The theater in Chilpancingo bears the name of **María Luisa Ocampo** (1905–1974), a lady who worked in the National Secretariat for Education's library division, but who is also remembered in Guerrero as a playwright and novelist. Sets for her play *El corrido de Juan Saavedra* (1929) were designed by the painter and muralist Diego Rivera.

Guerrero is known for its textiles, for which the Nahuas and Mixtecs have become particularly famous. Many Indian women go about their business in traditional dress of their own making. The Chilapa area is noted for its figures crafted from corn husks, for use at festivities and sometimes for household decoration. The village of Ayahualulco is renowned for woven articles made from *carrizo*, a type of reed; they make vases, baskets, and so forth. In general, the palm is widely used for all sorts of weaving purposes.

The importance of silverwork, especially in Taxco, has been enormous. Gold is also worked in a number of places, but mainly in Iguala. Iron and steel artifacts, such as machetes, are made in Ayutla, Tixtla, and other places, while tin crafts come from Tlacotepec, Tlalchipa, and Cuetzala del Progreso. Lacquer work (boxes, masks, frames, screens, and so on) comes from Olinalá and other sites. In Olinalá, about 80 kilometers (50 miles) northeast of Chilpancingo, linoleum, lacquer, and *esgrafiado* (a kind of bas-relief) are used, often applied to furniture and gourds. There are also wooden masks and marquetry. In Olinalá, they still work with an aromatic wood called *linaloe*, but that wood is becoming scarce, with the result that more common types of wood are being treated with liquids that impart the aroma of the linaloe, as a substitute.

In many places, especially in the central valleys, people make simple pottery from hand-molded and painted clay. The products range from useful to decorative. The basic technique comes from the Indian tradition and entails mixing the clay with broken-up pieces of cotton. Different techniques involving glazing are employed in San Juan (Chilapa), and in nearby Acatlán, they make small glazed toys that double as whistles. From near Ometepec come pitchers decorated with white veins and red floral or animal designs; the Tierra Caliente also produces such items, though with a somewhat different style of decoration.

Other crafts involve the use of leather for hats, belts, saddles, and sandals and of *papel de amate* (a kind of paper made from the bark of a type of fig tree) for paintings. This last is one of the craft activities that has met with most commercial acceptance and been most exported from the state. The most famous places for it are Xalitla, Huapan, Maxela, Ameyaltepec, and Tolimán. Costume jewelry is made in Acatlán.

Social Customs

The Feast of La Candelaria, in early February, is a major occasion in the northern mountains and in central parts of the state. San Isidro Labrador is celebrated on the Costa Chica and in the northern mountains in May. San Miguel Arcángel is celebrated in each of the regions in September; the custom is to go out and burn "Evil" using dry flowers and then to place crosses and fresh flowers behind one's door as protection.

Some other examples of festivities are Acapetlahuaya's celebration of the Feast of St. John in June with dances such as *pastoras*, *moros y cristianos*, and tecuanes, Carnival in Acapulco, and the celebration of the Virgen de Guadalupe. A less routine form of Carnival celebration is held in Xochistlahuaca, an Indian community, where a procession is headed by a wooden horse (the *macho mula*), the men wear red scarves over their faces, and the women show off the typical blouses of the Amuzgo Indians. There are dances, fireworks, and bullfights, but only with straw bulls. The Feast of

Musicians play in Zitlala. Every year, inhabitants of this town participate in a ceremony to ask for a good harvest and plenty of rain. At the end of the ceremony, men dressed as tigers battle each other. (AP Photo/Eduardo Verdugo)

San Juan is important for Acatlán, where, among other events, a particular dance called *las maromas* has the dancers jumping over ropes. Atoyac is known for its festivities on the occasions of the Day of the Dead and the Feast of the Virgin of Guadalupe. On this same feast day, Ayutla has a range of dances, including those of the tlacololeros, the moros, the *viejas* (old women), the gachupines, and the *siete sicios* (the Seven Sins).

In celebration of Mexican independence, in September, Ciudad Altamirano, like many places in Mexico, reenacts Hidalgo's cry for independence and has a procession, with floats, military bands, local musicians, and school groups. More unusually, there are also displays of gymnastics. Bullfights are a major element; the distinctive custom is for the bulls' horns to be decorated ahead of time with *guanachas*, and for people to rush down from their seats before the bullfight proper and steal them, in a kind of parody of bullfighting movements. There is a commercial fair at the same time.

On September 28 in Chichihualco, there is a festivity in honor of Santiago Apóstol, notable for the colorful costumes of the dancers, the procession of the Teopancalaquis, and the garlands of *zempazúchil*, a native plant. The Festival of the Rains in Mochitlán clearly dates from pre-Hispanic times, but the present-day celebration of it is a hybrid affair. Pilgrims and groups of dancers gather at night in response to the summons of the *teponaxtle* (an indigenous drum) and climb the local volcano (the Volcán Negro) in order to witness the dawn and pray for water (*agua para sus ranchos*). The festivities in Olinala on October 4 are also of pre-Hispanic origin. They focus on the sacred tiger, whose image is seen in people's dress. San Luis Acatlán is one of few places where the traditional turtle dance (*danza de la tortuga*) is still performed. Among Taxco's many festivities are those that are associated with the Blessing of the Animals (January), Palm Sunday, Holy Week, and Las Posadas (a pre-Christmas custom).

On a secular level, Taxco also holds a Silver Fair in December. In May, there is a major open-air tourist market (Tianguis Turístico) in Acapulco, the Festival Acapulco at the end of the month, and a waterskiing championship (Campeonato Internacional de Esquí). There is an international fishing contest in that same month in Ixtapa. Taxco holds its celebration of the playwright Alarcón throughout May, and Ixcateopan remembers Cuauhtémoc, whose remains were found there.

Noteworthy Places

Taxco (whose name comes from Náhuatl and means "The Place Where They Play Ball") is one of the finest colonial towns in Mexico and has been officially designated a national treasure. In honor of its most famous son, Juan Ruiz de Alarcón, his name was added to the Indian one, so that the full name of the town is Taxco de Alarcón. Alarcón's house is among its interesting buildings. Churches include the sixteenth-century San Bernardino, which was once part of a convent, and San Miguel (which has a plateresque façade); San Francisco, which dates from the seventeenth century; and the Cathedral of Santa Prisca, from the eighteenth, in the churrigueresque style. The Casa Borda is an interesting example of a civic colonial building, once the home of a rich miner who financed the construction of Santa Prisca; the Casa Borda includes a museum on mining. The Casa Humboldt houses the Spratling Museum; William Spratling was a U.S. national who became noted for his silverwork. San Juan Bautista is a former *hacienda*. About 8 miles from Taxco is a waterfall known as the Cascada de Cacalotenango.

Chilpancingo, the state capital, has a Museo Regional covering regional history since pre-Hispanic times. There is also a zoo. Close to the city lies the Juxtlahuaca Grotto, and the nature reserve associated with it. Another nature reserve, the Parque Natural de Guerrero, is some 80 kilometers (50 miles) to the northeast, and covers about 75 square kilometers (30 square miles) of forest.

Iguala, famous for being the place where Iturbide and Guerrero hatched the Plan de Iguala that led to Mexico's independence, has a Museo Histórico de la Bandera (Historical Museum of the Flag) on the main square. Among the flags on display is the one used by Cortés, bearing the image of "the Most Holy Mary crowned with gold and twelve stars."

Acapulco has a little to offer apart from its sixteen beaches and its famous cliff divers. For example, the San Diego Fort dates from the seventeenth century, when trade with the Orient was growing in importance. The fort now houses a historical museum; it was here that Morelos besieged forces loyal to Spain, during the movement toward independence. The Cathedral (Catedral de Nuestra Señora de la Soledad) has Byzantine-style towers and a Moorish-style dome.

Ixtapa-Zihuatanejo, whose name means "The Place of the White Sand," is another part of the so-called Sun Triangle (together with Taxco and Acapulco). It is 250 kilometers (150 miles) north of Acapulco and is a major, deliberately-developed tourist destination. Zihuatanejo itself is an old fishing village, in an area once inhabited by Tarascos. In the colonial era, it served as a refuge for pirates.

There are rock paintings at the Cueva de Oxtotitlán, most notably of human hands. Some fragments of ceramics have also been found there. There are other caves at the Parque Nacional Grutas de Cacahuamilpa.

The Tomb of Cuauhtémoc at Ixcateopan is almost a national sanctuary. In the presbytery of the Church of Santa María de la Asunción lie the remains of the last of the Aztec emperors, a fact that remained secret for many years. Fray Toribio de Benavente, one of the early Spanish missionaries, left a letter referring to the burial and the need to keep it secret. It was only during the presidency of Miguel Alemán, in the middle of the twentieth century, that the document was authenticated, the body was exhumed, and it was confirmed to be that of Cuauhtémoc.

There are many archaeological sites. La Organera is in the central region, close to Xochilapa. It has seventeen monumental structures and some ceremonial open areas covering a total of approximately 1,600 square meters (17,200 square feet). The structures date from the Classical Period (AD 200–900). At Huamuxtitlán, there is a pyramid, but the present-day town covers part of what is assumed to have been ceremonial and living quarters. It is one of several sites dotted along the Tlapaneco River, in the mountain region. The pyramid dates from the Postclassical Period. When the area was being excavated, in the upper part of it archaeologists found a flint knife, a skull with a jade bead in its mouth, and human bones. On the steps, they found a further twenty-three such knives, the remains of a jaguar, a rattlesnake, a hawk and an adult human, and a small, yellow-colored vessel containing jade beads. Teopantecuanitlán is one of the most important sites in the state, in terms of both size and antiquity. Its ceremonial center includes a sunken patio, a hydraulic system, and a number of tombs. There are also four monoliths shaped like an upended T that represent plump figures with the jaws of a jaguar and the eyes of a viper. Each holds an ear of corn, which has led to the supposition that they stand for agriculture. Pueblo Viejo, Ixcateopan, Los Tepoltzis, Texmelican, Ozumba, Palma Sola, and El Cerro de los Monos are other sites. Some sites have suffered considerable plundering.

Cuisine

Like most of Mexico, Guerrero has a cuisine that is the result of blending indigenous and European traditions. One could say that the indigenous tradition holds sway in that the staple foods are still corn, chiles, beans, and meat. The thick *mole* sauces that are associated with certain Mexican dishes and that typically involve chocolate are of pre-Hispanic origin. So, too, are the chile-based sauces and all the many corn-based dishes. Spain brought in wheat, pork, beef, and its already mixed culinary tradition, influenced by the Middle East. Then the invasion by the French was followed by an invasion of things French, including their cuisine.

Typical seafood dishes include fish-head soup, *ceviche* (marinated raw fish), octopus marinated in vinegar, stuffed squid, clams with *chorizo*, lobster tacos, snapper with pineapple, and fish in a host of shapes and forms—for example, in *tamales*. Meat and vegetarian dishes include iguana with chiles and garlic or with *mole*, *pozole* (a corn-based stew), *frijoles rancheros*, steak with *huauzontle*, and chicken curry with coconut and tamarind (evidence of the oriental connection). Among desserts, there are *dulce de tamarindo, tlaxcales, tamales de cuajada, arroz de leche tropical, cocada horneada, alfajor de coco acapulqueño*, and *tulipán con frutas tropicales*.

Local drinks are *tuba, sangre de baco, petaquilla*, and *amarguito*. There are many infusions that take advantage of local fruits and herbs, as well as a wide variety of fruit-based cold drinks, such as the *chilate* of the Costa Chica. Among the alcoholic drinks, Guerrero inevitably has its own type of *mezcal*, which is reputed to be of superior quality but is only made on a small scale. Huitzuca is known for its wine.

Ceviche Acapulqueño

Ingredients:

    1 lb. swordfish, filleted
    5 tomatoes
    8 limes
    $^1/_2$ onion
    $^1/_4$ cup cilantro
    3 tbsp olive oil
    $^1/_2$ cup green olives, finely chopped
    1 avocado
    10 capers
    A pinch of oregano
    Salt

Cut the fish into small chunks. Add the juice of six of the limes, cover and leave to marinate in the refrigerator for at least six hours, then drain. Chop the onion and combine it with the remaining lime juice, the olive oil, the olives, and the capers. Add oregano and salt to taste. Cut the tomatoes into small pieces. Mix all these things together and garnish with chopped cilantro. Serve with pieces of avocado.

Pozole

Pozole provides an economical one-dish meal. Varieties of it can be found in many parts of the country; the Guerrero version is distinguished by having egg, crackling, and avocado in it. It is served hot in a deep bowl and garnished according to taste with lime, chopped onion, oregano, ground chile, shredded lettuce, and pieces of radish. It is eaten with *tostadas*, the fried tortillas, which are coated with cream and sprinkled with grated cheese.

Ingredients:

    $^1/_2$ lb. *maíz cacahuazintle* (corn with large white kernels)
    $^1/_2$ lb. pork, cut into small pieces
    $^1/_2$ lb. pigs's head
    1 clove of garlic
    1 large onion
    Salt
    3 *ancho* chiles
    2 tbsp of oil

Soak the corn kernels overnight. Drain them the next day and rinse. Put them in a large pot to boil for about an hour (until the kernels start to open up).

Then add the meats, garlic, onion, and salt. Boil steadily for about 40 minutes, so that the meat is thoroughly cooked. Briefly roast the chiles (too long and they go bitter), then put them to soak in hot water for 10 minutes; drain them and clean out their seeds and veins. Puree them with a small amount of water and then fry them briefly in hot oil. Add the chiles to the rest of the ingredients, simmer for a while, and season as necessary.

Hidalgo

State Characteristics

Hidalgo, which is named after Miguel Hidalgo, the priest who issued the first public call for independence from Spain, is in central Mexico, northeast of Mexico City. The state of San Luis Potosí is to Hidalgo's north, Veracruz to its northwest, Puebla to its southeast, Tlaxcala and the state of México to its south, and Querétaro to its east. At 20,813 square kilometers (8,117 square miles), Hidalgo is not a large state—in fact, it is Mexico's twenty-sixth largest. Its population density is about average for Mexican states. In 2005, there were 2,235,591 inhabitants, of whom 91 percent were Catholic and 5 percent Protestant or evangelical.

The capital city is Pachuca, population 96,538. Hidalgo has eighty-four municipalities and is represented by a total of eleven members in the National Congress. Pachuca publishes four newspapers: *El Sol, Síntesis, Plaza Juárez,* and *El Reloj.* Huejutla de Reyes has *Zu-Noticia* and *Diario de las Huastecas,* and Tulancingo also publishes an edition of *El Sol,* a newspaper that has affiliates all over the country. There are seven institutions of higher education in Hidalgo, the largest of which is the Universidad Autónoma.

The varied terrain comprises three basic regions at different levels: in the east toward the Gulf of Mexico, lowlands called the Planicie Costera; the intermediate level of the Sierra Madre Oriental, where the altitude averages around 800 meters (2,600 feet); and the highest area, the Altiplano Meridional to the south, with an average altitude of 2,000 meters (6,500 feet). The Altiplano Meridional is the smallest of the three regions, but also the most heavily populated. There are many places where the altitude reaches 3,000 meters (10,000 feet); the highest point is the Cerro la Peñuela at 3,350 meters (11,000 feet). The rivers run eastward toward the Pánuco basin and the Gulf; the principal ones are the Amajac, the Tula, and the Metztitlán. There are a quite a few major lakes and dams and also several places with geothermal waters.

In the driest and hottest areas, such as the municipality of Pisaflores, maxima can reach 44°C (111°F) in the summer. Areas with more moderate and moist climates benefit from the cooling effects of winds; in the coldest areas, winter temperatures rise to only 5°C (41°F) in the daytime and drop to –15°C (5°F) at night. Average rainfall varies from 250 millimeters (10 inches) a year in the driest climate (Ixmiquilpan) to 2,800 (112 inches) in the wettest. Since it lacks the protection of trees, Pachuca is a windy city where the force of the wind can reach 120 kph (75 mph). It is nicknamed "La Bella Airosa"; *airosa* may suggest airy, but it also means graceful.

The highest regions of the state, which are the south and parts of the Huasteca region, have pines, firs, oaks, and junipers. At the other extreme, in the lowest areas, there are *copal*, mahogany, ebony, and poinciana trees. On the altiplano, that is to say in most of the state, there is desert vegetation of cactus, mesquite, *damiana*, and *huizache*. Hidalgo has over thirty different kinds of snakes and thirteen different types of ducks. Depending on the area there are doves, quail, parrots, hummingbirds, falcons, eagles, foxes, badgers, hares, tortoises, spider monkeys, wild boars, nutrias, and bears.

Cultural Groups and Languages

The 2005 census results state that 15.5 percent of the population over age five, that is to say 320,029 people, speaks an indigenous language. While this is by no means the highest proportion for a Mexican state, it is larger than most. Of the indigenous-language speakers, 81.4 percent also speak Spanish, which indicates the degree to which they have become integrated into the mainstream culture. If language were not the only criterion for identifying Indians, the number of people identified as Indians would no doubt be higher. There are three basic ethnic groups whose presence can be traced back to precolonial days: the Nahuas, Otomíes, and Tepehuas.

Náhuatl, the language of the Aztecs, is by far the most widely spoken language, accounting for about two-thirds of the indigenous-language speakers. Otomí accounts for most of the remainder. Other languages, such as Zapotec, are present as the result of migration into the state by Indians from other states, especially Oaxaca. The proximity of Hidalgo to Mexico City means that it is seen as a place with job opportunities.

The municipalities with the highest numbers of Indians are Huejutla de Reyes, Ixmiquilpan, San Felipe, Orizatlán, Tlalchinol, Yahualica, Huehuetla, Pachuca de Soto, Xochiatipan, Atlapexco, Tepehuacán de Guerrero, and San Salvador. There are Otomí Indians in the Mezquital Valley and Huastecos in the region that bears their name.

History

The area that is now Hidalgo was a transit zone for nomadic hunters and gatherers who came from the north. Some settled and took up agriculture. The Toltecs first settled in Xochicoatlán (in the modern municipality of Molango) early in the seventh century, and later they dispersed, some to Huejutla but more of them to Tollatzingo (the modern Tulancingo), and westward to Tollan (Tula), which by 900 had consolidated its position as the Toltec capital. Buildings were constructed, the arts flourished, and the god Quetzalcóatl was worshipped; Tula became one of the first great indigenous centers of Mesoamerica. These Toltec peoples were later overtaken by the Chichimecs, whose main settlement in Hidalgo was Metztitlán. In 1050, Otomí people settled at Njunthé, close to what is now Pachuca. About a hundred years after that, Tula was abandoned and then destroyed by the Pames. The Toltecs migrated to the east, as far as Yucatán. All these changes seem like a preamble to the arrival of the Aztecs. In the twelfth century, they came to Tula and established Mixquiahuala, and somewhat later Tizayuca and Tepehuacán; they also conquered Patlachihuacán (now Pachuca) and Huejutla, so that within quite a short period, Hidalgo had been assimilated into the Aztec federation.

Hernán Cortés first passed through the future Hidalgo territory (through Apan, to be precise) in 1520, when he was retreating to Tlaxcala after having been driven out of the Aztec capital, Tenochtitlán. A year later, the Spaniards had returned and conquered Tenochtitlán and also taken the kingdoms (*señoríos*) of Tototepec and Mextitlán. By 1527, they had control of the Tulancingo Valley and had taken Pachuca. Pedro Rodríguez de Escobar took Ixmiquilpan in 1530, and soon after that Nicolás de San Luis Montañez subdued the Chichimecs and Otomíes of Huichapan. Explorers such as these (including Cortés himself) often financed their own expeditions, and they were routinely rewarded by being granted control of lands and Indians, who were organized and exploited under the *encomienda* system. Indian numbers were severely depleted by their working conditions and also by diseases and fighting. One of the most notoriously cruel of the conquistadores, Nuño Beltrán de Guzmán, made his destructive way to Pánuco in 1528, where he acted as governor of what was then a province that included parts of the future state of Hidalgo.

Franciscan missionaries founded convents in the northern part of the territory, for example, at Apan and Tulancingo, and in the west at Tula and other places. The Augustinians, who came a little later, did the same in Atotonilco el Grande, Molango, and Metztitlán, after which they extended their influence to the Sierra Alta and Huejutla. At that time, the secular clergy (those who were not members of a religious order) worked in a narrow strip of land running from Tizayuca to the Huasteca area, including Pachuca.

By 1537, the Valle del Mezquital was full of sheep and pigs (introduced from Europe) that were being reared on the altiplano; this caused problems for the Indians, who found they could no longer drink the water and that their food was being eaten by the animals. The result was Indian unrest, stemming from which the Spaniards took control of even more lands. Pig farming became very important for the altiplano; for years, Tepeapulco and Apan had the reputation of being the best places for pigs. Moreover, the altiplano became famous for its production of *pulque*, a drink fermented from cactus.

The search for precious metals was one of the driving forces behind the settlement and development of new territories. It was in 1552 that Alonso Pérez de Zamora discovered silver at a place that is now called Real del Monte. More minerals were found at Plomo Pobre (Ixmiquilpan) and at Pachuca. In 1553, a rich merchant from Seville, Bartolomé de Medina, came to Mexico to exploit its mineral wealth; he made his way to Pachuca, where he established a settlement called Purísima Concepción, beside the Río Avenidas on the slopes of the Cerro de la Magdalena. It was there that Medina discovered the process of mixing mercury with common salt as a means of releasing silver, a technique that was soon being used all over the Americas and in Europe. The Indians were sorely exploited in the mines; in 1677, Otomí Indians killed their leader, Ixmiquilpan, because he wanted to make them work in such harsh conditions.

By the eighteenth century, the mines had become flooded and silver production had stopped, so the mining communities were in decline. At that point another entrepreneur, José Alejandro Bustamante y Bustillo, stepped in, offering to pump out the mines in exchange for being granted title to them. So it was that by 1762 the mining industry was entering a new phase, its golden age of silver production, so to speak. Workers came back, and soon Pachuca was the fourth most important silver-producing site in New Spain. Pedro Romero de Terreros, another Spaniard and a partner of Bustamente, did well enough to loan Spain a considerable sum of money and give it two warships; in recompense, he was given the noble title of Conde de Regla. He built a number of *haciendas*, of which his favorites were San Miguel, San Antonio, and Santa María Regla. In 1766, mineworkers at Vizcaína threatened to stop work unless their demands for better conditions were met, and since the authorities paid no attention to them, they went on strike; this has gone down in history as the first strike in the Americas. The strike did not last long, however, since the workers were forced back into the mines and their leaders thrown in jail.

By 1750, most of the Franciscan and Augustinian monasteries had passed into the hands of the secular clergy (those who were not members of religious orders) and effectively had come under the control of the archbishop of Mexico, but in 1777 the Franciscans in Pachuca established missions in the Sierra Gorda, where the Indians were most recalcitrant and difficult to find, many having taken refuge there. Not long afterward, Indians in several villages close to Zempoala rose up in protest at the taxes that were being imposed on pulque by the Spanish authorities, even if it was for Indian consumption. Then, in 1784, near the Hacienda de San Pedro Tultepec (also known as Vaquerías) in the Sierra Gorda, there was an Indian attempt to regain control of the land, led by a priest, Miguel de Molina. The ecclesiastical authorities put Molina on trial, and the lands were formally given to the family of the Conde de Regla, resulting in one of the largest and most powerful haciendas in the state. In 1807, the Indian leaders in Tulancingo were imprisoned when they refused to pay a supplementary tax intended to cover repairs to a local church.

When Father Miguel Hidalgo issued his call for Mexican independence in 1810, the local priests José María Correa of Nopala and José Antonio Magos of Huichapan were quick to rally behind him, and the Valle del Mezquital became a focal point of resistance to the Spanish authorities, though there were no big battles in Hidalgo during the independence movement. The first armed uprising was led by Miguel Sánchez and **Julián Villagrán** (1760–1813). Villagrán was an hacienda-owning *criollo* who had had taken part in the Querétaro conspiracy with Father Hidalgo. Villagrán gathered together an army of four thousand and attacked royalist convoys close to Huichapan. There came a time when Villagrán's son, also an insurgent, was captured, Villagrán *père* was invited to lay down his arms in exchange for his son's freedom, but he refused to do so and his son was shot. Later on, the father was also captured and shot.

After independence had been won, Hidalgo went from being part of the enormous administrative unit known as the Intendencia de México (under the direct jurisdiction of Mexico City) to being part of a newly created state of México. Three districts were created: Tula, Tulancingo, and Huejutla.

The first half of the nineteenth century was a turbulent period for the whole country, with constant fighting between federalist liberals and centralist conservatives; people who had fought side by side as insurgents against Spain now fought each other over whether power should be concentrated in Mexico City or devolved to the states. One of the most significant confrontations occurred in 1828, when Nicolás Bravo, the country's vice president and a centralist, holed up in Tulancingo, where he was attacked by the forces of Vicente Guerrero and defeated. **Pedro María Anaya** (1794–1854) was a soldier and a politician, a combination that seems to have been de rigueur in the politics of nineteenth-century Mexico. Anaya served as minister of war under President José Joaquín Herrera, president of the National Congress, and twice as interim president of the country in an era when presidents came and went with disturbing frequency. He also participated in the war with the United States, as did **Vicente García Torres** (1811–1894), who also made a mark by founding one of the most influential national newspapers of the century, *El Monitor Republicano*, and by publishing the *Semanario de las Señoritas Mexicanas*, an early illustrated magazine that evolved into quite a serious publication addressed not only to women.

Partly due to the conflicts between rival political factions, the mines of Pachuca and Real del Monte were ruined. The Count of Regla passed them over to a British company in 1824, resulting in the introduction of more up-to-date techniques, but the mines were not a financial success. They were again sold to Mexican entrepreneurs in the middle of the century, when they revived and once again became very important.

Another significant event during this period was Antonio López de Santa Anna's confinement to Tulancingo of a leading figure among the liberals, Melchor Ocampo, of Michoacán; Ocampo came into contact with **Manuel Fernando Soto Pastrana** (1825–1896), a distinguished writer and campaigner for reform—the man who led the campaign to have Hidalgo made a state.

One of the arguments was that Toluca, the capital of the state of México, was simply too far away. Eventually, in 1861, Toluca acceded to the arguments of the separatists. The threat of the French intervention led to the idea that the state of México should be made into three separate military districts; one of these, with its capital in Actopan, was to cover more or less the same area as the present-day state of Hidalgo.

In the middle of the century, there was also a local liberal group led by Gabriel Mayorga that drew up a document calling for the separation of church and state, freedom of worship, an end to the monasteries, and the introduction of land reforms. Many of their ideas were incorporated into Mexico's 1857 constitution, a constitution that unleashed a new round of armed confrontations between liberals and conservatives.

During the French Intervention, the government of Benito Juárez was forced out of the capital. French forces occupied the future Hidalgo, but were eventually beaten back by forces led by people such as Nicolás Romero, Antonio Reyes ("El Tordo"), and José María Pérez. In the end, France withdrew its troops from Mexico, and Maximilian and some of his conservative allies were imprisoned in Querétaro and shot. The return of the legitimate government provided conditions in which Soto was able to put the argument for statehood to the National Congress, and in 1869, the state of Hidalgo came into being. Juan C. Doria, a man appointed provisional governor by President Juárez, arrived in Pachuca early that year, and soon after, that city was declared the state's capital. Later in 1869, the first gubernatorial elections brought an hacienda owner, Antonio Tagle, to the governorship.

Political instability continued as conservatives and liberals jockeyed for control until the rise to the presidency of Porfirio Díaz. Politically, Hidalgo was dominated for a long time by the Craviotos, three brothers who held the governorship from 1876 to 1897. After that, Díaz brought in a fellow Oaxacan, Pedro L. Rodríguez, to govern the state until 1911. This was a period during which, as in other parts of Mexico, the telegraph, the telephone, and the railroad reached Hidalgo. Foreigners were given incentives to invest, and there were technological innovations, for example, in the mining industry. As everywhere during the *porfiriato*, these changes benefited people who were already rich and powerful, while the position of the majority poor became worse. Moreover, Díaz and his cronies used favors to ensure the acquiescence of people who might oppose them, and if that did not work, they used strong-arm tactics to silence them. Economically, the mining industry prospered, as did the haciendas producing pulque for Mexico City. With English capital, a new cement industry began; textile factories also developed. In 1906, the Compañía Minera Real del Monte y Pachuca was taken over by the United States Mining, Smelting, and Refining Company. Among the poor, there was continuing discontent with living conditions, especially among the Indians of rural areas.

On May 29, 1910, Francisco Madero, the national leader of the opposition to Díaz's reelection after some thirty years at the helm, held a meeting in Pachuca at the invitation of like-minded people. Díaz, concerned about Madero's popularity, had him put in prison the following July, which provoked Madero to call upon his supporters to take up arms. Early the next year, Huejutla fell to them. **Nicolás Flores** (1873–1934) gained control of Jacala and threatened to do the same with Zimapán and Ixmiquilpan. In May, Gabriel Hernández marched into Tulancingo and Pachuca, whereupon Díaz's appointee governor, Pedro Rodríguez, stepped down. Soon Díaz himself did the same thing.

Madero did not last long or achieve much as president. He was betrayed, imprisoned by Victoriano Huerta with the backing of the U.S. ambassador, and then assassinated. Hidalgo meanwhile went through another unstable period with several changes of governor. Madero sympathizers took to arms in Huasteca, Jacala, and Tulancingo, and more people demanded an end to Huerta's rule and a return to constitutional government. Towns in the Huasteca region fell successively into the hands of supporters of Huerta and Venustiano Carranza, and finally Carranza triumphed. In Aguascalientes, he convened a conference of revolutionary leaders, with the aim of reconciling their differences and laying the foundations for the postrevolutionary government, but agreement was not reached.

Felipe Angeles Ramírez (1869–1919) was yet another soldier-politician. He played a prominent role during the postrevolutionary years, as a representative of Pancho Villa at the Constituent Congress and later serving in Carranza's government, but then switched back to the side of Villa.

The governorship of Hidalgo now shifted from the supporters of one revolutionary leader to those of another, with some men lasting only a few days in the position. Nicolás Flores made a comeback in 1915, and another member of the Cravioto family, **Alfonso Cravioto Mejorada** (1883–1955), was active as a representative of the state in the National Congress. He was not only a politician but also a lawyer and a writer. Cravioto served in a number of national offices, such as secretary for education, director of Bellas Artes (the National Institute of Fine Arts), and ambassador to a half-dozen countries. In addition, he was a member of the Academy of the Language and also a journalist and poet.

A new constitution for Hidalgo was introduced in 1920. Despite political disagreements, during the following years, and particularly after the 1930s, there was progress in improving the state infrastructure: schools, hospitals, roads, and water supply.

Economy

More than a third of Hidalgo's population works on the land, and many people are employed raising livestock. Approximately 30 percent of the land is cultivable, and about two-thirds of that land is irrigated; 38 percent is pastureland, 22 percent forest. The principal crops are corn, barley, beans, oats, wheat, squashes, chiles, and tomatoes. Some crops are also harvested for forage. In the flatlands toward the Gulf Coast, there is rice, tobacco, sugarcane, cacao, coffee, and a variety of fruit. El Mezquital is one of the most productive agricultural areas in the state; among many other things, it produces about a quarter of Mexico's total crop of alfalfa and of green chiles. And yet this is one of the poorest parts of the state, one with high levels of malnutrition.

Apan, Tulancingo, Pachuca, Tizayuca, Actopan, and Ixmiquilpan are the areas where livestock is most concentrated. Beef, pork, and lamb are all produced, in that order of importance, and in addition there is extensive poultry rearing. Fish are a major factor in the state's economy; the main species are bream, tilapia, carp, trout, and *charal*, both wild and farmed.

There is a serious deforestation problem that has not been properly addressed. The most exploited woods are pines, firs, and oaks. Cuautepec is the most productive municipality in this industry, producing both sawn and dressed wood for furniture and construction and wood for particleboard and paper.

The most important products of manufacturing industry are metal goods, machines, and equipment, coupled with nonmetallic mineral products. Train carriages and trucks, for example, are made in an industrial complex known as Ciudad Sahagún. There is an important cement industry, involving four major firms, based at Tula de Allende, along with an oil refinery. There are textile factories at Tepeji del Río and Tulancingo. Tepeapulco is the *municipio* where most industry is concentrated. Hidalgo generates slightly more than average supplies of electricity. Overall, industry accounts for about a quarter of the state economy.

Mining is one of Hidalgo's oldest economic activities, one with an international reputation. There are rich deposits suitable for mining in several parts of the state, plus surface supplies of limestone, basalt, gravel, and sand. Nowadays, magnesium is the mineral that is produced in the largest quantities, followed by zinc, silver, limestone, and lead. Pachuca and Zimapan are the most important municipalities in this respect.

Wholesale food distribution is a significant component of the service sector, while tourism is less significant than it is in some neighboring states. Overall, the working population is distributed fairly evenly across the three economic sectors. In many ways, Hidalgo benefits from the closeness of Mexico City and the fact that there is no mountain barrier between the two.

Arts

Common musical genres in the Sierra Alta and Huasteca regions are *huapangos* (dances performed on a platform and usually characterized by alternating 6/8 and 3/4 tempi) and *sones*, ballads accompanied by the violin and *jarana*, a guitar-like instrument. There are also Indian songs here and in the Valle del Mezquital. More typical of the pulque-producing altiplano are working songs. Among the many traditional dances are *el tecomate*, *apaches*, *concheros*, *segadores*, *matachines*, and *Xochipitzáhuatl*. Wind bands are generally popular in towns, playing *corridos* and waltzes. The state has its own symphony orchestra.

There is a wide variety of crafts. *Tenangos* are items made of fabrics embroidered with images of local flora and fauna. The Valle del Mezquital is famous for its basketwork with fibers from the *maguey* and *lechuguilla* cacti. Miniature wooden instruments carved from juniper wood are also produced there and in the Huasteca, sometimes inlaid with pieces of tortoiseshell. Utilitarian wooden items are made with pine, oak, and cedar in the Sierra Gorda and the Sierra de Tenango, and furniture and decorative items with rattan in the Valle del Mezquital and the Huasteca. There is a range of leatherwork, from saddles and whips to belts and sandals. Potters in the Valle del Mezquital, Tulancingo, and other places make unglazed pots, dishes, and vases, while more elaborate earthenware comes from Tulancingo. In a number of areas, wool is woven into *sarapes*, blankets, mats, and so forth, while cotton is widely used for making clothing and white goods. There is metalwork with copper in the Sierra Alta, with iron both there and in the Valle del Mezquital, and with silver in the mining areas. Other craft products include fireworks, paper items, and candles.

Anastasio María Ochoa y Acuña (1783-1833) is regarded by many as one of Mexico's first satirical poets and dramatists. He was classical scholar and translator, a humanist, and a cleric, who wrote under several successive pseudonyms, the last of which was "Astanio." Another dramatist, belonging to the Romantic period, was **Ignacio Rodríguez Galván** (1816-1842), who was also cofounder of the *Calendario de las Señoritas Mexicanas*, an early illustrated magazine that grew into a serious one. He served in diplomatic posts in South America. A third writer, a dramatist and poet, was **José Ma. Rodríguez y Cos** (1823-1899), one of the group of positivist intellectuals who influenced the thinking of Porfirio Díaz. His epic poem "El Anáhuac" brought him considerable fame. Other poets (who also had distinguished professional careers) were **Ramón Monterola Bernal** (1848-1906), **Francisco César Morales Rivera** (1886-1947), and **Efrén Rebolledo** (1877-1929).

Aniceto Ortega del Villar (1825-1875) was an obstetrician by training but gained a reputation in music, being a founder of the Sociedad Filarmónica Mexicana, which in turn created the National Conservatory. Ortega was also a performing pianist, a music critic, and a composer, one of whose marches served for several years as the national anthem. **Abundio Martínez** (1864–1914) was another musician. His compositions became very popular at the end of the nineteenth century, but he died in abject poverty. **Adalberto García de Mendoza Hernández** (1900–1965) combined teaching and writing about philosophy and logic at the Universidad Nacional Autónoma de México with being a professor of piano and composition at the National Conservatory.

Social Customs

Religious and civic celebrations are usually characterized by processions, religious ceremonies, traditional dancing, food fairs, fireworks, bullfights, and cockfights. In larger towns, these are sometimes combined with sporting competitions and cultural events such as poetry contests, plays, and art shows. A great many celebrations have rituals that reveal the mixture of indigenous and Spanish heritages.

Apart from the key moments of the Catholic calendar that are observed all over Mexico, such as Holy Week, the Day of the Dead, and the Feast of the Virgin of Guadalupe, and others of a civic nature, such as the celebration of Father Hidalgo's call for independence, there are several regional festivities in Hidalgo. Acaxochitlán and Tecozautla both hold a Feria de la Fruta (Fruit Festival, in August and July, respectively). Acatlán has its Expo-Acatlán (in September) concurrently with the Feast of San Miguel Arcángel. Actopan hosts the Feria Anual de Actopan in July, commemorating the elevation of the town to city (featuring an agricultural show and a barbecue contest, Hidalgo style), and the Fiesta de San Nicolás Tolentino. Apan holds a Feria del Maguey y la Cebada (Maguey and Barley Fair).

Epazoyucan celebrates the Feast of San Andrés Apóstol in November, with masked popular dances called *mojigangas* and its own version of the running of the bulls, and also its Fiestas Patrias, an occasion for a civic parade, mariachis, and wind bands. Huejutla commemorates the defeat of the French by Antonio Reyes with a reenactment of the battle, and in December holds its Feria Regional. Omitlán de Juárez has a Fiesta de la Manzana (Apple Fest, in July).

Pachuca's Feria Internacional San Francisco (otherwise known as the Feria del Caballo, or Horse Fair, because of its equestrian events) is an event that probably dates back to the sixteenth century and is now the most important in the state, with its own dedicated premises. Santiago de Anaya celebrates the Fiesta del Señor Santiago in July, coinciding with the Feria del Ixtle and characterized by Otomí dances and pre-Hispanic foods, and regional competitions. Tehuetlán marks the Fiesta de San José, patron saint of the town, with dances such as *Xoxitines* and *Guaxopiates*. Tenango de Doria has an Otomí Carnival, with more indigenous dances and a predominance of wooden masks. Tula de Allende celebrates the Fiesta de San José, in March, together with the Feria Anual de Tula, attracting pilgrims and visitors from all over the state. Finally, Tulancingo has its Fiesta de Nuestra Señora de los Ángeles in August, an occasion for the usual religious and civic celebrations, plus sporting and cultural events; it is held at the same time as a commercial fair called Expo-Tulancingo.

Noteworthy Places

The main archaeological sites are at Huichapan, Tula, Huejutla, Tepeapalco, and Zacuala. The Tula site has a large square with monumental structures on three of its sides: on the northern one, Tlahuizcalpantecutli and the so-called Palacio Quemado (Burnt Palace); on the eastern, the main building; and on the western, a ball court. On the southern side, all that remains is a mound. Tula also has an archaeological museum.

Religious buildings of note include Eparoyucan's church and the former Convento de San Andrés, dating from the sixteenth century; the seventeenth-century church of Santa María de Regla; Huejutla de Reyes's

Stall selling religious items.

sixteenth-century church and former Augustinian convent; and Ixmiquil-pan's Ex-Convento de San Miguel Arcángel, also sixteenth century and Augustinian. In Pachuca, the main churches are the Templo de San Francisco (sixteenth century) and the Capilla de la Asunción.

Museums include Acaxochitlán's Museo de Arte Religioso and Museo Etnográfico; Pachuca's important Museo Nacional de Fotografía (which has valuable photos from the Casasola Archive); and the Museo de la Cultura Otomí in Ixmiquilpan.

The Cajas Reales building in Pachuca was the place where miners had to pay their dues to the Crown; it was built during the seventeenth century. During the porfiriato, Pachuca acquired a number of buildings in the neoclassical style. For example, its Teatro Bartolomé de Medina was inaugurated in 1887, but later demolished and replaced by another theater building in the middle of the twentieth century. Also from the time of Díaz are the train station, the School of Mining, the monumental clock (1910), the Banco de Hidalgo building (1907), and a monument to Miguel Hidalgo (1888). The Casa del Conde de Rule is now the town hall, but was built in 1890 by mining magnate Francisco Rule. Huichapan's town hall also dates from about that time and is again in the neoclassical style. The Teatro de la Ciudad (Teatro San Francisco) in Pachuca is a one of the best-equipped halls in the country, seating almost a thousand people; it was built in the modernist style early in the century and then renovated in 1993, to provide a venue for concerts and opera.

There are caves at Tolantongo, a national park at Mineral del Chico, a state park at Real de Huasca, and a natural conservation area at Laguna de Azteca.

Cuisine

The food of Hidalgo, as everywhere in Mexico, derives from a mixture of traditions, especially the indigenous and the Hispanic. Typical *hidalguense* dishes associated with particular regions include *quesadillas de flor de calabaza* (Altiplano), *tamales de frijol* (Tula), *tlacoyos enchilados* (Huichapan), *tamales de escamoles* (Tulancingo and Apan), and many others that are found all over the state and beyond, such as *sopa de tortilla, tortas de elote, mixiotes, pollo con nopales*, and *pipián de chilacayote*, plus sweet things like *mermelada de pepita de calabaza, mermelada de nopal*, and *atole de gualumbo*. Pulque, of course, is a common drink.

Barbacoa

In Hidalgo, barbecue (*barbacoa*), which is arguably *the* state dish, means meat steamed with onions, garlic, and spices and wrapped in cactus leaves. Any meat may be used, even iguana, but the most common is lamb; sometimes pieces of offal are included. The Indian method of cooking involved digging a hole in the ground, lining it with stones and cactus leaves, and putting the meat in a clay vessel on top, covered with more cactus leaves; a fire would then be lit on top and the meat left to cook slowly for as long as twelve hours.

Ingredients:

1 leg of lamb (4–5 lb.; Merino lamb is best)
2 lb. lamb chops or shoulder
1 lb. chickpeas
$^1/_2$ lb. carrots, chopped
3 bay leaves
5 cloves of garlic
5 green tomatoes, quartered
2 medium onions, halved
About 4 maguey leaves
6 avocado leaves
3 green chiles
2–3 pints pulque (or beer)
Salt and pepper

Soak the chickpeas overnight. The next day, drain them and put them in the pot with the pulque, carrots, bay leaves, garlic, tomatoes, onions, chiles, and two of the avocado leaves; season with salt and pepper. Roast the maguey leaves, then use them to line the tray or basket that is to sit above the liquid. Arrange the meat on top of them, together with the remaining avocado leaves, and then cover with more maguey leaves. Cover the pot securely. Steam slowly for 3–4 hours. A pressure cooker may be used instead.

Quesadillas de Flor de Calabaza

Ingredients:

2 *poblano* chiles
1 small onion
2 cloves of garlic
1 medium tomato
20 pumpkin or zucchini flowers
$^1/_2$ tsp dried *epazote*
$^3/_4$ lb. mild cheese (e.g., Monterey Jack), grated
Lard and/or oil
Salt and pepper
15 medium-size tortillas

Toast the chiles under a broiler, on a barbecue grill, or in a frying pan until their skins blister and begin to turn black. Then put them in a sealed plastic bag and leave them to cool. Once they are cool enough to handle, peel them, clean them out, remove the stalks, finely dice them, and set them aside. Chop the onion and garlic, and gently fry them in a little oil until they are soft. Then chop the tomato and add it to the mixture, and cook until the liquid reduces.

Add the chiles, the epazote, and the flowers, season with salt and pepper, and cook for another minute or so until the flowers have wilted. Stir well. Spoon the mixture onto half of the face of a tortilla, sprinkle with grated cheese, and then fold the tortilla in half so that it makes a semicircle, pressing the edges together to seal them. Fry the tortillas one by one on both sides until they are crusty and start to brown.

Mole de Olla

Ingredients:

> 2 lb. shoulder pork
> 2 *xoconoxtles* (fruit of the *nopal* cactus)
> 2 ears of corn
> $1/2$ lb. string beans
> 6 zucchinis
> 1 onion
> 4 cloves of garlic
> 2 sprigs of fresh epazote (or a pinch of dried leaves)
> 4 peppercorns
> 2 *pasilla* chiles
> 2 *ancho* chiles
> $1/2$ cup water
> Salt

Cover the pork with water and boil it, together with the xoconoxtles (peeled and diced), the corn (in cross-sections), the epazote, half of the garlic, the peppercorns, and some salt. Cut the chiles open, remove the seeds and the stalk, and then toast the chiles briefly in a frying pan, taking care not to let them burn. (If dried, soak the chiles in warm water before cleaning them and removing the stalks.) Chop up the chiles and blend them in half a cup of water with the onion and the remaining garlic. Put this mixture in the pot with the meat. Chop up the zucchinis and the beans and add those. Lower the heat and simmer until the meat and vegetables are tender.

Jalisco

State Characteristics

Jalisco's name is thought to come from the language of the Aztecs, Náhuatl, and to mean "Upon the Surface of the Sand." The state is in central western Mexico, south of Nayarit, Zacatecas, Aguascalientes, and San Luis Potosí. Guanajuato is on its eastern flank and Colima and Michoacán to its south. It also has a Pacific coastline. Jalisco's area is 80,137 square kilometers (31,253 square miles), which is 4.1 percent of Mexico and makes it the sixth largest state in the country. There are 126 administrative municipalities, grouped into twelve regions, each with a particular municipality serving as its capital. The state elects twenty-three people to represent it in the National Congress. Officially, the adjective used to identify people and things from Jalisco is *jaliscense*, but *tapatío* is in popular use.

Jalisco is one of the most heavily populated states: according to the 2005 census, the total was 6,752,113 people. More than 95 percent stated that they were Catholic, and only 2 percent Protestant or evangelical. The metropolitan area of Guadalajara, the state capital, has over four million inhabitants, making it the second biggest city in Mexico. In general, the state's population has grown rapidly since the middle of the twentieth century.

The University of Guadalajara is one of Mexico's oldest (1791) and best; there are about fifteen other institutions of higher education. Guadalajara has a similar number of newspapers; examples are *El Informador, Público, El Occidental*, and *La Jornada*. Puerto Vallarta publishes five more, including *Tribuna de la Bahía* and *Vallarta Opina*, and one other is published in Jalostotitlán: *Diario de los Altos*.

This is a state peppered with mountain ranges. From the standpoint of physical geography, it has four basic areas: the Sierra Madre Occidental is in the northern part of the state; the tableland of the Mesa del Centro lies in the far northeast; the Eje Neovolcánico (Neovolcanic Axis) is the most extensive area and occupies the central part of the state; and the Sierra Madre del Sur is in the west, comprising a relatively flat zone, followed by steep mountains and limited coastal lowlands. The highest elevations are at Nevado de Colima (4,260 meters/14,000 feet) and Volcán de Colima (3,820 meters/12,600 feet); there are many other parts of the state where the altitude exceeds 2,500 meters (8,000 feet).

The climate in the north and northwest is fairly dry, with annual rainfall below 700 millimeters (28 inches). In the mountains, where the rainfall is between 700 and 1,000 millimeters (28-39 inches) annually, it is temperate. In central parts of the state and near Chapala, the climate is moderately hot, with average temperatures always above 18°C (64°F) and good rainfall (800-1,200 millimeters/32-48 inches). The hottest climate is found along the coast, where average temperatures range from 22°C to 26°C (72-79°F) and rainfall levels are between 1,000 and 1,500 millimeters (40-60 inches) per annum. For coastal areas and those on the western side of the mountains, the dominant winds are from the south; elsewhere they are from the west in winter and spring and veer to the east in summer and autumn.

The rivers all run westward or southwestward, some of them converging into the Lerma-Santiago system and others flowing directly into the Pacific; the Ameca is one of the latter. Lake Chapala is the largest body of water in the country, fed by the Lerma, Sahuayo, and Moras rivers and emptying into the Santiago River, which feeds the Juanacatlán Falls. The Río Grande de Santiago is fed by several other rivers in the central part of the state. Apart from Chapala, there are three other major lakes: Cajititlán, Colorada, and Santa Rosa.

The state has eight conservation areas, encompassing some beaches. The largest protected area is the Reserva de la Biosfera Chamela-Cuitzmala, covering 13,143 hectares (32,463 acres). Jalisco is Mexico's sixth most diverse state in terms of living species. In the mountains, there are pines, firs, and oaks; in the valleys, mesquite, agave, *palo dulce*, and *pochote*; and on the coast, coconut palms, *casahuates*, *nanches*, and other fruits. The fauna of the higher areas includes squirrels, foxes, mountain cats, and deer. In the valleys and flatter areas, there are weasels, wild boars, hares, coyotes, and wolves, and on the coast, common species are peccaries, alligators, spider monkeys, armadillos, ocelots, herons, ducks, gulls, and kingfishers. Prominent sea species are lobster, snapper, grouper, shark, and bream.

Cultural Groups and Languages

The 2005 census reports that a low percentage of the population over five years of age speaks an indigenous language, only 0.7 percent, that is to say 42,372 people in all. The leading language is Huichol, with more than

12,000 speakers, followed by Náhuatl (7,664); these are the two indigenous languages that are native to the state. Others, such as Purépecha, Otomí, Zapotec, and Mixtec, are present because of recent inward migration of Indians from other parts of Mexico in search of work. The Huichol people live in the municipalities of Mezquitic and Bolaños in the north of the state. Other municipalities with significant numbers of Indians are Zapopan, Guadalajara, and Tlaquepaque.

History

Remains found in Jalisco indicate that people were there at least 15,000 years ago: arrowheads and pieces of bone were found in the area of lakes Zacoalco and Chapala. In addition, rock carvings have been found in a number of places. Archaeologists believe that the earliest settlements in western Mexico, signaling the development of agricultural practices and the making of pottery, date back to 5000 BC. This is part of Mexico that has become famous for its underground burial shafts known as *tumbas de tiro*, which date from that era. A second major phase in the development of western Mexican civilization was the one during which the Toltecs became dominant, at which time ceramics became more advanced, metalwork with gold, silver, and copper began, and there was widespread commerce with other areas and peoples. Monumental structures were built and irrigation systems developed. What is now Jalisco was inhabited by fifteen or twenty different peoples.

In the sixteenth century, all fell subject to Spain, for the most part without a fight. The Spaniards mounted several expeditions into these lands, led by the conquistadores Cristóbal de Olid (in 1521), Alonso de Avalos (1521), Juan Alvarez Chico (1521), Gonzalo de Sandoval (1522), Francisco Cortés de Sanbuenaventura (1524), and Nuño Beltrán de Guzmán (1530), the last of whom became notorious for his willful destructiveness and cruelty. In 1530, on the banks of the Río Lerma, Beltrán dubbed his campaign the Conquista del Espíritu Santo de la Mayor España (Great Spanish Conquest of the Holy Spirit); a year later, he founded a town similarly called Villa del Espíritu Santo de la Mayor España, as capital of those lands. However, a royal decree imposed different names: Provincia de Nueva Galicia (Province of New Galicia) and, for the capital, Santiago Galicia de Compostela.

By 1548, Nueva Galicia had its own bishop and its own legal authority (*audiencia*). It was always to be important in the commercial and administrative life of New Spain. Between the sixteenth and eighteenth centuries, this province grew to encompass what are now the states of Nayarit, Zacatecas, and Aguascalientes, most of Jalisco and Sinaloa, plus parts of San Luis Potosí and Durango. In 1786, King Carlos III of Spain reorganized New Spain, creating three provinces and a dozen new and powerful administrative and political entities called *intendencias*; these entities were to survive until the early nineteenth century. The Provincia de Nueva Galicia became the Intendencia de Guadalajara, and its territorial limits were modified so that it covered what are now Jalisco, Aguascalientes, Nayarit, and Colima. In 1804, the intendencia had 520,000 inhabitants and enjoyed a good deal of autonomy.

Throughout the colonial period, there were signs of discontent among the Indians, who were exploited by being put to work on *encomiendas* and saw their numbers decline due to imported diseases and other factors. During the sixteenth century, major uprisings occurred at San Miguel de Culiacán, Coaxicori, El Mixtón, and Guaynamota; during the seventeenth, there was another led by a man called Cogoxito, and early in the eighteenth, one led by an Indian named Mariano.

The *criollos* also grew dissatisfied with the privileged status of people born in Spain, so when Father Miguel Hidalgo issued his call for independence, he found a sympathetic ear in criollo circles. Not long after his call, two groups of insurgents advanced into New Galician territory, one toward Jalostotitlán, Atotonilco, and La Barca and the other toward Sahuayo, Tizapán el Alto, Atoyac, and Zacoalco. The leader of the latter incursion was **José Antonio Torres** (d. 1812), whom Hidalgo had directed to take Guadalajara; this he did, on November 11, 1810, only two months after the *Grito de Dolores*. Loyalists to Spain organized a defense force to resist the insurgent advances, the clergy mounted a "crusade" against them, and the bishop of the day declared that the rebels were to be excommunicated, but it was all in vain. Soon the parish priest of Ahualulco, **José María Mercado** (1781–1811), joined the rebels, and by the end of the month, Hidalgo marched triumphantly into Guadalajara. While there, he took a number of significant initiatives, such as proclaiming the end of slavery, establishing a number of new government agencies, and naming a representative of the new Mexico to the United States.

At Hidalgo's instigation, Guadalajara began to publish an influential newspaper called *El Despertador Americano* (The American Awakener), whose editor was **José Francisco Severo Maldonado** (1775–1832). The colonial authorities forgave Maldonado for having acted in that capacity and instead put him in charge of *El Telégrafo de Guadalajara*, which was pro-Spain. Maldonado was elected New Spain's representative to the new Spanish government that had established itself in Cádiz, following Napoleon's invasion of Spain, but he never took up the post since independence soon became a reality. Instead he took part in the Constitutive Congress and then ran a paper called *El Fanal del Imperio Mexicano*.

Nueva Galicia witnessed a number of bloody battles during the movement for independence. One of the longest took place on the island of Mezcala, ending in 1816, when the rebels, led by Marcos Castellanos, capitulated.

By 1821, after Hidalgo's death, Vicente Guerrero, an insurgent leader, and Agustin de Iturbide, a criollo soldier, agreed on a program for an independent Mexico, the Plan de Iguala, which was formally signed at San

Pedro Tlaquepaque. In New Galicia, both the army and the clergy supported this plan, and they even had the backing of the bishop, **Juan Cruz Ruíz de Cabañas y Crespo** (1752-1824), who had by now come around to the rebel cause. A public proclamation of independence followed, on June 23, a day that also saw the start of a new government newspaper, the *Gaceta del Gobierno de Guadalajara*. In the Mexico City cathedral, Iturbide was crowned emperor by Cabañas, but his rule was to be short lived: within a year, he had been denounced by Antonio López de Santa Anna and others and forced to abdicate. Guadalajara took a leading role in demanding that a national congress be convened and a federal system of government be established. June 16, 1823, is traditionally held to be the birth date of the state of Jalisco, even though the Constitutive Congress that recognized the founding states of the federal republic did not take place until the following year. The state's first governor was Prisciliano Sánchez.

Not everyone was in favor of the change. Those who had benefited most from the colonial order, especially powerful landowners, formed the core of opposition in a Mexico whose first century of independence was marred by constant struggles between conservatives who wanted to maintain the status quo and centralize power and liberals who favored change and a freer federal structure. In Jalisco, the liberals remained in power, despite hostilities, for about a decade, at which point Santa Anna became president, supported the centrist conservatives, and imposed limitations upon political activities. José Antonio Romero was an influential conservative governor of Jalisco at this time.

The liberals rallied in 1846, incensed by the conservative idea that a foreign prince might rule the country. A group of liberals took to arms, calling for the defense of the republic, whereupon the government in Mexico City sent troops to lay siege to Guadalajara. **José Justo Corro** (1794-1864) was serving as interim president of Mexico when Santa Anna was defeated in Texas, so he suspended relations with the United States and took steps to reinforce Mexico City's control.

Another man who occupied the presidency of the country around this time was **Valentín Gómez Farías** (1781-1858). A physician by profession and a teacher at the University of Guadalajara, Gómez Farías created the Dirección General de Instrucción Pública (Department of Education), nationalized church properties on the grounds that they were part of the national heritage, and opposed the idea of ceding Mexican territory at the end of the war with the United States. In the final battle of that war, at Chapultepec Castle in Mexico City, **Francisco Márquez** (1834-1847) was the youngest of the military cadets—the "Niños Héroes"—to die.

By 1852, the conservatives and Santa Anna were back in power. The liberals responded by drawing up the Plan de Ayutla, to which Jalisco and the garrison at Guadalajara subscribed. Santa Anna fled the country in 1855, a reformist government came to power, and two years later a revised constitution was promulgated, giving greater powers to the states and restoring civil liberties. But this was to herald the three years of renewed fighting between liberals and conservatives known as the Reform War.

With Mexico severely in debt to others, the country had to face the possibility of foreign intervention. In 1861, the governor of Jalisco called upon his fellow jaliscenses to be ready to take up arms in defense of the republic. Napoleon's forces did invade, and Maximilian was imposed as emperor, backed by Mexican conservatives. French troops came to Guadalajara in 1864, and violent confrontations ensued, increasing in frequency in 1866. There were two major victories for the resistance: at the Hacienda de La Coronilla, near Santa Ana Acatlán, there was a battle between French forces and troops led by Gen. Eulogio Parra, while **Gen. Ramón Corona** (1837–1889) took Guadalajara. Twenty years later, Corona, as governor of the state, introduced significant improvements in educational provision and inaugurated the railroad link with Mexico City, but in 1889, while on his way to the theater, he was assassinated, and his death opened the way for President Porfirio Díaz to install his cronies in the governorship.

The *porfiriato*, which lasted about three decades, was a time of significant economic development and modernization. Foreign investment was expedited, often at the cost of selling the national jewels, the rich became richer, and the gap between them and the poor grew ever larger. Díaz silenced his opponents with bribes or by force. Contrary to Jalisco's aspirations, Nayarit was separated off from it and became a territory in its own right (and later a state). Signs of resistance were evident in Jalisco in 1903, with minor protests against Díaz's rule. When the aging dictator announced his intention to continue for yet another term in office, many intellectuals and professionals began to get organized in opposition to his reelection, and thus was born the Partido Anti-reeleccionista, led by Francisco Madero, whose plan of action, the Plan de San Luis, called for an armed uprising. The response in Jalisco was only a few controllable disturbances in the southern and central parts of the state, but the balance of public opinion was clearly in favor of an end to the porfiriato.

After the betrayal and assassination of President Madero, and in opposition to Victoriano Huerta, Jalisco's poor declared their support for Venustiano Carranza with uprisings in quite a few places, but not on a sufficient scale to be thought a threat to Huerta's rule. There were also confrontations in the state between supporters of Pancho Villa and Carranza, though these, once again, were not enough to threaten stability. In 1914, Carranza appointed Gen. Manuel M. Diéguez as governor of the state; then, in 1916, when Carranza convened the Constituent Congress in Querétaro, Diéguez organized the election of Jalisco's representatives to it. One of the men chosen, **Luis Manuel Rojas** (1871–1949), who had supported Madero, presided over the congress. Rojas later served as director of Bellas Artes (the National Institute for the Fine Arts) and of the National Library and as ambassador to Guatemala. He founded a major literary review and was editor of two important newspapers, *El Universal* and *El Siglo XX*.

During the years that followed the fall of Díaz, Jalisco's economic, social, and political life underwent radical changes that included a devolution of power to municipal level and a restitution of political freedoms. The next major hurdle was to be the Rebelión Cristera of 1926–1929, a conservative and religious backlash provoked by the reduction of long-standing powers and privileges. More steps in that direction came in the ideological 1930s, when land was redistributed, the powers of the church attacked, and education and health provision extended to rural parts of the country. **Wistano Luis Orozco** (1856–1927), a native of Jalisco, was the chief ideologue behind the agrarian reform.

Starting in about the middle of the century, the disparities in development between Jalisco's various regions grew more apparent. There were widening gaps between the standards of living of town dwellers and of people in the countryside, and there was increasing conflict between the demands of urbanization and the need to protect natural resources. In the 1970s and 1980s, attempts were made to give the municipalities greater control of and responsibility for their own affairs, but their freedom of action continued to be constrained by the national and state governments, and economic development continued to be concentrated in Guadalajara and other major towns. In 1974, a guerrilla group kidnapped former governor José Guadalupe Zuno, releasing him a few days later. In 1985, Ciudad Guzmán in Jalisco was severely affected by the major earthquake that caused large-scale destruction in Mexico City, and in 1995 another earthquake struck the town of Cihuatlán.

Toward the end of the twentieth century, widespread dissatisfaction with political corruption and with uneven economic conditions revealed itself via the ballot box rather than by the violent means that have clouded so much of Mexico's internal political history. In local elections held in 1988, the balance of power changed quite significantly: until that time the Partido Revolucionario Institucional (PRI) had enjoyed almost unrivaled power in Jalisco, as it had in most of the country, but the effect of the 1988 elections was to put a few of Jalisco's municipalities in the hands of the opposition parties, especially the Partido de Acción Nacional (PAN). A different picture was in the making, such that by the end of the century the political map would be far more diverse.

Economy

Jalisco is one of the more prosperous Mexican states. Approximately 16 percent of the working population is engaged in the primary sector (agriculture, livestock, and fishing), 30 percent in the secondary (mining, industry, and construction), and 54 percent in the tertiary (commerce, tourism, and services). The state's varied geography and climate make for quite a wide range of resources.

The number working in agriculture and raising livestock has been declining. However, almost 24 percent of the land is still cultivated. Corn, sugarcane, sorghum, *maguey* (of the type used for making tequila), and beans are the major crops, but there are many others. Pasture accounts for more than 9 percent of the land, providing forage for the usual range of animals. Woods, mostly of pines and oaks, cover 31 percent. Scrub covers 9 percent, and in these areas, cacti and acacias are exploitable natural resources. Nearly 25 percent is jungle, providing some forage and several usable woods.

The main focal points of commercial fishing are the ports of Barra de Navidad and Puerto Vallarta, together with Lake Chapala. Viable species include snapper, shrimp, shark, catfish, carp, and bream.

Jalisco produces about a fifth of the nation's corn, a quarter of its eggs, a tenth of its sugarcane, a fifth of its milk products, a tenth of its honey, and a fifth of its pork. It is the nation's leading producer of chocolate goods and number two for processed foods, drinks, tobacco, nonmetallic minerals such as cement and gypsum, transport, banking, and hotels. It also accounts for about 5 percent of Mexico's income from tourism. It is significant in terms of craftwork destined for export.

There are several industrial zones around Guadalajara, the largest of which are at Tlajomulco, and there are some in other parts of the state, at Tala, Villa Hidalgo Arandas, and San Miguel el Alto. Industrial activity includes smelting and the production of metal goods, machines, vehicles, chemicals, wood, textiles, electronics, photographic materials, processed foods and drinks, and footwear. Jalisco is also known as the cradle of tequila.

Arts

There is a wide range of craftwork. Tlaquepaque, Tonalá, Tuxpan, and Talavera de Sayula are known for their pottery and ceramics, Concepción de Buenos Aires for its sandals (*huaraches*), Colotlán for its work with *pita* (a cactus fiber), Tlaquepaque and Tonalá for glassblowing, Zacoalco de Torres for leatherwork, Talpa and Los Altos for *jorongos* (woven woolen articles, such as shawls), Chapala and Tuxpan for their cotton fabrics, and the Huichol region for its embroidery. There is basketry and weaving in many places. Marquetry is associated with Jalostotitlán and metalwork with Ocotlán and other places. Figures are made with corn husks in Acatlán de Juárez, wooden articles are carved in Teocaltiche, and, last but not least, *chicle* is used to make things in Talpa.

Turning now to music and dance, the *jarabe*, a song/dance genre found in many parts of Mexico, is particularly associated with Jalisco. Its local version, the *jarabe tapatío*, is known in the English-speaking world as the Mexican hat dance. Jarabes have become linked to the national identity and were used, for example, as morale boosters among revolutionary troops. Some famous examples are "Los Enanos," "El Gato," "El Palo," and "El Perico." However, the origins of the jarabe are in Andalusia, Spain, and the name comes from an Arabic word that means "syrup" or "sweet thing."

The *son jaliscense*, a typical regional song/dance form, has a distinctive ending that goes from dominant, to subdominant, to supertonic, to two brief notes on the tonic. Mariachi music is very popular; some people believe that mariachi bands started in Jalisco, although others claim they began in Nayarit. Traditional mariachi music has a religious side as well as a secular one. Where dancing is involved, *mariachi-fandango* dances are performed informally in the open air, whereas *mariachi-tarima* is performed on a stage, often with a lot of foot stamping. In addition to jarabes and sones, the popular repertoire includes waltzes, polkas, and mazurkas.

Rock musician **Carlos Santana** (1947-) was born in Jalisco. The state has Mexico's oldest symphony orchestra, the Orquesta Filarmónica, founded in 1915 at the instigation of a **José Rolón** (1876-1945), a leading composer whose best-known work, a symphonic poem called *Cuauhtémoc* (1930), is in the romantic vein. **Blas Galindo Dimas** (1910-1993) was a composer of a later generation. A protégé of Carlos Chávez, a member of the "Group of Four" and an acquaintance of Aaron Copland, he made continuing attempts to marry the popular tradition with art music; his most famous work is *Sones de Mariachi* (1940). He was director of the National Conservatory of Music.

In the early colonial era, there were several men of the cloth who wrote creative works or accounts of their experiences in New Galicia, such as Bishop Antonio de la Mota y Escobar (1546-?), Bernardo de Balbuena (1568-1627), and Matías López de la Mota Padilla (1688-?). In the modern era, Jalisco has given Mexico some outstanding literary figures. **Mariano Azuela** (1873-1952) was a doctor and a politician who turned to writing, for which he won the National Prize for Literature. He supported Pancho Villa for a while and served as a doctor for the revolutionary forces. By far his most famous literary work is the realistic novel *Los de abajo* (The Underdogs), which is generally regarded as the archetypal novel of a genre called the "Novel of the Revolution." **Agustín Yáñez** (1904-1980) was a politician and diplomat as well as one of the leading Mexican novelists of the first half of the century; his most famous work is *Al filo del agua*.

While the reputations of those two writers are strongest in Mexico itself, the fame of **Juan Rulfo** (1918-1986) is international, and that despite the fact that his meager output is unmistakably Mexican in its setting and worldview. Rulfo was orphaned at an early age, and after working for a while as a sales representative, he became a civil servant, working on immigration and Indian affairs. He wrote only one short novel, *Pedro Páramo* (set against the background of the Cristero Rebellion); a book of short stories, *El llano en llamas*; and one screenplay, but that was enough for him to come to be regarded as one of the great writers of twentieth-century Latin America. He was awarded a number of major prizes but suffered from alcoholism and depression.

Juan José Arreola (1918-2001) was an actor before he made a reputation as the writer of a novel and many short and eccentric fictional pieces, most of which are gathered in *Confabulario total*. In contrast to the reclusive Rulfo, Arreola was outgoing by nature; he was a prominent figure in the arts and the media, and a writer whose works have altogether a more cosmopolitan feel.

There have also been at least two major figures in Mexican visual art. **Gerardo Murillo** (1875–1964), better known as Dr. Atl, was an active revolutionary who supported Carranza and then Alvaro Obregón, and who served Carranza as an emissary to Emiliano Zapata. He organized workers' battalions and wrote for revolutionary publications. As an artist, Murillo directed the Academia de San Carlos, the country's premier art school, but he began the movement to make art more accessible to the general populace. In his own works, he used experimental techniques. He also wrote a number of books.

José Clemente Orozco (1883–1949) was one of the three leading muralists. In contrast to Diego Rivera, who was above all an astute self-promoter, and David Alfaro Siqueiros, a political activist and something of a slave to political dogma, Orozco was independent minded and somewhat skeptical. He began as a cartoonist in the tradition of José Guadalupe Posada and then turned to easel painting and murals. His work is all over Mexico (for example, at the Casa de los Azulejos, the Escuela Nacional Preparatoria, and the Suprema Corte de Justicia in Mexico City and at the Hospicio Cabañas and the Palacio de Gobierno in Guadalajara) and the United States (for example, Pomona College in California and the New School for Social Research in New York City).

Social Customs

Many religious festivities such as Carnival and the Feast of the Virgin of Guadalupe are celebrated all over the state. Some other local highlights are the fiestas of El Señor de los Rayos in Tenamaxtlán (in January), La Candelaria in the Los Altos region (February), the Virgen de los Dolores in Teocaltiche (November), San Pedro in Tlaquepaque (June), and Santiago in Tonalá (July). Tonalá also has an important Easter event that is two hundred years old, called Judea en Vivo (Judea Live). There are a great many town and regional fairs, some tied to local products, many coinciding with religious celebrations, and most involving a mixture of parades, dancing, and entertainments such as fireworks, carnival rides, bullfights, cockfights, and the inevitable mariachis and *jaranas*. Typical traditional dances for such occasions include the *aztecas*, the *sonajeros*, the *nachtes*, and the *baile de la conquista* (dance of the Conquest).

April brings the Feria de Abril to Tepatitlán and the Fiestas del Sol to Tonalá. Ocotlán's Feria Regional is in May, as are Puerto Vallarta's Fiestas, the Fiesta Nacional de Maíz in Zapopán, and the Feria Nacional de la Caña (Sugarcane Festival) in Tala. August is time for a two-week *feria* in Lagos de Moreno for the Fiesta de la Virgen de la Candelaria. Zapotlán has its feria in

October, which is also the time of Guadalajara's monthlong Fiestas. Shortly
before that, the capital hosts the Encuentro Internacional del Mariachi
(International Mariachi Festival). The Feria Internacional del Tequila, in the
town so named, is in December. Perhaps the most interestingly different of
all festivities are those of the Huichol people, in Mezquitic and Huejuquilla
el Alto; these coincide with a handing over of authority in January, a Fiesta
del Sol (feast in celebration of the sun), a Fiesta del Esquite (Corn Festival)
that takes place before the spring rains, and a Fiesta del Peyote in June,
before the corn is sown.

The *vestido ranchero* is a traditional form of women's dress derived
from the Spanish tradition, imitating the high style of the royal court, with
complicated lacework, stays, silks, and velvets, but in Mexico it became
enlivened with bright adornments and was simplified, at least in the countryside. Such clothing became popular all over Mexico at the time of the
Revolution. The version worn by the *soldaderas* (camp-following women)
has led to the dress that is commonly worn by women at festivities: a simple full skirt and a frilly, high-necked blouse. The colors are usually bright
and often there is floral embroidery. They wear a sash, low-heeled slippers,
and showy necklaces and have their hair in two pigtails that come together
to form a bun. There is also a form of dress known as *florecitas*, which
draws on the Indian tradition, suppressing the lace and adding an extra
flounce to the skirt. For dances, men tend to wear white clothing, together
with a bright kerchief and sash, sandals, and a straw hat.

Noteworthy Places

Many of the most important buildings in the state are religious. Examples
are the Santuario del Señor del Rayo, in Temastián, which contains a fourteenth-century sculpture of Christ; the parish church of Santiago Apóstol at
Ameca; the former Franciscan convent at Eztatlán; the eighteenth-century
Church of San Francisco at Tepatitlán, and the Templo de San José in Guadalajara, whose 1543 façade is in the plateresque style. Other eighteenth-
century churches are the basilica and the parish church at Lagos de Moreno, Talpa's Santuario de la Virgen del Rosario, Sayula's Santuario de Guadalupe, and Guadalajara's Templo de Nuestra Señora de Aránzazu, which is in
the highly decorated baroque style known as *churrigueresque*. Guadalajara's cathedral is imposing and in the Gothic style, though, like one or two
other churches, it was begun early but is basically a nineteenth-century
structure (the original building having been severely damaged by
earthquakes).

The fact that Guadalajara was the most important city in western Mexico
during colonial times has left it with a rich history and architectural heritage. Among its notable civic buildings are its baroque Palacio Legislativo,
dating from the eighteenth century, and the Palacio de Gobierno. The latter
was first built in 1650 out of adobe and was the seat of government for

Guadalajara cathedral. Courtesy of Tibor Bognar/Art Directors & TRIP Photo Library.

New Galicia; in 1750, the building was destroyed by an earthquake and a new stone one constructed with money raised from liquor taxes, being inaugurated in 1790.

What was once the Hospicio Cabañas has become the Instituto Cultural Cabañas; it has no less than twenty-three patios and houses many works by José Clemente Orozco, including his masterpiece mural "El Hombre de Fuego" (Man of Fire). Begun in 1805 and dedicated five years later, the Hospicio was built on the initiative of Bishop Cabañas and intended as a refuge for orphans and homeless people. The architect was Manuel Tolsà.

A number of buildings whose style reveals a fashionable French influence date from the time of Porfirio Díaz, such as the Pantheon and the Treasury Building. Lagos de Moreno has a theater, the Teatro Rosas Moreno, that was built in the nineteenth century, as was Guadalajara's Teatro Degollado, in the neoclassical style. An example of modern architecture is the Arcos Vallarta, a pair of matching arches that mark the entrance to Puerto Vallarta.

There are about fifty archaeological sites in Jalisco, such as Ixtépete, Ocanahua, Amatitlán, Ezatlán, and Tuxcacuezco, though what remains in them is not a great deal. Many places have petroglyphs. The Ixtépete site has a pyramid, built between 600 and 900, that shows signs of the influence of Teotihuacán. Close by are two smaller pyramids leading onto a patio with a wall around it, possibly once a ball court.

Naturally, many of the state's museums are in the capital. The Museo Regional began life in the early eighteenth century as a seminary, and it now traces history from pre-Hispanic to colonial times, with some additional items from the nineteenth century and a good collection of art. The Museo del Periodismo y de las Artes Gráficas is where Jalisco's first printing press produced *El Despertador Americano*, the newspaper that backed the movement for independence from Spain. The Casa-Museo López Portillo shows how luxurious was the life of this family, which supplied an early twentieth-century governor of the state and later one of Mexico's most notoriously corrupt presidents, José López Portillo. The Museo de las Artes de la Universidad de Guadalajara includes works by Orozco in its permanent collection.

Close to Chapala lies the Museo Arquelógico de la Sociedad de Alumnos Avanzados. The main modern art museum is the Museo de Arte de Zapoapán. Tlaquepaque has a Regional Ceramics Museum and Encarnación de Díaz a museum devoted to the Cristero Rebellion.

Places of natural beauty include Guadalajara's Parque Mirador Independencia, the coast around Puerto Vallarta (a place that was put on the tourist map by John Huston's 1963 film *Night of the Iguana*), the Costalegre (an area of ecotourism), Lake Chapala, and the southern mountains with their canyons and waterfalls.

Cuisine

Like the rest of Mexico, Jalisco draws on the indigenous and Spanish traditions. Corn is the prime example of an essential ingredient from the Indian tradition, milk products part of the Spanish one. Some common dishes in Jalisco are *gorditas*, *enchiladas de mole*, *borrego al pastor* (particularly in Tapalpa), *birria*, *menudo*, *pozole*, *charales* (Chapala), and the spicy *tortas ahogadas* (which are typical of Guadalajara). Apart from tequila, drinks include *raicilla* on the coast and a variety of fruit concoctions, plus *aguamiel*, *pajaretes*, *tepache*, and *mezcal* all over the state, *tuba* in Autlán de Navarro, and *tejuino* in central regions. Chapala is known for its milk-based desserts. *Cocadas* and sweets made with tamarind are popular along the coast, guava rolls in Atenguillo and Mascota, *palanquetas de nuez* in Ciudad Guzmán, and fritters in Guadalajara.

Birria

Birria is a meat stew that comes in many varieties and is found in many parts of Mexico. This particular version comes from Jalisco.

Ingredients:

   6–7 lb. meat (e.g., brisket, shoulder of lamb or mutton, pork shoulder, goat)
   5 or 6 tomatoes

4 *ancho* chiles
1 cup pineapple vinegar (or wine vinegar)
$1/2$ cup rice vinegar
4 cloves of garlic
2 long sticks of cinnamon
$1/2$ tsp cumin seeds
$1/2$ tsp peppercorns
2 tsp oregano
$1 1/2$ oz. chocolate
Salt

This is two-day procedure. Put the chiles in water and simmer for about 5 minutes, then let stand for another 5 minutes before draining. (If using dried chiles, soak them first.) Grind the cumin seeds. Blend the vinegars, garlic, salt, spices, and oregano together, slowly adding the chiles and chocolate, plus a little water as necessary to form a thick paste. After cutting the meat into largish chunks, coat it with the paste, cover it, and leave it overnight. On the following day, steam the meat on a rack above water in a covered pot or pressure-cooker; in a conventional pot, this will take about 4 hours. Check the water level from time to time to make sure it does not evaporate alto-gether. Heat oven to 400°F. Place the cooked meat in a dish (reserving the broth below it) and roast it for about half an hour, turning it over once, so that it begins to get crusty. Boil the tomatoes whole in the reserved broth, then take them out, puree them, and return them to the pot of broth; heat a little longer, reducing as necessary to make a sauce. Serve with rice, shredded cabbage, finely chopped onion, and pieces of lime.

Pozole de Camarón

Ingredients:

1 lb. white corn (strip kernels off cob before weighing)
$1/2$ lb. fresh shrimp
$1/2$ lb. dried shrimp
4 ancho chiles
4 *guajillo* chiles
4 cloves
Pinch of ground cumin
4 cloves of garlic, peeled and halved
Olive oil
Salt

Boil the corn until the kernels begin to open (about 3 hours). Clean out the chiles and remove their stalks. Put each kind in separate pans of hot water and simmer them for about 5 minutes, leave them to soak for a further 10 until they are soft, and then drain them. Use a blender to grind together the cloves, cumin, and garlic, adding a little water, the aim being to make a thick sauce. Add the ancho chiles and blend those in. Fry this sauce in olive oil in a deep pan for about 3 minutes, stirring so that it does not stick. Now use the blender to combine the guajillos with a little water, and then strain this blend into the pan with the sauce in it. Continue to fry the mixture a little longer, then add the corn and the water in which it was cooked. Peel the fresh shrimp; wrap the heads in a muslin bag, tie it, and add it to the pan. Simmer for a quarter of an hour before removing the bag, adding the fresh and dried shrimp, and continuing to cook for a further 10 minutes. Salt to taste. The pozole is commonly garnished with finely chopped onion, slices of radish, shredded cabbage, pieces of lime, and a pinch of oregano.

Palanqueta de Nuez

Ingredients:

- 2 cups granulated sugar
- 1 cup honey
- 2 cups walnuts
- 2 tsp bicarbonate of soda
- 2 tbsp butter

Dissolve the sugar in water. Add the honey and heat until the liquid shows signs of getting stringy as it drips from a spoon. Add the nuts and stir until the mixture has a light coffee color, then remove from the heat and immediately stir in the bicarbonate of soda and the butter. Keep stirring. Pour the mixture evenly and quickly into a slightly warm, buttered dish and leave to cool completely. When cool, cut into pieces.

México

State Characteristics

The state of México is not to be confused with México D.F. (the Distrito Federal), in which the heart of Mexico City lies. The two are governed as separate entities within the republican federation, although to the casual observer it is hard to see the dividing line, because the suburbs of Mexico City extend well into the state of México. The state would completely surround the city were it not for Morelos, which shares the city's southern border. México has borders with several states apart from Morelos: Queretaro and Hidalgo to its north, Guerrero to its south, Puebla and Tlaxcala to its east, and Guerrero and Michoacán to its west. The capital of the state is Toluca, with a population 467,713, according to 2005 official figures; Toluca is only 63 kilometers (39 miles) from Mexico City.

The total state population is 14,007,495, which is by far the highest of all the states. In 1990, the state of México had less than 10 million people, and the rapid growth in population in recent decades has brought the state to the point where something like half of its inhabitants were born outside it. In 2005, Catholics accounted for 91 percent of the population, Protestants and evangelicals for 4 percent. There are 124 administrative municipalities, and the state is represented by forty people in the National Congress. People and things from this state are referred to as *mexiquenses*, which is a way of avoiding confusion with the adjective *mexicano*, used in reference to the country as a whole.

About twenty newspapers are published in the state of México. Apart from *Adelante en la Noticia*, which is published in Tlalnepantla de Baz, all of them come out of Toluca; examples are *Amanecer, Columnas, Cambio,*

Milenio Toluca, and *Impulso*. Some of the newspapers, such as *El Sol*, are part of national chains. México also has a large number of higher education establishments, one of the best known being its Universidad Autónoma.

Despite its huge population, México is a relatively small state in terms of the land covered—just 22,500 square kilometers (8,750 square miles), or 1.9 percent of the country—making it number 25 among states by this yardstick. The land is varied, giving the state five natural regions: the Valley of Anáhuac with its volcanoes, the flatlands and hills of the north, the mountainous peaks of the west, the Balsas basin, and the mountains and valleys of the southwest. The Toluca Valley lies at about 2,440 meters (8,000 feet) above sea level. The highest elevation is Popocatépetl, a volcano on the border with Puebla, at 5,452 meters (17,890 feet); the second highest is Iztaccíhuatl, at 5,286 meters (17,340 feet). There are many other points where the altitude is over 3,000 meters (10,000 feet).

Three of the country's most important river systems dominate the state: the Lerma, the Balsas, and the Pánuco. The source of the Lerma, which runs for about 125 kilometers (78 miles), is in the municipality called Almoloya del Río. The whole of the southern region is part of the Balsas basin. The Pánuco basin is shared with the D.F. and has links with Lake Texcoco, in which the Aztecs built their capital. There are also several major lakes, thermal springs, and dams.

About 70 percent of the state enjoys a moderate climate, with average annual temperatures ranging between 10°C and 16°C (50–61°F) and annual rainfall of 500 to 1,500 millimeters (20–60 inches). Most of the rain falls in the summer months. The higher elevations (that is, the central and eastern mountains) have cold or moderately cold climates. Low-lying areas to the south, covering about 5 percent of the state, have warmer and wetter conditions, while areas close to Tlaxcala and Puebla, also covering about 5 percent, are a good deal drier. May is usually the hottest month, but May averages for the state as a whole are only in the region of 24°C (75°F).

There are pines, oaks, cedars, and firs in the mountains; pastures, cacti, *ocotillo*, and *damiana* in the valleys; and *uña de gato* (a thorny vine), *huizache*, *casahuate* (morning glory tree), *copal* (which produces an aromatic resin), and *leucaena* in the Balsas basin. Mammals include hares, rabbits, mountain cats, and deer in mountainous areas, and muskrats, badgers, coyotes, weasels, and foxes in other parts. There is also a wide variety of birds, reptiles, amphibians, and insects. The Parque Nacional Bosencheve, close to Michoacán, is a refuge for monarch butterflies. There are forty-nine protected natural areas in the state, including the Parque Nacional del Nevado de Toluca and several state parks—the Otomí-Mazahua, the Sierra Morelos, and the Nahuatlaca-Matlatzinca, for example.

Cultural Groups and Languages

The area now occupied by the state of México and the Distrito Federal was one of the most vital in pre-Columbian times, developed by successive

Mesoamerican civilizations. Though the descendants of indigenous peoples have become very integrated into mainstream society and their cultural habits fused with imported ones, evidence of the indigenous heritage is everywhere.

The 2005 census listed a total of 312,319 people over the age of five as speakers of indigenous languages. This was 2.6 percent of the population of the state, down from 3.3 percent in the 2000 census. The decline is not a surprise, given the pressures toward integration and the constant influx of immigrants from other parts of the country. Several neighboring states registered much higher figures in the 2005 census (Puebla, 11.7 percent; Hidalgo, 15.5; and Guerrero, 14.2). The dominant indigenous languages in the state of México were Mazahua (95,411 speakers), Otomí (83,411), and Náhuatl (45,972).

History

Archaeological evidence found on an island in Lake Chalco indicates that humans were present there 20,000 years ago. In many other places, evidence has shown that hunters and gatherers became increasingly organized and that, between 5000 and 2500 BC, they evolved into settled groups that cultivated maize (corn), beans, and squashes. There are ceramics dating from the end of that period, when villages such as Tlapacoya, Atoto, Malinalco, Acatzingo and Tlatilco were established.

Between 100 BC and AD 100, the major buildings of Teotihuacán were constructed: pyramids, temples, a fortress, and a market area. By about 800, the Mazatlincas had built a walled city with squares, temples, and a ball court at Teotenango. These people were conquered during the fifteenth century by the Mexicas (Aztecs) and the Purépechas, and the names of their villages were changed. But the Mazatlincas were only one of several peoples who had established themselves in the region; others were the Chichimecs, the Acolhuas, the Mazahuas, and the Otomíes, all of whom were conquered by the Spaniards in 1521.

After the fall of the Aztec capital, Tenochtitlán, Hernán Cortés and his cousin Juan Altamirano gained control of the Toluca Valley and *encomiendas* were granted to several of the conquistadores. Missionary work began in 1523, first by the Franciscans and later by Augustinians, Dominicans, and Jesuits. The Jesuit convent at Tepozotlán became one of the most influential in the whole of Latin America.

The Indian population declined disastrously during the first two hundred years of the colonial period, from an estimated two million to about two hundred thousand. The reasons for this were war, slave-like working conditions, and European diseases such as smallpox, to which the Indians had not developed a resistance. Indeed, problems with epidemics and droughts recurred during the eighteenth century. During the colonial era, the main role of the areas surrounding the ever-expanding Mexico City was to supply it with food and other services. There were silver and gold mines in several locations. *Haciendas* produced sugarcane and *pulque*, a drink fermented from cactus. Textiles were made at San Felipe del Obraje, Texcoco, and Sultepec; soap at Toluca; tack for animals at Valle de Bravo; saddles at Almoloya de Juárez, and so on. For the natives, it was a time of great poverty and injustice.

In 1810, soon after Father Miguel Hidalgo issued his call for independence from Spain, his rebel army came down from the mountains that divide México and Michoacán and took Toluca before moving on to Mexico City. Forces loyal to Spain were defeated in a fierce battle that took place at the Monte de las Cruces on October 30. Meanwhile, in the southern part of México, royalists were shooting insurgents and people they thought might become rebels. There were confrontations in several towns, such as Sultepec, Amanalco, Temascaltepec, and Lerma, in which insurgents such as José María Oviedo, Antonio Rosales, Isidoro Montes de Oca, Father José Manuel Izquierdo, and Pedro Ascencio de Alquisiras distinguished themselves.

After Emperor Agustin de Iturbide's empire failed, independent Mexico held a congress at which the foundational states of a new republic were identified. The state of México was created at that time, with Melchor Muzquiz as its first governor, but its borders at that time were very different from those of today. Initially, there were eight administrative districts to the state, and it included Mexico City and territory that later became other states. About five months after the initial boundaries were set, the D.F. was established. It was agreed that the state authorities would remain for the time being in Mexico City, until a state capital could be decided upon. In 1827, Texcoco was chosen for that role, a state constitution was promulgated, and elections were held for a new governor. Lorenzo de Zavala, the winner of that election, proposed that instead the capital should be in San Agustín de las Cuevas. Three years later, it was moved again to its current place, Toluca.

The first few decades of the nineteenth century all over Mexico were characterized by struggles between federalists and centralists, liberals and conservatives. In the case of México, after some changes of governor, in 1835 Carlos María de Bustamante drew up the so-called Plan de Toluca, which called for the restoration of central power and a modification of the constitution of the state. Toluca lost its power, and authority moved to Mexico City, with Toluca reduced to the status of a department. It remained so until 1846, when the liberal governor, Francisco de Olaguíbel, had the seat of power moved back to Toluca. In the interim, Toluca's prestigious Instituto Literario had been closed, but it now reopened. One of the most distinguished intellectuals associated with it, Ignacio Ramírez, served in Olaguíbel's local government. In 1848, when invading U.S. troops occupied Toluca, Olaguíbel was obliged to move the seat of power to Sultepec, but it was not long before the war was over. Yet the shifts of identity and of power were to continue for much of the century, making it difficult to achieve social and economic progress.

The period that ran from the conclusion of that war to the end of the last presidency of Gen. Antonio López de Santa Anna saw eleven different governors in México. During that period, a presidential decree took away a large part of the territory to create the state of Guerrero. Constitutional rule in the country was suspended more than once, eventually leading to the Reform War (sometimes called the Three Years' War). Violent struggles occurred between liberals, who wished to reduce clerical and military privileges that had been in place since colonial days, and conservatives, who wished to retain them in their own interests. Then came the intervention of the French, causing the displacement of the national government. With support from the conservatives, an Austrian prince, Maximilian, was installed by Napoleon III as emperor. One of the most distinguished fighters for liberal reform during this period was **Plutarco González** (1813–1857). The state also provided the country with a president, albeit a brief one: **Manuel de la Peña y Peña** (1789–1850).

After the withdrawal of French troops and the defeat of Maximilian, President Benito Juárez's liberal national government was restored to power and more reforms ensued. The states of Hidalgo and Morelos were created, and a new constitution for the state of México was drawn up. Under Governor José Vicente Villada during the late 1880s, primary education was extended to cover the whole of the state, and there were other initiatives to improve education—better secondary schools, a boost for the Instituto Científico y Literario, and a new school for arts and crafts. Textile factories became mechanized, and mining reached a new level of development.

This was at the beginning of the era of Porfirio Díaz, the man who occupied the country's presidency for almost thirty years. It was typical of his time for industry to modernize and expand and for there to be progress in communications, but Díaz encouraged foreign investors to exploit natural resources and the labor force, and he took a hard line against those who opposed him. State governors, in general, were people who toed the line—his appointees. Although Díaz had enough power to take on influential landowners and the church, in fact what happened was that the rich became richer and the poor were left further behind than ever: the size of haciendas grew, while humble people, especially Indians, lost their lands. In the second half of the nineteenth century, México provided the country with an archbishop: **Próspero María Alarcón y Sánchez de la Barquera** (1825–1908).

In 1909, Andrés Molina Enríquez, a native of Jilotepec, published a book called *Los grandes problemas nacionales* (Major Problems Facing the Nation), in which he criticized the system of land tenure. As the Mexican Revolution developed, starting a year later, the relevance of this book to the struggle, especially as envisaged by the southern forces under Emiliano Zapata, became very clear. Inspired by the opposition movement led by Francisco Madero, in 1910 the brothers Alfonso and Joaquín Miranda took up arms, supported by hundreds of Indians in Ocuilan and Malinalco. After

Madero, as president, had been betrayed and killed, Zapatista activity in the state of México increased. In opposition to Victoriano Huerta, who had usurped the presidency, an accord was signed in Teoloyucan in 1914, demanding the restoration of power to constitutional revolutionary forces; on two separate occasions during the following year, Toluca was the site of a convention of revolutionary governors and leaders.

The governments of the first two decades of the twentieth century made some progress in righting the wrongs of the past, but personal rivalries, political instability, and the conservative and clerical uprising that became known as the Cristero Rebellion slowed progress. Labor organizations began to take shape, and there was some redistribution of land. Real changes began in the 1930s, especially under President Lázaro Cárdenas.

In 1933, a law was passed exempting basic industries from taxes. An industrial zone was set up at Naucalpan in 1940, encouraging exponential growth in the municipalities close to the D.F. In 1956, the highly respected Instituto Científico y Literario became the core of a new Universidad Autónoma del Estado de México.

As in most of Mexico, the politics of the state were dominated by the Partido Revolucionario Institucional throughout the twentieth century. One of the country's twentieth-century presidents, **Adolfo López Mateos** (1910–1969), was born in Atizapán de Zaragoza.

Economy

Outside the urban areas, the principal activities in México are agriculture and raising animals to feed Mexico City. In general, the state is extremely well connected with its markets, by road, rail, and air.

Roughly 47 percent of the land is devoted to agriculture, and 15 percent to pasture; 28 percent is forested and a further 6 percent can be described as jungle. The predominant agricultural crops are corn (the state being one of the country's largest producers), followed by beans, barley, oats, and potatoes. Sugar, one of the main products of the nineteenth-century economy, is still important, as is the alcoholic pulque. Flowers and fruits are also grown. Although the usual variety of animals is reared, pigs account for nearly half of livestock. As for forestry, the main exploitable woods are pine, fir and oak. There is some mining of gold, silver, lead, copper, and zinc, but not on a grand scale.

México is one of the most industrialized states in the country. Industrial development first gained pace during the governorship of Isidro Fabela in the 1940s. The leading industries now are chemicals; textiles and clothing; the manufacture and repair of machines, electrical equipment, and automobiles; and food processing. Toluca is a major industrial center and has its own airport. Other industries tend to be closer to Mexico City. There are about a dozen industrial parks in the state. Some of the major companies represented are Bacardí, Bic, Bimbo (the leading Hispanic maker of U.S.-style factory bread), BMW, DaimlerChrysler, Holiday Inn, Nestlé, Panasonic, Bosch, and Yakult.

In the service sector, hotels and restaurants loom large. The state's natural attractions, such as its conservation areas and the Popocatépetl volcano, combined with archaeological sites and the proximity of Mexico City, make tourism a significant contributor to the economy.

Arts

Among the state's crafts, there are textiles made by traditional methods of cotton and wool, including carpets (particularly in Temoaya). Wood carving, pottery, metalwork, and basketry are other examples. Glass is blown and engraved, and mosaics are made in the Byzantine style. Metepec is known for its clay figures and especially for the production of representations of the Tree of Life. Tultepec is famous for making fireworks.

México has its own orchestra, its own traditional dance company (the Ballet Folklórico), and other such companies. It is well supplied with theaters. In the popular musical tradition, wind bands are prominent, as are mariachi ensembles. *Corridos* are an essential part of the musical repertoire. Common instruments from the indigenous heritage are *sonajeros* (rattles) and drums such as *teponaxtles* and *huéhuetles*. Popular dances include the *concheros*, which has indigenous roots, the *moros y cristianos* and *Santiagos*, which have Spanish ones, and others of European provenance such as *doce pares de Francia*. The *danza de los arrieros* is of local historical significance, since the state was a main transition point for arrieros (mule drivers) taking goods between Acapulco and Mexico City. The Matlatzinca *danza de la pluma* is a ritual indigenous dance performed by an indeterminate number of children.

Musicians and composers born in the state have included **Agustín Caballero** (1815–1886) and **Felipe de Jesús Villanueva Gutiérrez** (1862–1893). Painters have included **Felipe Santiago Gutiérrez Cortés** (1824–1904) and **Pastor Velázquez** (1895–1960). By far the most famous of mexiquense painters was **José María Velasco** (1840–1912). Velasco was a world-class artist, the country's leading landscape painter, and also the contributor of a major collection of lithographs of flora and fauna to the Natural History Society. One of his most famous paintings is a small study of Oaxaca Cathedral, a picture that was presented to Pope Leo XIII. Velasco did a great many landscapes of the hills close to Mexico City, always attentive to detail and respectful of the countryside's grandeur.

Juan Bautista Pomar (1540–?), born in Cuautitlán, was an important chronicler of the early colonial era, as was **Juan Tovar** (1543–1623), born in Texcoco. Similarly, **Fernando de Alba Ixtlixóchitl** (1568–1648), from Teotihuacán, was a hispanicized Indian who is now regarded as a major writer of that time.

There have been many poets from this region, one of the earliest and most famous being the Indian king **Nezahualcóyotl** (1402–1472).

Nezahualcóyotl governed the kingdom of Texcoco. He wrote poetry in Náhuatl that was translated into Spanish and even so gives some insight into the coded language of Aztec poetry, an art that they prized highly. His writing has a strangely modern quality to it. It deals with some timeless themes, such as the transience of human existence. **Angel María Garibay Kintana** (1892–1967) was a priest and a humanist who was a leading authority on the Náhuatl language and made translations of the poetry of people like Nezahualcóyotl.

Another celebrated poet was the nun **Sor Juana Inés de la Cruz** (1648–1695). Despite being of illegitimate birth, Juana de Asbaje became a valued presence at the viceregal court, but she suddenly withdrew to a convent, took vows, and became Sor Juana. Her cell became a place for discussions with her literary friends, and her writings, which are deeply thoughtful, witty, and skillfully put together, were sometimes controversial. She wrote suggestive love poems, made fun of men, and ruffled a few theological feathers. Apart from poetry, she also wrote plays. Sor Juana is generally regarded as the greatest colonial writer of all Latin America.

Social Customs

Major festivities are frequently associated with key moments in the Catholic calendar, such as Lent (Carnival), Holy Week, and Christmas. More characteristically Mexican are the celebration of the Day of the Dead (All Saints' Day) and the Feast of the Virgin of Guadalupe in December. Important saints' days for most parts of the state are San José in March, Santa Cruz in May, San Pablo in June, Santiago Apóstol in July, San Miguel Arcángel in September, and San Francisco in October. Such occasions are typically marked by religious ceremonies, processions, bullfights, cockfights, fireworks, concerts of popular and traditional music, dancing, food stalls, and cultural events. One of the most characteristic features of Santa Cruz festivals is the *tecamacada*, the celebration that occurs in the municipality of Tecámac.

Agricultural and trade fairs are held all over the state. Prime examples are the one that coincides with the Feast of San Isidro in Metepec, or those of Jilotepec and Texcoco.

Noteworthy Places

El Salto is a 50-meter (165-foot) waterfall in the municipality of Tonatico. Los Venados Park in Zinacantepec is one of several nature reserves; so-called because of the proliferation of white-tailed deer. The two main volcanoes are part of the Parque Nacional Izta-Popo. Other places of natural beauty are El Oro, Sultepec, and the Valle de Bravo.

The state has many museums. In Toluca, there is one devoted to watercolors and another to modern art, as well as a science museum, a stamp museum, and an anthropological museum. Acolman has a Museo Colonial,

View along the Avenue of the Dead, at Teotihuacán.

Tepexpan a Museo de la Prehistoria, El Oro a Museum of Mining, and Temascalcingo a museum devoted to the painter José María Velasco. Archaeological museums are found in Chalco and Chimalpain. Tepotzotlán houses the important Museo Nacional del Virreinato, and there is also a Museo Virreinal in Zinacantepec.

Teotihuacán stands out among archaeological sites, not only because of its scale and historical significance but also because of the flocks of tourists. Its dominant structures are two pyramids dedicated to the sun and the moon. A long ceremonial avenue leads past other imposing monuments, such as the Temple of Quetzalcóatl. Teotihuacán, "The Place Where Men Become Gods," was a burial place for kings—hence the name given to its 4-kilometer (2.5-mile) central avenue: "The Way of the Dead." In Aztec mythology, this was the place where the gods created the sun and the moon. Historically, it was the center of one of the first great Mesoamerican cultures, traceable back to 150 BC and known to have thrived until about AD 750, when it was abandoned for unknown reasons.

At about 60 meters (200 feet) high, the Pyramid of the Sun is second in size only to the one at Cholula in the state of Puebla. The Mural del Puma is a multicolored mural of a feline animal, and the Temple of Quetzalcóatl has elaborate statues and stonework representing both Quetzalcóatl (the Plumed Serpent) and Tlaloc (the God of Rain). Another temple, the Templo de los Jaguares has a mural of two jaguars holding up a snail, while the oldest structure on the site, known as the Caracoles Emplumados (Plumed Snails), is approached by a tunnel and consists of a temple set on a platform and decorated with images of snails, flowers, and birds. The Teotihuacán site has a modern archaeological museum also.

Other archaeological sites in the state are Calixtlahuaca, Tlatilco, Tlapacoya, Tenango, and Malinalco.

Historic buildings from the colonial era include the open chapels (open in order to accommodate large numbers of Indians in the sort of sacred space with which they were familiar) and the often simple and unadorned Franciscan convents. Two major haciendas are Atenco and La Gavia.

Among the most important convent buildings are those at Tepotzotlán, Acolman, Zinacantepec, Malinalco, Ozumba, Amecameca, Metepec, and Toluca. The former convent at Zinacantepec, for example, is a Franciscan building dating from the sixteenth century. It has a fine wooden carving at its entrance, and inside the church are a later, neoclassical altarpiece and an impressive pulpit. There are vestiges of frescoes. The entrance to the *capilla abierta* (open chapel) shows signs of the plateresque style. It has a particularly fine stone baptismal font, one of the most important of the colonial era; carved into it are images that are clearly the work of Indian craftsmen.

Toluca is a modern industrial town. One of its interesting buildings is the Cosmovitral, originally intended to be a market and built of stone and iron between 1909 and 1933, under the influence of Art Nouveau. It did serve as a market until 1972, when it was renovated and made into a botanical garden. Its name is due to the extensive use of leaded glass to represent, among other things, the figure of a man becoming the sun.

Cuisine

As in much of the country, the mexiquense cuisine is a hybrid based on several traditions, especially the indigenous and the Spanish. The former provided chiles, beans, and corn in many forms, together with rich and complex sauces. Spain provided new meats, olives, almonds, and raisins, among other things. Typical dishes include *chorizo en salsa verde, mixiote* (pit-barbecued meat), *carnitas, mole rojo con guajolote, escamoles* (ants' eggs), and *acociles* (similar to crawfish). Sweets include *requesón* (cream cheese), limes stuffed with coconut, *garapiñas toluqueñas,* and *dulce de pepita y cacahuate. Mosco* is a fruit liquor, and pulque is fermented from cactus; several other drinks are based on corn. Cheeses from Ayapango and Aculco are highly prized.

Carnitas

Ingredients:

  1½ lb. boneless pork shoulder
  2 tbsp brown sugar

1 tbsp tequila (or orange juice)
1 tbsp molasses
2 cloves of garlic
1 green onion
Salt and pepper

Lay the meat out flat in a frying pan and cover it with the rest of the ingredients (minus the green onion). Add some water, heat to boiling, and then reduce to a simmer. Cook for about 40 minutes, until the water evaporates and the pork begins to caramelize. Serve sprinkled with green onion.

Sopa de Huitlacoche

Huitlacoche is a fungus that grows on corn and is widely used in México.

Ingredients:

1 lb. huitlacoche, washed and drained
1 large ear of corn
6 cups chicken broth
1 small onion
2 cloves of garlic
Grated cheese
3 *serrano* chiles
Oil
Epazote
Salt and pepper

Heat some oil in a pan and gently fry the chopped onion and garlic. When softened, add the huitlacoche and the corn from the cob, sauté them for a few minutes, and then add the broth, the chiles, and a pinch of epazote leaves (or better still, a sprig). Season and let simmer for 5 minutes. Serve with cheese sprinkled on top.

Mole Rojo

Ingredients:

6 dried *pasilla* chiles
10 dried *ancho* chiles
8 dried *mulato* chiles (or dried *poblanos*)
4 *tomatillos*
5 plum tomatoes
1/2 cup raisins
2 tbsp sesame seeds
2 corn tortillas
6 cloves of garlic
2 tsp cinnamon
2 cloves
1/2 tsp allspice

5 oz. bitter chocolate
Peanut oil, or fat from the bird
Salt and pepper

Dry the tortillas in the oven at about 150°F, then break them into small pieces and set aside. Roast and peel the garlic. Soak the raisins in warm water. Remove the stems and seeds from the chiles, then roast them for a moment in a dry frying pan, taking care not to burn them. Add a little water to the pan and simmer the chiles very slowly for about half an hour. Strain them and leave them to cool. Clean the husks from the tomatillos. Roast them and the tomatoes in the same way as the chiles, or over a gas flame. Roast the sesame seeds in a dry frying pan until they pop. Briefly sauté the almonds in a little oil. Now put all these things, together with the spices, in a blender and make a puree. Melt the chocolate in a little water, then blend it into the mixture. Add water slowly, bringing the volume up to about 5 cups. Heat some oil in a deep pan; once the oil is hot, add the mixture from the blender and refry it over moderate heat for about 10 minutes, stirring constantly and making sure that it does not thicken too much. Serve warm over cooked poultry.

Michoacán

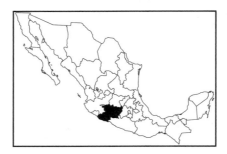

State Characteristics

Michoacán de Ocampo is in central western Mexico. "Michoacán" is thought to derive either from a word in the Náhuatl language that means "the place of the fishermen" or from one in the Tarasco language that means "the place by the water." Indeed, the state sits beside the Pacific and has about 200 kilometers (125 miles) of coastline. Following that coast toward the southeast one comes to Guerrero, and toward the northwest to Jalisco. Directly north of Michoacán are the states of Jalisco and Guanajuato, to the west of it Jalisco and Colima, and to the east Guerrero and México. Mexico City is about 320 kilometers (200 miles) away. Michoacán covers 59,864 square kilometers (23,300 square miles), which is about 3 percent of Mexico's total.

The population of the state accounts for a higher proportion of Mexico's total. The state population, according to the 2005 census, was 3,966,073 people, 95 percent of whom were Catholic and 2 percent Protestant or evangelical. Michoacán has 113 administrative municipalities and is represented by a delegation of seventeen in the National Congress. The capital city, with a population of over 600,000 people, is Morelia.

The state's principal institutions of higher education are the Instituto Tecnológico and the Universidad Michoacana. Most of its eighteen newspapers emanate from the capital, including *La Voz de Michoacán*, *El Sol*, *Cambio*, and *La Jornada*. *La Opinión* is published in Uruapan del Progreso, *El Clarín* in Zitácuaro, *El Heraldo* in Zamora de Hidalgo, *Panorama del Puerto* in Lázaro Cárdenas, and *El Día* in Apatzingan.

Taking into account differences of culture and climate, the state of Michoacán can be divided into six regions: Costa, Sierra Madre del Sur, Tierras Calientes, Balcones, Eje Volcánico, and Bajío. The land comprises two major mountain ranges, the Sierra Madre del Sur and the Sistema Volcánico Transversal, with its several valleys. The Sierra Madre del Sur, a prolongation of the Sierra Madre Occidental, runs parallel to the coast and quite close to it. The Sierra is almost 100 kilometers (60 miles) wide; its highest point is the Cerro de las Canoas (3,000 meters/9,850 feet), and there are many other places that approach that altitude. The Sistema Volcánico Transversal (sometimes called the Cordillera Neovolcánica) lies in the south of the state, on the *meseta*. It runs for 300 kilometers (180 miles) and is about 130 kilometers (80 miles) wide. Tancítaro, at 3,857 meters (12,650 feet) is its highest point. The rivers east of the Sierra Madre contribute to two of Mexico's most important systems: those of the northern part feed the Lerma, and those of the southern part, the Balsas. There are a number of sizable lakes, some with islands in them. One vital river is the Tepalcatepec, because it supplies water for agriculture and also generates electricity. The mountains along the coast sometimes fall quite sharply toward the ocean, interrupted by bays and lagoons. On this western side, there are many minor rivers that flow southwest into the Pacific.

The climate in Michoacán is extremely varied, due to its physical geography. In the north, annual average temperatures are around 13°C (55°F), while in coastal areas to the south, they reach 29°C (84°F) or higher. The southern area, like neighboring Guerrero, is referred to as the Tierra Caliente (Hot Country). The high temperatures range from 27°C (81°F) in the north to 48°C (118°F) in the south, and the lows from 7°C (45°F) to 18°C (64°F). Similarly, rainfall averages between 600 and 1,600 millimeters (24–64 inches), with the higher levels of precipitation occurring in the north and other mountainous locations, especially Uruapan. Most of the rain falls during the summer months. Simplifying somewhat, one can say that there are three main climates: tropical along the coast and in the Balsas basin, though with some dry areas; moderately wet in some places with high elevations; and elsewhere moderate to fairly dry.

There are conifers in the high mountains, pines and oaks a little lower down, mixed vegetation including bushes and pastures at lower levels, and tropical vegetation along the coast. Among the state's mammals are foxes, *mapaches*, rabbits, armadillos, *cacomixtles*, mountain cats, and *tlacuaches*. Birds include ducks, *cercetas*, *chachalacas*, pheasants, *huilotas*, *torcaces*, doves, and seabirds. Amphibians and fish in lakes and rivers include *axolotls*, *acúmaras*, *achoques*, catfish, tilapia, trout, crawfish, frogs, and toads; there are reptiles such as turtles and many types of snakes, some of them poisonous. Common marine species are snapper, bream, grouper, oysters, squid, sharks, and swordfish, plus sea turtles of various kinds.

Cultural Groups and Languages

The 2005 census states that in Michoacán 3.3 percent of those over five years of age spoke an indigenous language. Of these 113,166 people, 96,966 spoke the Purépecha language, 4,009 Náhuatl, and 3,472 Mazahua; other languages had fewer than a thousand speakers. Indigenous-language speakers are distributed over about a quarter of the municipalities and comprise four ethnic groups: the Purépechas, Mazahuas, Otomíes, and Nahuas. The overwhelming majority of indigenous-language speakers also speak Spanish, which shows how far they have become assimilated into the dominant culture.

History

Archaeological evidence shows that the region was inhabited in the Pre-classical Period of Mesoamerican civilizations, that is to say from about 1500 BC, by Nahuas, Otomíes, Matlazincas (or Pirindas), and Tecos. Many languages were spoken, the principal one being Purépecha. During the Postclassical Period, three or four centuries before the Spaniards came, the area of Lake Pátzcuaro was inhabited by Purépechas and Nahuas who were settled and engaged in agriculture and fishing. In the thirteenth century, groups of Purépecha hunters and gatherers arrived from the north, encountering others who shared their language and some of their beliefs and customs, but there was conflict between them. Eventually a Purépecha state was formed, probably over the course of seven generations, with a seat at Pátzcuaro and two other foci, Ihuatzio and Tzintzuntzán.

During the fifteenth century, the Purépechas extended their control over other peoples, creating an empire that ranged over what are now the states of Michoacán, Colima, Nayarit, Querétaro, Guanajuato, Guerrero, and Jalisco and parts of San Luis Potosí and Sinaloa. The Purépechas were skilled craftsmen, famous for their work with hummingbird feathers, for example, but not builders of lasting monuments. They fought off attacks by those other imperialists, the Aztecs. When the latter realized that the Spaniards represented a serious threat, they attempted to make an alliance with the Purépechas, but the Purépechas rejected any such arrangement. However, in the process of negotiating with the Purépechas, the Aztec emissaries had brought a new disease: smallpox. An epidemic followed, and thousands died, lacking immunity to this European disease.

The Spaniards gave the Purépechas a new name, "Tarascos,"—a name that still can have pejorative overtones. Ironically, the term had first been used by the Purépechas themselves as a pejorative way of referring to the marauding Spaniards. After the fall of the Aztec capital Tenochtitlán, Hernán Cortés assured the king of the Purépechas, Tangaxoan, that if his people submitted to the invaders, they would be well treated. The Spaniards were then allowed unopposed entry to the Purépecha capital. When

Cristóbal de Olid arrived there, in 1522, with a few hundred Spaniards and several thousand Indian allies, he found a city of some 40,000 people. He also found evidence of idolatry and of the sacrifice of hundreds of people, with the result that the Spaniards and their allies destroyed and looted the Purépecha temples and occupied the city.

When gold was discovered in western Mexico, more invaders flocked in. The Tarascans were organized into *encomiendas* and put to work in mines or tending the land in order to feed the miners. In 1524, the Tarascan king was baptized in Mexico City, and he asked for more priests to be sent to Michoacán to help convert others. A year later, six Franciscans arrived and set about constructing a monastery in Tzintzuntzán, the Tarascan capital, tearing down the Indian temples and using the stone to build the monastery. Augustinian friars arrived in 1533, and the Jesuits twenty years later. The Jesuits made their headquarters in Pátzcuaro and set up six colleges to provide basic education.

Spain's lack of control over New Spain was becoming a cause for concern, and the colony was increasingly anarchic. There were also concerns about the mistreatment of the Indians, the assault on their ways, and the decline in their numbers. In an attempt to reassert the authority of the Crown, King Carlos I (Holy Roman Emperor Charles V) set up a new regulatory body—an *audiencia*—and put a lawyer, Nuño Beltrán de Guzmán, in charge of it. Unfortunately, Beltrán proved to be a ruthless, cruel, and destructive man. He willfully destroyed things that the Indians valued, demanded tribute, sold some of them into slavery, and stole their women. He also took over some of the encomiendas for himself. There was soon conflict with Bishop Zumárraga of Mexico City, who had been charged with protecting the Indians, and by 1529, Beltrán had been excommunicated. At about that time, Beltrán arrived in Michoacán and demanded that King Tangoxoán hand over all his gold. Beltrán then tortured the king and had him burned at the stake. A revolt ensued, with many Tarascans losing their lives. Having previously submitted peacefully but in vain to the Spanish order, many now fled to the hills, while Beltrán proceeded to plunder and destroy everything in his path. He then declared himself king of the Tarascan Empire and turned his attention to Jalisco. Eventually the authorities caught up with him, arrested him, and sent him back to Spain to be tried.

Beltrán had all but destroyed the Purépechas, but there now emerged one of the shining figures of the colonial era. **Vasco de Quiroga** (1470?–1565), in his sixties, had been sent to New Spain to be a judge in the audiencia and was instrumental in putting an end to the misdeeds of Beltrán. In an effort to compensate for the wrongs done to the Indians, Quiroga used his own resources to found hospital-schools near the capital and in Michoacán. When King Carlos pulled back from an earlier ruling that the Indians should not be treated as slaves, Quiroga sent him *Información en derecho* (1535), an energetic defense of the Indians and an attack on the way they were being abused by Spanish settlers. Late in life, Quiroga took religious vows, and by 1537 he had risen to the rank of bishop of Michoacán. Inspired by the writings of Sir Thomas More, Quiroga was now in a position to try to build a utopia. He convinced the Tarascos to return to their homelands and established a number of communities where the Indians were housed, fed, and taught not only about Christianity but also practical skills and principles of communal living. He became known as "Tata Vasco," the protector of the Indians, and it is thanks in part to him that Michoacán prospered economically and artistically during the following years; however, the fact remained that about a third of its indigenous population had been lost due to warfare, disease, or harsh labor conditions, and the loss would grow in later years to about 50 percent.

Another initiative of Vasco's was the construction of the Cathedral of Santa Ana, begun in 1540. By that time, King Carlos had already made Tzintzuntzán into the city of Michoacán. After using Pátzcuaro for a while as the administrative seat, the viceroy ordered the creation of a new town, to be called Valladolid, in a location the Indians called Guayangareo. With royal approval, the city of Valladolid came into being in 1545. About two hundred years later, it would be the birthplace of **José María Morelos y Pavón** (1762–1815), a leading light of the movement for independence from Spain, and so, some time after his death, the town was renamed Morelia in his honor.

The eighteenth century saw an Indian uprising in Tlazazalca and La Piedad, in 1707, and 1767 brought the expulsion of the Jesuits by order of the Spanish king, Carlos III, on the grounds that they were subversive. In 1776, the Spaniards introduced new administrative regions; what had been a wide-ranging province now became the *intendencia* of Valladolid, covering present-day Colima and Michoacán. Later, Colima was made part of the intendencia of Guadalajara, and Michoacán assumed more or less its present-day limits. In 1786, Fray Antonio de San Miguel began the construction of roads and an aqueduct, providing funds at a time when the people were struggling against sickness and food shortages; that year became known as the "Year of Hunger."

The first conspiracy in favor of independence took shape in Valladolid, in 1809, led by García Obeso, Soto Saldaña, Juan José de Lejarza, José Ma. Izazaga, and Vicente Santa María. After Father Miguel Hidalgo's open call for independence from Spain, these conspirators were joined by the López Rayón brothers, and by Morelos, who was the parish priest in Carácuaro. On the death of Hidalgo, Morelos took up the torch and the focus of the struggle became Michoacán. In Zitácuaro, **Ignacio López Rayón** (1773–1832) established the Primer Congreso Nacional Gubernativo (First National Government Congress) in 1811. López Rayón went on to distinguish himself in the fight for independence. At one point, he was captured and sentenced to death, and yet his execution was delayed and somehow he managed to continue to be active in public life, becoming a delegate to the Constituent Congress of the Republic. Three years after the Primer Congreso, the first constitution (Primera Constitución o Decreto Constitucional para la Libertad de la América Mexicana) was proclaimed in Apatzingán. It was there that Morelos read out his *Sentimientos de la Nación*, an expression of the desire for independent nationhood and an end to the system of *castas* (racial castes). Morelos engaged in many campaigns, especially in the state that bears his name, where at one stage his troops held out under siege in Cuautla for more than two months. He was later captured and executed, and the campaign torch passed on to Vicente Guerrero.

While Michoacán generally was in favor of independence, Valladolid stood out as the remaining stronghold of the royalists. It finally fell to troops led by **Agustín de Iturbide** (1783–1824), a *criollo* soldier and, like Morelos, a native of that city. Iturbide had remained loyal to Spain at the beginning of the independence movement, but then he had made a pact with Guerrero and together they had devised the Plan de Iguala, which laid down the basis for an independent country. Although it was not quite part of that plan, after a while Iturbide insinuated himself into the position of emperor of Mexico, and in 1822 he was crowned amid much pomp. But his empire proved to be short-lived: he reigned for exactly a year before being forced to abdicate, going briefly into exile, and then returning to Mexico, to be captured and shot.

In 1824, a national Constituent Congress was held, and at that point Michoacán became a state of the Mexican Republic. A year later, it had its first governor and the name of Valladolid, its capital, was changed to Morelia. The nineteenth century was a time of constant and often bloody fights for power between conservatives, who favored strong centralized authority in Mexico City, and liberals who were federally minded. In the case of Michoacán, the struggle was intimately linked with the question of whether or not it was to continue to be a state. Under conservative influence, for a while Michoacán became a department of the nation and was once again lumped together with Colima. In 1846, it recovered its former status, and Colima was separated from it for a second time. But that was not the end of the story: after a period under liberal control, the conservatives came back to power and Michoacán again reverted to department status.

Anastasio Bustamante (1780–1853) was president on three separate occasions. Having supported the royalist cause and Iturbide, Bustamante became vice president under Guerrero, only to take up arms against him and become president himself in 1830. After two years, he was unseated by Santa Anna, but was reelected in 1836 and 1842.

The middle of the century brought war between the two factions. Prominent among the liberals, and on more than one occasion governor of the state, was **Melchor Ocampo** (1814–1861) whose credits include organizing an army to fight in the war with the United States, representing the state in the National Congress, and serving as a government minister. He was a leading reformer, responsible, for example, for a law permitting civil marriage. Having been expelled from the country by Antonio López de Santa Anna, Ocampo organized a rebel force against him, and later, when he could return to the country, Ocampo helped draft the Reform Laws. In 1861, he retired from public life, but his enemies hunted him down and shot him.

During the French Intervention, Michoacán declared itself against the new regime, refusing to accept its authority. Morelia was taken by the French in 1863, so the state government moved to Uruapan. During the fighting with the French, some parts of the state suffered a great deal; Zitácuaro, for example, was looted and burned. Eventually, in 1857, the French were driven from Morelia. Nationally, President Benito Juárez was restored to power, and warring continued between reformists, who favored reducing the long-standing privileges of the church and the military, and conservatives, who wished to keep those privileges. After a troubled period, Juárez died while in office. Soon the country would enter the long era that became known as the *porfiriato*.

Porfirio Díaz ruled in an authoritarian manner, putting his own appointees into state governorships. His sway lasted for some thirty years; for most of that time, he was president, and even when not in the presidency himself, he was pulling strings from behind the scenes. Díaz brought progress and modernization to Mexico, improved communications, welcomed foreign investors, and granted land and other assets to them. Natural resources were exploited without control. The rich became richer and their estates grew larger, while the poor made no progress or lost what little they had. He silenced opposition by buying people off or by strong-arm tactics.

The revolutionary movement in Michoacán began in May 1911, when the then subprefect of Santa Clara del Cobre, Salvador Escalante, announced his support for Francisco Madero, the leader of the opposition nationally, and traveled to a number of towns to spread the message, meeting with little resistance. By September, the pro-Díaz governor of the state, who was in his fourth term in that office, stepped down. Escalante and others supported the candidacy of the liberal Miguel Silva, who faced fierce opposition from a Catholic faction led by José Ugarte, until Silva was elected governor in 1912. By this time, Díaz had vacated the presidency and slipped out of the country, and Madero had become president. Following Madero's assassination, Gen. Gertrudis Sánchez became governor of Michoacán, took over some church property, and made improvements affecting agriculture and education. He was followed in office by another military man, General Alfredo Elizondo, appointed by President Alvaro Obregón; Elizondo brought about additional improvements in the educational sphere.

Although democratically elected governor in 1920, **Francisco J. Mújica** (1884-1954) did not enjoy the support of Mexico City, which attempted to withdraw state powers, only to find itself obliged to restore them due to the level of public support behind Mújica. Mújica was nevertheless criticized and subjected to harassment by Obregón until he stepped down from the governorship. During his tenure, there were confrontations between workers' and religious associations, and one of the workers' leaders, Isaac Arriaga, was assassinated. Mújica represented the state at the Constituent Congress of 1917 and later served in the Cárdenas government.

The next hurdle was the Rebelión Cristera, a violent uprising born of an alliance of *hacienda* owners and Catholic organizations, aimed at halting the redistribution of land, the organization of labor, and further curtailment of church powers. It began when the seminaries at Morelia and Zamora were shut down. The task of calming things down fell to **Lázaro Cárdenas del Río** (1895-1970), who was elected to the governorship in 1928. He reorganized the state government, gave greater powers to local authorities, and redistributed 400,807 hectares (a million acres) of land as *ejidos* to 24,000 people. He also organized the Confederación Revolucionaria de los Trabajadores (Revolutionary Workers' Confederation).

Cárdenas would go on to become a national icon and probably the most significant president of twentieth-century Mexico, and his influence would be felt in Michoacán long after he ceased to lead the country. Nor was he the only governor of Michoacán to become president; **Pascual Ortiz Rubio** (1877-1963) occupied that office for two years shortly before him, having also served in Obregón's government and as ambassador to Germany and Brazil. Two of Ortiz's most significant initiatives during his brief period in the presidency were to give official recognition to the Spanish Republic and to bring Mexico into the League of Nations.

Cárdenas was the most distinguished in a long line of national and state leaders who were members of the Partido Revolucionario Institucional (PRI), which had emerged after the Revolution and dominated Mexican politics throughout the twentieth century. Only during the closing years of the century were there real signs of change, of a rejection of the comfortable and often corrupt political strategies that the PRI had evolved. The conservative Partido de Acción Nacional (PAN) began to win more support among people disaffected with entrenched habits and corruption, and the national elections in 2000 brought a member of that party, Vicente Fox, to the presidency. More importantly for the state of Michoacán, a new "Cardenismo" also emerged, a movement that attempted to be faithful to the revolutionary ideals while cleaning up the PRI's politics. A leading figure in this was Cárdenas's son **Cuauhtémoc Cárdenas Solórzano** (1934-), who went from governor of the state to being one of the most prominent national politicians, a voice in favor of political renewal in Mexico. The close of the century saw the election of his son, Lázaro Cárdenas Batel, to the governorship, and he in turn was replaced by Leonel Godoy; both are members of the new PRD, the Party of Democratic Revolution.

In recent years, Michoacán has been an unsettled place due to serious problems with violence related to the drug trade.

Economy

Approximately a third of the economically active population is involved in agriculture, livestock raising, fishing, or forestry. Manufacturing and the construction industries employ about a quarter of the population. The remainder works in the service sector.

Avocados (of which Michoacán is number-one producer in the world), sesame, strawberries, rice, mangoes, cotton, sorghum, wheat, sugarcane, garlic, alfalfa, chiles, beans, potatoes, and tomatoes are among the most prevalent agricultural products. About 20 percent of the land is devoted to agriculture, and about a third of that is irrigated. Some 40 percent of the agricultural land is used for raising all types of animals, many of them by traditional methods. Pig farms are particularly concentrated in the municipalities of La Piedad, Puruándiro, Yurécuaro, Huandacareo, and Numarán. As far as the fishing industry is concerned, the major catch is of tilapia, catfish, and carp.

Woods and forests cover something like 60 percent of the state. Forestry is a very important part of the state economy, providing fir, ash, oak, and pine that is prepared in the many sawmills for building and for making furniture.

There are a large number of hydroelectric facilities. Factories process sugarcane, make textiles with cotton and wool, and produce flour and vegetable oils. Chemicals, plastics, cellulose and paper, iron and steel, and bottled drinks are major industrial products. Industry is concentrated in the central region of the state near Morelia, in the west near Apatzingán, and in the Ciénaga de Chapala near Zamora.

Mining exploits deposits of iron, copper, zinc, cadmium, lead, silver, and gold, in addition to nonmetals such as sand, gravel, limestone, marble, kaolin, and gypsum. Nationally, Michoacán is a significant producer of copper and iron.

Arts

From the earliest days of colonization, the Spaniards were aware of the artistic skills of the Indians. The Spaniards trained them in new skills, too, resulting in distinctive hybrid products, for which a new term was devised: *tequitqui*. An example is the use of traditional Indian appliqué techniques with feathers in the production of Catholic images. There is still a rich tradition of handmade pottery and ceramics, often characterized by a distinctive pre-Hispanic glaze. Traditional methods are also used in glasswork, copperwork, ironwork, and weaving. Mats, baskets, and hats are made with sedge and straw. Leather riding gear is made in Apatzingán, and sandals and fine hats in Sahuayo, to name a couple of examples. Gold and silver are worked in several places. Religious effigies are carved in hardwood, lacquered, and sometimes decorated with gold, while softer woods are used to make masks, boxes, toys, and paper artifacts. Artisans produce several distinctive styles of furniture. Paracho and Ahuiran are known for their stringed instruments.

Michoacán has produced a number of significant artists and intellectuals. **José Rubén Romero** (1890–1952) fought for the Revolution, served as private secretary to Ortiz, and was ambassador to Brazil, but he is also remembered as a writer of poetry and especially of a picaresque novel called *La vida inútil de Pito Pérez.* **Samuel Ramos Magaña** (1897–1959) moved to Mexico City while still quite young, studied at prestigious universities in Europe, and returned to Mexico to serve in high-ranking positions in education. His writings concern philosophy and education; one of his most important and controversial books was *El perfil del hombre y la cultura en México*, a critique of Mexico's cultural dependence on Europe. **Homero Aridjis** (1940–) is a leading poet and literary journalist.

In the musical field, **Marcos Jiménez A.** (1882–1944), who was also a significant journalist, became known for writing songs, including one of the country's most popular: "Adiós Mariquita Linda." **Miguel Bernal Jiménez** (1910–1956) was a teacher, musicologist, composer, and promoter of choral music in general. Among his compositions are suites, symphonies, and a concertino for organ, plus an opera entitled *Tata Vasco.* Bernal Jiménez was active in the Conservatorio de las Rosas de Morelia, the oldest conservatory of music on the continent.

Morelia has a boys' choir that has a significant reputation; there is also a women's choir from Santa Fe de la Laguna. There have been many successful folk music groups from Zirahuén, Tarímbaro, Paracho, Pichataro, and Apatzingán. The group called Erandi has had some international success. Other successful groups are Los Originales de San Juan, Los Morros del Norte, and Los Razos.

Some popular musical genres are *trecuas* on the meseta and in the central region of the state, *sones* in the Bajío region, and *valonas* in the Tierra Caliente. Dances in the central region include the *danza de los viejos* (dance of the old men) and *danza del pescado* (dance of the fish). On the meseta, they perform the *canacuas*, *iguiris*, and *paloteros* dances. The ensembles of Michoacán play in all sorts of styles, sometimes using accordions and sounding like *norteño* bands.

Morelia has its concert and opera seasons and its October film festival. There is also an international organ festival in May and a choral festival in December.

Alfredo Zalce (1908–2003) participated in the muralist movement and was an active member of the League of Revolutionary Writers and Artists, but unlike some other muralists, he was not given to self-promotion. He also made easel paintings, ceramics, engravings, and sculptures. Works of his are displayed all over the world. **Rodolfo Amezcua** (1937–2002) was a theater director, playwright, and painter who also worked in films.

Social Customs

There are perhaps four hundred popular fiestas and social and cultural events every year in Michoacán. Some of the most important or distinctive are mentioned below.

In 1943, the Paricutín Volcano began a prolonged eruption, driving the inhabitants of the closest village to take refuge in San Juan de las Colchas; each January, they remember this event with civic ceremonies and a dancing contest for which people don traditional dress. Several towns mark the anniversary of their foundation, such as Nuevo Urecho in March, with processions, music, cultural events, fireworks, and merrymaking. At about the same time of year, a cultural festival in honor of Vasco de Quiroga takes place at Pátzcuaro, which also has a major fair in November. The Expo-Feria Lázaro Cárdenas is also in March, as are the feasts of El Señor de Araró in Zinapécuaro and San José in San José de Gracia.

Maiapita is otherwise known as the Feria del Atole. It takes place in Tarecuato, a community of Purépecha artisans famous for its textiles and

Woman sells flowers during preparations for the Day of the Dead celebrations in Tzintzuntzán. (AP Photo/Claudio Cruz)

embroidery and its garments called *guanengos*. *Atole* is a drink made with corn, and on this occasion it is flavored in all sorts of different ways.

Still in March, the Feria del Geranio is a flower, craft, and food festival in the town of Timngambato. Expo Arena is an excuse for dance competitions, a sandcastle-making contest, exhibitions, and beach sports held at Playa la Soledad in the municipality of Lázaro Cárdenas. Palm Sunday is a major occasion for several places, including Periban; it is marked by open-air markets in many parts of the state. Holy Week is widely observed, as are other major moments in the Catholic calendar, including, of course, the Day of the Dead.

Ticla holds the National Surfing Tournament. The arrival of the monarch butterfly is celebrated in Angangueo, starting in November. There is an international fishing competition in Lázaro Cárdenas during the early summer. Michoacán's Expo-Feria—the equivalent of a state fair—takes place in May.

Noteworthy Places

Huandacareo, Pátzcuaro, Tzintzuntzán, Tingambato, and Zitácuaro are all archaeological sites. Tzintzuntzán, for example, was a principal ceremonial center for the Purépecha people during the Postclassical Period that immediately preceded the arrival of the Spaniards. The central part of the site has a large platform with sloping walls and staircases made of stone slabs. Near this are vestiges of squares and a housing area. Some of the stones have geometric engravings on them. Tingambato, by contrast, predates the heyday of the Purépechas and shows signs of the influence of Teotihuacán. It has a platform in the typical two-tiered style and a ball court, squares, and sunken patios. Zitácuaro's site at San Felipe de los Alzati is of Matlalzinca origin. It has two pyramids, the larger of which is about $11^1/_2$ meters (38 feet) high, with the ruins of staircases and higher structures. There are stone carvings of spiral shapes and tortoises. This site is also from the Postclassical Period.

Many of the remains and artifacts found on these sites have made their way into the state's museums, such as the Museo Michoacano in Morelia, which is located in a sumptuous house once occupied by Emperor Maximilian. Apart from pre-Hispanic exhibits, this museum has colonial art and historical documents, plus paintings by regional artists, notably Alfredo Zalce. The Museo del Estado traces state history; it is housed in a building where the wife of Iturbide once lived. The Casa Museo José María Morelos y Pavón remains as it was when Morelos was alive. Morelia also has art museums devoted to the colonial and contemporary periods; the latter of the two includes works by José Clemente Orozco and José Guadalupe Posada.

The sixteenth-century building in Pátzcuaro that once was the seat of the Colegio de San Nicolás, founded by Vasco de Quiroga, is now a folk art museum. Sahuayo has a museum of works by painter Luis Sahagún that also houses a small but important collection of pre-Hispanic items. Salvador Escalante's Museo del Cobre displays artwork in copper that ranges from pre-Hispanic to modern times. In addition to tracing the lives of the López Rayón brothers, Tlalpujahua's Museo Hermanos Rayón covers other history, especially the history of mining in the state. The Museo de la Constitución is in Apatzingán, and the Museo Lázaro Cárdenas in Jiquilpan.

Charo has what was once an Augustinian monastery, built by Indian labor; later it was a meeting place for Morelos and Hidalgo. Its Ex-Convento de Capuchinas was built on the orders of Philip V during the eighteenth century. The Iglesia de las Rosas, dating from the same period, is on the site of a former Dominican convent. Morelia's cathedral was begun in 1660 but finished more than a hundred years later, and in the baroque style; the sacristy has two paintings by Juan Cabrera, one of the leading early colonial artists.

Among the state's most interesting civic buildings is Maravatio's Teatro Morelos, a popular venue during the porfiriato. Morelia's Palacio de Gobierno is located in an early eighteenth-century building that was once the Colegio Seminario Tridentino de Valladolid; its interior has murals by Zalce. The Palacio Clavijero, formerly the Jesuit Colegio de San Francisco Javier, is another baroque building that was begun in the seventeenth century.

The Colegio de San Nicolás de Hidalgo, founded by Quiroga and first located in Pátzcuaro, was transferred to another building in Valladolid and thereafter administered by the Jesuits. Both Hidalgo and Morelos were students there, and Hidalgo became its rector. Having been closed during the struggle for independence, it was reopened by Ocampo, who appended Hidalgo's name. The eighteenth-century building that houses the Conservatorio de Música de las Rosas was once a convent, then a school for destitute girls; it is now one of Latin America's leading musical conservatories.

Pátzcuaro has the Palacio de Huitziméngari, which is said to have belonged to Antonio de Huitziméngari, son of the last Purépecha chieftain and adopted son of Viceroy Antonio de Mendoza. Its public library, situated in a former convent church, has a mural by Juan O'Gorman. The church of Nuestra Señora de la Salud was built on a sacred pre-Hispanic site and served as the cathedral see until 1580, when power shifted to Valladolid. In 1924, the church was upgraded to a basilica. The Casa de los Once Patios (House of Eleven Patios) was once the Convento de Monjas Dominicanas de Santa Catarina (XVIIIC). There is also a seventeenth-century chapel called El Humilladero; it is the oldest in Pátzcuaro and is so named because it is where the natives are said to have humbly submitted to Christian authority.

La Huatapera is the name of a hospital in Uruapan that Fray Juan de San Miguel established to take care of the Indians; it has plateresque and *mudéjar* architectural features. Zacapu's sixteenth-century Franciscan convent is an outstanding example of the plateresque style.

Natural attractions include a monarch butterfly reserve, where as many as 500 million migrating butterflies arrive from the north between November and March of every year. South of Uruapan lies a 30-meter (100–foot) waterfall called the Cascada de Tzaráracua; the Chorros del Varal, which are of slightly greater height, are five waterfalls on the Iturria River. There are national parks at Lago de Camécuaro and Barranca del Cupatitzio. Michoacán also has a good number of beaches.

One outstanding natural phenomenon is the Volcan Paricutín, which suddenly began to grow from nothing in 1943, rose well over 300 meters (1,000 feet) in that year while covering two villages in lava, and continued to erupt for ten years. Since then, it has been dormant. Its height is now over 2,700 meters (9,000 feet).

Cuisine

As in most states, the cuisine of Michoacán is a lively hybrid of Indian and European traditions. From the Indians came the use of corn and a range of fruits, vegetables, and condiments, and from the Europeans came beef, pork, olives, almonds, and many other things, some of Middle Eastern origin. Most regions of the state are associated with typical dishes: for example, Apatzingán with *morisqueta* (rice with pork and chiles), Ario de Rosales with *olla podrida* (meat stewed in *pulque* with jalapeños and cactus fruit), Ciudad Hidalgo with *tacos de cabeza con salsa de ciruela fresca y chile verde* (meat tacos with a plum and chile sauce), coastal regions with *pescado a la talla* (fish barbecued over mangrove wood), Paracho and the whole of the meseta with *atapacua* (a corn-based stew, like *pozole*), San José de Gracia with *minquiche* (cheese fried with chiles and cream), Tocumbo with a variety of desserts made from fruits, Zamora also with its sweets, and Zirahuen with its fresh trout and other fish dishes.

Cerdo con Salsa

Ingredients:

2^1/$_4$ lb. boneless shoulder or rib pork
8 cloves of garlic
^{1}/$_4$ lb. *pasilla* chiles
1 cup pumpkin seeds, stripped
2 peppercorns
2 allspice fruits
2 cloves
Oil
Water
Salt

Cut the pork into small cubes and put it in a large pan, covering the meat with water. Add six crushed cloves of garlic and some salt, cover, and boil for about 20 minutes. Then take out the garlic and reserve half of the liquid, while keeping the meat cooking until done. Remove any remaining liquid and continue cooking the meat so that it browns in its own fat. In another pan, fry the chiles lightly all over, taking care not to burn them. Take them out, rinse them, and then soak them in some of the reserved water for about 15 minutes. Scrape out the chiles and briefly fry their seeds until they begin to brown, then grind them in a blender. Gently fry the pumpkin seeds until they start to pop. Add them, together with the spices and the remaining garlic, to the blender, put in a little of the broth, and make a puree. Add the puree to the meat in the pot. Blend the flesh of the chiles with more broth, add this to the pot, and continue cooking for 5 or 10 minutes. The aim is to have a fairly thick sauce.

Caldo Michi

Ingredients:

> 4 lb. catfish
> 1 *chayote* (prickly pear)
> 2 zucchinis
> $1/2$ small cabbage
> $1/2$ lb. fresh peas
> $1/2$ lb. potatoes
> $1/2$ lb. carrots
> $1/2$ lb. green tomatoes
> 10 *guajillo* chiles
> 2 *serrano* chiles (canned)
> 2 *chipotle* chiles (canned)
> 2 bay leaves
> A pinch of oregano
> 1 medium head of garlic
> 10 *xoconoztles* (the bitter fruit of the *agave* cactus)
> 1/3 cup wine vinegar
> Lime juice
> Salt

Cut the fish down the middle and open it up; rinse and drain. Coat it all over with salt and lime juice and leave it in the sun for 15 minutes to reduce the fishy smell. Wash it again in lukewarm water. Chop up the vegetables and cactus fruit, sauté them briefly, and then put them to boil. Add the whole head of garlic, the bay leaves, and the guajillo chiles. When all this is well cooked, add the fish. Boil for about half an hour. Just before serving, add the vinegar, the canned chiles, and the oregano.

Chongos Zamoranos

Ingredients:

> 4 pints milk
> 2 tablets rennet

2½ cups unrefined brown sugar
2 two-inch cinnamon sticks
Water

Heat the milk as advised by the rennet manufacturer. Stir in the rennet evenly, pour into a shallow dish, cover, and leave in a warm place for at least 2 hours. Make sure the mixture has set; when set, it will not stick to one's fingers. Leaving it in the pan, cut it into triangles or rectangles, sprinkle them with ½ cup sugar, and insert flakes of cinnamon along the cuts. Put the dish into the oven at a low temperature until the mixture is quite solid and begins to shrink. Leave it to cool down completely. When cool, lift out the pieces (*chongos*) and drain off any liquid. Make a syrup by dissolving 2 cups of sugar in water, adding one of the cinnamon sticks, and heating slowly while stirring frequently for about a quarter of an hour until the syrup thickens and clarifies. Leave to cool. Place the chongos on a serving dish (by this time they should be fairly soft on top and have brownish bubbles underneath). Pour the cool syrup over them and leave them in the refrigerator for an hour before serving.

Morelos

State Characteristics

Morelos is named in honor of the insurgent leader José María Morelos, who took up the torch of independence after the demise of Father Miguel Hidalgo in the early nineteenth century. Morelos was active in the state, but not a native of it.

The state is located in the middle of the country, with Mexico City and the state of México to its north, Guerrero to its south, and Puebla to its east. It has thirty-three administrative municipalities and is represented by eight people in the National Congress. The capital is Cuernavaca, population 332,197. Morelos is not a large state: at 4,958 square kilometers (1,934 square miles), it covers only 0.25 percent of the country and ranks number 30 among states in terms of area. However, the population of Morelos, according to the 2005 census, was 1,612,899, which is relatively high and ascribable to a benign climate coupled with proximity to the nation's capital. The census showed that 83.6 percent of the state population was Catholic and 7.3 percent Protestant or evangelical. Morelos has seven newspapers, six of them published in Cuernavaca, including *Diario de Morelos*, *Unión de Morelos*, and *El Regional del Sur. El Sol* is published both in Cuernavaca and in Cuautla. Morelos has two universities.

To the west of the state lie the mountains and valleys of the southern Sierra Madre, which cover about half of the state. The rest of it falls within the so-called Neovolcanic Axis, and its most important area is Anahuac, an area of lakes. Among the volcanoes is Mexico's most famous, Popocatépetl, which rises to almost 5,500 meters (18,000 feet) above sea level. Other

Countryside.

major volcanoes are Volcán Ololica (3,280 m/10,760 ft.) and Volcán Tesoyo (3,180 m/10,430 ft.). In several other places, the elevation exceeds 3,000 meters (10,000 feet).

Morelos is part of the Río Balsas system, which is one of the most important in Mexico. The major river in the state, flowing into the Balsas, is the Río Grande de Amacuzac; others are the Bajo Amacuzac, Cuautla, Apatlaco, Patlán, and Alto Amacuzac. For most of the state, the climate is moderate and very pleasant, with annual rainfall ranging between 800 and 1,000 millimeters (32–40 inches) and temperatures averaging from spring maxima of around 27°C (80°F) to winter lows of 20°C (68°F). In spring, the prevailing winds are from the east, in summer they veer to the southwest, and during the rest of the year they are from the northwest. The climate has made this state a popular retreat for the wealthy of Mexico City, which is only an hour away. Cuernavaca is dubbed "The City Where Spring Is Eternal."

In the higher reaches of the mountains, there are pines, *oyamel*, and other evergreens, while lower down one finds myrtles and *palo blanco*. Predominant varieties in the valleys are willows, bays, *ahuehuetes*, *amates*, and bracken. Coyotes, *tlalcoyotes*, foxes, hawks, eagles, and quail live in the mountains. In the valleys, there are many *chichichuilotes*, doves, and ducks. El Tepozteco, the Corredor Biológico Ajusco-Chichinautzin, and Xochicalco are conservation areas.

The state is said to have four main cultural regions: Zona Norte (north), Zona Oriente (east), Zona Sur Oeste (southwest), and Zona Centro (center).

Cultural Groups and Languages

The use of indigenous languages in modern Morelos is quite limited. In 2005, 1.8 percent of the population (24,757 people over age five) claimed to speak an indigenous language. Náhuatl was overwhelmingly the most widely spoken and accounted for about two-thirds of the total. The next most important language groups were the 3,576 speakers of Mixtec and the 1,361 speakers of Tlapaneco. Indigenous language use is largely restricted to the home context. However, some indigenous cultural practices do survive in the broader social context. Work on the *haciendas* during the second half of the nineteenth century, coupled by the homogenizing effects of the Revolution, drew the Nahuas into the wider community, moving them away from a culture based on the cultivation of corn simply for their own consumption. Bearing these factors in mind, some thirty communities are currently identified as "Indian," if not because of language use, then because they have managed to preserve some of their cultural practices. The municipalities with the highest Indian numbers are Ayala, Cuautla, Cuernavaca, Jiutepec, Puente de Ixtla, Temixco, Tepoztlán, and Tetela del Volcán.

Ayala exemplifies how immigrant Indian peoples (Tlapanecos and Mixtecs) have come to outnumber the Nahuas. The immigrants tend to work as agricultural day laborers (*jornaleros*). In the most economically advanced areas, such as Cuernavaca and Jiutepec, and generally in the northern part of the state, the Indians tend to live in great poverty. The mountainous areas to the north are where traditional indigenous practices are the strongest.

History

The first place known to have been inhabited in the area that is now Morelos was Tamoanchán. There is evidence of an Olmec presence from about 1500 BC, particularly in the reliefs found at the Cerro de Cantera in Chalcatzingo. Another important piece of archaeological evidence is the temple of the god Quetzalcóatl (dating from AD 650) in Xochicalco, suggesting influences from Teotihuacán, the Mayas, the Mixtecs, and the Zapotecs. After the fall of the Toltec empire (between 1250 and 1300), groups from the north came into Morelos, among them the Xochimilcas and the Tlahuicas. The former founded Hueyacapan, Tepoztlán, and Xumiltepec in the south, while the Tlahuicas settled in an area that came to be known as Cuauhnáhuac. A century later, the Mexicas were in control, and they would remain so until the arrival of the Spaniards. Under the Mexicas (more commonly known as the Aztecs), Morelos had two administrative regions: Cuernavaca and Oaxtepec.

Hernán Cortés and his conquistadores reached Texcoco in late December 1520, made an alliance with the Indian chieftain Ixtlilxochitl, and turned his attention to conquering the peoples of the surrounding lands, prior to making a definitive attack on the Aztec capital, Tenochtitlán. Cortés occupied Yautepec without a fight, engaged in battle at the Cerro de Zacapalótzin, and moved on to Jiutepec and the fortified Cuauhnáhuac, where there was more fighting. It appears that the inhabitants of Cuernavaca fled upon seeing the Spaniards approach. Having control of these places, Cortés proceeded to conquer Tenochtitlán in 1521.

During one of his visits to Cuernavaca, in 1523, Cortés founded the church of San José, which he put in the hands of Franciscan friars; at the same time, he brought water to the town and set up the first sugar plantation. As part of the process of evangelization, the Franciscans built the church of San Francisco and then a convent dedicated to Nuestra Señora de la Asunción, which would become Cuernavaca's cathedral. In 1529, Emperor Charles V made Cortés the Marquis of the Valley of Oaxaca and gave him vast (though scattered) lands that included 4,000 square kilometers (1,500 square miles) in Morelos, encompassing Cuernavaca and Oaxtepec, eighty communities, and 23,000 Indians. Cortés built himself a palace in Cuernavaca. The Augustinians came to the Tepoztlán region in 1533, and a little later the Dominicans evangelized central parts of the state.

During the eighteenth century, Cuernavaca became an essential staging post on the route to Acapulco and the Pacific, and a distribution center for products that came to Mexico from the Orient. It also became the home of some of the rich merchants of Taxco.

The favorable climate and the lie of the land—self-defining, enclosed, flat, and fertile—made the area one of rich agricultural production. The Tlahuicas had developed a calendar based on the agricultural cycle and were skilled farmers, specializing in cotton, which was the main currency with which they satisfied the tributes demanded of them by the Aztecs. After the arrival of the Spaniards, the Tlahuicas had to modify their activities and turn to growing and refining sugarcane. In the absence of slave labor of the kind used in the islands of the Caribbean islands, the Spaniards made the Indians slaves in all but name and developed the large haciendas that persisted well into the twentieth century.

At the time of the movement in favor of independence from Spain, a number of local people swelled the ranks of the insurgents. Francisco Ayala joined José María Morelos's army, and other prominent insurgents included Mariano Matamoros, Apolinar Matamoros, Joaquín Camacho, and Ignacio Noguera. During his campaign, Morelos went from Izúcar to Cuautla, Jojutla, Ixtla, the Hacienda de San Gabriel, Amacuzac, and Huajintlán and thence to Taxco. After his victory at the battle of Tecualoya, he moved on to Cuernavaca and back to Cuautla, hoping to launch a final attack on Mexico City. In 1812, however, forces loyal to Spain set out from Mexico City to engage the rebels at Cuautla. After two and a half months of fighting,

Cuautla lay in the hands of the loyalists and Morelos withdrew his troops and headed for the state of Puebla. Morelos, a native of Valladolid in the state of Michoacán, was a priest, like his mentor Miguel Hidalgo, the first leader of the insurgent movement. In 1815, Morelos was captured by the loyalists and, again like Father Hidalgo, defrocked and shot by a firing squad. However, Agustin de Iturbide and Vicente Guerrero then led the insurgent movement into Mexico City, and by 1821 Mexico's independence was secured.

The second and third quarters of the nineteenth century were difficult for Mexico, with often violent struggles for power between conservatives and liberals, the loss of Texas, and invasions by the United States and France. Sometimes the liberals looked to the United States for support, and the conservatives to Europe. During the war with the United States (1846–1847), Cuernavaca suffered severe losses and fell for a while to the invaders. Later, when the country was undergoing a process of reform that threatened vested interests, many conservatives welcomed the French Intervention. Napoleon III made Mexico an empire once again and installed an Austrian, Maximilian of Hapsburg, on its throne. Maximilian discovered the delights of Cuernavaca's Jardín Borda and made it his summer residence. A while later he acquired another tract of land in Acapantzingo, where he installed a lodge he called Olindo. One result of Maximilian's presence was that the road between Cuernavaca and Mexico City was upgraded; another was the early arrival of the telegraph. A few months later, in 1866, Maximilian was in Acapantzingo when he received news of Napoleon's withdrawal of French troops.

When the republic had first been constituted in 1824, Cuernavaca and Cuautla were lumped with the state of México. It was in 1869, under President Benito Juárez, that they were combined with parts of Guerrero and Puebla to make the new state of Morelos, partly as a means of fragmenting potential political opposition. Gen. Francisco Leyva (1836–1912), who had led republican forces against the French, was elected as its first governor, and the state constitution was ratified a year later. Leyva's period of tenure as governor was essentially a democratic one, during which he attempted to defend workers despite attacks by landowners; later, Leyva would be prominent in opposition to the reelection of Porfirio Díaz.

In the last half of the nineteenth century, the sugar industry made Morelos one of the richest states in the republic, with substantial exports to Europe. The haciendas that produced the sugar were quite self-contained and self-governing, their owners living in the lap of luxury and their workers in misery and debt. They grew in size as common land was sold off to them by the government, and their need for water led them to take control of the supplies on which smaller enterprises depended. By 1909, a mere twenty-eight hacienda owners held title to three-quarters of the state's land. As a result of hacienda growth, many communities lost their autonomy and were swallowed up.

The year 1873 saw the opening of the interoceanic railway line, which ran as far as Yautepec, but another twenty-five years passed before the first train arrived in Cuernavaca along a line from Mexico City. Improvements in communications were a trademark of the Díaz era. This was a time when foreign investment in Mexico dramatically increased, industry grew and modernized, and a small group of people became richer, especially those who had been rich in the first place. Poor people, and Indians in particular, were left behind. Díaz put his cronies in positions of power, bought the silence of some intellectuals, and recruited an army of ex-bandits, called the Rurales, to crush any opposition to him. In the later years of his long and authoritarian regime, rumblings of discontent became louder. **Agustín Aragón y León** (1870–1954) was an engineer who also wrote historical and sociological studies following the positivist philosophy that underlay Díaz's thinking, indeed Aragón served in government positions under Díaz before joining the opposition to his reelection and advocating reform of the 1857 Constitution.

The state went through a period of social unrest during the first decade of the twentieth century. Toward the end of 1910, in Villa de Ayala, a group of malcontents gathered in the house of **Pablo Torres Burgos** (1878–1911); among them were **Emiliano Zapata Salazar** (1879–1919), Rafael Merino, Catarino Perdomo, and Gabriel Tepepa, all sympathizers with the opposition led by Francisco Madero. A year later, Zapata, Merino, and Torres Burgos met in Cuautla at the time of its traditional fair, and a day later they staged an armed revolt in Villa de Ayala, after which Torres Burgos read out Madero's Plan de San Luis and publicly announced the start of the Revolution. Zapata was chosen as military commander for the south.

In 1911, Díaz stepped down from the presidency, and, after a short period with an interim president, Madero came to power. Though Madero spoke of the triumph of the Revolution, asking people to lay down their arms, the social realities of the country were largely unaffected by the change of power: the old order remained intact. In Morelos, Zapata claimed that, unless land and agricultural issues were addressed, there would be no peace. After failed negotiations between Madero and Zapata, the latter reaffirmed his opposition to the president, met with other revolutionaries, and drew up the Plan de Ayala, which called for Pascual Orozco to become president. Later, this plan was modified, depriving Orozco, an ally of Victoriano Huerta, of authority and giving more to Zapata.

In 1914, with both Madero and Huerta out of the picture, Venustiano Carranza, one of the major revolutionary leaders of the north, became president. He refused to accept the Plan de Ayala, however, whereupon Zapata refused to recognize Carranza's authority. At a convention of revolutionary leaders held in Aguascalientes that year, things did not go Carranza's way; he left Mexico City and headed for Veracruz, while other revolutionary forces occupied the capital. Then, in 1915, the revolutionary government moved its seat to Cuernavaca, while Carranza and his constitutionalists returned to Mexico City. Within two months, the Zapatistas had control of Cuernavaca, Cuautla, Yautepec, Villa de Ayala, Jonacatepec, Iguala, Taxco, Jojutla, and Tlaltizapán. In 1917, as the country acquired a new constitution, Zapata, the champion of peasants' rights, was betrayed and killed at the Hacienda de Chinameca.

With Alvaro Obregón in the presidency, José Parrés, Zapata's former doctor, became governor of Morelos. Although he and Obregón were both aware of how crucial the question of land redistribution was, and although he did create a number of *ejidos*, redistribution was not brought about as advocated in the Plan de Ayutla. In 1930, a peasant leader called Rubén Jaramillo asked that the sugar mills of Zacatepec be reorganized as a cooperative, but Mexico had to wait until the presidency of Lázaro Cárdenas for real change to come about. Jaramillo had fought alongside Zapata; he went on to found the Partido Agrario Obrero Morelense (Morelos Agricultural Workers' Party).

Economy

Morelos is one of the more prosperous states in Mexico, and one with an excellent infrastructure. It grows rice, sugarcane, beans, corn, wheat, coffee, avocados, mangoes, guavas, plums, *jícamas*, peanuts, and many vegetables. Its forestry provides pine, oak, and other woods. The rearing of livestock involves all the usual animals, plus donkeys and mules, and there is a wide range of poultry. There is also some fish farming.

Apart from sugar, the state's industries process wheat and cotton, make artificial fibers and textiles of cotton and wool, and produce chemicals, pharmaceutical products, and cars. Quite a large portion of the industrial production is sent abroad, mostly to other parts of North America, to Japan, and to Europe. Wood is dressed for construction or furniture making, drinks (both alcoholic and nonalcoholic) are made, foods are canned, and leather is tanned. Both Cuernavaca and Cuautla have industrial parks. About a third of the working population is involved in industry in one form or another.

Although mining is not a major activity, there is some production of gold, silver, and lead. Tourism is significant, but mostly domestic.

Arts

Crafts in Morelos include the ceramics of Tlayacapan, Tetela del Monte, and Salto de San Antón. There is also jewelry made from gold and silver, and metalwork using tin. Fabrics are used to make *rebozos*, *sarapes*, and traditional Indian clothing. There is some furniture making involving sedge.

Wind bands are common all over the state, performing in public squares. The most popular musical genres are *sones* and *corridos* (though locally they are called *bolas*) and, among dances, the *chinelos, apaches, moros y cristianos,* and *pastoras.* The dancers of chinelos are noted for their complicated jumps and somersaults.

Cuernavaca has attracted a number of internationally known Mexican artists and writers to live, such as David Alfaro Siqueiros and Carlos Fuentes. Two musicians of note who were born in Morelos are **Manuel León** (1882–1940), a composer with a highly varied output that includes the state anthem, and a sometime violinist in the Mexican Symphony Orchestra, and **Augusto Novaro** (1891–1960), who was self-taught and brought acoustic science to bear on music, inventing instruments characterized by having a spiral sound-chamber designed to purify sound and make it last. Novaro invented a system of tuning that was adopted by piano manufacturers such as Steinway and Baldwin, and he wrote theoretical works about music.

Social Customs

Major fiestas celebrated in the valleys include La Candelaria (in February) and Holy Week. May's Feast of Santa Cruz is important all over the state, as is September's San Miguel Arcángel. There is a regional fair in Cuautla during Lent, a Flower Festival in Cuernavaca in May, a Feria Comercial in Jojutla in January, and a *feria* in Tulanzingo to coincide with Holy Week. The Tepalcingo fair is the main one for Morelos, and it brings in visitors from other states. In June, Tequesquitengo holds a triathlon. The 25th of January and of July are the dates of festivities in Axochiapan, the first being the Día de San Pablo and the second Santiago Apóstol; both days are marked by fireworks, processions, and traditional dances such as the aztecas, moros y cristianos, *tecuanes, locos,* and *doce pares.*

For the chinelos dance, the impressive traditional dress appears to have Moorish origins. It begins with a large funnel-shaped hat whose widest part is at the top and which is ringed with arched wire strings of "pearls." There are tassels threaded through thin tubes of plastic that run down the body of the hat and are arranged into letters or figures. Embroidered parts represent animal or human figures or Indian deities. A scarf is worn around the neck and a mask on the face. This mask is also made of covered wires; it has exaggerated features that usually include a pointed beard and a wide moustache. The cloak runs full length and has long sleeves; it is usually made of black velvet, which contrasts with a bright border in a single color that traditionally is made of rabbit fur or feathers.

On May 19, Cuautla recalls the battle that took place there in the days of José María Morelos. Also in May, Cuernavaca celebrates the Día de San Isidro Labrador, and Ixcatepec the Día del Señor de Ixcatepec, which has its roots in pre-Hispanic times, when the ruler of the town would make a pilgrimage to greet the ruler of another, Milpa Alta. Carnival is widely celebrated, for example, in Tepoztlán and in Yautepec. Yeccapixtla has a procession and dancing, including the characteristic *chinelos*, to mark the Feast of San Marcos in April; in October it hosts the Feria del Gran Tianguis, a huge open-air market conveniently supplied with, *inter alia*, things used for celebrating the Day of the Dead.

On the last Sunday in September, Zacualpan has its Festival de las Mojigangas, which is full of color and merrymaking. Children dress up as women and play the *mojigangas* (giant papier mâché figures) in a procession headed by three women on horseback, one of them bearing the standard of the town's patroness, the Virgen del Rosario—all of which is a preamble to her feast day in early October. There is a crafts and food fair at the same time.

A good example of a hybrid of indigenous and Hispanic practices is the so-called Reto del Tepozteco (Tepozteco Challenge). On September 8, a procession leaves Morelia and heads for the Tepozteco pyramid, where offerings are made in remembrance of the conversion of King Tepoztécatl to Catholicism.

Noteworthy Places

About a thousand places of archaeological interest have been identified in Morelos. Among them are Chalcatzingo, Cuernavaca, Coatlán del Río, Coatetelco, Gualupita, Xochicalco, Teopanzolco, Tepoztlán, Tepozteco, Las Pilas, and Olintepec. Teopanzolco, one of the principal sites, was ceremonial, a place of many human sacrifices on its pyramid dedicated to the gods of war (Huitzilopochtli) and rain (Tláloc). Other structures at the site are in honor of minor deities. The Zona Arqueológica de Xochicalco is a fortified site set on a hill, with terraces, squares, and platforms connected by stairs and porticos. It has three ball courts, an observatory, a major pyramid with an imposing staircase, and smaller ones, including the Pyramid of the Plumed Serpents. A slope displays more than 250 carved stone reliefs of animals. There are a governors' palace and a number of other structures whose function is less clear.

Cortés's palace in Cuernavaca (Cuauhnáhuac) was begun in 1530 and set on a Tlahuica ceremonial site. It remained in the hand of Cortés's family for a long time. For a while after that, it was used as a state legislative building, and now it is the state Regional Museum. In addition to pre-Hispanic and colonial exhibits, it has murals by Diego Rivera. Other early colonial buildings in Cuernavaca are the cathedral, once a Franciscan monastery, the Iglesia de la Tercera Orden, and the Iglesia de Guadalupe. The cathedral was completed in 1552 and is much like a fortress; it contains some interesting sixteenth-century frescoes. Robert Brady was a U.S. artist and art collector who traveled to Italy and then made his home in Cuernavaca, where his former residence, once part of a monastery, is now a private museum, with pieces ranging from the pre-Hispanic era to modern times. The Muros Museum displays works from the Gelman collection. South of the center of Cuernavaca is another museum set in a restored residence that once was used by Emperor Maximilian for trysts with his Indian lover; it now displays regional flora, with information on their medicinal and nutritional properties. The garden called the Jardín Borda, also in central Cuernavaca, dates back to the late eighteenth century. José de la Borda was a silver magnate from Taxco who made it his summer residence; on his death, it became a botanical garden, and later it was taken over by Maximilian and his wife, Carlota. The Casa Estudio de David Alfaro Siqueiros is the painter's house, preserved as it was at the time of his death in 1974.

Close to Cuernavaca there are the remains of sugar mills, for example at Atlacomulco. The Hacienda de Temizco has been turned into a spa. Elsewhere, Cuautla has the Casa de Morelos, Coatelco and Tepoztlán their archaeological museums, and Jantetelco a historical museum. Among places of natural interest are the San Antón waterfalls, the Parque Nacional Lagunas de Zempoala, and the Parque Natural Las Estacas.

Cuisine

Tlacoyos rellenos de frijol (large, stuffed tortillas), *cecina con guacamole* (rehydrated dried beef with guacamole), *torta de nopales* (pieces of cactus with eggs, chiles, garlic, and onion), *guajolote en mole verde de pepita* (turkey in a green *mole* sauce), *tamales de iguana*, and *quesadillas de flor de calabaza* (quesadillas filled with pumpkin blossoms) are examples of Morelos's typical dishes. It is claimed that the best cecina in Mexico comes from Yecapixtla. Typical of the desserts are *alegrías*, *nieves de frutas* (fruit slushies), sometimes made with avocados, *jamoncillo de pepita* (ground pumpkin seeds mixed with milk and brown sugar), and *palanqueta* (a sort of peanut bar). Drinks include *pulque*, which is fermented from cactus; *mosco*, a liqueur based on oranges; and *nanche*, which is a complicated liqueur involving alcohol from sugarcane, chiles, and the fruit of the loquat tree.

Cerdo en Salsa de Cacahuate

Ingredients:

2 lb. lean pork, in one piece
$^1/_2$ cup peanuts, ground into a paste
1 *chipotle* chile, cleaned and deveined
2 *poblano* chiles, cleaned and deveined
2 medium tomatoes
$^1/_2$ onion, chopped
2 cloves of garlic, chopped
2 peppercorns
2 bay leaves
Ground cinnamon

1 tsp sugar
Vegetable broth
Vinegar
2 oz. red wine
Oil
Salt

Prick the pork all over and rub cinnamon and salt over it. Brown the meat evenly in oil, then lift it out. Puree the peanuts, chiles, garlic, onion, tomatoes, peppercorns, bay leaves, and sugar together, then fry the mixture gently in the oil and juice left by the meat. After a few minutes, return the meat to the pot, add some broth, the wine, and the vinegar, cover and leave to simmer for about 45 minutes, making sure that it does not dry out.

Jamoncillo de Pepita

Ingredients:

4 cups pumpkin seeds
4 cups milk
3 cups unrefined brown sugar

Soak the seeds overnight in water. Drain them and rub them to remove any husk, then grind them with half a cup of milk until they turn into a smooth paste. Put the rest of the milk to boil in a pan, along with the sugar. When it begins to thicken, take it off the heat, add the pumpkin seed mixture, stir well, and put it back on a low heat, stirring until it begins to clarify. At that point, remove the pan from the heat. As it cools, beat it vigorously until it reaches the point where it is possible to shape it with one's hands. Make a ball or log with it and leave it to cool for several hours before cutting and serving.

Clemole

Ingredients:

1 large hen
10 *cascabel* chiles
$1/2$ lb. *ancho* chiles
$1/2$ lb. tender corn kernels
$1/2$ lb. green beans
$1/2$ lb. zucchini, chopped
$1/2$ tsp black pepper
1 large onion
2 cloves of garlic
4 cloves
Pork lard
Salt and pepper

Cut up the bird. Boil the pieces in water, adding half an onion in large pieces, one crushed clove of garlic, and some salt. Tie the cloves and peppercorns in a muslin bag and put the bag into the pot. While the meat is cooking, prepare the sauce. Roast the chiles, then soak them in warm water. Remove them, clean them out, and then grind them with some garlic, clove, and black pepper. Finally, fry the mixture briefly in the lard with some slices of onion. Once the meat is thoroughly cooked, add the corn, the green beans, and the zucchini. After a short time, add the sauce and leave to simmer for five or ten minutes.

Nayarit

State Characteristics

The name Nayarit comes from a revered leader of the Cora Indians, Nayar, who founded a kingdom high up in the mountains of the Sierra Madre Occidental. Nayarit means "Son of God, close to the heavens and the sun." The state is roughly halfway down Mexico's west coast. Sinaloa, Durango, and Zacatecas are the states to its north, and Jalisco is to the south and east. Nayarit covers 27,864 square kilometers (10,871 square miles) including the Islas Marías and Isla Isabel. With only 1.4 percent of Mexico's total area, Nayarit is one of the country's smallest states, the twenty-seventh in size.

The 2005 census gave the total state population as 949,684 and the percentage of indigenous-language speakers as 5 percent. Nayarit has seven representatives in the National Congress. There are twenty municipalities, grouped into five districts: Acaponeta, Tepic (the most populous), Santiago Ixcuintla (the second most populous), Compostela, and Ixtlán. The state capital is Tepic, whose population in 2005 was 295,204. The main port is San Blas. The religious breakdown in Nayarit is 93 percent Catholic, 2 percent Protestant or evangelical, 0.1 percent Jewish, and the rest unspecified or atheist. For a small state with a modest population, Nayarit has an extraordinary total of fourteen newspapers; one of these, *El Eco de Nayarit*, is published in Acaponeta, and all the rest in Tepic, including *Express*, *El Meridiano*, *El Tiempo de Nayarit*, *El Sol de Nayarit*, and *Avance*.

Nayarit has five regions: Centro, Norte, Sierra, Sur, and Costa Sur. From the standpoint of physical geography, the dominant features are the Sierra Madre Occidental mountains, the Llanura Costera del Pacífico (Pacific lowlands), the Eje Neovolcánico (Neovolcanic Axis), and the Sierra Madre del Sur (southern Sierra Madre). The highest elevations are the Cerro El Vigía at 2,760 meters above sea level (9,050 feet), Sierra El Pinabete (2,500 m/8,200 ft.), Cerro Dolores (2,460 m/8,070 ft.), Sierra Los Huicholes (2,400 m/7,870 ft.), Sierra Pajaritos (2,360 m/7,740 ft.), Volcán Sangangüey (2,340 m/7,675 ft.), and Volcán del Ceboruco (2,280 m/7,524 ft.).

This state is unusually well supplied with rivers: there are twenty, of which the principal ones are the Grande (or Santiago), the San Pedro, the Acaponeta, the Ameca, and the Cañas. In addition, there are many dams—the main ones being the Presa de Aguamilpa, Presa San Rafael, and Presa Amado Nervo—and saltwater lagoons such as Laguna de Agua Brava and the Laguna de Santa María del Oro.

Despite cold temperatures in the mountains, much of the state has a warm and relatively moist climate that favors an agricultural economy. Rainfall along the coastal plains and over about half the state can be quite substantial, between 900 and 1,500 millimeters (36–60 inches) annually. The average annual temperature for the state is 21°C (70°F).

In the mountain areas, conifers (pine, *ocote*, *oyamel*) are predominant, along with more valuable woods such as cedar and oak. In the valleys, there are fruit trees, and in the lowlands, crops such as corn, tobacco, cotton, and beans. Among fauna there are deer, coyotes, pumas and other wild cats, and boars; there are also quail, ducks, macaws, geese, and many small birds. Coastal areas have a wide variety of seabirds, fish, and shellfish.

Cultural Groups and Languages

Among the population over five years of age, there were 41,689 speakers of indigenous languages, according to the 2005 census. Numerically speaking, the principal cultural groups that are still found in Nayarit are the Huicholes and the Coras, with the Tepehuanes in a distant third place. Most of the Indians are in the municipality of El Nayar, but there are also some in Huajicori, La Yesca, Jala, Santa María del Oro, Tepic, Rosamorada, Ruíz, and Acaponeta. Approximately 12 percent of speakers of indigenous languages do not also speak Spanish. Huichol is spoken by 19,722 people, Cora by 16,569, and Tepehuano by 1,649. Less common languages are Náhuatl, Purépecha, Mazahua, and Tlapaneco. Almost 2,000 people are listed as speaking "unspecified" indigenous languages.

The Tepehuanes are also found in the states of Durango and Zacatecas. Another group, the Mexicaneros, coexists with them in Nayarit, in the same areas. The coastal Coras are found in the municipality of Ruiz. There are more Huicholes in northern Jalisco than there are in Nayarit, but those who do live there are in the municipalities of El Nayar and La Yesca. In addition to being in the mountains and in one or two towns, some Huicholes live close to the coast. These have largely lost their traditional customs, though they may still speak the language.

The traditional basis of the economy for all these groups is agriculture; they cultivate maize (corn) and to a lesser extent beans, sugarcane, squashes, sweet potatoes, peanuts, and chiles, almost exclusively for their own consumption. Their lands are communal and their farming implements simple. The Huicholes also raise cattle for sale to the *mestizos*. Some Indians work in very poorly paid jobs on lands belonging to non-Indian people. Malnutrition and consequently diseases among the Indians are fairly common; infant mortality is quite high.

History

Designs carved or painted on rocks at Huajicori, the Cerro de Cuamiles, the Cañón de Boquillas, and El Tambor suggest that the earliest inhabitants of Nayarit were there between 5000 and 1000 BC. Further evidence—ceramics, tombs, clay figurines, and metal vessels—indicates a developing culture that reached its zenith in Ixtlán from about 900 to 1200. The Indian tradition speaks of a north–south migration and suggests links between the peoples of western Mexico and others to the north, such as the Apaches and the Seris. There was constant warfare among the various peoples. Some groups lived in relative isolation from the rest; this was favored by the mountains, and it helped them maintain their different languages, traditions, and practices.

One result of the diversity and independence of so many Indian peoples was that they did not present a united front against the Spanish invaders. It appears that when the latter arrived, the peoples of Nayarit had not become subject to the Aztecs, despite which Náhuatl, the Aztec language, was something of a lingua franca among them. The Spaniards encountered Coras, Huicholes, Huaynamotas, Tepehuanes, Jaliciences, and others in the mountains. To the south, in Ixtlán, there were Nahuas. The lowland peoples of Aztatlan and Acaponeta were both numerous and prosperous, and they were sworn enemies of the mountain groups.

After conquering the Aztec capital Tenochtitlán, Hernán Cortés had turned his attention to the west, sending a relative, Francisco Cortés de San Buenaventura, to explore the realm of Xalisco. Francisco Cortés proved to be a peaceful and moderate man, in stark contrast with a later and infamous explorer of western parts of the country, Nuño Beltrán de Guzmán. Cortés was received royally in Xalisco and without any real resistance elsewhere, except in the case of the mountain region, whose inhabitants had so long fought against the indigenous peoples of the lowlands.

Beltrán, a rival of Hernán Cortés, left Mexico City in 1530 with a sizable army of Spaniards and very many more Indian allies, to murder and plunder his way toward Michoacán and beyond. Any peaceful coexistence there may have been between Spaniards and lowland Indians under Francisco Cortés was sabotaged by Beltrán's forces, whose destructive advance provoked an uprising by Ixtlán, Ahuacatlán, and coastal tribes. This rebellion only gave Beltrán an excuse to overwhelm them by force and destroy or confiscate their possessions. Those Indians who survived did so by surrendering to the conquerors or by fleeing to the hills or swamps. In July 1532, the Spaniards founded a settlement they called Compostela, which was to become today's Tepic. Six Spaniards were allotted *encomiendas* there, which meant that they had control of the Indians and of the benefits of their labors, but also the duty to see to their conversion to Catholicism. Beltrán's cruelty, together with the mistreatment of Indians by Spaniards under the encomienda system, were the motivating factors behind the protests of Fray Bartolomé de Las Casas, one of a number of friars who spoke up for the Indians, drawing the attention of the authorities to what had been happening.

In 1538, the people of Ahuacatlán, Jocotlan, and Hostotipaquillo made an alliance with Xocotepec, believing that the time had come to confront the invaders. They took to arms, using the deep ravines of Mochitilic as a natural defense. Fearing that other peoples might join the resistance, the Spaniards quickly engaged them in a bloody battle, but did not destroy them completely. The possibility of further uprisings engendered concern for the safety of the inhabitants of Tepic, so the Spaniards resolved to move the town to its present-day location. In 1540, they built the first of Nayarit's monasteries, the Convento de Xalisco.

In 1541, the Indians rebelled again. This time, they took advantage of the fact that Spanish forces had been depleted by the departure of a new expedition heading north in search of greater riches. The rebel Indians refused to pay their tribute to the *encomenderos*, defeated Indian allies of the Spaniards, and beseiged the center of Tepic. Meanwhile another campaign of resistance was being waged in the mountains. The viceroy himself, alarmed at these rebellions, arrived with thousands of reinforcements, and after fierce fighting, both uprisings were crushed. But this did not mean an end to rebellions. For example, communications between the highlands and lowlands improved, but they were subject to occasional outbreaks of violence. The mountains became a haven not only for rebel Indians but also for criminals and for the persecuted.

From the early days of colonization, the Franciscans had been traveling the mountain areas and dealing peacefully with the Indians, trying to persuade them to abandon their bellicose ways, but with only partial success. An exceptional example of a constructive and peaceful friar was **Andrés de Medina** (fl. late sixteenth century), of the Acaponeta Monastery. Over a period of twenty years, and with the help of Christianized Indians, he persuaded mountain rebels to come down to Acaponeta, change their lifestyle, live in townships, and cultivate the land. When the authorities transferred him to Guadalajara, the Indians protested; some returned to the mountains, and a delegation of about sixty went to Mexico City, where they successfully petitioned the viceroy for his return. In subsequent years, Father Medina founded several more townships.

By the early seventeenth century, the disastrous decline in Indian numbers due to disease or hostilities had slowed. Towns were growing and becoming more prosperous, and roads, bridges, and schools were being built. The economy was based on agriculture and livestock; on the *haciendas* grazed cattle that were driven in huge herds down to Guadalajara or Mexico City. Gold and silver mining attracted people of all sorts to the region, but prospectors who invaded the hills in search of riches disturbed the mountain dwellers, who responded by burning down their settlements. Unrest of this kind continued for many years until the Spanish authorities were emboldened by the development of the region and came to regard the Indian resistance as scandalous. The Spaniards were obsessed with the possibility of finding a mythical gateway through the mountains, to what they imagined was an uncharted and promising land. (Curiously, the Huicholes also have a myth of a magical gateway as part of their ritual pilgrimage to Viricota, during which they must pass through five passages that are guarded by blue stags.)

Early in the eighteenth century, there was a last attempt to convert the Indians and bring them under control by peaceful means, but they wished to be left to their ways. They came down from the mountains to attack Spanish towns and then found themselves cut off, under a blockade and without the salt that was so essential to their way of life. The Spanish Crown instructed that they be brought into the fold once and for all, entrusting the task to Juan de la Torre, a man who had the Indians' trust and spoke their language. De la Torre managed to convince an Indian leader to take a delegation to Mexico City and pay their respects to the viceroy, but having done so, on their return they were confronted by their people, who accused them of betrayal. Following the failure of this and other peaceful initiatives by de la Torre, the authorities sent a military expedition to put an end to the matter, and after a lot of fighting, the Sierra was pacified. For good measure, the skeleton of the King of Nayarit was sent to Mexico City, along with some valued artifacts. In order not to lose control, the Spaniards now built forts and towns in the mountains.

Nayarit's first port, Matachén, was founded in 1744. By 1768, it had been replaced by San Blas, which from then until 1792 enjoyed its golden years as one of the principal west coast ports in Mexico, a period during which seven Jesuit expeditions left from San Blas, heading for the Californias or the Philippines. In Nayarit itself, the Jesuits had done a great deal to help the Indian transition from traditional mountain life to life in settled missions, with their own cultivable land, helping them also to improve their nutrition and encouraging them to coexist peacefully with others. But the Jesuits were banned from the New World in 1767; in their eight missions in Nayarit they left three thousand people, of whom only about three hundred were not Indians. The mission work was taken over by the Franciscans, but it was not long before the missions faced decline. There were some disturbances in Nayarit during the second half of the century, but none major enough to rock the Spanish boat until rumors began to circulate about the appearance of an Indian leader called El Indio Mariano, alias "Máscara de Oro," who was seeking independence for the region. Some historians have seen this man as a precursor of Mexico's independence movement, while others have doubted his very existence. What does seem clear is that the rumors unsettled the authorities, who even suspected some form of foreign conspiracy might be involved.

They had reason to be worried, in view of the unrest among the poor masses, the resentment felt by the *criollos*, and what had been going on in Europe—namely, Spain's political instability and the rise in revolutionary thinking. In September 1810, Father Miguel Hidalgo issued his call for Mexican independence from Spain. The Franciscan friar who was in charge of the missions in the mountains of Nayarit tried to stop news of the insurgency from spreading, but it was a vain attempt.

The outstanding local figure among the insurgents was the young parish priest of Ahualulco, **José María Mercado** (1781–1811), with the backing of a wealthy and influential landowner, Juan José Zea, added his voice to Hidalgo's. A month after Hidalgo's call for independence, Mercado set out with fifty men and peacefully occupied Tepic's main square, after which his army grew to two thousand men and he went on to take San Blas. Despite the fact that this last Spanish stronghold was far better equipped with weaponry and professional soldiers, within seventeen days it was under Mercado's control, and not a single person had been killed. However, this was not the end of the affair. Royalist troops defeated Hidalgo, and Mercado's forces were infiltrated by royalist sympathizers, who launched a surprise attack on San Blas. Mercado was shot and Zea hanged in 1811; Zea's body was left on show on the edge of Tepic for more than six months.

Now Tepic and other towns fell back into royalist hands and there followed a period of bloody civil war. As in the past, the mountain region proved to be one of the most difficult for those loyal to Spain to control, and a place where rebels could hide. The movement toward independence lasted eleven years, until 1821, when criollos led by Agustín de Iturbide and rebel forces led by Vicente Guerrero came to an agreement that led to Mexico becoming independent. As the republic took shape, Nayarit was designated a canton of Jalisco in the Constituent Congress that took place in 1824. At that time, Jalisco had some 650,000 inhabitants and the area that is now Nayarit only about 55,000; it was decided that there should be approximately one representative for every 20,000 people, so that Nayarit was allotted three.

The nineteenth century in Mexico was turbulent and insecure, with frequent confrontations between liberals and conservatives on the political front, problems with other nations (the United States and France) and continuing social inequalities. The middle of the century was when Mexico lost Texas and found itself being invaded by the United States. In the concluding battle of that war, **Juan Escutia** (1827–1847) was one of the

military cadets, the "Niños Héroes," who sacrificed themselves at Chapultepec Castle in Mexico City.

A more complex distinguished son was **Manuel Lozada** (1828–1873).
Lozada first gained a reputation as a bandit. In 1857, a group of Cora Indians led by Lozada, who became known as "El Tigre de Álica" (the Tiger
from Álica), attacked an hacienda in the municipality of Santa María del
Oro; it seems that Lozada had a personal grudge to settle there. But Lozada,
a man from a humble background, was also a fighter for the rights of poor
mountain people. He became prominent at a time of great rivalry between
two local factions, Los Barrón and Los Castaños. Lozada went from being a
bandit to making an alliance with the Barrón faction, which helped finance
his operations. In 1857, he declared his support for the conservatives,
against Benito Juárez. Then he seemed to shift to the side of the liberals
when in 1862 he signed a peace treaty with the governor of Jalisco. Two
years later, Lozada signed another document, recognizing the legitimacy of
Maximilian, the emperor who had been installed by the French, and he
was decorated by the French in recognition of his support in fighting the
liberal opposition. Once it became clear that the empire was at an end,
Lozada declared himself to be neutral. With the republic restored and
Juárez back in power in Mexico City, Lozada managed to keep in the president's favor until Juárez's death in 1873. However, in 1870 Lozada took up
arms once again, calling on the poor and needy to fight for autonomy. After
Juárez's death, Lozada felt threatened, so he decided to take matters into
his own hands by gathering an army of six thousand men and marching on
Guadalajara. But the authorities had decided that it was time to put an end
to his activities; close to Guadalajara, federal troops halted Lozada's
advance, his army disbanded, and he was eventually tracked down and
shot.

In 1859, Maximilian had divided up his empire into fifty departments,
one of which was named Nayarit—the first time that name had been used
to refer to a political entity, although it had previously been in use for a
geographical one, the Sierra de Nayarit. Tensions between Jalisco and
Nayarit were considerable; once Lozada was out of the way, Jalisco wanted
to reassert its control, but from 1868 on there were arguments by Jalisco's
opponents that the central government should create a state of Tepic.
Juárez acceded to neither interest, and instead he created a Distrito Militar
de Tepic, directly answerable to Mexico City. To the extent that it now
became governed by its own elected official, it was a de facto state. Despite more attempts by Jalisco to regain control of Tepic, the latter was
later elevated to the status of a territory, and eventually it became an autonomous state, but not until 1917.

The armed conflict that lasted for a decade after the start of the Reform
Movement in 1857 made for a settling of accounts between the rich and
the poor, and between the lowland and highland people; it was as if there
were a continuation of the earlier colonial conflicts. In the nineteenth

century, the mountain dwellers and the people in the missions were in abject poverty, while the lower areas were being transformed by large haciendas, such as those devoted to sugar, whose demands threatened the supply of water. Rival liberal and conservative forces signed a peace treaty in 1880, and then Porfirio Díaz became president. There had been continuing rebellions since the days of Lozada, but they had been put down. In 1884 came the last of them, a rebellion provoked by the fact that land was in the hands of so few people.

The authoritarian era of Díaz ushered in many developments, such as increased investment in industrialization, improved communications, and better education. Unfortunately, these changes benefited only a minority of Mexicans, and the rural communities in particular were left behind. The more stable environment encouraged immigration: between 1843 and 1910—the end of the *porfiriato*—the population almost tripled. In 1894, a labor movement, led by women, took shape at one of the state's major textile factories, Bellavista; in 1896, there was another one in Jauja, and in 1905 a second at Bellavista. The beginning of the new century found Tepic undergoing a slow and difficult development, in part because of bad communications. While for many parts of Mexico the porfiriato had meant the arrival of the railroad, in Nayarit it came only in 1912, after Díaz's long rule was over. A rail connection with Guadalajara had to wait until 1926.

In 1911, when the Revolution in the north of the country gained impetus, Ixtlán and Ahuacatlán—towns that had been at loggerheads since the days of Lozada (the first being liberal, the second conservative)—became allies. The inhabitants of Ixtlán took up arms but did not have to engage in any fighting until after the departure of Díaz. The same cannot be said for neighboring Ahuacatlán, which suffered serious losses. Revolutionary groups, including people from Sinaloa, marched into Tepic in May of that year. Not long after Francisco Madero came to power, there was a women workers' rebellion in Jauja in protest against the twelve-hour day and low wages; the women lost their jobs. Then, in 1912, on the day the railroad first came to Tepic, workers at the Casa Aguirre seized the chance to demand better conditions of the visiting vice president, José María Pina Suárez; their demand was unsuccessful, so they then went on strike.

After the assassination of Madero, Victoriano Huerta took over the presidency of the country. Huerta was denounced by Venustiano Carranza, then governor of Coahuila, and thereafter a number of rebel groups engaged federal forces in the northern states. For example, in Acaponeta in March 1913, there was a fierce battle from which the revolutionaries had to retreat, but in November of that year they defeated the federal troops at Sauta and Navarrete, and by May of the following year they had taken the strategic prize, Tepic.

With Alvaro Obregón in the presidency, there were reforms, and punishments for some who had supported the old order. The way began to open up for the creation of labor organizations; in 1916, workers in several towns celebrated their first "Labor Day," and the first union was established—for the textile workers at the Bellavista factory. Soon after that, the factory was turned into a workers' cooperative. At the Constituent Congress that Carranza called in Querétaro, in December of 1916, he proposed the creation of a new state of Nayarit, a proposal that bore fruit in the new year.

The Revolution, however, was by no means over; the Cristero War had yet to come, and chaos would last into the 1930s. According to the terms of its new constitution, during the period 1918–1934, Nayarit would normally have had four governors; in fact, it had thirty-two, some of them lasting for only a matter of days. Francisco Parra (1934–1937) was the first governor not to be ousted by a coup or some other form of rebellion. This was the period during which the social and economic structures associated with the vast old estates broke down; many people lost their lives in the fight for land redistribution. Even after President Lázaro Cárdenas came to power, there were still occasional outbreaks of violence.

The late 1940s saw some further modernization. By 1969, Nayarit had a university, by 1972 an institute of technology. Toward the end of the twentieth century, dams to aid the generation of hydroelectric power were built, an airport was opened at Tepic, and major new highways went into service.

Economy

The discovery of gold in California gave a boost to the port of San Blas, as did the closure of the port of Acapulco early in the movement for independence from Spain. For some fifty years thereafter, San Blas prospered as the main west coast port through which goods were shipped in and out of Guadalajara to Europe, the Orient, and the north. The increased trade meant that Tepic, for which San Blas was the port, grew rapidly; many people would migrate from the latter to the former during the summer months to avoid disease and bad weather. The importance of San Blas and Tepic did not escape the British, who opened a consulate in 1823. Signs of the former prosperity and international significance of these places could be seen in the presence of the Barrón family, which was of Irish descent, in the existence of a Forbes College, and in the prominence in commercial activities of Spanish, French, German, and Italian nationals. The affluence also drew many Mexicans from other states. The prosperity of San Blas did not last, however. Later in the nineteenth century, it was beset by political and military crises, and for a while Mazatlán became the most active port. Not only was Tepic a divided city, but there were problems with bandits along the roads.

By the beginning of the twentieth century, Tepic was undergoing slow modernization. The great estates on the coast were producing tobacco and cotton, and those inland, coffee, which were of sufficient value to compensate for the difficulties in transportation, but low prices meant that it was not profitable to ship out quantities of such plentiful commodities as corn, beans, and barley. Thousands of workers were employed in the mines, but here too the transportation problem limited the extent of exploitation of natural resources. The main factories were in Tepic; they were well equipped and produced textiles, soap, sugar, and distilled liquor. However, their workers were poorly paid and much exploited, and this provoked a number of organized protests. As was the case all over Mexico, the years under President Díaz had brought some progress, but the benefits had gone to a minority or to foreign interests. In the territory of Tepic, a large part of the wealth lay in very few hands: seven families and two companies controlled 75 percent of the land and its riches.

The Revolution did not change the lot of the poor a great deal, but it did bring a change in the balance of activity; for example, there was a decline in sugar production and an increase in other agricultural products, such as coffee and corn. While the state in general had water, it did not have the irrigation systems that would allow full use of the land, and the problem of isolation remained. A third of the state belonged to Casa Aguirre, a Spanish company that had control of thirty haciendas, the main electricity plant, the two main textile factories, and the water, gasoline, and lumber supplies. It was during the time of President Cárdenas that agrarian reforms came, albeit in a some-what irregular way: the lands were occupied and the haciendas dissolved. By 1939, Nayarit was being referred to as the *ejido* state. However, the towns siphoned off resources, with the result that the rural people's newly acquired lands did not resolve their problems. Some peasants were ill-equipped to man-age their own land, and in any case, many of the lands they now owned were neither very fertile nor extensive enough to be economically viable.

Only with the arrival of the train and with better roads could economic progress begin, and when it did come, it came very slowly. Agriculture con-tinued to be the state's main occupation. In industry, there was even a slight decline during the first half of the twentieth century, although textile production picked up during World War II. Between 1940 and 1980, the population of Nayarit grew, as did that of the country at large, by about 350 percent. There was greater development of natural resources—and the depletion of some, such as forests.

Modern Nayarit is still predominantly an agricultural state, and in many respects it is still an unspoiled one. The central region (Centro) has most of the industry and commerce; the northern one (Norte) has high-tech farming, especially livestock, and also fishing; the mountain region (Sierra) provides lumber; the southern region (Sur) has seasonal crops, livestock, and exploit-able lagoons; and the southern coastal region (Costa Sur) is the main focus of the tourist industry, in addition to having agriculture and livestock.

Currently, approximately 20 percent of the land is given over to the culti-vation of beans, sorghum, sugarcane, corn, and tobacco; 6 percent is pas-tureland; 35 percent is highland forest; and a similar percentage is lowland woods. Seventy-three percent of all cultivable land is planted with annual crops, and the rest with perennials. In addition to the crops already listed, there are rice, chiles, peanuts, melons, tomatoes, coffee, mangoes, bananas, and avocados. The state accounts for 2.6 percent of national production in this sector. A good deal of the produce is shipped to Guadalajara and Mexico City, Mexico's two biggest cities, and some of it (especially fruits) goes to the United States and Europe. Honey production is also significant.

Cattle are the most important livestock, followed by pigs, goats, horses, and sheep. Chickens dominate poultry production. Nayarit accounts for 1.2 percent of national livestock production. There are usable woods ranging from mountain varieties such as pine and oak to more temperate varieties such as cedar and mahogany. Pine and oak are the most widely available. Nayarit produces 1.6 percent of Mexico's lumber for industrial purposes and has the potential to produce more.

Nayarit's 289 kilometers (180 miles) of coastline, with its broad continental shelf offering estuaries and saltwater lagoons, favor prosperous fishing and aquaculture. There are seventy-five cooperatives and many labor organizations related to the fishing industry. Aquaculture (of catfish, tilapia, and shrimp) is strong in San Blas, Santiago Ixcuintla, Tecuala, Tuxpan, and Rosamorada. Among the many varieties of seafood that are exploited are swordfish, shark, bass, snapper, and oysters. Fishing represents about 2.4 percent of national production. Nayarit receives a significant number of migratory workers who come to the most productive agricultural areas (Tepic and the coast) for seasonal work.

The most important industrial activities are food and drink processing, together with making tobacco products. About a third of the annual tobacco production is exported as cigarettes. Sugarcane growing allows the production of alcoholic drinks. There is a certain amount of mining, mainly of nonmetallic substances such as limestone and kaolin. Salt production is also quite important. There are several *maquiladoras* that assemble goods from U.S.-made components for sale north of the border. Nayarit is a major and increasingly important provider of energy to other parts of Mexico.

Tourism is a key and growing component of the service sector; restaurants and hotels provide about 40 percent of the gross income of this sector. The main coastal destinations for tourists are in the municipalities of San Blas, Santiago Ixcuintla, Tecuala, and Compostela. There are fears that rapid development in these and other towns during recent years might bring as much harm as benefit.

From a socioeconomic standpoint, the state continues to grapple with real inequalities, inadequate provision of health care, and insufficient educational opportunities.

Arts

Nayarit is proud of the creative products of its indigenous peoples. These include waxed wooden objects, such as masks and animal heads, decorated with several colors. Gourds are put to decorative and practical use. The Tepehuanes make cloth rucksacks that are in some demand outside their communities. The Mexicaneros make useful objects such as baskets, wooden kitchen implements, and nets from *ixtle*. Ixtle, a silky fiber from a cactus, is dyed yellow and used to make bows for musical accompaniment at their agricultural ceremonies. They also make reed or clay pipes, *comales* and simple pottery dishes, and clay toys. From wood, the Mexicaneros produce carts that can be as much as a meter (three feet) in length, as well as unpainted masks for fiestas.

The crafts of the Coras are quite varied; one of their distinctive items is the *talega*, which is another type of backpack that comes in many sizes, can be of wool or cotton, and can vary in color from a dull plain gray to brightly contrasting designs that symbolize the Cora worldview. For ceremonial occasions, these bags have tassels. The Coras also make hats from jute, and sandals (*huaraches*) with leather uppers and soles made from old tires.

Huicholes who follow their own cultural traditions place great importance on the design of clothing, the construction of shrines, and ceremonial trappings such as musical instruments. The Huicholes are famous for their paintings, representing religious beliefs and rites. Some are made from natural products such as reeds, bound together with wax. They also make *ojos de Dios* (God's eyes), which they believe protect children from harm; these objects have blue centers and are otherwise white and red. When a child reaches the age of five, the family ceremoniously casts the eyes into the sea in gratitude for the child's survival. There are also wooden or clay effigies of their gods, necklaces, wristbands, and other jewelry. Huichol clothing is much valued.

The *muveri* is a small arrow made from bamboo and feathers that a shaman can use to call upon the gods; in Huichol paintings, these muveris are sometimes represented as horns. The *niérika* is a piece of cloth with a hole in the middle, or sometimes a mirror; the shaman uses this object in his search, and as an offering to the gods. The *tepo* is a sacred drum made from the trunk of an oak tree and covered with deerskin; it has holes in its wooden sides to let out the smoke that is used to tension the skin. Huichol paintings are often stuck on wood or used to decorate objects such as violins. These paintings vary in quality, many being produced for tourists; the best examples are personal expressions of the artist's religious experiences.

The principal crafts among the *mestizo* communities are wooden furniture, basketry (in the municipality of Jala), pottery (in Ixtlán del Río and in Ahuacatlán), and rock carving (in Santiago Ixcuintla).

Nayarit has produced one distinguished individual in the mainstream arts, the poet **Amado Nervo** (1870–1917), one of the leading figures of Mexican literature in the late nineteenth century. The fact that Nervo first studied to become a priest is reflected in some of the writing he turned to later. For example, his poetry is sometimes influenced by the mystics. But

Nervo was also very interested in poetic forms and exotic imagery, both of which are typical characteristics of the Spanish-American *modernista* style with which he is usually associated. Nervo wrote a great deal and met with considerable acclaim in artistic circles during his lifetime.

Social Customs

Nowadays, the religious and social customs of Indians such as the Coras and Huicholes derive from a mixture of their Pre-Hispanic traditions and imported Hispanic ones. Both Coras and Huicholes continue to observe religious rites such as making offerings to their gods and seeking their blessing in hopes of rain, a good harvest, and general well-being. For the Huicholes, the principal festivities are at the beginning of the new year and on the feasts of Saint Sebastian and Saint Francis. There are also festivities associated with maize and *peyote* (also known as *jícuri*). The Huichol people believe that the elements of nature can take personal and supernatural forms: gods can turn into plants or animals, and they are revealed supernaturally in rituals. Each year, the Huichol people make an arduous pilgrimage (about 400 kilometers/250 miles) from their home territory across the central plateau into the state of San Luis Potosí, in search of a small, well-camouflaged cactus with a button-shaped growth at the top that yields peyote, a hallucinogen that is an essential part of their culture. Small amounts of peyote help them ward off hunger and fatigue, but larger ones, such as those taken by their shamans, bring visions that make sense of the world and can inspire paintings and designs.

Among the Coras, the great celebration is a maize festival called the *mitote*; corn is their staple food and the very basis of their existence. They consider soft red corn sacred. The mitote involves several phases related to the life cycle of corn. The Coras also have a major celebration during Holy Week, an example of the fusion of their own traditions with Catholic ones.

In the dominant mestizo community, there are many festive traditions. Tepic's National Fair (La Feria Nacional de Tepic) takes place in March. In August, Jala and Xalisco have their Feria del Elote, also known as La Purísima Concepción. Spring fairs are held in Tuxpan and Santiago Ixcuintla. The Feast of the Virgen de la Candelaria is a major festivity for Huajicori, as is that of the Virgen de Guadalupe in the small town of El Pichón.

Typically, these occasions are marked by parties and dances in public places prior to the key day, when there are pilgrimages and processions with allegorical floats. People in traditional clothing perform dances that have a supposedly pre-Hispanic flavor, and there are also more mainstream traditional Mexican dances, such as the *baile de la conquista* and *matachines*. There are usually plenty of fireworks. The dominant music is provided by *bandas* (Mexican big bands), mariachis, and traditional trios. One example of such a festivity is the Feast of Santiago, which is celebrated on July 25 in Compostela: men self-consciously ride around town on horseback on one day, and women do the same on the next. On the first Friday in December (Día del Señor de la Misericordia), the four suburbs of Compostela engage in competitions involving pageantry and dancing. In October, in Ixtlán del Río, dances such as the *danza de la pluma* and *danza de los quetzales* are performed in the atrium of the church, and then there is a procession of carriages and floats.

Examples of popular song/dance numbers are the *buey*, a mountain dance with indigenous roots, in which the woman's foot movements are accompanied by skirt swinging and gestures with a palm fan; the *ardillo*, which is performed on a stage after the tequila has been flowing and is an excuse for the dancer to show of his foot-stamping skills while balancing a bottle or a glass on his head; and the *gallito*, which is a couples dance also performed on a platform, with a foot-stamping cock courting a foot-stamping hen, and a "crowing" violin to mark his success. The typical dress for men on such occasions consists of breeches, a close-fitting shirt, a red sash, a scarf, and a cloak over the shoulders. They wear a narrow-brimmed hat and huaraches. The women wear brightly colored satin blouses with frilly necklines, and wide skirts with flounces along the bottom edge that pick up the colors of the blouses. A *peineta* (high comb) is worn in the hair and a small gathering of flowers on the right side of the head. They wear bracelets and a chain with a cross on it and carry a fan made from palm. The wide skirt is manipulated in order to accentuate the dance movements.

Noteworthy Places

Nayarit has more natural attractions than man-made ones. Even official state publications acknowledge that there is no risk of Tepic, its capital, being mistaken for a colonial gem. But the state does have approximately 300 kilometers (180 miles) of coastline with many beaches that encourage recreational activities such as diving and sailing. In addition, there are islands, lagoons, mountains, springs, and waterfalls. El Novillero beach, in the north of the state, is Mexico's longest.

At Coamiles, there are petroglyphs dating from well before the arrival of the Spaniards. Scattered over an area of about 2 hectares (5 acres) are sixteen rocks with such markings. The designs vary from geometric or hieroglyphic to stylized floral to human forms in hieratic poses.

Far richer is Los Toriles (Ixtlán), which is one of the most important archaeological sites in western Mexico. Los Toriles dates from the Postclassical Period and was built about AD 650 by Nahua peoples who had been influenced by the Toltec culture. The site has two parts. One has the Palace of Tláloc, the rain god, which is L-shaped and still has pillars and two decorative staircases. In front of the palace is an altar approached by steps, with a small shrine beside it. The other part has a dwelling believed to have housed a priest, and beside that a small shrine. Then there is the highly original Temple of Quetzalcóatl, identified by a bas-relief of this god (the

Plumed Serpent) on one of its corners. This temple is a circular structure set on a platform and approached by five elaborate staircases; at its top are shrines dedicated to the sun and the moon. These shrines have similar staircases that lead to square platforms and parapets with cross-shaped openings. Finally, there is a further shrine that faces the temple and has three staircases; it sits in the middle of a broad square on whose southern flank lies another palace, called the Palacio de Tezcatlipoca.

Ixtlán has a small pyramid, but the cultures of western Mexico in general did not leave a great deal in the way of monumental structures. What is distinctive about western Mexican Indian cultures is the presence of *tumbas de tiro*, which are thought to date from the period between 500 BC and AD 500. These are vertical, shaftlike tombs with side chambers containing human remains, arrowheads, ceramic effigies of humans and animals, and musical instruments. Ixtlán is one of the places where excavations have been most productive.

Most colonial buildings reflect the times when trade via the port of San Blas was prosperous. The remains of the San Blas customhouse, dating from the late nineteenth century, are of some interest. Also in San Blas are the ruins of the Church of the Virgen del Sagrario and the Contaduría. The church was begun in 1769 and finished in 1788. The Contaduría is of the same period and similar in style; it was laid out in such a way as to accommodate various branches of the financial administration of the colonial port, and it has its own defenses. This was the place José María Mercado captured during the movement toward independence.

Tepic's cathedral is a neo-Gothic edifice dating from the eighteenth century but subsequently modified. Its original architect also designed the penitentiary that later became the seat of state government (Palacio de Gobierno). The Nayarit Regional Museum (Museo Regional de Nayarit) is housed in an eighteenth-century house that once belonged to the Count of Miravalle. In addition to temporary exhibitions, this museum has a permanent collection of native artifacts (ceramics, jade, and ritual and votive objects), in which the Cora and Huichol cultures are strongly represented. One outstanding piece is a two-thousand-year-old circular stone bearing the image of a bird with a snake in its clutches, a reminder of the story of the origins of the Aztec Empire. Other noteworthy buildings in Tepic are the former Bellavista Textile Factory, the former Convento de la Cruz, and the Casa Fenelón.

Tuxpan has the Casa Aguirre. There are several ex-haciendas. Museums include the Casa-Museo de Juan Escutia, the Museo Amado Nervo, the Museo de los Cuatro Pueblos, the Museo Aramara, and the Museo de Mexcaltitán, located on the island of that name.

Cuisine

Nayarit cooking draws overwhelmingly on local products, including the bounty of the sea (shrimp, clams, lobsters, oysters, octopus, and fish).

Popular dishes include shrimp broth, the local variety of *ceviche*, and *pescado zarandeado* (a grilled fish dish). *Tamales de camarón* come wrapped in palm leaves. The state's livestock production makes for meat dishes, which are on the whole very simple, such as charcoal roasted beef, *birria* (a kind of stew, sometimes of goat), and roast pork, lamb, or chicken. Such dishes are usually served with vegetables and beer. *Cocadas* (coconut cakes) and banana bread are examples of common sweet preparations. Many dishes that are popular all over the country are given a local spin, such as *pozole*, the hominy-based thick soup, and *quesadillas*. Arguably one of the most distinctive of Nayarit's dishes is plantain fritters (*bollos de plátano*), which are served with pieces of radish and lettuce leaves, and with a sauce made from cheese, tomatoes, and onions. Among local drinks one finds a liqueur made from a fruit called *nanche*, a barley-water *horchata*, and a pineapple drink called *tepache de piña*.

Marlin Ahumado Estilo Nayarit

Ingredients:

> 2 lb. smoked marlin, chopped
> 1 small cabbage, shredded
> 3 stalks of celery, chopped
> 2 carrots, grated
> 1/4 cup preserved jalapeños
> 2 cloves of garlic
> 1 cup olive oil
> Salt

Finely chop the garlic and soften it in some of the olive oil, then add the cabbage, celery, carrots, peppers and a little salt. Cover and allow the cabbage to become soft, then add pieces of marlin and warm through, stirring occasionally.

Pescado Zarandeado

Ingredients:

> 1 Large whole bass, snapper, or similar fresh catch
> Salsa Huichol (a hot sauce, to taste)
> 1 bottle of beer
> Soy sauce (to taste)
> 1 lime (for juice)
> Butter (for basting)
> 1/2 Onion, sliced
> 1/4 Cucumber, sliced
> 2 Tomatoes, sliced

Clean the fish and split it down the middle so that it lays flat. Brush it with a sauce made by combining Salsa Huichol with beer, lime juice, and soy sauce. Grill the fish on both sides over coals (e.g., mesquite), basting it occasionally with the sauce. When it starts to dry out, brush butter over it on both sides and let it turn golden. Serve topped with slices of onion, cucumber, and tomato.

Jugo de Camarón

Ingredients:

   $^1/_2$ lb. fresh shrimp
   1 cup water
   4 pints fish stock
   4 medium potatoes, chopped
   4 carrots, chopped
   1 onion, chopped
   A generous spoonful of jalapeños, chopped
   Salt

Boil the shrimp in the stock and puree in a blender. Add the vegetables and water and cook until they are about to disintegrate. Season with salt.

Nuevo León

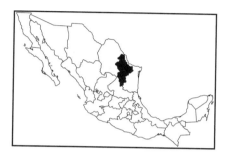

State Characteristics

A small portion of Nuevo León's northern border is shared with Texas but most of it with the states of Coahuila and Tamaulipas. Tamaulipas runs down its eastern side. On the west lie Coahuila, San Luis Potosí, and Zacatecas. The state covers 64,210 square kilometers (25,000 square miles), making it the thirteenth largest state, with 3.3 percent of Mexico's total area. The capital city is Monterrey, one of the largest cities in the country, with 1,693,691 inhabitants (commonly referred to as the *regiomontanos*). The total state population (according to the 2005 census) is 4,199,292; a large proportion of that total is around Monterrey, if not actually in it. The populace is 88 percent Catholic and 6 percent Protestant or evangelical.

The state is named after León, once a kingdom of northern Spain. Nuevo León (New León) has fifty-one administrative municipalities. It is represented in the National Congress by fifteen people. There are eight institutions of higher education. One of these, the Instituto Tecnológico de Monterrey, is a system with campuses in several parts of the country. Eleven newspapers are published in the state, one in Guadalupe and all the rest in the capital city. Examples are *El Norte*, *Milenio*, *El Porvenir*, *Crucero*, and *El Gráfico de Nuevo León*.

It is customary to view Nuevo León as having three geographical regions. The Sierra Madre Oriental dominates the western side of the state, and also the south of it. A second major feature is the Great Plains of North America, which begin in Nuevo León. Third, the lowest-lying section of the state is part of the coastal plain that runs along the Gulf of Mexico.

In the mountains, there are many places with elevations in excess of 3,000 meters (10,000 feet): the Cerro el Morro, the Cerro el Potosí, the Picacho San Onofre, the Sierra el Viejo, the Sierra Potego de Abrego, the Sierra los Toros, and the Cerro Grande de la Ascensión. Most of the rivers run eastward toward the Gulf. The San Juan and Salado rivers, together with the waterfall known as the Cola de Caballo, feed into the Río Bravo system. The Conchos River system also has its source in Nuevo León, in the Sierra Madre Oriental. However, Nuevo León is generally distinguished by its lack of waterways.

Thirteen distinct climate zones have been identified, most of them dry to very dry. The mean annual temperature is 14°C (57°F) in the Sierra Madre and 24°C (75°F) in the lowlands. At 1,010 millimeters (39.8 inches) a year, the highest rainfall is in the municipality of Villa de Santiago; the lowest, 217 millimeters (8.5 inches), is in Mina. Prevailing winds are generally from the east, but come from the north in winter.

Pines, cedars, *oyamel*, oaks, and *zacatonales* grow in the Sierra. The flatlands are dominated by varieties of cactus. Typical fauna in the mountains are eagles and pumas; on the *meseta*, there are *cacomixtles*, prairie dogs, desert foxes, and badgers, while in the lowlands there are white-winged doves, wild boars, and white-tailed deer.

Cultural Groups and Languages

According to the 2005 census, only 0.8 percent of the population over age five spoke an indigenous language. This is a low proportion by comparison with many Mexican states, though in line with others located in the north. By far the largest proportion of the 29,538 indigenous-language speakers, 44 percent, spoke Náhuatl, the language of the Aztecs; 12 percent spoke Huasteco, 4 percent Otomí, and 2 percent languages of the Zapotec family. The predominance of Náhuatl is explained by two things: the disappearance of the original indigenous inhabitants and the importation by the Spaniards of their Indian allies from Tlaxcala, a Náhuatl-speaking area.

History

What is known of the early peoples of Nuevo León comes primarily from archaeological investigations, but also from the observations of Alonso de León, a Spanish settler of the seventeenth century. The inhabitants were nomadic hunters and gatherers. Important groups among them were the Hualahuises in the south, the Coahuiltecos in the west, the Borrados in the east, and the Catujanes in the north; these and other peoples were collectively referred to as the Chichimecs. They left rock paintings but no great cities, unlike the indigenous peoples of south and central Mexico.

In 1544, Fray Andrés de Olmos reached the territory that is now Nuevo León, but it would be more than thirty years before another explorer,

Alberto del Canto, founded Villa de Santiago de Saltillo, before continuing northeastward and discovering the valley that the Spaniards named the Valle de Extremadura. Close by some natural wells, to the north of the Sierra de la Sila, Olmos founded a settlement he called Santa Lucía.

By the time Spain was ready to turn its attention to these remote lands, the viceroys in Mexico City were looking to private entrepreneurs to finance explorations. **Luis de Carvajal** (1539–1595) was one such entrepreneur; in Toledo, Spain, King Philip II granted him a *capitulación*, the right to conquer and name a large part of these northern lands. Carvajal then set out for the New World in the *Santa Catarina*, but when he and his fellow travelers arrived in Mexico they were disillusioned with what they found; there was resentment against Carvajal for having raised expectations of something better. After some months in the southern part of the territory, where he soon had control of the settlements and established *encomiendas* in accordance with the king's directives, Carvajal renamed the San Gregorio mine settlement Ciudad de León. He then went on to found San Luis Rey de Francia—the future Monterrey—in 1582.

By 1585, Carvajal controlled vast stretches of land, with three lieutenants under him governing different regions. Carvajal was accused of encroaching on the lands to which others had acquired rights, but escaped any retribution for that; however, his killing of one of his subordinates provoked a revolt in 1587, and as a result San Luis was almost abandoned for a while. Carvajal, who was imprisoned for a time, later reappeared on the scene and made one of his lieutenants, **Diego de Montemayor** (1530–1611), governor of Coahuila, charging him with repopulating Ciudad de León. Carvajal took other initiatives, but it was not long before the authorities caught up with him and took him to Mexico City. He was tried by the Inquisition and later died in prison.

Following the period of abandonment, Montemayor returned to what was then called the Nuevo Reino de León and on September 20, 1596, founded the Ciudad Metropolitana de Nuestra Señora de Monterrey. In effect, Monterrey was founded three times; the definitive name was chosen in honor of the then viceroy of New Spain, the Count of Monterrey. Lands and privileges were granted to settlers. One was the Hacienda de los Nogales. This repopulation process was viewed as illegal by the Crown, however, so in 1599 Montemayor made a trip to Mexico City to argue his case. In the end, he received official approval and was named governor of the territory.

For a long time, the Nuevo Reino de León consisted of little more than the rather isolated city of Monterrey. Saltillo was the closest town of any size, and Zacatecas the nearest one of real importance, but that was a long way away. The first few years were ones of poverty and hunger for the inhabitants of Monterrey. In some ways it was a closed society, made up of a few families, several of which were related to Montemayor; to join the community, a written application was necessary, accompanied by an undertaking not to leave if admitted to the fold. The principal economic activities were agriculture and raising livestock. Montemayor made further efforts to populate the territory, but these failed. There was further depopulation prior to Montemayor's death in 1611. Floods did away with many of Monterrey's houses in that year, and the authorities in Mexico City, in an attempt to avoid such problems, relocated it farther south. They gave lands to those who still remained and provided them with seeds and food over the course of a period of ten years, all in an attempt to save the area from depopulation.

Among the earliest friars to arrive and begin the process of evangelizing the natives were Juan de la Magdalena and Pedro Infante. During the seventeenth century they were joined by many more who founded missions and built churches and convents. Fray José de San Gabriel is an interesting case; as a miner, he had taken full advantage of his position and treated the Indians as slaves, but then he turned to religion, changed his name, and became a staunch defender of Indian rights.

In 1646, Alfonso de León was charged with establishing the town of Nuestra Señora de San Juan de Tlaxcala; the plan was to resettle four hundred families of Indians from Tlaxcala, near Puebla, because early during the conquest of Mexico they had become allies of the Spaniards. The Nuevo León settlement lasted for about fifty years, suffering constant attacks from the Chichimecs, until it was finally destroyed and the inhabitants taken into the missions. There the Tlaxcaltecas helped instruct local Indians in Spanish ways, including their methods of agriculture. The Hualahuises were particularly bellicose and reluctant to submit to the new order, but in 1655 they were overcome and installed in a mission built for them, the Misión de San Cristóbal; however, by 1685 the only person there was Fray Juan de Menchaca. In 1710, the governor distributed lands to the Tlaxcaltecas, and in 1715 some of them repopulated the San Cristóbal mission; about a hundred years later, it became a town. The checkered history of this mission is in some ways typical: many were founded, but by no means all of them survived.

At the Convento de Nuestra Señora de la Concepción was a priest named Francisco de Ribera, who upon arriving there in 1632 denounced the mistreatment of the natives by his fellow Spaniards and, together with other friars from the San Luis Potosí convent, supported Indian rebellion. The system of privileges and the granting of encomiendas, coupled with the greed and cruelty of many settlers, conspired to make life intolerable for the Indians. Many died of disease; some even committed suicide or killed their children rather than have them become slaves. When labor ran short, the settlers sent out raiding parties into areas where there were known to be more Indians, to capture more of them to work their lands. For this, the settlers were rewarded with payments, discreetly masked as religious titles.

In the northeast, one of the most important missions was Santa Teresa del Álamo, founded in 1659 near Cerralvo. In the north, the Boca de

Leones Mission was founded in 1687, only to be eliminated shortly afterward because mineral deposits were discovered there; the place then became Real y Minas de San Pedro de Boca de Leones, a major social center.

The Franciscan Order, which had been responsible for the many missions, lost authority in 1712, when the bishop ordered that the missions be "secularized," that is, put in the hands of clergy who were not members of the Catholic orders. Further decline in the missions followed, which provoked protests from friars and Indians alike. Rebellious Indians took refuge in the Sierra de Tamaulipas, while the friars argued in the courts for their reinstatement as the people responsible for the missions. The Mexico City authorities sent Francisco Guadalupe Barbadillo y Victoria to mediate in the conflict with the Indians. Barbadillo appointed Fray Juan Losada as administrator of the Franciscan convents of Linares and the Pilón Valley, and Losada is credited with the repopulation and founding of some missions. Under his authority, peace was established, and subsequently Barbadillo was appointed governor.

In 1786, Spain decided that New Spain should be reorganized into twelve administrative units called *intendencias*; one of them was to be the Intendencia de San Luis Potosí, and it was to include Nuevo León, Zacatecas, and Sonora. Then, in 1787, another administrative reorganization brought Coahuila, Nuevo Reino de León, and Nuevo Santander under the Comandancia de Oriente. By this time, the inhabitants of the Nuevo Reino de León had settled into a simple, peaceful, and patriarchal lifestyle. Nuevo León had two regional seats of government, in Linares and in Monterrey.

In 1805, the then governor, Simón Herrera y Leyva, passed the baton on to his brother Pedro. They were concerned about the northern frontier and the implications of the recent Louisiana Purchase by the United States. But events in Spain and within Mexico itself were to overtake such concerns: Mexico was on the verge of becoming independent.

News of Miguel Hidalgo's rebellion reached Nuevo León weeks after the event. Poor people were quick to join the rebel movement, while the governor sought reinforcements to combat it and the local bishop ruled that sympathizers with the rebellion should do penance. Initially, Governor Manuel de Santa María sent troops to stop the advance northward of the insurgent troops, but eventually he and his commander, Juan Ignacio Ramón, decided to switch sides. Saltillo and Monterrey soon came under rebel control, but the defeat of Hidalgo's army put a halt to their advance. Meanwhile, in Texas a counterrevolutionary movement was beginning under José Ramón Díaz de Bustamante, Ignacio Elizondo, and others. It was not long before the rebel leaders were captured and shot, as were Santa María and Juan Ignacio Ramón. A governing junta was then established in Monterrey. It lasted until 1813, but rebel activity continued, led by people such as Rafael and Ramón González, Juan de Villerías, José Herrera, and Policarpo Verástegui. A year later, the loyalist authorities had control of the situation and were more concerned about Indian attacks, but elsewhere the independence movement was very much alive.

It is at about this time that the rebel priest Fray **Servando Teresa de Mier** (1765–1827) appeared on the scene, together with Francisco Javier Mina. They came by boat to Soto de la Marina, Mier after a period in exile in Europe. On hearing of their arrival, Joaquín de Arredondo, the governor, sent troops to confront them; many of the rebels fell prisoners, Mier among them, but Mina escaped into the mountains. Mier was taken to be tried by the Inquisition. However, 1821 brought the Plan de Iguala, and with it the conversion of Mexico into an independent empire. At this point, Arredondo fled to San Luis Potosí, to be replaced by Gaspar López, who declared his allegiance to the new empire.

The empire lasted only a year, and in 1824 Mexico became a federal republic, with Nuevo León as one of its founding states. Its first governor, **José María Parás** (1794–1851), later became a member of the National Congress and fought against the U.S. invasion. As governor of the state, he published its first newspaper, the *Gaceta Constitucional*, and he took steps to develop agriculture, mining, and trade and to improve education. However, it was not long before the country became embroiled in rivalries, sometimes violent, between conservatives who wanted to concentrate power in Mexico City and preserve the social status quo and liberals who favored a freer, more federal structure. Monterrey did not escape the feuding between conservatives and liberals, changing hands between them several times.

Against this background of decades of strife in Mexico, the United States began to take steps to extend its territory. Texas, pointing to the despotism of President Antonio López de Santa Anna and alleging that Mexico could not govern itself properly, sought to break away. Santa Anna tried to impose his authority, winning the Battle of the Alamo, but was then defeated in San Antonio and forced to cede Texas in 1836. Then came war with the United States, at the end of which Mexico lost almost half of its territory to its northern neighbor. The U.S. invasion brought Gen. Zachary Taylor and his army to Monterrey, where they took control despite spirited resistance. Among those who fought the U.S. invasion were two notable women, María de Jesús Dosamantes and María Josefa Zozaya. After the war, Nuevo León suffered an outbreak of cholera and lived in fear of a bandit called Agapito Treviño, alias "Caballo Blanco."

After years under Santa Anna, the reformist Plan de Ayutla won support all over the country. In Nuevo León, **Santiago Vidaurri** (1809–1867), the government secretary, left Monterrey in 1855 and went to Lampazos, where, with the help of **Juan Zuazua** (1821–1860), he launched a plan for reform. They then came back to Monterrey, where Vidaurri declared himself governor and made Zuazua a colonel. Zuazua had fought against the U.S. invasion, and he went on to support the liberals during the Reform War.

By August 1855, the whole country was under the control of Santa Anna's opponents. Vidaurri eased restrictions on trade and encouraged other reforms, but after the new national Constitution of 1857 had been adopted, his powers were curtailed; he had gained control of Coahuila and become so powerful in the northeast that there were fears that some of its states might try to break away from the rest of Mexico.

The reformist 1857 Constitution threatened entrenched interests and provoked the era of the Reform War, a civil war that lasted for several years. The liberal Benito Juárez became president, and after the country was invaded by the French, he came to Monterrey in 1864, whereupon Vidaurri, who had previously supported Juárez, withdrew to Ciudadela; they did talk, but they did not agree. Juárez then made Coahuila separate from Nuevo León and declared Vidaurri a traitor for having dealt with the French, because Vidaurri had aligned himself with Maximilian and served in his government. Pursued by Juárez's troops, eventually Vidaurri fled across the Río Bravo. Juárez settled his exiled government in Monterrey for some months, but always had to contend with threats from supporters of Vidaurri and with imperialist advances. In 1865, Nuevo León was taken by the imperialist forces, then recovered, and then lost to them once again, until finally Emperor Maximilian was defeated. Vidaurri meanwhile had made his way to Querétaro; from there he approached Mexico City, as did the forces loyal to Juárez. As the result of a betrayal, Vidaurri was captured and shot.

With Juárez's government back in power, new elections took place in Nuevo León. More civil unrest led to a financial crisis, but the new governor, **Gerónimo Treviño** (1836–1914) managed to bring about some improvements in communications and educational provision. He opposed Juárez's reelection and fought against forces loyal to the president at the Battle of Zacatecas. The Reform War continued, fueled by Juárez's new laws limiting the powers of the church and nationalizing some assets. Juárez was reelected president, but died not long afterward.

After the presidency of Sebastián Lerdo de Tejeda, Gen. Porfirio Díaz became president, an office which he held or managed from offstage for about thirty years. During this time, state governors tended to be people put in the position by Díaz. It was an era of great expansion in communications and industry, of foreign investment and modernization, but also one during which the rich became richer and the poor were left behind, with national assets being sold off to foreign interests. Nuevo León acquired a railroad line, but in the process it ceased to be place where people bought local goods, instead becoming a place of transit for imported ones. Nevertheless, industry increased.

A dominant political figure in Nuevo León was Bernardo Reyes, an ambitious opportunist who had long wielded power in the state and who some speculated might even succeed Díaz as president. On hearing these rumors, Díaz had Reyes leave the country, ostensibly on a mission to study European military forces. In fact, Díaz had more to worry about in the person of Francisco Madero, who had widespread support among those who felt that it was time for an end to Díaz's long rule. Two prominent local opponents of Díaz's reelection were **Antonio I. Villarreal** (1879-1944) and **Pablo González** (1879-1950).

By 1911, Díaz and his vice president, Ramón Corral, had stepped down, and Díaz slipped out of the country. In July of that year, Madero triumphantly arrived in Mexico City, and a few months later he was elected president, though he was assassinated not long after. In the confusion of those revolutionary years, there were a number of outbreaks of violence in Nuevo León. At one point, Bernardo Reyes reappeared on the scene and was arrested; after his release from prison by rioters in Ciudadela, he tried to storm the government palace and was killed during the fighting. A distinguished figure during the Revolution was **Pablo A. de la Garza** (1876-1932), a lawyer and military man who held a number of official posts before joining the revolutionary campaign. After seeing action in Tamaulipas and Coahuila, he was responsible for taking Monterrey, following which he was made commander and military governor of Guanajuato, and then of Nuevo León. He also served as procurator general of Mexico and as a military commander in Campeche, Yucatán, and Quintana Roo.

Following the Convención de Aguascalientes, in which President Venustiano Carranza tried to settle his differences with the supporters of Pancho Villa, the latter occupied Monterrey. The new state governor was Madero's brother, Raúl. Later, Villa was ousted from Nuevo León and Carranza's troops occupied Monterrey, installing another governor who shortly afterward died at the hands of supporters of Villa. Amid much political maneuvering, the state adopted a new constitution that was almost an exact copy of the one that had been introduced nationally in 1917.

During the presidency of Plutarco Elías Calles, there were several improvements in Nuevo León, among them the definition of workers' rights and the building of schools and a university, roads, and the first dams. When Lázaro Cárdenas became president, there were more changes, including land redistribution. Agriculture and livestock breeding advanced as the inescapable problems of droughts, disease, and theft were confronted.

Economy

Corn, sorghum, wheat, beans, oats, and other crops are sown over 211,000 hectares (521,000 acres) in Nuevo León, generating a total production in the region of 430,000 tons, and a further 169,000 hectares (418,000 acres) are given over to orchards such as of citrus fruits and walnuts. For the most part, agriculture relies on flood irrigation. The northern and central parts of the state concentrate on livestock, of which there are more than 13 million head; goats lead the list, followed by cows and pigs. Huge numbers of chickens and other birds are raised for their meat, and egg production is also significant.

Nuevo León calls itself the industrial center of Mexico. It is well linked to other states, and it is the second biggest rail center in Mexico. In the nineteenth century, it had textile factories, and these were joined by beer production at the Cervecería Cuauhtémoc and smelting at the Compañía Fundidora de Hierro y Acero. Another major enterprise dealing with metals, dating from 1942, was Hojalata y Lámina. Many industries, mostly manufacturing, are now located in or around Monterrey; their products include cement, glass, chemicals, domestic appliances, furniture, and clothing. Among the firms involved are Alfa, Axa, Cydsa, Gamesa, Protexa, Cementos Mexicanos, Imsa, Vitro, and Visa. Nuevo León is number four in the world for cement production, and number one in Latin America for glass.

The Monterrey media industry has also been significant; the proprietors of *El Norte* have been responsible for the creation in recent years of *Reforma*, a leading Mexico City newspaper that prides itself on avoiding the customary channels of corruption that dog the Mexican press.

As far back as 1918, the Junta de Conciliación y Arbitraje was created to give workers, bosses, and government representatives a forum for exchanging views and ideas.

Arts

Nuevo León's crafts reveal the skills brought by the Tlaxcalteca Indians: wood carving (of chairs, for example), pottery, structures made with reeds and adobe, and so forth. Palm is woven to make hats, baskets, and mats, and leather is used to make clothing and bags.

During the second half of the nineteenth century, the popular music of the northern states was influenced by the arrival of immigrants from Germany and Eastern Europe. Prior to that time, the standard instruments used in popular festivities had been the guitar and the violin. To these were added the accordion and a large derivative of the guitar called the *bajo sexto*. New dance forms such as the polka and the mazurka became popular. Moreover, the simple narrative ballads known as *corridos* were given a boost by the Revolution, which provided colorful people such as Pancho Villa to sing about; the corrido soon became popular over much of the country.

One consequence of the fusion of new musical instruments and genres with more traditional ones was a new, northern style called *norteño*. The related, brass-based *banda* music usually involves woodwinds and percussion also, and a signature instrument is the *tambora*, a type of bass drum that provides the insistent rhythmic drive. The ensembles are relatively large, of up to fifteen people. The repertoire for norteño and banda ensembles is both instrumental and vocal and usually ranges from *canciones rancheras* and corridos to *cumbias* and *boleros*. Electronic music has also been entering the mixture.

Among the people who have made a mark on music are **Belisario de Jesús García** (1892–1952) and **Armando Villarreal** (1903–1976), both musicians and composers; **Eulalio González** (1921–2003) was a singer and dancer; and famous groups include Los Cadetes de Linares and Los Alegres de Terán.

Two significant visual artists from Nuevo León were **Alfredo Ramos Martínez** (1876–1946), considered one of the founding fathers of modern Mexican art, and **Federico Cantú** (1907–1989) a painter, engraver, and sculptor.

One of the most significant historical figures associated with Mexico's independence from Spain, the aforementioned Fray Servando Teresa de Mier, was a writer to boot. He was an intriguing figure of Enlightenment literature, a very unorthodox Dominican priest who claimed to be related to Moctezuma and even suggested, in *Notes for the Sermon on the Appearance of the Virgin of Guadalupe*, that Mexico had been evangelized in the sixth century, long before the arrival of the Spaniards. Mier was forced into exile, to spend ten years in a Spanish monastery. He escaped and was recaptured several times and traveled widely, ending up penniless in London, where he wrote one of his most important works, *Historia de la revolución de Nueva España* (1813). His most interesting work from a modern standpoint is *Apología y relaciones de su vida* (Apology and Accounts of His Life), which he wrote after his return to Mexico, in prison. But with independence came recognition for his patriotism. At the end of his life, ever true to his unorthodox style, he orchestrated the run-up to his own funeral.

Alfonso Reyes (1889–1959) was a lawyer, teacher, diplomat, journalist, writer, and one of the leading intellectuals of his day. He cofounded the Ateneo de La Juventud, one of Mexico's most important cultural institutions, working with major figures of the time, such as José Vasconcelos, Pedro Henríquez Ureña, and Antonio Caso. He represented his country in France, Spain, Argentina, and Brazil. Reyes was the founder and first president of the Colegio de México, Mexico's premier research institution in the humanities and social sciences; president of the Academy of the Language; and a recipient of the National Prize for Literature and many other honors. Among his many books are *Visión de Anáhuac* and *La experiencia literaria*.

Social Customs

Villaseca, a part of Linares, holds its fiestas each year during the first half of August. There are craft exhibitions, commercial and industrial shows, rodeo events, processions, cockfights, and horse races. In the town theater, there are concerts and dance competitions, and in the open air, rides, food stalls, and fireworks. For Abasolo, December 12, the Feast of the Virgin of Guadalupe, is the major celebration, marked by similar events. The same day in Ciudad Anahuac has a more religious and popular flavor; *matachines* (mummers) are key participants. San Pablo (in late January) is the major fiesta for Galeana, the March Fiesta de Fidencia for the municipality of Mina, Santa Cruz (in May) for Villalda, and the Fiesta de Villaseca (in August) for Linares.

In Monterrey, an Agricultural and Trade Fair takes place in May, and the celebration of independence in September is a major occasion. Monterrey also hosts a number of arts festivals: the Muestra de Teatro Español, the Festival Alfonsino, the Temporada de Conciertos de Otoño, and the Festival de Artes Monterrey.

Noteworthy Places

The city of Monterrey is one of the largest in Mexico, a modern industrial and administrative center with a strong educational tradition. Created in 1985, the Macroplaza de Monterrey is said to be the largest such square in the world. It covers about a hundred acres and is six times the size of the square in front of the cathedral in Mexico City. It is home to a large number of monuments and major buildings, such as the Explanada de los Héroes, the Parque Hundido, the Teatro de la Ciudad, the Tribunal Superior de Justicia, the Biblioteca Central Fray Servando Teresa de Mier, and the Secretaría de Educación y Cultura, and beneath it is a shopping center. Close by are several museums, such as the Museo de Arte Contemporáneo, Museo de Historia Mexicana, and Museo de Historia Metropolitano. La Explanada de los Héroes is an open area that leads to the Palacio Municipal, an area for celebrations and demonstrations. Under the square lie the remains of state worthies such as Pablo González, Juan Zuazua, and Antonio I. Villarreal. Luis Barragán, one of Mexico's most distinguished architects, designed part of the Macroplaza; Rufino Tamayo, one of the country's leading artists, designed another part. The Palacio de Gobierno (Government Palace) was begun during the *porfiriato*, while Bernardo Reyes was the governor, and it took thirteen years to complete the stone building in the neoclassical style. The cathedral (Catedral Metropolitana de Monterrey) dates from the eighteenth century. The Centro Cultural Alfa is a high-tech facility that includes a planetarium.

In Zuazua lies the former Hacienda San Pedro, also known as the Casa de Melchor. It was constructed in 1666 and resembles a fortress, complete with turrets at its corners. It now belongs to the Universidad Autónoma de Nuevo León and is a venue for cultural events.

The Parque Cumbres de Monterrey is one of the oldest protected natural areas in the state, covering more than 240,000 hectares (600,000 acres). Other natural attractions include the Cañón de la Huasteca, the Mesa Chipinque, the García and Nevada caves, and the Cola del Caballo waterfall. A little surprisingly, given the state's liking for things on a grand scale, the Parque Nacional El Sabinal is the smallest state park in Mexico.

Rock paintings and carvings can be seen at Boca de Potrerillos in the municipality of Mina. There are some four thousand carved stones and eight thousand images, mostly of fauna and solar and geometric designs.

Cuisine

Influences from the Spanish and the Tlaxcaltecan traditions have shaped the cuisine of Nuevo León. The Indian contribution comes in the form of tortillas, chiles, and certain herbs and other plants, such as cacti. One valued dish for the Spaniards was (and still is) roast lamb, but given the relative lack of sheep, the early colonial inhabitants of Nuevo León turned to goat instead. Apart from roasting goats, they made things with their entrails, such as *machito*, based on a Castilian dish called *zarajos*. Another inheritance from the conquistadores was *cemitas*, which are sweet rolls containing walnuts. Meats were often dried as a way of preserving them; from that tradition comes *machaca*, which is common all over the northern states. A characteristic cut of beef for grilling is the *arrachera*, which is now found all over Mexico but originated in Nuevo León. Another common dish is *carne zaraza*, which consists of strips of meat served with guacamole. Nuevo León eats more meat per inhabitant than any other Mexican state.

Linares is known for its *tortas* (sandwiches) and for its cakes known as *glorias* (for which it has about fifteen factories). Galeana has a national reputation for its potatoes. Common sweets are *besitos indios* (containing cinnamon and cream) and *bolitas de leche* (made of goat's or cow's milk and with pumpkin and orange in it). *Pan de Bustamante* is a sweet homemade bread. Beer is the favored drink.

Cabrito Asado

Ingredients:

> 2 kid goats
> Salt
> 1 cup vinegar
> 2 cups guacamole
> $1/2$ cup finely chopped onion
> 1 cup finely chopped tomato
> $1/4$ cup chopped cilantro
> 3 tbsp chopped *serrano* chiles
> Beans (*frijoles de olla*)
> $1^1/2$ cups grated Monterey Jack cheese
> Fried wedges of tortilla

Put the goats in a large pot and cover with water, adding some salt and the vinegar. Let this stand for a couple of hours. Then remove the meat and roast it slowly over coals (preferably mesquite) for at least 2 hours, basting it only with salt water. Using a rotisserie is ideal. When cooked, cut the meat into portions and serve garnished with the guacamole, onion, tomato, cilantro, and the chile pieces, with beans sprinkled with the grated cheese, and wedges of tortilla.

Huevos Estilo León

Ingredients:

6 eggs
6 tortillas
2 oz. lard
2 *serrano* chiles
12 medium tomatoes
1 onion
1 clove of garlic
1 sprig of cilantro
Salt and pepper

Make a sauce by blending the tomatoes, onion, chiles, cilantro, and garlic together, seasoning it with salt and pepper, and frying it briefly in some of the fat. Then fry the tortillas, lay them on a dish, and put a fried egg on each one, topped with some of the sauce.

Capirotada

Ingredients:

10 to 12 pieces of French bread
1 tsp ground cinnamon
1 tsp chopped tomato
$1/4$ tsp finely chopped onion
5 cloves
6 peppercorns
$1/2$ lb. cheese
$1/2$ cup brown sugar
2 tbsp of grated orange peel
Raisins
Walnuts, chopped
1 bay leaf

Boil the sugar with the tomato, onion, and spices until it has the consistency of honey. Toast the bread in a pan until it is golden. Place the bread in a casserole dish, making layers of bread and grated cheese and sprinkling them with a few raisins and walnut pieces until the bread is all in place and the cheese used up. Pour the sauce over it and cook it gently. When the bread has thoroughly absorbed the sauce, leave the dish to cool, then serve. It is customary to drink milk with this dish.

Glorias

Ingredients:

2 pints goat milk
$2 1/2$ cups sugar

3 tsp vanilla essence
3 tsp honey
1 cup chopped walnuts
$^1/_2$ tsp bicarbonate of soda

Mix together the milk, sugar, vanilla, and honey. Cook over a medium heat until the mixture bubbles, then add the bicarbonate of soda and stir well. Reduce the heat and stir until the mixture clarifies. Take it off the heat, add the nuts, and beat to help it cool to the point where it can be shaped with floured hands into individual portions.

Oaxaca

State Characteristics

Oaxaca is in the south of the country. It borders on the states of Puebla and Veracruz to its north, Chiapas to its east, Guerrero to its west, and the Pacific Ocean to its south. Oaxaca covers 95,364 square kilometers (37,192 square miles), which is 4.8 percent of Mexico, making it the fifth largest state in the country. According to the 2005 census, there were 3,506,821 inhabitants, of whom no less than 35.3 percent were speakers of indigenous languages. This is the highest proportion for any state in Mexico; the only other state that even approaches such a level is Yucatán. The population density in the state of Oaxaca in 2005 was 37 per square kilometer (95 per square mile). Its capital city, with a population of 258,008, is also called Oaxaca. Fifteen people make up the state's delegation to the National Congress. Regarding religion, the 2005 census reported that 85 percent of the population was Catholic and 8 percent was Protestant or evangelical.

Traditionally, the state has been seen as having seven regions: Valle, Sierra, Costa, Cañada, the Mixtecas (Alta and Baja), Papaloapan, and Istmo. Politically, the organization is among the most complicated in Mexico. There are 570 municipalities, grouped into eight regions: Cañada, Costa, Istmo, Mixteca, Papaloapan, Sierra Sur, Sierra Norte, and Valles Centrales.

Oaxaca has seven institutions of higher education, the most well-known of them being the Universidad Autónoma Benito Juárez. Fifteen newspapers are published in the state, and the great majority of them in the capital city; among the latter are *El Imparcial*, *Noticias*, *Expresión*, *Tiempo*, *Extra*, and *A Diario*, while *El Sol del Istmo* is published in Salina Santa Cruz.

This is one of Mexico's most interesting and varied states in terms of geography. Altitudes range from sea level to a highest point of 3,750 meters (12,300 feet) at the Cerro Nube, also known by its Indian name, Quie Yelaag. At many other places, the elevation exceeds 3,000 meters (10,000 feet). As if to tie a knot, the Sierra Madre del Sur, Sierra Madre de Oaxaca, and Sierra Atravesada converge in this state. The first of these ranges runs along the coast from northeast to southeast, with an average width of 150 kilometers (93 miles) and an average altitude of 2,000 meters (6,600 feet). The Sierra de Oaxaca has an average elevation of 2,500 meters (8,200 feet).

Apart from its mountains, Oaxaca also has beaches, valleys, and plains. Of the many ravines and canyons, the most important are Cuicatlán, Cortés, Galicia, María, Chiquini, Yucuxina, Ixtlayutla, and Tomellín. The picture as far as rivers are concerned is no less complex: not only are there many of them, but they go under several names. They can be grouped according to whether they run toward the Pacific or the Gulf of Mexico. The main rivers of the Gulf group are the Papaloapan and the Coatzacoalcos. On the Pacific side, there are three main river systems: the Río Mixteco, Río Verde (or Atoyac), and Río Tehuantepec. Many rivers are used to generate electricity, and some for irrigation. There are lagoons in coastal areas.

Despite being at a tropical latitude, Oaxaca has a predominantly mild climate, thanks to the high altitude of much of its terrain. The average temperature for the state as a whole is 18°C (64°F), but that generalization masks considerable variation: the Pacific coastal region, Yautepec, Putla, and parts of Huajupan and Silacayoapan have a hot, dry climate, while a hot but moist one is to be found in Villa Alta. In the Oaxaca Valley, the climate is mild, and in the mountains, it is cool. Rainfall ranges widely, from an annual average of 431 millimeters (17 inches) to 2,710 millimeters (108 inches) according to region; while some areas are quite dry, in the Sierra Mazateca, Tuxtepec, and the border area between Juchitán and Veracruz rain falls throughout the year.

Plants in the valleys include *framboyán* (royal poinciana), casuarina, *palo mulato*, *ahuehuete*, *cazahuate*, sage, *huamanche*, thyme, fennel, and bay. In the hills, one finds pines, ashes, and oaks, and in coastal areas, there are palms, mangroves, coconut trees, pineapples, *guayacanes*, and *zapotes*. In several places, cacti such as *agave* grow. Among the birds of the region, there are doves, quail, pigeons, eagles, linnets, and *tzenzontles*, plus aquatic varieties on the coast. Common among the mammals are red squirrels, deer, and mountain cats. Insects and arachnids include bees, scorpions, and a variety of spiders. Turtles and crabs are found on the coast, together with the usual varieties of Pacific fish and shellfish. There are many types of lizards and snakes.

Cultural Groups and Languages

Oaxaca has a high proportion of indigenous people. Evidence of an Indian presence is felt all over the state, in festivities and hybrid traditions, in the variety of languages spoken and the importation of some indigenous terms into Spanish, in the cuisine, and in the varied styles of dress.

Recent government surveys have taken the ability to speak an indigenous language as the sole criterion for classifying people as Indian, though the reality is that, for practical purposes, being Indian is a matter of whether one sees oneself or is seen by others as such; it is a question of how deeply one embraces indigenous cultural habits or how far one has assimilated into the dominant Hispanic culture. Using the language criterion alone, however, the 2005 census concluded that more than 35 percent of people over the age of five were Indians; many of those people also spoke Spanish. The Indian language that is strongest in Oaxaca is Zapotec, which was the language of the major civilization once centered on Monte Albán. According to the National Indian Institute, there are now sixteen different ethnic groups in Oaxaca. In descending order by numbers, they are Zapotec (approximately 31 percent of the total), Mixtec (27), Mazatec (15), Mixe (10), Chinantec (5.5), Chatino (2), Chontal (2), Cuicatec (1.5), Triqui (1.3), Chocholtec (1), Huave (0.9), Zoque (0.8), Nahua (0.6), Amuzgo (0.5), Tacuate (0.2), and Ixcatec (0.1).

The residents of Chacahua, a place known for its national park and lakes, are predominantly black. Its people (locally known as *morenos*) are descendents of a community of former slaves, and their culture is clearly influenced by Africa.

History

The earliest traces of a human presence—stone tools and preserved plants found in a cave near Mitla—date back to 11,000 BC. It is assumed that nomadic peoples eventually gave way to peoples who settled in the valleys, where they began to cultivate crops and raise animals. Evidence suggests that this transition had taken place by 2000 BC. For example, close to the town of Yanhuitlán, there appears to have been a fishing community that left behind artifacts, including figurines of women, that resemble those found in the central uplands; nearby were found ceramic remains in the style of the Olmecs. Elsewhere, ceramic remains suggest links with peoples of Guatemala.

Monte Albán, which is fairly close to the modern city of Oaxaca, was the focus of one of the outstanding cultures of the Preclassical Period in Mesoamerica. Monte Albán's first phase, roughly from 650 to 200 BC, has distinctive characteristics but also displays a marked Olmec influence, while during a second phase it came under the influence of peoples from Chiapas, Guatemala, and Teotihuacán. The resulting culture, the Zapotec, lasted until the arrival of the Spaniards in the sixteenth century.

It was the commercial success of another people, however, the Mixtecs, that motivated Aztec expansion into Oaxaca. During the rule of Moctezuma I, the Aztecs began their conquest of the south, taking control of the

Isthmus of Tehuantepec and a large part of the coast. In the fifteenth century, an Aztec settlement was established beside the Río Atoyac, in an area where they had to cut down a number of acacia trees, and so they called it Huaxyacac, "The Place of the Acacias," which later became Oaxaca.

The Spaniards first came to this area in search of gold. In 1519, soon after reaching Mexico, the conquistador Hernán Cortés sent Diego Pizarro with four men to Tuxtepec. Bernal Díaz del Castillo, a chronicler of the conquest, notes that this expedition came as a result of Cortés asking Moctezuma about the source of his supplies of gold. Other Spaniards explored Mixtecapan, the Valle de Huaxyacac (Oaxaca Valley), and the coast of Tehuantepec. A further aim of the Spaniards was to gain access to the Mar del Sur (Southern Sea) and establish a trade route to the Far East.

In general, the natives provided considerable resistance. On one occasion, for example, they took advantage of an unguarded moment to annihilate the Spanish troops who had occupied Tuxtepec. The Mixtecs defeated Francisco de Orozco, but soon Cortés sent reinforcements, and with the help of Zapotec allies, Orozco took Huaxyacac in 1521. Gonzalo de Sandoval and Pedro de Alvarado were then sent to complete the conquest of the area. The Indian chieftain of Tututepec paid Alvarado a sizable sum in gold, only to find himself imprisoned—but that was only typical of Alvarado, who has gone down in history as a ruthless man of great cruelty. Emperor Charles V, the Spanish monarch, rewarded Cortés with the rights to huge tracts of land, including what is now Oaxaca.

The first representative of the Church to arrive in Oaxaca and engage in the business of evangelization was Father Juan Díaz, Orozco's chaplain. Along with Father Olmedo and Dean Minaya, Díaz accompanied Alvarado as he went about subduing the Indians, and ostensibly they converted some of them. One of the principal Indian leaders, Cosijoeza, was baptized. In 1528, the Dominicans came to the city of Oaxaca, to a modest church that for a while served as the city's cathedral and is now the church of San Juan de Dios; after that, they spread out across the state. Oaxaca received its first bishop in 1535: Juan López Zárate. The Jesuits arrived in 1596, followed by other religious orders.

As commercial life in the colony developed, silk, duly dyed and woven, became one of Oaxaca's prized products. During the colonial era, there was some discontent with Spanish control: for example, 1681 brought a rebellion against taxes on trade that had been imposed by the colonial authorities. But by 1810, when there were rumblings about independence, the people of the city of Oaxaca, now numbering in the region of 18,000 and mostly *mestizos*, were generally loyal to the colonial regime. When Miguel Hidalgo's representatives José María Armenta and Miguel López de Lira came to Oaxaca to spread the message about independence, they were hanged, and their heads put on display to warn the inhabitants, in streets that now bear their names. Felipe Tinoco and Catarino Palacios were local men who also tried to light the torch of independence; their fate was to be shot. Still, by 1812, the movement for independence had gained strength. At Huahuapan de León, insurgent forces were under siege for several months before José María Morelos sent troops to defeat the colonial forces. More battles followed until independence was eventually proclaimed at Huahuapan de León, in June 1821.

Once installed in Oaxaca, Morelos took steps to curtail the interests of some of its richest people, among them the dealers in *grana*, a valued natural dye. He imprisoned some Spaniards and shot some soldiers who had supported the colonial order. He also founded the most important newspaper of the times, the *Correo Americano del Sur*. During the skirmishes between rival forces, the main churches were pressed into service, and they suffered some damage, but they suffered more from earthquakes. In some ways, things did not change a great deal as compared with the colonial order; for example, a census dating from 1824 indicates that at that time approximately half of buildings in the capital city belonged to the Church.

After the demise of Agustín de Iturbide's short-lived Mexican Empire, Antonio de León and Nicolás Bravo took control of the city of Oaxaca and aligned themselves with the emerging federal republic. Struggles between liberals who were generally in favor of federalism and conservatives who preferred strong central government clouded the first half of the nineteenth century. The liberals became known as the Vinegar Party and the conservatives as the Oil Party, and each espoused different Masonic rites. The result of the rivalry between the two was political and economic chaos; unrest and discontent were the order of the day. For example, the people of the Isthmus made an attempt to break away, and did so for a while. As if political instability were not enough, the 1830s brought a major epidemic of cholera, followed by a serious drought. The economic situation worsened still further when the currency was devalued and the production of grana collapsed. After Antonio López de Santa Anna first came to power in 1834, some laws restricting the powers of the Church were rescinded, and a campaign ensued in Oaxaca, led by Luis Quintanar, to persecute the liberals. At the time of the U.S. invasion, Oaxaca sent a battalion under Gen. Antonio de León to fight in Mexico City.

During the nineteenth century, two very different local sons distinguished themselves, both becoming president of Mexico: Benito Juárez and Porfirio Díaz. **Benito Juárez García** (1806–1872), a lawyer and teacher by training, was Mexico's first president of real stature, and he was a major force for reform. Along the way, his authority as president was usurped by the French Intervention, and his government had to leave Mexico City and travel the country, finally to be restored after the defeat of the French. In 1847, the liberal Juárez had assumed the governorship of Oaxaca and taken significant steps to foster peace and prosperity in the troubled state. He was reelected for a second term, during which he encouraged improvements in educational provision. His successor, Lope San Germán, renewed the attack on the liberals, but after the Ayutla rebellion, Juárez once again became governor, in 1856. A year later, the 1857 Constitution was formally adopted in Oaxaca, and at the invitation of President Ignacio Comonfort, Juárez left the state to become a minister in the national government. The conservatives now began to take control of some local communities and eventually attacked the capital of Oaxaca, but the liberals managed to regain control. Once Juárez became president of Mexico, he issued a law nationalizing Church assets (the Church being one of the richest property owners in the country), upon which the conservatives rose up in arms, beginning a civil war that lasted several years, known as the Reform War.

Porfirio Díaz Mori (1830–1915) became famous as a soldier and then as a politician, but he began as a professor of law, rather like Juárez. During the Reform War, Díaz fought against the conservatives; he became the political chief of Tehuantepec and then represented Oaxaca in the National Congress. As a senior military man, he took part in the Battle of Puebla (celebrated today in Cinco de Mayo festivities) against the French. When Puebla fell, he was taken prisoner, but he escaped, to take charge of military resistance in the states of Oaxaca, Puebla, Chiapas, Veracruz, and Tabasco. Díaz was imprisoned for a second time after French forces took the city of Oaxaca, but once again got away. He persuaded Gen. Carlos Oronoz, in Miahuatlán, to join him and retake the capital.

The French Intervention soon came to an end, the Republic was restored, and Juárez resumed power for a period that lasted until 1872. During his last years in office, there was some unrest in Oaxaca, and Díaz was a driving force behind it. Although once an ally of Juárez, Díaz drew up the Plan de la Noria in opposition to him and later he devised the Plan de Tuxtepec, in opposition to President Sebastián Lerdo de Tejada. He was unsuccessful with the first, but successful with the second.

Díaz himself became interim president in 1876 and was elected to that office a year later. Following his initial period in office, he became a minister (an extremely powerful one) under President Manuel González and then governor of Oaxaca (in which capacity he promoted the construction of the Tehuantepec railroad). By 1884, Díaz was president once again, and this time he managed to keep hold of the office until the Revolution, in 1911.

Díaz's long rule, commonly referred to as the *porfiriato*, was characterized by progress and authoritarian control. Unfortunately, the progress did not significantly better the lot of the majority poor, and it adversely affected the position of indigenous peoples in particular. In the case of Oaxaca, oil lamps were installed in the capital, several railroad lines started up, new crops were introduced, and trade was revitalized. Communications improved, industry blossomed, as it did in many parts of the country, and foreign investment was encouraged. But Mexico's rich became richer, national assets were sold off to foreigners, and there was unbridled exploitation of natural resources. Moreover, Díaz used strong-arm tactics to silence any opposition.

A new generation of liberals opposed Díaz, among them some other famous sons of Oaxaca, the Flores Magón brothers. The most influential of these was **Ricardo Flores Magón** (1873–1922), a politician and journalist who was imprisoned by Díaz in 1892. He was editor of *El Demócrata* and, together with his brothers, he founded *Regeneración*, the main mouthpiece for opposition to Díaz, and a paper that was published for a while in Texas, where the brothers were living in exile. There, Flores founded a political party called the Partido Liberal Mexicano and supported the leading light of national opposition to Díaz, Francisco Madero. Later, Flores attempted to set up an anarchist community in Baja California. (He also protested peacefully against U.S. participation in World War I, for which he was once again imprisoned. He died in a prison in Kansas.)

Madero visited Oaxaca in 1909 to spread the opposition's message: it was time for Porfirio Díaz to go. In January 1911, Sebastián Ortiz and others took the government building in Oaxaca, captured its officials, stole arms, and then retreated to the hills. Mexico City sent troops to put out this army, which called itself the Ejército Libertador Benito Juárez. Back in Oaxaca, a number of anti-Díaz figures were detained, while the archbishop, Eulogio Gillow, called upon the faithful not to support the Revolution. But soon the Revolution had gained momentum; rebel groups from Guerrero and Puebla came to the coastal area and the Mixtecas, and there were uprisings in Jamiltepec and Cañada. By the middle of the year, the revolutionaries had control of most of the main towns along the railroad lines; they were ready to take the capital and demanding the appointment of an opposition leader as governor.

Although Díaz slipped into exile and Madero came to power in Mexico, within the year the latter had been assassinated and the country found itself in the dubious hands of Victoriano Huerta. There followed years of political convulsions, with various revolutionary leaders jockeying for power and no lack of armed confrontation. During this period, Oaxaca lost its autonomy and then recovered it, acquired a new state constitution in 1922, and then found itself under a military governor imposed by Mexico City.

After the controversial election of Onofre Jiménez to the governorship of the state, there began an era of uneasy calm that saw some improvements. Yet **José Vasconcelos** (1882–1959), Jiménez's unsuccessful rival for the governorship, was to prove a far more influential figure. He was a lawyer, writer, and teacher, as well as a politician and diplomat. He had campaigned against the reelection of the eighty-year-old Díaz, and he had supported Madero and represented him in the United States and elsewhere. Vasconcelos was a journalist, an editor, and a writer of books (of which probably the most famous is *La raza cósmica*, which proposes that in Mexico is to be found a groundbreaking new "race," the mestizos). As an educator, Vasconcelos became director of the prestigious Escuela Nacional Preparatoria, cofounded the influential Ateneo de la Juventud, ran Bellas Artes (the National Institute of Fine Arts), and was a member of the Academy of the Language. While he was minister of education, he promoted the national university (giving it its motto, "My Race Shall Be the Voice of the Spirit"), promoted education for the masses and its provision in remote areas, established libraries across the country, and sponsored the art of muralists such as Diego Rivera.

In 1929, the leftist parties of Oaxaca united behind the new National Revolutionary Party (later to become the Partido Revolucionario Institucional or PRI). Soon the state had introduced the eight-hour working day as norm. By 1936, under the influence of the policies of President Cárdenas, workers began to organize themselves into associations. The year 1946 was a troubled time, marked by widespread protests by tradesmen and students against rising taxes, and leading to the demise of the then governor, Sánchez Cano.

Starting in the early twentieth century, the population of the city of Oaxaca had grown rapidly, spilling over the established boundaries and encompassing what had previously been separate Indian communities—places such as Jalatlaco and Santa María del Marquesado. There was another major earthquake in 1931, one that destroyed some old buildings. For years after that, the historic city of Oaxaca suffered neglect, until in the 1970s there began to be attempts to restore or preserve its architectural heritage. Civil unrest in 2007, however, once again in protest against the governor's policies, did new damage to the façades of some of Oaxaca's finest buildings.

Economy

The primary sector (agriculture, livestock, and fishing) accounts for about 40 percent of the Oaxaca economy, the secondary (mining, industry, and construction) for 20 percent, and the tertiary (commerce, tourism, and services) for the rest.

Much of the state has plentiful water. Over 80,000 hectares (200,000 acres) of land are irrigated. A wide variety of fruit is cultivated. Most seasonal agriculture is carried out in the Valles Centrales (especially corn, beans, wheat, sorghum, alfalfa, and peanuts), the Mixtecas (the same crops, plus coffee and millet), Tuxtepec (corn, beans, wheat, rice, sesame, sorghum, barley, sugarcane, pineapples, and coffee), the Isthmus (corn, beans, sesame, sorghum, rice, and coffee), and the Coastal Region (corn, beans, sesame, cotton, peanuts, coffee, and copra).

About 30 percent of the land is used to rear livestock, predominantly cattle in the Tuxtepec, Isthmus, and Coastal regions and pigs, sheep, goats, and poultry in the Valles Centrales, on the coast, and in the Mixtecas. Most of the beekeeping takes place in the Coastal region.

Fishing brought in approximately 8,000 tons in 2004. The principal species caught are *jurel, barrilete, pargo,* snapper, shrimp, tuna, and catfish. The first four of these are caught in sufficient numbers to be significant in terms of national production.

Oaxaca accounts for 7 percent of Mexico's total production of wood. Ninety-eight percent of Oaxaca wood production is of pine.

Mining has a long tradition here. Etla, Ixtlán, Taviche, Pápalo, and Salina Cruz have deposits of coal, graphite, titanium, silver, gold, and lead. Marble, salt, gypsum, mica, lime, and stones for the construction industry are also produced. Salina Cruz also has a refinery for oil and liquid gas that meets demand along the coast.

Food processing, tobacco products, and the manufacture of drinks are the backbone of the state's industry. The second most important area of industrial activity involves chemical products derived from oil and rubber.

Tourists are attracted by the city of Oaxaca (which has been declared a World Heritage site by UNESCO), by Monte Albán and Mitla; and by the state's natural splendor and its coast. The most visited regions are the Valles Centrales, the Mixtecas, Papaloapan, and the coast. In 2005, 2.2 million tourists came to the state, 88 percent of them from within Mexico.

Arts

The rich variety of arts and crafts in Oaxaca includes gold and silverwork, pottery, weaving and embroidery, metalwork, leatherwork, basketry, the making of fireworks and paper artifacts and decorations, and articles of onyx, wax, or wood.

Alebrijes are handmade figures of animals, sometimes fantastic ones, that are made of wood and intricately painted in bright colors; the origin of this kind of craftwork is quite recent, dating back only to the 1970s. Arrazola, where the art was invented, is most famous for it, along with La Unión Tejalapan and San Martín Tilcajete.

There are two characteristic types of indigenous pottery: the vitreous green clay artifacts associated with Atzompa and the black ceramics of San Bartolo Coyotepec. The former are made by hand, without a wheel; the background is usually white or light brown, and the designs floral. Once fired, the black ceramics acquire their distinctive hue and a crystal-like ringing sound when tapped.

Basketry with reeds is mostly associated with the Oaxaca Valley (producing cages, lampshades, screens, and so forth), and the use of palm with the Mixtecas. Knives have been made since colonial times and have a national reputation; quite often they are inscribed with sayings. Similarly, ironwork has been practiced since the colonial era, for example, gates and railings in Tlacolula and machetes on the coast. Another craft that dates from that era is tinwork. Some of the goods produced are utilitarian, but many are decorative, too. There are many types of jewelry; a good deal of the work with gold is devoted to reproducing the treasures of Monte Albán. Leatherwork has reached sufficient production levels to justify some exporting to other countries.

Mantillas, tablecloths, curtains, and other such cotton goods are associated primarily with the state capital. Many textiles have colors or designs that identify the region of origin. Wool, colored with natural dyes, is used to weave mats, blankets, and carpets; Teotitlán del Valle, Mitla, and Tlacolula make these. Mitla and Santo Tomás Jalieza make shawls, *huipiles*, blouses, bags, and many other items. San Antonino Castillo Velasco is known for its dresses and blouses embroidered with silk.

Oaxaca has produced at least two painters of national stature, the one early colonial and the other modern. **Miguel Cabrera** (1695–1768) was one of the most prominent painters of the colonial era and official artist to the archbishop of Mexico and to the Society of Jesus. His works can be seen in many places, including the cathedrals of Mexico City and Puebla. He was also a portrait artist. **Rufino Tamayo** (1899–1991) was one of twentieth-century Mexico's most distinguished painters; he worked at the National Archaeological Museum in Mexico City, the Ministry of Education, and the Brooklyn Museum, among other places. Tamayo was important in part because he won national recognition despite not being one of the muralists whose art was so favored by official Mexico during the early part of the century. Some of his works indirectly invoke the pre-Hispanic tradition through their style and colors and their animal and vegetable motifs. He often painted in a two-dimensional, rather abstract style. Among his more nationalistic works are "Juárez" (1932) and "Zapata" (1935), but unlike the works of the muralists, these are not part of a political agenda. In the 1940s, Tamayo became more expressionistic (for example, in "Muchacha atacada por un extraño pájaro," 1941), and thereafter his work became increasingly abstract (as in "Sandías," 1968). By the early 1950s such was Tamayo's stature that he had been invited to add his own contribution to the walls of the Palacio de Bellas Artes in Mexico City, alongside the works of the muralists. The canvases he produced for this are called "The Birth of Our Nationality" and "Mexico Today," both of them striking displays of color and geometry. Apart from the museum he himself founded in Oaxaca, there is also one in his name in Mexico City's Chapultepec Park. **Francisco Toledo** (1940–) and **Rodolfo Morales** (1925–2001) are other significant Oaxacan painters.

On the popular musical front, José López Avalés is remembered for having composed "Canción Mixteca," Chuy Rasgado for "Naila," and Alvaro Carrillo for "Sabor a mi" and "Pinotepa." As far as musical genres and ensembles are concerned, wind bands are characteristic of the Sierra region, *chilenas* (a musical genre deriving from the Chilean *cueca*, imported into southwestern Mexico during the gold rush) of the coast, and marimba music and songs of Zapotec origin of the Isthmus. The well-known song "La llorona" is an example of the local ballad form known as the *son istmeño*.

Among the most usual dances at religious and civic celebrations are the *danza de la pluma* (feather dance), and the *danza de los moros* and *danza de Santiago* (both inherited from Spain and based on the quadrille). In addition to the dancing associated with festivities in general, Puerto Escondido hosts an annual Festival of Dance in November.

Social Customs

The Fiesta de Guelaguetza dates back to the Aztecs, for whom it was a celebration in honor of Centéotl, the goddess of fertility. It would begin in mid-July and last for eight days, during which there would be dancing and offerings; on the eighth day, they would perform a dance of nobles and soldiers and sacrifice a virgin to the goddess. When the Spaniards arrived in Oaxaca, they destroyed the temple of Centéotl and replaced it with a shrine to Santa Veracruz. However, the Indians continued to come to the place at the appointed time and celebrate, albeit in a modified way. In 1697, the Carmelites put a church in place of the shrine, the Carmen Alto Church, introducing the cult of the Virgen del Carmen, whose date coincides with the Aztec one. The ancient tradition of climbing up a hill to what is now called the Cerro del Fortín was allowed to continue, but with an Hispanic overlay. With official promotion, eventually the festivity grew into what is now the Fiesta de Guelaguetza, focused on the last two Mondays in July and therefore sometimes called the Fiesta de los Lunes del Cerro. In the present day, a dedicated open-air auditorium with a capacity of 10,000 hosts a large-scale celebration of the state's seven regions, with music and dance, including *sones*, *fandangos*, and *jarabes*. It is the most important festivity in the state.

The Jueves de los Compadres is another major celebration, one associated with El Marquesado; it takes place on the Thursday before Ash Wednesday, when it is customary to venerate El Señor de Santa María and to prepare *moles* to give to one's neighbors. Noche de Rábanos (Radish Night) is another Oaxaca tradition, one that is shrouded in mystery; it comes a couple of days before Christmas and is marked by huge and lavish stalls with radishes sculpted into strange, sometimes monstrous shapes. Many other types of local produce are also on display, and prizes are awarded to the best of them. Part of the tradition of the day, inherited from Spain, is to eat *buñuelos* (fritters) and then to toss the plate into the air so that it shatters.

Carnival is important in a number of places, such as Huaxpaltepec, Juxtlahuaca, and Cacahuatepec. In Cacahuatepec, it involves the dances of the *mascaritas*, the *tortuga*, the *tigre* (which has hunters and a dog in it), and the *viejitas* (performed by men in drag). Carnival in Zaachila means enacting a battle between priests and devils: the devils use ribbons to "whip" the priests, who fend them off with wooden crosses and buckets of water. The priests naturally emerge victorious, amid general cheering. Both groups wear wooden masks for the performance. The Day of the Dead, which is important all over Mexico, is particularly so for Chiltepec. Huautla de Jiménez, a place renowned for its use of hallucinogens to cure ailments, has a major celebration on the third Friday in Lent, when Mazatec Indians march down from the hills wearing traditional dress. One typical festive practice in certain areas is fruit throwing. For example, it is part of the celebration in honor of San Isidro Labrador in Juchitán, a place also noted for its candlelight processions. Juquilla, an Indian community, is the focus of a popular festivity coinciding with the Feast of the Immaculate Conception in December, when representatives of many different Indian groups converge to enact their various rituals, finally joining in a common celebration. March 21 sees the celebration of the birth of Juárez, in Gueltao. These are only a small sample from among the many festivities that take place in the state.

With so many different peoples, the state of Oaxaca has a number of traditional styles of dress. These can be seen on social occasions and at festivities, are sometimes donned for work in tourist venues, and are to some extent seen in less elaborate forms in rural communities. Tlaxiaco, Tuxtepec, and Huautla de Jiménez are famous for their striking regional costumes of pre-Hispanic origin: huipiles, *enredos*, and *quexquémitls*. From the Isthmus come brightly colored garments of silk and velvet with floral embroidery. In everyday situations, Indian women may be seen wearing blouses and full, long, dark skirts, with or without footwear, while for celebrations they might have sandals and full-length white shifts overlain with shorter ones and decorated with elaborate, geometric, floral, or animal designs in strong colors. During festivities, men wear less interesting outfits of white cotton pants, jacket shirts, a straw hat, and a kerchief.

Noteworthy Places

Monte Albán and Mitla, both of which are quite close to the capital city, are the two main archaeological sites and are among the most significant in the country. The former is set impressively on a hilltop at 1,950 meters (6,400 feet), with commanding views over the surrounding countryside. Though there is no clear account of the original name of the place, Monte Albán became known as such in the seventeenth century, due simply to the fact that the land had been acquired by a Spaniard named Montalbán.

Archaeologists have identified five different stages in Monte Albán's development, covering the period from 500 BC to the time of the arrival of the Spaniards. For 1,400 years, the site was continually occupied. Work began on a reconstruction of the Monte Albán site in 1932. The restored area represents the center of the Zapotec community, an area of approximately 2,000 hectares (8 square miles). Its main square is surrounded by pyramids, terraces, patios, and temples, all made of stone. Most date from the later years, but some appear to have been superimposed on earlier

Ruins of Monte Albán.

structures. Most of the buildings are wide and relatively low, with steps up to a flat area that is sometimes in the shape of an E. The most notable structures are the ball court and the palace on the eastern side, the temples of the main square, and the observatory, which was probably the first in Mesoamerica. The platform to the south is particularly imposing and is decorated with numbers, hieroglyphs, and human figures that mark the evolution of the site and its conflicts. Probably most famous are the monoliths with relief representations of humans, known as Los Danzantes (The Dancers); given their physical characteristics, these are believed to be Olmec in origin. To the north, there is another monumental platform and a sunken patio. There are also dwellings and tombs where murals and artifacts were discovered, including the so-called Treasure of Monte Albán, which is now housed in the regional museum in Oaxaca.

Mitla is another of Oaxaca's major archaeological sites. The Mexicas (Aztecs) called it Mictlán, the "Place of the Dead"; for the Zapotecs, its name was Lyobaa, which meant "Place of Rest," and indeed, one of its features is its burial grounds. It is believed that Mitla was occupied at the time of the first phase of Monte Albán, between 600 and 200 BC. However, it appears to have developed and prospered to a greater degree after the decline of Monte Albán, around AD 700. Most of the structures that survive today date from the thirteenth and fourteenth centuries. They are Zapotec

Oaxaca Cathedral.

with Mixtec influence, the Mixtecs having invaded the Central Valley under pressure from the Aztecs. The most striking aspect of the Mitla buildings is their distinctive geometrical decorative motifs. Some of the buildings at the site were ceremonial and are set beside squares. Others were residential, with palaces set around patios. There is a tomb to the north of the site that has a column now known as the "Pillar of Life"; legend has it that if one embraces it, the space between one's hands indicates the span of life remaining. Mitla provides an excellent illustration of how the Spaniards superimposed their own structures, especially churches, on Indian religious sites.

Among the colonial-era religious buildings, some of the most outstanding are the monasteries or convents at Cuilapan, Tlaxiaco, Coixtlahuaca, and Yanhuitlán; Cuilapan features a *capilla abierta* (open chapel), a large church, and a fortress-like monastery. Teposcolula has one of Mexico's best examples of a capilla abierta. The Convento de Santo Domingo and the Iglesia de la Soledad, in the capital, are also very significant; the church of the former, just inside its entrance, has an arched roof with an elaborate representation of the Tree of Life. Oaxaca's cathedral, which was immortalized in a famous painting by José María Velasco, the country's foremost landscape artist, was completed in 1574. It was modified and extended about a hundred years later, severely damaged by an earthquake in 1714, and as a result closed for reconstruction until 1733, though building work continued for some time thereafter. As cathedrals go, it is not large. It is a harmonious structure in greenish-gray stone with walls 2 meters ($6^1/_2$ feet) thick, a distinctive octagonal dome and vaults, and finely worked wooden choir stalls and chancel, and it is home to some significant paintings.

The state has many museums, notably the Museo Rufino Tamayo and the Museo Regional, both of which are in the capital. The Tamayo museum's building was once the colonial Casa de Villarraza; it houses a major collection of pre-Hispanic artworks. The Museo Regional (also known as the Museo de Las Culturas) is located in the former Convento de Santo Domingo de Guzmán, which is itself of considerable interest. The museum collection includes archaeological artifacts tracing the evolution of peoples up to and including the heyday of the culture of the Oaxaca Valley. Part of the museum is devoted exclusively to displaying the Treasure of Monte Albán; among the five hundred pieces on display that were found at tomb number 7 are personal adornments made of obsidian, turquoise, rock crystal, pearls, and jade. Another part of the museum is devoted to the clothing worn by the many different indigenous peoples of Oaxaca.

The house in the capital that once welcomed Benito Juárez has become the Museo Casa de Juárez; it has personal items, including his printing and binding equipment, and some important documents. The city of Oaxaca's main square and the adjacent open area beside the cathedral are the focus of social life and celebrations, and in the evening of a cacophony of mariachis, brass bands, and marimbas. The Fuente de las Siete Regiones, also in the capital city, is a modern fountain, a monument that has sculptures representing the seven regions of the state. The Benito Juárez Market (once called the Porfirio Díaz Market) is one of the most famous in Mexico; it is a permanent installation near Oaxaca's main square.

Santa Cruz de Huatulco is a legendary place. It is said that when the Spaniards arrived at Huatulco, they were impressed to discover a large wooden cross on the beach, said by the locals to have been venerated for years prior to colonization and to have been brought by a bearded white man from the sea, who taught them to worship Christ. This cross acquired new prominence in 1567, when the English pirate Thomas Cavendish took the port of Huatulco and tried unsuccessfully to destroy the cross. It was subsequently taken with much ceremony to the capital and made into a number of smaller crosses, one of which was sent to the pope, one back to Huatulco, one to a church in Puebla, and another to Oaxaca's cathedral. In 1895, a replica of the original was returned to Huatulco.

Among the state's natural attractions, Las Regaderas, in Huautla de Jiménez, is one of many waterfalls; it is about 40 meters (130 feet) high. Somewhat more unusual are the Cascadas Petrificadas de Hierve el Agua (Petrified Falls of Boiling Water), near San Lorenzo. The effect, as the name suggests, is of boiling water, but in fact the water is only tepid; the boiling impression comes from the cascade of deposited calcium carbonate that seems to spill down toward an almost desert landscape. Caves in Oaxaca include Nindo-Da-Gé in San Antonio Eloxochitlan and the Sótano de San Agustín in Huautla de Jiménez; the latter is 800 meters (half a mile) deep and ranks as the second deepest in Mexico.

One curiosity is the Arbol del Tule, which sits beside the modest church of Santa María de la Asunción, not far from Oaxaca. It is an immense *ahuehete* (*Taxodium mucionatum*) with a height of 40 meters (132 feet) and a girth of 42 meters (138 feet), estimated to be two thousand years old. Local people have given parts of it names, such as "The Elephant" and "The Pineapple."

An example of a major conservation area is the Parque Nacional Lagunas de Chacahua, with its rivers, lakes, jungle, mangroves, and beaches. The coastline is long, with many beaches; its principal tourist areas are Puerto Escondido, Puerto Angel, and Bahías de Huatulco.

Cuisine

Oaxaca is sometimes the butt of a joke: "*En Oaxaca todo lo hacen tamal*"—"It's all tamales." Referring to politics as much as food, the phrase also implies that in general they do things badly. Neither implication is entirely justified. While tamales are common in Oaxaca, the cuisine is varied and rich, benefiting from the differences in climate and terrain and also from several traditions. Dishes that have an Indian origin include a variety of *moles* (thick and complex sauces of different hues), *tlayudas* (open tortillas topped with ingredients, pizza-style, and somewhat like the *guaraches* one finds in more northerly states), *chapulines* (insects cooked with garlic, salt, and lime), and *memelitas* (cooked tortillas dressed with lard, beans, mild cheese, and salsa). From the Hispanic tradition come such things as *cecina* (cured pork), *tasajo* (lightly salted beef), and *queso fresco* (a very mild cheese, rather like ricotta).

Among local drinks, there is the famous and highly potent *mezcal* (distilled from the *maguey* cactus), *champurrado* (a corn-based drink that contains chocolate), *tejate* (another corn-based drink, of pre-Hispanic origin, also with chocolate or brown sugar, plus crushed flowers and seeds), and fruit drinks such as *jicotilla* and *chilacayota*.

Sweet items include *alegrías* (made with toasted almond seeds), *mangate* (candied mango—the *-ate* suffix attached to the name of a fruit indicates that it has been candied), *mamón* (a sweet cinnamon-flavored sponge cake), and *gollorías* (made with nuts and chocolate). *Marquesote* and *pan de yema* are local breads.

Tlayudas

Ingredients:

5 large tortillas
1 lb. tasajo (beef)

3 tbsp pork fat (*asiento*)
1 lb. mild cheese, shredded
3 cups black beans, ground and drained
Chopped lettuce
Salsa verde

Grill strips of the meat. Brush one side of each tortilla with some melted fat and spread beans on the other. Place greased side down on a hotplate, in a frying pan, or, better still, on a barbecue. Sprinkle cheese on top. When the cheese starts to melt, add the beef. Finally, add some salsa verde and lettuce. The tortilla can be folded, like a calzone.

Mole Negro

This dish improves if prepared a day before eating.

Ingredients:

1 young turkey (around 5 lbs.)
3 cloves of garlic
1 onion
2 oz. each of *chilhuacle negro, chilhuacle rojo, mulato negro,* and *pasilla* chiles
1 tortilla
2 oz. chocolate
1 tbsp sugar
3 avocado leaves, roasted
6 tomatoes
1 oz. pumpkin seeds
2 tbsp peanuts, skinned
2 oz. chopped walnuts
3 oz. chopped almonds
4 oz. sesame seeds
4 oz. raisins
1 tbsp oregano
1 tsp thyme
Pinch of aniseeds
Pinch of cumin
4 peppercorns
2 cloves
4 *pimientas*
1 cinnamon stick
Oil or lard
Salt

Cut the turkey into pieces, wash it, and brown it in oil with half the garlic and onion, and a little salt. Cover the turkey with water and boil gently for about 40 minutes. Soak the raisins in water. Top, devein, and deseed the chiles (greasy hands help avoid skin irritation). Fry the chiles one by one until they begin to brown. Then toast the nuts and pumpkin and sesame seeds with a little salt added (to stop them from popping). Toast the tortilla until it turns black, then rinse it in water so it does not become bitter. Roast the tomatoes with the remaining garlic and onion. When cool, grind everything except the turkey, the chocolate, and the sugar into a paste. Put some fat or oil into a deep pan and fry the paste, stirring frequently. Add the toasted avocado leaves, herbs, chocolate, and sugar. Add salt and water as needed and leave to simmer over a low flame for about an hour. If necessary, the sauce can be thickened with a few dried breadcrumbs. Now remove the turkey pieces from the liquid. Remove the avocado leaves from the sauce before serving over the turkey. Rice goes well with this.

Nieve de Tuna (Cactus-Fruit Slushy)

Ingredients:

> 20 *tunas* (otherwise known as *higos chumbos*, the fruit of the *agave* cactus)
> 2 pints water
> 10 oz. sugar

With gloves on, carefully remove the spines from the tunas and peel and chop them up well. Put them in the water and pass the mixture through a sieve in order to eliminate the seeds. Add the sugar. Put in the freezer for about 3 hours, until set.

Puebla

State Characteristics

The state of Puebla is set in the southwestern part of Mexico's central *mesa*, between the Sierra Nevada and the eastern range of the Sierra Madre (Sierra Madre Oriental). To the north and east of the state lies Veracruz, to the south, Oaxaca and Guerrero, and to the west, Morelos, México, Tlaxcala, and Hidalgo. Puebla covers 1.7 percent of the country, a total surface area of 33,919 square kilometers (13,228 square miles).

There are 217 *municipios*. The state has the fourth highest population in Mexico; in 2005, its official population stood at 5,383,133—5.2 percent of the national total. Approximately 94 percent of the population of Puebla identifies itself as Catholic, 4 percent Protestant. The number of representatives for Puebla in the National Congress is fifteen.

The city of Puebla, with close to a million and a half inhabitants, is one of Mexico's most important, as its grandiose full name seems to suggest: Heroica Puebla de Zaragoza. In terms of urban area occupied, Puebla is Mexico's fourth largest city. The second biggest town in the state is Tehuacán, with 238,229 inhabitants; other major towns are Atlixco (86,173), San Martín Texmelucan (72,505), Tezuitlán (60,579), and Huauchinango (51,898). Cholula is another important focus of population, though its 82,964 people are scattered over two conurbations, San Andrés and San Pedro.

After Mexico City, Puebla is Mexico's most important center for tertiary education. It has no less than thirty universities or other institutions of higher education, such as its Conservatory of Music. The enrollment for all these institutions taken together is approximately 118,000, comparable to the enrollment at Mexico City's huge Universidad Nacional Autónoma. The most famous of Puebla's universities are the capital city's own Universidad Autónoma and Cholula's Universidad de las Américas.

Puebla has no less than fourteen daily newspapers; of these, twelve are based in the capital city and two in Tehuacán. They include *El Sol de Puebla* (*El Sol* is one of a chain of newspapers, and each state has its own), *La Opinión*, *Diario de Puebla*, *La Voz de Puebla*, and *El Mundo*.

Given the broad variety of climatic zones, geographers distinguish eleven different regions in this state, but for present purposes, these can be grouped into five. The mean annual temperature for the state as a whole is 16°C (61°F). In much of the state, including the capital, the high elevation makes for warm to hot days and chilly to cold nights. The rainy season begins in May and lasts until October, giving an average annual precipitation of 801 millimeters (32 inches). Details for each of the five regions are as follows: Central and southern parts of the state have moderate temperatures and a moderate average rainfall of 858 millimeters (34 inches). In the southwest, it is warmer (22°C/72°F) and the rainfall is slightly lower (830 mm/33 in.). The north is similarly warm (22°C/72°F), but the rainfall is much higher (2,250 mm/90 in.). The southeast is quite dry (550 mm/22 in.), and again warm (22°C/72°F). Lastly, the mountainous areas vary from cold to very cold, and there are mountaintops that are snowcapped year-round.

There are many high mountains, including five volcanic peaks that reach more than 4,500 meters (15,000 feet) above sea level. The highest and most famous are Citlaltépetl (often called the Pico de Orizaba) at 5,610 meters (18,513 feet) and Popocatépetl at 5,452 (17,890 feet). From the mountains, water runs either toward the Gulf or toward the Pacific. Running east toward the Gulf are the Pantepec, Nautla, Necaxa, and Papaloapan rivers. On the Pacific side, the Temixco, the Huajuapan, and the Nexapa feed into the Atoyac basin. There are several important dams and two major lakes, El Salado and Totolcingo. Natural springs, rich in minerals, can be found, for example, in the Valley of Tehuacán.

One can speak of three ecosystems in Puebla: the mild to cold, the tropical, and the dry or semidry. Their flora ranges from mountain pines, oaks, and conifers, through deciduous trees in the valleys and hills with more moderate climates, to subtropical vegetation on the eastern flanks of the Sierra Madre, and finally to scrub, cacti, yucca, mesquite, and *huizache* in the driest areas. Depending on the terrain, one can find wild boars, margays (wild cats related to leopards), porcupines, squirrels, and badgers; various reptiles, including rattlesnakes and coral snakes; and a wide variety of brightly colored birds, including goldfinches and *tzentzontles*. There are conservation areas at La Malinche, the Pico de Orizaba, Zoquiapan, Yanexas, and Iztaccihuatl-Popocatépetl.

Cultural Groups and Languages

The 2005 census states that 11.7 percent of the Puebla population over the age of five speaks an indigenous language. Historically, the state has received cultural influences from the Olmecs, Teotihuacanos, Toltecs, Chichimecs, and Mexicas. Nahua peoples are today in evidence in the northern sierras and to the south of Totonacapan. In the latter area, there are also Totonacs, and in the former, Huastecs. Popoluca people can be found in the Teotihuacán Valley and in parts of the central and southern valleys, Mazatecs in the southeast, Chochos in the southern central area, and Otomíes in the northern mountains. There are nearly 400,000 speakers of Náhuatl (the language of the Mexicas), and approximately 100,000 speakers of Totonac, out of a total of 548,723 speakers of Indian languages for the state as a whole. Popoloca and Mazateco are the next most widely spoken languages (at about 15,000 and 13,000 speakers, respectively).

History

The oldest evidence of a human presence in the region that is now Puebla has been found in the area of Valsequillo, dating back as far as 22,000 BC. Signs of early cultivation of maize (corn) have been found in the Valley of Teotihuacán from around 3000 BC. Evidence of the presence of the great preclassical civilization of the Olmecs suggests they were in the area from 1600 to 800 BC. Shortly after that time, irrigation was being practiced and corn, beans, squashes, chiles, and cotton were being cultivated.

Some people related to the Olmecs founded a sacred city to which they gave the name of Tlachihualtépetl, on the site of a spring. At Tlachihualtépetl, they constructed the largest human-made structure on the continent: a pyramid whose sides measured 450 meters (1,480 feet) at the base and whose height was 65 meters (213 feet). In the twelfth century, the Toltecs sought refuge there, leaving their cultural imprint on it and changing its name to Tolla Chollolan Tlachihualtépetl. This revered place—now Cholula—would also grow into a major commercial center. Náhuatl-speaking peoples settled in other places, too, such as Huejotzingo and Tepeaca; in the latter, the Mexicas established an open-air market (*tianguis*) that by the fifteenth century was the most important in the whole mesa. The Aztecs had a special relationship with Cholula, Huejotzingo, and especially Tlaxcala, for these were the places from which they captured people to sacrifice to their gods.

Thus, prior to the conquest by Spain in the early sixteenth century, various indigenous peoples—the Otomíes, Mixtecs, Ixtaaltecos, Zapotecs, Totonacs, and, most importantly, the Mexicas (Aztecs)—had settled in the north, south, and east of the state. By the fourteenth century, the Mexicas had taken control of the area, and that remained the case until the arrival of the Spaniards.

In 1519, Hernán Cortés, having reached Tlaxcala, sent Pedro de Alvarado and Bernardino Vázquez de Tapia to Cholula, Atlixco, and Huaquechula. On October 12, Cortés issued an order for a massacre of Indians to take place at Cholula. With the Indians under their control, the Spaniards then set about building convents and churches, often putting their structures on top of native ones, as in the case of the famous pyramid at Cholula, which is now simply a grass-covered hill topped by a Catholic church.

In 1531, Fray Julián Garcés, Bishop of Tlaxcala, and Fray Toribio de Benavente (also known as Motolinía), founded Puebla de los Angeles in an area formerly known as Cuetlaxcoapan, located between Cholula and Tlaxcala. Plans for a town were carefully drawn up by Hernando de Elgueta, in accordance with royal directives that also determined land and property ownership. The Indians were put to work in construction. By the next year, Puebla was deemed a city, and soon thereafter its inhabitants moved to the western bank of the San Francisco River, with new plans being drawn up and more land distribution. By 1538, Puebla the city had its own coat of arms, and two years later so did the town of San Pedro Cholula, not far away. Administrative units called *audiencias* were set up in New Spain. The Puebla project was in some ways a Utopian one, designed to bring some order to New Spain, to counterbalance the *encomienda* system, and to facilitate the campaign to convert the natives.

Many convents or monasteries were built in the sixteenth century, first by Franciscans and later by other Catholic orders. The first major diocese, established in Yucatán in 1526, soon functioned not from there but from Tlaxcala. In 1550, its seat was transferred to Puebla, by which time its jurisdiction ranged widely, over much of what are now the states of Puebla, Veracruz, Tlaxcala, and Guerrero.

By 1700, Puebla was already a sizable city of around 70,000 people. It was basking in prosperity and visibility, thanks in good measure to the energies of its bishop, **Juan de Palafox y Mendoza** (1600–1659). Palafox had been born in Spain and would also die there. The son of the Marquis of Ariza, he studied at the University of Salamanca and rose quickly to positions of power in Spain. However, he relinquished his privileges, resigned from membership of the Consejo de Indias (the king's most senior advisory group on matters concerning the New World), and entered the priesthood. In 1639, Palafox was appointed bishop of Puebla de los Angeles and also visitor general to Mexico. Later he would be offered the post of archbishop of Mexico, a post he declined to accept. Briefly, in 1642, he served as acting viceroy.

Bishop Palafox did much to correct financial abuses in Mexico, and he came into conflict with those with vested interests and also with members of the religious orders, whom he viewed as a threat to his authority. During his brief period as viceroy, he drew up statutes for the University of Mexico, took steps to root out idolatry among the Indians, rounded up prostitutes, banned public dancing, and had many priceless antiquities collected by previous viceroys destroyed. A tireless and determined man, he also wrote a great deal, and in general helped to enhance learning and promote Puebla. In the eighteenth century, there was a campaign to have him canonized. Though Palafox saw the Indian rites as idolatrous, he also extolled native virtues, and he founded libraries, schools, hospitals, and asylums. Puebla's place in New Spain's commercial and cultural life grew yet stronger.

The Plan de Iguala, which laid down the basis for an independent Mexico, was formalized in Puebla in 1821. It brought Agustín de Iturbide to power as emperor of the new Mexican state, but Iturbide's rule was not to last for long, and by 1823 Puebla had set up its own independent congress in defiance of him. In 1824, the new Federal Republic of Mexico was constituted; Puebla became a part of it in October of that year. A year later, Puebla had its own state constitution and its first governor was in place. In 1827, the State Congress decreed that the Spaniards should be expelled from Puebla. However, loyalist troops occupied the city in 1829, and it was several years before Antonio López de Santa Anna took Puebla for Mexico for good.

In 1847, without a shot being fired, U.S. troops under Gen. Winfield Scott invaded and took Puebla. They withdrew a year later, after the Treaty of Guadalupe Hidalgo had been signed and the United States had gained almost half of Mexico's territory.

Then, in 1862, it was the turn of French troops under the command of the Count of Lorencez to attack, but this first French attack was defeated by forces led by Gen. Ignacio Zaragoza. This occurred on May 5, the famous "Cinco de Mayo," a date now celebrated nationally. Zaragoza was duly declared a local hero—hence the full name of the city. But the euphoria was relatively short-lived, for in 1863 the French attacked the city for a second time. It found itself under siege for sixty-one days, after which it surrendered, having run out of ammunition and food. A year later, Emperor Maximilian and Empress Carlota were received in Puebla, amid much pomp. In 1867, Porfirio Díaz, then a soldier but later to be a longtime president of Mexico, retook Puebla from the French. Two years later, President Benito Juárez was opening Puebla's railroad link with Mexico City, a link that in 1873 would be extended eastward to Veracruz, the country's principal port.

A decade into the twentieth century, Díaz was still president, having kept himself in office for some thirty years. Local opposition to the possibility of his reelection led to the formation of the Club Antireeleccionista Luz y Progreso, whose most prominent member was **Aquiles Serdán** (1876–1910). Along with his brother, Serdán lost his life because of his opposition to Díaz, but his death provoked outrage, fueling support for the Revolution. Over the course of the ten years of the Revolution (1910–1920), Puebla found itself under the control of one faction after another. However, 1917 was promising, for it brought the crystallization of

Venustiano Carranza's new national constitution, under which Puebla was to be a state comprising 222 municipalities. But violence and instability continued for years after that. It was in Puebla, in a place called Tlaxcalantongo, that Carranza was assassinated in 1920. Only in the late 1930s did Puebla (and Mexico) begin to settle down and recuperate.

Puebla has naturally produced a number of people who have distinguished themselves in national politics. One notable figure in the insurgency against Spain that characterized the start if the nineteenth century was **Juan Nepomuceno Rossains** (1782–1830). He became secretary to José María Morelos, who named him general commander of Puebla, Veracruz, Oaxaca, and Northern Mexico. In 1830, Rossains he took part in a conspiracy against the government of Anastasio Bustamante, as a result of which he was taken prisoner and shot. Another nineteenth-century figure was **Martín Carrera Sabat** (1806–1871), a military man who rose to government office and briefly occupied the presidency of the country. Similarly, **Ignacio Comonfort** (1812–1863) fought on the side of Santa Anna, against Bustamante and against the U.S. invasion. He too was president, from 1835–1838, and he died fighting the French.

José María Lafragua (1813–1875) was a lawyer and politician whose distinctions include being minister of foreign affairs, ambassador to Spain, and founder of the National Library. **Rafael Martínez de la Torre** (1828–1876), a lawyer, orator, and national congressman, was one of Mexico's first urban planners. **Juan N. Méndez** (1820–1894) was another soldier; he fought the U.S. invasion, supported the reform movement, organized resistance against the French invaders, served as a senator in congress, and briefly was president of Mexico (1876). **Manuel González** (1833–1893) also fought against the U.S. invasion and served as a minister under Díaz. While president himself, González decreed that primary schooling should be obligatory. He also founded the National Bank of Mexico.

Vicente Suárez Ferrer (1833–1847) was the first to die among the six military cadets who became national heroes (Niños Héroes) after throwing themselves from the Castle of Chapultepec during the final battle with U.S. forces. **Juan Crisóstomo Bonilla** (1835–1884), again a soldier-politician, fought on the side of Juárez and Zaragoza, twice represented his state in the National Congress, and also became governor of the Distrito Federal (Mexico City). He is remembered for the support he gave to education.

During the revolutionary years, **Pastor Rouaix** (1874–1949) was a supporter of Madero and became governor of Durango, where he was responsible for land reform and the appropriation of some church possessions. He also served as one of President Carranza's ministers and wrote pamphlets about political reform. **Luis Cabrera** (1876–1954), a lawyer and writer, was another supporter of Madero and another of Carranza's ministers.

In more recent times, Puebla has supplied two presidents in **Manuel Ávila Camacho** (1879–1955), who, inter alia, sealed the nationalization of the oil industry and started Mexico's social security system, and **Gustavo Díaz Ordaz** (1911–1979), another lawyer, who after a spell as a professor at the University of Puebla represented the state in the National Congress, occupied ministerial and diplomatic positions, and then became president. His major achievement as president was to secure agreement that Latin American nations would remain nuclear free. **Vicente Lombardo Toledano** (1894–1968) was once again a lawyer and politician, but above all he was active as a labor leader, union official, and journalist.

Economy

Not long after the Conquest, Puebla was New Spain's second city, and the most important from an agricultural standpoint. Following its establishment, European fruits and cereals were introduced, along with metal implements and beasts of burden; the Indian irrigation system was developed and expanded. By 1531, Puebla had its first mill, and a few years later it was fully engaged in the production of silks, linens, and cottons. There was a tanning industry, and other manufactures included soap, ceramics, and glass, metal, and wooden objects. Puebla grew into Mexico's major commercial city. Then, during the seventeenth and eighteenth centuries, the economy came under financial pressure. There was a reduction in the supply of goods to Peru, which had been a considerable function for Puebla. There were also epidemics and shortages, and some migration to Mexico City took place.

After independence, Puebla was one of the first cities in the country to industrialize. It remains the most important city by road or rail between Veracruz, the country's main port, and Mexico City, its capital, which is about two hours away from Puebla by road.

Nowadays, roughly 70 percent of the state's population lives in urban environments. The service sector, manufacturing, and commerce each account for about 22 percent of economic activity, the finance sector and housing for another 13 percent, and agriculture for a mere 4 percent. The principal crops are corn, coffee, carrots, tomatoes, squashes, and citrus fruits, but peanuts, potatoes, beans, avocados, and garlic are also grown. Puebla is also a source of flowers—Mexico's number-one grower of gladioli. Honey is another important product. Among livestock, poultry is prominent, along with pigs, sheep, and goats; Puebla is Mexico's primary egg producer, and ranks third and fourth for goats and sheep, respectively.

Mining is not particularly significant, although there is some lead, gold, and silver, and some oil and natural gas are produced. Puebla's great industrial strengths are in textiles and car manufacturing. Volkswagen has a huge facility on the outskirts of the capital city that provides employment to a considerable portion of the population; its presence has also given rise to other enterprises that serve and supply it. The Puebla plant is the only one the company has in North America. (Volkswagen cars, including the Old

Beetle, are generally very much in evidence in Mexico.) Other industries in the state are cement, food processing, alcoholic beverages, and chemicals. Cholula and Tezuitlán have iron and steel industries, there are petrochemical plants in San Martín Texmelucan and paper in Moyotzingo. Tehuacán has bottling facilities and also processes animal fodder. Cider is made in Cholula, Huejotzingo, and Zacatlán. In other places, there is a range of craft industries based on the use of onyx, palm, glass, paper, and leather, and there is pottery production in the capital.

Arts

One tradition stemming from places such as Izúcar de Matamoros and Acatlán (and also from places in the state of México) is the making of the Arbol de la Vida (Tree of Life). This is a representation of the creation of natural phenomena, animals, and human beings, together with good and evil. The precise style and mode of production varies from place to place. In the small provincial town of Izúcar de Matamoros, for example, the tree is made in earthenware and painted in several colors.

Chignahuapan is famous for its handmade glass objects, especially decorative glass balls. San Andrés Hueyapan maintains its tradition of embroidering shawls and other items, such as bedspreads; natural dyes are used for the materials, and the designs typically involve animal and plant imagery. Tecali, a well-preserved and quiet town, is full of workshops that produce artifacts made of onyx.

Papel de amate is made from the bark of a variety of *ficus* tree; it was used in pre-Hispanic times rather like parchment, for writing and painting. In modern times, if the painter is a shaman, then the painted images on this "paper" are often anthropomorphic and allude to deities and spirits, with white signifying good and dark colors evil; such paintings may be used in rituals. If the painter is an ordinary person, however, the ritual significance is absent and the probable destiny of the product is the tourist market. San Pablito Pahuatlán, located in the northern mountains, is known for *papel de amate* art.

Since the sixteenth century, Amozoc has been a place of metalworkers, producing utilitarian objects (spurs, knives, and so forth), as well as decorative ones with ivory, mother-of-pearl, or bone inlays. The techniques show signs of having been inherited from the city of Toledo, in Spain.

Finally, the pottery of Puebla is known as Talavera due to its similarity to pottery from the town of that name in Spain (also in the province of Toledo). Like the metalwork of Toledo, Talavera's pottery drew on Arab techniques and motifs. Puebla Talavera is highly regarded in Mexico and is used for the decoration of walls as well as for freestanding objects. The base material is clay, and this is covered with a lead glaze. Typically, the background color is white or off-white, and the decoration in a rich blue, with the result that Puebla's ceramics sometimes have a Chinese look about them. The ceramic tradition began in Puebla after it was imported by the Dominicans in the sixteenth century.

Puebla has its own Orquesta Filarmónica (symphony orchestra) and strong traditions in theater and dance. The Teatro Principal, which dates from the middle of the eighteenth century (though reformed in the early nineteenth), is one of Latin America's oldest. Puebla also holds a summer arts festival. Traditional popular music typically involves the use of the violin and guitar, sometimes with flutes or more obscure instruments such as the *chirimía* (a shawm-like wind instrument) and the *teponaxtle* (a type of drum). There are songs in the mountain style and lowland style, *huastecas* and *huapangos*, ballads and *fandangos*. Dances include the *danza de la flor de naranjo* (orange blossom dance), the *danza de los voladores* (dance of the flying men), the *quetzal*, the *danza de los negritos huehues* (dance of the old black men), *tocotines*, *santiagueros*, and *toreros*.

Distinguished *poblanos* (people from Puebla) in the arts and sciences include **Manuel Orozco y Berra** (1816–1881), an engineer, topographer, and lawyer who occupied a number of public offices and also wrote about matters geographical and historical, and **Gabino Barreda** (1818–1881), a doctor and intellectual who introduced the philosophy of positivism into Mexico and also wrote about moral issues. Positivism had an immense effect on nineteenth-century thinking in Latin America.

Juan Cordero (1822–1884) was a painter and muralist who studied at Mexico City's Academia de San Carlos and also in Europe. Among his works is a mural at Mexico City's Escuela Nacional Preparatoria, a major show-place for muralists. **Manuel Centurión Sabat** (1883–1952) was a sculptor; one of his works, an equestrian statue of the South American liberator Simón Bolívar, can be seen in Mexico City's Chapultepec Park. He also produced a medal for the national celebration of the centenary of the *Grito de Dolores*, the "Cry from Dolores" that marked the start of Mexico's break-away from Spain.

One of the most famous people to have emerged from Puebla in recent years is the novelist **Angeles Mastretta** (1949–), one of many prominent women writers in modern Mexico, but one of the few whose works have become best-sellers. Her breakthrough work, *Arráncame la vida* (1986) (translated into English under the title *Mexican Bolero* [1989]) is the story of a girl from Puebla who is swept off her feet by an older man, an unscrupulous soldier and politician.

Social Customs

Huey Atlixcáyotl is a grand flower festival held by the villages of Atlixco, a time for them to make a show of their cultural heritage. It is said that in the center of the town of Atlixco there is a hill where the Toltecs-Chichimecs once settled and where they paid homage to the god

Quetzalcóatl. There would be dancing and singing in honor of the lord of spring, with festivities and happiness. In the colonial era, the inhabitants of one of the towns, Villa de Carrión, built a little hermitage which was dedicated to "the Lord of the Celestial Army," and there they would hold celebrations in late September. In Náhuatl, "Atlixcáyotl" means "the Great Atlixco Tradition."

Many places celebrate the Day of the Dead with rituals that reflect their particular heritage. In Huaquechula, for example, elaborate altars are set up in the homes of the families of deceased persons. These altars have several levels, supported by a structure that is covered in pieces of white paper. On the lowest level, food and drink are placed; on the second, memorabilia relating to the deceased; and on top, a cross or a saintly image. The fact that an offering is being made inside a house is made public to anyone outside it by laying out a path to its door, made of the yellow petals of a flower called *cempasúchil*.

It is held by some that on the spring equinox, March 21 or 22, one's body is infused with energy if one enters the vicinity of any sacred pre-Hispanic pyramid. At the Cholula pyramid known as Tlachihualtepetl ("the Man-made Hill"), each year there is a ritual in honor of Quetzalcóatl, the Plumed Serpent, that draws pilgrims from a wide area to celebrate a tradition dating back to before the arrival of the Spaniards.

Puebla's International Fair begins in late April and lasts for three weeks. It includes industrial, agricultural, and craft displays, regional dances, artistic performances, cockfights, food, and rides. May 5, Cinco de Mayo, the day when Mexican forces fought off the French, is marked in the capital by military processions, bands, and fireworks. On August 26 comes the Feast of Saint Augustine, with its music, dancing, and more fireworks.

Carnival is a major event for a number of places, including Huejotzingo. Its inhabitants don showy costumes decorated with palm fronds and feathers, along with masks, representing the Spanish conquistadores, demons, or animals. The celebration begins on the Saturday prior to Ash Wednesday and ends on Shrove Tuesday with a reenactment of the events of the Cinco de Mayo and the legend of Agustín Lorenzo, a seventeenth-century Robin Hood figure.

A Coffee Festival is held annually in Cuetzalan, on October 4, the Feast of Saint Francis. Coffee is the major product of the area. There are (supposedly) pre-Hispanic dances dedicated to the gods, and a Coffee Queen is chosen—two sample activities that amply illustrate the hybrid nature of this festival. The gradual fading or contamination of Indian traditions led to the creation in 1962 of a simultaneous Huipil Fair, in a conscious attempt to revive Indian traditions. It has dancing and music, fancy dress, fireworks, and a lot of excitement. Cuetzalan is in the northern mountains, a long way from Puebla itself, and its native festivities have upstaged the imported Hispanic ones ever since the sixteenth century.

Huauchinango, another mountain location, holds a Fiesta del Santo Entierro y Feria de las Flores. This is ostensibly a religious festivity ("The

Feast of the Holy Burial") that begins on the eve of the first Sunday of Lent, but is also a flower festival, a major event that draws growers from all over the country. On the first day, a Flower Queen is crowned. There is an agricultural show, dancing, rides, processions, fireworks, cockfights, cowboy displays, films, theatrical performances, and lectures. In addition to the Flower Queen, an India Bonita (Pretty Indian Girl) is chosen, and there is a *son et lumière* event with a pre-Hispanic spin. The region is famous for its naturally wide variety of flowers.

Among other festivities, Zacatlán has an Apple Festival, Tetela de Ocampo a Peach Festival, and Atlixco an Avocado Fair, to cite a few examples.

Puebla has produced one of Mexico's national icons in the figure of the *china poblana*. The origins of this figure, or at least of her name, are a little confused. In colonial times, the word *china* was an Indian one that was commonly used to mean domestic servant, but in Spanish it also means "Chinese." It happens that there was a china in early colonial days who was not Chinese, though indeed oriental, and who became well known for her good deeds. She lived in Puebla. *Poblana* means "from Puebla" but also "from among the ordinary folk." The image of the china poblana has crystallized over the years into that of virtuous young lady of modest means. She has acquired a traditional appearance, too: an off-the-shoulder white cotton blouse with heavy embroidery, a full green skirt, silk shoes, a shawl, and swept-back hair. Quite often her clothes echo the colors of the Mexican flag; from the point of view of national propaganda, at least, one could say that the china poblana is the very representation of Mexican womanhood. There is a monument to the china poblana on the outskirts of Puebla.

Noteworthy Places

The state has many natural attractions, especially the thermal waters at Chignahuapan, the monumental stones of the Valle de Piedras Encimadas at Zacatlán, the springs at Tehuacán, and the mountains and volcanoes. Cholula has massive historical significance and is one of the oldest settlements in the continent, while the city of Puebla is full of architectural and historical interest. There are many convents or monasteries across the state, and innumerable churches with interesting decoration.

In 1977, the Mexican government designated the city of Puebla a *Zona de Monumentos Históricos* (place of historic interest), and ten years after that, UNESCO made it a World Heritage site. Puebla is a city laid out according to a rigid grid pattern with uniformly sized blocks; its dull predictability is relieved by a plethora of exuberant façades and interesting interiors. Outside the gridded area lies the Barrio Alto, which was designated in colonial times for Indian occupation, and which has a more characterful and unpredictable layout. The streets here are cobbled. The Iglesia de la Cruz is said to be where Motolinía celebrated the first Catholic Mass.

The Zócalo.

Puebla has a great number of impressive churches. Arguably, the jewel among them is Santo Domingo, a Dominican church that houses a side chapel called the Capilla del Rosario. The latter is widely regarded as one of the very greatest works of baroque architecture. Its dome is festooned with gold relief work, and its walls are covered with human figures and abstract and floral motifs. It receives a constant flow of visitors. The main body of the church contains an impressive pulpit in black and white marble, with emblems of the Dominican Order. The lower parts of the interior walls are decorated with tiles in the local style. The church was begun in the late sixteenth century, with Francisco de Becerra as architect, while the Capilla del Rosario dates from about a century later. The church occupies a corner site and is approached via a spacious front courtyard. Many of Puebla's churches are eye-catching from the outside, and this one is no exception. It has a striking array of windows.

Many other churches are attached to convents. Dominican nuns occupied the Convent of Santa Catalina de Siena, the first such convent in New Spain. As was customary with convent churches, the nave of this one runs parallel with the street. The parish church of San José is part of a group of colorful sixteenth- and seventeenth-century buildings that also exemplify the local baroque predilection for covering façades with brick and tiles. The interior of the church has a notable sacristy and baroque altarpieces.

Quiet corner of Puebla.

The exterior of the Franciscan Convento de la Concepción, begun in 1539 and dedicated in 1617, is ringed with distinctive, high buttresses, painted white and blue; the interior has a spacious cloister. The Santa Clara convent, also Franciscan and dating from 1642, has a tiled dome and also sports buttresses, a defense against earthquakes rather than heathens. Another convent, completed much later, in 1731, is Nuestra Señora de la Soledad. Its church has a fine pulpit and baroque altarpieces, while the outside aspect is a vivid combination of yellow, black, and white, with neoclassical elements in its structure. The Convento de Santa Inés, dating from the eighteenth century, is beside the seventeenth-century Iglesia de la Concordia and the Casa de Ejercicios that houses the famous Patio de los Azulejos (Tiled Patio), another example of wall decoration with an elaborate combination of brick and tiles, this time in floral and geometric patterns upon neoclassical structures.

There are many other interesting churches and convents. La Compañía is a church that was established by the Jesuits soon after their arrival in

Puebla in 1578, though reconstructed in the eighteenth century. This church contains the tomb of Catarina de San Juan, the archetypal china poblana. The adjacent Jesuit college buildings still have an educational function as the main buildings of the Universidad Autónoma de Puebla.

Last but not least among the religious buildings is the cathedral. Having been first begun by Francisco de Becerra and Juan de Cigorondo in 1575, plans to modify it were drawn up by the architect of Mexico City's cathedral during the first half of the seventeenth century, but it took Bishop Palafox to see that the project was carried through. He entrusted the job to an artist, architect, and sculptor from Aragón (Spain) named Mosén Pedro García Ferrer. Palafox consecrated the cathedral in April 1649. It stands beside Puebla's central square, an imposing and somber building by comparison with Puebla's other churches. Among its treasures, it houses paintings by Cistóbal de Villalpando and Baltasar de Echave, two of the most distinguished colonial painters, Flemish and Italian art in its Capilla Ochavo (Octagonal Chapel), memorable altarpieces, and fine choir stalls.

The dean of the cathedral once occupied a large and rambling house very close to the cathedral, the Casa del Deán, whose interior walls were covered in murals. Thoughtless and unscrupulous development led to the destruction of most of this property and its conversion into a cinema, but two rooms remain much as they were in the sixteenth century, when their walls were painted. Running the full circuit of the walls of the first room are images representing the Sybils, and the life of Jesus Christ that these prophetesses foretold. The walls of the other room tell a secular story drawn from the writings of the Italian poet Petrarch. This building is a unique example of mural painting for private purposes, rather than public and propagandistic ones.

The buildings of the Seminario Tridentino house four seminaries, in one of which the Biblioteca Palafoxiana is located. Palafox donated his personal library to it in 1646. It is an elegant group of buildings, and the library, whose collection was subsequently enriched by other sources, includes some priceless works.

Other notable places in Puebla include the bishop's palace, the Teatro Principal (Main Theater), and many private houses or museums with elaborate façades, such as the Casa de Alfeñique. Puebla has a Barrio del Artista, where stalls sell artwork of various kinds, and nearby El Parián, which is more oriented toward the tourist market. The Callejón de los Sapos is known for its street market of antiques, trinkets, and crafts. What is now known as the Palacio de Gobierno was built as a bank at the beginning of the twentieth century and changed hands several times before it became the Government Palace in 1940; after 1968, it became the seat of the City Treasury. It is a modern structure but one that shows marked evidence of a Renaissance influence. The Antiguo Edificio de la Ciudad de México is huge, a nineteenth-century complex that was redeveloped in the early twentieth century by French immigrants and became Puebla's first large-scale shopping center. Others have followed, notably one beside a new convention center and a complex of restaurants and cultural facilities, built around the vestiges of ancient structures.

Puebla also has a large number of interesting museums, such as the Railway Museum, the Museum of the Mexican Revolution, the Museum of Religious Art and Museum of Popular Art (both in former convents, the latter in Santa Rosa, which has a famous tiled kitchen), the Museum of Contemporary Art, the Puebla Museum of Viceregal Art (in what was once a hospital), the University Museum (in a famous eighteenth-century building called the Casa de los Muñecos), the Regional Museum, and the fine Amparo Museum.

After Puebla itself, one of the most interesting places is neighboring Cholula, which has been settled for almost 25,000 years. The pyramid on which the Spaniards placed a church has already been mentioned. In the center of modern Cholula stand the Franciscan Convento de San Gabriel and the adjacent Templo de los Remedios. The convent was built between 1529 and 1552 on the site of a temple dedicated to Quetzalcóatl. Another church was added beside the Templo de los Remedios. This second church, known as the Iglesia de la Tercera Orden (Church of the Third Order), is highly unusual in design, and unique in Mexico; it has sometimes been compared to a mosque. It has no fewer than seven naves, each feeding toward a central point, so as to accommodate a great number of worshipers.

Not far from Cholula is Santa María Tonantzintla, a small church with a profusely and brightly decorated interior displaying many examples of the sort of hybridization that characterizes Mexican colonial art and architecture. The church is dedicated to the Virgin Mary and was put there because the local Indians were accustomed to worshipping Tonantzin ("Our Mother"), a protective goddess who watched over maize. Another nearby church, known above all for its tiled façade, though also having sumptuous interior plasterwork, is San Francisco Acatepec.

Several important monasteries can be found in other parts of the state, among them Huejotzingo, Calpan, Tochimilco, and Huaquechula. Huejotzingo's Franciscan Convento de San Miguel, for example, was built in the mid-sixteenth century. On the outside it offers a mixture of the plateresque and *mudéjar* styles. Among its distinguishing characteristics inside are a rare *retablo* by Flemish artist Simon Peyrens and a mural depicting the first twelve friars sent by the pope to begin the process of converting indigenous peoples to Catholicism. There are four *capillas posas* with elaborate stonework. All four of these convents have been singled out by UNESCO as World Heritage sites.

Farther afield lies Teteaca, where there is yet another Franciscan monastery, though in this case with a fortress-like appearance. It was from here that Cortés sent one of his reports back to the Spanish monarch. Though Acatzingo also has a monastery, it is more memorable for its Parroquia de

San Juan Evangelista (Parish Church of St. John the Evangelist) and the Chapel of the Virgin within it, which has early eighteenth-century retablos. Cuauhtinchan was a powerful Indian realm before the Conquest, and therefore a prime candidate for locating another monastery; the resulting structure is somber, but inside, it has a fine stone baptismal font, a small museum, and paintings attributed to Peyrens. The Templo de la Merced at Quecholac is in ruins, but still serves as an impressive example of the popular baroque style, whereas the Convento de Santa María at Tecamachalco, once the leading settlement of the Popoluca people, is another example of hybrid styles that mix the Spanish and the indigenous, especially visible in a series of wall paintings on themes from the Old Testament and the Apocalypse. San José Chiapa has a curious history. After a confrontation with the Jesuits, Bishop Palafox took refuge here on an estate whose chapel was given a century later to the Bishopric of Puebla. The bishop at that time, Francisco Fabián y Fuero, had the chapel embellished with exceptional onyx and alabaster decoration, and with columns like votive candles.

Tepapayeca, Tepexi, Yohualichan, and Cantona are archaeological sites. There are also rock paintings at Zapotitlán de Méndez, with human and animal figures and some geometric shapes.

Yohualichan reveals that coastal peoples (from Tajín, now in Veracruz) had come to the mountains and that these peoples gave way to more bellicose peoples from central Mexico. This was an influential ceremonial and monumental center. Its tiered, pyramidal architecture has characteristic double niches (one inside another), some of them still with a stucco facing, and they are protected by protruding flat pieces of stone.

The Cantona site, in the north between the municipalities of Tepeyahualco and Coyoaco, covers 12 square kilometers (4.7 square miles). The southernmost portion is the best preserved, with an area for the buildings that housed dignitaries and priests. It is believed that Cantona was occupied from 600 to 1000, reaching its zenith at the time of the decline of the Classical Age of Mesoamerican civilizations. Possibly it was involved in the demise of Teotihuacán, thanks to a location that made it able to hinder the passage of goods to the west. There is evidence of there having been a great many large patios, probably housing different peoples or groups of families, and specialized work areas, for example, for the production of articles made from obsidian. The humbler the inhabitant, the lower his dwelling on the site's many tiers. At the top were temples, a ball court, and the houses of the leaders.

Puebla's natural attractions include the Parque Nacional Izta-Popo, beside the two major volcanoes, snowcapped Iztaccíhuatl and Popocatépetl. It has sulfur springs, an attractive range of hues, spectacular views, and facilities for walkers and climbers. There are thermal springs at Chignahuapan, waterfalls at Cola de Caballo near Zacapoaxtla, and the Karmidas Caves at Zapotitlán de Méndez. The Valle de Piedras Encimadas has impressive natural stone sculptures that stand as high as 4 meters (13 feet) and suggest human faces and poses, animals and birds, and even flying saucers; they have led the locals to weave elaborate tales about them.

Cuisine

Puebla cuisine is a hybrid of the indigenous and the Hispanic. In homes and convents, the two culinary traditions were combined, so that corn, turkey, and chiles, for example, confronted pork, olives, and cheese. Probably the most famous dish is *mole poblano*, a thick, complex sauce made with dozens of ingredients, including chocolate, and served with poultry; it is said to have been invented in the kitchen of the Convento de Santa Rosa. Another signature dish is *chiles en nogada*, peppers stuffed with a mixture of meat and fruit and served with a milky walnut sauce; it is sometimes claimed to be a patriotic dish because it has the colors of the Mexican flag. *Chalupas* are a common form of greasy fried tortilla that is served with shredded chicken, cheese, and a sauce. *Tinga* is a sauce made with pork, chicken, and spicy sausage fried with tomatoes. *Molotes* are the local version of *quesadillas*, filled in this case with brains and pumpkin blossoms. *Tlatapas* are made with yellow beans, sausage, and chiles. For dessert, one finds *camotes poblanos* (sweet potato puree flavored with coconut, pineapple, or orange), *yemas reales* (cooked egg yolks with syrup), and *dulces de almendras*. As far as drinks are concerned, there are many liqueurs made with fruits, such as *acachul*, *chumiate*, and *zacualpan*.

Chiles en Nogada

This dish was created by Augustinian nuns in Puebla in honor of Agustín de Iturbide, to mark the occasion of his signing the treaty of independence for Mexico. Ever since, it has been customary to prepare it at the time of the Feast of San Agustín. The right kind of walnuts is available during August and September.

Ingredients:

 $^1/_2$ onion, finely chopped
3 cloves of garlic, peeled and finely chopped
Olive oil
1 lb. ground, lean pork
3 tomatoes, roasted and chopped
1 plantain, diced
2 peaches, diced
2 pears, diced
2 apples, diced
 $^1/_2$ cup raisins
1 *acitrón* (candied *nopal*), finely chopped
 $^1/_2$ cup pine nuts
 $^1/_2$ cup chopped almonds
1 tsp sugar

Salt and pepper
12 *poblano* chiles, roasted and cleaned out
6 eggs
Flour
2 cups walnuts (*nueces de Castilla*)
$^1/_2$ cup creamy goat cheese
3 oz. sherry
$^1/_2$ pt. milk
2 deseeded pomegranates

Nogada is a walnut sauce. Purists skin the walnuts, and soak them so that they do not spoil; the sauce is made later by grinding the walnuts with goat cheese, milk, and sometimes sherry. Soften the garlic and onion by frying them in a little oil, then add the meat. When it starts to brown, add the tomatoes. When fairly dry, add the fruits, acitrón, pine nuts, almonds, sugar, and salt and pepper to taste. Cook gently for about 20 minutes. Stuff the chiles with this mixture. Beat the whites of the eggs to soft peaks and then fold in the yolks; roll the chiles in flour and dip them in the egg. Fry them until golden. Puree the walnuts with the cheese, milk, and sherry to make a thick sauce; add a little sugar, salt, and pepper according to taste. Pour this over the chiles and sprinkle with pomegranate flesh.

Mole Poblano

Ingredients:

10 to 12 lb. turkey or chicken
8 *chipotle* chiles
$^1/_4$ lb. *ancho* chile
2 lb. *mulato* chile
3 oz. *pasilla* chile
3 oz. almonds
3 oz. peanuts
$^1/_2$ cup sesame seeds, toasted
1 lb. raisins
1 head of garlic
1 small onion
$1^1/_2$ oz. ground cinnamon
2 tsp aniseed
2 tortillas, toasted and broken into small pieces
2 lb. plantains, chopped
6 large squares of dark chocolate, grated
Salt
Sugar
Pork lard

Cut up the turkey (or chicken) and boil the pieces. The chiles (apart from the chipotle) must be opened, deseeded, and then briefly roasted or fried in pork fat. Then fry the chipotle. In separate operations, fry the plantain pieces then the nuts, then the raisins, aniseeds, and cinnamon. Soften the garlic and onion by frying them. Put all these ingredients, plus the chocolate, and pieces of tortilla together in a greased pan and heat for a short while before pureeing to make a paste. Thin the paste with some of the turkey broth, making sure that it stays fairly thick. Season with salt, pepper, and sugar to taste. Simmer the sauce gently with the turkey for about half an hour. Serve with sesame seeds sprinkled on top.

Camotes

Ingredients:

2 lb. sweet potatoes
2 lb. sugar
$^1/_2$ pint water
5 drops of lemon or orange essence (or some zest)
A drop or two of food coloring (green or orange are usual)
Powdered sugar

Boil the sweet potatoes, then peel them, mash them thoroughly, and put them through a sieve. Dissolve the sugar in the water, heating it to make a syrup; remove any scum. Mix the syrup into the sweet potato, then heat, stirring constantly, until it is thick and somewhat sticky. Allow it to cool a little, then mix in the lemon essence and food coloring. Lay out the mixture on a flat surface and allow it to cool completely. Make balls with the cold mixture, roll them in powdered sugar, and let them dry. Once fairly dry, they can be kept in greaseproof paper.

Querétaro

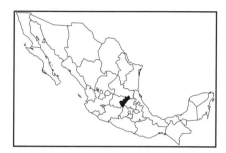

State Characteristics

Two explanations have been offered for the name of Querétaro: one, leaning on the Otomí language, gives as its meaning "the Great Ball Game"; the other, attributing it to roots in the Tarasco (Purépecha) language, glosses it as "Place of Stones." The formal name of the state is in fact Querétaro Arteaga; Arteaga was the name of a distinguished governor of the state during the nineteenth century. Querétaro is considered the birthplace of Mexican independence.

This state is roughly in the middle of the country, about 160 kilometers (a hundred miles) northwest of Mexico City. The states of México and Michoacán make up its southern border, and San Luis Potosí lies to the north, Guanajuato to the west, and Hidalgo to the east. At 11,450 square kilometers (4,465 square miles), Querétaro is not one of the largest states. The capital city is Santiago de Querétaro (and is often called, rather confusingly, "Querétaro" for short); it has a population of 596,450, while the total state population is 1,598,139, according to the 2005 census results. The state is ranked seventh in terms of population density. Its other populous cities are San Juan del Río, which approaches 200,000, and Corregidora and El Marqués, each over 70,000. There are eighteen administrative municipalities. Seven people represent Querétaro Arteaga in the National Congress. In the 2005 survey, 95 percent of the population said they were Catholic, and 2 percent said Protestant or evangelical. The state has six institutions of higher education and publishes just five newspapers: *Diario de Querétaro*, *Noticias*, *El Corregidor*, and *A.M. de Querétaro* in the capital, and *El Sol* in San Juan del Río.

It is customary to think of the state in terms of three geographical regions: the Región Sur (Southern Region), the Región Serrana (Mountain Region), and the Región Semidesierto (Semidesert Region). Two major mountain systems meet in this state: the Sierra Madre Oriental and the Sistema Volcánico Transversal. The Sierra Gorda, which is the north, is a part of the former; it has high elevations, small valleys, and deep canyons. Similarly, in the south there is the Sierra Queretana, which is part of the Sistema Volcánico Transversal.

The central Semidesert Region covers about 14 percent of the state. Its *mesetas* run north–south at an average altitude of 2,000 meters (6,500 feet) above sea level, with some peaks reaching 3,000 meters (10,000 feet). The Mountain Region to the northeast accounts for about 36 percent of the land and has many peaks that reach over 3,000 meters (10,000 feet). The Southern Region is crossed by the volcanic range and covers the remaining 50 percent of the state. Elevations again range between 2,000 and 3,000 meters (6,500–10,000 feet). The highest elevation in the state is at the Cerro de Zamorano: 3,360 meters (11,020 feet).

The state's rivers are part of two major systems, the Lerma and the Pánuco. The Lerma system is fed by Querétaro's Pueblito and Querétaro rivers, which run southeastward but are not large. They are controlled by the Santa Catarina Dam. The Pánuco system is fed by the westward-flowing San Juan and Extoraz Rivers, which are fuller. Given that this is a volcanic area, there are geothermal waters in several spots. The capital of the state, and therefore the majority of the population, depend on the Lerma watershed, which has to meet the needs of much of central Mexico, including Mexico City. Water has always been a problem for Querétaro, which draws heavily on underground aquifers that are not adequately replenished.

For much of the year, the average temperatures range between 18°C and 21°C (65°F to 70°F), but the climate varies quite a lot according to region. In the south, it is temperate and fairly dry; in the center, dry or moderately dry; and in the north, hot or moderately hot. There are frequent frosts during the winter in the mountains. Rainfall on average is between 500 and 600 millimeters a year (20–24 inches) a year. The highest average rainfall is on the eastern side of the Sierra Madre, at 1,500 millimeters (60 inches); the lowest, less than 500 millimeters (20 inches), is in the basin of the Extoraz River. Prevailing winds are from the northeast in winter and from the east during the remainder of the year.

Vegetation varies considerably. In the mountains (in Amealco), there are oaks and pines; in the central meseta, cacti and thistles; in the Sierra Gorda, there are several types of trees, including oaks and bays; and in the Sierra Madre, there are *ceiba*, *palo de rosa*, red cedar, and varieties of bracken. Squirrels, *tuzas*, *güicos*, *huilotas*, woodpeckers, and doves can be seen in the Sierra de Amealco; foxes, *tlacuaches*, sparrows, and pigeons on the central plains; white-tailed deer, mountain cats, *mapaches*, and falcons in the Sierra Gorda; and lynxes, weasels, deer, herons, and kingfishers in the Sierra Madre. Protected areas are the Biosphere of the Sierra Gorda (which has six different ecosystems), the Cerro de las Campanas, and El Cimatario.

Cultural Groups and Languages

In the 2005 census, a mere 1.7 percent of the population over the age of five (23,363 people) claimed to speak an indigenous language. Otomí speakers are located in the south of the state (in the municipality of Amealco), in the central region (in Tolimán, Cadereyta, Colón, and Ezequiel Montes), and in the northern mountains (in Jalpan and Arroyo Seco). The first two regions are traditional lands of the Otomíes, but the third was once the land of the Pames, who are still there in some numbers, along with some Huastecos.

History

Evidence of inhabitation by agricultural communities around 500 bc has been found near San Juan del Río and Huimilpan. This area was part of the network of communities that made up the empire of Teotihuacán. Later it came under the influence of Tula, as shown by vestiges of that culture found in El Cerrito, in the Querétaro Valley. For a lengthy period, perhaps three centuries, the region was more or less abandoned as peoples migrated toward the south, until, in the twelfth century, it was populated by two types of peoples, hunters and gatherers on the one hand and small agricultural communities on the other. During the fifteenth century, the region was affected by warring between the Tarascos and the Mexicas (or Aztecs). As a result, pre-Hispanic Querétaro was not homogeneous in organization and culture. Peoples of the hills contrasted with those of the valleys, the former having more in common with other peoples to the east and the latter more in common with those of the west—and even within each of these two broad groups, there were regional distinctions. By the time the Spaniards arrived, the dominant groups were the Pames, practicing agriculture in the valleys, and the Chichimecs (Jonaces), a hunting and gathering people, occupying the mountains.

The Spaniards founded Huimilpan in 1529 and San Juan del Río and Querétaro in 1531. The leading figures in this process were two Indians who had converted to Christianity and adopted Spanish names: Nicolás de San Luis Montañés, a descendent of the lords of Xilotepec, and Fernando de Tapia, otherwise known as Conín, an Otomí chieftain also from Xilotepec. There was a battle on July 25, the Feast of Santiago, at the Cerro del Sangremal (in today's Barrio de Santa Cruz). It was the only one necessary for the Spaniards to secure control. Father Jacobo Daciano, a Franciscan, proceeded to baptize the defeated Pames Indians.

The seventeenth century saw the consolidation of Spanish power. Churches were built, and links were established between rural communities and the town. In 1655, the king of Spain elevated the town of Querétaro to city status, which attracted more Spaniards, *criollos*, and *mestizos* to it, so that soon they outnumbered the indigenous population. Querétaro became an inevitable point of transit for anyone heading north, and by 1671 it was officially the third most important city in New Spain (after Mexico City and Puebla).

Cattle ranching, agriculture, textiles, and trade turned Querétaro into a prosperous place during the eighteenth century. Querétaro became the leading producer of wool in the whole of Spanish America. It had New Spain's second biggest tobacco factory, and mining for mercury and silver also became important. Thanks to this prosperity and to the enterprising Franciscans, during this time Querétaro acquired valuable objects such as artworks and liturgical accoutrements, and it exuded an impression of richness. This was the period when the city settled its urban design and when many of its most imposing buildings were constructed. It was also the time when its aqueduct was built, to bring water into the city.

During the eighteenth century, the Chichimecs of the Sierra Gorda, who had long resisted the Spanish invasion, were put down by forces commanded by José de Escandón, who went on to bring parts of the northeast of New Spain into the administrative fold. Fray **Junípero Serra** (1713–1784) led a group of Franciscans in converting the Chichimecs, resulting in the establishment of missions at Jalpan, Concá, Tilaco, Tancoyol, and Landa.

The prosperity of eighteenth-century Querétaro contrasts with its decline in the next century, perhaps because it was so entrenched in the colonial order of things. Yet Querétaro was the state where the movement for independence from Spain began. When France occupied Spain and the Spanish king was dethroned, reactions in New Spain were varied. In Querétaro, the criollos, seeing this as a justification for breaking free of Spain, became involved in conspiracies. One venue that facilitated such activity was the Club Literario, run by **Josefa Ortiz de Domínguez** (1768–1829), the wife of the *corregidor* (a high civil office). Eventually the authorities learned of the plans of the conspirators, who, under cover of her literary *tertulias* (discussion groups), had been planning a breakaway from Spanish control; on hearing of this, Doña Josefa sent a warning to Miguel Hidalgo, the priest who was the leader of the conspiracy, prompting him to issue his famous call for independence. From the small town of Dolores (in what is now the state of Guanajuato), he demanded an end to colonial rule and then set out with a motley army of peasants to do battle with the authorities. Shortly after the start of the campaign, Querétaro fell into the hands of the *realistas*, the forces that remained loyal to Spain, and it proved to be the last place to fall to the rebels. In the meantime, the fighting moved elsewhere and the mountains became the refuge of the insurgents. After a bloody ransacking of Guanajuato and some victories in other places, Hidalgo's army was defeated by royalist forces, and he was taken prisoner, defrocked, and shot, along with some fellow rebel leaders. But the tide of the independence movement was flowing too strongly for the authorities to stop it.

Once independence became a fact in 1821, there was a short-lived empire presided over by Agustín de Iturbide. Thereafter, Querétaro was made an independent state in the new republic, despite attempts to incorporate it into the states of San Luis Potosí and México. By 1825, Querétaro had a state constitution and its first governor, José María Díezmarina. But there now began a period of great instability, both locally and nationally. There were constant struggles between conservatives seeking to centralize power in Mexico City and liberals who favored federal freedoms. Between 1824 and 1855, Querétaro had twenty-five governors. Nonetheless, there was a revival in some parts of the local economy.

At the end of the war with the United States, the peace treaty between the two countries was signed in Querétaro. In 1857, the year in which a new liberal constitution was introduced in Mexico, local elections brought Gen. **José María Arteaga** (1827–1865) to the governorship of the state, though he was not a native of it. Arteaga organized a coalition with Jalisco, Guanajuato, Michoacán, Aguascalientes, and Zacatecas, to defend the constitution against its conservative opponents. Further trouble arrived in 1861 in the form of an invasion by France and the imposition by Napoleon III of Maximilian of Austria as emperor of Mexico. Republican opposition to him was such that Maximilian left Mexico City and came to Querétaro, occupying the city from 1863 until it was besieged and retaken by the republicans four years later. Maximilian was then taken prisoner, tried, and shot by a firing squad at the Cerro de las Campanas.

With the restoration of the republic and the presidency of Benito Juárez, Querétaro promulgated a new state constitution that was in harmony with the national one. A new round of elections made Julio M. Cervantes governor of the state. The Era of Reform brought with it the nationalization of Church assets; some churches were destroyed, and others were pressed into service for different purposes, changing the face of Querétaro. In 1870, there were revolts in the state, which was put under military control. More unrest followed the death of Juárez.

Gen. Porfirio Díaz, a former ally of Juárez and fellow Oaxacan, had drawn up a plan in opposition to Juárez and now espoused a more successful one against his successor, President Sebastián Lerdo de Tejada. Díaz then defeated another aspirant to the presidency, José María Iglesias, who had taken refuge in Querétaro, and Díaz later assumed the presidency of the country. Querétaro then acquired a governor who remained in office for twenty-seven years, twenty-four of them consecutively, almost as long as Díaz held on the presidency of Mexico; this new state governor was Francisco González de Cosío. Another state constitution was promulgated in 1879, identifying the limits of six districts. At about that time there were 192 large *haciendas* and 292 smallholdings.

As everywhere in Mexico, the *porfiriato* brought progress in communications and industry to Querétaro. Drinking water came to the capital and to San Juan del Río, a monument was built at the Cerro de las Campanas, a teachers' college was founded, the telephone arrived, the Compañía Hidroeléctrica was set up to improve water resources, and an ice factory was begun. The number of companies involved in mining grew, and existing mills and textile factories were modernized, one of them being the largest in the country. The early twentieth century was also a time of improvements in educational provision and health. However, the porfiriato did all these things at the expense of selling off national assets, allowing foreign investors to exploit resources unbridled; the rich became richer, and the poor poorer. Moreover, Díaz brooked no opposition, using strong-arm tactics to silence any recalcitrants.

Opposition to Díaz came to a head with unrest among workers in 1909 and riots in Jalpan and Cadereyta. Once Díaz was ousted and Francisco Madero was president, Cosío resigned from the governorship, in 1911. He was replaced by the authoritarian Joaquín F. Chicarro, who press-ganged peasants into joining the army and fighting against Victoriano Huerta. Only after Governor Federico Montes came to power did things begin to change for the better; he instituted trade restrictions and price controls and took measures to deal with health issues, guarantee the water supply, and protect the rights of workers. On February 2, 1916, President Venustiano Carranza made Querétaro the capital of the country, and a year later he convened the Congreso Constituyente (Constituent Congress) that produced the 1917 Constitution, which is still in effect today, despite many amendments. A new constitution for the state followed shortly after.

In 1941, a law was introduced to protect Querétaro as a place of historic interest. It was around that time that industrialization began to take off. The capital grew substantially; by the 1960s its population stood at about 60,000, but by 1990 it was ten times as high. In 1996 UNESCO declared the city center a World Heritage site, and it was at that time that Querétaro reverted to its original name of Santiago de Querétaro, recalling its foundation on the Feast of Santiago.

Modern Mexico's Partido Revolucionario Institucional (PRI) was founded in Querétaro, and after the Revolution, it dominated state politics for many decades, as it did the rest of the country. In 1997, the conservative Partido de Acción Nacional (PAN) gained control of the state, which is now considered a stronghold of that party. In 2005, a nongovernmental watchdog organization concerned with political corruption declared Querétaro to have the lowest levels of political corruption in Mexico.

Economy

From an economic perspective the state has five regions: Amealco de Bonfil, Cadereyta de Montes, Jalpan de Serra, Querétaro, and San Juan del Río.

Amealco has almost 36,000 hectares (over 88,000 acres) devoted to the cultivation of grains. Industrial activity is on a modest scale, apart from the existence of some *maquiladoras*, the assembly plants that put together consumer products to be sent to the United States. There is also some forestry, but it is not high-tech. Basic services and primary education are generally available, but illiteracy continues to exist among indigenous people. Production of crafts is not on a significant scale.

Cadereyta lies in the center of the state. An area similar in size to Amealco's grain fields is devoted to agriculture and livestock. The crops are seasonal, depending on rainfall, and livestock includes goats and pigs. Once again, the methods employed are not very modern. Mining is limited, but sophisticated and capable of further development; traditionally, the principal mineral has been silver, followed by gold, mercury, and others. The natural vegetation does not provide wood, although there is some exploitation of cacti and of the herb *damiana*; nevertheless, as much land is devoted to tree-farming as to agriculture and pasture. There is little by way of industry, although maquiladoras have made an appearance in recent years, together with recycling plants. There are problems with illiteracy, malnutrition, and health.

Three percent of Jalpan is cultivated, supplying local needs; citrus fruits, mangos, peaches, apples, and coffee are the principal crops. Livestock is of increasing importance. There is underutilization of forests and little industry. Many people migrate to other places in search of work.

The Querétaro region, by contrast, is the second most important agricultural area and has good irrigation. Crops cultivated intensively include sorghum, wheat, barley, alfalfa, oats, and, to a lesser extent, vegetables, corn, and beans. There are extensive pasturelands accommodating all types of animals and providing many of the state's milk products. Production methods are modern. Industrial production is even more important. More than half the state's industry is located in this region. Preference has been given to "clean" industries that have relatively low water demands. Major activities include the production of metal goods, auto parts, cables, chemicals, clothes, and electrical appliances. The infrastructure is sophisticated, and the capital city is connected by a major highway to other parts of the country.

San Juan is pre-eminent among the state's agricultural regions, growing much the same things as Querétaro, with major livestock and milk production. Wine production is also significant. This is the second most important region as far as industry is concerned; its varied products include paper and processed foods. San Juan has suffered from environmental pollution due to its industrial activities, but steps are being taken to address the problem. Some parts of the region are significant for tourism. The infrastructure is generally adequate, except in some isolated areas.

In the national context, Querétaro State has become one of Mexico's leading chicken producers. Its reputation as a relatively safe and stable place has attracted increasing foreign investment. Tourism, both by Mexican nationals and by foreigners, has been increasing. Querétaro now has about a third of Mexico's manufacturing industry.

Arts

Querétaro's craftwork includes embroidery, Otomí dolls, furniture, clothing, pottery, jewelry, and objects made from stone, osier, and rattan. Ixtle, a fiber from a type of cactus, is woven into such things as mats and baskets. The central valleys are known for their basketwork and their artifacts made from palm; textiles, pottery, and rag dolls are associated with the Sierra de Amealco, jewelry with the lowlands, and metalwork with the Sierra Gorda.

The local musical tradition favors *sones*, marches, waltzes, and mazurkas, which tend to be performed by wind bands in the central lowlands and the Sierra de Amealco. In the Sierra de Amealco, the *danza de los concheros* and the *matachines* (mummers' dances full of stock characters) are often accompanied by indigenous instruments: the *huéhuetl*, the *chirimía*, and the *teponaxtle*. In the Bajío area, mariachis are popular, along with dances such as *apaches*, *pastoras*, and *aztecas*. *Corridos* are often performed, to guitar accompaniment. In the mountains, there are Chichimeca dances and *huapangos*.

Mariano Arce (d. 1816) was a *queretano* visual artist, a sculptor and follower of Manuel Tolsà. His sculpture of St. James can be seen in the cathedral in Mexico City. Among writers, **Heriberto Frías** (1870–1925) became known for his novels, especially *Tomóchic*, based on his experiences as a soldier fighting Indians in the state of Chihuahua, and *Aguila o sol*. As a journalist, Frías edited *El Correo de la Tarde*, a Mazatlán newspaper. He was prominent in the opposition to Porfirio Díaz's reelection. **Alfonso Aguilar** (1879–?) was a musician—a cellist, pianist, and composer who was active in promoting opera and who worked at the National Conservatory of Music. Querétaro is home to the Escuela Nacional de Laudería, a national institution specializing in the making and repair of stringed instruments (a *laúd* is a lute).

Social Customs

Tequisquiapan holds an annual International Wine and Cheese Fair in late May; apart from displays and tastings of the local products, there are dances, concerts, rodeos, fireworks, and rides. The Feria Internacional de Querétaro is one of Mexico's most important livestock shows. It is accompanied by industrial and craft exhibitions, popular theater, and cockfights. Freixenet, the Spanish firm that makes sparkling wine by the Champagne method, has premises in the state and holds an annual Feria de la Vendimia (Grape Harvest Festival), which includes flamenco dancing. September brings a celebration of independence, in which Querétaro played an important part; a cavalcade leaves the capital for San Miguel de Allende and Dolores. San Joaquín holds a Concurso Nacional de Baile de Huapango Huasteco and Querétaro has its Festival Santiago, both in April. The town of Bernal, in Corregidora, celebrates the spring equinox, a tradition that has pre-Hispanic roots.

There are a great many religious festivities, most of them involving a mixture of Catholic ceremony and elements such as indigenous dances and fireworks. Holy Week is important—for example, the live Via Crucis held at Tolimán—as is the run-up to Christmas in the capital. Other religious festivities of note are the celebration of the Virgen de Belén in the central lowlands in February; San Isidro Labrador in the Sierra Madre in May; Santiago Apóstol in Amealco in July; La Santísima Virgen de los Dolores de Soriano, in Colón in April; and the Virgen del Pueblito in the municipality of Corregidora in February.

Noteworthy Places

Toluquilla is a place of archaeological interest that reveals the influence of the Huastecos and connections with peoples of Veracruz. Set on a hill (the name means "Hunchback Hill") with restricted approaches, Toluquilla is in a strategic position and was used as a defense post and ceremonial center. The structures are built of flat stones and clay. The site also has ball courts set on pyramidal bases. Other archaeological sites are at Ranas, the Cerro de las Campanas, the Cerro del Sapo, Lobos, and Sabino.

The five eighteenth-century Franciscan missions are located in the municipalities of Jalpan de Serra, Arroyo Seco, and Landa de Matamoros. The most decorated of them is the Misión de Santa María del Agua (in Landa).

Querétaro City has a great deal that is of architectural interest. It is full of churches, civic buildings, and private houses that bear witness to its historical importance, many dating back to the sixteenth and seventeenth centuries. Construction of the city's aqueduct was begun in 1726 and took nearly ten years. It is made of quarried pink-hued stone and has seventy-four arches. Most of it was paid for by a private benefactor, the Marqués de la Villa del Villar. The Fountain of Neptune (Fuente de Neptuno) was built in 1797.

Among many old churches of note is the Templo de Santa Clara, which was once part of a seventeenth-century convent; its interior offers a fine example of the baroque style called *churrigueresque*, and there is an elaborate choir and an ancient organ. Other significant churches are the Templo de San José de Gracia, the Templo y Ex-Convento de las Teresitas, the Templo de San Sebastián, la Iglesia de San Antonio, la Iglesia de Santo Domingo, la Iglesia de la Congregación, and the Templo de San Francisco.

Ornate façade.

The neoclassical theater called the Teatro de la República was finished in 1852; initially called the Teatro Iturbide, it was renamed in 1922. Quertaro's town hall, another impressive building, overlooks an elegant though small square, the Plaza de Armas. There are several fine squares in the city, and they serve as the centers of social life. Other notable civic buildings include the Casona de los Cinco Patios, the Casas Reales, the Casa de Don Bartolo, the Casa de los López de Ecala, the Casa del Diezmo, the Casa de los Perros, and the Casa de la Marquesa.

Querétaro's former Convento de San Francisco includes an area devoted to art exhibitions and concerts, and the Museo Regional is set in this same building. The museum has artifacts of the various indigenous peoples associated with the state, the mummified body of a woman found in one of the convents, and furniture, objects, and documents associated with the state's history, such as the table on which the peace treaty with the United States was signed. There are works by Miguel Cabrera and other major colonial painters. Querétaro also has a Museum of Art, a City Museum, located at the place where Maximilian was shot, and, more unusually, a Museum of Mathematics.

At Jalpan de Serra is the Museo Histórico de la Sierra Gorda, with historical details of the indigenous peoples and of missionary work. San Joaquín has its Museo Arqueológico y Minero de la Sierra, covering its ancient history and especially the development of mining in that area. San Juan del Río has a Museum of Death (Museo de la Muerte), which illustrates cultural practices regarding death in the state. The historic center of San Juan del Río also has important buildings. All told, there are 2,345 sites on Mexico's National Register of Historic Buildings in the state of Querétaro, approximately half of them in the capital.

Among the state's natural attractions, there are numerous waterfalls and caves.

Cuisine

The cuisine could be called *mestiza*—that is, a hybrid built upon the many indigenous traditions and the influence of Spain, with subsequent contributions from other places. Typical foods include *zacahuil* (a kind of *tamal*), *pan de pulque* (bread made with *pulque*, a fermented liquor made from cactus), *mamanxa* (made with corn, cheese, and cinnamon), *enchiladas queretanas*, *chilacayote frito* (fried squash), *nopales en penca*, *atole* (a corn-based drink), *chivo tapeado*, and desserts made with fruits, milk products, and honey.

Nopales en Penca

Ingredients:

6 lb. *nopales* (cactus leaves), cooked and sliced
1 oz. garlic, finely chopped
3 onions, sliced
Oil
Salt
Chicken stock
5 *árbol* chiles
Oregano
Cilantro
3 medium tomatoes, chopped
2 nopales, whole
8 corn *gorditas* (tortillas)
3 oz. mild cheese
1 avocado
2 oz. radishes

Soften the garlic and onion in some hot oil, together with the chiles. Add the cooked pieces of nopal and stir. Add the tomatoes and a little chicken stock, season with cilantro, oregano, and salt, and simmer for a while. Use this to fill the whole nopal leaves, then wrap them in aluminum foil and bake them at 350°F for about 30 minutes. When done, place the whole leaves on a serving dish, laying the gorditas around them and decorating with cheese, slices of the avocado and radishes, and more cilantro.

Chivo Tapeado

Ingredients:

  1 kid goat
  Salt
  Oil
  1 medium onion
  6 oz. each of *pasilla*, *ancho*, and *mulato* chiles, deseeded and deveined
  5 cloves of garlic
  1/4 tsp each of cumin, cinnamon, and oregano
  Chicken stock
  12 oz. each of red and white wine (24 oz. of either, or a rosé may be used)
  Epazote (a common Mexican herb)
  Grated cheese

Rub the goat all over with salt, then brown it in the oil. Place it in the oven to bake at 400°F for 1 hour. Briefly roast the onion. While the goat is baking, puree the chiles with the garlic, onion, seasonings, and a little chicken stock. Then fry this mixture in hot oil, add the wine, and mix well. Once the goat has baked for an hour, take it out of the oven, pour most of the mixture over it, and then put it back in the oven for another 45 minutes. Before serving, pour the remaining sauce over the meat and sprinkle with *epazote* and a little grated cheese for decoration.

Sopa de Aguacate

Ingredients:

  4 avocados
  1 *poblano* chile, cleaned and deseeded
  1/4 cup dry white wine
  2 small canned red bell peppers, chopped
  3 or 4 pints chicken stock
  Juice of half a lime
  1 tbsp of finely chopped onion
  Salt and pepper

Peel the avocados and remove the seeds. Blend the flesh together with the chile, lime juice, and onion. Season with salt and pepper. Heat the stock, mixing in the blended ingredients and the wine. Decorate with small pieces of red pepper before serving.

Quintana Roo

State Characteristics

This state is named in honor of Andrés Quintana Roo (1787–1851), a writer and politician who became famous as a journalist and a supporter of the drive toward independence from Spain. Quintana Roo was a signatory to Mexico's declaration of independence. However, he was a native of Mérida, the capital of Yucatán, not of this state (for more on Andrés Quintana Roo, see the Yucatán chapter).

The state of Quintana Roo is one of the youngest in the country, created only in 1974, at the same time as Baja California Sur. Located at the eastern end of the Yucatán Peninsula, it has the Gulf of Mexico to its north, the state of Yucatán to its northwest, Campeche to its west, Guatemala and Belize to its south, and the Caribbean to its east. It is Mexico's nineteenth largest state, occupying a total of 50,212 square kilometers (19,583 square miles), or 2.6 percent of Mexico's total area. In 2005, it had a population of 1,135,309, which was only twenty-sixth in Mexico; 73 percent were Catholics, and 11 percent Protestants or evangelicals. There are eight administrative municipalities in Quintana Roo. The capital of the state is Chetumal, but thanks to tourism, the largest city is now Cancún, whose resident population includes many immigrant workers from neighboring states. Quintana Roo has nine daily newspapers, of which five are published in Cancún, including *Novedades de Quintana Roo*, *La Voz del Caribe*, and *Quequi*; one is in Chetumal: *Diario de Quintana Roo*. The state is represented by six people in the National Congress. There are four institutions of higher education.

Quintana Roo is a low-lying and predominantly flat state that slopes gently down from west to east. Its highest elevations are near Belize and Guatemala, but there are only two places where the elevation exceeds 200 meters (660 feet): El Cerro del Charro (230 m/755 ft.) and El Cerro el Gavilán (210 m/690 ft.). As in other parts of the Yucatán Peninsula, the waterways are largely underground. However, the Río Hondo is an exception; it is about a 210 kilometers (130 miles) long and has an average depth of some 9 meters (30 feet) and an average width of about 45 meters (150 feet). This river marks the border with Belize. Other surface rivers, though less important, are the Escondido, the Azul, and the Ucum. There are a number lakes, of which the major ones are the Laguna de Bacalar, the San Felipe, the Virtud, the Guerrero, and the Milagros in the municipality of Othón P. Blanco; the Laguna Chichankanab and the Esmeralda in José María Morelos; the Kaná, Noh Bec, Paytoro, Sac Ayin, X Kojoli, Ocom, and Chunyaxché in Felipe Carrillo Puerto; the Laguna Cobá in Solidaridad; and the Laguna Nichupte in Cancún. *Cenotes* (or *dolinas*) are natural wells or ponds formed by rainwater eroding the limestone bedrock and causing it to cave in. In some low-lying places where there is clay, rain can accumulate at times to form large ponds called *aguadas*.

Two tropical climates dominate Quintana Roo. The mainland is generally hot and fairly humid, whereas the island of Cozumel is even more humid. Everywhere, rain falls mainly in the summer, but on Cozumel it is more abundant; the average annual rainfall ranges from 1,100 to 1,500 millimeters (44–60 inches). Over the year, the average daily temperature ranges from 26°C (79°F) down to 10°C (50°F); in the hottest months, the temperature can exceed 35°C (95°F). The trade winds are dominant for most of the year, blowing from the east, but in winter, the wind can blow from the north, lowering temperatures. The region is subject to hurricanes.

Vegetation consists of tropical forests of evergreens, reeds, fruit trees, orchids, and creepers. Some deciduous trees, usually not exceeding 24 meters (80 feet) high, are found in the relatively drier areas. Along part of the southeast coast, there is low vegetation with many thorny plants. Aquatic plants can be found in the lagoons and swamps. There are many valuable hardwoods, including cedar and mahogany.

Quintana Roo has an abundance of fauna. Mammals include spider monkeys, jaguars, armadillos, boars, and *tepezcuintles*; manatees are distinctive and endangered. Among the many birds, there are wild turkeys, pheasants, toucans, flamingoes, vultures, *cojolites*, and *chachalacas*. Some of the numerous reptiles are dangerous, such as the *nauyaca*, rattlesnake, coral snake, boa, yellow-bearded snake, *oxcan*, and crocodile. There are also lizards, turtles, frogs, and hosts of insects. Aware of the great biodiversity and the need to protect it, the state government has sought federal aid to designate no less than 25 percent of the state as wildlife protection areas.

It has become customary to consider the state as having three regions. The Northern Region (Región Norte) consists of the municipalities of Isla

Mujeres (so called because Mayan sculptures of women were found on the island that gives the municipality its name), Benito Juárez, and Cozumel and the coastal portion of the municipality of Solidaridad. This region covers just 6 percent of the state, yet has 60 percent of the population, most of them living in the larger towns. Many residents come from other parts of the peninsula during the last fifteen or twenty years, due to the development of the tourist industry. The influx of people into the region has put great pressure on the infrastructure.

The Mayan Area (Zona Maya) comprises the municipalities of Felipe Carrillo Puerto, José María Morelos, and Lázaro Cárdenas and the inland part of Solidaridad, covering 57 percent of the state but being home to only 13 percent of the total state population. Whereas about two-thirds of the population of the Northern Region is concentrated in large urban areas, in the Mayan Area, 64 percent of the population lives in communities with fewer than 2,500 inhabitants. There has been some emigration, especially by young people, from this area to the tourist areas and to the state capital. Basic services and facilities in the Mayan Area are not as good as elsewhere, partly because of the scattered nature of communities and the inclination to move about.

Finally, the Southern Region (Región Sur), made up of the municipality Othón P. Blanco, covers 37 percent of the state and has 27 percent of its population. Rather like the Northern Region, 70 percent of the Southern Region's population is urban. The population of this region consists largely of people of Mayan descent, but there are also immigrants from other parts of Yucatán and farther away, some of them having come in as a result of a federal repopulation program dating from the 1960s. The indigenous portion of the population is estimated at 23 percent. In urban areas, the services are good; in rural ones, they are not.

Cultural Groups and Languages

In 2005, 19.3 percent of the population over age five was listed in the census as speakers of an indigenous language. In the 2000 census, that figure had been about 23 percent, so there has been a decline, as one would expect. Among the 170,982 people so identified in the more recent of the two surveys, 155,960 were speakers of Mayan dialects; the next most widely used indigenous language, at just 1,958 speakers, was Tzotzil. Six other languages had between 762 and 1,444 speakers; in descending order, they are Kanjobal, Chol, Tzeltal, Náhuatl, Mame, and Zapotec. A further 2,621 people are listed as speaking unspecified indigenous languages. There are more speakers of Mayan in the state of Yucatán than in the other peninsular states.

The cultural heritage and present-day influence of the Mayas is felt everywhere, and there are many signs of their continued life, in customs and language use. Mayan culture is reflected in the way people dress, in the cuisine, and perhaps above all in the impact of the Mayan language on local Spanish. For example, in the pronunciation of Spanish in the Yucatán Peninsula, there is sometimes a lengthening of stressed vowels and a tendency to turn a final [n] into an [m]. In most parts of Mexico, when indigenous terms enter Spanish, their form is adapted to the host system. This happens in Yucatán, for example, with the verb *anolar* (to gnaw), which is adapted from the Mayan verb *anolah*. However, this sort of adaptation is unusual in Yucatán, where more commonly the original Mayan term is imported into Spanish without modification; examples are *chich* (grandmother), *pepén* (butterfly), *xik'* (armpit), *chuchul* (dry), *k'olis* (bald), *popots'ki* (slippery), *chen* (only, simply), and *han* (quickly). The influence of the Mayan language is largely a local phenomenon and it contrasts with the influence of Náhuatl, the language of the Aztecs; whereas the Aztecs were imperialists and had an influence on many parts of Mexico, the Mayas did not expand their empire and aggressively spread their culture.

One important sociolinguistic difference regarding the use of Mayan here, as compared to the use of indigenous languages elsewhere in Mexico, is that it is found in several strata of society and generally does not suffer the same stigma as do indigenous languages in other states. Knowing Mayan can actually be a feather in the cap of the bourgeoisie and those in authority; one hears priests, businesspeople, and public officials speaking it, for instance. In rural contexts, Mayan is not simply the language of the peasants but also the language of those with authority and influence. In some places, it is almost an official language, while in others its use is characteristic of relaxed situations and family life.

Nevertheless, the modernization of rural areas, where traditions are changing and Spanish is growing in strength, has had an influence on Mayan. Education in Spanish, including well-intentioned campaigns against illiteracy, has reduced the number of monolingual Mayan speakers, as has increasing exposure to the media. Aware that this is the case, some institutions and individuals have been taking steps to preserve the use of Mayan. The culture of today's Mayan peoples is a lively hybrid with the Hispanic, but they remain deeply rooted in their own traditions.

History

The history of what is now Quintana Roo can be understood only in the context of the overall evolution of the Yucatán Peninsula. Although Quintana Roo has had some autonomy since the early twentieth century, prior to that its history was largely shared with neighboring states, particularly Yucatán.

The story begins with the arrival of the Mayas. There were two successive geographical foci of Maya civilization. The first was southern Mexico, Guatemala and Honduras, where the Mayas thrived around the end of the first millennium. Then, for reasons that have not become fully clear (perhaps strife or disease or a natural disaster) they abandoned those lands and migrated to the Yucatán Peninsula. Between 415 and 435, Mayan people had already settled in a place they called Siyancaan Bakhalal (today's Bacalar), and there they remained for some sixty years, after which they founded Tulum and Ichpatún (close to Chetumal). Legend has it that the god Kukulkan established the Liga de Mayapán (League of Mayapán), comprising Uxmal, Chichen-Itzá, Mayapán, Itzamal, Tulum, and other places in the peninsula. This federation lasted approximately two hundred years from the end of the first millennium. At that stage, internecine struggles began to undermine it, leading to the establishment of separate kingdoms, and so it was that the Mayas were in a politically weakened condition by the time of the arrival of the Spaniards in the early sixteenth century.

The first Spanish expedition reached Mexico in 1511; 1517 saw Francisco Hernández de Córdoba arrive at what are now the Isla Mujeres and Cabo Catoche; and a year later Juan de Grijalva disembarked in Cozumel. On the coast of Quintana Roo, a Spanish shipwreck had left two survivors, Gonzalo Guerrero and Jerónimo de Aguilar, in 1511. The former was rescued by the Indians and became fully integrated in their society, marrying an Indian princess and having three children by her. Aguilar also lived with the Mayas and learned their language, but when Hernán Cortés came in 1519 to begin the expedition that would lead to the conquest of Mexico, Aguilar joined him and served as interpreter. Cortés soon moved on along the coast and northward to establish a settlement that became Veracruz, and thence he marched to Tenochtitlán, the Aztec capital.

In 1526, Francisco de Montejo was authorized by Emperor Charles V, the king of Spain, to carry out the conquest of the Yucatán Peninsula. He arrived in Cozumel in 1527 and attempted to advance into the peninsula from the east, setting up several settlements that were later abandoned due to Indian hostility. The first Spanish settlement set up by Montejo was in Xel-Ha; this and the town of San Felipe Bacalar became the most important centers during the early colonial period. The difficult terrain and the resistance of the Mayas made colonization slow.

In view of the difficulties, Montejo retreated to Mexico City, where he agreed with his son that they should now approach the task from the west. Between 1530 and 1535, both men fought in Mayan territory but failed to take control. In 1531, a royal decree ordered that help be given to Montejo, who duly received provisions, arms, and reinforcements. One of their captains, Alonso Dávila, explored Nachancán and Tulum and went on to Bakhalal, which had been abandoned. Dávila established a settlement at Chetumal, which he named Villa Real, but the Indians drove him out of it.

On the advice of Guerrero, the shipwrecked Spaniard who had lived among the Mayas, the local chieftain at Bakhalal had retreated into the jungle. Faced with the Spanish invasion, many Mayas retreated to places in the interior that were difficult to reach, thus preserving their independence and their traditions. Indeed, the Spaniards never really gained control of them during the colonial era, and even afterward, independence for the people of the peninsula was always on the agenda.

Montejo turned his attention to Tabasco and then to Honduras, but his son made a renewed effort to complete the conquest in 1537. This attempt was successful and was marked by the surrender of the principal chieftains in 1541 in T-Hó (Mérida). Only the province of Bakhalal continued to resist, until it fell to the Spaniards in 1545 and was turned into Villa de Salamanca de Bacalar.

At the start of the colonial era, the Yucatán Peninsula was administered by the Audiencia de los Confines, whose seat was in present-day Guatemala, but in 1560 a royal decree determined that it should come under Mexico City's jurisdiction. It is at about that time that **Fray Diego de Landa** (1524–1579) appeared on the scene; he was a friar chosen by the Franciscans to direct their operations in the peninsula, and he was to go down in history as a man who destroyed a large part of the Mayan culture. In 1562, Landa issued an official condemnation of the Indians for idolatry, and in a place called Maní he had many of their priceless documents and artifacts burned as a form of retribution for their practice of human sacrifice. Also in 1562, the peninsula received its first bishop, Francisco del Toral, who complained to the Spanish authorities about Landa's behavior, with the result that the latter was forced to return to Spain. Landa later set about writing what was to become an invaluable source of information about Mayan life, religion, and language, his *Relación de las cosas de Yucatán* (Account of Things in Yucatán). After Toral's death, Landa returned to Yucatán, as bishop. His work was published three hundred years after he wrote it.

The peninsula was a place of constant Indian uprisings during the colonial period, and the revolts consolidated Yucatán's reputation as a fierce and indomitable region, something of a thorn in the side of colonial Spain. Moreover, the Spaniards had to contend with pirates. By the middle of the seventeenth century, there was open warfare with the natives of Chetumal, and Bacalar was the only place that remained in Spanish hands. It was only in 1697 that the Spaniards finally gained control of it when they took Petén Itzá, the last pocket of resistance. (After almost disappearing, Bacalar was reconstructed and fortified against attack during the eighteenth century.)

A remarkable early figure who has entered peninsular mythology was **José Jacinto Uc de los Santos Canek** (d. 1761), a Mayan in the service of the Catholic friars. From them, Canek acquired a good education, but this did nothing to reduce his loathing of the invaders. Once expelled from the religious order, he began to appear at local festivities and celebrations, where he would use his historical knowledge and bilingual skills to drum up support for violent rebellion. In 1761, Canek was taken prisoner by the Spaniards and sentenced to be hung, drawn and quartered; afterward, his body was burned in Mérida's main square. He thus became a symbolic figure for Mayan resistance over the centuries.

Isolation from Mexico City meant that the Yucatán Peninsula enjoyed a certain degree of liberty; indeed, at several points in its history, there were drives for peninsular independence from central control. One result of Yucatán's remoteness was that the movement for independence from Spain, early in the nineteenth century, did not have any real military effect, though the spirit of independence was certainly alive there.

A group of *yucatecos*, inspired by the liberal constitution that had been drawn up in the city of Cádiz in opposition to Napoleon III's control of Spain, had been pressing to have its provisions in favor of greater social equality in matters of taxes and land tenure put into effect in the Yucatán Peninsula. This group of liberals were known as the Sanjuanistas. In 1820, a Confederación Patriótica (Patriotic Confederation) was set up, but it soon split into two factions, one that was in support of adopting Spain's new constitution and the other in favor of complete independence from colonial rule. Lorenzo Zavala, a leader of the Sanjuanistas, was sent to Madrid to represent Yucatán's interests, but events overtook him: elsewhere in Mexico, the Plan de Iguala was drawn up, and in 1821 that plan ushered in an independent, if short-lived, Mexican Empire, of which Yucatán formally became part. Yucatán continued to be part of the republic that followed, but control by Mexico City of the remote parts of the peninsula was so poor that in 1823 Guatemala took over 36,000 square kilometers (14,000 square miles) of the Petén Itzá district.

The period 1840 to 1848 saw a struggle for power between Miguel Barbachano and Santiago Méndez Ibarra, the former wanting unity with Mexico and the latter independence from it. In 1841, the major landowners had control, and they promulgated a decree establishing a Republic of Yucatán, but other countries failed to grant it recognition, and Yucatán was therefore obliged to return to the Mexican fold. After that there arose a conflict between Mérida and Campeche, leading to the latter's breakaway; President Benito Juárez responded by creating a new state of Campeche. Yucatán was politically weakened, though economically quite prosperous, thanks to sisal.

A dramatic development began in 1847 in Tepich and Tihosuco: a Maya rebellion led by **Jacinto Pat** and **Cecilio Chí** that was once again to destabilize the peninsula. This was the Guerra de Castas, the Caste War. For more than fifty years the Mexico City authorities effectively lost control. Quite early in that rebellion, the Mayas attacked Bacalar and killed most of its inhabitants, though some fled to Belize. Soon only Mérida, a few coastal settlements, and the main road to Campeche remained under the control of the Yucatán authorities. The governor, Barbachano, made a pact with Pat, eliminating personal taxes, reducing charges for baptisms and marriages, granting the Indians certain rights to cultivate land, absolving people of debt, and confiscating arms; however, Chí, the leader of the eastern Mayas, rejected this agreement, being determined to get rid of the whites. In 1850, there was another attempt to secure a peace agreement: the proposal was that the Indians should lay down their arms in exchange for being allowed to have control of their own lands and choose their own authorities. This time, though, it was the government that proved unwilling to agree, and so the violence continued.

It was in 1895, under President Porfirio Díaz, that Quintana Roo's strategic importance was recognized. An agreement was reached with Great Britain, the colonial power that controlled Belize, to police the shared border along the Río Hondo, across which the Mayas were receiving arms in exchange for mahogany and cedar. That agreement went into practical effect three years later, when **Capt. Othón Pompeyo Blanco** (1868–1959) was sent by Díaz to ensure that the frontier was being respected and that the arms traffic was being stopped. It was Blanco who founded the town of Payo Obispo, which later became Chetumal. He was a peacemaker who, though he had arms and forces at his disposal, sought reconciliation with the Mayas.

Much to the chagrin of the *yucatecos*, a new administrative territory of Quintana Roo was then established by presidential decree and granted certain privileges and protections relating to the exploitation of natural resources and the importation of goods. Officially, the Mayan unrest had finally been contained, but guerrilla activity continued until the Mexican Revolution. As in other parts of the country, Díaz's three-decade rule had brought stability and some industrial progress, but it was an authoritarian regime that did not tolerate opposition and, above all, the benefits of the material progress went to a privileged minority of Mexicans, or to foreigners. Some three hundred large *haciendas* were established in Yucatán during the nineteenth century, with the land controlled by only a few people, and the distribution of wealth did not improve. Such inequalities, coupled with the traditional exploitation of Mayan labor, favored a revolutionary spirit.

In 1913, President Venustiano Carranza returned Quintana Roo to Yucatán, and many of Quintana Roo's trade concessions were rescinded. But in 1915, Carranza gave Quintana Roo back its status as a separate territory. **Francisco May** (1884–1969) was a Mayan from Quintana Roo who became a general in the federal army. On Carranza's orders, he took on the task of organizing the commercialization of resources such as *chicle* and mahogany in the Southern Region. Quintana Roo's status was still not definitive, however. In 1931, President Pascual Ortíz Rubio divided the territory up, giving part of it to Yucatán and part to Campeche; then, in 1935, President Lázaro Cárdenas acceded to local pressure that it become a separate territory once again.

In the early twentieth century, Quintana Roo was still a remote and poorly connected part of Mexico. After the Revolution, there was some change in the social and economic fabric. The first chicle cooperatives were set up in the late 1920s, and the large estates that were in the hands of a small group of people began to be broken up. The Indians began to come around to the idea of formal education. In the late 1930s, there was friction with neighboring Campeche, stemming from the encroachment of Campeche-based commercial interests on local ones. A territorial dispute followed, and President Cárdenas was obliged to intervene to resolve it. The 1940s saw some industrial development and greater limits on foreign exploitation of natural resources. Hurricane Janet brought devastation to Chetumal in 1955, but the 1960s saw considerable progress and development, thanks in part to **Javier Rojo Gómez** (1896–1970), a native of Hidalgo who was appointed governor of the territory of Quintana Roo.

Quintana Roo was declared a state in 1974, during the presidency of Luis Echeverría, and a year later it had its own constitution in place. The development of tourism took off a decade later. The state went through a difficult period during the 1990s, when its administration developed relationships with Colombian drug traffickers. Such was the scale of the problem that President Ernesto Zedillo was prompted to bring the governor of the state, Mario Villanueva Madrid, to justice; the governor fled the country but was later arrested and brought back to Mexico to answer the indictments against him.

Economy

Quintana Roo is the only Mexican state with a Caribbean coast—a fact much exploited by the burgeoning tourist industry. The Northern Region is the main focus of tourism, with places like Cancún, Cozumel, Isla Mujeres, Playa del Carmen, and the historical site of Tulum. Trade and fishing are also significant in this region, which is home to the state's main ports, of which Puerto Morelos is the most important. Shrimp, lobster, and fish are exported, if not destined to feed the tourists.

The main economic activities in the Mayan Area are agriculture, livestock, beekeeping, forestry, chicle, and fishing. Antiquated techniques and poor soil mean that agriculture and livestock are not very prosperous activities. The region is relatively depressed economically. The fishing takes place mostly in northern parts of the region, but also on the Caribbean coast.

As for the Southern Region, which contains the state capital, the principal economic activities are agriculture, livestock, beekeeping, forestry, chicle, fishing, small industries, and trade and public administration. Ecotourism is also growing in this region.

The state's main agricultural crops are sugarcane, chiles, corn, oranges, rice, watermelons, vegetables, and tropical fruits. Overwhelmingly, these crops are seasonal. The most important agricultural area is the south. In the municipality of Jose María Morelos, in the center of the state, there is some mechanization and irrigation. Production is generally low and meets only local needs. Cattle and pigs are the main livestock; other animals are only reared for family use. The livestock are found in the municipalities of Othón P. Blanco and Lázaro Cárdenas, and there is available land that is suitable for further development of the livestock industry. The state has over a hundred thousand beehives, mostly in its central part.

Forestry is quite important for Quintana Roo's economy, carried out in the municipalities of Felipe Carrillo Puerto, Othón P. Blanco, Lázaro Cárdenas, and José María Morelos. For a long time, the exploitation of precious woods such as mahogany was the backbone of the economy, but abuse of these resources during the nineteenth and early twentieth centuries led to serious deforestation. The state has been taking steps to redress the balance by replanting and encouraging the exploitation of other resources. Currently, precious woods account for about 20 percent of forestry production.

With 860 kilometers (533 miles) of coast and 264,000 hectares (652,000 acres) of bays and lagoons that are suitable for aquaculture, the state is well supplied with conditions that would favor a major fishing industry, but that potential has yet to be realized. Fishing is generally uncoordinated and relies on antiquated methods; much of it is carried out by small boats close to the coast. There are several places that freeze the catch, but little in the way of processing plants.

Mining and industry are on a very modest scale. Mining is limited to the limestone along the coast facing the island of Cozumel; all of the stone is exported to the United States. A lot of the industrial activity is carried out by family businesses, especially in manufacturing, making clothes, or processing foods or wood. Most industry is located in the municipality of Benito Juárez. In Othón P. Blanco, there is a sugar plant that is the biggest single industrial enterprise in the state.

Quintana Roo's tourism has grown on a massive scale over the last thirty years and now accounts for 11.3 percent of Mexico's gross national product. More than a third of the foreign money that makes its way into Mexico due to tourism comes from Quintana Roo. Millions of visitors flock in on flights from the United States, as well as some from Belize and many on cruise ships. They come to Cancún, Cozumel, Playa del Carmen, or the so-called Riviera Maya, and while there, they perhaps see an archaeological site or two. Cancún was made for them: it is a product of the 1970s, a formerly uninhabited place that was developed specifically for tourists, and its success led to the development of Cozumel, now a port of call for cruise ships.

Arts

In its short life as a separate state, Quintana Roo has not produced outstanding figures in the arts who have made their mark nationally or internationally. The state's culture has two salient elements: the vestiges of Mayan culture and the contrasting culture of tourism.

Reeds and wood are the basis for many Mayan artifacts; the Mayas also embroider *huipiles* and weave hammocks. Crafts on the coast naturally involve the products of the sea, such as shells and snails, but the most valued products are made with black coral.

In general, the area's crafts, music, dance, and other creative activities are the same as those of the Yucatán region of which Quintana Roo was a part for so long. However, there are some distinctive aspects to the dancing and music of Quintana Roo. In the course of the Pig's Head Dance the participants dance with trays on their heads, and on those trays are decorated pigs' heads. Those watching may bid for the pigs' heads; if a person receives one he may take it home, but in doing so he enters into an obligation to supply two for the following year's celebration. The Pig's Head Dance has its origins in Yucatán. Also shared with that state is a sort of maypole dance called the *baile de las cintas*. *Jaranas* are popular, here as elsewhere. A distinctive traditional dance of Quintana Roo is the *danza de los chicleros* (dance of the chicle harvesters), which evokes the camps set up in the jungle to exploit the resin that comes from the *chicozapote*.

The local music is much influenced by Yucatán and the Caribbean. Closeness to Belize and to Cuba are significant factors; for example, for a long time, the best radio reception was from Cuba. Tourist development has further internationalized popular music. Cancún has an annual jazz festival, for instance. In the Mayan Region, the Maya Pax is the typical ensemble, using native instruments such as drums, shells, and rattles, combined with others imported from the European tradition, such as the violin, the guitar, and the trumpet.

Social Customs

In the municipalities of the Zona Maya, there are religious celebrations that tend to reflect their closeness to the land: Lol Cah is a ritual blessing of the community; another ceremony surrounds the planning of the *ceiba*, which is held to be a sacred tree. Offerings are made to the rain god Chac to ward off droughts.

Religious celebrations of Catholic origin involving the wider community include Carnival, the Day of the Dead, and other such events that are much celebrated in Mexico, though sometimes with a particular local significance. Carnival Sunday in Cozumel is a lively and disorderly affair, with dancing on the main square, processions, and bands. In Isla Mujeres, celebrations last for many days. The Isla Mujeres Festival that coincides with Carnival, despite taking place in a popular tourist area, has much of the traditional flavor of Yucatán peninsular culture. A festival queen is elected and crowned, after which masked dancers perform *jaranas*. The Carnival celebrations close with a gala during which an effigy of Juan Carnaval is burned, though he leaves behind a satirical lampoon for everyone to enjoy.

According to legend, in 1890 three fishermen at Ecab, an old colonial settlement, came across three virgin sisters, who were then taken to three towns, including Kantunilkín. December 3 in Kantunilkín marks the Feast

Atlante's fans cheer their team outside Quintana Roo stadium before the Mexican Soccer League final match in Cancún, 2007. (AP Photo/Claudio Cruz)

of the Immaculate Conception, which brings in visitors from all over. Five consecutive days of merrymaking involve dances, processions, fireworks, bullfights, and the like. The traditional way to begin the celebrations is to dance the pig's head dance, and the traditional way to end it is with a procession of boats, songs in honor of the Virgin, and a grand ball.

International regattas and fishing competitions take place in the tourist areas.

On festive occasions, particularly when dancing, women typically wear huipiles, simple white cotton shifts embroidered with broad bands of striking and brightly colored floral patterns that run around the skirt below the hips and along the square neckline. There is also a shawl-like section that goes over the shoulders and is similarly embroidered. They wear sandals or white shoes with medium heels. The men wear a white outfit, too: loose trousers, long-sleeved shirts, and broad-brimmed hats, together with a red neckerchief.

For some festivities, women may wear an outfit called a *terno*, which involves finer fabrics and lace, with cross-stitched embroidery and a shawl, accessorized with gold chains, earrings, and rosaries made with coral. The men, correspondingly, wear tailored trousers of finer cloth, occasionally with gold buttons, a high-collared jacket-shirt known as a *filipina*, sandals, and fine straw hats, again with a red neckerchief. In regional festivities, this clothing is often seen when jarana dancing competitions are being held.

Noteworthy Places

Tulum is the third most visited of all the archaeological sites in Mexico. Located on the coast, it is a walled compound that features a temple called El Castillo set on a rise, another in ruins called the Templo del Dios, and the Templo de los Frescos, which still has Mayan wall paintings in their original colors. Cobá is a site that is considered more important by archaeologists because of the discoveries made during excavations there. It has Nohoch Mul, the highest pyramid in the peninsula, a complex castle, a ball court, and a network of pathways. Kohunlich is in the south of the state. It is distinguished by the stucco figures that grace the façades of its principal buildings. There is also a ball court. Dzibanché and Kinichná, both in the Othón P. Blanco municipality, also have vestiges of the Mayan civilization.

The Museo de la Ciudad in Chetumal evokes life in the capital at the beginning of the twentieth century. Chetumal also has the Museum of Mayan Culture. In Cancún, there is a Museum of History, which also deals with the Mayas. The Museo Arqueológico-Marino in Cozumel displays vestiges of the Mayan civilization that have been found on that island, as well as illustrating aspects of its marine life. The Museo Marino de Xel Ha does the same on a much smaller scale. More about the Mayas can be seen in Bacalar's Museo del Fuerte de Bacalar, which also covers aspects of colonial life in that town. The Museo del Centro de Estudios y Deportes Acuáticos de México (CEDAM) is in Akumal and has the remains of boats that were shipwrecked locally during the colonial period. Tihosuco, more originally, offers a museum devoted to the Caste Wars, the nineteenth-century indigenous rebellion against the authorities; it, too, has details of present-day Mayan life. Historically, one of the most interesting churches in the state is the Templo de la Santa Cruz in Sabán, where a massacre of old people, women, and children by Indian rebels took place during the Caste Wars.

Cuisine

The cuisine of Quintana Roo is strongly influenced by Mayan practices, with some Caribbean elements. It is generally much the same as the cuisine of the state of Yucatán. Corn is a staple, as it is almost everywhere in Mexico. There are many dishes involving wild game, such as deer, boars, turkeys, and other rather more exotic animals. Cooking is often carried out using a *pib*, a kind of oven consisting of a hole in the ground that is filled with coals, after which marinated meat is wrapped in banana leaves, put in the ground, and left to cook.

Belize influences the cooking of the south of the state, giving dishes like rice and beans cooked in coconut milk and usually accompanied by fried chicken. On the coast, there are many seafood dishes, including *ceviches* made with sea snails, and fish *al Tikinxic* (dressed with annatto and then baked or cooked over embers).

Poc Chuc

Ingredients:

6 fillets of pork, 10 oz. each
16 oz. fresh orange juice
$^1/_2$ cup lime juice
$1^1/_2$ oz. annatto paste
1 tsp chopped oregano leaves
1 tsp chopped thyme leaves
1 tsp black pepper
5 cups water
5 red onions
8 oz. white wine vinegar
1 sprig of cilantro
1 tsp finely chopped *habanero* chile

Mix all but the pork, water, chile and onions in food processor and liquefy, adding salt to taste. Chop most of the onion, reserving a few slices for later. Boil the chopped onion, drain off the water, then add the onion to the mixture. Marinate the pork in the liquid prior to roasting or grilling it. Garnish with cilantro, slices of onion, and the chile. This dish is usually served with yellow rice.

Ceviche de Caracol de Mar

Fish or shrimp may be used instead of the conch meat, or in combination with it. *Serrano* chiles can be substituted for the habaneros, for a less spicy effect, but the habaneros are traditional.

Ingredients:

1 lb. fresh conch meat
$^1/_2$ cup fresh lemon juice
$^1/_2$ cup fresh lime juice
$^1/_4$ cup chopped cilantro
1 medium habanero chile, finely chopped
1 cup finely chopped onion
1 cup fresh tomatoes, peeled and chopped (and deseeded, if preferred)
$^1/_4$ cup olive oil
Salt and pepper

While tasty, conch meat can be tough, so it is best tenderized before use; this can be done by beating it flat on a cutting board. After that, cut the conch meat into small pieces, place it in a shallow pan, and cover with the citrus juices. Cover and leave to stand in the refrigerator for at least 2 hours, then add the chile and let stand for a further 2 hours. Drain, put in a deeper bowl, and mix in the onion, cilantro, tomato, olive oil, salt, and pepper. Squeeze half a lime over it just before serving. The ceviche may be garnished with slices of avocado.

Pan de Chetumal (Pan de Espiga)

Ingredients:

For the dough:
6 oz. milk
Pinch of salt
2 oz. butter
3 egg yolks
1 oz. dried yeast
14 oz. flour
For the filling:
$^1/_2$ lb. diced ham
1 cup mayonnaise
$^1/_2$ a cup chopped green olives
1 boiled egg, chopped
$^1/_2$ cup chopped onion
1 tbsp chopped parsley

Blend the milk, salt, and butter together and mix well. Add the yolks and yeast, then add the flour and continue to blend for 2 minutes. Roll out the dough so that it makes a rectangle, then brush with melted butter. Mix the ingredients for the filling and then place the filling on top of the dough. Roll it up, make a few cuts across it, and shape it into a crown. Let it rise to about double its size and sprinkle a little grated cheese on top. Place a bowl of hot water in the oven, then bake the dough on a baking tray at 350°F until golden (about 45 minutes).

San Luis Potosí

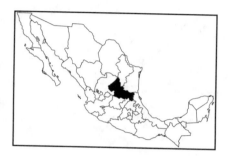

State Characteristics

This state was originally named in honor of King (Saint) Louis IX of France. At a later date, once its importance for mining had been recognized, the name of the most important silver town in South America (Potosí, Bolivia) was appended, although it is still often referred to simply as "San Luis."

San Luis Potosí is located in the high *mesa* of northern Mexico and has four regions: Altiplano, Centro, Media, and Huasteca. It shares borders with many other states: Coahuila to its north; Nuevo León and Tamaulipas to its northwest; Veracruz to its east; Guanajuato, Querétaro, and Hidalgo to its south; Jalisco to its southwest; and Zacatecas to its west. The surface area of San Luis is 60,550 square kilometers (37,540 square miles), about 3 percent of the country. The state comprises fifty-six municipalities and has a total population (in 2005) of 2,410,414. Of that number, 4.6 percent declared themselves to be Protestants or evangelicals, 92 percent Catholics. The capital city, situated at an altitude of 1,860 meters (6,138 feet), has the same name as the state; approximately 30 percent of the population lives in the capital city or its associated municipality. The state is represented by seven people in the National Congress.

There are five institutions of higher education, including the Universidad Autónoma and the Universidad Potosina. Ten newspapers are published in the state, eight of them in the capital city; among them are *San Luis Hoy*, *Huasteca Hoy*, *La Prensa del Centro*, *Pulso*, and *Tribuna*.

This is a mountainous state. The Sierra Madre Oriental (Eastern Sierra Madre) runs through it from northeast to southeast, and there are

Rural garden fence.

extensions of the Sierra Gorda de Guanajuato that run from south to north. The highest elevations are in the latter: San Miguelito, Bocas, Venado, Guadalcázar, Coronado, Charca, Catorce, and Cedral, with the average running to 3,100 meters (10,170 feet) above sea level. There are several major valleys, such as the Salado, Villa de Reyes, Cedral, Vanegas, Ciudad del Maíz, Villa Hidalgo, and Alaquines.

Due to the complications of the terrain, the picture as far as water is concerned is one of marked contrasts: in the northwest, there are no significant rivers, whereas the southeast has an extensive river system that feeds the Pánuco basin. One important river in it is the Río Verde, which meets the Río Santa María flowing out of Guanajuato; another is the Río Bagres. In other parts of the state, the rivers are seasonal and apparent only after heavy rains. There are many lakes, including Santa María del Peñón Blanco, Santa Clara, Tequesquite, El Lagarto, Tabasaquiche, and the Laguna Grande. There are also many hot springs, among them Ojo Caliente, Los Manantiales de Lourdes, Agua Grande, Amapolas, Estancia, Gogorrón, San Diego, Ojo de Agua Caliente, Taninul, and Los Bañitos. Waterfalls of note, as the rivers make their way toward the Gulf of Mexico, are El Salto (which drops 90 meters [297 feet]), Micos, Puente de Dios, and Tamuín (which is 105 meters [345 feet] high and as much as 300 meters [985 feet] wide). The falls at El Salto and Micos generate electricity.

Since the terrain varies so much, so does the climate. Broadly speaking, about 10 percent of the state is hot and humid, with summer rains; a similar amount is warm and humid, with abundant summer rain; around 20 percent is semidry and warm to fairly hot; roughly 50 percent is dry and fairly hot; and the remainder of the state ranges from very dry and hot to mild and moist. In the highest areas, temperatures range from 0°C (32°F) to 18°C (64°F). On the *meseta*, they average 18°–20°C (64°–68°F). Most of the state has an average rainfall of less than 750 millimeters (30 inches). The driest area is El Salado. Tropical cyclones sometimes sweep across the mountains, bringing humidity to much of the state and sometime creating dangerous conditions in the eastern part of it. On the coastal plains, thanks to the effects of the trade winds, the average rainfall is closer to 1,000 millimeters (40 inches), and the weather is warm and humid all the time.

There are nine ecologically protected areas. The predominant flora in San Luis is desert scrub on the meseta, which covers about 40 percent of the land. There are cacti, yuccas, and mesquite on another 10 percent of the land. At the other extreme, about 17 percent is tropical forest, with mulberry trees, palms, and tropical fruits such as papaya and custard apple. In addition, there are smaller proportions with mountain or coastal vegetation. Many of San Luis Potosí's wide range of species of wildlife have disappeared or are under threat. There are still many insects, reptiles (turtles, snakes, and lizards), frogs and toads, birds—from vultures and eagles to quail and doves to swallows and sparrows—and mammals such as rodents, coyotes, mountain lions, badgers, boars, armadillos, foxes, and deer. The waters are home to a variety of freshwater species, including eels, catfish, and trout.

Cultural Groups and Languages

The 2005 census reported that 11.1 percent of the population over the age of five were speakers of indigenous languages, totaling 234,815 people. Speakers of Náhuatl accounted for some 60 percent of them; they are mostly concentrated in the southern area, in the municipalities of Tamazunchale, Matlapa, Tampacan, Xilitla, San Martín Chalchicuautla, Axtla de Terrazas, Coxcatlán, Tampamolón, and Tancanhuitz de Santos.

The Tenek or Huasteco people accounted for approximately 35 percent of the total and are in the central and northern Huasteca area, in Aquismón, Huehuetlán, Tanlajás, San Antonio, Tampamolón, Tancanhuitz de Santos, Valles, Tanquian de Escobedo, and San Vicente Tancuayalab.

The Pames represent only about 3.5 percent. However, this figure is based on language use, and the fact is that these are migratory people who may lose the language while preserving other cultural manifestations, so the spread of Pames culture is wider than this percentage implies. The Pames are most numerous in Santa Catarina, Rayón, and Tamasopo.

In parts of the state, covering the municipalities of Ébano, Tamuín, and San Vicente Tancuayalab and a portion of Valles, the creation during the twentieth century of *ejidos* (communal farms) on what had been large private estates led to the resettlement there of considerable numbers of Indians of various ethnicities.

History

Prior to the arrival of the Spaniards, the northern and central western portions of San Luis had been inhabited by Otomí and Chichimec Indians, and the east and southeast by Huastecos, Pames, and Mexicas. The most influential of the early peoples were the Chichimecs, Huastecos, and Pames. The term *Chichimec* is in fact a blanket one that applies to a number of nomadic hunter-gatherer peoples; they were belligerent and conflictive, and they spoke several different languages, but they are grouped under the term due to their shared customs. For a long time, they would attack Spanish travelers and missionaries, sometimes scalping their prisoners, but in 1589 a peace agreement was negotiated with them by Rodrigo Río de la Loza and others.

The Huastecos, on the other hand, were sedentary, related to the Mayas and influenced by the Toltecs. Their culture was more sophisticated than that of the Chichimecs. They were cultivators of the land and produced some impressive art. Huastec culture thrived for about a thousand years, from 100 bc. The Aztecs subjugated the Huastecos during the first half of the fifteenth century, and the Spaniards controlled them after that, organizing them into *encomiendas*. Their main communities were Tamazunchale, Coxcatlán, Tampamolón, Tancuayalab, and Tamuín.

As part of their strategy to integrate the local indigenous peoples, the Spaniards transplanted four hundred families of Indians from Tlaxcala to populate newly conquered regions of the north; the Tlaxcalteca Indians had become allies of Spain against their oppressors, the Aztecs, shortly after the Spaniards arrived in New Spain. In 1591, Indians from Tlaxcala came on the orders of the viceroy to what are now Mexquitic, San Luis Potosí, Moctezuma, Venado, and Saltillo. Early in the seventeenth century, the Franciscans arrived to begin the process of evangelization of the natives.

In 1592, the Spaniards discovered mineral deposits at a hill they named the Cerro de San Pedro. Since there was no water, they established a settlement in the valley below and called it San Luis de Mezquitique, which later became the city of San Luis Potosí. Spaniards flocked in, and it grew to become the third most important city in New Spain, a very prosperous place during the eighteenth century. The city of San Luis was laid out on a grid pattern, with nineteen blocks emanating from a central *plaza* (square) out toward the cardinal points. As the city grew, Indian workers settled in outlying barrios. In 1766, San Luis was the site of Los Motines, a popular uprising in protest about the living conditions of some of the city's marginalized inhabitants. The expulsion of the Jesuits, who had done much to educate and support native people, only aggravated the situation, and eventually the protest was quashed by force. This had an effect on other parts of the country, fueling Indian resentment against the Spaniards. In 1786, New Spain was reorganized into twelve *intendencias*, and San Luis found itself part of one whose jurisdiction extended as far as Texas.

At the time of Miguel Hidalgo's cry for independence from Spain, San Luis responded with its own insurgency led by Luis Herrera, Father Juan Villerías, and Father Gregorio de la Concepción. Another leading light of the rebellion was **Mariano Jiménez** (1781–1811), who was shot by a firing squad in Chihuahua, along with Hidalgo and other prominent insurgents. In 1817, a rebel Spaniard named Francisco Javier Mina defeated loyalist forces at Ciudad del Maíz and at the Hacienda de Peotillos. By 1821, San Luis was proclaiming its independence from Spain; Agustin Iturbide's ill-fated Mexican empire was about to come into being.

Once the republic was established, San Luis was soon incorporated into it. Its first state constitution dates from 1826 and served until 1835, when the central government reasserted its authority, effectively taking control until the liberal reforms of the middle of the century. San Luis played quite a prominent part in the war over Texas in 1836 and then against the U.S. invasion in 1846–1847.

Ponciano Arriaga (1811–1863) was a lawyer and passionate federalist who had been banished more than once during the struggles between centralists and federalists that characterized the first half of the nineteenth century. His opposition to the U.S. invasion was very strong, and he rejected the terms of the 1848 peace treaty, given the losses it entailed for Mexico. Arriaga served as a government minister under President Mariano Arista, but later President Antonio López de Santa Anna found him too liberal and had him exiled. Following the implementation of the Plan de Ayutla, Arriaga returned to Mexico, where he presided over the Constituent Congress of 1856 and then represented several states in Congress. Because of his role in drafting the 1857 Constitution, he is sometimes called the "father" of it. Arriaga also served as interim governor of Aguascalientes and of Mexico City.

At the time of the French Intervention, President Benito Juárez transferred the national seat of power to San Luis, and for a short while, it was the capital of Mexico. Then the city fell into imperial hands, and under Emperor Maximilian the area became a department of Mexico. When Juárez returned in 1867, Republican forces took Querétaro, and Maximilian and two of his associates were taken prisoner and executed. After the restoration of the Republic, San Luis had a progressive governor in Gen. Carlos Diez Gutiérrez, who extended educational provisions and encouraged agriculture and mining.

The Mexico City–Laredo railway line was inaugurated in 1888, passing through San Luis, and lines connecting the city with other places followed; President Porfirio Díaz came to San Luis to bask in publicity. In 1901, oil was discovered in Ébano, and a year later the dam at San José became operational. Indeed, the era of Díaz was generally one of progress and stability, but the progress was often brought about at the expense of selling the family jewels, and only a minority of people really benefited from it. It was in that same year of 1901 that the first public anti-Díaz rally took place, with **Camilo Arriaga** (1862–1945), Librado Rivera, Ricardo Flores Magón, and Antonio Díaz Soto y Gama among its leading participants. Arriaga was a civil engineer by training but distinguished himself by championing the Reform Laws. He was a member of the National Congress and founder of a liberal club from which fierce opposition to Díaz emerged, resulting in Arriaga's imprisonment. Francisco Madero later offered him a government post, but he declined it. Arriaga supported anti-fascist causes. In his later years, he worked as a journalist in Mexico City. **Juan Sarabia** (1882–1920) was a lawyer and another fierce opponent of Díaz. He founded and wrote for a number of major newspapers, both in Mexico and in the United States, notably *El Demócrata*, *El Porvenir*, and *Regeneración*. He was imprisoned for his opposition to Díaz, and later by Victoriano Huerta. He died while serving as a senator for San Luis.

In 1910, with Díaz seeking to extend his thirty years in office yet further, Madero became the standard-bearer of opposition. Madero was arrested in Monterrey and imprisoned in San Luis before fleeing to the United States, where he published his Plan de San Luis, which bore the date of his final day spent in San Luis Potosí. This document was to become the inspiration for the early stages of the revolution that then swept across the country. The first armed revolutionary to march into San Luis was Cándido Navarro, on May 26, 1911.

Once Madero was at the helm of the nation, there was a rebellion by brothers Cleofas, Magdaleno, and **Saturnino Cedillo** (1890–1939), who switched allegiance from Venustiano Carranza to Huerta and then to Pancho Villa; only Saturnino survived the violence, switching again to Carranza and rising to high military office. He was appointed operational head of the state in 1924, then became its governor and a regional strongman who engineered the appointment of some subsequent governors.

Another regional strongman arising from the revolutionary era was **Gonzalo N. Santos** (1896–1979). As a soldier during the Revolution, he rose to the rank of general. After that, he became active in politics and was a founder of the political party that eventually came to dominate twentieth-century Mexico, the Partido Revolucionario Institucional (PRI). He was a member of the National Congress and sometime governor of the state, which allowed him to become very powerful, especially in the Huasteca region, where his private lands were more extensive than any others in the state and among the most extensive in the whole of Mexico.

Economy

Mining is still a major occupation in San Luis. The state is Mexico's most important producer of fluorite, of which it has the largest deposits in the world. Nationally it is third in the mining of zinc and copper, sixth in gold, eighth in lead, and ninth in silver. The mining of manganese, gypsum, cement, dolomite, silica, marble, and phosphorus is also significant. Mining companies are found especially in the municipalities of San Luis Potosí, Zaragoza, Villa de la Paz, Charcas, Ciudad Valles, Tamuín, Catorce, and Guadalcázar. Exports go to other parts of the Americas, to Asia, and to Europe.

In the agricultural sector, corn, beans, and sorghum are the principal crops sown annually, while sugarcane and oranges are the main perennials. Cattle, sheep, and goats outnumber pigs. There are many horses, and poultry and bees are also important.

A major industry for San Luis is food, especially bread production, drinks, chocolates, and sweets. Most of the food industry is concentrated in the municipalities of San Luis Potosí, Ciudad Valles, Matehuala, Rioverde, and Soledad de Graciano Sánchez. The products of this industry are exported to Latin America, the United States, Canada, and Europe.

The textile industry makes fabrics and finished articles of clothing; this sector is growing and is complemented by *maquiladoras*. There are also some sixty enterprises engaged in the production of leather goods. The textile industry is found mainly in San Luis Potosí, Matehuala, Soledad de Graciano Sánchez, and Rioverde and it exports to the same places as the food sector, plus Japan.

Furniture making is a traditional occupation that employs some three thousand workers in a large number of small enterprises, mostly in the municipality of San Luis. The products are sometimes exported to the United States. Also in the San Luis area, a similar number of workers is employed in the chemicals industry, which accounts for about 7 percent of industrial revenues; plastics and pharmaceuticals predominate and are exported in significant quantities. A comparable contribution comes from other manufactured items, which include electrical goods, domestic appliances, cars parts, water tanks, machinery, and so forth. Smelting is also an important part of the economy.

Finally, San Luis is one of Mexico's more interesting colonial towns, which, coupled with the attractions of some other parts of the varied landscape, brings in many tourists.

Arts

San Luis Potosí's array of crafts varies somewhat by region. There is goldwork, wood and stone carving, barrel making, ironwork, leatherwork, pottery, pyrotechnics, macramé, and shawl making on the meseta. In the center, they make mesquite furniture, palm hats, *huaraches* (sandals), rattan furniture, saddles, baskets, embroidery, wooden and stone artifacts, and ceramics. In the Huasteca, tough fibers are used for weaving, together with palm; there is also leatherwork, mask making, woodwork, paperwork, fireworks, earthenware, and textiles ranging from coarse to fine.

As far as music and dance are concerned, the *son huasteco* is a *mestizo* genre that is deeply rooted in the Huasteca, a region that spills over into Hidalgo, Tamaulipas, and Veracruz. The *huapango* is a dance that is traditionally performed on a platform, accompanied by instrumentalists and singers. There are huapango dancing contests, but the dance is also performed informally at social events. Examples of popular huapangos are the numbers known as "El Sonsolito," "El Taconcito," "El Gusto," and "El Sombrerito." To make a show of their skills, some dancers perform on their knees or with glasses of water balanced on their heads.

Another traditional form, found in central parts of the state, is the *son arribeño* or *valona*. This is also performed on a platform, with a hollow beneath it to augment the sound made by the feet. The musicians sit on benches along the sides of the platform and engage in a kind of competition of verses and song. After a while, people join in dancing together.

Other popular dances are *las varitas*, which is a little like a Morris dance; *los chichimecas*, for which the dancers carry wooden bows and gourd rattles, with one of them going masked; and *zacamson* (*tzacam son*), which is accompanied by stringed instruments and which the Indians dance in honor of the bounties provided by Mother Earth. In the mountains and in the rural communities of the municipality of Rioverde, people perform *décimas* and *valonas*, which are simple poems expressing desires and hopes or telling stories. Sometimes these poetical exchanges can be competitive, with the versifiers "attacking" each other. *Jarabes* and *sones* are usually accompanied by a couple of violins, a *bajo sexto* (a form of bass guitar), and another stringed instrument called a *jarana*.

Manuel José Othón (1858–1906) was a lawyer, writer, and member of the National Congress. He contributed to Mexico City's influential periodicals *El Mundo Ilustrado* and the *Revista Azul* and to literature of every genre. **Francisco González Bocanegra** (1824–1861), a poet, became famous as the author of the words of Mexico's national anthem.

Julián Carrillo Trujillo (1875–1965) was a musicologist, composer, and sometime director of the National Conservatory. **Antonio Castro Leal** (1896–1981), a lawyer and a professor of literature, was briefly rector (president) of the Universidad Nacional Autónoma de México (UNAM), Mexico's largest university. He later served as the director of Bellas Artes (the National Fine Arts Institute) and president of the National Film Commission. Castro Leal became a high-ranking official in UNESCO and also as a member of the Mexican National Congress.

Social Customs

On September 28, the Feast of St. Michael Archangel, Aquismon attracts the faithful from all over the Huasteca region, as does Axila two months later for the Feast of St. Catherine. The Feast of St. Francis, in early October, is celebrated in Catorce. In this case, the festive dancing takes place inside the church. This event usually coincides with the arrival of Huichol Indians, who come in search of *peyote*. Matehuala celebrates the Epiphany on January 6 on a grander scale, with fireworks, trade shows, performances, and exhibitions, in addition to dancing; similar celebrations take place in many places.

In the capital, one main event occurs in January and is associated with the Feast of St. Sebastian; over the course of ten days, there are a great many processions and pilgrimages, and parents dress their children up as Indians and take them to church to be blessed. On July 25 (the Feast of Santiago) pilgrims flock to San Luis bearing flowers and candles to church, and a month later, for the Day of San Luis, the whole town lets its hair down in honor of its patron saint. There are floats, bands, fireworks, a fair, and all shorts of entertainments.

The Day of the Dead is important all over Mexico, but in the town of San Martín Chalchicuautla, it is marked by dancing the *danza de los viejos* (dance of the old men), whose participants sometimes dress up as women and dance from one house to another, led by a figure known as "El Cole," who is dressed as an Apache.

The *quechquémitl* is a heavily embroidered white cotton shawl worn by Huasteca women. The embroidered motifs may be of crosses, flowers, animals, or plants. The shawl has a fringe that echoes the colors of the embroidery, which are typically red, orange, pink, and green. This shawl is worn over a puffy pink blouse. The most striking element in this traditional garb is the *petob*, a kind of crown made by weaving locks of hair around a colored hoop. The full, paneled skirt goes to ankle level, is usually of black woolen fabric, and is topped by a colored sash. Sometimes women carry a woolen bag (*talega*) that also reflects the designs of the embroidery on the shawl. Men traditionally wear long-sleeved white shirt-jackets and white trousers, both of cotton, plus a red kerchief and a straw hat.

Noteworthy Places

San Luis Potosí has a rich architectural heritage. Towns that are especially interesting are the capital San Luis, Cerro de San Pedro, Armadillo de los Infante, Alaquines, Guadalcázar, and Real de Catorce.

Among the archaeological sites is El Consuelo, in the municipality of Tamuín, one of the most important of the Huasteca region. This Huasteca commercial center is where a famous sculpture called "The Huastecan Adolescent" was found; it is believed to be a representation of the god Quetzalcóatl. The site of Tantoc and its pyramid are major features. Another archaeological site is Tzintzin, in the same municipality. In other parts of the state, there are vestiges of different cultures.

Among the many important religious buildings in the capital city are its cathedral, the Templo y Convento de San Francisco, the Templo de la Tercera Orden, the churches of Sagrado Corazón, San Miguelito, San Sebastián,

Tlaxcala (Nuestra Señora de la Asunción), San Cristóbal del Montecillo, Santiago del Río, San Juan de Dios, San Juan de Guadalupe, and Espíritu Santo, the Templo de la Compañía de Jesús, the Capilla de Loreto, and the convent of the Carmelitas Descalzas. San Luis also has a number of attractive gardens and squares; the main one is the Plaza de Armas. Its principal civic buildings include the Government Palace, the Municipal Palace, the Palacio Martí (which houses Museum of Masks), the old money exchange (Casa de Moneda), the corn exchange (Lonja), theaters, the penitentiary, the railroad station, and the post office. An example of its historic residences is the Casa de la Virreina.

In other municipalities, important structures include Ahualulco's Templo Parroquial and the former Hacienda de San Francisco Javier de la Parada, Armadillo's Templo de la Purísima Concepción and Hacienda Pozo del Carmen (also once a Carmelite convent), and Cerro de San Pedro's San Pedro and San Nicolás churches and Hacienda de Monte Caldera. Mexquitic de Carmona has its Templo de San Miguel Arcángel and the Santuario del Desierto, Santa María del Río has the Templo de la Asunción, and Soledad de Graciano Sánchez has the Templo de la Soledad. Villa de Reyes is the site of half a dozen interesting former haciendas, and Cedral and Charcas have their parish churches. In addition to churches, Matehuala boasts at least three imposing old houses. Most municipalities have buildings of architectural value.

Besides the Museum of Masks, in a neoclassical rose-colored stone building from the late nineteenth century, the capital offers a Museum of the Revolution, set in a house that once belonged to Mariano Jiménez. There is the Museum of State Culture (Museo de Cultura Potosina), which also serves as an educational center, Casa Museo de Manuel José Othón, and Museo de Culturas Populares. The Museo Regional Potosino concentrates on Huasteca culture and history and colonial art; it is housed in an eighteenth-century convent building. Huasteca culture is also the focus of the Museo Regional de Valles.

One curiosity, located deep in the Huasteca jungle, is Las Pozas de Xilitla, a fantasy garden built by an eccentric and very wealthy English aristocrat, Sir Edward James, who rubbed shoulders with many of the fashionable artists and intellectuals of his day and was the greatest patron and promoter of surrealism, and in particular of Salvador Dalí.

Cuisine

San Luis Potosí's cuisine draws on Huasteca tradition as well as the Spanish one. *Zacahuil* (a huge *tamal* filled with spiced chicken or turkey and wrapped in banana leaves) is a dish taken from the Indian tradition, as are *nopales con papas de monte*, which are filled with palm shoots, and *cabuches; cabrito al pastor* (roast kid goat) derives from the Spanish heritage. Other favored dishes include *enchiladas potosinas* and *queso de tuna* (made with the fruit of the *agave* cactus). *Coloche* is an alcoholic drink made from the *nopal* cactus.

Enchiladas Huastecas Potosinas

Ingredients:

> 1 lb. dried salt beef (*cecina*)
> 1 lb. carrots
> 1 lb. potatoes
> 1 chicken
> 1 medium onion
> $\frac{1}{2}$ lb. (or 2 cans) roasted sardines
> $\frac{1}{2}$ lb. mild cheese, grated
> 3 *ancho* chiles
> 3 tomatoes
> 1 clove of garlic
> Pinch of ground cumin
> 15–20 corn tortillas
> 1 head of lettuce
> 6 oz. pork fat
> 4–5 oz. refried black beans
> Salt and pepper, to taste

Cut the chicken into pieces and boil with the onion and some salt. When cooked, strip the meat from the bone. Cut up the dried beef, rinse it, and put it to soak in warm water to get rid of most of the salt. Roast the chiles gently, then clean them out and put them to soak in hot water. After about 20 minutes, grind or puree the chiles together with the garlic, tomatoes, cumin, and a dash of salt. Fry this mixture in a little of the fat, then slowly add water to it until it makes a fairly runny sauce. Cut up the potatoes and carrots into small bits and parboil them, so that they are still firm. Remove the beef pieces from the water, drain well, and brown. Heat the refried beans in a little fat.

Lay some lettuce leaves on serving plates. Dip the tortillas in the sauce and fry each one briefly in plenty of fat or oil, without allowing them to get crisp. Put some cheese on each tortilla and roll them up, laying three or four on each plate, on top of the lettuce leaves. Around the tortillas lay a portion of chicken, a portion of beef, some sardines, and some beans. Now fry the carrots and potato pieces and scatter these on top. Pour the sauce over all this and sprinkle with cheese.

Pemoles

Ingredients:

> 2 lb. fine cornmeal
> 1 lb. vegetable lard (or equivalent in oil)
> 1 tbsp baking powder

1$\frac{1}{2}$ cups sugar
1 cup strong coffee

Use a food mixer to blend the cornmeal, lard, baking powder, and sugar together thoroughly. Then blend in the coffee. Shape the dough into rounds and put them in the oven to bake for 10–15 minutes at 375°F until they start to turn brown.

Sopa de Cabuches con Yerba Santa

Ingredients:

2 lb. *cabuches* (cactus flowers)
1 lb. green tomatoes
1 medium onion
2 cloves of garlic
5 leaves of *hierba santa* (*Piper auritum*, a large-leaved plant with a flavor somewhat like anise)
1 lb. zucchinis
3 pints chicken stock
Salt

Clean and rinse the cabuches and boil them with water and a little salt. Drain and discard the water. Chop up the tomatoes, onion, garlic, and zucchinis, and boil; when cooked, drain them and puree them, then pass the mixture through a sieve. Remove the main veins from the centers of the hierba santa leaves, then put the leaves to soak for 30 seconds in boiling water. Drain them and puree them with the green tomato mixture. Add the liquid to the chicken broth and heat through.

Sinaloa

State Characteristics

Shaped rather like a leg, Sinaloa lies in the northwest of Mexico, on the coast. The states of Sonora and Chihuahua border it to the north, Nayarit to the south, Durango to the east, and the Gulf of California and the Pacific Ocean to the west. There has been a good deal of speculation about the origins of the name of the state; the one that has won official recognition attributes it to roots in the Cáhita language; according to this explanation the name means "The Place of the Round *Pitahaya*" (pitahaya is a local variety of cactus).

Sinaloa occupies 2.9 percent of Mexico's surface, covering 56,500 square kilometers (22,000 square miles). It has eighteen administrative municipalities and a total population (according to the 2005 census) of 2,608,442. Catholics accounted for 87 percent of the population, Protestants and evangelicals for 3 percent. The state has twelve representatives in the National Congress.

The capital city is Culiacán de Rosales (commonly known simply as Culiacán), population 605,304; the main port, Mazatlán, has a population of 325,471. There are only three other towns in the state that have a population in excess of 50,000. Sinaloa publishes a total of thirteen newspapers, in the capital, in Mazatlán, and in Los Mochis, such as *El Sol de Sinaloa, Noroeste, Adelante, Demócrata, El Debate*, and *La Voz de Sinaloa*. There are ten institutions of higher education, of which the most important is the Universidad Autónoma de Sinaloa.

The main geographical features are the Sierra Madre Occidental and the coastal plains. The highest elevations are at the Picacho de los Frailes, the Mesa San Bartolo, and the Cordón el Copo Alto, all of which rise to around 2,520 meters (8,265 feet). About half the state has a warm climate with summer rains; the rest is hot and arid. The average annual temperature is about 25°C (77°F), with January's temperatures around 17°C (63°F) and July's around 32°C (90°F). In some places, summer highs can reach 42°C (108°F). Along the coastal plains, annual rainfall averages 700 millimeters (28 inches); the highest rainfall, 1,188 millimeters (46.8 inches), occurs in parts of the mountains. The main rivers, running westward, are the Fuerte, Sinaloa, Mocorito, Humaya, Tamazula, Culiacán, Elota, Baluarte, Presidio, Quelite, and San Lorenzo; most of these are controlled by dams. Of the 650 kilometers (400 miles) of coastline, 90 percent is on the Gulf of California. There are bays in the northern stretch and lagoons in the southern. The Islas del Golfo de California, the Playa Ceuta, El Verde Camacho, and the Meseta de Cacaxtla are the major nature reserves.

The mountains have forests of pines and oaks, while on the plains there are coconut trees, linden trees, *huizaches*, oaks, myrtles, and pasturelands, and along the coasts there are mangroves, *tules*, and *guamúchiles*. The fauna of the mountainous areas includes white-tailed deer, foxes, coyotes, panthers, and pumas. On the plains, there are armadillos, rabbits, *mapaches*, and *tlacuaches*, and birds such as ducks, quail, and parrots. The mangroves are home to reptiles of various sorts, including crocodiles, and there is a variety of coastal birds. Common among sea dwellers are shrimp, grouper, bream, bass, sardines, and turtles.

Cultural Groups and Languages

Only 1.3 percent of those over the age of five speaks an indigenous language. Indigenous peoples whose historical roots are in the state are limited to the Mayos, who are still found in the municipalities of Choix, El Fuerte, Ahome, and Sinaloa. Other indigenous peoples have migrated into the state, including Tarahumaras, Mayas, Mixtecs, Coras, Mexicas, and Zapotecs. In a 1940 census, 9,327 indigenous-language speakers were identified, a figure that declined until the 1970s, when migrants from other states, actively recruited to work on the land, boosted the Indian numbers. For 2005, the total figure was 30,459 speakers, with 26 percent of these speaking Mayo, 21 percent Náhuatl, and 16 percent Mixtec or Zapotec.

History

Sinaloa's history is bound up with that of its neighbor Sonora. For a long time during the colonial era, the two were administered as a single unit, and before the arrival of the Spaniards, they were both occupied by scattered indigenous groups who spoke mutually comprehensible languages, dialects of the Cahíta group. In the case of the area that is now Sinaloa, the dominant groups were the Tahues in central parts of the state, from Mocorito to Piaxtla; the Totoranes on the border with Nayarit; the Pacaxees around Culiacán; and the Acaxees and Xiximes in the hills close to Durango. These were hunters and gatherers, not creators of highly organized settlements such as those found in central and southern Mexico. The indigenous groups of Sinaloa were in three clusters, determined by the characteristics of the land, and after the Spanish invasion, these clusters became the basis for three provinces: Chiametlán, Culiacán, and Sinaloa. The Indians made ceremonial ceramics, buried their dead in pots that probably symbolized a return to the womb, wove blankets, made pipes, and left rock paintings.

Their lives were disrupted by the arrival of the Spaniards, especially by the ravages of one notorious conquistador, Nuño Beltrán de Guzmán. One consequence was a transformation of their relationship with nature; they learned to practice agriculture and faced an invader for whom land was a private possession. They were put to work for the Spaniards on the land or in mines, and they were "reduced"—in other words, settled in missions.

In 1531, Beltrán founded the Villa de San Miguel de Culiacán. The invaders' sojourn in Sinaloa was spoiled by an epidemic that killed a large number of their Indian allies, and so Beltrán returned to the south, leaving an outpost that was besieged by Indians, about 150 kilometers (a hundred miles) north of the closest Spanish settlement. The local Indians also suffered from measles and smallpox during the first five years of the decade, and their numbers declined dramatically during the first decades of the colonial era. There was generally a great deal of Indian resistance to Spanish expansion, but inexorably more settlements were established.

One explorer, Diego de Alcaraz, had had an extraordinary surprise in 1536. While exploring his way along the Río Petatlán, he came across a large group of Indians who were accompanying four Spaniards. It transpired that these Spaniards were survivors of a shipwreck in Florida, and that they had made their way across the southern United States to Mexico. Their leader was Alvar Núñez Cabeza de Vaca, who later wrote of his experiences and how he had become acculturated to native ways. Cabeza de Vaca and his friends spoke of the existence of seven fabulous cities in Cíbola and Quivira. When these tales reached the viceroy, his appetite for further riches was whetted. He sent Francisco Vázquez de Coronado to be governor of Nueva Galicia. Vázquez then sent Father Marcos de Niza to explore, and following Niza's reports, he then set out himself in 1540 to conquer more lands. Vázquez founded the town of Villa de San Jerónimo de los Corazones (later destroyed by the Yaquis) and went as far as Arizona, Colorado, New Mexico, and even Arkansas, before returning in disillusionment to Culiacán in 1542.

Capt. Francisco de Ibarra, a peacemaker, came in 1564. He founded Villa de San Juan Bautista de Carapoa on the banks of the Río Fuerte and then turned south to revive Villa de Chametla and found Villa de San Sebastián, today's Concordia. Toward the end of 1583, Capt. Pedro de Montoya left Culiacán with a small detachment of soldiers and founded Villa de San Felipe y Santiago—a town that would be abandoned, revived, and abandoned again in the face of Indian attacks. In 1590, the first Jesuits arrived in Sinaloa, which at that time the Spaniards called New Aragón. The first Jesuits to begin the process of evangelization of the natives were Gonzalo de Tapia and Martín Pérez. Thereafter a determined campaign was begun to subdue the Indians of the Fuerte River area.

In 1601 came a revolt by the Acaxee Indians, who lived in the canyons of the Sierra Madre Occidental in northwestern Durango and eastern Sinaloa. Jesuit missionaries had worked to bring them together in a controlled way and to change their customs, but a leader called Perico, taking a page out of the Christian book and presenting himself as the savior of his people, incited them to reject the falsehoods of the Jesuits and kill all Spaniards. After some Acaxee attacks, negotiations ensued but failed, and ultimately reinforcements were summoned, the rebellion put down, and many Acaxees killed or sold into slavery.

Another important group, the Mayos, had voluntarily become acquainted with the Jesuit missions, and many had converted to Christianity. In 1609, the Mayos signed a peace treaty. Spanish dealings with the Yaqui peoples, who lived along the river of that name, were less straightforward, however. The Yaquis had fought against Beltrán, but had welcomed the peaceful Ibarra in 1565. It appears that they hoped to forge an alliance with the Spaniards, but instead found themselves forced into two bloody battles, against both the Spaniards and Mayos. The Spaniards were defeated. In time, the Yaquis also made approaches to the missions, using their old rivals the Mayos as intermediaries. The Jesuits were clearly concerned for the well-being of the indigenous peoples, and they tried to defend them from exploitation by settlers. Between 1617 and 1619, about 30,000 Yaquis were baptized, and it was only a few years before the Jesuits had about eighty of their scattered communities organized into a tenth as many missions.

Both Sinaloa and Sonora were part of a vast administrative territory that colonial Spain called Nueva Vizcaya. In 1733, after mining and ranching had made Sinaloa and Sonora important, the authorities detached them both from that larger territory and established them as the province of New Spain.

Although by the middle of the eighteenth century the Yaquis, the Mayos, and the Spaniards had coexisted peacefully for almost 150 years, Indian dissatisfaction had grown, due to the way in which they were managed and their lack of control of their own affairs. Around 1740, two spokesmen emerged from the Indian community—El Muni and Bernabé—and took the Yaquis' grievances to local civil authorities, they were promptly arrested. In response to Indian protests, the governor of the province then invited the Yaqui leaders to go to Mexico City and present their case to the highest authorities, as a result of which they were granted the right to elect their own officials, preserve their lands, receive payment for work, and not be forced to work in the mines. But these rights were not respected, and that triggered Indian violence, with churches burned and priests and settlers fleeing. By the time the rebels had been subdued, about six thousand lives had been lost, a thousand of them Spanish. After that, the governor of the province began a drive toward secularization, set up military garrisons, and encouraged settlers to return.

In their efforts to educate and protect the Indians, the Jesuits were often at loggerheads with the Spanish authorities, so much so that they came to be viewed as subversive of the colonial power. As a result, in 1767 the Spanish king, Carlos III, resolved to banish them from the New World, and their missionary work passed into the hands of the Franciscans. The government thereupon began to take over Yaqui lands. There were many more Indian uprisings, and not only by the Yaquis. Sinaloa became isolated from the rest of New Spain, while landowners increasingly exploited the indigenous people. As for the question of Yaqui land tenure, that dragged on well into the twentieth century.

The year 1776 brought the creation of a new administrative order, with Sinaloa, Sonora, the Californias, Nueva Vizcaya, Coahuila de Zaragoza, Texas, and Nuevo México all grouped together as the Comandancia General de las Provincias Internas. Arizpe, in Sonora, was the capital of this huge new administrative entity.

In 1810, the leader of the movement for independence from Spain, Miguel Hidalgo, called upon José María González de Hermosillo, a native of Sonora, to promote the movement in the north of the country. After Mexico had become independent from Spain, Sonora and Sinaloa, which had been administered for some time as a single unit, were separated—only to be reunited six months later as the Estado de Occidente (Western State). In 1831, they were once again separated, and each became a state in its own right. Sinaloa's first Constitutive Assembly (Congreso Constituyente) met formally for the first time in the Villa de Culiacán on March 13, 1831.

A distinguished native son of Sinaloa during the early years of independence was **Pablo de Villavicencio**, "El Payo del Rosario" (1796-1832), a liberal journalist and *costumbrista* writer who attacked many of the leading figures of the moment, from Hidalgo to Agustín de Iturbide to Vicente Guerrero, Nicolás Bravo, Anastasio Bustamante, and Guadalupe Victoria, taking all of them to task for unfulfilled promises.

Much of the nineteenth century in Mexico was marred by political instability and by fighting between conservatives and liberals. Between 1836 and 1846, when the conservative centralists were dominant, there were powerful military commanders in Mazatlán and Culiacán, which alternated as the effective seat of government (Culiacán was finally made the state capital in 1873). Mazatlán, the most strategic city, was also prominent in the confrontation with the United States, when it was threatened by a naval blockade, surrendered without violence, and was occupied until the end of the conflict in 1848. Mazatlán then underwent a difficult period that began with an epidemic of cholera in 1851. In 1852, it witnessed a rebellion by tradesmen who were opposed to certain economic reforms; government forces were brought in to control them, but the government was forced to compromise. Mazatlán was the focus of trade for the state, the major port via which raw materials, especially precious metals, were exported and manufactured goods imported.

By the time the French Intervention took place, the liberals were in power in Sinaloa. The governor of the state, Gen. **Plácido Vega** (1830–1878), organized a brigade that joined with forces from other states to fight against the French, while troops in Mazatlán defended the port against French attacks from the sea, until the French finally took control and Gen. **Antonio Rosales** (1822-1865), the commander of the Mexican troops, was obliged to retreat to Culiacán. Shortly after that, he defeated other French forces who had landed at Altata. Meanwhile, Gen. Ramón Corona was successfully defending the state in the south, and in 1866 he recovered control of Mazatlán, a development that signaled the end of the French presence in Sinaloa.

The restoration of Benito Juárez's national government was followed by the Reform War, which brought the Church and landowners into conflict with reformists. There were fierce rivalries between Rosales and Corona, and between Rosales and Gen. **Domingo Rubí** (1824-1896). Sinaloa elected the reformist Rubí to the governorship, but at the time of the Plan de la Noria, drawn up in Oaxaca by Porfirio Díaz in opposition to Juárez, Rubí had to call on support from neighboring Sonora in order to regain control of Culiacán from supporters of Díaz. The death of Juárez encouraged conservative military men to seize power once again until the acting president of Mexico, Sebastián Lerdo de Tejada, ordered an end to the hostilities.

One of the most successful liberal governors of the state during this era was **Eustaquio Buelna** (1830-1907), who assumed the post in 1871 at a time of considerable unrest. Despite political troubles, Buelna introduced major improvements in the state's educational system and promoted cultural activities, even finding time to write historical studies himself. Although he also became a minister at national level, his life ended in obscurity.

Political troubles were not all that Sinaloa had to contend with: in 1877, there was a severe drought, causing hunger for many people. During this convulsive period, a new figure appeared on the political stage, the legendary **Heraclio Bernal**, "El Rayo de Sinaloa" (1855-1888). Bernal began to take part in politics at the age of sixteen, supporting Juárez, and went on to be a leading opponent of Díaz and a champion of the interests in mineworkers. As commander of the forces opposing Díaz, in 1880 he took over the port of Mazatlán.

One of the effects of the *porfiriato* was to remove states' rights to elect their governors. Instead, Díaz chose people who would promote his policies. Mariano Martínez de Castro and Gen. **Francisco Cañedo** (1839–1910) were two appointees to the governorship of the state of Sinaloa. Cañedo held that office for almost as long as Díaz did the presidency of the country, which explains why in Sinaloa the politics of the period are commonly referred to as *cañedismo*. The pro-Díaz governors of Sinaloa promoted the president's national strategy, which favored the rich, allowed foreign interests to exploit resources and the labor force, and made the poor poorer, silencing any opposition with strong-arm tactics. For example, a recalcitrant journalist named José Cayetano Valadés was assassinated.

Among the major foreign concerns that came into the state were the Sonora-Sinaloa Irrigation Company, the United Sugar Company, and American Smelting. A more utopian development, resulting from an agreement signed in 1886 by the government of Mexico, the Texas Topolobampo, and the Pacific Railroad and Telegraph Company, was that Albert K. Owen was able to acquire lands and bring in U.S. settlers to create an agricultural cooperative. This project failed, but it did lead to the development of the area known as Los Mochis. The Topolobampo initiative came under the umbrella of a general policy that favored opening up more lands and bringing in foreign capital and labor to exploit them. The official view was that the locals were lazy and unambitious, entrenched in outdated practices. *Compañías deslindadoras* such as the Sinaloa Land Company were established to open up land that in many cases had belonged to the Church or to the Indians. Vast estates were created, with land sometimes purchased at laughable prices, to expand sugarcane production and raise cattle. Most of the state fell into the hands of a very few people, such as the Almada, Redo, and Johnston families. These estates were largely autonomous, producing food for their workers, which they sold to them in their own shops; they had their own churches and prisons and effectively ran the lives of the people employed in them.

In 1910, there was a rebellion against the porfiriato by **Gabriel Leyva Solano** (1871–1910). A rural schoolteacher, Leyva opposed Díaz's reelection and sought to champion the rights of poor workers, but having once defeated pro-Díaz forces, he himself was defeated and was shot "while trying to escape." **Manuel Bonilla** (1867–1957) was a politician, military man, and writer who joined the supporters of Francisco Madero and founded the Club Antirreeleccionista de Culiacán, in opposition to Díaz's reelection at the age of eighty, after some thirty years in power. Bonilla also edited an opposition newspaper, *El Correo de la Tarde*. He later served as a minister in Madero's national government and then as an aide to Pancho Villa, taking charge of matters of land tenure.

By 1911, revolutionary forces had gained control of a number of strategic locations and laid siege to Culiacán and Mazatlán, successfully occupying the capital. Another unsettled period ensued. Madero became president of

Mexico and then had his authority usurped by Victoriano Huerta. **Benjamín Hill** (1877-1920), another of the people who had openly opposed the reelection of Porfirio, was among many who fought against Huerta; he later served under Venustiano Carranza. **Francisco R. Serrano** (1889-1927) served under Alvaro Obregón, was governor of Mexico City, and became a presidential candidate before being shot. During the Revolution, Culiacán and Mazatlán were both taken by Obregón.

Another Indian rebellion erupted in 1915, this time by the Mayos, under the leadership of **Felipe Bachombo** (1883-1916), an illiterate worker on one of the big *haciendas*, whose fate was also to be captured and shot.

Sinaloa had a series of provisional governors until 1917, when the new national constitution was introduced under President Carranza. At that time, another general, Ramón Iturbe, was properly elected to the post. Once again political rivalries made progress difficult, but Iturbe did make improvements on the administrative and legal fronts and in educational provision. The state was reorganized into sixteen municipalities (to which a further two were added many decades later).

Obregón took to arms in order to unseat Carranza. In 1920, Obregón, who was from Sonora, published the Plan de Agua Prieta, one of whose signatories was **Angel Flores** (1883-1926), a rival of Iturbe's. The conflict between Obregón and Carranza led to the death of the latter, and Obregón, once president, appointed Flores to the governorship of Sinaloa, at the same time making him a senior military commander. Flores set about eliminating any opposition to Obregón. Whatever revolutionary credentials he may have had, Flores did not take steps to redistribute land to the poor, although he did promote the state's first major irrigation project. With the support of some rich landowners, he stood unsuccessfully against Plutarco Elías Calles in the next presidential elections. Disillusioned, Flores then retired from public life. The precise circumstances of his death were never clarified; some suspected he had been murdered.

The rivalry between Flores and Iturbe was only one of several that characterized this epoch. As the country recuperated after the disruptions of the Revolution and the era of *caudillos* waned, Sinaloa had more military governors, but these were every bit as much administrators and men of letters as they were soldiers; perhaps above all they were people who knew how to play their cards right. Labor organizations grew, especially in the 1920s, education improved, and there was agricultural development, but, even though many of Sinaloa's governors were from humble backgrounds, they tended to forget the poor. The main promise of the 1917 Constitution—that land would be redistributed—had not been fulfilled; in the Sinaloa of the 1920s, the same landowning families were in control as in the days of cañedismo.

In the 1930s, during the presidency of Lázaro Cárdenas, there was some expropriation and redistribution of land. Then, under Governor Pablo Macías Valenzuela, there was more progress in the educational field and in improving conditions for agriculture. A crucial step in the development of agriculture was the construction of the state's dams, the first of which was built in 1939. Over the years, more land was designated for *ejidos*, so that by 1972, 62 percent was under that system of tenure. However, the old landowning families—for example, the Redo family—weathered the changes and were still influential and powerful at the close of the century.

Sinaloa developed as an agricultural state, and industrialization came only slowly. In 1970, 51 percent of the working population was occupied in agriculture or fishing, and only 1.3 percent in industry. As in other parts of Mexico, problems arose in the 1970s and 1980s with civil unrest and the collapse of the national economy. On the political front, the stagnation and corruption scandals that rocked the dominant Partido Revolucionario Institucional (PRI) had their local repercussions, with the opposition Partido de Acción Nacional (PAN) making advances. One of the most active and controversial figures in the politics of the late twentieth century was **Maquío Clouthier** (1934–1989), a businessman who undertook a personal campaign to enhance democracy in Mexico, stood unsuccessfully as a candidate for the presidency of the country, and participated in a hunger strike in Mexico City.

Economy

During the colonial era, the economy had relied on the mining of precious minerals and on cattle ranching. By the middle of the nineteenth century, there were three textile factories engaged in producing mostly cotton fabrics for the use of humbler folk, since the wealthy imported theirs. There was a little cultivation in a few areas that had adequate rainfall; the products of this served local needs. The mines were supported by a factory that made metal implements and tools, and there were one or two minor manufacturing businesses besides. With the porfiriato came modernization, industrialization, and better communications, such as the telegraph and the railroad. More land was put in the hands of the rich, foreign investment flowed in, and agriculture acquired a new face, beginning a long and significant process of development, although the issue of land tenure remained unaddressed for many years.

The state has had some difficulty in industrializing. Agriculture is still the backbone of the state's economy, although in recent decades it has become more modern and mechanized than almost anywhere else in Mexico. Government aid has encouraged new technologies and improved irrigation systems. About two-thirds of the state's exports are of fresh agricultural products, mostly to the United States but also to South America, Japan, and Europe. Sinaloa is one of Mexico's leading producers of cucumbers, tomatoes, squashes, peppers, eggplants, corn, beans, soybeans, rice, wheat, safflower, sorghum, and fruits such as mangos, melons, and watermelons. Some 10 percent of the state's working population is engaged in agriculture.

Approximately 37,000 square kilometers (14,500 square miles) of land is devoted to rearing animals. The Sinaloan livestock industry is the biggest in Mexico, with something like three million head of cattle, pigs, sheep, and goats and a good deal of poultry.

About 5 percent of the working population is engaged in fishing and related industries. Sinaloa's fishing activity is among the most important in Mexico, in terms of both offshore fishing and fish farming, whose importance increases as natural stocks are depleted. The highest-volume catch from the sea is of tuna, shrimp, varieties of white fish such as snapper, crabs, sardines, and shark; the dominant farmed varieties are tilapia, bass, catfish, and shrimp. Turtles are now protected and have reserved breeding grounds. The infrastructure has been greatly strengthened by private and government investment, providing dedicated port areas (at Perihuete and Altata) and storage and processing facilities. A good deal of the catch goes for export, and there has also been a campaign to encourage greater fish consumption within the state.

Forestry is a relatively minor sector. Sinaloa has a number of factories that process wood for use in construction and packaging, as well as making furniture. The state has been making efforts toward reforestation.

Mining reached its zenith at the end of the nineteenth century, when there was investment by Britain and the United States, leading to modernization. The most important mines today are in the municipalities of San Ignacio, Culiacán, Rosario, Cosalá, Badiraguato, Mazatlán, El Fuerte, Choix, Concordia, Mocorito, Elota, Escuinapa, Sinaloa, and Navolato. Overwhelmingly, the production has been of precious metals (gold, silver, lead, zinc, copper). Recent decades have seen the development of mineral processing facilities.

Approximately 13 percent of the workforce is in industry. Food processing is the second most important economic activity in the state after agriculture; seafood is the most important category, followed by drinks, fruits, and vegetables. The assembly plants known as *maquiladoras* are quite plentiful, putting together finished products for shipment north of the border, especially auto parts and clothes.

Tourism is growing, though not as developed as in some other states. Approximately a quarter of the labor force is employed in the service sector, in activities related to tourism.

As in every part of Mexico, there is also a widespread and diverse informal economy. A dominant component of that, especially in the northern states, is the drug trade.

Arts

Craftwork includes basketry and pottery, which are found all over the state. In the northern mountains, cotton and woolen textiles are woven. Lower down, there is embroidery; the *deshilado* technique, which is of

European origin and involves drawing threads out of the fabric, is quite widely used.

Sinaloa is the birthplace of *banda*, the big band version of *norteño* music, which is popular all over the north of Mexico and in the southwestern United States. The banda repertoire includes *rancheras*, *boleros*, and *cumbias*. Banda is distinguished from norteño largely by the broader and noisier instrumentation. Among the most successful performers have been Chalino Sánchez, El Chapo de Sinaloa, Los Tigres del Norte, and El Veloz de Sinaloa. Norteño musicians have come in for some criticism because of their *narcocorridos*, songs that approvingly recount the exploits of drug traffickers.

Sinaloa was something of a magnet for *modernista* poets at the end of the nineteenth century, attracting several of the leading national figures. A major local poet of the early twentieth century was **Jesús G. Andrade** (1879-1928), who was much influenced by Baudelaire. **Genaro Estrada** (1887-1937), a historian, poet, and diplomat, made his reputation as undersecretary for foreign affairs, ambassador to Spain and Turkey, and a delegate to the League of Nations. He became known for advocating nonintervention in the affairs of other countries. As a writer, Estrada published poetry and a novel. He was a member of the Mexican Academy of the Language and founder of the Mexican Academy of History. **Alejandro Quijano** (1883-1957), a writer and journalist, was the director of the Mexican Academy of the Language for almost twenty years. He contributed to national newspapers such as *El Imparcial* and *El Universal* and was editor of *Novedades*. Quijano published a number of academic works. **Gilberto Owen** (1907-1952) was a politician and diplomat, but also a writer who contributed to two seminal literary magazines of the early twentieth century, *Ulises* and *Contemporáneos*. He was primarily a poet. The short fiction of **Inés Arredondo** (1928-1989) is highly regarded, though she was not especially prolific. **Oscar Leira** (1946-1990) was a theater director and a major dramatist with a national reputation, three times winner of the Ruiz de Alarcón Prize for best theatrical work. A theater in Culiacán bears his name.

A number of *sinaloenses* moved to the United States and made their careers there in films. One who returned to work in Mexico was **Beto González** (1969-); he trained in the United States and Canada and worked with major filmmakers in Spain before making his own in Mexico. The Mexican-trained writer and director **Oscar Blancarte** (1949-) has made a number of successful documentaries and feature films, including *Dulces compañías* (1995).

There have been several stars of Mexican cinema who started life in Sinaloa. Easily the most famous is **Pedro Infante** (1917-1957). Born the fourth of fourteen siblings in Mazatlán, after working locally as a singer, Infante rose to be one of Mexico's most famous film stars of all time, the essential male lead of the *cine de arrabal* of the 1940s and 1950s. He made a total of forty-five films, of which some of the most famous are *Nosotros los pobres*, *Escuela de vagabundos*, and *Pepe el Toro*. He was not the only actor to make a mark in the Mexican cinema of that time, however; others included **Luis Pérez Meza** (1918–1981) and **Amelia Wilhelmy** (fl. 1940s).

José Limón (1908–1972) was a dancer and choreographer who danced with the Humphrey Wederman Company and became artistic director of the Latin American Dance Theater at the Lincoln Center in New York City. He was considered the best modern dancer of his time and was awarded the Premio Nacional de la Unión Americana in 1950. **Lola Beltrán** (1932–1996) was a nationally famous singer of ranchera songs who appeared in a great many films of the 1950s and 1960s. She was nicknamed "Lola la Grande." Other famous popular singers were **Chayito Valdez** (1945–), nicknamed "The Mexican Thrush," and **Manolita Arriola** (1922–2004). **Miguel C. Castro** (1869–1948) was a prolific composer of popular dances and songs, such as waltzes and polkas. He is particularly remembered for a song called "¿Por qué lloras?" **Aldo Rodríguez** (1966–) is one of the state's leading modern musical composers. In the visual arts, the painter **Alvaro Blancarte** (1934–) has been prominent.

Social Customs

In the village of Boca, near Choix, September 28 is time to celebrate the Feast of San Miguel Arcángel. Pilgrims come from surrounding communities to witness traditional dances. Dancing figures of Moors bear the wooden effigy of St. Michael along the road from Choix to Boca.

Carnival is a major event for Los Mochis, Guamuchil, Culiacán, and Mazatlán, characterized by processions, instrumental groups, folk dancing, masked balls, displays and exhibitions, and a flower fight. Carnival at Mazatlán has a national reputation. It begins on the Thursday with a masked ball and a prize for the best mask. On Friday, there are floral displays and a poetry contest; a Carnival queen is selected, after which she parades around town to a background of band music and fireworks. On Saturday, a cardboard figure representing Bad Humor—and resembling a prominent local personage—is ceremoniously burned and poems are read, making fun of the person being lampooned. Then there is the "naval encounter" during which the boats of the coast guard launch rockets (fireworks) attacking those on the land, who fight back with more rockets. That day also sees concerts by major national artists. On Sunday, there is a grand procession, and on Monday, the election of a child queen who duly processes around with her ladies-in-waiting. Carnival reaches its climax on the seafront, with general celebration and dancing to local bands. A trade fair takes place at the same time as Carnival.

Although there is traditional dancing, the Feast of the Immaculate Conception in December is a more sober event in Mazatlán, with effigies, processions of floats, and displays of flowers.

A major religious procession takes place in Guasave, in honor of the Feast of the Virgen del Rosario, in October. The Feast of San Juan Bautista is important for the small town of Mochicahui, with hundreds of the faithful taking part in a pageant and featuring mummers' dances, the *pascolas* dance, and the dance of the deer. There is a strong Mayo cultural contribution on this occasion. The Bay of Topolobampo holds a grand civic Day of the Sea (Día Marina). A most unusual event is San Ignacio's annual Día de la Taspana (Town Cleanup Day), an event that dates from the mid-nineteenth century, when local people agreed that they should clean the town of the agricultural debris that tended to accumulate during the rainy season. This they now do to the accompaniment of bands and while imbibing large quantities of beer. Culiacán has a livestock fair in November. Among many the cultural events in Sinaloa, there is an annual dance festival named after José Limón (Festival Internacional de Danza José Limón); it takes place in the capital, Mazatlán, and Los Mochis. The Feria de las Artes Sinaloa is one of the most significant events for the theatrical arts in northern Mexico, and an international affair. A recent creation is the Festival Internacional de Guitarra.

There is a traditional sinaloense style of dress for women that consists of a loose blouse and a wide, flowing skirt in matching material. The neckline is broad, the sleeves gathered. The skirt is typically held in the hands to dramatize dancing movements. The colors are those of the Mexican flag, arranged in horizontal bands on a floral background. Men in northern states tend to dress up in cowboy clothes for festivities.

Noteworthy Places

The Teatro Angela Peralta, in Mazatlán, was built in 1874, when opera was quite popular. It was originally called the Teatro Rubio. The opera company headed by Mexico's diva Angela Peralta (aka "The Mexican Nightingale") was scheduled to perform there in 1883, but the star was unable to do so because she contracted yellow fever during the voyage there and died shortly after her arrival, in a house next door. In later years, the theater served as a venue for Carnival celebrations, as a boxing arena, and as a cinema. A hurricane in 1975 all but destroyed it, yet in its ruined state, it continued to be used for Sinaloa's Festival of Culture until it was declared a historic monument and renovated. The new theater, which has all the advantages of modern technology, was inaugurated in 1992; it now serves for orchestral concerts, operas, classical and folk ballets, and other cultural events.

One of the most important churches in the state is the Templo de Rosario, considered to be a key example of ecclesiastical architecture in western Mexico, especially because of its ornate baroque altarpiece. The church was begun in 1665, as Rosario was becoming the richest town in northern New Spain. Its entrance was designed by Dominican friars.

Completed only in 1759, the church later was threatened with collapse due to the mineshafts beneath. In 1932, the decision was made to relocate it stone by stone and restore it.

In Nio, there is an interesting unfinished church begun by the Jesuits in 1760, shortly before their expulsion from the New World. Some of the old haciendas have also been renovated and become hotels or museums.

There are rock paintings at Ocolome (El Fuerte). These are on separate rocks set about 5.5 meters (18 feet) from each other. One has anthropomorphic figures, others a circular design with geometric figures within them (thought to be of Toltec origin). They have been compared with similar stones found in Utah. Near Ocolome, at the Cerro La Máscara, there are more representations of human figures.

Culiacán's Centro de Ciencias de Sinaloa, inaugurated in 1993, is one of Mexico's best science centers. It includes a planetarium. Mazatlán has one of the country's best aquariums.

The Laguna de Chiricacueto is one of many places where wildlife can be watched, or hunted. The many beaches and bays accommodate recreational fishermen, divers, and sailors.

Sinaloa's Museum of Art has been created in a building, built in 1837, that formerly served as a bishop's palace and later as state administrative offices. Its patio was occasionally used for performing plays and light operas. The museum's art collection is one of the most important in the north; it includes a self-portrait by Diego Rivera, plus works by leading Mexican artists such as Juan Cordero, Francisco Goitia, Roberto Montenegro, Gerardo Murillo (Dr. Átl), José Luis Cuevas, Francisco Toledo, Rufino Tamayo, and Pedro Coronel. Culiacán's Museo Regional de Sinaloa has archaeological remains and objects of interest from the Indian cultures, plus relics from the time of the independence movement and the Revolution. Cosala has a Museum of Mining.

Cuisine

The hundreds of kilometers of coastline make fish and seafood central to the state's cuisine. Mazatlán in particular is considered the place for shrimp, in all sorts of guises. Turtle used to be commonly eaten, but is now protected and has been replaced by a dish called *caguamanta*, made with stingrays. Also common are tacos made with smoked marlin. All this does not mean that meat dishes are lacking in Sinaloa; *chilorio*, for example, is a traditional meat casserole. Other popular dishes are *colacho*, made with pumpkins; *caldillo de machaca*, a beef broth; *sopa de elote con chiquelites*, a corn-based soup; *caldo zuzule* (a soup made with beans); and roast meats. Sweeter products include *empanadas con relleno de guayaba* (guava-filled pastries) and *turrón de miel y cacahuate*. A regional drink is *damiana*, an alcoholic liqueur made from herbs and rumored to have aphrodisiacal properties.

Frijoles Puercos

Ingredients:

2 lb. kidney beans
1 lb. pork fat
1 lb. *chorizo*, finely chopped
1 lb. mild cheese, grated
$^{1}/_{2}$ lb. bacon
1 can (6 oz.) tuna (optional)
About 15 green olives, chopped
1 medium-hot chile, deseeded and cut into strips
Hot sauce, according to taste
Tortillas

Put the beans to soak, then thoroughly cook and drain them. Blend them into a thick paste. Heat the fat in a heavy pan. When it is very hot, put in the chorizo and bacon. Once the meat is cooked, add the contents of the blender and stir carefully so that the mixture does not burn. When it bubbles, add the chopped olives, the strips of chile, the tuna (if used), and the cheese, and keep warming until the cheese melts. Serve with hot sauce and tortillas.

Pollo Estilo Sinaloa

Ingredients:

2 whole chickens
1 onion, thickly sliced
8 cloves of garlic
$1^{1}/_{2}$ cups orange juice
$^{1}/_{2}$ tsp each of oregano, thyme, and marjoram
4 bay leaves
Salt and pepper

Cut the chickens lengthwise and open them flat. Briefly grill them on both sides to seal in the juices. Place them in wide cooking dish. Use a blender to combine the orange juice with everything else except the onion. Pour this mixture over the chicken and leave it all to marinate in the refrigerator for at least 4 hours, turning the chickens over once or twice during that time. Remove the dish from the refrigerator at least half an hour before continuing the preparation. Grease the grill well and grill the chickens over hot charcoal, turning them over every so often. They can be basted with any remaining marinade. Shortly before the chicken is ready to eat, grill the slices of onion, or fry them in a little olive oil. Put them on top of the chicken and serve.

Ceviche de Camarón

This dish is served with *tostadas* and mayonnaise.

Ingredients:

    2 lb. raw shrimp, peeled
    1 lb. tomatoes (plum tomatoes work well)
    $^1/_2$ purple onion
    1 white onion
    7 *serrano* chiles
    Cilantro
    Salt and pepper
    15 limes
    1 generous tsp Tabasco sauce

Chop the shrimp into small pieces, add salt and pepper, and stir well. Cut up and juice the limes. Add the juice to the shrimp and refrigerate. Chop the tomatoes into small chunks. Dice the onions and chiles into small pieces and add chopped cilantro according to taste. Stir the shrimp to make sure that they have all turned red, then drain off and reserve any excess juice. Combine all the ingredients and mix them together. Add a generous spoonful of the reserved juice, plus salt if necessary. Let the dish stand for 10 minutes or so before serving.

Turrón de Miel y Cacahuate

Ingredients:

    1 lb. sugar
    1 lb. honey
    1 pint warm water
    Whites of four eggs
    Juice of half a lime
    4 oz. chopped peanuts

Melt the sugar and honey in the water until it reaches the state where, when a small quantity is dropped into a bowl of cold water, it makes a ball that can be shaped with the hands. (If using a thermometer, bring it to between 112°C and 116°C). Allow it to cool. Beat the egg whites to soft peaks and add them to the sugar-honey mixture. Add the lime juice and most of the peanuts. Pour it into a flat dish, sprinkle the remaining peanuts on top, and allow it to cool before serving.

Sonora

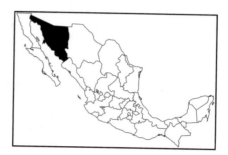

State Characteristics

The northern border of Sonora, 588 kilometers (365 miles) long, is shared with Arizona and New Mexico. To the west are the state of Baja California and the Gulf of California (Mar de Cortés), to the south Sinaloa, and to the east Chihuahua. The name of Sonora has generated a number of possible explanations. One assumes that it is related to the fact that explorers habitually named places according to saints' days. Explorers reached the Yaquí River on the day of Nuestra Señora del Rosario, and this explanation holds that the name results from mispronunciation of "señora" by indigenous peoples. Yet another theory is that it is from the mispronunciation by Spaniards of an indigenous term. One explanation suggests that the name reflects the discovery of gold (*oro*) in southern parts of the state.

This is a large and arid state, a land of mountains (the Sierra Madre) and vast desert expanses. It covers 184,934 square kilometers (72,124 square miles), which at 9.4 percent of Mexico's total area makes it the nation's second largest state. There are seventy-two administrative municipalities. Five regions are commonly distinguished: Río Colorado, Sonora Norte, Sonora Sur, Sinaloa, and Cuencas Cerradas del Norte.

According to the 2005 census, the total population of the state was 2,394,861. The capital city is Hermosillo, located more or less in the middle and with a 2005 population of 641,791. There are many institutions of higher education in the state, and some twenty newspapers, six published in the capital (e.g., *El Imparcial*, *Expreso*, *Crítica*, and *El Independiente*), three in Ciudad Obregón (e.g., *Tribuna de Yaqui*), three in Heroica

Nogales (e.g., *El Diario de Sonora*), three in San Luis Río Colorado (e.g., *La Tribuna*) and the others in Navojoa, Guaymas, and Caborca (*El Informe del Mayo*, *La Voz del Puerto*, and *Diario del Desierto*). Eleven people represent the state in the National Congress.

Much of the state is quite flat. In the mountainous northwest and northeast, there are wooded areas covering a little more than 6 percent of the state, but 70 percent of Sonora has desert vegetation. The forested areas have pines, cedars, and oaks, and to a lesser extent mahogany, ebony, and cypress.

The principal rivers are the Colorado (now much less full than it once was, since so much water has been diverted from it north of the border), Concepción, San Ignacio, Sonora, Mátepe, Yaqui, and Mayo. Most rivers flow sporadically westward into the Gulf of California; a large amount of the water is drawn off for irrigation and does not reach the gulf. There are also several very important dams, mostly named after presidents of Mexico. Many areas are severely short of water and their aquifers depleted. Climate ranges from desert to moderately humid; 90 percent of the state is dry. The mildest areas are limited to higher elevations in Yécora and some parts of the mountains to the north of Cananea; there is also a strip that has a moderate climate in the southeast, near Chihuahua. The mean annual temperature ranges from 13°C (55°F) in Yécora to 26°C (79°F) in Navojoa. The lowest average monthly temperature recorded is 6°C (43°F) in Yécora, and the highest 35°C (95°F) in Hermosillo. Average annual rainfall for the state as a whole is in the neighborhood of 400 millimeters (16 inches). The dominant winds are from the northeast, but from the south in summer.

There are fifty-four native species of mammals, including white-tailed deer, wild sheep, bats, hares, squirrels, moles, badgers, wolves, coyotes, bears, and mountain cats of various kinds. There are amphibians such as frogs and toads, reptiles such as desert tortoises, chameleons, Gila monsters, and rattlesnakes, and hundreds of bird species, of which prominent examples are the roadrunner, the quail, the partridge, the wild turkey, and the vulture. The many miles of coastline offer fish species such as tuna, bream, tilapia, pompano, and sardine; other seafood includes varieties of shrimp, crab, lobster, clams, abalone, snails, octopuses, and oysters.

Cultural Groups and Languages

A low proportion of Sonora's population, 2.5 percent of those over five years of age, speak an indigenous language. However, the Indian population is concentrated in fourteen of the municipalities, and in those it can approach 20 percent of the population. The highest numbers are in Etchojoa and Guaymas, each of which has nine thousand to ten thousand speakers, followed by Huatabampo with about seven thousand, and Navojoa and Hermosillo with five thousand to six thousand each.

In the 1895 census, Sonora was found to have approximately 30,000 people who spoke an indigenous language, and a Spanish-speaking population of about 160,000. By 1930, the official number of indigenous-language speakers was just 6,024. In the present day, the Yaquis still have some cultural identity, and about 12,000 people speak their language; the Mayos number about 25,000. Other indigenous languages that are still spoken, such as Zapotec and Mixtec, have been imported from other parts of Mexico. Sonorans have a dichotomous attitude to the native peoples: the Indians are admired as representatives of the roots of regional identity but also in many ways despised. Migrations, intermarriage, and the advance of the prevailing national culture are putting Indian cultures at risk of extinction.

History

The first Spaniards to set foot on Sonoran territory were those who were shipwrecked in 1529 during an expedition led by Diego Hurtado de Mendoza. It was in 1531 that the notorious conquistador Nuño Beltrán de Guzmán, having already wrought havoc while making his way through Michoacán, Jalisco, Zacatecas, and Nayarit, led an expedition to explore coastal parts of what is now the state of Sinaloa. His expedition of a few hundred soldiers and several thousand Indian allies engaged in a major confrontation with an estimated 30,000 Indian warriors at Culiacán. The local Indians, who were decisively defeated, were speakers of the many dialects of the Cáhita language. The Cáhita peoples were the most numerous in northern Mexico, numbering perhaps 115,000, and they were scattered about coastal areas of the northwest. Among them were the Opatas, the Pimas, the Pápagos, the Yaquis, the Mayos, and the Seris. Unlike the highly organized indigenous peoples of south and central Mexico, these peoples were hunters and gatherers; they learned agriculture only after the arrival of the Spaniards. An epidemic eventually depleted Beltrán's army, so he retreated southward, leaving Culiacán as an isolated outpost surrounded by hostile forces.

In 1540, another conquistador, Francisco Vázquez de Coronado, set out to conquer the seven mythical cities of Cíbola. The Spaniards were driven by such myths—by the belief that there were riches to be found and indigenous people to bring into the Catholic fold. The Yaqui Indians, who were among those who fought against the ravages perpetrated by Beltrán, welcomed a later arrival, the peacemaker Francisco de Ibarra, who came in 1565. It seems that the Yaquis hoped to forge an alliance with Spain against their enemies, the Mayos, but the latter, in the early seventeenth century, sent delegations to visit the Jesuit missions and eventually signed a peace treaty with the Spaniards, voluntarily converting to Catholicism and coming into the missions. The Spaniards, with the Mayos as allies, were later to lose two major battles against the Yaquis, but in time the Yaquis also made approaches to the missions, using the Mayos as intermediaries. The Jesuits were clearly concerned for the well-being of the indigenous peoples and tried to defend them from exploitation by settlers. Indeed, the Jesuits were often at loggerheads with the Spanish authorities.

Once there was peace with the Yaquis, the Spaniards set about the business of "reducing" the Indians, that is to say settling them in missions and educating them in Spanish ways. The Mayo mission was founded in 1614 and that of the Cumuripas ten years later, both by Jesuits. In 1687, Father Francisco Eusebio Kino, also a Jesuit, founded the mission of Nuestra Señora de Dolores de Cosari, and in 1700 the Spaniards founded a number of towns (Nuestra Señora del Pópulo, Nuestra Señora de los Angeles, and La Santísima Trinidad del Pitic) that would later grow into Hermosillo, the state capital. In 1703, yet another famous Jesuit, Jesús Salvatierra, founded the Misión de San José de Guaymas.

Until 1733, Both Sinaloa and Sonora were part of a vast administrative territory that colonial Spain called Nueva Vizcaya. In that year, because of their mining and ranching importance, the authorities detached them both from Nueva Vizcaya and created the new province of Nueva España. By 1760, important deposits of gold and copper had been discovered at Cananea.

By the mid-1700s, the Yaquis, the Mayos, and the Spaniards had coexisted peacefully for almost a hundred and fifty years, but Indian dissatisfaction had grown, due to the way in which they were managed and their lack of control of their own affairs. A poor harvest in 1739, followed by floods a year later, seem to have been the immediate causes of an Indian rebellion in 1740. From the Indian community emerged spokesmen called El Muni and Bernabé who took the Yaquis' grievances to local civil authorities. However, the indignant authorities had them arrested. In response to Indian protests, the governor of the province then invited the Yaqui leaders to go to Mexico City and present their case to the highest authorities. There, they received a more sympathetic response and were granted the right to elect their own officials, preserve their lands, receive payment for work, and not be forced to work in the mines. Nevertheless, these rights were ignored. Indian violence ensued, with churches burned and priests and settlers fleeing. By the time the rebels had been subdued, a thousand Spanish and five thousand Indian lives had been lost. After that, the governor of the province began a drive towards secularization, set up military garrisons, and encouraged settlers to return. In 1768, the government began to take over Yaqui lands, leading to many further Indian uprisings. The question of Yaqui land tenure dragged on well into the twentieth century.

About a decade after the 1740 Yaqui uprising, there was unrest among the Pimas, who were scattered over parts of Sonora and southern Arizona. They were subdued, and as they faced defeat, their leader, Luís Oacpicagi-gua, offered to die in an attempt to save his people from future mistreatment. Between 1751 and 1774, there were Apache raids in Sonora and Chihuahua; mines and ranches were destroyed, livestock stolen, and missions burned. In its defense, New Spain established armed garrisons in frontier regions, twenty-three of them by 1760. There were also problems with the Seri Indians, who were neighbors of the Yaqui and lived along the central coast of Sonora.

For political reasons, in 1767 Carlos III of Spain banished the Jesuits from the New World. Their missions and schools were transferred to the control of other religious orders or used for different purposes. In Sonora and Chihuahua, the missionary work was taken over by the Franciscans. That year also brought the start of a government campaign to pacify the coastal Indians of Sonora, a costly and unsuccessful campaign that lasted until 1771. In 1777, peace negotiations with the Apaches and Comanches of the frontier areas began, but these negotiations had a checkered history, and it was the end of the century before an uneasy peace came. A year earlier, in 1776, a new administrative order was put in place, with Sinaloa, Sonora, the Californias, Nueva Vizcaya, Coahuila de Zaragoza, Texas, and Nuevo México all grouped together as the Comandancia General de las Provincias Internas; Arizpe, in Sonora, was designated the capital of this huge new administrative entity.

In 1810, the leader of the movement for independence from Spain, Miguel Hidalgo, called upon **José María González de Hermosillo** (d. 1819) to promote the movement in the north of the country. Having fought in Sonora, Sinaloa, Nayarit, Jalisco, Michoacán, and Zacatecas, Hermosillo was appointed commander of the forces in Nueva Galicia at the Congreso de Chilpancingo, and it was in his honor that a later congress named the state capital. After Mexico became independent from Spain, Sonora and Sinaloa, long administered as a single entity, were separated. They were reunited only six months later as the Estado de Occidente (the Western State), but in 1831 were once again separated, and each became a state in its own right.

Much of the nineteenth century in Mexico was marked by political instability and by fighting between conservatives and liberals. There was a setback for Sonora in 1836, when a centralist (conservative) constitution deprived it of its statehood, resulting in bloody fighting between rival factions.

José Urrea (1797–1849), born in Tucson, was a military commander who participated in (and wrote about) the Texas campaign and the war against the United States. Although initially he had fought against the insurgents at the time of the movement for independence, he later resisted Spanish attempts to reassert control over Mexico. He was twice governor of Sonora and was a prominent champion of federalism.

As a result of the war with the United States, in 1847 Sonora, then the largest state in Mexico, had to give up more than a quarter of its territory (and towns such as Nogales and Tucson). With the subsequent gold rush, opportunists like William Walker, Gastón Raousset de Boulbon, and Henry Alexander Crabb ventured into Mexico, but they were driven back at Guaymas in 1854.

The next problem was to be the French Intervention. The reformist government led by Benito Juárez, Mexico's first president of real stature, was forced into exile when the French invaded the country and Napoleon III installed Maximilian of Austria as emperor. **Ignacio Pesqueira** (1820–1886) was a military man who had fought against the United States and later served for three terms as governor of Sonora. A defender of liberal interests, Pesqueira refused to acknowledge the new imperial power. However, in 1865 the French took the port of Guaymas, and in July of that year the state capital fell into their hands.

The end of the French Intervention and the return of Juárez to power ushered in reforms that threatened the entrenched interests of landowners and the Church, and the civil war known as the Reform War began. This was followed by a long era of peace under Porfirio Díaz, but it was a peace achieved at some cost. While industry developed and work opportunities increased, tight controls were maintained and oppositional voices were silenced. Moreover, much of the economic progress came at the expense of allowing foreign interests to exploit Mexico's resources freely. Inequalities between the rich and the poor were exacerbated, and at the end of the century, a great deal of the land lay in the hands of a very few people, who frequently exploited their workers. In the case of Sonora, Guillermo Andrade controlled 15,700 square kilometers (6,100 square miles) of land, Manuel Peniche about half as much, and William Cornell Greene about a third as much. Moreover, the government set up developmental companies (*compañías deslindadoras*) whose role was to bring in foreign workers, in the belief that they would be better at cultivating the land than were its traditional inhabitants. As a carrot, the foreign workers would receive title to a third of land they developed. The Richardson Company was one of the most influential of these companies.

Indian uprisings had continued throughout the nineteenth century; for example, according to a government report, between 1831 and 1849, thirty *haciendas*, ninety ranches, and twenty-six mines had been abandoned due to Apache raids. There were also Comanche raids deep into Mexico from north of the border, and on a number of occasions, the Yaquis tried to reassert their rights. At the end of the century, a new leader emerged, a Mexicanized Yaqui named **José María Leyva Cajeme** (1857–1887), who had acquired an excellent reputation while serving in the Mexican army and was named mayor of the Yaqui River area by Governor Pesqueira. In that capacity, he demanded autonomy for the Yaquis, but their lands were among the most fertile in the state and Díaz's government had plans to allow foreign interests to exploit them. Cajeme then assembled an army and began attacking strategic sites along the Sonora railroad, and Díaz authorized a campaign against the rebels. In 1886, Cajeme sought a truce, but the government took over all Yaqui territory and Cajeme was detained; he was held for some time before being shot, supposedly while trying to escape. His death coincided with the expulsion from Sonora of the last Apache chief, Gerónimo.

Some Yaqui rebels hid by merging into the general community, others fled to Arizona (there are perhaps 10,000 Yaquis living in the United States today), and armed guerrilla activity continued. Eventually, in 1897, a peace treaty with the Yaquis was signed, but its provisions were not respected by either side and confrontations continued until the end of the century, when the rebel leader Tetabiate was killed and the few hundred surviving rebels hunted down. Following this, the government rounded up other Yaquis and deported thousands of them, perhaps a third of the Yaqui population, to the south of the country, mostly to work in Yucatán on the sisal plantations. Yaquis were required to have passports and were arrested if they did not carry them. The Yaquis had been more or less continuously at war with the Mexican authorities from 1825 to 1902, and their last battle was not fought until 1927. In 1939, long after the Revolution, President Lázaro Cárdenas officially recognized the Yaqui people and gave them title to about a third of the land that had once been theirs.

The first real threat to the Porfirian order was in Cananea, in 1906, when there was a strike at the Consolidated Copper Company over inequalities in salaries between native and foreign workers. That strike was put down by government forces, aided by Texas Rangers, and nineteen people were left dead. After that, intellectuals and workers began to close ranks behind Francisco Madero, the leader of the opposition to Díaz, who by 1910 had been in power for some thirty years and was seeking reelection. As soon as Madero was elected president, he faced problems with regional leaders, and it was not long before he had been betrayed and killed, his authority usurped by Victoriano Huerta, whom Sonora was the first state to denounce.

Sonora was the birthplace of **Alvaro Obregón Salido** (1880–1928), one of the leading revolutionaries and a president of Mexico. A farmer, teacher, and soldier, Obregón led the northeastern revolutionary forces that took Guadalajara, Querétaro, and Mexico City, defeated Pancho Villa at Celaya and León, opposed Venustiano Carranza, and in 1920 became president. In that capacity, he created the Secretaría de Educación Pública (Department of Education), began agrarian reform, and negotiated the resolution of outstanding disputes with the United States. He was reelected for a second term, but was assassinated by a religious fanatic.

Among the protesters at Cananea in 1906 had been **Arnulfo R. Gómez** (d. 1927), an ardent *antireeleccionista* who supported Madero. At one point, Gómez was himself a candidate for the presidency of the country. He took up arms against Obregón and was shot.

After the Revolution had run its long course, Sonora produced more major political figures. **Adolfo de la Huerta** (1881–1954) established the state's first workers' association and later became Carranza's successor as president. As a military man, **Plutarco Elías Calles** (1877–1945) had resisted Villa's attempts to take Hermosillo. One of Calles's initiatives while he was governor of Sonora was to introduce a minimum wage, and he went on to become one of early twentieth-century Mexico's most significant presidents. As president, he promulgated the Ley de Cultos, a law curtailing religious privileges, sparking off the long rebellion known as the

Man climbs over the international border fence into Nogales,
Arizona, from Nogales, Sonora. (AP Photo/Matt York)

Rebelión Cristera (Cristero Rebellion). Calles was also instrumental in
founding the Partido Nacional Revolucionario, the political party that
became the Partido Revolucionario Institucional (PRI) in later years. He
acquired the nickname of "Jefe Máximo de la Revolución," Supreme Leader
of the Revolution.

In accordance with the legal provisions of the new Ley de Expropiación
(Law of Expropriation), in 1936 President Cárdenas expropriated more
than 90,000 hectares (225,000 acres) of land from the Colorado River Land
Company, to return it to the peasants. The year 1947 then saw the founda-
tion in Sonora of the Unión General de Obreros y Campesinos de México
(Mexican National Union of Workers and Laborers).

Economy

Agriculture is the backbone of state's economy. Sonora is thought of as the
nation's breadbasket. The principal areas where agriculture is carried out

are the Yaqui, Mayo, Guaymas, and San Luis Río Colorado valleys and the Hermosillo and Caborca coasts, all of which have water supplies that are adequate to sustain significant agricultural activity. Sonora contributes significantly to the nation's cattle raising. Pigs, horses, and sheep are also raised, and there is large-scale production of poultry.

Given the state's long coastline, fishing is naturally important for the economy. Sonora has a somewhat better infrastructure for its fishing industry than do most Mexican states, allowing it to meet the demands of Mexicans and also export significant quantities of shrimp and other species to the United States. There are cooperatives that farm certain species, such as shrimp and oysters.

Mining has always been significant for the state. Figures for 2002 show that Sonora produced 6,635 kilograms (14,596 pounds) of gold and 153,834 kilograms (338,435 pounds) of silver. It also produced 5 metric tons of lead, 267,171 of copper, 3 of zinc, and 7,176 of barite, as well as making 18,961 tons of steel.

Most industrial activity is concerned with the packaging and processing of agricultural and farm products. There are a number of *maquiladoras* in the northern part of the state, assembly plants for consumer goods that are shipped north of the border. Hermosillo has a Ford assembly plant, and there are similar plants in other places.

The long and often unspoiled coastline attracts tourists. Popular places include San Carlos and Puerto Peñasco.

Arts

The Seri people are known for their artifacts made with things like conchs, snails, seeds, and shark bones. They also carve human and animal figures from a wood called *palo fierro*. A fiber from the *torote* plant is used to make baskets and vases. Others in the mountains work with leather, and the Mayos with wool.

Popular music is dominated by *norteño* and its cousin *banda*, as is the case with the northern states in general. Norteño music uses instruments such as the bass, the accordion, and the saxophone, and sometimes brass instruments also. The typical repertoire is of waltzes, polkas, and *corridos*, which are narrative ballads that usually tell of the exploits of famous people like Pancho Villa. In a different area of music, **Rodolfo Campodónico** (1866–1926) was a local composer and band director. More unusually, **Alfonso Ortiz Tirado** (1894–1960) was a surgeon who made a continental reputation as a tenor, singing both opera and popular songs.

Two major movie stars have come from Sonora. **María Félix** (1914–2002) succeeded Dolores del Río as the leading lady of the golden age of Mexican cinema, starring in many successful movies and acquiring notoriety for her lively and varied love life. **Silvia Pinal** (1931–) was a star of theater and television, but above all of some of Luis Buñuel's greatest films, including *El angel exterminador* and *Viridiana*. She also became a member of the National Congress, representing the PRI.

Social Customs

Carnival is an international affair in Puerto Peñasco, with a Carnival queen, processions, sporting events, fireworks, rides, craft stalls, and a good deal of merrymaking. Puerto Peñasco also hosts international jazz festivals in both May and October; in addition to jazz, there is folk dancing. San Carlos hosts an international fishing competition. Caborca has a grape festival (Festival de la Uva) and Hermosillo a wine fair (Feria de la Vendimia). Cananea has a copper fair (Feria del Cobre) and Ciudad Obregón an agricultural one.

Festivities include the Feast of the Immaculate Conception (December 8) in Alamos, when hundreds of pilgrims visit the local church, bearing candles and offerings to the Virgin. Holy Thursday in Cocorit, which is primarily a Yaqui community, is marked by dancing *matachines* (mummers) and also by performances of the traditional dance of the deer (*danza del venado*). Two important occasions for Guaymas are the Día del Señor San José on March 19 and the Día de San Juan Bautista on June 24. The first of these is celebrated in a small town that bears the saint's name, and it combines religious rituals with fireworks and festivities. The second is known for its traditional dances.

Magdalena has a fair on the occasion of the Feast of San Francisco Javier in October. Navajoa celebrates San Juan in June, and of course the Day of the Dead, but its most important festivity is the one in honor of the Virgin of Guadalupe, on December 14. Celebrations of this start on the 12th, when dancing begins, continuing until the time of a grand procession of hundreds of people.

For Potam, the key time of the year is Holy Week, during which a series of well-established Catholic ceremonies takes place, beginning with Tinieblas, when the lights are dimmed and chains are heard to sound, in remembrance of Christ's capture. On the following day, there are processions (including the Chapayecas, a distinctive local addition), and on the last day an effigy of Judas is burned. Once again, there are traditional dances, too, such as the *pascolas*, matachines, and venado.

Noteworthy Places

Sonora has a major nature reserve at the Pinacate and the Gran Desierto de Altar, in the extreme northwest of the state, covering terrain that ranges from mountainous and volcanic to desert and includes a significant area of sand dunes. Isla San Jorge, also known as Isla de los Pájaros (Bird Island), is situated close to Puerto Peñasco in the Gulf of California; it is a rocky archipelago that is also a nature reserve. The Ejido Luis Encinas Johnson is another area of natural interest. Hermosillo's Centro Ecológico is primarily an educational facility.

Civic architecture of interest includes the capital's Government Palace, dating from 1859. The building now occupied by Hermosillo's Museo de Sonora was a penitentiary until 1979. It currently houses an archaeological and historical collection, arranged chronologically. About half of it concentrates on the development of the state. Hermosillo has an elegant cathedral, but it dates only from the nineteenth century. Another modern church is Bacum's Iglesia de Santa Rosa de Lima; this twentieth-century church is distinctive because it is decorated with Yaqui paintings.

Many of the colonial mission buildings were abandoned or destroyed. Two Jesuit ones that survive are San Antonio de Padua (in Oquitoa) and San Ignacio de Loyola (in Caborca). A prominent Franciscan one is the Misión de San Pedro (Aconchi). Notable churches from the colonial era include Bacanora's Iglesia de San Ignacio de Loyola, Magdalena de Kino's Iglesia de San Ignacio de Caborca (it is said that the remains of the Jesuit Father Kino were discovered in the church), and Moctezuma's Iglesia de la Candelaria.

Ciudad Obregón is home to the Museo de los Yaquis, detailing the culture and difficult history of the Yaqui people. There is also a museum devoted to the Seri people.

There are cave paintings at the Cueva de los Monos, in Cucurpe, showing men mounted on donkeys, or hunting deer, and of hands and geometrical figures.

Cuisine

Like most northern states, Sonora bases its cooking above all on meat. The climate encouraged settlers to dry their meats—hence the frequent use of *carne seca*. Typical dishes include *carne asada, machaca con huevo, tamales de pitahaya* (a cactus), *yumaré*, and *guacavaquí*. Fish and shrimp appear in various guises. Beef, pork, lamb, and goat are all commonly eaten. Burritos are popular. Desserts include *capirotada, champurro* (a chocolate custard), and *coyotas* (a cookie). A drink that is specific to Sonora is *bacanora*, a clear, distilled liquor made from a type of *agave* that grows in certain parts of the state.

Burros de Machaca

Ingredients:

- ¹/₂ lb. *machaca* (rehydrated dried beef)
- 2 tbsp flour
- 2 tbsp lard
- 10 *colorado* chiles

3 tbsp vinegar
Salt
A generous pinch of oregano
10 flour tortillas

Put the chiles to boil in 3 cups of water. When cooked, clean them out and puree them. Fry the flour in the fat, add the machaca and fry, stirring so that it does not burn. Add the chile paste and season with vinegar, oregano, and salt. Allow to simmer for a few minutes, then fill the tortillas.

Capirotada Sonorense

Ingredients:

1 French loaf (*bolillo*)
About 5 leftover tortillas
5 oz. of walnuts
2 oz. of prunes
3 oz. of raisins
6 oz. of peanuts
3 oz. of dried apricots
1 plantain
3 oz. of ricotta-style cheese (*queso fresco*), unsalted if possible
Grated peel of 1 orange
2 oz. of butter
A pinch of salt
Equal quantities (approximately two cups each) of brown sugar and water

Make a syrup by boiling the water and dissolving the sugar in it; add a pinch of salt (unless the cheese is salted). A little cinnamon may also be added. Cut the bread into slices that are about an inch thick, toast them lightly and spread a little butter on them. Briefly fry slices of plantain in butter. Line a deep pan or baking dish with the dry tortillas and set the slices of bread on top, a little spaced from each other. Lay the plantain pieces on top. Arrange successive layers of dried fruit and nuts over the bread and plantain, and sprinkle cheese and a little grated orange peel over the last layer. Pour the syrup over the ingredients in the pan until they are covered. Place the pan, uncovered, in a warm to moderate oven (250 to 300°F) until the syrup has been absorbed (about 30 or 40 minutes), but take care that the dish does not dry out.

Guacavaquí

Ingredients:

1 oxtail
4 cloves of garlic
2 lb. pork

3 green chiles
1 lb. squirrel
3 tomatoes
1 lb. corn
1 Chinese cabbage
1 cup chickpeas
Large slice of pumpkin
6 carrots
Handful of fresh, chopped cilantro
2 onions
Salt

Put the chickpeas in water to soak. Roast the chiles and then clean them out. Strip the kernels from the corn cobs, and chop up the vegetables. Put the meats in water to boil, and when fairly well done, add the chickpeas and some salt, then the rest of the ingredients. Leave to simmer until everything is tender.

Botana de Pescado en Mostaza

Ingredients:

2 lb. fish fillet (snapper or bream are good choices)
10 cloves of garlic
1 tbsp powdered mustard
Vinegar
2 large onions
1$^1/_2$ cups olive oil
Salt and pepper

Add enough vinegar to the mustard to make a fairly thick paste. Finely chop the onions and garlic. Cut the fish into small chunks and fry in the oil. When brown, add the onions and garlic, then the mustard, and salt and pepper to taste.

Tabasco

State Characteristics

Tabasco is in southeast Mexico. It has a long northern coastline along the Gulf of Mexico, and part of its northern border is with the state of Campeche. Guatemala is to the southeast, the state of Chiapas to the south, and that of Veracruz to the west.

There has been a good deal of debate about the origin of Tabasco's name. Bernal Díaz del Castillo, a soldier who chronicled the conquest of Mexico in the sixteenth century, attributed it to the existence of a Tabasco River, whose name had come from that of an Indian chieftain. Others have suggested that the name comes from adapting Mayan words meaning "Our Lord of the Eight Lions," or that it has roots in other Indian languages and means "The Place with a Lord," "The Place Where the Land Is Wet," or "The Land of *Pastle*" (referring to a plant that hangs from some local trees). It has also been suggested that the name was given to the place after the fall of the Mayan city of Mayapán, when a community called Taabscoob (meaning "We Were Deceived") was established by some survivors of that event.

There are seventeen administrative municipalities in the modern state, and it has six people in the National Congress. Tabasco covers 24,661 square kilometers (9,618 square miles), 1.3 percent of the national territory. The capital city is Villahermosa, population 335,778 (2005). In recent decades, the population has grown in parts of the state where the oil industry has developed, and the standard of living there is generally much higher than in rural locations inland. According to the 2005 official figures,

Country road.

the total state population at that time was 1,989,969. Approximately 70 percent of the state population regards itself as Catholic, about 20 percent as Protestant. Fourteen newspapers are published in Villahermosa, including *Tabasco Hoy, Novedades de Tabasco, Diario Olmeca, El Heraldo*, and *El Sol*. There are five institutions of higher education.

This is a flat, low-lying state, whose highest elevations (to the south, in the Sierra Madrigal and Sierra Tapijulapa) are only 900 meters (about 3,000 feet) above sea level. Nor is there a great deal of variation in climate: three-quarters of the state is warm and humid with heavy summer rains; a fifth of it is similarly hot and humid, but with rain more evenly spread throughout the year; and the remainder is a little less humid, with some summer rain. In the municipality of Teapa, the average annual rainfall is 3,133 millimeters (roughly 125 inches), in Villahermosa 2,159 millimeters (86 inches), and in San Pedro 1,595 millimeters (64 inches). Mean annual temperatures for the state as a whole are approximately 27°C (80°F). The prevailing winds blow from the north in spring and from the east during the rest of the year. The main river systems are the Grijalva and the Usumacinta, each of which has a number of tributaries. The Grijalva and Usumacinta come together at a place called Tres Brazos (Three Branches), forming a river that is about a kilometer and a half (about a mile) wide. The River Tonalá is also important, and there are sea and freshwater lagoons in many places.

Vegetation in the south and southeast consists of trees such as *ceiba*, *guapaque*, and *canchan*, and others that provide valuable woods, such as cedar and mahogany. There are also pasturelands and fruit trees (tamarind, naseberry, mango, and so forth). In the swampy areas, there are herbaceous and aquatic plants such as *tasiste*, and on the coast *icaco*, coconut palms, *majagua*, and mangroves. The forest and savannah fauna includes many insects, exotic birds such as parrots and *zentzontles*, deer, ocelots, and snakes. In watery territory, one finds nutrias, manatees, lizards, turtles, and freshwater varieties of fish, catfish and gar among them; both the manatee and the gar are species threatened with extinction. The sea provides many species: shrimp, snapper, and bream, for example. There are 17,138 hectares (42,330 acres) of state parks, with ecologically protected areas at Pantanos de Centla, Yumká, the Laguna de las Ilusiones, the Laguna de la Lima, the Casacadas de Reforma, Chontalpa, the Laguna del Camarón, and Yu-Balcah.

Cultural Groups and Languages

According to the 2005 official statistics, 3 percent of the state population spoke an indigenous language (as compared with a national average of 6.7 percent). Of the 52,139 speakers of indigenous languages, over 95 percent also spoke Spanish. The municipalities with the highest number of indigenous-language speakers are Centro, Centla, Macuspana, Nacajuca, Tacotalpa, and Tenosique; 62 percent speak the Tabasco varieties of Chontal (that is, the varieties associated with Macuspana, Centro, and Nacajuca), 16 percent Chol, and 9 percent Zapotec.

The Chontales are a Mayan people (not to be confused with the Chontales of Oaxaca) whose main territory is in the center of the state, a swampy area where the two main rivers come together. Mangroves and other forms of vegetation and wildlife that are natural to such an environment have declined significantly due to increased cattle grazing, the commercial exploitation of wood, and the growth of the oil industry. Traditionally, the Chontales have been farmers, hunters, and fishermen, but in modern times they have been drawn into work associated with petroleum. Although traditional structures of authority among the Indians have fallen into disuse, a High Council of the Chontales still attempts to assert the people's aboriginal land rights.

Ix Bolom, the ancient goddess of fertility for the Chontales, has become associated with the Virgin Mary and is celebrated on her feast day, July 16. The Chontales also believe in supernatural "lords" of the lakes, the mangrove swamps, and so forth, whose mission is to protect the environment from those who would harm it: the lords are believed to be able to drive such people mad or make them fatally ill.

History

Tabasco has strong Mayan cultural roots and can also claim to have been home to the seminal Olmec culture, on which other indigenous cultures of Mesoamerica drew. The story begins about 1000 BC, when the Olmecs appeared in the western part of the state, reaching their peak at La Venta two hundred years later. The Mayas came much later, in about AD 300, and they established cities at Comalcalco, Pomoná, Morales, Santa Elena, El Tortuguero, and Jonuta, which reached their zenith in the sixth and seventh centuries.

The first contact between Indians and Spaniards took place during the second expedition that the Spaniards undertook from Cuba, which in 1518 reached the mouth of a river that acquired the name of the expedition's leader, Juan de Grijalva; they landed at Potonchán, which was part of the kingdom of Chontal de Acalan. A year later, Hernán Cortés led another expedition to the Río Grijalva, where he engaged the natives at the Battle of Centla, using horses and firearms for the first time in the Americas. He marked the victory by founding Villa de Santa María de la Victoria, which was to become the provincial capital. It was then that Cortés received the gift of twenty women from a local chieftain; among the women was Malinche, who would serve him as interpreter, become his mistress, and bear him a son who became symbolically the first of a new mixed race of Mexicans.

It took the Spaniards most of the century to gain full control of the region from the natives, after which they had to deal with the problem of English pirates who had occupied an island called the Isla del Carmen, together with other strategic points along the Gulf Coast. The pirates were launching attacks on the Spanish settlements, stealing their goods, destroying their houses, and abusing their women. Since Villa de Santa María de la Victoria was a prime target, its inhabitants decided to move inland, founding a new town called San Juan Bautista on the bank of the Grijalva. In 1598, King Philip II of Spain decreed this to be Villa Hermosa de San Juan Bautista, granting it a coat of arms that is one of the oldest in the Americas and still serves the state. The pirates proceeded to destroy Villa de Santa María and then headed for Villa Hermosa, which they attacked and burned several times, driving its inhabitants farther into the hills. So it was that the capital was transferred to Tacotalpa, where it remained for more than a century.

At the start of the eighteenth century, Tabasco organized a militia that, with the aid of similar forces from Veracruz, managed to drive the pirates out of Isla Carmen, thus regaining control of the coast and of a major commercial sea route. The authorities now turned their attention to the town that had been established at San Juan Bautista, which by then was commonly known as Villahermosa del Puerto. In 1795, the decision was made to relocate the capital there.

The movement toward independence from Spain might have passed almost unnoticed in Tabasco were it not for José María Jiménez, who raised his voice in support of freedom and was soon jailed for it by local authorities who were anxious to express their loyalty to the colonial order. Another prominent figure of the time was **José Eduardo de Cárdenas y Romero** (1765–1821), a writer, politician, and priest who served as Tabasco's representative to the liberal Spanish government (the Cortes de Cádiz), where he explained the rationale for the independence movement and drew attention to the way the colonial authorities had neglected the region. The province of Tabasco was lagging behind others, for example in its provision of schools and hospitals.

After the Plan de Iguala was drawn up in 1821, laying the basis for an independent country, Gen. Antonio López de Santa Anna, who was a senior officer in Veracruz, sent a deputy to Tabasco to claim it for this new Mexico. In 1823, Tabasco was one of the first provinces to commit to the federation. A year later, it had its first state constitution, replaced in 1831 by its second, which was decidedly liberal.

Like other parts of the country, Tabasco was subject to destructive rivalries between centrists and federalists during the first half of the nineteenth century; fighting and instability did not make for economic and social progress. In 1840, following violent confrontations between the two sides, the federalists established a Junta Renovadora del Federalismo, and once again Tabasco asserted its right to self-government. A year later, the state congress decided to break away from the Mexican Republic, when Yucatán invited it, together with Chiapas, Oaxaca, and Veracruz, to form a new country. However, the central powers weighed in, forcing Tabasco's federalists to flee to Veracruz. Two decades later, Tabasco once again formed a political alliance with the states mentioned.

In 1846, following the declaration of war by the United States, U.S. forces took the port of Frontera, made their way along the Grijalva River, and tried to take the capital of Tabasco, which was successfully defended by troops led by Col. Juan Bautista Traconis. The United States then brought in reinforcements to bombard and seize the city. Lacking federal support, the *tabasqueño* army resorted to guerrilla tactics. As the struggle continued, U.S. forces began to succumb to local diseases, and the result was that they had to abandon the city a month after capturing it.

The next act in the nineteenth-century drama of Mexican history was to be confrontation with France. In 1862, President Benito Juárez declared that Mexico could no longer repay its significant debts to Great Britain, Spain, and France. The former two agreed to compromise, but France refused and invaded. The French took the capital of Tabasco and installed Eduardo González Arévalo as governor. There were soon rebellions in Villa de Cárdenas, Comalcalco, Jalpa, Tacotalpa, Teapa, Jalapa, and Pichucalco. In a show of force, González Arévalo confronted the rebels and put a price on the heads of some of their leaders, but he underestimated the strength of support for the rebels, and in 1863 he suffered an ignominious defeat. After this, the republican forces marched on San Juan Bautista and drove the interventionists out.

It was at about this time that the destruction of the Tabasco jungle began to become serious, due to the exploitation of wood by entrepreneurs such as the Romanos, the Bulnes, the Valenzuelas, and the Schindlers. The capital city of the state became the focus of the trade in lumber, and an important commercial center for imported goods besides. The unthinking greed that drove the abuse of natural resources became more widespread during the era of Porfirio Díaz; as happened all over the country, a small number of people, especially major landowners, benefited from such exploitation, while the majority were destined to work and live in poor conditions, sometimes bound by inescapable debts to the landowners.

In the Ríos region, where the exploitation of wood and *chicle* was being carried out on a large scale, a woman named Salomé Marín Virgilio took steps to improve the lot of the workers, founding schools and spreading progressive ideas that led to her being persecuted by Díaz's lackeys. She became the inspiration for one of Tabasco's most significant political figures of the late nineteenth century, **José María Pino Suárez** (1869-1913), a lawyer, journalist, poet, and politician who rose to the rank of vice president of Mexico and was assassinated at the same time as Francisco Madero.

A local figure who had become ineluctably associated with support for Díaz was Gen. **Abraham Bandala Patiño** (1838-1916), who was reelected as governor of Tabasco on no less than sixteen occasions. In 1906, he jailed a group of protesters against authoritarian rule, an act that only served to feed what by then was widespread discontent with Díaz's regime.

Shortly after the outbreak of the Revolution in November 1910—at which time Tabasco was being governed by one of the landowning wood barons—there was an armed uprising in the municipality of Cárdenas. Once Madero came to power, there were rebellions against him in some parts of Mexico, including Tabasco, where one of his leading opponents was José Gurdiel Fernández, a Spaniard and former priest who founded a newspaper, *El Correo de Tabasco*, that was loud in its criticism of Madero. Gurdiel was imprisoned, apparently for publishing personal details about the governor of the state, **Manuel Mestre Ghigliazza** (1870-1954); however, Gurdiel escaped to Texas, where he gathered together a group of mercenaries, and afterwards he returned to fight in Balancán, where allies of Pino Suárez had him hunted down and killed. This notorious incident was something of an exception during the generally benign rule of Madero, and it was hotly debated in the National Congress.

The ouster of Madero by Victoriano Huerta's coup was followed by resistance from a number of people in Tabasco who allied themselves with Venustiano Carranza—but when the latter came to power, things did not calm down, since he named a cousin of Pino Suárez as governor, unleashing a bloody struggle for power between rival local interests. However, this governor, General Luis Felipe Domínguez, can be credited with at least one major reform: he decreed that the system of *peonaje* that tied workers to a life of dependency on abusive landowners should come to an end. Rivalry between the Domínguez faction and their rivals, led by another general, Carlos Greene Ramírez, came to a head in 1919, when the "reds" took on the "blues" in a bloody electoral contest. Greene declared himself the winner, but the supporters of Domínguez refused to concede and set up an alternative state government in Amatitán, as a result of which Greene had to seek support from Mexico City. To resolve the impasse, Carranza recognized Greene's authority and dispatched Dominguez to the Isthmus of Tehuantepec to be chief military officer. But that was not to be the end of the affair. A new opposition faction, the *guindas*, sprang up, and violence and political instability continued—so much so that in 1920 the National Congress suspended Tabasco's authority as a state.

Félix Fulgencio Palavicini (1881-1952) had been among the opponents of Díaz's campaign for reelection. Palavicini was an engineer, a politician, a writer, a teacher, and a diplomat. He ran a newspaper called *El Antireeleccionista* and supported Madero, later served in President Carranza's government as secretary of education (during which time he brought in new standards for the teaching of Spanish, took steps to encourage university autonomy, and improved education in rural areas), represented his state in the Constituent Congress, and later served as Mexico's ambassador to Belgium, Great Britain, France, Italy, Spain, and Argentina. Palavicini also founded a number of other newspapers, among them *El Universal*, a paper of national significance. One of his collaborators, both in opposition to Díaz and as a journalist, was the doctor and writer Mestre, who, in addition to serving as governor of Tabasco, became director of the National Library.

In 1924, Adolfo de la Huerta took up arms against the government of Alvaro Obregón. He came to the port of Frontera, set up his own government, and then headed for New York, ostensibly to secure U.S. recognition. However, the officers he had appointed to his new government fell into disagreement and de la Huerta's rebellion, although it did lead to the flight of the state governor to Guatemala, otherwise came to nothing. De la Huerta's forces, which had had control of much of the southeast of the Yucatán Peninsula, were defeated, and some of its leaders put to death.

Once they and the Greene supporters were out of the way, the state was pacified and **Tomás Garrido** (1890-1943) became governor. Garrido made a number of changes that improved educational and social services, and in time, workers' organizations were begun. There was also a youth movement with a diverse portfolio involving combating fanaticism, the Church, and alcoholism; they were known as the "red shirts." Garrido's influence lasted for about sixteen years. Among other things, he was something of a showman, a promoter of trade fairs, festivities, contests, and social campaigns. After Obregón's assassination, Garrido became President Plutarco

Elias Calles's right-hand man. Then, with Lázaro Cárdenas in the presidency, Garrido returned to Tabasco to serve as director of education, until another spell of civic unrest once again led to the suspension of Tabasco's state authority, at which point Garrido went voluntarily into exile, to Costa Rica.

In subsequent years, there were further improvements in the educational system, health care, and nutrition. Tabasco's traditional isolation began to be overcome and its economy was transformed by the discovery of oil in the Gulf. It was in 1974 that the oil industry began to leave its mark on Tabasco, encouraged by developmental aid from the national government. Road networks were developed so that communications within the state became better, as did links between the state and other parts of Mexico. A Technological Institute was established, together with libraries and museums, and there was increasing building and agricultural and industrial development. This led to improvements in social services and local facilities; however, the demand for services exceeded the state's ability to provide them, and the capital city, in particular, suffered an onslaught of immigration and cultural change. The old, relaxed, quiet lifestyle was lost.

In response to these pressures, local governments took initiatives to support traditional culture, for example by founding Casas de Cultura in the main towns, taking steps to preserve historic buildings, setting up a research center on the Mayan and Olmec cultures, and sponsoring a state theater. Problems arising from changes brought about by the oil industry generated some social tensions, but such problems have increasingly been dealt with by democratic and community-based actions, for which Tabasco has acquired something of a national reputation. There have been difficult political times, too; for example, a hotly contested election in 1989 heralded a new period of political instability and confrontation.

In 2007, Tabasco suffered the most destructive floods ever recorded in its history.

Economy

In contrasts with many parts of Mexico, Tabasco does not need more water but rather the means to drain away an excess of it. Natural pastureland is supplemented by drained lands, for free-range livestock rearing, especially those varieties of cattle that prosper in a tropical climate. Most of the cattle are raised for meat. In addition to cattle, which account for about three-quarters of the livestock, pigs and poultry are important. About 30 percent of the land is pastureland.

Approximately half of the 25 percent of the state that is cultivable is devoted to perennials and most of the rest to cyclical crops. Principal among the latter are corn, beans, sorghum, rice, and watermelons; among the former are cacao, bananas, coconut, sugarcane, and oranges. Compared with production levels for other states in Mexico, Tabasco's levels for cacao, black pepper, bananas, papayas, coconuts, pineapples, watermelons, and rice have been the most significant.

Fishing, whether along the two hundred kilometers (120 miles) of coast or in the many lagoons and waterways, is naturally quite significant for the state economy, but in the early 1980s accounted for only 1.8 percent of Mexican production. Tabasco has moved up in the ranking since that time, increasing production significantly. Shellfish and crustaceans are exploited, along with typical sea and freshwater fish, such as shark, swordfish, bream, gar, and catfish. Most fish is destined for human consumption.

Family businesses still account for about 90 percent of the industrial activity that is associated with processing food and other natural products; in this sector, Villahermosa is most important. There is also some production of textiles, leather goods, rubber, soap, and dressed woods such as mahogany and cedar. Above all, Tabasco is a major player in the Mexican petroleum industry. Pemex, the nationalized oil company, has a large petrochemical plant in the municipality of Macuspana. There are over eight hundred wells scattered across the state, producing crude oil and natural gas.

Tourism has some significance in Tabasco.

Arts

Like other parts of the Yucatán Peninsula, Tabasco has a healthy theatrical tradition. The State Library (Biblioteca Central del Estado) is one of the largest in Latin America. Tabasco has produced some distinguished individuals in the arts and entertainment, such as the actress and singer **Esperanza Iris** (1888–1962). After successful appearances at the beginning of the twentieth century, Iris founded her own theatrical company and toured Europe and the Americas with it, being dubbed the "Queen of Operetta." She also appeared in films.

Carlos Pellicer (1899–1977) was one of Mexico's leading poets. He taught poetry at the Universidad Autónoma in Mexico City, where he also served as director of Bellas Artes (the National Institute of Fine Arts). He was responsible for setting up the Frida Kahlo Museum in Coyoacán, the Diego Rivera one at Anahuacalli, and the La Venta archaeological park in Tabasco. Pellicer was a member of the National Congress and of the Academia de la Lengua (Academy of the Language), a man whose creative writing and contributions to major literary reviews brought him widespread recognition and several prizes, including the Premio Nacional de Literatura (National Prize for Literature). Among his books are *Exágonos* and *Sonetos*.

José Gorostiza (1901–1973) was another poet who achieved a national reputation. He was a politician and diplomat as well as a writer. In the former capacity, he served as Mexico's ambassador to Great Britain, Italy, and the United Nations, and nationally he was prominent in the Ministry of

Foreign Affairs. He, too, directed Bellas Artes and became a member of the Academy of the Language. His books include *Canciones para cantar en las barcas* and *Muerte sin fin*.

Traditional *tabasqueño* dances include *el gigante* and *el caballito* (or *baile gigante*), which are performed in Nacajuca on the 14th of August. At various times of the year, the *baile viejo* is danced in Tucta, Nacajuca, Guaytalpa, and Atasta de Serra. *El pochó*, a dance with pre-Hispanic roots, is the most distinctive and mysterious of the Tabasco dances and is a regular at the time of Carnival in Tenosique. Also characteristic of Tenosique is *los blanquitos*, which is a symbolic representation of the struggle of black slaves against their white masters. Somewhat similarly, *el caballito blanco* represents the struggle between indigenous peoples and the Spaniards; this dance is found in Tamulté de las Sabanas and in Quintín Arauz Centla (where a major battle between the two peoples once took place). Particularly characteristic of the Tabasco dancing style is the use of *zapateo*, a foot-stamping technique brought over from Spain; it was first performed to the accompaniment of small instrumental ensembles, and lyrics were added later. These dances are traditionally interrupted by *bombas*, which are short and flirtatious rhymes exchanged between male and female dancers.

Percussion instruments (for example, drums and turtle shells) and wind instruments (conchs, reed flutes) derive from the time of the Olmecs and the Mayas, but as usual in Mexico, the pre-Hispanic musical practices have long since become mixed with imported ones, so there is no "pure" indigenous music. The marimba is quite popular.

Artisans in Nacajuca produce showy bags, hats, fans, mats, baskets, and lamps, all made out of palm and similar natural fibers. There are also ceramics, wooden boats (*cayucos*), and drums from a town called Tucta. Jalpa de Méndez has *jícaras* (carved gourds), living lamps, vases, maracas, and other such items. Tacotalpa is known for its decorative objects and furniture (especially rocking chairs) made from a type of osier. Centla and Tenosique are known for their leather goods, such as bags and boots, and more fancy personal articles made from the skins of all manner of creatures, from cattle to manatees, sharks, monkeys, and iguanas.

Social Customs

The typical traditional dress for tabasqueña women seen on festive occasions, consists of a cotton blouse with brightly colored embroidery together with a wide floral skirt. A red sash runs from the right-hand side of the waist down the skirt, and a brightly colored shawl is also worn. The shoes are black and low heeled. A woman may wear her hair in a bun, with a red tulip on the left side and a *peineta* (comb) on the other. Her jewelry is usually gold colored. When dancing, men often wear their Sunday best: a long-sleeved white cotton shirt and white trousers, a bright kerchief about the neck, a Chontal hat, and leather boots. Such clothing is made in most of the state's municipalities.

In November, the dead are honored, as they are all over Mexico; the tradition in Tabasco is to eat *tamales* at this time. Grijalva, in the municipality of Villahermosa, is known for its allegorical *flotillas*. There is fishing for blind sardines in the grottoes of Villa Luz (Tacotalpa).

The Feria de Tabasco, the state fair, is the biggest event in the state and has been held in Villahermosa since 1982; it acquired its own dedicated premises in 2000. It has the usual mix of commercial and agricultural shows, plus song and dance contests, artistic displays, and various forms of merrymaking. One of the high spots is the election of the beauty queen, called the Flor Más Bella de Tabasco (Tabasco's Most Beautiful Flower). Villahermosa is also known for its Carnival, which typically has processions, fireworks, street entertainers, masked balls, and much merriment.

Important among the religious events is the Via Crucis at Tapijulapa (Tlocatalpa). Among other major festivities that have a Catholic origin is the Feast of San Antonio de Padua, celebrated in Cárdenas in June with a fair and processions led by trade associations and social groups, who carry their standards to the church and lay gifts at the altar. May in Teapa brings the Feast of Santa Cruz, which is the festivity associated with construction workers; the laborers raise crosses where they are working, and the owners and technical personnel put on a banquet for them.

Religious celebrations and rituals in the Indian communities are hybrids of the Catholic and the pre-Hispanic, of the religious and the secular. They commonly entail music and dancing, stalls selling all manner of goods, and amusement areas. Examples are the Feast of Santiago in the Chontalpa and Zoque communities, and Lent in Atasta and Tamulté.

Noteworthy Places

Tourists are drawn to Tabasco by its beaches, waterways, and wildlife, and also by two main archaeological sites, Comalcalco and La Venta. Among the state's natural attractions are waterfalls and caves, for example, the Grutas de Coconá. Agua Selva is an ecological reserve of natural beauty, in the hills about 142 kilometers (88 miles) from Villahermosa. Another is the Pantanos de Centla, a swampy nature reserve that lies in the most important delta in the country and is of interest for its vegetation and wildlife: 39 fish, 50 amphibian and reptile, 60 mammal, and 125 bird species. The area covers 302,706 hectares (747,700 acres).

Comalcalco is the most westerly of the major Mayan archaeological sites. It dates from the Classical Period, roughly from 100 BC to AD 900, which means that it was contemporary with Palenque in Chiapas. Comalcalco had important ties with Mayan cities in Yucatán and with the Toltec culture. Its buildings were made of compressed earth covered with stucco, and its temples built on weak pyramidal foundations and made of tree trunks, palm, and guano, until in the seventh century they discovered the process of firing bricks. Comalcalco is believed to be the first place in the Americas to have used that process. Many of the bricks were decorated to illustrate the inhabitants' customs and beliefs, but not on the outside of buildings. Comalcalco has three main parts: the Great Acropolis, the Northern Square, and the Eastern Acropolis. The Great Acropolis has a 35-meter-high (115-foot) platform supporting buildings on several levels, such as the Palace, the Sunken Patio, the Stucco Tomb (Tomb of the Nine Lords of Night), and a number of temples. The Palace is the biggest structure, 80 meters (262 feet) long and 9 meters (30 feet) high, with vaulted galleries, niches, and altars. Its façade is reminiscent of Palenque. The Sunken Patio is below the Palace and on its northern flank has the remains of what are presumed to have been living quarters. There is a temple on another side of it, a chamber with stucco figures, a staircase with hieroglyphs, and to the southeast an altar. The Stucco Tomb of the Nine Lords of Night is the most important of several burial places that have been unearthed at Comalcalco; it is 3 meters (10 feet) long and almost as high, and inside are stucco representations of nine figures, together with inscriptions.

La Venta is the key site for the Olmec culture, which archaeologists regard as the "mother culture" of Mesoamerica. What is now the Parque Museo La Venta began in 1958 on the initiative of a famous Tabascan poet called Carlos Pellicer. Successive modifications and developments have made it a recreational area, with a natural history museum and other facilities, but the park still offers a glimpse of the Olmec culture, in particular the huge basalt sculptures of human heads with unusual features. The sculptures were made over a span of some six hundred years, but they have been arranged thematically, not chronologically. Some represent social customs and human types, others refer to heavenly bodies, and some to revered animals, such as jaguars and snakes.

The Casa de los Azulejos is one of Villahermosa's most opulent houses, with an intensely colored façade that contrasts with its white stuccowork. It was constructed between 1890 and 1915 following the demolition of an earlier house. The building brings together a range of architectural styles—Gothic, Arabic, baroque, and Renaissance—in a manner that was fashionable during the time of Porfirio Díaz. Initially it served as both a residence and commercial premises. It takes its name from its tiled façade and interior, which contrast with its mostly white adornments and statues, which are mostly in white—some of family significance, and others representing classical personages, such as Mercury, the god of commerce. Upon the death of the man who built the house, it was converted into a hotel, and some of its features were spoiled in the process, but later it was restored, and it now houses Tabasco's Museum of History.

The history of Villahermosa's cathedral starts in 1776, when a church was built in what is now the Parque Morelos; this church was replaced by a cathedral whose construction began in 1884. Anticlericalism during the nineteenth century led to the ruin of number of religious buildings; at one point, the cathedral was put to use as a school, and in the 1920s it was totally destroyed. Construction of a new cathedral began in 1960 and is ongoing.

Villahermosa is also home to the Centro de Investigación de las Culturas Olmeca y Maya (CICOM), a cultural complex that includes a library, a gallery, a research center, a bookshop, the Regional Museum of Anthropology, and a theater.

The Iglesia de Cupillo, in Comacalco, has an impressively lurid façade. The state has sixteen museums, nine of which are in the Centro municipality. Villahermosa houses the Museo Carlos Pellicer, the Museo de Cultura Popular, and the Museo de Historia, among others, plus a number of art galleries. There are museums devoted to Mayan culture in Huimanguillo, Comalcalco, Balancán, Emiliano Zapata, and Jonuta, while Teapa has one devoted to both the Mayas and the Olmecs.

Cuisine

Thanks to the Mayan and Hispanic traditions and to the range of local products—fish, meat, and a wide variety of fruits and vegetables—Tabasco's cuisine is quite varied. A large number of local plants and herbs are used, including *achiote, epazote, chaya, muste,* and *chipilín;* banana leaves are commonly used for roasts, as are the leaves of the *tó.* Exotic local dishes include iguana casserole, civet of turtle, marinated *tepezcuintle,* and roast udder. A great number of sweets are made with fruits: *cocoyol, chigua, nance,* coconut, papaya, red currants, *huapaque,* lemons, and pumpkins. Others without fruit include *salsa borracha, buñuelos, panetelas,* and *zizguá. Pozol* and other corn-based drinks, *agua de Magali, pinol, mistela, cacaotada, silbache, guarapo,* and a number of fruit drinks are common beverages.

Filete de Pescado a la Tabasqueña

Ingredients:

6 fillets of catfish or similar fish
2 cloves of garlic, chopped
1 medium onion, chopped
6 tomatoes, peeled and chopped
1 oz. yellow chile, finely chopped
6 oz. sweet red bell pepper, finely chopped
$^1/_2$ lb. octopus, cooked and cut into strips
$^1/_2$ lb. small shrimp, cooked and peeled
6 pieces of banana leaf (each large enough to wrap a fillet)
1 tsp mixed herbs
Flour
Juice of 2 limes
Oil
Salt and pepper

Lightly salt and pepper the fish, sprinkle them with the lime juice, and roll in flour. Fry briefly over a hot flame until golden, and then set aside. Sauté the onions and garlic. Add the tomatoes, peppers, and herbs, and then the octopus and shrimp. Cook briefly and season as necessary. Place a piece of fish on each banana leaf, cover with some of the sauce just made, wrap the leaves around the fillets, and then grill or broil for 5–10 minutes. Serve with refried beans or fried plantain, radishes, and parsley.

Pollo en Chirmole

Ingredients:

    1 young chicken
    4 large *ancho* chiles
    4 corn tortillas
    4 peppercorns
    1 medium onion
    1 sprig of epazote
    2 oz. pumpkin seeds
    3 tbsp lard (or oil)
    2 cups broth
    Salt

Clean and rinse the chicken. Brown it, then boil in water with the epazote and some salt. Roast and clean the chiles. Toast the pumpkin seeds. Brown the tortillas well, and then grind them up with the chiles, the pumpkin seeds, the onion, and the peppercorns. Fry this mixture in the fat. Once it is well done, add the chicken and broth. Leave to simmer until the sauce thickens a little.

Zizguá

Ingredients:

    20 tender ears of corn
    $^1/_2$ lb. pork fat
    1 lb. butter
    8 eggs
    $^1/_2$ lb. mature cheese
    1 pint milk
    $^1/_2$ cup sugar

Strip the corn kernels off the ears and blend them together with the eggs, cheese, milk, sugar, the fat, and most of the butter. Line a pan with grease-proof paper and rub with butter. Pour the mixture into the pan and bake at 400°F for 2 hours.

Tamaulipas

State Characteristics

The state of Tamaulipas lies at the eastern end of the border with the United States, below southern Texas. The Gulf of Mexico runs along the eastern flank of Tamaulipas. Neighboring Mexican states are Nuevo León to the west, San Luis Potosí to the southwest, and Veracruz to the south. Tamaulipas takes its name from a group of Indians, the Tamaulipecas; it is thought to mean "High Mountains."

The state is the seventh largest in Mexico; it occupies a total of 79,829 square kilometers (31,133 square miles) and has a population of 3,025,238. Twelve people represent the state in the National Congress. Tamaulipas has forty-three administrative municipalities. Its capital, set in the central southern part of the state, is Ciudad Victoria, home to approximately 5 percent of the total state population. Three of the principal towns, Matamoros (population 460,598), Reynosa (540,207), and Nuevo Laredo (367,504), are on the U.S. border, and Bravo is not far from it. Over 80 percent of the population is Catholic, and about 10 percent is Protestant.

Tamaulipas has an extraordinary number of newspapers—more than thirty in all. The towns of Matamoros, Ciudad Victoria, and Reynosa each have seven, including *El Diario de Matamoros* and *El Regional*, *El Mercurio de Tamaulipas* and *La Verdad*, and *La Prensa de Reynosa* and *El Mañana*. Tampico (population 313,409) and Nuevo Laredo each have five, with *El Sol de Tampico* and *El Mundo* in the former and *El Diario de Laredo* and *El Eco* in the latter. Ciudad Mante has four, including *Debate* and *El Tiempo*.

The main university is the Universidad Autónoma de Tamaulipas. There is also a satellite campus of the Monterrey Technological Institute, one of Mexico's most important systems of higher education.

The Faja Fronteriza, the border region, consists of the strip that runs across the north of the state; it is quite mountainous and has a hot, dry climate, although there can be sudden deluges and the temperature drops significantly in winter. This is an area that is quite industrial, especially because of the many *maquiladoras*, assembly plants for goods to be shipped north. The Faja Fronteriza is also quite populous.

The Alta del Poniente (or Alta de San Carlos) is a second region, set in the sierras (in the Sierra de San Carlos and the Sierra de Cruillas), where the mountains can reach 1,680 meters (5,500 feet) high. In this region, the climate is relatively humid and mild. It is predominantly a cattle-raising region, with some agriculture, forestry, industry, and mining. The municipality of San Carlos, which is part of this region, is the most sparsely populated in the state.

Los Llanos de San Fernando is the region located along the coastal plain in the Conchos and Chorreras river basins. The climate is predominantly mild and moist, and the land supports a number of seasonal crops such as corn and cotton, as well as pig and poultry farming.

The Cuenca Central (Central Basin) is the largest region, encompassing part of the coastal plain with the Soto La Marina River basin and extending across to the Sierra Madre Oriental on the eastern side. The climate is warm and quite dry, except in winter, when temperatures can drop to freezing. This is the region where the capital city is located.

The Huasteca Tamaulipeca region runs across the south of the Cuenca Central, again from the coast to the Sierra Madre. South of it lie the states of San Luis Potosí and Veracruz. This region contains the Tamesi, Barberena, Tigre, and Carrizal basins. Its climate is warm and fairly humid. Commerce and industry (especially the oil industry) are concentrated in the towns of Tampico and Madero. There is also the port of Altamira. The sugar industry is important in this region.

Finally, the Old Fourth District (Antiguo Cuarto Distrito) is a region comprising a number of isolated valleys and plateaus within the Sierra Madre. There, the climate is mild and moderately moist, although hotter in the lower reaches. There is no significant river, but a number of springs allow for some irrigation of the land. There are forests and some minerals, but livestock is on a small scale and agriculture is at subsistence level. There is some exploitation of varieties of cactus.

Annual average temperatures for the state range from 16°C (60°F) in the municipality of Joya de Salas to 31°C (88°F) in Los Uvalle. Rainfall averages run from 37 millimeters (1.5 inches) a year in Los Uvalle to 1,540 (61 inches) in Ocampo. The state has a number of mountains that exceed 3,000 meters (10,000 feet) in height; the highest (in the Sierra El Pedregoso) is 3,280 meters (10,760 feet) above sea level.

Much of Tamaulipas, with its low annual rainfall, has flora that mimic the varieties found in similar conditions in other states of northern Mexico, such as Coahuila and Nuevo León. In the highest northeastern parts of Tamaulipas, the vegetation is sparse and consists largely of thorny plants, bushes, and cacti. In the more southerly parts, there are mahogany and palms at low elevations, and oaks and pines at higher ones. Closer to the border with Veracruz and along the coastal plain, where there is much more rain and there are also lagoons, vegetation is generally abundant. Sample plant species include mahogany, cedar, rubber plants, cacao, and fruit trees such a *mamey*. The state's mammal population features squirrels, jaguars, coyotes, wild boars, armadillos, badgers, deer, and spider monkeys. There are also several types of lizards and snakes, such as rattlesnakes. Birds include quail, parrots, owls, hawks, and partridges. Common fish and shellfish varieties are shrimp, crab, trout, sea bass, and bream.

Cultural Groups and Languages

Only 0.8 percent of the state population (22,221 people) speak an indigenous language, and most of them also speak Spanish, according to official 2005 figures. Despite this low proportion, a surprising number of languages—as many as fifty—are involved. The most widely spoken among them are Náhuatl (spoken by about 8,500 people), Huasteco (4,000), Totonaca (1,300), Mazahua and Zapotec (each of which has over 400), and Mayan (200). Evidence of the Huasteca culture, which was once the most advanced and dominant in the area, can also be found in parts of the states of San Luis Potosí, Veracruz, Puebla, Hidalgo, and Querétaro.

History

It is believed that, prior to the arrival of the Spaniards, sixty-two different and often conflictive indigenous groups had settled in the area that is now Tamaulipas. Among them were the Huastecos and the Tamaulipecas, who gave their name to the state. The Huastecos are thought by most historians to be related to the Nahuas, though some have held that there is a connection with the Mayas, basing this assumption on certain similarities of language. The area became known as the land of the Huastecos, since by the time the Spaniards came, the Huastecos had become dominant from the coast across to San Luis Potosí.

Gonzalo de Sandoval, a Spaniard sent by Hernán Cortés in the 1520s to bring the Huastecos under control, defeated them at the pass of Coaxcatlán. The Spaniards then made the area into a province they called Pánuco (after the Río Pánuco), with Villa de Tampico as its capital. Some Spaniards settled the land, but many more Mexica and Tlaxcalteca Indians from other parts of Mexico, and later some Olives, were imported to help colonize it. (Some have contended that the name of the state is of Olive origin, not Tamaulipeca.) In the middle of the century, a Franciscan missionary, Fray Andrés de Olmos, arrived to mitigate the aggressive tendencies of the Spaniards. A speaker of several indigenous languages, he made contact with groups of natives, and in about 1544, he brought many of them into a mission he called Tama Holipa. After Olmos's death, other missions were established at Tula and Jaumabe. Some Indians were organized by the Spaniards into *encomiendas*, but the missions were more important, and it was around them that a number of today's towns grew.

In the first half of the eighteenth century, Lt. **José de Escandón y Helguera** (1700–1770), who had already built up a reputation for extending the colonial order elsewhere, having put down Indian uprisings in Guanajuato and Querétaro, was charged by the viceroy with doing the same with more northerly territories. By midcentury, he had freed Nuevo Reyno de León, Pánuco, Tampico, Villa de Valles, Guadalcázar, and Charcas from the threat of the Chichimecs. He then drew up a plan for the population and development of what was to become the Provincia de Nuevo Santander.

The people who came in to settle the province—most of whom arrived from rural Guanajuato, Querétaro, San Luis Potosí, Coahuila, Nuevo León, and Las Huastecas—were generally unsophisticated and illiterate, with few skills. They were attracted by the promise of lands of their own, even though they might have to risk their lives to defend them. These people worked the land and looked after animals, while the missionary friars attended to the education of their children. There were permanent garrisons to defend the settlements, though at times the settlers themselves had to join the ranks of the soldiers in order to fight off Indian attacks. A vast castle-like governor's house was built in Nuevo Santander, the provincial capital established in 1749, by laborers brought up from Mexico City; from there, the governor ruled like a feudal lord. His house was in marked contrast to those of the many towns that were formally established by him in the middle of the century: such towns may have been given grand titles, but they generally consisted of clusters of crude structures roofed with palm. Many of the newly established towns were given names that have since passed into history; an example is Villa Escandón, named after the governor himself, but now called Xicohténcatl (after an Indian leader from Tlaxcala). Laredo, Texas, was one of the towns founded by Escandón; it dates from 1755 and was the twenty-second town founded by him.

At the start, the new colony was answerable to Mexico City in matters of law and economy and depended on it for military aid. This was the situation until 1785, when the Comandancia General de las Provincias Internas (General Command of the Provinces of the Interior) was set up. It was administered in three divisions, the eastern one of which took over jurisdiction of Nuevo Santander, Texas, Nuevo León, and Coahuila. However, that lasted for only two years before Nuevo León and Santander once again became directly subject to the authority of the viceroy in Mexico City. The nomadic Tamaulipeca people did not adapt well to all these new developments and structures; their communities began to fragment, and they eventually disappeared as a separate ethnic group. Meanwhile, Escandón, the great colonizer of the territory, had run into legal troubles and been replaced in 1767 by Fernando de Palacio. Escandón died in 1770 and was posthumously pardoned for any wrongdoing.

By the time the movement for independence began in 1810, the province of New Santander was under the governorship of Col. Manuel Iturbe, who attempted to assemble a force that could combat the insurgency. However, those very troops declared themselves in favor of independence, occupied the capital, and drove Iturbe out. Not that the insurgents escaped setbacks. For example, there was a particularly strong popular uprising in Tula and Palmillas: in December 1810, insurgents occupied the barracks at Tula. But a year later, the building had been ceded to troops loyal to Spain, an event that marked the beginning of a series of defeats for the insurgents, as a result of which a number of their leaders were executed. One man to distinguish himself at the time of the rebellion against Spain was **José Bernardo Gutiérrez de Lara** (1780–1843); after collaborating with Miguel Hidalgo, in 1813 he declared Texas independent of Spain, in an attempt to undermine Spanish authority. Gutiérrez later became the governor of Tamaulipas and commander in chief of the Eastern Division of the Provinces of the Interior.

One curious development had its origin in a meeting in London between Francisco Javier Mina and Fray Servando Teresa de Mier, one of the most interesting and unusual figures associated with Mexico's drive for independence. In 1816, Mina, Fray Servando, and thirty-two Italian officers set out from Liverpool on a naval expedition in support of the insurgent rebellion. They landed at a place called La Pesca, in the modern municipality of Soto la Marina, occupied the town, announced their arrival, and set up a printing press, the first in a very wide area. They then divided their forces in two, one part becoming responsible for the defense of the town and the other for incursions into other parts of the territory. The latter force first attacked a major *hacienda* that was in royalist hands and then went on to San Luis and over the mountains to Guanajuato, where Mina was taken prisoner and shot. Tamaulipeca Indian volunteers played an important role in this campaign. When Agustín de Iturbide and Vicente Guerrero agreed upon the Plan de Iguala, supporters of independence in Tamaulipas were quick to sign on to it, the governor was pressed to resign, and independence for a new Departamento del Nuevo Santander was proclaimed. Iturbide did not last long as emperor before being forced into exile. When he returned to Mexico, he was captured and shot at Padilla, a small Tamaulipeca town that at the time was the capital.

Tamaulipas then participated in the 1824 congress that laid the groundwork for a Mexican republic. Within a year, it had its own state constitution, and the town of Aguayo, one of the leading insurgent communities, was renamed Ciudad Victoria and became state capital. Tamaulipas was then caught up in the political rivalries between centralists and federalists during the early nineteenth century, as was all of Mexico to some degree. Naturally, Tamaulipas was at the forefront when the question of a breakaway by Texas came onto the agenda. Separatists occupied Matamoros, Laredo, and Guerrero, and by 1844 the United States had recognized the independence of Texas, soon afterward incorporating it into the union. Once the war that ensued with the United States was over, the border between the two countries became the Río Bravo.

Juan José de la Garza Galván (1826-1893) was one of the leading figures of the nineteenth century: a strong supporter of Benito Juárez, six times governor of Tamaulipas, holder of some of the highest legal offices in the nation, including that of chief justice, and ambassador to Guatemala. His statue is one of those that now grace the grand Paseo de la Reforma in Mexico City.

Another famous son of Tamaulipas was **Ignacio Zaragoza Seguín** (1829-1862), a soldier who became a national hero. Zaragoza distinguished himself in several military campaigns and held high offices under President Juárez, but became known for his defense of Puebla against the French; as a result, Puebla is now officially "Puebla de Zaragoza."

At the time of Mexico's Reform War, Garza and others opposed the conservative governor of Tamaulipas. Attempts to implement the reformed 1857 Constitution failed, however, and a violent confrontation followed between liberals and conservatives, one that eased up only when the country was facing invasion by the French. The governor of Nuevo León, who was acting as a mediator between the two local political factions, appointed Ignacio Comonfort to gather together the first northern division that would confront French forces; Garza organized a second, and together they headed south. After the liberal triumph, there was an ill-fated accommodation between President Juárez and conservatives in Tamaulipas in 1864. Generally, political instability and violence in the state continued until Porfirio Díaz came to power.

Other distinguished people during the era of reform and the time of the French invasion were **Pedro Hinojosa** (1822-1903) and **Carlos Salazar** (1829-1865). Hinojosa was a politician and a military man who fought against the United States and against the French, led the reformist forces in the northern states, was governor of several of them, and served Mexico a member of the National Congress and a minister under Díaz. Similarly, Salazar fought against the United States and at Puebla against the French; he also served as governor of Michoacán, before being shot there by people loyal to the French.

Like most states, Tamaulipas benefited economically during the more stable period of the *porfiriato*. It shipped goods between Mexico, the United

States, and Europe. Investors, pioneers, and adventurers, especially from the United States, made their way into Mexico's less developed areas. The railway came, linking the border towns with Monterrey and Tampico and encouraging development and investment by foreigners, who bought mines, introduced new technologies, and began to exploit the natural reserves of coal, gas, and oil. Díaz's regime encouraged the process and made great concessions to such investors, allowing them to acquire large tracts of land and develop huge ranches, for example, those of Río Bravo S.A. near the border, and those of Manuel González further south. Late in the porfiriato, six institutions of higher learning were established, and an important paper, *El Progresista*, began publication.

When Francisco Madero began his revolt in 1910, among his notable supporters were two brothers from Tula—Francisco and Emilio Vázquez Gómez—and a rural primary schoolteacher named **Alberto Carrera Torres** (1887-1917), who was one of the first people to publicly denounce Victoriano Huerta and who began the process of land redistribution. **Francisco Vázquez Gómez** (1860-1933) is an interesting case because he was President Díaz's personal physician before opposing Díaz's reelection. Like others who were against reelection, he went into exile in the United States; he also became one of Madero's ministers.

Given its frontier location and the possibility of securing arms there, Matamoros was a key place for the rebels; the city was taken over by them in 1913 and thence came the troops who later took control of the north and central parts of the country. Lucio Blanco, who had led the attack on Matamoros, made the first redistribution of land to peasants working on one of the vast ranches, the Hacienda de los Borregos.

At the time of the Revolution, Tampico, which was under Huerta's control, became the scene of an international incident involving the United States: eight U.S. troops were forced to leave their boat, which naturally was displaying the U.S. flag. An apology was immediately given, but the United States used the incident as an excuse to occupy Veracruz, Mexico's main port.

Postrevolutionary governments in Tamaulipas have been at pains to develop industry and communications and to foster trade across the border. They founded a state university, introduced reforms into the oil industry, and continued the program of land reform so that economically viable lands might be placed in the hands of more people. Nonetheless, poverty levels have remained high for many people, who still live in very basic conditions.

One of the most distinguished political figures (also a writer) of the twentieth century was **Emilio Portes Gil** (1891-1978), a champion of the rights of workers in the oil industry, who were in conflict with the foreign companies that owned the operations. He served in the government of Plutarco Elías Calles before becoming interim president himself from 1928 to 1930.

Economy

At the Jamaube mission, there was some commercial exploitation of a variety of cactus commonly called *lechuguilla* as early as the seventeenth century. The fiber from this cactus, used in particular for making toothbrushes, became known as *fibra Jamaube* and provided as much as 90 percent of world consumption until synthetic fibers displaced it quite late in the late twentieth century. Tamaulipas's modern claim to economic importance stems from its oil industry, livestock, crops, and fishing industry. In addition, near the U.S. border there are now more than 350 assembly plants of the kind known as maquiladoras. The beaches of the Gulf attract tourists.

There are oil refineries in Reynosa and Ciudad Madero. The deposits of oil and natural gas lie in the northern municipalities of Reynosa, Matamoros, Río Bravo, Valle Hermoso, and Camargo, and in the southern ones of Altamira and Ciudad Madero. There is some mining for lead, zinc, asbestos, phosphorite, and talc in the municipalities of San Nicolás, Llera, Victoria, and Bustamante, and in San Carlos there is marble. Manufacturing accounts for approximately 20 percent of the state's economy.

Twenty-one percent of the land is devoted to agriculture, about a third of it requiring irrigation systems, as in the Faja Fronteriza; 58 percent is used for livestock; and 11 percent is forested. The most important

Village street.

agricultural product is sorghum; other important crops are corn, sugarcane, cotton, soybeans, wheat, sisal, melons, avocados, and citrus fruits. Over a million hectares (2,500,000 acres) are used as pastureland, with cattle and sheep predominating. In the southeast, there is industrial activity associated with the important fishing industry, which yields varieties such as snapper, drum, oysters, crabs, and shrimp.

Arts

Craftwork in Tamaulipas includes the production of leather and suede goods, such as clothing and other personal items and riding gear. Articles are also made with *ixtle*, the fiber that comes from the lechuguilla cactus, and with sisal. There is some glassblowing, and furniture is made out of wood and palm.

Tampico is known for its theater. It has several companies, one of which specializes in mime.

The state has an interesting popular musical tradition. Traditional dance genres in Tamaulipas include the *redova*, a $3/4$ dance with stress on the last beat and with movements somewhat like those of a subdued polka. Like other genres from Germany and Eastern Europe, this one made its way to Mexico (from Czechoslovakia) during the late nineteenth and early twentieth centuries. The *chotís* is also popular; it has a binary rhythm and is more sedate than the redova, but again it is the last of the beats that is stressed.

The local style of dancing involves a good deal of heel-stamping. One of the most characteristic dances of Tamaulipas is *la picota*, a hybridized dance that has its roots in ancient rituals celebrating the earth's fertility. In its modern version, it is danced barefoot, with the dancers wearing cloaks embroidered with flowers and moving to the accompaniment of a drum and a clarinet. The word *picota* refers to the stake or column that once marked the place where miscreants were put to shame by having their misdeeds proclaimed in public, with a military drum sounding all the while. The dance is sometimes performed at weddings, in which case the drum announces the arrival of the newlyweds, who are greeted by family members, gathered around an aged oak "wedding" tree (the Encino de los Novios); then they all make their way to the place where the fiesta is to take place.

Norteño music, found all over the northern states, is popular in Tamaulipas. It employs instruments such as the bass, the accordion, and the saxophone, and sometimes brass instruments. But the state has some musical and dance features of its own. For example, the use of drum and clarinet is typical of the mountain culture, where many popular forms commonly found in northern states—such as the *huapango*, polka, redova, chotís, and waltz—are performed on these two instruments. The huapango and the *son huasteco* both derive from the *fandango* and the *jota* that were brought over from Spain in the colonial era; these are more characteristic forms on the Gulf Coast and the south of the state. The huapango is both a song and dance form and is often performed on a stage or platform in competitions. Once accompanied by harp and guitar, it and the *son* can now be accompanied by a variety of instruments, including the *jarana* and the violin.

The state has produced some popular singers and entertainers, but few other creative artists who have made their mark outside Tamaulipas. **Celedonio Junco de la Vega** (1863–1948) was a journalist and writer of some note and a member of Mexico's national Academia de la Lengua. **Ciro R. de la Garza Treviño** (1905–1973) was a lawyer and historian who wrote a good deal. **Ernesto Cortázar** (1900–1953) was a composer and performer of popular music, some of it for the cinema, for which he also wrote screenplays. One of the classic films of Mexico's golden age of movies, *Allá en el rancho grande*, had music by Cortázar. Also in the musical field, **Juan Diego Tercero** (1895–1987) was a composer, musicologist, pianist, and choral director of note.

In the visual arts, **Ramón García Zurita** (1927–1965) studied at the national San Carlos Academy of Art, was influenced by José Clemente Orozco, and produced figurative paintings, portraits, and murals. **Gabriel Saldívar Silva** (1909–1980) left Tamaulipas for Mexico City to study medicine, but soon found himself charged with writing a history of the university's Faculty of Medicine, a task that sparked an interest in meticulous library research and led to his writing about twenty books about this and other topics, including art and the national musical traditions, particularly the indigenous. (A widely respected compilation by him from indigenous musical sources is commonly referred to as the Saldívar Codex).

Amalia González Caballero (1902–1986) studied at the National Conservatory and became extremely active in encouraging and promoting cultural associations, in particular those related to the involvement of women in intellectual and cultural life. She lectured at home and abroad, represented her country at international cultural events, was the founding president of the Ateneo Mexicano de Mujeres, founded the International Women's Club, served as undersecretary for culture under Jaime Torres Bodet, sponsored the creation of the Comedia Mexicana, was ambassador to Austria and Sweden, and besides was a significant writer of creative and critical works.

Social Customs

Suede and leather clothing has been in evidence since early colonial days, first among soldiers and riders and later among cowboys. It evolved from the utilitarian to the decorative. At festivities, men and women might now wear white shoes and tan or yellowish leather jackets with frills in the Apache style and with white decoration around the neck and the waistline;

the men wear matching leather trousers and hat, and the women skirts with half-moon patches of white on the front and a band of white at knee level.

Among religious celebrations, the Feast of the Virgin of Guadalupe, in December, is especially important in the municipalities of Güemes, Llera, Ocampo, and Palmillas. In July, Altamira celebrates the Feast of Santiago and in November that of San Martín de Porres, both being occasions for dancing *matachines*. San Martín de Porres is revered in Tampico, too, where Carnival is also a major event. Tula celebrates the Day of the Holy Cross in May and the Feast of San Antonio de Padua in June; the latter is known for its performances of *pastorelas*, religious playlets involving angels, devils, and Indians. A typical dance for the occasion is the *danza del patriarca*. On July 16, Tula marks the Feast of the Virgen del Carmen, when devotees of the Virgin bring gifts to her church altar and place hundreds of candles at her feet. They also engage in the traditional dances of *la Malinche*, *el viejo*, and the patriarca. In general, all such celebrations are marked by processions and pilgrimages, fireworks, food, and frolicking.

Among the principal secular festivities in the state, El Mante holds a Sugar Festival in February, and the founding of Tampico is celebrated in April. There are regional fairs at Matamoros in July and at Reynosa in August. Nuevo Laredo hosts an agricultural fair in September. There is an annual Expo at Tampico in late October, at which time Bagdad Beach, which is close to Matamoros, holds its Festival of the Sea (Festival del Mar). The Festival Internacional de Tamaulipas, in October, coincides with the commemoration of the creation of the state; this festival typically offers more than six hundred cultural events scattered over the state, including theatrical performances, opera, dance displays, concerts, and art exhibitions. Matamoros hosts a similar festival, though on a more modest scale, at that time. Tampico has literary, musical, theatrical, and visual arts festivals twice a year. Nuevo Laredo holds a Festival Ofrenda arts festival and, together with Matamoros and Reynosa, has a thematic Festival de la Frontera (Border Festival). Dance is the main focus of Ciudad Victoria's May Festival de Música y Danza "Janambre."

Noteworthy Places

The long coastline provides beaches and aquatic entertainments that draw tourists from Mexico and abroad; one example is the beach known as La Barra del Tordo. Inland there are several canyons and other natural attractions. There is also a planetarium and observatory at a recreational park called the Parque Cultural y Recreativo Siglo XXI.

Among museums, Matamoros has a Museum of Contemporary Art and the Museo Casa Mata, which deals with local history and includes some Huasteca artifacts. Ciudad Madero has a more substantial Museo de Arte Huasteco. Ciudad Victoria and Ciudad Mante both have anthropological museums. Archaeological sites are at Tula, Tanco, and Las Flores (Tampico); La Palma (Altamirano); La Alberca (Ocampo); and Tanxillab (Mantel Pueblito). Matamoros has a theater, the Teatro de la Reforma (popularly referred to as the "Teatro de la opera" [Opera Theater]), the place where Mexico's national anthem was premiered. The Catedral de Nuestra Señora del Refugio in Matamoros dates from 1832. The port city of Tampico also has a cathedral and a historically interesting customs building.

Cuisine

As in most northerly states, meat plays an important role in the cuisine of Tamaulipas, especially beef and pork, and game when in season. The coast offers seafood such as snapper and bass, shrimp and crabs. The cuisine varies somewhat by region. Typical breakfast dishes are *guayín, chochas de sotol,* and *flor de pita con huevo*; for main meals, *empanadas de nopal, asado de puerco, mole de papas con camarón, chilpachole de jaiba, jaibas rellenas,* and *cabrito en su sangre* are typical. Desserts rely heavily on fruits and include *camote con piña, calabaza en tacha, cocada con piña y nuez, mermelada de nopal, pipitorias,* and *adepitas*. Representative drinks are *champurrado de maíz de Teja, miel seba, mezcal de San Carlos,* and *agua de huapilla*.

Cabrito en Su Sangre (Civet of Young Goat)

Ingredients:

    1 kid goat (including its blood)
    3 cloves of garlic, chopped
    2 red bell peppers
    2 bay leaves
    Jalapeño chiles, sliced, for garnish
    1 onion, sliced
    Salt and pepper
    Cornmeal

The blood of the goat must be reserved at the time of slaughtering, for later use. First brown the meat in a heavy pan, add the garlic and about half the onion, then the red pepper and bay leaves, the blood, plus salt and pepper to taste. Simmer until tender, thickening with a little cornmeal if necessary. Serve garnished with jalapeños and slices of onion.

Mole de Papas con Camarón

Ingredients:

    4 lb. potatoes
    2 lb. shrimp

> 1 red bell pepper, sliced
> 2 or 3 large tomatoes, sliced
> Pinch of *epazote*
> 2 hardboiled eggs, chopped
> Olive oil
> Black pepper and salt to taste

Peel the potatoes and cut them into chunks, then boil until tender but without allowing them to disintegrate. Fry the red pepper and tomatoes, season with salt and pepper, and add the shrimp and epazote. After a couple of minutes, add the potatoes and the hardboiled egg.

Pipitorias

Ingredients:

> 2 lb. sesame seeds
> $1/4$ lb. shelled peanuts
> $1/4$ lb. pumpkin seeds
> 1 lb. brown sugar
> 2 oz. butter

Briefly toast the peanuts together with the seeds. Melt the butter in a pan and dissolve the sugar, then add the other ingredients and allow to thicken before pouring the mixture into a shallow pan or onto a flat surface, to cool and harden.

Tlaxcala

State Characteristics

Tlaxcala—officially Tlaxcala de Xicoténcatl—is a small state located in southwest central Mexico, amid volcanic mountains. *Tlaxcala* comes from a term in the Náhuatl language and means "Place of the Corn Tortilla," while Xicoténcatl was the name of a prominent local indigenous leader at the time of conquest by Spain.

Much of Tlaxcala is surrounded by the state of Puebla, with which it has been closely linked historically. To the north of Tlaxcala lies Hidalgo and to its west the state of México. Tlaxcala has forty-four *municipios*, but it is the smallest state in the country in terms of surface area: at 4,061 square kilometers (1,584 square miles), it covers only 0.2 percent of Mexico's total area. Its population total is also modest—1,068,207, according to the 2005 census—putting it at number 27 in the rankings of state populations for the country as a whole, but Tlaxcala's population density is relatively high, given the small area covered. Tlaxcala sends seven representatives to the National Congress. The state has three newspapers of its own: *El Sol de Tlaxcala*, *ABC Noticias*, and *El Periódico de Tlaxcala*. The state university (Universidad Autónoma de Tlaxcala) is young, having been founded in the 1970s, and there are two other institutions of higher education.

The only towns whose population exceeds 50,000 are the state capital, also called Tlaxcala (63,335), and Apizaco (50,593). The most important of Tlaxcala's municipios are Tlaxcala, Apizaco, Chiautempan, Huamantla, Calpulalpan and Tlaxco. The capital city is located only about 32 kilometers (20 miles) north of the city of Puebla, and indeed, some parts of the state seem like satellites of that city. The state has two main regions, the north and the southern-central; the natural characteristics of each have determined their resources and influenced production, population patterns, communications, and social structures, modifying the latter considerably and leading to the loss of some traditional practices.

The mean altitude for the state as a whole is 2,230 meters (7,315 feet). Rainfall is not particularly high; central parts, where annual precipitation reaches between 600 and 1,200 millimeters (24–48 inches), receive the most, whereas in the northeast and east rainfall is less than 500 millimeters (20 inches). The main sources of water are the Atoyac-Zahuapan basin and the Atlangatepec Dam. There are a few rivers, such as the San Martín and the Zahuapa, and lagoons such as the Atocha and the Acuitapilco; there are also springs at Atotonilco and Tepellanco. Except in one or two high places, covering approximately 10 percent of the state, the climate is generally mild and quite dry, with temperatures rarely exceeding 30°C (86°F). The average annual temperature in the city of Tlaxcala is about 17°C (63°F).

The land comprises plains and volcanic mountain ranges with rocky slopes. The highest mountain is the volcano known as Malinche (or Matlalcuéyetl), at 4,461 meters (14,636 feet), and there are a further eight peaks that are at least 2,750 meters (9,000 feet) high. Some 25 percent of the state is mountainous. At the higher elevations, there are pines, oaks and junipers; lower areas feature cacti such as *maguey* and *nopal*. Like many states in Mexico, Tlaxcala has suffered from deforestation and erosion, but some attempts have been made to make good the loss and prevent further deterioration. There is a conservation area around the Malinche Volcano. The state fauna includes quail, hares, eagles, falcons, squirrels, and coyotes in the hills, and in the valleys and plains, pigeons, rabbits, *cocomixtles*, badgers, and skunks.

Cultural Groups and Languages

Tlaxcala has a distinguished indigenous past, but has become a state characterized by *mestizaje*, in both the racial and cultural senses. Most people in Tlaxcala, as in Mexico at large, are of mixed European and Indian heritage. According to the 2005 census, Tlaxcala had 23,807 people over five years of age who were speakers of an Indian language, and of these only 1.2 percent did not also speak Spanish. Náhuatl is overwhelmingly the most widely spoken of the Indian languages, with 20,149 speakers; the next most spoken is Totonac, with 1,105. At least six other Indian languages are spoken.

History

Small though it is, the state of Tlaxcala has had a very special place in Mexico's history. There is evidence of a human presence in the area dating from 10,000 BC. As in other parts of Mexico, the first people are believed to have been nomadic hunters and gatherers, but time brought with it the rearing of animals and the beginnings of agriculture, encouraging settlement. Tlaxcala was successively settled by a number of peoples, including the Olmecs (Olmec-Xicalanca). By AD 900, they had declined and control had been taken over by the Teo-Chichimecs. Indeed, the history of Tlaxcala before the Conquest is a history of many peoples jostling for position.

About 450 years later, the Tlaxcaltecas were the dominant people; by 1348, they had founded Tepectícpac, their first city. These were people who shared the language and the cultural roots of the Mexicas (Aztecs), but who were at loggerheads with them. The Tlaxcaltecas subdued most of their neighbors, demanded tribute from them, and set up a strong federation of four "republics" or *señoríos*—Tizatlán, Tepetícpac, Ocotelulco, and Quiahuixtlán—each with a good deal of autonomy and led by its own chieftain; history has dubbed these four chieftains the "*cuatro señores.*" The Tlaxcaltecas were preeminent, but there were at least twenty señoríos in the area, for example, the Otomí señorío of Tliliuhquitepec in the north-central area.

The Tlaxcaltecas were constantly attacked and harassed by the powerful Mexicas, whose empire dominated the Valley of Mexico. In fact, the four señoríos of Tlaxcala became a major plundering ground for the *Guerras Floridas* (Flower Wars), which the Mexicas fought with the goal of taking live captives for subsequent sacrifice to their gods. By the time Hernán Cortés arrived in 1519 with his band of Spanish conquistadores, the Tlaxcaltecas were surrounded by enemies, under a blockade that was depriving them of some of life's essentials, struggling to survive, and deeply resentful of the Aztecs. Understanding this, Cortés proposed an alliance with the Tlaxcaltecas to defeat the Aztecs. At first, the Tlaxcaltecas refused, but Cortés's power gave them little choice in the matter, so an alliance was forged that helped the Spaniards to take control of Mexico. Principal among the four señores of Tlaxcala was Xicoténcatl, who acceded to the alliance; however, his son resisted it, and he paid for that resistance with his life.

In none of the four señoríos of the Tlaxcaltecas was there a town or other place that served as the shared seat of government. The city of Tlaxcala was founded by the Spaniards because they wanted a means of bringing the four together, centralizing power, implanting Spanish institutions and ways, and consolidating the alliance. In recognition of their compliance and help, the Spaniards granted the Tlaxcaltecas certain privileges, and they respected these privileges for most of the sixteenth century: the Indians were exempt from taxes, and they kept their traditional lands. In the early colonial years, the Spaniards set up a Cabildo de Naturales, a Native Town Council, answerable to a provincial governor. In name at least, the people of Tlaxcala were duly converted to the "true faith" of Catholicism. Later they were to serve in other parts of Mexico and Central

America by helping to populate new territories conquered by the Spaniards and promoting the "civilizing" mission. As part of this process, on
June 6, 1591, four hundred families were dispatched—or perhaps it would
be more correct to say induced to go with the promise of privileges and
protections—to Jalisco. From there they moved farther north, even into
lands that are now part of the United States.

Once the Spaniards had control of New Spain, they divided it into five
major administrative regions, of which Tlaxcala was one. Toward the end
of the sixteenth century, the Spanish authorities decided to exact tribute
from the Indians and take over their lands. This contributed to Indian
revolts during the seventeenth and eighteenth centuries, but the Tlaxcaltecas were kept in hand by the Spaniards. The special role played by the
Tlaxcaltecas, and the privileges granted them because of it, help to explain
why the territorial limits of Tlaxcala itself have changed rather little over
the years; until 1860, when the additional region of Calpulalpan was
annexed to the state of Tlaxcala, its boundaries had barely changed since
before the Conquest.

During the colonial era, Tlaxcala went through several changes of status:
the authorities designated it a territory, then a district, and then a territory
once again. In the early nineteenth century, when there was growing interest among Mexicans in general in the possibility of independence from
Spain, Tlaxcala was no exception, but forces loyal to the Spanish crown
successfully kept control of the area until 1821, when the Plan of Iguala
sealed Mexico's independence. Three years later, under the Constitution of
1824, Tlaxcala was declared a constituent state of the new federal
republic.

At the time of the drive for national independence, **José Miguel Guridi
y Alcocer** (1763–1828) was a priest, politician, and writer who participated in the Constituent Congress of 1822 and was a signatory of the declaration of independence and of the 1824 Constitution. He was one of the
people who were active in promoting Tlaxcala to statehood. **José Manuel
Herrera** (1776–1831), a soldier, politician, and journalist, supported José
María Morelos, participated in the taking of Oaxaca, and served as an envoy
to the United States. Herrera was the editor of the newspaper *El Mexicano
Independiente*. He represented Tlaxcala in the National Congress and
became minister of home and foreign affairs.

Political and social instability characterized much of the nineteenth century in Mexico. There were conflicts between federalists and centralists
and between liberals and conservatives; there were military confrontations
within Mexico and between it and foreign countries. France and the United
States both had to be contended with. **Felipe Santiago Xicoténcatl**
(1805–1847) is remembered in Tlaxcala as a soldier who fought on the side
of Guadalupe Victoria in Puebla and later died defending his country
against the United States at the Battle of Chapultepec. The political instability of the nineteenth century delayed economic development until the time

of Porfirio Díaz, but by the end of the century, Tlaxcala had become an important commercial and textile center.

Juan Cuamatzi (1879-1911) is one of many Tlaxcalans who were against Díaz and the idea of his possible reelection after years in power. Cuamatzi supported Díaz's rival, Francisco Madero; he was taken prisoner and shot. Another supporter of Madero, and a man who was active during the Revolution of 1910-1920 and was shot in Calpulalpan, was **Domingo Arenas** (1888-1915). Arenas was a seminal figure in modern Tlaxcalan politics and was instrumental in securing land for the peasants of Tlaxcala and Puebla. In subsequent years, those who followed in his footsteps were dubbed *arenistas*.

By the late 1920s, Tlaxcala was beginning to recover from the revolutionary violence and was becoming more stable. The population of the capital then stood at only about six thousand; thereafter the population base strengthened, along with educational opportunities.

During the 1920s, the economy was in the doldrums; the old *haciendas* had lost their vibrancy, and the *pulque* and textile industries were in decline. On the political front, 1926 saw a socialist governor, Ignacio Mendoza, come to power. This was a time of increasing unionization of the workers, a process furthered by another governor, Adolfo Bonilla, who had earlier fought on the side of Arenas. Steps were taken to encourage development, and communications were improved.

By the end of the 1930s, Tlaxcala—given its plentiful supply of labor and its favorable location—seemed ready to industrialize. But that industrialization did not take place. World War II intervened, without benefit to Tlaxcala, and the economy stagnated. Faced with this, many Tlaxcalans headed for other states, or across the U.S. border taking advantage of the *bracero* program. And so things continued until the 1960s, when, frustrated by legal constraints on land use, some desperate peasants invaded the haciendas. By 1970, almost all the old factories had closed their doors. In view of these developments, the authorities, both local (Governor Emilio Sánchez Piedras) and national (the government of Luis Echeverría), redoubled their efforts to encourage industrialization in Tlaxcala.

Economy

Tlaxcala has benefited from its geographical position, being the axis of communication by road and rail between Veracruz (the country's main port) and Mexico City (the country's capital city), not to mention its proximity to Puebla, another of Mexico's major cities. Topography and climate have also affected Tlaxcala's economic development.

In colonial times, the main square of the town of Tlaxcala served as an open marketplace (*tianguis*), especially on Saturdays. Tlaxcala became known for providing the prized cochineal, a dye that comes from a beetle. Cocoa beans, wool, salt, cotton clothing, chickens, ducks, hares, and rabbits were also traded, along with seeds and vegetables, articles made from wood, and jewelry. **Diego Muñoz Camargo** (1529–1599), a contemporary historian, wrote of the natives' subtlety and wiles in dealing with the Spaniards.

In modern times, almost 84 percent of the land is devoted to agriculture. Some fruit is cultivated, mostly on the hillsides of the dominant volcano. In flatter areas (and in order of importance), one finds corn and barley, wheat, pulses, oats, broad beans, potatoes, and alfalfa, among other things. Some of the crop production serves as forage. A further 2.6 percent is pastureland; cattle are raised for meat and for bullfighting, and there are also pigs, horses, goats, and poultry. Beekeeping is a significant occupation, too. Agricultural activity is strongest in the municipalities of Tlaxco, Terrenate, Altzayanca, Calpulalpan, and Nanacamilpa de Mariano Arista. Forests cover 13.4 percent of Tlaxcala, providing pine and oak for commercial use. Some furniture is made, and there is craft production of walking sticks, earthenware cooking vessels, woolen textiles, painted wooden masks, pottery, and baskets.

Major industries, developing largely in the last quarter of the twentieth century, include car production, chemicals, electronics, and the making of alcoholic drinks (especially of the distilled variety). Tlaxcala also has great historical and architectural interest, and so it draws in "cultural" tourists.

Arts

Craftwork in Tlaxcala includes the making of *sarapes* (wraps, of a type worn largely by men) and *tapetes* (tablecloths) in the traditional style, characterized by an uneven texture that comes from the way the material jumps as it moves on the wooden loom. Various municipalities are known for their crafts. San Sebastián Atlahapa is particularly known for its burnished clay pottery. Carnival masks are made in Tlatempan. In the municipality of San Pablo del Monte, they make articles out of onyx and also produce Talavera-style pottery in the colonial tradition, but with a very Mexican spin. In the municipality of Xaltocan, stone is worked for fountains and monuments, and in San Juan Ixtenco, cotton clothing is made, freely embroidered in the Otomí Indian style. Ixtenco is known for rugs and also for pictures made by assembling various kinds of seeds, as in a mosaic. Ixtacuixtla makes cardboard figures, masks, and *piñatas*, while Españita makes figures of all kinds from corn husks. The municipality of Altzayanca produces fine psalteries, following an eighteenth-century tradition. Finally, the city of Tlaxcala is famous for its silversmiths and for styles combining the Spanish and the indigenous.

It is especially difficult to separate Tlaxcala's culture from its history and social customs. Ancient pagan rituals mix with Christian ones. In the music that is reconstructed or at least partly derived from the Indian tradition, instruments called the *chirimía, huehuetl, tarola,* and *teponaxtle* are employed. Drawing on the European instrumental tradition, Tlaxcala is also well known for its local brass bands. The psaltery is popular in the Tlaxco-Caldera-Huamantla mountain range. Traditional dances called *xochipizahu mahuizontrintli* and *pistoro* are performed in the region of the Malinche Volcano and on the Huamantla plain, and the *manzontini* in the Puebla-Tlaxcala valley. There are other traditional songs and dances inherited and adapted from Spain, such as *moros y cristianos*.

Among the region's notable cultural figures, **Xicoténcatl** (Xicoténcatl El Viejo; d. 1522) was an orator and poet, in addition to being one of the cuatro señores. A revealing poem of his has survived, expressing his wish to put an end once and for all to the Flower Wars and have a final confrontation with the Mexicas. In that poem, Xicoténcatl calls upon his people to go the canals of Tenochtitlán and steal the Aztecs' water—a metaphor for saying that Tenochtitlán should be deprived of life. He calls on the gods to look benevolently on the Tlaxcaltecas, helping them find their way to that water.

An early important cultural figure after the Conquest was Fray **Diego de Valadés** (1533-1582), who was born in the city of Tlaxcala, son of a conquistador and an Indian woman and thus a *mestizo*. Having already distinguished himself as a writer, he joined the Franciscan order, became private secretary to the influential Pedro de Gante, and taught art at the Colegio de San José de los Naturales, which the Spaniards set up to train the Indians in European ways. In 1570, Valadés was the guardian of the San Francisco Convent in Tlaxcala. He was the first Mexican to publish a book in Europe, his *Rhetorica Christiana* (Perugia, Italy, 1579); this compendium of culture, history, and theology is one of the most important books of the century.

Diego Muñoz Camargo was a historian of the early colonial period, an indigenous governor of Tlaxcala, an interpreter for the Spaniards, a student of local antiquities, and most significantly the author of a much valued history of Tlaxcala, dating from 1576. **José Agustín Arrieta** (1802-1824) was a painter noted for his *costumbrista* works, full of local color. **Próspero Cahuantzi** (1834-1915) was a soldier and later governor of the state from 1885 to 1911. He was also a scholar of Náhuatl who published the *Lienzo de Tlaxcala*, a major historical document. More recently, **Miguel N. Lira** (1905-1961) was a poet, novelist, playwright, and lawyer.

Social Customs

There are still vestiges of ancient Indian festive rituals in honor of the vital gods, such as Tláloc (the god of rain), Chicomecóatl (maize), Xochiquetzalli (flowers), and Echécatl (wind). As with so many things Mexican, these vestiges appear in hybridized form, mixed with Christian rituals.

Carnival is a big affair in many parts of Mexico. Brought to New Spain by the Franciscans, in Tlaxcala it acquired a rather special character—a character that is rooted in the sumptuous festivities indulged in by the seventeenth-century colonial landowners, and the fact that the Indians were debarred from them. Instead, the Indians used to dance and cavort in the streets, making fun of the extravagant dress and curious gyrations of their masters; for this, they would don a mask with a white face and blue eyes. The landowners were so troubled by this that they attempted to ban the Indian parody. Nowadays, Carnival is celebrated in more than sixty towns and villages, each giving the celebration a local color, with distinctive characteristics of dress or particular combinations of dances.

The proceedings normally begin on the Friday before Ash Wednesday with the *tragafuegos* ceremony, in which, to a background of funereal music, an effigy representing Bad Temper is burned from foot to head. This is followed by the burning of the coffin of sadness, resentment, and anger. The outcome is a display of joyfulness. One typical dance is the *danza de los huehues*, to whose preservation many clubs are devoted; it is a dance that entails wearing showy dress and indulging in a lot of whip-cracking. Another dance is the *cuadrilla de catrines*, which stems from the French *quadrille*; here, humble folk engage in a burlesque at the expense of the rich and powerful.

On the Carnival weekend in the city of Tlaxcala, the Virgin of Ocotlán is dressed and brought down the hill from her church to be paraded about a Tlaxcala that is festooned with flowers, streamers, and colored sawdust. She is taken to visit the parish church of San José and then to the San Francisco Convent, where a Mass is celebrated. On her way back, she stops at another small church called the Capilla del Pósito, which is where she is believed to have made her very first appearance one Sunday before Carnival. Finally, on the Sunday after Carnival, there is another popular ceremony called El Ahorcado ("The Hanged Man"), in which a mock trial of the authorities and other targets of criticism is held.

Fairs and festivals are held in Tlaxcala, Huamantla, Santa Ana Chiautempan, Tlaxco, Calpulalpan, Zacatelco, and Apizaco. Calpulalpan has a food festival in mid-June, with typical treats such as *maguey* worms and pulque. Chiautempan has a sarape festival in late July. In mid-August, Huamantla holds its Humantlada—a running of the bulls, Pamplona style, through flower-strewn streets. Tlaxco's fair, in mid-September, is noted for bullfights, cowboy displays, and overeating.

Noteworthy Places

There are rock paintings dating back six thousand years at Abrigo Rocoso, close to the Atlihuetzía Falls. These paintings represent heavenly bodies, mammals, spiders, anthropomorphic figures, and solar symbols; the principal medium is iron oxide. Among several archaeological sites—Cacaxtla, Tlaxco, Tlaxcalian, Ocotelulco, Xochiatécatl, Tizatlán, and Quiahuatztlán—the first is the most important. Cacaxtla, which was discovered only in the

1970s, was first developed between 600 and 700 AD by the Olmec-Xicalanca people, who came to dominate a good part of the Puebla-Tlaxcala valley. They set the ceremonial center at Cacaxtla on a hill looking over the valley, perhaps for defensive purposes. Over a period of years, new structures were superimposed on others, as many as seven layers deep. The surviving structures are surrounded by a substantial trench, and there are some significant pre-Hispanic paintings, the most important of which is a mural that is larger than any other known from pre-Hispanic times; it covers 200 square meters (2,150 square feet) and represents a battle and human sacrifices. Archaeologists have suggested a Mayan influence, and some have also seen signs of the influence of Teotihuacán and Monte Albán. What seems fairly clear is that this was a place of confluence through which several cultures passed.

"The Most Noble and Loyal City of Tlaxcala," as the Spaniards dubbed it, is one of New Spain's oldest, having been founded in 1525. The modern city is small and has a distinctly provincial feel. It has narrow streets,

Parish church of San José.

largely laid out on a standard grid pattern, and its center is relatively traffic-free, with fine, harmonious, and well-kept buildings, thanks to an awareness on the part of the authorities of the value (and the tourist potential) of Tlaxcala's historical heritage. The sprawling outskirts, however, are predictably disorderly and unattractive.

What is now the Regional Museum was once the Convent of San Francisco, founded in 1537 by Fray Martín de Valencia and attached to Tlaxcala's Catedral de Nuestra Señora de la Asunción (Cathedral of Our Lady of the Assumption). Among many other historical relics, the museum includes four anonymous early paintings, each portraying one of the cuatro señores; from their mouths come ballooned captions of their cries in honor of the Virgin and the saints. No doubt these paintings were part of the Catholic propaganda machine. (Significantly, there were twelve convents established in the region of Tlaxcala, just as there had been twelve Franciscans initially charged by the pope with converting the natives.) The cathedral itself is small but notable for the quality of its beamed ceiling in the *mudéjar* style, for a pulpit with an inscription stating that the process of evangelizing the New World began there, and for a baptismal font where it is believed that the highly symbolic act of baptizing the four señores was carried out. The convent complex also includes a tower, a cloister, a *capilla posa* (corner chapel), and a fine example of a *capilla abierta* (open chapel) designed to accommodate large numbers of natives in a sacred open space of the kind with which they were familiar in their own traditional rituals.

The striking colored and decorated exterior of the Parroquia de San José (Parish Church of Saint Joseph) includes an elaborate, wedding-cake façade and areas covered with Talavera tiles. This church was begun in the seventeenth century and finished in the eighteenth. Inside, there are two sculpted fonts, one displaying the Spanish imperial coat of arms and the other an image of Camaxtli, the war god of the ancient Tlaxcaltecas. There is also a canvas beside the altar, depicting the baptism of the señores.

It is unusual, given the typical colonial Spanish town layout, for the main church not to be on the main square. What does dominate Tlaxcala's main square is its principal civic building, the Government Palace, which was begun in 1545, and which at one time or another during the colonial era housed important figures such as Cortés and visiting royals. Its interior arches on the ground floor are in a Portuguese mudéjar style and are original. However, the overall structure has undergone several modifications over the years, for example as a result of a fire in 1692 (an anniversary year) when there was a native rebellion, and later because of an earthquake in 1711. The façade of this building was redecorated in a French rococo style in 1929. Nonetheless, it is a fine building. Murals inside it, representing historical scenes from the pre-Hispanic era through the time of the Conquest, are by local artist **Desiderio Hernández Xochitiotzin** (1922–2007), who lends his name to a local art museum also. Another important building on the main square is the Palace of Justice, once the

Capilla Real de Indios (Royal Indian Chapel), whose original construction began in 1528 in honor of Emperor Charles V and was financed by the four señores.

Tlaxcala's museums are generally on a small scale. An interesting one is the Museo de la Memoria, set in an old building that has been refurbished and redesigned to accommodate a homage to Tlaxcala's Indian heritage. A curiosity is the small Museo Nacional del Títere (National Puppet Museum).

Not far from Tlaxcala is Ocotlán, a small village on a hill with a disproportionately large church set behind an ample forecourt with imposing entrances. This church has one of Mexico's most impressive baroque façades and an important baroque gold altarpiece. Ocotlán is a place of pilgrimage.

San Esteban de Tizatlán, also close to Tlaxcala, is the place where, on September 23, 1519, the alliance between the Indians and the Spaniards was agreed. In this place, there is a sixteenth-century capilla abierta with fine frescoes, sitting on what was once part of Xicoténcatl's palace. The chapel was made with adobe, using pre-Hispanic techniques, and dates from 1550; it is portrayed in the famous *Lienzo de Tlaxcala*. There is also a modern botanic garden at Tizatlán.

At Panotla, the church of San Nicolás de Bari has an extravagant baroque façade. At Contla, there is the church of San Bernardino, with a plateresque entrance, a baroque *retablo*, and fine plasterwork. Huamantla is a town of simple façades and balconies, with a certain French flavor deriving from the fashions of the *porfiriato*. Huamantla's Franciscan convent has a *churrigueresque* altarpiece.

Fifteen kilometers (9 miles) from Tlaxcala is La Trinidad, founded in 1880 as a textile factory and now a recreational center. The La Malintzín National Park, an area beside the main volcano that was designated a national park in 1938, is about 32 kilometers (20 miles) from Apizaco. It covers 45,711 hectares (112,926 acres) and is the highest national park in Mexico. There are thermal waters at the Manantial Santa Cruz el Porvenir, about 16 kilometers (10 miles) from Tlaxcala.

Cuisine

As can be said of most Mexican food, Tlaxcalan food is the product of a fusion of indigenous and Spanish traditions. Corn—believed by the Indians to have divine qualities—is the staple. Cornmeal is used for many things, such as making *tlatloyos*, *pozoles*, and *tlaxcales*. From the corn plant also comes a widely used fungus called *huitlacoche*. One effect of the Aztec blockade of Tlaxcala was to deprive its inhabitants of salt, so they took to using an alternative condiment that is still employed sometimes: *tequesquite*.

There is an abundance of local herbs and plants, such as *epazote*, *pápalo quelite*, *quintoniles*, *verdolagas*, *huauzontle*, *pipitza*, and *xoconoxtle*. Squash blossoms and the leaves of the nopal cactus are widely used, as they are in many parts of Mexico. Insects provide seasonal delicacies, such as the red worms from the *maguey* (*chinicuiles*) and the ants' eggs (*escamoles*) that are harvested in spring at the base of the *agave*. The *charal* is a freshwater fish, the *axolotl* a small lizard, and the *acocil* a variety of freshwater shrimp.

Pulque, a cactus-based alcoholic drink, is used to preserve fruit and in cooking. Apart from pulque, there is *capulín* (a kind of wine) and there are many fruit and other nonalcoholic drinks, such as *agua de jamaica*, made from hibiscus leaves, a drink that is popular all over Mexico.

Though the rich and complex sauce known as *mole* is usually associated with Puebla, it and its close relative *pipián* are every bit as much a specialty of Tlaxcala. *Pollo Tocatlán* and *pollo Calpulalpan* are two typical chicken dishes. Desserts include fritters with cream, cheese, and honey; *muéganos* from Huamantla; and *alegrías*. The Indians sweetened their food with honey from wild ants; the use of honey from bees, and sugar, came with the Spaniards.

Muéganos

Ingredients:

    1 lb. flour
    6 eggs
    4 tbsp milk
    Oil
    1/2 lb. brown sugar
    1 1/2 cups water
    1 cinnamon stick

Mix the flour with the eggs and milk to make a smooth dough (adding more milk if needed). Roll out the dough into a thin sheet. Cut it into small squares and fry them until they pop up. Drain and put on paper towel. Dissolve the brown sugar in water, bringing it to a boil, then add the cinnamon, making a thick syrup. Remove the cinnamon stick and pour the rest over the squares; leave them to dry.

Pollo Tocatlán

Ingredients:

    2 chickens, cut into pieces
    Salt and pepper
    Mixiote leaves (the outer leaves of the maguey cactus)
    3 tbsp pork fat or oil
    1 large onion, finely chopped
    6 *serrano* chiles, chopped
    1 or 2 cloves of garlic

3 lb. tomatoes, chopped (ideally, the wild ones found in some cornfields: *toma-titos de milpa*)
8 *nopalitos* (cleaned nopal leaves), in strips
1 cup chopped cilantro
Chicken broth
Salt

Wash and dry the chicken pieces and season with salt and pepper. Make a sauce by first softening the onion, garlic, and chiles in a little fat, then adding the chopped tomatoes, the cilantro, and strips of nopalito. Leave this to simmer over a low heat; add a little chicken broth if it becomes too dry. Now lay the chicken pieces in the mixiote leaves, cover them with the sauce, wrap the leaves around them, and tie them up well. Steam for about an hour until thoroughly cooked. Serve with dry refried beans.

Pipián Verde

A pipián is a sauce made of pumpkin seeds, nuts (sometimes peanuts), and chiles that is usually served lukewarm with chicken. It used to be common in Tlaxcala to serve it with duck, but ducks are no longer so readily available.

Ingredients:

1 cup pumpkin seeds
2 tbsp peanut oil
$^1/_2$ cup onion, finely chopped
3 *poblano* chiles
Chicken stock
2 cloves of garlic
Handful of raddish tops
Handful of watercress
$1^1/_2$ cups chopped cilantro
1 tsp sugar
$^1/_2$ head of lettuce
1 tbsp duck fat
$1^1/_2$ tsp aniseeds, roasted
A pinch of salt

Briefly toast the pumpkin seeds in a dry frying pan, until they have popped. Remove a few of them for later use. Brown the onion in the oil. Clean, deseed, and devein the chiles. Put these together with the pumpkin seeds and some stock in a blender and blend into a paste. Add $^1/_2$ cup of the cilantro and the other ingredients, except for the duck fat. Blend. Put the duck fat in a deep pot and on a high heat; when very hot, put in the contents of the blender and fry this for 3 to 4 minutes. Then return the sauce to the blender, add the rest of the cilantro and blend again.

Veracruz

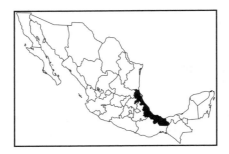

State Characteristics

Much longer than it is broad, the state of Veracruz curves from north to southeast along the Gulf of Mexico. The full name of the state is Veracruz de Ignacio de la Llave. It is quite a large state, covering 72,815 square kilometers (28,398 square miles), which accounts for 3.7 percent of Mexico's total area. Veracruz has the states of Tamaulipas to its north, Oaxaca and Chiapas to its south, Tabasco to its southwest, and Puebla, Hidalgo, and San Luis Potosí to its west. There are seven geographical regions to Veracruz, but the state is administered in 210 municipalities.

According to the 2005 government census, the state population totaled 7,110,214, making it one of the most heavily populated states in the country. Nine towns have 50,000 inhabitants or more. The largest city in the state is the port that bears the same name, Veracruz, which has approximately 700,000 inhabitants; the state capital, however, is Xalapa (sometimes spelled Jalapa; full name Xalapa Enríquez), with a population of about 550,000. Regarding religion, the census recorded that 83 percent of the population is Catholic and 7 percent is Protestant or evangelical. The state of Veracruz is represented by twenty-seven people in the National Congress.

Broadly speaking, the climate can be described in terms of bands that run parallel to the coastline. To the west, the land rises from a wide coastal plain to the *serranías*, the mountain ranges, parts of which are given to seismic activity. A small area directly west of Xalapa, halfway down the state, has a climate that is semidry and mild. Approximately 80 percent of

Veracruz, however, has a hot, humid, tropical climate, with plenty of rain, especially in the summer. A further 8 percent is moderately hot, about 6 percent is temperate, 0.5 percent is cool (but still humid), and a very small portion (0.02 percent) has a truly cold climate. Mean temperatures for the state range from 10°C (50°F) in the colder areas to 26°C (79°F) in the hotter places. In Xalapa, the capital, which sits in the hills, the average annual temperature is about 19°C (65°F); the port city of Veracruz is hotter and steamier. Coastal regions of the state are victims of occasional *nortes*, northerly winds that are strong enough to cause damage and that bring major drops in temperature; however, these winds rarely blow for more than a couple of days. There are also occasional hurricanes.

The variety of topography and climate sustains a plethora of vegetation and wildlife. For example, there are oaks and pines in the hills, palms and cacti in drier areas, and near the coast, mangroves and *amates* (a *ficus* whose bark has a long history of use in the manner of parchment, for writing and painting). There is pastureland in some areas and banana plantations in others. A whole array of tropical plants and fruits is cultivated. The waters are home to herons, martins, pelicans, gulls, oysters, crabs, shrimp, snapper, pompano, and many other species. In the hills, one can find hares, squirrels, deer, and *cacomixtles* (raccoon-like carnivores). At lower elevations, typical animals include rabbits, coyotes, parrots, and iguanas, to mention only a few examples.

From a geological standpoint, there are four regions in the state: the northern coastal plains, the Sierra Madre Oriental, the volcanic axis that cuts across the latter, and the Sierra Madre del Sur. There are conservation zones at the Sierras de Santa Marta, the Volcán de San Martín, and the Cañón del Río Blanco, which is a national park; there is also the Los Tuxtlas Biosphere.

At 5,610 meters (18,400 feet), the highest elevation in the state—and in the country—is found at the Volcán Citlatépetl, a volcano otherwise known as the Pico de Orizaba (often featured, snowcapped and smoking, in tourist posters). Other major peaks are the Volcán Cofre de Perote (4,200 meters/13,780 feet), Cerro Tepozteca (3,140 m/10,300 ft.), and Cerro Cuamila (2,980 m/9,775 ft.). There are many rivers, most of them short, that run from the hills eastwards, down to the Gulf. Some of them are navigable, at least in their coastal reaches, though silt deposits limit navigation in some instances; among these are the Pánuco, Tuxpan, Cazones, Tecotutla, Nautla, Actopan, Jamapa, Papaloapan, Coatzacoalcos, and Tonalá.

Inhabitants of Veracruz are known as *jarochos*—a term whose origins are in the colonial caste system, where it was first used pejoratively to refer to people who were of mixed race, Indian and black; such people were invariably farmworkers. By the end of the eighteenth century, the pejorative associations had gone, the use of the term had widened racially, and it now suggested a person with a lively and happy disposition. Nineteenth-century visitors who wrote about Mexico, such as Daniel Thomas Egerton and Fanny Calderón, use the term as a synonym for *veracruzano*, meaning simply from or of Veracruz.

Cultural Groups and Languages

According to the 2005 census, 9.5 percent of the population over the age of five spoke an indigenous language. Apart from Spanish, fourteen different Indian languages are noted in the state, the most widespread being Náhuatl, Totonac, Huasteco, Popoluc, and Otomí. The indigenous cultures are most vital in La Huasteca (Huastecos), the Sierra de Huayacocotla (Otomíes and Tepehuas), Totonacapan (Totonacs), Las Grandes Montañas (Nahuas), and Los Tuxtlas and the Isthmus (Popolucs).

The Spanish of Veracruz has some similarities with dialects spoken in the Caribbean islands, and in some ways is quite different from the Spanish of other parts of Mexico; it is a long way from the Cantinflas stereotype. (Cantinflas, a native of Mexico City, became popular as a resourceful and cheeky character in movies. His accent was an exaggeration of the speech style found primarily in northern Mexico.) Similarly, the state's ethnic composition could be compared with that of the Caribbean: because Africans came to Veracruz in more significant numbers than they did to other parts of Mexico, the so-called "third root" (black) has been more important in Veracruz. Today, the various races are so intermingled that any attempt to draw clear racial distinctions is largely pointless.

History

The oldest archaeological remains found in Veracruz date back to 1500 BC. In the early days, there were three significant indigenous cultures in the area that this state occupies: the Huasteca, the Totonac, and the Olmec. The area occupied by the Huastecos stretched well beyond the confines of the present-day state: it ran from Tamaulipas to San Luis Potosí, Querétaro, Puebla, and Hidalgo and extended southward as far as the Cazones River. Huasteca development, however, was hindered by constant incursions by other peoples from the north. The oldest remnants of the Huasteca culture have been found near Pánuco.

The Totonacs developed in the central part of the state, during the late Classical Period. These were the people who built the ceremonial centers of El Tajín, Yohualichán, Nepatecuhtlán, Las Higueras, Nopiloa, and El Zapotal. They also produced sophisticated artifacts such as yokes and axes, images of smiling faces, and large earthenware sculptures. The Totonacs are believed to have been part of the Tula Empire until, in 1450, they fell subject to the Nahuas.

The Olmecs prospered along the Gulf Coast, especially in the southern parts of the state and in the state of Tabasco. These have come to be viewed by historians and anthropologists as developers of the seminal culture of Mesoamerica. The influence of the Olmecs extended to many other peoples (though not into Yucatán, nor far north). Rather than being wanderers and hunter-gatherers, the Olmecs practiced stable agriculture, for example, in Tres Zapotes and La Venta, from around 1200 BC. The Olmecs are famous for their huge monumental stone sculptures of heads, whose human features (such as heavy lips and broad noses) do not reflect the realities of the physical characteristics of indigenous peoples of Mesoamerica.

The first Spanish expeditions to make a mark on Veracruz were led by Juan de Grijalva, Alonso Dávila, Pedro de Alvarado, and Francisco de Montejo. Grijalva gave his name to a river, as did Alvarado (though his was subsequently renamed Papaloapán). The Spaniards bartered with Indians at Boca del Río, and they discovered and named a number of islands, including Isla de Sacrificios (so named because they found evidence of human sacrifice there) and the important islet that was to be San Juan de Ulúa ("San Juan" because it was found on the day of the Feast of St. John and "Ulúa" because the Spaniards thought they had heard natives saying that word). It was across from San Juan de Ulúa that Hernán Cortés, Mexico's conqueror, first set foot on the mainland on April 22, 1519; because that day was Good Friday, he called the place Villa Rica de la Vera Cruz ("True Cross"). There, the Spaniards would establish the first town hall in the Americas. But because they wanted better terrain and a better climate for this first settlement, they soon moved it north to Quihuiztlan, a Totonac site; there it remained until 1525, when it was again transferred, this time to Huitzilapan (now called La Antigua), only to be brought back to the original site in 1599.

In the summer of 1519, Cortés began his march toward Tenochtitlán, the Aztec capital, leaving some of his captains to keep control of the local natives. Few Spaniards in fact settled in Veracruz in the early years, since most of them preferred the less humid climate of the central *meseta*, but as a port, Veracruz became ever more crucial, both commercially and politically. It was soon designated by the Crown as one of few officially approved points of entry and egress for trade between the Americas and Europe. From Veracruz to the Old World went precious metals, turkeys, corn, avocados, beans, and cotton, while into Mexico came wheat, rice, domestic animals, fabrics, wine, and so on. After the sixteenth century, the port was repeatedly attacked by pirates and by rival nations who were aware of its importance and keen to get in on the American act.

As far as religious jurisdiction was concerned, initially the area was made subject to the diocese of Tlaxcala. In 1527, it was put under that of Huasteca, and from 1535 part of it was answerable to the bishop of Oaxaca.

Largely as a result of disease and exploitation, the Indian population declined dramatically in the years after the Conquest, and so, during the seventeenth century, numbers of black people were brought in, for example to work in the salt marshes. This was also a time of increasing economic instability, social unrest, and insecurity, with unrest among the

Indians, attacks on communities, and highway robberies. In response to this turmoil, the town of Córdoba was founded in 1618 to protect travelers en route between Mexico City and the port of Veracruz. In addition to the trade route via Córdoba and Orizaba, a second one developed via Xalapa and Perote. So it was that in the port of Veracruz there grew a class of prosperous and influential merchants.

Famous natives of Veracruz include two eighteenth-century Jesuits associated with the Enlightenment: **Francisco Xavier Clavijero** (1731–1787) and **Francisco Xavier Alegre** (1729–1788). Clavijero was also a significant historian, driven into exile when the Jesuits were officially banned from the New World in 1767.

The city of Xalapa, which is now the state capital, was founded in 1739 on the site of four Indian settlements. For a while, this city was known as "Xalapa de Las Ferias" due to the fact that, somewhat paradoxically, it came to house the annual Fair of the Fleets, which had been transferred there from Veracruz because the latter was regarded as an unhealthy place. Xalapa became a major clearinghouse for trade between Europe and New Spain.

In 1821, with the revolt against Spain gathering momentum, the last Spanish viceroy, Juan de O'Dónoju, arrived at the port of Veracruz. O'Dónoju was a realist and a conciliator who understood that times were changing. He signed a treaty with Agustín de Iturbide granting Mexico sovereignty and independence, and in so doing no doubt avoided a war that would otherwise have been costly for both countries. Veracruz soon ceased to be an *intendencia*, as it had been under colonial rule, and under the national Constitution of 1824, it became a state; a year later, its own constitution was promulgated. At about that time, the fort of San Juan de Ulúa, the last bastion of Spanish power, was surrendered. This was not quite the end of the story of independence, however; in June 1829, a Spanish brigadier, Isidro Barradas, disembarked at Tampico with three thousand men, intent on retaking the country for Spain, only to be defeated a year later by forces led by Manuel de Mier y Terán and **Antonio López de Santa Anna** (1794–1876).

Santa Anna was born in Xalapa and was destined to become one of the most controversial figures in the history of Mexico. President of the country on several occasions, he was exiled and brought back to power more than once. He dominated much of the country's politics during the first half of the nineteenth century and was prominent at the time of conflict with the United States.

Ignacio de la Llave (1818–1863), who gives his name to the state, had a distinguished legal and political career; spent a while as state governor, during which he reduced taxes on the poor and opened up educational possibilities, stood up to the American invasions, championed the liberal cause against the authoritarian Santa Anna, and eventually became one of President Benito Juárez's government ministers.

During the war with the United States (1846–1847), the port of Veracruz came under a blockade and was heavily bombarded by U.S. forces.

Veracruz was then occupied for a year by the invaders, until the Treaty of Guadalupe Hidalgo was signed in 1848 and Mexico ceded almost half of its territory to the United States. Later, during the Reform War, Juárez set up his liberal government in Veracruz, and from there he promulgated the famous Reform Laws. On May 28, 1864, Maximilian, the surrogate sent by Napoleon III, arrived in Veracruz as Mexico's new emperor, and the Juárez government was forced to migrate inland.

The state enjoyed considerable modernization and growth in the second half of the nineteenth century: among other positive developments, a railway line was opened linking Veracruz, Xalapa, Perote, and Puebla, and electricity and phone services were installed. Under President Porfirio Díaz, there was some unrest in the factories of Orizaba, with workers protesting about their conditions; then, in 1906, textile workers from the state of Veracruz joined with others from Tlaxcala and Puebla, forming the Gran Círculo de Obreros Libres (Grand Circle of Free Workers) and provoking what came to be known as the "Textile War." When Díaz came down on the side of management, the workers refused to go back to work, went on the rampage, and were brutally put down by the police and the military, with a great deal of bloodshed. Disaffection with Díaz was already running high nationally; events in Veracruz encouraged local sympathy with the opposition and ultimately with the national revolution that broke out in 1910. The Revolution had many supporters in places such as Orizaba, Nogales, Río Blanco, and Paso del Macho. Before long, Xalapa and other important towns were in revolutionary hands.

The port of Veracruz was again occupied by U.S. forces in 1914, the justification being that eight naval personnel from the battleship *Dolphin* had been illegally detained after disembarking at Tampico. A number of people lost their lives resisting this new invasion. It was also in 1914 that Veracruz became the seat of Venustiano Carranza's constitutional government; for a while, Veracruz was the country's capital. An imposing statue of Carranza, in a square close to the waterfront at Veracruz, now marks his association with the city. It was from Veracruz that major postrevolutionary social and agrarian reforms were promulgated. In March 1915, the first Preliminary National Congress was held there and the Mexican Confederation of Labor was set up. Indeed, Veracruz has since been a place noted for its labor movements and campaigns for social reform. For example, its unions played an important part in asserting the rights of Mexicans to the benefits of the country's oil.

Distinguished jarocho figures in twentieth-century society and politics included **Miguel Alemán Valdés** (1905–1985), who was born in Sayula, in the southern part of the state, at a time when disaffection with Díaz was rife and there was a good deal of social unrest. He rose via the state governorship to national political office and eventually to the presidency of the country. During his time in office, he introduced some major developments and reforms, such as the construction of the campus of the Universidad

Nacional Autónoma de México, Latin America's largest university. When his six-year term was over, Alemán was still relatively young, and he continued in politics for years. His successor was another native of Veracruz, **Adolfo Ruiz Cortines** (1889–1973). Ruiz Cortines was a revolutionary soldier, then state governor, and eventually president of Mexico from 1952 to 1958. His motto while president was "Austerity and Labor"; he is remembered for his financial discipline, for bringing in agrarian reforms, and for introducing legislation that gave the vote to Mexican women (albeit somewhat later than in other parts of Latin America). **Ursulo Galván** (1892–1930) is remembered as a defender of workers' rights and first president of the Liga Campesina (League of Peasants).

Economy

Approximately 43 percent of the state is given over to the cultivation of corn, sugarcane, chiles, rice, cotton, *chicle*, and tropical fruits such as pawpaw, mango, and citrus. Another 27 percent is pastureland for horses, goats, sheep, and cows. About 4 percent is woodland that produces pine, oak, and so forth, and some 24 percent is jungle that is exploited for tropical woods and palms, providing materials used especially for basketry. An example of craft production is the leather goods (saddlery) of Tantoyuca, a town also known for the baskets, hats, and other articles woven from natural fibers, made by jail inmates. The Gulf waters produce a wide variety of fish and seafood, of which Veracruz is a major national supplier. Major coastal lagoons for food production include Tamiahua, Tampamachoco, Mandinga, and Alvarado.

The oil industry is significant; Veracruz's Cerro Azul 4, one of the country's most productive wells, opened in 1912, and there are others. Oil production in the Gulf states has attracted national and foreign investment since the end of the nineteenth century, when foreign interests were allowed to import machinery and set up operation (for example, the American-owned Huasteca and Aguila companies).

Veracruz also has beer production (Sol), mining (e.g., for sulfur), textile production (especially cotton), and tobacco growing. A number of products are derived from sugarcane.

The tourist industry is significant; quite apart from its historic and cultural interest, Veracruz has many natural attractions, including areas of lush and verdant beauty and a good number of beaches. Visitors come not only to see the scenery but also to practice "extreme" sports. The beaches attract many Mexicans.

Arts

Huasteca is known for its goods woven from natural fibers, such as palm, and also for its musical instruments; Totonacapan for its vanilla figures; the

Isthmus and Las Grandes Montañas for earthenware, and Las Grandes Montañas also for woolen textiles; and the Llanuras de Barlovento (Windward Plains) for wool and tortoiseshell products.

The coastal culture is sometimes described as "Caribe Afroandaluz" (Afro-Andalusian Caribbean). An example of the African influence is the *chuchumbé*, a satirical song/dance form whose usual target during colonial times was the Church. The popular dance known as the *danzón* made its way into the area from Cuba; it was first brought to the city of Veracruz from Cuba in the 1870s by refugees fleeing a war-torn country, and though at first viewed as scandalously sensual, it was eventually adopted by Veracruz high society. Now it can be found in dance clubs throughout the Americas. The Andalusian influence can be seen in the *fandango*, another song/dance form, which is particularly associated with the south of the state and neighboring areas. Fandango performances can last as much as an hour and engage as many as a hundred musicians. There is a state-sponsored traditional dance troupe called the Ballet Folklórico, whose members are aged between 15 and 25, and a state symphony orchestra.

The *huapango* (*son huapango*) is traditional in the Huasteca region and also popular in the state of Tamaulipas. It is an example of a hybrid form that has evolved from the admixture of Indian and Spanish cultures—some say with African input also. Among the many huapangos that exist, four are especially traditional; they are called "El caimán," "La presumida," "La huasanga," and "El caballito." The huapango is purely a social dance and has no other ceremonial significance. Its music is characterized by simultaneous or alternating $6/8$ and $3/4$ rhythms, often fast but sometimes with relaxed, waltz-like interludes during which the musicians are the focus of attention. The accompanists may consist of a violin trio, sometimes with the addition of a *jarana* or *quinta* (both stringed instruments related to the guitar) and a harp, or even a mariachi ensemble. The dance involves complicated changes of position, dramatic gestures, and foot-stamping.

There are many types of *son*. The *son jarocho* is associated primarily with the southern half of the state. Urban versions of the son have also evolved, but not to match the danzón, which is altogether more calm and quite often danced with a full orchestral backing. Other regional song-and-dance forms in the Huasteca region are the *tigrillo* and *gavilanes espejos*. In the Grandes Montañas, there are the *tocotín* and the *huehue*; in Totonacapan, the *negritos* and *guaguas*. The tocotín dance has Totonac and Nahua roots and represents the arrival of the Spaniards and their passage through Xico Viejo.

Perhaps the pre-Hispanic tradition of the *voladores*, the flying men, which is associated with the town of Papantla, is the most intriguing regional phenomenon. Traditionally, the leader of the group of performers of this ritual would make an expedition into the hills in search of a suitable tree for a post. On finding one, he would engage in ritual dance and song and would bow before it, before drinking to each of the cardinal points.

After a path was cleared to ensure that it could be removed without being damaged, the tree was felled and stripped. It would then be rolled on smaller logs and dragged to the ceremonial site, with no one being allowed to step on it, nor any woman to touch it. Once installed in its rightful place, with its platform and ropes, a sacrifice would be made (of a cockerel or seven live chicks, as well as tobacco and *tamales*) to ensure the safety of the flyers. The ceremony, in honor of the sun god, begins with the playing of a small drum and a red flute that represent the deity and a bird. Then four men, symbolizing the earth's cardinal points, fall backward from high up on a small platform and swing upside-down around the post, hanging from the ropes attached to it. The post stands for the connection between heaven and earth, and the rope suggests an umbilical cord. Each of the four flyers goes around thirteen times—four times thirteen makes fifty-two, a very significant figure according to the indigenous worldview, which held that it represented a complete cycle of existence for the universe.

In the visual arts, **Joaquín Santamaría Díaz** (1890–1975), a photographer, left a valuable record of the social classes of the early part of the century and documented the arrival of refugees from Gen. Francisco Franco's Spain.

One of Veracruz's most famous sons is **Agustín Lara** (1900–1970), a songwriter, pianist, and singer known to all Mexicans. Lara was a larger-than-life figure who had a colorful and very successful career that included playing the piano in brothels and being a bullfighter. He had eight wives, one of whom was the Mexican screen goddess María Félix, and many lovers besides. Lara once said that there was little to distinguish a native of Veracruz from an Andalusian, and he often spoke of his fondness for southern Spain; his songs dedicated to the capitals of Andalusian provinces, particularly "Granada," have become widely known; they so pleased Spain's dictator, Franco, that he gave Lara a house in Granada.

Salvador Díaz Mirón (1853–1928), from Xalapa, was a major national poet during the *porfiriato*, a transitional figure on the path toward *modernismo*; he was also active in politics. Díaz Mirón was a passionate individualist whose life had its share of drama and violence; he eventually found himself exiled in Spain and later in Havana. **Jorge Cuesta** (1903–1941) was another poet, associated with the *Ulysses* literary review and with the important group of intellectuals known as the Contemporáneos. His most famous poem is a long one entitled "Canto a un dios mineral."

Sergio Pitol (1933–) is another veracruzano who has close ties with Spain, where his work as a writer has achieved as much recognition as it has in his native country. Pitol is a sophisticated, cosmopolitan writer, one of the most engaging voices in recent Mexican literature, and his own man, not a member of any literary movement or trend. Among his works are the collection of stories *Vals de Mefisto* and the novels *El desfile del amor*, *Domar a la divina garza*, and *La vida conyugal*. Apart from his literary activities, Pitol has worked as a diplomat, including a five-year spell as ambassador to Czechoslovakia. He has won several prizes for his writing, including Spain's prestigious Premio Cervantes.

Social Customs

At Eastertide in 1519, the Spanish explorer Hernán Cortés arrived and founded Villa Rica de la Vera Cruz, the city of the True Cross. It was to grow into a city with ways and rhythms of its own, unlike any other city in Mexico. The port of Veracruz is Mexico's oldest and grandest, a city full of history that has been occupied for one reason or another by people from all sorts of places. This variety is reflected in its present-day communities of Italians, Lebanese, Spaniards, and others. Racially, culturally, and linguistically, this is essentially a Caribbean town, with an atmosphere that is a little like the New Orleans of the mid-twentieth century: steamy, laid-back, and noisy—except that here the music is not jazz, but a cacophony of marimba bands, mariachis, danzón music, and other varieties. To these sounds are added the cries of street vendors and traffic noise, plus the sounds associated with the comings and goings of sea vessels.

Social life begins around noon in the main square, which is surrounded by galleried *portales*, and in cafés such as the Gran Café del Portal (begun by some Spaniards in a former monastery building in 1835, and a favored haunt of Mexican presidents) and the Café de la Parroquia, beside the promenade. In both, the custom is to summon a waiter by tapping one's glass with a spoon. It is said that the habit arose because a trolley car driver would ring his bell a block from one of the cafés to let the waiters know that he was on his way.

Festivities in Veracruz include Carnival, for which the state, and especially the port city, are renowned; La Candelaria on the coastal plains (February); San José (March) and Santa Cruz (May) in the sierras; Corpus Christi, especially in Papantla (June); the Feast of Santiago in Santiago Tuxtla (July); the Virgen del Carmen in Catemaco (July); and the Virgen de Guadalupe everywhere (December). Fairs are held in Boca del Río (the Cattle Fair in May or June), Coatepec (a coffee fair in April and May), Córdoba (a trade fair in May), and Fortín de las Flores (the Flower Festival in April/May).

As an example of the festivities, the Feria de la Virgen de la Candelaria in Tlacotalpan involves popular contemporary music and dancing, traditional folkloric dancing, religious ceremonies, bullfights, races, and other sporting competitions, cockfights, *charrerías* (rodeos), old-time entertainments like greased poles, flour fights, and cats in sacks, and, of course, parades and parties.

In Veracruz during the Christmas season, children go through the streets bearing branches and entoning passages from the scriptures, in a custom called "Las Ramas." After that comes "El Viejo," in which people dress up as old men, or parade effigies of them, to symbolize the passing of the old year.

Catemaco hosts an annual Congreso de Brujos. Wizards and witches believe that their powers increase on the first Friday of the third month of the year, enabling them to purge themselves of evil influences. Hence they convene at that time and celebrate a White Mass, starting at midnight Thursday night. The chosen place is cordoned off to prevent intruders from entering, and then the ground is marked out with lines to indicate where the ceremony is to be conducted. Unlit torches are strategically located around this area and a star is drawn, also highlighted with torches. Another star is made from sticks and cloth, to be set alight with purifying fire. The five points of this star, the pentagram, serve to summon evil and the Devil. In comes the wizard celebrant, clad in white, to order that the fires be lit; then he utters some ritual words, and a black chicken, representing evil, is sacrificed. In adjacent areas, other minor rites of purification are carried out, and there are stalls with magic herbs and potions on sale.

At night in Veracruz City, in front of the Palacio Municipal, bands of old men play for couples who dance the deliberate and elegant steps of the *danzón*; in fact, Veracruz is credited with launching it. Many people stroll in the evening along the *malecón* (promenade), which stretches for miles along the Gulf of Mexico to the outlying suburbs and the beaches of Boca del Río. Veracruz is popular vacation territory for Mexican nationals.

The traditional women's dress has Spanish roots, but heavy European fabrics have naturally given way to lighter ones, such as muslin and cotton. Relatively simple styles in the early colonial period evolved into more elaborate ones. What has come to be viewed as traditional jarocha dress is in fact a nineteenth-century style: pastel colors are sometimes the basis for this clothing, but it tends above all to be white, with half-sleeves and a full skirt with flounces. There is a single-colored silk shawl (*rebozo*) to match a headband with a bow on top of it, a gathering of roses over one ear (the precise position reflecting the woman's status—on the left for single, on the right for married), and finally an elaborate tortoiseshell *peineta* (hairclip). The woman normally carries a fan and wears jewelry handed down by members of her family.

Another form of typical dress is used for dancing the huapango, based on traditional Huasteca Indian clothing. For women, it consists of a simple sleeveless white blouse and a wide, pleated, calf-length skirt. On top is a *quechquemitl*, a wide shawl that runs around the shoulders and crosses at the front, making a V shape at the waist; the basic white of this shawl contrasts with a thin, vividly colored band along its upper edge and a broader band of the same colors, together with tassels, along the lower edge. Necklaces are worn and a fan is held. Men wear a *guayabera* shirt, from which four strings of saddlebags hang. Around their necks, they wear red kerchiefs, and the outfit is completed with white trousers, boots, and a straw hat with an ornamental band.

All over Mexico, soccer is overwhelmingly the most popular team sport. However, baseball also has a significant following in Veracruz.

Noteworthy Places

Veracruz City's many elegant buildings, painted in lively, even outrageous colors, speak of its historical importance. Much of the city has a run-down appearance, and some of its historic buildings are now juxtaposed with unsightly modern structures. Nevertheless, Veracruz has a number of points of interest, including the Museo de la Ciudad (City Museum), a naval museum, a modern aquarium (the largest in Latin America), and a neoclassical post office building (from the time of the porfiriato, like Mexico City's). A little way along the coast to the south is a museum in a house given by a state governor to an internationally known son of Veracruz, the musician Agustín Lara. Lara's song "Veracruz" has become a sort of local anthem.

The weather-beaten Fort of San Juan Ulúa bears testimony to the dark days of piracy and the Spanish Inquisition. It was first built as a castle in the 1500s, but the danger of attack from foreign powers prompted the Spanish authorities to begin fortifying it in 1635. It was finished in 1707 and later served as a prison. Narrow stone-lined passageways lead to a

Steet in the old section of Xalapa.

On the main square in Veracruz.

labyrinth of dungeons with walls as much as 7 meters (24 feet) thick; the more serious the crime, the hotter and darker the cell. Among its famous inmates were Benito Juárez (before he was exiled to Louisiana), Fray Servando Teresa de Mier (a rebel writer just before independence), and "Chucho el Roto," a Robin Hood–style bandit of the 1700s. San Juan de Ulúa ceased to be a prison under Carranza. Between about 1880 and 1910, the population of the city quintupled, with immigrants from China, Syria, and Lebanon, as well as from the more traditional sources.

The capital, Xalapa, in many ways a rival of Veracruz, boasts luxuriant vegetation, several parks (among them the Parque Juárez, one of Mexico's finest town squares), a cathedral, some cobbled streets, an anthropological museum, a modern art museum, the University of Veracruz (Universidad Veracruzana), and above all a lovely location. It also lends its name to the famous *jalapeño* peppers. At Xico, not far from Xalapa, are the picturesque Falls of Texolo. There are other interesting towns in Veracruz, as well, such as Tlacotalpan and Papantla.

Archaeological sites can be found at Tres Zapotes, Zempoalla, El Tajín, Cacahatenango, and Tabuco. The most important of these is El Tajín, a Totonac site near the town of Papantla. *Tajín* means "thunder" in Totonac, although it is not certain that this was its original name nor indeed that the place was built by Totonacs. El Tajín was lost from sight for a long time, and it was only in the eighteenth century that a tobacco inspector drew it to public attention. Diego Rivera later made it the focus of one of his murals for the National Palace in Mexico City. The modern site has a museum, in front of which the ritual of the voladores is performed. El Tajín developed late in the first millennium, when a rural settlement became associated with the worship of Quetzalcóatl (the Plumed Serpent). Solid constructions were built, with a ceremonial ball court. In its heyday, El Tajín, including its outlying suburbs, is estimated to have had a population of 20,000 to 25,000, and its influence extended to more people yet. El Tajín has a "square" with a pyramid called the Pirámide de Los Nichos due to the fact that it has 360 niches, one for each day in the solar year. There is a second group of buildings called the Plaza de Tajín Chico (Little Tajín Square), one of whose components has polychromatic paintings with ritual themes.

Cuisine

The state of Veracruz is the source of the best coffee in Mexico. A favored drink is the *lechero*, which is comparable to an Italian *latte*. One place that thrives on coffee production is the small and attractive town of Coatepec, near Xalapa, which has its own coffee festival. The state's fish and seafood also have a national reputation, and dishes such as *huachinango a la veracruzana* (snapper Veracruz style) or that same fish with mango sauce (*con salsa de mango*) can be found on the menus of some of the country's classiest restaurants. Very much in evidence are *neverías*, which are establishments that sell crushed ice flavored with tropical fruits.

Arroz a la Tumbada

This is a poor people's dish that has become fashionable in the best restaurants of Mexico, a seafood and rice dish somewhat like the Spanish *paella*. Its identity varies according to whatever seafood is available and the preferences of the cook. Traditionally, the dish is prepared in earthenware vessels and is *tumbado*, that is, put briefly into a wood-fired oven, just before being served.

Ingredients:

> Seafood: any combination of shrimp, baby clams, crab, squid, oysters, octopus, sea snails, fish, and fish roe
> Tomatoes
> Onions
> Garlic
> *Chipotle* chiles
> Olive oil or lard
> Water or stock
> Salt and pepper
> Herbs (cilantro, *epazote*, mint, oregano)

The basic technique is to shell and cut the seafood (except the fish) into manageable pieces, then briefly sauté them in lard or olive oil. Crush or blend the tomatoes together with the garlic, onion, and chiles and add to the shellfish. Cook for a few minutes, stirring frequently, then add the pieces of fish, together with warm water or stock, and simmer. Meanwhile, fry the rice briefly in a separate pan. Combine the two dishes, season to taste, and leave to simmer until the rice is cooked. Garnish with slices of green chiles.

Pescado a la Veracruzana

Ingredients:

> 6 thick slices of filleted white fish (e.g., snapper or grouper)
> 1 onion, sliced
> 2 tomatoes, peeled and chopped
> 1 clove of garlic, crushed
> 1 green pepper, cut into strips
> 1 *curtido* chile, cut into strips
> 2 tsp capers
> 10 whole green olives
> 1/2 glass dry white wine
> 1 tbsp parsley, chopped
> 3 bay leaves
> Salt and pepper

Place all ingredients except the fish in a pan and simmer gently until the volume of liquid has reduced by half. Add the fish and cover. Reduce heat to low and let simmer for 20 minutes, or place in a moderate oven. The broth should be fairly thick by the time it is served. This dish improves if kept for a day.

Calabaza en Tacha

Ingredients:

> 10 cups water
> 2 lb. brown sugar
> 8 cinnamon sticks
> 1 tsp aniseeds
> 1 tsp cloves
> 2 large pumpkins
> 4 tbsp lime (*cal*)

Heat the water in a large pot and add the sugar and cinnamon. Place the aniseeds and the cloves in a small muslin pouch, tie it securely, and put it in the pot. Cook gently for about 3 hours until it is like honey. Meanwhile, cut up the pumpkins into chunks and put these in a pot with enough water to cover them. Add the lime and leave to soak until the first pot is ready. Now drain and rinse the pumpkin, combine it with the syrup, and cook over a low heat until the pumpkin is tender.

Veracruz

This is a cocktail invented in the city.

Ingredients:

    2 parts tequila
    2 parts melon liqueur
    4 parts pineapple juice
    2 parts grapefruit juice

Mix vigorously in a cocktail shaker and serve in a tall glass over ice, or in the bowl of half a melon from which the flesh has been scooped out.

Caldo Largo

Ingredients:

    2 lb. fish heads and bones
    6 fish fillets
    1 celery stalk
    1 onion, finely chopped
    1 clove of garlic
    3 tomatoes, chopped
    1½ cups peeled and diced potatoes
    1½ cups diced carrots
    Pickled jalapeños (or *serrano* chiles)
    1 *guajillo* chile
    1 tsp fresh cilantro
    2 bay leaves
    Pinch of *epazote*
    2 pinches of oregano
    Salt
    Olive oil
    Enough water to cover ingredients when boiling

In a deep pan, heat a little olive oil, then add the garlic, onion, and celery and fry them gently for 2 to 3 minutes. Add the chopped-up fish bones and heads, water, cilantro, bay leaves, and a little salt and bring to boiling. Cover and simmer for about half an hour. Take out the bones and heads, saving any flesh. When cool enough, strain through a sieve. Clean out the guajillo chile and blend it with a little of the stock, then strain this before sautéing it in a little olive oil. Add the tomatoes and, after a few minutes, the fish stock and the epazote. When this comes to a boil, add the potatoes and carrots. Simmer for 15 minutes, season, and then add the oregano and the fish fillets. Cook a little longer until the fish becomes flaky. Garnish with the jalapeños.

Volovanes de Cangrejo

Ingredients:

4 vol-au-vents
1 pint fish stock
1 tbsp cream
$1/4$ lb. crabmeat
Juice of 1 lime
1 glass dry white wine
1 bay leaf
1 oz. butter
Flour
Dill
Salt

Boil the crabmeat in the fish stock, together with the lime juice, the bay leaf, and some salt. Make a roux with the butter and a little flour, then, stirring all the while, slowly add the wine and finally the cream. Season. Fill the vol-au-vents with the drained crabmeat and cover with the sauce. Place in the oven at 350°F for approximately 10 minutes. Serve sprinkled with dill.

Yucatán

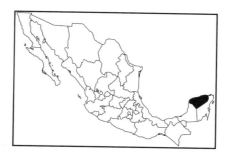

State Characteristics

It is said that when Hernández de Córdova, a Spanish explorer, arrived on the coast of Yucatán and asked the natives what the place was called, they responded by saying that he was speaking too quickly and they could not understand. The Spaniards, not understanding that response, adapted some of the sounds they heard and came up with the name "Yucatán." Some, however, have argued that the name has its origin in the language of the Aztecs, Náhuatl, and that it means "Place of Riches."

The modern state of Yucatán shares the Yucatán Peninsula with two other states, Campeche and Quintana Roo. Campeche is to its west and southwest, Quintana Roo to its east and southeast, and the Gulf of Mexico to its north. The state of Yucatán occupies 43,379 square kilometers (16,918 square miles), which is equivalent to 2.21 percent of Mexico. The capital city is Mérida; with a population of 734,153, this is the thirteenth largest city in Mexico, and the only city with more than 50,000 inhabitants in the whole of the state of Yucatán. Yucatán's newspapers are all published in Mérida: *Diario de Yucatán, Por Esto, Diario del Sureste, Milenio, Novedades, El Mundo al Día, Diario de la Tarde, De Peso,* and *LAI.*

The 2005 census gives the total state population as 1,818,948. At approximately 40 people per square kilometer (16 per square mile), the population density is fairly low. Yucatán has 106 administrative municipalities, grouped into nine regions. The state is represented by nine people in the National Congress. Approximately 84 percent of the population is Catholic and 11 percent Protestant. There are four institutions of higher education.

Yucatán is an exceptionally flat and uniform state, although it does have minor ranges of hills; the highest elevation is only 210 meters (693 feet). Yucatán is a limestone table with little by way of topsoil and no surface rivers, but with copious underground supplies of water, in aquifers that make up a system that feeds into the sea. The underground waters are at depths of 2 to 3 meters (7-10 feet) near the coast but can be as deep as 115 meters (350 feet) in the southern part of the state. Although there are no rivers as such, water is sometimes visible from the surface at points where the limestone covering has collapsed, forming sizable wells or lakes; locally, these are called *cenotes, rejolladas,* or *aguadas*. Twelve percent of the land is devoted to agriculture and almost 6 percent to pastureland; 3 percent is mangrove swamp, and 78 percent is jungle.

The climate is generally very warm and humid, though somewhat less humid along the northern coast. Depending on location, the average annual temperatures range from 25° to 28°C (76°–82°F) and the rainfall averages between 470 and 930 millimeters (19-37 inches) annually. In the capital city of Mérida, temperatures range from daily maxima of 40°C (104°F) to minima of 14°C (57°F), and the average humidity from 61 percent to 83 percent. In most areas, rain falls primarily at the end of the spring, is moderate, and is generally accompanied by winds from the east. In the south, the rainfall is heavier, while on the coast, rain is relatively infrequent.

There are more than 320 kilometers (200 miles) of coastline (3.3 percent of the country's total), most of which has shallow seas, sandy beaches, lagoons, and sandbanks. About 48 kilometers (30 miles) north of the coast from Progreso lie the Arrecife de Alacranes and the Cayo Arenas—several small, barren crescent-shaped islands that are home to thousands of birds that feed on the abundant fish stocks. Yucatán is a place for birds—it has been estimated that there are 443 different bird species in the state, which is almost half of the total number of species found in Mexico. Of these, 233 species are resident and about a dozen of those are endemic to the state, including the ocellated turkey and Yucatán varieties of the yellow-lored parrot, poorwill, nightjar, woodpecker, flycatcher, jay, wren, black catbird, rose-throated tanager, and orange oriole. Yucatán is also famous for its colonies of flamingos. Among other common forms of wildlife are rabbits, deer, foxes, pumas, jaguars, crocodiles, snakes, iguanas, and turtles. Over much of the terrain, the vegetation consists primarily of deciduous tropical jungle, with thorny undergrowth.

Cultural Groups and Languages

Of the people over five years of age, more than a third were reported in the 2005 census to be speakers of indigenous languages; only the state of Oaxaca has more indigenous-language speakers than Yucatán. The cultural heritage and present-day influence of the Mayas is felt all over the state.

Remnants of the past Mayan civilization can be seen in a great many places, while the role of Mayan culture in our own times is omnipresent. It is to be seen in the way people dress, in the cuisine, and perhaps above all in the impact of Mayan language on local Spanish. For example, in *yucateco* Spanish pronunciation, there is sometimes a lengthening of stressed vowels and a turning of a final [n] into an [m]. In most parts of Mexico, when indigenous terms enter Spanish, their form is adapted to the host system. This happens in Yucatán, for example, with the verb *anolar* (to gnaw), which is adapted from the Mayan verb *anolah*. However, this sort of adaptation is unusual in Yucatán, where the norm is for the original Mayan term to be accepted into Spanish without modification; examples are *chich* (grandmother), *pepén* (butterfly), *xik'* (armpit), *chuchul* (dry), *k'olis* (bald), *popots'ki* (slippery), *chen* (only, simply), and *han* (quickly). The Mayan influence is largely a local phenomenon, and it makes Yucatán different; whereas the Aztecs were imperialists and had an influence on many parts of Mexico, the Mayas did not expand their empire and aggressively spread their culture.

The Mayan language has far more speakers in Yucatán than in the neighboring states. It is overwhelmingly the dominant indigenous language in the state of Yucatán, accounting for over 97 percent of all indigenous-language speakers. The remaining 3 percent is largely made up of speakers of Chol, Tzeltal, and Zapotec, of whom there are perhaps a thousand in all.

One important sociolinguistic difference regarding the use of Mayan in Yucatán, as compared to the use of indigenous languages elsewhere in Mexico, is that it is found in several strata of society and generally does not suffer the same stigma as do indigenous languages in other states. Knowing Mayan can actually be a feather in the cap of the bourgeoisie and those in authority; one hears such people as priests, businesspeople, and public officials speaking it. In rural contexts, Mayan is not simply the language of the peasants but also the language of those with authority and influence. In the corn-growing area of Cantamayec, for example, it is almost an official language, used both in relaxed social situations and in formal meetings. In other places, the use of Mayan is restricted to the family context.

The Mayan language in Yucatán has suffered a decline, partly as a result of emigration of Mayan speakers to other parts of the country or abroad. Many have gone to neighboring Quintana Roo to work in the tourist industry. Another factor is the "modernization" of rural areas, where traditions are changing and Spanish is growing in strength. Education in Spanish, including well-intentioned campaigns against illiteracy, has reduced the number of monolingual Mayan speakers, as has increasing exposure to the media. Aware that this is the case, some institutions and individuals have been taking steps to preserve the use of Mayan; one example is Mérida's Centro de Estudios del Mundo Maya (Center for the Study of the Mayan World). The culture of today's Mayan peoples is a lively hybrid with the Hispanic, but they remain deeply rooted in their own traditions.

History

There were two Mayan empires. The first, which reached its peak about AD 700 during the Classical Period of Mesoamerican civilizations, was centered on parts of what are now Guatemala and Honduras and the Mexican state of Chiapas. For reasons that have never become fully clear—perhaps war, a natural disaster, or disease—quite suddenly the Mayas abandoned those lands and moved northeastward to the Yucatán Peninsula. This they made the site of their second empire, which lasted from 987 until well after the arrival of the Spaniards.

From the time of their transfer to Yucatán, the Mayas came under the influence of other indigenous peoples, in particular the Toltecs, who were then dominant in central Mexico. The result is that the Yucatán empire became a cultural hybrid, as can be deduced from the architecture of its most famous cities, Chichen-Itzá and Uxmal. Not only are the reasons for abandoning the territory of the first empire unclear, but nor is it clear why the second empire had gone into decline before the Spaniards arrived: the Mayan astronomers and architects had disappeared, their cities had been abandoned, and the people were scattered and disorganized or in conflict with one another.

The Spaniards' first contact with the peninsula was made in 1511, when there was a shipwreck off the coast. Two men, Gonzalo de Guerrero and Jerónimo de Aguilar, survived and lived among the Mayas. Guerrero became fully integrated into the indigenous society, while Aguilar rejoined the Spaniards after encountering Hernán Cortés on the latter's arrival in the peninsula in 1519; Aguilar served Cortés as an interpreter during the conquest of Mexico.

Prior to that, in 1517, an expedition headed by Francisco Hernández de Córdoba had come to Isla Mujeres and Cabo Catoche—an event that marks the start of the exploration of the Yucatán Peninsula, today home to three states: Campeche, Quintana Roo, and Yucatán. Hernández de Córdoba's men were defeated by the natives and had to retreat to Cuba, which at the time was Spain's base for westward explorations.

A second expedition, under Juan de Grijalva, nephew of the governor of Cuba, sailed along the eastern coast and disembarked in Cozumel. After a more fortunate battle, he established the town of Campeche in 1518. Grijalva's name was given to one of the most important rivers of the state of Campeche. After that, the Spaniards moved on to explore and conquer other parts of Mexico, and it was some time before they paid serious attention to the Yucatán Peninsula. Francisco de Montejo, who had been empowered by Emperor Charles V of Spain to colonize it, headed a third expedition that led to the foundation of the city of Mérida in 1542, on the site of a former Mayan settlement called Ichcanzihó.

At the start of the colonial era, the Yucatán Peninsula was administered by the Audiencia de los Confines, whose seat was in present-day

Guatemala, but in 1560 a royal decree determined that it should come under Mexico City's jurisdiction. It is at about that time that Fray **Diego de Landa** (1524–1579) appeared on the scene; he was a friar chosen by the Franciscans to direct their operations in the peninsula, and he was to go down in history as a man who destroyed a large part of the Mayan culture. In 1562, Landa issued an official condemnation of the Indians for idolatry, and in a place called Maní he had many of their priceless documents and artifacts burned as a form of retribution for their practice of human sacrifice. Also in 1562, the peninsula received its first bishop, Francisco del Toral, who complained to the Spanish authorities about Landa's behavior, with the result that the latter was forced to return to Spain. Landa later set about writing what was to become an invaluable source of information about Mayan life, religion, and language, his *Relación de las cosas de Yucatán* (Account of Things in Yucatán). After Toral's death, Landa returned to Yucatán as bishop. His work was published three hundred years after he wrote it.

The peninsula was a place of constant Indian uprisings during the colonial period, and It was only in 1697 that the Spaniards finally gained control of it when they took Petén Itzá, the last pocket of resistance. A remarkable early figure who has entered peninsular mythology was **José Jacinto Uc de los Santos Canek** (d. 1761), a Mayan in the service of the Catholic friars. From them, Canek acquired a good education, but this did nothing to reduce his loathing of the invaders. Once expelled from the religious order, he began to appear at local festivities and celebrations, where he would use his historical knowledge and bilingual skills to drum up support for violent rebellion. In 1761, Canek was taken prisoner by the Spaniards and sentenced to death. He was hung, drawn, and quartered, after which his body was burned in Mérida's main square. He thus became a symbolic figure for Mayan resistance over the centuries.

Isolation from Mexico City meant that Yucatán always enjoyed a certain degree of liberty; indeed, at several points in its history, there have been drives for peninsular independence from central control. One result of Yucatán's remoteness was that the movement for independence from Spain, early in the nineteenth century, did not have any real military effect, though the spirit of independence was certainly alive there.

Andrés Quintana Roo (1787–1851), a native of Mérida, was a lawyer who moved to Mexico City, where he actively supported Father Miguel Hidalgo's call for independence from Spain and published an influential paper called *El Ilustrador Americano*, together with a manifesto on the subject of independence. At the first Mexican congress in 1813, Quintana Roo was elected vice president, and it was he who signed the formal declaration of Mexican independence. He served as a Supreme Court judge under Agustín de Iturbide, and thereafter as a member of congress and government minister. Quintana Roo was a leader of public opinion and one of the first individuals to offer financial support for the fight against the French invasion. He also found time to write poetry and translate the Psalms.

In Yucatán itself at the time of the beginnings of the independence movement, a group of yucatecos, inspired by the liberal constitution that had been drawn up in the city of Cádiz in opposition to Napoleon's control of Spain, had been pressing to have its provisions in favor of greater social equality in matters of taxes and land tenure put into effect in the peninsula. This liberal group became known as the Sanjuanistas, and one of its leading lights was **Lorenzo de Zavala** (1789–1836), an energetic advocate of democratic reforms whose activities put him in prison for three years. In 1820, a Confederación Patriótica (Patriotic Confederation) was set up, but it soon split into two factions, one that was in support of adopting Spain's new constitution and the other in favor of complete independence from colonial rule. Zavala was sent to Madrid to represent Yucatán's interests, but in the meantime the Plan de Iguala had been hatched elsewhere in Mexico, and in 1821 that ushered in Iturbide's independent Mexican Empire, of which Yucatán formally became part. After the demise of that short-lived empire, Yucatán became a state of the new Mexican Republic under the 1824 Constitution.

The constitution of the state of Yucatán was ratified in 1825, when the governor of the state was none other than Antonio López de Santa Anna. Zavala had by then returned to Mexico and taken part in the Constituent Congress, becoming a member of the Mexican Senate. He went on to serve as governor of the state of México, finance minister under President Vicente Guerrero Saldaña, and ambassador to France under Santa Anna. However, because he felt Santa Anna was not showing due respect for the constitution, Zavala left his service and moved his family to Texas, where he had been authorized to settle five hundred families. Thus he made his way into Texas politics, where he actively supported federalism, in opposition to Santa Anna.

The first half of the nineteenth century was characterized by political instability, with struggles between centralists who wished to see power concentrated in Mexico City and federalists who sought greater regional and state autonomy. The possibility of an independent Yucatán Peninsula was rarely off the agenda. In 1835, a movement led by **Miguel Barbachano** (1806–1859), five times governor of the state, led to Yucatán becoming free of Mexico City's control for a number of years. In 1841, the state constitution was amended to grant greater religious and press freedom and to enhance individual legal rights.

Yucatán was obliged to return to the fold when it needed support in dealing with the Caste War (*Guerra de Castas*) in 1848. The Caste War arose because of the desperate living conditions of the Mayas and their abuse by the *criollos* and mestizos, who considered themselves the legitimate yucatecos and regarded the Mayas as a separate and generally inferior people. Incited by opponents of the central government and resentful about unkept promises of reforms, the Mayas took to arms, led by Cecilio Chí and Jacinto Pat. The war began in 1847 in a town called Tepich. The Mayas went on to take over most of the peninsula, and Barbachano had to ask Mexico City for help. It was a very drawn-out conflict whose official end came only in 1901.

The midcentury also saw two foreign invasions of Mexico. In the concluding battle after the U.S. invasion in 1846, one of Yucatán's heroes was Lt. Col. **Juan Crisóstomo Cano y Cano** (1815–1847), who lost his life at Chapultepec Castle in Mexico City. However, back in Yucatán, there were those who saw the United States as a possible ally. **Justo Sierra O'Reilly** (1814–1861) was, as his name suggests, of Irish and Hispanic descent. Born in Yucatán, he had made a name as a lawyer, politician, and writer, and he was legal adviser to the state's General Assembly at a time when it declared Yucatán independent of the central Mexico City government—a move that was crushed by Santa Anna. When the Mexican-American War broke out, Yucatán declared itself neutral, and U.S. forces occupied one of its islands. O'Reilly was sent as a special envoy to Washington to negotiate U.S. evacuation of the island, but also to offer the peninsula to the United States in exchange for military assistance in dealing with the rebellious Mayas. That mission did not succeed, although it was seriously debated in the U.S. Congress. At the same time, Mérida also made similar overtures to Spain and Great Britain.

After Mexico's internal struggle known as the Reform War, the country suffered a second invasion, by the French, starting in 1862. Soon it found it was no longer a republic with a president but was being ruled by Maximilian of Austria, an emperor installed by Napoleon III. True to its independent spirit, Yucatán sided with the invaders.

The first step in the reduction of Yucatán to the territorial limits of today's state was taken in 1857, when Campeche was separated off and became a state in its own right. The second came some fifty years later, when President Porfirio Díaz took a part of Yucatán that was occupied by Mayas and made it into a new territory, called Quintana Roo; this, too, would eventually become a state.

As in other parts of the country, Díaz's long rule brought stability and industrial progress, but it was an authoritarian regime that did not tolerate opposition, and the benefits of the material progress went only to a privileged minority of Mexicans or to foreigners. Some three hundred large *haciendas* were established in Yucatán during the nineteenth century, with the land controlled by only a few people, and the distribution of wealth did not improve. Such inequalities, coupled with traditional exploitation of Mayan labor, favored a revolutionary spirit.

A significant sign that the 1910 Revolution, which had so dramatically affected other parts of Mexico, was reaching even as far as Yucatán was the arrival in Mérida in 1915 of Gen. Salvador Alvarado at the head of seven thousand troops—an event that marked the start of a series of social and political reforms. In 1922, Felipe Carillo Puerto became governor of Yucatán and introduced radical changes, particularly affecting land tenure. He also founded the Universidad Nacional del Sureste, later to become the Universidad de Yucatán. Carillo Puerto was assassinated by federal troops in 1924. In 1937, President Lázaro Cárdenas, one of Mexico's most significant presidents and reformers, came to Yucatán and spent almost a month working personally on land redistribution to create *ejidos*, cooperative land holdings under the control of the rural poor.

The first Mayan person to be elected to the governorship of the state was Francisco Luna Kan, in 1976. At the end of the twentieth century, Yucatán elected its first woman governor, Ivonne Ortega.

Economy

For much of the colonial period, some people in Yucatán had prospered, thanks to the exploitation of Mayan labor and of one crop: *henequén* (sisal), sometimes referred to as "green gold." Trade had to be via the sea. Even well into the twentieth century, trade with the Caribbean, the United States, and Europe was more significant than with other parts of Mexico. The railroad made its first run in Yucatán in 1865, between Campeche and Mérida, but only in 1950 did Mérida get a train link to Mexico City; a rudimentary air service, begun in 1929, was upgraded to jet service in the 1960s, but the cheapest means of transportation was undoubtedly still by sea, through the ports of Río Lagartos, San Felipe, El Cuyo, and Las Coloradas.

Sisal is a tough, coarse fiber used for making durable articles such as ropes and mats. It was the very basis of the peninsular economy until after World War II, when competition increased as other parts of the world also began to grow sisal, and artificial fibers began to become available. Thanks to the prosperity brought by sisal, though, Mérida had electric lights before Mexico City did. It is said that at the beginning of the twentieth century there were proportionally more rich people in Yucatán than in any other part of Latin America. Some evidence of the prosperity of those times can be seen in Mérida's Champs Elysées–inspired Paseo Montejo, with its imposing mansions. Cordemex, a national enterprise that set about industrializing the production of sisal, ostensibly for the benefit of the workers, was created in 1961. In 1984, the state was signatory to a new economic plan agreed upon with Mexico City, the Programa de Reordenación Henequenera y Desarrollo Integral de Yucatán (Program for the Reorganization of the Sisal Industry and the Economic Development of Yucatán).

The almost total reliance on henequén caused serious problems when the market slipped away, but state agriculture diversified thereafter, to produce such things as corn, beans, sugarcane, melons, avocados, mangoes, and citrus fruits. Yucatán is one of Mexico's important states for livestock, in particular for cattle, pigs, and horses. Fishing is important in Progreso, Celestún, Yucalpetén, Telchac Puerto, Dzilam de Bravo, San Felipe, Río Lagartos, and El Cuyo; common species caught are grouper, snapper, bream, bass, anchovies, sardines, shark, swordfish, crustaceans, and shellfish. The few hilly areas have valuable woods, such as cedar and mahogany, but most sea-level forest consists of low trees and thorny undergrowth, with mangroves and swamps along parts of the coast. Celestún is one of several places where sea salt is extracted.

Apart from sisal products, industrial firms in Yucatán produce textiles, process foods and tobacco, and make beer. Mayan clothing is quite popular abroad, but a lot of production is hand-embroidered on an artisan level. By the end of the eighteenth century, the *guayabera* was the standard garment of the upper-class male in Yucatán, and it generally came from Cuba. After the rise of Fidel Castro to power in Cuba, Yucatán took to making its own guayaberas and creating its own characteristic designs for them, only to be undercut by competition from the Far East. The textile factories that survived did so by diversifying their production.

Cultural tourism is a very significant contributor to the economy, and recreational tourism is on the increase. The state is culturally rather different from the rest of Mexico; it has archaeological sites that are richer and more interesting than those of most states, and it also has natural attractions such as cenotes, grottoes, and sandy beaches.

Arts

One of the skills of the ancient Mayas was stone carving, to meet both practical domestic and ritual needs. There are still places today where one can find people who make *metates* and other such useful objects, using only chisels. Others make decorative objects such as figures of animals and reproductions of ancient ceremonial artifacts. Two animals that were much revered by the Mayas are the deer and the jaguar, whose skins they would cure with lime and the bark of local trees before using them as clothing or for decoration. With the arrival of the Spaniards, they also turned to curing the skins of livestock, using the same techniques to make horse-riding gear as well as accessories such as belts, shoes, and bags. In present times, there are places that specialize in these crafts also.

Another craft is the making of rope sandals. *Bejuco* is a thin liana that grows in the hills; it is used in the construction of houses and to make household objects such as baskets, sometimes taking advantage of its different natural colors to make fine patterns. The embroidery for which Yucatán is famous is done by men as well as women, using several quite complex techniques, some from the Mayan tradition, some European. Hammocks are the traditional places to sleep, though the origin of the practice is not quite clear. These brightly colored and attractive creations are mostly made in the municipalities of Tixkokob, Chumayel, and Teabo.

There are some distinctive aspects to the dancing and music of Yucatán and its former possession, Quintana Roo. In the course of the pig's head dance, for instance, the participants dance with trays on their heads, and on those trays are decorated pigs' heads. Those watching may bid for the pigs' heads, and if a person receives one, he may take it home, but in doing so he enters into an obligation to supply two for the following year's celebration. Another example is a sort of maypole dance called the *baile de las cintas*.

Yucatán has its own traditional musical genre, the *trova*. This is a type of popular romantic song that rose to prominence in the early part of the twentieth century, having migrated to Yucatán from eastern Cuba at a time when musical serenades performed as duets and accompanied by the guitars were in vogue, and reaching its heyday in the 1920s. The genre underwent a similar development in countries such as Puerto Rico and Colombia. The traditional instrumental ensemble for the *trova yucateca* is a trio consisting of two guitars (one to carry the rhythm and one for the bass line) and a *requinto*, another, higher-pitched string instrument. Trovas can be in various forms, such as waltzes, *pasillos*, or *habaneras* (the last two revealing Colombian and Cuban influence, respectively). Subgenres are the *bambuco*, the *clave*, and the *bolero*. The most famous exponents of the trova yucateca have been Ricardo Palmerín, Guty Cárdenas, and Narciso Serradel. In 1909, Luis Rosado Vega, a local poet, published the first collection of trova lyrics, including some by **José Peón Contreras** (1843–1907), a leading poet and dramatist and the founder of Mérida's Teatro Principal. The trova genre is, of course, a reflection of Yucatán's close commercial ties with Havana and Cartagena, Colombia's northern port. Many of the songs are about love; others praise nature, lament tragic events, or speak of melancholy; and some are even allegorical. In its most traditional form, the trova melody is shared by two voices, but after the middle of the twentieth century the traditional duet was replaced by a trio.

The *jarana*, a song/dance genre found in many parts of the country, is also much in evidence in Yucatán. The best-known musical composer and performer of jaranas from Yucatán was **José Jacinto Cuevas** (1821–1878).

Yucateco painters include Fernando Castro Pacheco, Manuel Lizama Salazar, and Sergio Cuevas. The state art collection includes sculptures by Enrique Gotdiener, as well as canvases from the colonial period and by modern artists such as Armando García Franchi. In the Bishops' Gallery of Mérida's cathedral, there are portraits of the early evangelists of the colonial era.

After Mexico City, Yucatán has one of the strongest theatrical traditions in the country, traceable back to the ceremonial spectacles of the ancient Mayas. In the twentieth century, there was a revival of this tradition, mostly in the form of short plays full of local color, often incorporating music and dance. In fact, Yucatán became a sort of haven for theater people—so much so that in 1917 there were more theaters in Mérida than in Mexico City. One of the dramatists involved was **Ermilo Abreu Gómez** (1894–

1971), who brought the Teatro del Murciélago theater company to Yucatán from Mexico City. Abreu Gómez worked for a while as a professor in the United States. His best known work is *Canek*, an imaginative piece of social criticism based on the Mayan experience. Other writers of note are **Antonio Ancona Albertos** (1883–1954), **Antonio Mediz Bolio** (1884–1957), and **Delio Moreno Cantón** (1863–1916), all of whom doubled as politicians, as was common during the nineteenth century. **Pablo Moreno Triay** (1733–1833) was a poet, essayist, and dramatist.

Social Customs

The Yucatán custom for the Day of the Dead is to make an improvised altar at home and to place *mucbil pollo*, *atole de maíz nuevo*, and a homemade chocolate drink on it—these being thought the preferred foods of the departed.

The *vaquería* is one of the most widespread celebrations. It dates back to the colonial period and takes its name from the time of the year when cattle would be branded on the haciendas. Like most festivities in Yucatán, it involves a mixture of religious and secular events and shows signs of the blending of Hispanic and Mayan traditions. The vaquería typically has three components: the Mass, the bullfight, and the dances. The celebration begins at the home of the organizer, who is called the *diputado*, and from there the dancers and musicians make their way to the end of the town, where they search for *ceiba* branches and palm fronds (the ceiba has a key place in the Indian worldview). They dance their way to the center, where these are symbolically "planted." During gaps between the dances, the performers engage in mock verbal battles, throwing *bombas* at each other; in this context, the "bombs" are suggestive dialogs in rhyme, usually four lines long, that court or make fun of the opposite sex.

An example of a popular dance is *el degollete*, which is closely tied to the history of the Mayas and became an expression of solidarity among them at the time of the Caste Wars. El degollete has three sections, each consisting of eight rhythms; each of the three sections is associated with ethnicity: the criollos, the mestizos, and the Mayas. During the dance, the Mayas make fun of the others. *El tunkuluchu-hu* is a dance that represents the courtship of owls and the noises they make. By contrast, the *danza de las cintas* has its origins in fourteenth-century Bavaria and is related to the maypole dances still found in Europe. It came to Yucatán with Austro-Hungarian immigrants at the time when Maximilian was emperor of Mexico and has since become hybridized with indigenous practices.

Every place has its saint's day or some other excuse for festivities. For example, many places enjoy Carnival, including Tixkokob, which elects a Carnival queen and an "Ugly King," who act as stand-ins for the town authorities until Ash Wednesday, when there are the usual festivities, accompanied by the reading of the final testament of Juan Carnaval and his subsequent immolation. Chumayel, another place that is known for its Carnival, also celebrates the Day of the Holy Christ (April 28), though the day turns into a week, with religious processions, bullfights, and dancing.

January in Dzitas brings a ritual that predates the arrival of the Spaniards: A dozen locals gather at two o'clock in the afternoon, dressed traditionally and each carrying a turkey on his shoulders. After some ceremonial words, the turkeys are slaughtered and plucked, to the accompaniment of dancing.

Tekoh celebrates a Hammock Fair in March. In Mérida, the September Feast of the Santo Cristo de las Ampollas is important, together with the August Feria de Santiago and the Feria de Xmatkuil. Also in Mérida, the Virgin of Guadalupe is revered on December 12 in the Templo de San Cristóbal, and the founding of the city is celebrated on January 6, which is the important Feast of the Magi, the traditional day for children to receive Christmas presents in the Hispanic world.

Valladolid is known for its celebration of the Feast of the Virgen de Candelaria, a celebration that dates back a century and a half to the time when workers asked the Virgin to rid them of an epidemic that had killed many people, and promised to honor her in return. There are regional dancing, a bullfight, food and craft stalls, and entertainments. February 2 is the day of the Virgin and the high spot of the event. Since 1992, there has also been a trade fair each year, in September.

On festive occasions, particularly when dancing, women typically wear *huipiles*, simple white cotton shifts embroidered with broad bands of striking and brightly colored floral patterns that run around the skirt below the hips and along the square neckline. There is also a shawl-like section that goes over the shoulders and is similarly embroidered. They wear sandals or white shoes with medium heels. The men wear a white outfit, too: loose trousers, long-sleeved shirts, and broad-brimmed hats, together with a red neckerchief. For some festivities, women may wear an outfit called a *terno*, which involves finer fabrics and lace, with cross-stitched embroidery and a shawl, accompanied with gold chains, earrings, and rosaries made with coral. The men, correspondingly, wear tailored trousers of finer cloth, occasionally with gold buttons, a high-collared jacket-shirt known as a *filipina*, sandals, fine straw hats, and a red neckerchief. In regional festivities, this clothing is often seen when jarana dancing competitions are being held.

The Ch'achaak is one of the most important Mayan ceremonies, an invocation of the god of rain and a plea for water in the cornfields. Presided over by a high priest, it is primarily a male affair, since women are considered sinners whose presence might hinder the response of the deity. Frogs, symbols of rainfall, are represented in this ceremony by children who are tied to the legs of the table while the ceremony is in progress. Its climax comes at the point where the prayers of the celebrants are heard, together with whistling that summons the benign gods that inhabit the hills and the croaking of the frogs. Should there be thunder at the end, the ceremony is deemed a success. The proceedings conclude with a celebratory meal called *chok'ob*. Later on, once the corn begins to ripen, the owner of the cornfield (*milpa*) is under an obligation to give thanks; the best ears of corn are roasted in a *pib* (a hole dug in the ground and filled with coals) and offered to the gods for about a half an hour, so that they can absorb their essence, while the people present enjoy *atole*, a type of corn soup.

Noteworthy Places

Mérida has many fine buildings. Its cathedral dates back to 1599, and the Templo de San Juan de Dios is similarly old. From the seventeenth century are the Templo de la Mejorada and the Iglesia del Jesús, and from the

Palacio Municipal and Ayuntamiento, Town Hall, Plaza Mayor, Zocalo, Mérida. Courtesy of Mel Longhurst/Art Directors & TRIP Photo Library.

eighteenth the Iglesia de San Cristóbal, the Iglesia de San Sebastián, the Ermita de Santa Isabel, and the Iglesia de San Juan Bautista. El Moro Muza is a Mayan sculpture that was transported from the ruins at T-Hó. Among the most impressive civic buildings in Mérida are the Casa de Montejo (dating from 1549), the Palacio del Ayuntamiento (Town Hall; 1735), the main building of the Universidad Autónoma de Yucatán (1864) and the Palacio de Gobierno (Government House; 1892). Also from the era of Porfirio Díaz are the Teatro Mérida, the Teatro Peón Contreras, the Palacio Federal de Correos (Post Office Building), and two former hospitals, Ayala and O'Horán. The Estación Central dates from 1920 and the Casa del Pueblo from 1928; an interesting example of "neo-Mayan" architecture, the Casa del Pueblo is actually the work of an Italian architect, Angelo Bachini, that combines elements of the French baroque style with Mayan and Toltec motifs. The Monumento a la Patria (Monument to the Fatherland) is an imposing pink limestone structure on the Paseo de Montejo, the work of a Colombian sculptor and a Mexican architect.

In the town of Valladolid, the Church of San Gervasio has imposing towers and also displays the cannons that were used to recover the town from the rebellious Mayas in 1848. The Convento de San Antonio, in Izamal, was built upon the ruins of an Indian ceremonial site; its church has the longest enclosed atrium of any church in Mexico, approaching the length of St. Peter's in Rome. There are many picturesque ex-haciendas in the state, some of which have become hotels or museums.

Museums include Mérida's Contemporary Art Museum, Natural History Museum, Museo de la Ciudad, and Museum of Yucateca Song. Dzbilchaltún has the Museum of the Mayan People; Valladolid, the Museo San Roque; Motul, the Museo de Felipe Carrillo Puerto; and Santa Elena, the Museo de las Momias (Mummy Museum). There are also museums at the principal archaeological sites: Ek Balam, Labná, Sayil, Dzibilchaltún, Mayapán, Uxmal, and Chichen-Itzá.

Uxmal dates from around 600 and prospered until about 900. Some of its buildings have rich stone reliefs decorating parts of their outside walls, displaying images of serpents, snails, and deities, together with geometric designs. The so-called Nun's Quadrangle consists of four buildings set on a platform and providing a complex of patios and retreats. The Casa del Enano (Dwarf's House) is believed to have housed a mythical leader. The Palace of the Governor is about 90 meters (300 feet) long, 12 meters (40 feet) wide, and 8 meters (27 feet) high. The Pyramid of the Magician is some 18 meters (60 feet) high and is climbed via precipitous stone staircase that has steps so shallow that one has to make one's way up in crisscross fashion, perhaps in order to show due respect for the shrine on top. Strikingly, this pyramid has rounded corners.

To the southwest of Valladolid lies Chichen-Itzá, one of Mexico's most famous archaeological sites, whose name means "The Mouth of the

Cenote Where the Itzá People Live." Chichen-Itzá was founded early in the sixth century. The sacred cenote was used for sacrifices to the rain god Chac Mool, whose recumbent effigy graces one of the site's major buildings. The site was abandoned in 670 but reconstructed some three hundred years later, to become the most important city in northern Yucatán. About 1200, Chichen-Itzá was occupied by the Toltecs and further developed. The ruins cover about 4 square kilometers (one and a half square miles). Many of the buildings are set on pyramid-shaped platforms and approached by wide stone staircases; the buildings themselves have vaulted roofs, and their walls are covered with relief stone carvings, hieroglyphs, and brightly colored paintings. There is a ball court to accommodate a game that had ceremonial and religious significance, a huge pyramid, and a circular building known as the Caracol (Snail), which is thought to have been an observatory. Near the ball court, a series of stakes supports a line of carved stone skulls, suggesting that human sacrifices took place there. The dominant building is the Castle or Temple of Kukulcán, a wide pyramid only about 30 meters (100 feet) high with the temple on top. Kukulcán was the Mayan name for the benign god Quetzalcóatl (the Plumed Serpent). Another major building is the Temple of the Warriors. By the time the Spaniards arrived, Chichen-Itzá had been abandoned for about a century.

Celestún has a national park with many varieties of native flora and fauna. There are grottoes at places such as Loltún and Waaybil Actún, and picturesque cenotes at Bolonchohol, Kankirixché, and Santa María. Excavations at Loltún have revealed the remains of extinct species and a past time when the climate was very different from that of today. Human artifacts, stone carvings, and paintings were also discovered, indicating that the caves were in use as long as 10,000 years ago; they have also been used by the Mayas at various stages in their history, for example as a refuge during the Caste Wars.

Cuisine

Like its language, the cuisine of Yucatán is a quite distinctive hybrid, and one appreciated as such all over Mexico. Local specialties include *panuchos* (tortillas filled with dry black beans and garnished with tomatoes, lettuce, shredded chicken, and jalapeños), *papadzules* (small corn tacos that have been soaked in a cream thickened with ground seeds and are filled with egg), *pavo en relleno negro* (turkey stuffed with sausage meat and with a rich *recado* sance), *queso relleno* (a cheese ball filled with pork sausage), *cochinita pibil*, and *sopa de lima*. Sweets include *torta del cielo* (a kind of almond tart), *atropellado de coco* (made with sweet potatoes and coconut), *postre de frijol*, and the delightfully named *caballeros pobres* ("poor gentlemen"—fritters drenched in syrup and flavored with cinnamon, cloves, and raisins). *Xtabentún* and *balché* are typical yucateco drinks, and there are many others that are made from fruit juices.

Recado Negro

Recado is a generic name for a thick and spicy sauce like a *mole*; indeed, sometimes it is called a *chilmole*. This recipe is for black recado; there is also a red variety. It is a paste made by charring dried chiles over a naked flame and then grinding them up with a mixture of spices. The paste is typically rubbed over meats when preparing dishes, or used as a sauce thickener.

Ingredients:

> 1 lb. dried chiles (a mixture of different types can be used, according to taste and tolerance for spiciness), seeded and de-veined
> 2 tbsp *achiote* (annatto) seeds (or paste)
> 5 whole cloves
> 5 whole allspice berries
> 1 tbsp black peppercorns
> 1/2 tsp cumin seeds
> 1 tbsp sea salt
> 1 tbsp oregano leaves
> 10 cloves of garlic
> 1 tsp vinegar

Char the chiles over an open flame, such as a barbecue, but take care not to burn excessively. Place them in a pot of water to cool, then drain thoroughly and put them in clean water. Drain once again but this time leave a small amount of water. Char the garlic, then peel. Grind up the spices to a fine powder, sift, and discard any solid residue. Put the garlic and the chiles with their small quantity of remaining water into a food processor, together with the spice mixture and the vinegar. Blend well. Thoroughly drain off liquid and then shape the mixture into a ball, which can be kept in plastic wrap in a refrigerator for as much as a year.

To prepare a red version of the recado, use the following ingredients: 1 white onion, 2 roasted and peeled heads of garlic, 3 tbsp achiote, 1 1-inch cinnamon stick, 8 cloves, 6 allspice berries, 1/2 tsp cumin seeds, and 1/2 tbsp dried oregano.

Cochinita Pibil

Traditionally, the meat for this dish would be cooked in a pib, a hole in the ground with hot coals in it. The modern alternative is to put the meat in a Dutch oven or similar pot.

Ingredients:

> 1 banana leaf
> 2 purple onions
> 1/4 lb. achiote paste (this can also be bought in dried granules, which go further)
> Juice of 2 oranges

3 cloves of garlic
1/4 cup white vinegar
Salt and pepper
2 lb. leg of pork
For the accompanying sauce:
1 purple onion, finely chopped
1/2 cup white vinegar
Habanero chiles (according to taste—this type is very hot), finely chopped
A pinch of oregano
Salt
Juice of 3 limes
Corn tortillas

Dissolve the achiote (annetto) paste with the orange juice and mix with other ingredients. Coat the pork with the mixture and let it sit for 2 to 3 hours. Briefly roast or fry the banana leaf and set aside. Put the meat in a Dutch oven, cover with the banana leaf, and cook for at least 45 minutes, until the meat begins to fall apart. In a separate operation, mix the sauce ingredients together. Serve the meat with the sauce and tortillas.

Pescado en Tikin-Xic'

This recipe is for grilled fish with red recado. The recado is made ahead of time (see the end of the recado negro recipe above). Ideally, the fish should be cooked over wood or charcoal, but a gas grill will work.

Ingredients:

2 whole red snappers or similar fish (total weight: 3–4 lb.)
2 tbsp vegetable oil
1 cup orange juice (from bitter oranges)
4 bay leaves
1 cup preserved onions (*cebollas curtidas*)
Salt
4 small tomatoes, chopped
2 limes, cut into wedges

Dissolve red recado in a bowl, using the oil and orange juice, until there is enough to coat the fish. Rub the fish with the mixture and put in a baking dish. Put the bay leaves on top, cover, and leave to marinate for several hours or overnight. When ready to cook, remove the fish from the marinade, reserving the liquid. Place the fish on a banana leaf, with the rib of the leaf facing downward and the skin of the fish up. Grill for about 15 minutes, turn the fish over, and baste with the reserved marinade. Repeat as necessary until the fish becomes flaky. Lift away the backbone of the fish, starting at the tail end, and remove the fins. Then garnish the fish with the onion, tomatoes, and lime wedges.

Papadzules

For this dish, first prepare a pumpkin seed sauce (*recado de pepita*), then a *chiltomate*, and finally the *papadzules* themselves.

Ingredients:

For the sauce:
10 oz. pumpkin seeds

For the chiltomate:
1 large onion, chopped into large pieces
5 firm medium tomatoes, cut into halves
2 cloves of garlic
1 or 2 fresh hot chiles (habaneros or jalapeños)
$1/2$ tsp oregano
$1/2$ tsp chopped fresh cilantro
Salt
Lard (or oil)

For the papadzules:
1 white onion, quartered
3 cloves of garlic
1 hot chile
$1/2$ tsp *epazote*
4 cups water
12 small corn tortillas
6 hardboiled eggs
2 cups preserved onions
Fresh cilantro

Begin with the recado de pepita by putting the pumpkin seeds in a skillet and toasting them for 5 minutes over a medium-low flame, until they begin to swell and pop. Put them in a blender and grind finely until they begin to form a paste. Press the paste through a sieve into a bowl and then regrind any solid pieces left behind. (This will keep for some weeks, if refrigerated).

For the chiltomate, roast the onion, tomatoes, garlic, and chiles. Put them into a blender, add the oregano and cilantro, plus a dash of salt, and blend. Melt a little lard in a frying pan and then warm the mixture.

Prepare the papadzules by putting the onion in a pan with the garlic, chile, and epazote. Add water, bring to a boil, and then reduce heat to simmer for 15 minutes. Strain and discard the solids. Allow the liquid to cool, then use a little of it to make a paste with the recado de pepita. Squeeze the mixture so that the seeds impart their flavor and release their oil; spoon off the oil and reserve. Slowly add more water to the mixture until it becomes a thick sauce, and warm it up. At the same time, warm the tortillas, wrapped in foil, in the oven (set at 350°F) and warm some plates. Put a heaping tablespoon of chopped egg on each tortilla and then roll them up. Place two or three on each plate, cover with the recado sauce, and then top with hot chiltomate. Drizzle the reserved oil over them and garnish with chopped cilantro.

Dulce de Frijol

Ingredients:

- 2 lb. kidney beans
- 4 lb. sugar
- 4 oz. raisins
- 2 oz. chopped almonds
- $1/2$ cinnamon stick
- 10 eggs
- Oil
- 2 tsp bicarbonate of soda
- 1 can condensed milk

Soak the beans in water, together with the bicarbonate of soda. Leave for about 10 hours. Then peel the beans, wash them, and grind them, adding the eggs and the can of milk, to make a thick paste. Shape the mixture into frying portions and make fritters. Now prepare the syrup, dissolving the sugar in 2 pints of water. When it is warm and thick, put the fritters in it, along with the almonds and raisins.

Zacatecas

State Characteristics

Zacatecas takes its name from that of the Indians who once lived there. The state lies in the north-central part of Mexico and is bordered by Coahuila to the north, Nuevo León to the northwest, San Luis Potosí to the east, Aguascalientes and Jalisco to the south, and Nayarit to the southwest. It is a state with a very irregular shape whose borders have changed a number of times over the course of its history. It now has a total area that accounts for 3.8 percent of Mexico (75,040 square kilometers/29,266 square miles), making it the tenth largest state in the country. Its population, according to the 2005 census, was 1,367,692; half of that population was under twenty years of age. The population density was low, at 18 per square kilometer (7 per square mile), the twenty-sixth highest among the states of Mexico.

Zacatecas is represented by nine people in the National Congress. The state has fifty-seven administrative municipalities and a capital city that bears the same name, with a population of 118,562. The next most populous city, Sombrerete, has approximately half as many people. Recent years have seen an increase in the concentration of the population in some municipalities, apart from the capital, and Sombrerete is one of them; others are Fresnillo, Guadalupe, Pinos, Río Grande, and Jerez. In the 2005 census, over 80 percent of the state's population identified themselves as Catholic, while fewer than 5 percent claimed another religious affiliation. Zacatecas has six newspapers, five published in the capital (*El Sol*, *Imagen*, *La Jornada*, *El Heraldo*, and *Página 24*) and one in Fresnillo (*La Voz*).

Zacatecas is a mountainous state with an average elevation of 2,230 meters (7,315 feet). It comprises the Sierra Madre Occidental on its western side, the Sierra Madre Oriental to the north and over part of the middle of the state, a central *meseta*, and a volcanic mountain range that crosses over the southwestern part. The Sierra Madre Occidental has steep mountains that reach higher than 2,500 meters (8,200 feet) and more gentle ranges that run from the southwest to the northeast; this last region encompasses the Juchipila and Tlaltenango canyons. Contained within the mountains are a number of small plains and valleys. In the center of the state is the Sierra de Fresnillo, which includes Proaño Hill, a place that became world famous for its deposits of lead, silver, and zinc. Similarly, the Sierra de Sombrerete, to the northeast, has a mountain called Sombreretillo, at the foot of which sits one of the richest mining towns in the state. Other important mountains are the Cerro de la Bufa, east of the town of Zacatecas, and Cerro del Ángel, in the north. There are peaks in the Sierra el Astillero, Sierra de Sombrerete, and Sierra Fría that exceed 3,000 meters (10,000 feet) in height.

Such rivers as there are—and there are not many—are relatively insignificant. Most of them rely on runoff from the mountains during the rainy season and dry up at other times. The main river that runs toward the Gulf of Mexico is the Río Grande, which passes through the state of Coahuila and changes its name in the process, to Aguanaval; flowing toward the Pacific, the main rivers are the Valparaíso and the Colotlán. There are several dams.

The climate is predominantly dry, although there are a few temperate areas. In the dry and often desertlike areas—for example, in the northeastern part of the state—the annual average temperature is over 18°C (65°F), with January being the coldest month and June the hottest. Rainfall averages about 400 millimeters (16 inches) a year, and most of that falls as rain in the summer. There are frosts from November to March. The southeastern areas are more temperate, with an average annual rainfall that can reach 800 millimeters (31 inches).

The extensive arid areas support a surprising variety of plants that are able to weather the dryness, in particular varieties of cactus. In the north, for example, there are *nopal*, palm, mesquite, *gobernadora*, *lechuguilla*, *candelilla*, yucca, *guayule*, and *huizache*. The fauna of that area includes deer, coyotes, wild boars, rattlesnakes, and rodents. The central region has pastureland, with some oaks and conifers, and wildlife such as coyotes, jaguars, *tlacuaches*, bats, armadillos, eagles, parrots, wild turkeys, and small mammals. In southern parts, there are more deciduous trees; mesquite, ebony, *palo verde*, and *palo fierro* are the predominant varieties. The wildlife is much as in the other regions.

Cultural Groups and Languages

Very little survives of the pre-Hispanic cultures that once characterized this area, although there are several archaeological sites. The Huicholes and

Tepehuanes, who lived in the far western parts of the state, have survived but are now found largely in other states, such as Durango and Nayarit. The indigenous peoples of Zacatecas have assimilated into the dominant culture, their blood mixed with Spanish blood and their languages lost. According to the 2005 census, only a small proportion of the population (0.3 percent) spoke an indigenous language; this is one of the lowest proportions in Mexico, and furthermore most of the people so identified also knew Spanish. There are now perhaps two thousand speakers of indigenous languages in the state, but most of those are people who have come into it from other states. In descending order of frequency, the languages concerned are Tepehuán, Huichol, Náhuatl, Otomí, Mazahua, and Purépecha.

History

Prior to the arrival of the Spaniards, agricultural societies had settled parts of the area that is now southern Zacatecas, with its gentler and more favorable climate. Northern parts were inhabited by hunters and gatherers comparable to the North American Indian peoples. The predominant cultural foci were at Chalchihuites and La Quemada. The former arose between AD 100 and 200 along the banks of the Súchil, Graceros, and Guadiana rivers, and its most important site was an astronomical observatory now known as Alta Vista. La Quemada, on the other hand, was a residential and commercial center that dates from about AD 300; meaning "The Burned," it acquired that name because the Spaniards found evidence that it had suffered a great fire. By the time of the arrival of the Spaniards, the region was occupied by a number of groups whom the Aztecs referred to collectively as Chichimecas. The Zacatecas Indians were one such group.

Late in 1529, a force of 10,000 men set out from Mexico City under the command of the conquistador Nuño Beltrán de Guzmán. Beltrán was an able but ruthless man who terrorized the natives, destroyed their homes and crops, and killed a great number of people. Reports of his brutality reached Mexico City and he was arrested, but his brutality had so enraged the natives that they would not let the Spaniards rest.

In 1530, Juan de Oñate, one of Beltrán's men, had started a town in what is now the southern part of the state, near Nochistlán. He named it Villa de Espíritu Santo de Guadalajara. From the start, it came under attack by the Indians, who destroyed churches and attacked settlers. After it became apparent that this was a problematic site, Beltrán decided to move Villa de Espíritu Santo to a more central location, where it eventually became the city of Guadalajara, Mexico's second biggest city and capital of the state of Jalisco. (In the sixteenth century, the states of Aguascalientes, Jalisco, and Zacatecas were administered as a single unit, called Nueva Galicia.)

A fierce Indian revolt in western Mexico, known as the Mixtón Rebellion, began in 1541, but by the end of the year reinforcements sent by the viceroy from Mexico City, consisting of a few hundred Spaniards and some 30,000 Aztec and Tlaxcalan Indians, had crushed the rebellion. The Chichimeca people who acquired the reputation for being most ferocious and indomitable were the Guachichiles; they occupied the largest area and were the ones who incited rebellion on the part of others.

In 1546, Juan de Tolosa came to Zacatecas in search of minerals, having had his appetite whetted by a stone that had been shown to him by an Indian. The three loads of stone that he gathered and sent to the authorities to be analyzed revealed significant deposits of lead and silver and interested the governor of the area, Cristóbal de Oñate. Together with Tolosa, Diego de Ibarra and Miguel Ibarra explored farther and established the first Spanish settlement, which became Zacatecas. The town's first buildings are generally held to date from 1547. The first significant silver mine was San Bernabé. By 1553, the town was known as Minas de Nuestra Señora de los Remedios, in the province of the Zacatecas.

Development was rapid but full of difficulties and dangers. The lure of riches brought prospectors, opportunists, and laborers flocking into the place. Over the next few years, ore deposits were discovered in several other places, such as San Martín, Sombrerete, and Nieves. Among other problems, the influx of people and the founding of new towns outstripped the provision of an adequate infrastructure of services. As a result, new routes were established to supply the new colonial settlements and to facilitate outward transport of their riches. Understandably, these routes, seen as lifelines by the Spaniards, became symbols of European intrusion as far as the Indians were concerned, and so they became the focus of attacks.

Assaults on travelers and merchants characterized the forty-year long Chichimeca War that began in 1550; it was the longest and most costly conflict of the colonial period. The Spaniards lost lives and goods; by the last decade of the war, thousands had died and the mining towns were becoming depopulated. The turning point came with the appointment of a new viceroy, the Marqués de Villamanrique, who introduced major changes in policy, outlawed enslavery of the Indians by Spaniards, and engaged in peace negotiations with the Chichimecs. Villamanrique's approach was maintained by his successor as viceroy, Luis de Velasco, who brought in missionaries and aid for the Indians, together with four hundred families of Tlaxcalan Indians, who by then had long been allies of the Spaniards and would aid the process of acculturation.

Conversion of the Chichimeca peoples—not an easy task considering their wide variety of languages and fierce resentment of the Spanish intrusion—was entrusted to the Franciscan order. In 1558, the Franciscans founded a hospice, and in 1567 a huge monastery. Later, the Augustinians, Dominicans, and Jesuits helped with the evangelization process and with gathering the Indians into stable settlements built around their churches and their monasteries, of which there were fourteen by 1596; these settlements were to be the basis for the towns of the present day.

Although the area prospered, its economic course was not always smooth. The period from 1690 to 1752 was one of prosperity, but then came a slump in the value of silver and with it a fifteen-year period of economic depression. Another period of prosperity ensued, bringing in many more people (the city of Zacatecas grew from 15,000 people in 1777 to 33,000 in 1803), but it declined again in the years following Father Miguel Hidalgo's call for independence in 1810. Local insurgent heroes of this period included **Ramón García** (1772-1812), **Víctor Rosales** (1776-1817), **Juan Valdivia** (1777-1811), and **José María Coss** (d. 1819), who was also a journalist.

Hidalgo's army first took Guanajuato and then occupied Zacatecas; despite his subsequent defeat by royalist forces, Spain was now on its way to losing its prized colony. In 1823, Zacatecas was declared a state of the new Mexican Republic. **Francisco García Salinas** (1786-1841) was one of Zacatecas's most distinguished and progressive political figures at this time, a man whose personal integrity and capacity for hard work earned him the reputation of being a model governor. He represented the state at the Constituent Congress and also served as finance minister under President Guadalupe Victoria.

Zacatecas did not acquire the degree of autonomy that it wished, however, and there were tensions with the central government in the following years. During the tenure of the conservative President Anastasio Bustamante, liberals in Zacatecas rebelled, but were defeated at the Battle of Gallinero (1832). There was another revolt against the powers in Mexico City three years later, and this time it was Antonio López de Santa Anna's troops who crushed the rebels, at the Battle of Guadalupe (1835), after which his forces sacked the city of Zacatecas and the silver mines at Fresnillo. To rub salt into the wound, Santa Anna took away Aguascalientes, which had hitherto been a part of the state; by 1857, Aguascalientes was a state in its own right.

Conservatives and liberals fought again during the Reform War (1858-1861), and Zacatecas once again became a battleground; at one time or another, its capital fell into the hands of both factions. Such conflicts continued when the French invaded and installed Maximilian as emperor in 1861. The conservatives, who had favored the invasion, rallied behind the invaders, while the liberals opposed them. Having occupied Mexico City, the French took control of Zacatecas in 1864 and kept control of it for two years. Prominent local figures in politics and the defense of the country against the U.S. and French invasions were **Trinidad García de la Cadena** (1813-1886), **Jesús González Ortega** (1822-1881), **Miguel Auza** (1822-1892), **Antonio Rosales** (1822-1865), and **Felipe Berriozabal** (1829-1900).

During the second half of the nineteenth century, the silver industry again picked up, and by about 1880 it alone accounted for 60 percent of Mexican exports. The *porfiriato* brought a number of improvements in transportation and communications. The train came to Zacatecas, making it safer and faster to move goods in and out. The Mexican Central Railway, which ran from Mexico City through Zacatecas and up to the United States, also encouraged emigration north of the border.

With opposition to Porfirio Díaz growing, **Roque Estrada Reynoso** (1883-1966) became a prominent leader of the *antireeleccionista* movement that supported Francisco Madero as an alternative presidential candidate. Later, Estrada became private secretary to Venustiano Carranza and a member of the National Congress. He was also a writer. **Enrique Estrada** (1889-1941) and **Joaquín Amaro** (1889-1952) also supported Madero and had significant political careers.

Zacatecas became a major battleground for the Mexican Revolution (1910-1920), particularly when it was taken by Pancho Villa—an event known as La Toma de Zacatecas and one that became the subject of a famous *corrido*. The fighting against the forces of Gen. Victoriano Huerta was particularly bloody, leaving some seven thousand soldiers dead and a further five thousand wounded, not to mention the numbers of civilian casualties. **Luis Moya** (1855-1911) and **Pánfilo Natera** (1882-1951) were local revolutionaries who also participated in this battle.

Economy

Mining, and particularly the silver trade, was the backbone of the Zacatecas economy during the colonial era, though it did suffer some flat periods. Modern Zacatecas produces raw materials through both mining and agricultural activities. Though the lack of rain does not favor agriculture, the state nevertheless grows a number of crops and raises a variety of animals, whether for meat or bullfights. Industrial activity, apart from mining, is modest in scale. There is some food processing and manufacturing, both of metallic and nonmetallic articles.

It is estimated that, over the years, Zacatecas and Fresnillo together have produced more than 1.5 billion ounces (42.6 million kilograms) of silver. Mining in the state is not as dominant now as it once was, but is still extremely important; zinc, copper, lead, silver, and gold are all mined, although the last two now only in modest quantities. That said, thanks primarily to Zacatecas, Mexico still produces 17 percent of the world's silver, more than any other country. There are about fifteen mining districts in all, the most important being Fresnillo, Zacatecas, Concepción del Oro, Sombrerete, and Chalchihuites. The state also has significant, though not fully exploited, nonmineral deposits of resources such as kaolin, fluorite, and barium.

Agriculture is possible on 27 percent of the state's surface. The principal crops are corn, beans, oats, chiles, and peaches. Pastureland accounts for 16 percent, and 13 percent is forested, giving pine and oak for construction and fuel, respectively, plus pine nuts for human consumption. Almost

40 percent of the state consists of dry, desert terrain that supports some plants, especially cacti, that are useful to humans: *ocotillo* is used in construction, *hojasén* and *gobernadora* for medicinal purposes, and *candelilla* and *guayule* in industry. Figures dating from 2000 list 1,037,287 head of cattle, 245,762 pigs, 310,023 sheep, 546,414 goats, 209,707 horses (or similar animals), and 1,862,726 poultry birds. There were almost 50,000 beehives, and about 5,000 metric tons of freshwater fish were harvested in that year.

Arts

Leatherwork is the major craft industry of this state, producing personal items such as bags and belts, as well as tack for cowboys and horse riders. Various articles are woven from *pita*, a fiber that comes from cactus. Villa García is known for its brightly colored *sarapes* (blankets).

The popular musical tradition of the *mestizo* and *criollo* populations includes the polka, a genre that gained popularity following an influx of East European immigrants in the late nineteenth century. In some places, they still dance the *chotís* and the *cuadrilla*, both of which are also European in origin. One of the most popular of all song/dance forms is the corrido, a type of ballad that generally extols the exploits of revolutionary heroes or tells tales of love. Mariachi ensembles are found all over Mexico, but *norteño* and *banda* groups are prevalent in northern states; Zacatecas has one of the most successful banda ensembles, Banda Jerez. Distinctive in the field of popular music is the *tamborazo zacatecano*, a freely assembled group of instruments of European origin, such as clarinets, trumpets, saxophones, *redobletes* (a type of guitar), and *tamboras* (a drum thought to derive from the indigenous *huehuetl*), but lacking the customary instruments that supply the harmonies and the base line. The music always begins with the drum, hence the name of the ensemble. Tamborazos are de rigueur as accompaniment for the typical *jarabes*, *sones*, and corridos of the state's musical repertoire.

Straddling the popular and classical genres is one of the key figures in the history of Mexican music, **Manuel M. Ponce** (1882-1948), who is claimed by both Aguascalientes and Zacatecas. Apart from his compositional achievements, Ponce is credited with being the first person to document popular Mexican musical forms in a serious and professional manner. Ponce studied in Europe before becoming director of Mexico's National Symphony Orchestra and of the National Conservatory of Music. Other musicians from the state are **Candelario Huízar** (1883-1970), **Carlos Estaban Lozano** (1888-1918), **Genaro Codina** (1851-1901), and **Ernesto Elorduy** (1854-1913). Elorduy studied with Clara Schumann and Anton Rubinstein and became an accomplished pianist. He was also a composer and arranger.

The mainstream Hispanic culture has produced a few distinguished figures in literature. **Ramón López Velarde** (1888-1921) was one of the outstanding poets of the turn of the twentieth century, as well as a lawyer and journalist. Like his friend, the composer Manuel Ponce, López Velarde is claimed by both Aguascalientes and Zacatecas. Both were in fact born in Zacatecas but moved to its neighbor at an early age. Though above all a great stylist and innovator, López Velarde turned from writing about exotic and refined things to writing about more ordinary matters of family and provincial life, and so he has sometimes been thought of as a literary herald of the Revolution. **Enrique Fernández Ledezma** (1888–1939) was another poet and journalist, but also a politician who represented the state in the National Congress and became director of the National Library.

Perhaps it is to painting that Zacatecas has made its most striking artistic contribution. The second half of the nineteenth century saw the emergence of **Julio Ruelas** (1870–1907), who, after having been expelled from a military college, studied art and became one of the most individualistic exponents of Romanticism and a transitional figure to modern art. Among other activities, he was the principal illustrator of a groundbreaking literary review called the *Revista Moderna*. Ruelas used figurative forms, but used them symbolically. More or less his contemporary, though he lived much longer, was **Francisco Goitia** (1882–1960). Goitia studied at Mexico City's principal art school, the Academia de San Carlos, went to Europe for some years, and then returned to sign up with Pancho Villa's army. His art is marked by anguished, surreal images of the effects of war. **Pedro Coronel** (1923–1985) was a painter, sculptor, and engraver who achieved a certain international recognition, won several Mexican prizes, and was named a favored son (*hijo predilecto*) of Zacatecas.

Social Customs

The Feria Nacional de Zacatecas commemorates the foundation of the city and is in honor of the Virgen del Patrocinio. It takes place over a period of three weeks during September, with dances, fireworks, religious ceremonies, the crowning of a queen of the fair, agricultural shows, concerts, sporting events, bullfights, street entertainments, and rides. Holy Week in Zacatecas coincides with a major cultural festival involving art exhibitions, literary events, theater, and music. In late August, Zacatecas holds its Día de la Morisma, when the conflict between the Moors and the Christians in Spain is reenacted close to the Cerro de la Bufa, with the whole town dressed up for one part or another; the key roles include Charlemagne, Mohammed, and John the Baptist. Once the leader of the infidels has been decapitated, to victorious cheers, there is general revelry.

On December 8, the Feast of the Immaculate Conception, there are festivities with all-day dancing in the small town of Concepción del Oro, a place that was important for mining during the colonial era. On Good Friday, Chalchihuites displays a figure of Christ that was given to it by King Philip II at the height of the empire; judgment takes place in the morning

Funeral at the Zacatecas cathedral. (AP Photo)

before knights of the Order of Santiago (Spain's patron saint) while the rest of the inhabitants of the town play the roles of Jews, Pharisees, and so forth. In late July, this same town celebrates the Feast of St. Peter, with religious processions, dancing by *matachines*, and young people engaging in a Batalla de las Flores (Flower Battle). Other local festivities involving similar celebrations include Easter Sunday and the Feast of the Virgen de la Soledad (September 8) in Jerez (Ciudad García); the day of Nuestra Señora de Loreto (December 10) in the town of that name; and Christ the Savior in Mazapil (August 5).

On the Wednesday after Corpus Christi, Juchipila celebrates a festivity that has pre-Hispanic origins, the Festival de Súchil. In its present-day form, floral arrangements are presented to the town's worthies and there are popular dances, such as the *jarabe tapatío* (Mexican hat dance) and the *paliacates*. For the Feast of Santiago in late July, people come from all around to Juchipila to see the *danza de los tastuanes*, which commemorates a sixteenth-century battle. The Apostle Santiago (St. James) rides a white horse and confronts the Cazcano Indians, who wear wooden masks and complicated headdresses made from hair from cow tails.

January 20, the day of Saint Sebastian, is a big day for Nochistlán. Dancers come in from Toyahua and perform a dance similar to Juchipila's tastuanes. October (San Francisco) is occasion for a larger-scale celebration in Nochistlán, one that continues for most of the month, with dancing, bullfights, cockfights, and fireworks. Zacatecas hosts an international folklore festival in the summer.

Noteworthy Places

The city of Zacatecas was founded in 1546 and originally called Minas de los Zacatecas. In 1993 UNESCO declared it a World Heritage site. Like other colonial mining towns, such as Taxco and Guanajuato, it sprang up because of the riches that were to be had locally, rather than as the result of a thoughtful choice of location taking into account the terrain and climate, and it grew for similar reasons rather than as a result of deliberate town planning. Thus it is not laid out on a grid system, as are many of Mexico's towns, and as a result it is less predictable and more interesting than most.

The city's cathedral (the Catedral Basílica de Zacatecas) has some of the finest baroque façades in Latin America. It was built in the eighteenth century, on the site of a modest church dating from 1567. The main façade, completed in 1745, is like a massive altarpiece set between two towers, with elaborately sculpted columns whose designs are sometimes cut as much as 10 centimeters (4 inches) deep into the stone. This busy surface has three niches accommodating Christ and his apostles, and there are elements that allude to the Trinity and the Eucharist (grapes, angels, and musical instruments).

Many of Zacatecas's buildings date from the same period, reflecting the town's economic importance and growing population. Other significant churches are Santo Domingo, San Agustín (now a museum), and San Francisco. Among its civic buildings, the Palacio de la Mala Noche (used as the Palace of Justice), the Presidencia Municipal, the Rectoría de la Universidad, and the Casa de la Condesa are noteworthy. The Palacio de Gobierno was built at the beginning of the eighteenth century to house one of the town's richest families; in view of its favored position on the main square, in 1829 it was made the Government Palace. Apart from its architectural interest, it has a mural depicting the state's history, painted in 1970 by a local artist, Antonio Pintor Rodríguez. The municipal market (Mercado González Ortega) dates from the time of Díaz, as does the building that houses the Museo Goitia. There is a highly unusual hotel set in what was the San

Pedro Bullring. An important focus for the artistic life of Zacatecas is the Teatro Calderón; located on the Plaza Goitia, this nineteenth-century theater hosts all kinds of performances.

The Museo Pedro Coronel houses the private collection of the painter so named. It is in what was once a Jesuit college, founded in 1616, that later came into the hands of the Dominican order before becoming state property. It then served as a barracks and a prison. The museum also houses a major theological library of 20,000 volumes, drawn from the holdings of the various Catholic orders and dating back to early colonial days. The art on display includes works by Coronel himself and other pieces, both ancient and modern, collected from all over the world. One room is devoted to Mexican colonial art, another to pre-Hispanic artifacts. At the other historical extreme are originals by painters such as Georges Roualt, Pablo Picasso, Joan Miró, Salvador Dalí, and Antoni Tàpies.

The Mina del Edén, beside Zacatecas, was first opened in 1588, when it was called the Mina San Eligio; the name change arose because the deposits were exceptionally rich and the mine seemed to be a paradise. However, in view of constant flooding and the proximity of the city, mining there was later abandoned and the mine became a place for sightseers to visit.

The Cerro de la Bufa is not only an impressive natural site but has also been of historical significance. The name the Spaniards gave it derives from a Basque word that means "pig's bladder" and was chosen because of the shape of the hill. This was once a place of refuge for pre-Hispanic peoples. It also became the scenario of the bloody Battle of Zacatecas, during which the forces of Pancho Villa defeated those of General Huerta, in 1914.

The Museo de Guadalupe, in the town of that name, is in what was one of the first religious foundations in New Spain devoted to spreading Catholic propaganda. This particular one began its work in 1707. It has been a museum since 1918. Apart from its architectural interest and beauty, this museum offers a major collection of colonial art distributed over twenty-seven rooms, featuring painters such as Miguel Cabrera, Cristóbal de Villalpando, José de Ibarra, and Luis Juárez.

Alta Vista, an archaeological site, is about 225 kilometers (140 miles) northwest of Zacatecas. It is a ceremonial and astronomical place rooted in the Chalchihuites culture that lasted for about eight centuries, though the site itself is assumed to have been occupied from around AD 100 to 1400.

La Quemada is the most important archaeological site in the state. It is about 55 kilometers (35 miles) south of the capital in the municipality of Villanueva. Previously called Chicomostoc, according to some archaeologists, it dates from the ninth to twelfth centuries and is thought to have been occupied by at least seven different nomadic peoples. The core of the site appears to have been reserved for the nobles, with the commoners living on the outskirts. The ruins are located on a hill and surrounding slopes, with natural and man-made terraces that give the impression of a fortress made of rocks, stone slabs, and mud. There is a four-sided, walled area with eleven huge columns, each about 65 meters (20 feet) high, which is presumed to have housed a palace or temple. On the same level, there is a small square that was probably the marketplace and also a ball court and a pyramid dedicated to the sun. A stone staircase leads to another level, where there is a labyrinth of rooms, including some believed to have been for the priests, where as many as three hundred human skeletons were found during excavations of the site. On the third level is another large, possibly sacrificial area, with annexes and passageways. The fourth level has an open area and the observatory, from which one can look down on the valley below, while the fifth has a citadel protected by double walls. This is one of Mesoamerica's most important pre-Hispanic sites.

At the Linares Dam, south of Fresnillo, there are some rock paintings in abstract, hieroglyphic styles.

Cuisine

The leaves of the nopal cactus, and its fruit, the *tuna*, are quite prominent in local markets, evidence of pre-Hispanic culinary traditions that still survive in Mexican food. Zacatecas ranks first in the country for the production of beans, chiles, and nopales; it is also second in guavas and third in grapes. But the Spaniards encouraged the raising of livestock in this region, too, and so meat figures quite prominently in the cuisine. One of the most typical dishes is a kind of roast pork loin, *asado de boda*, so called because it is served at weddings. *Birria*, a kind of stew, is also popular, together with the thick corn-based soup known as *pozole*, *menudo* (an offal-based dish), and *enchiladas*. Although they may have the same names as dishes served in southern states, the dishes of Zacatecas are relatively simple, involving fewer ingredients.

Particular towns have particular specialties: Jerez, for example, has its drinks made from fruit such as peaches and plums, its *figadete jerezano* (savory pork rinds), and its *bacalao jerezano* (a local version of the Basque Country's salt cod dish). Juchipila is known for its chicken in fruit sauce and its chickpea croquettes.

Common desserts and sweet foods in Zacatecas include *cocadas jerezanas*, *melcochas*, and *charamuscas*, *ates* (jellies) made of *tuna*, guava, or quince, and *jamoncillos de leche* (a milk-based candy). A favored local alcoholic drink is Huitzila *mescal*. Zacatecas also makes table wines.

Puchero Vaquero

This hearty Cowboy Stew serves 8–10. (Amost any piece of meat from a cow can be accommodated in this dish.)

Ingredients:

3$\frac{1}{2}$ lb. beef steak or other cut, cubed
2$\frac{1}{2}$ quarts water or beef stock

4 tsp annatto paste, dissolved in a little water
1 cup rice
4 oz. thin noodles
2 prickly pears (*chayotes*), chopped
3 zucchinis, chopped
1 bunch of spinach, chopped
1 medium white onion, chopped
Cilantro (to taste)
5 *güero* chiles, soaked in vinaigrette
Salt and pepper

Put the meat in a large saucepan and add the water or beef stock. Bring to a boil and add the annatto paste. Once the meat is tender, add the rice, noodles, and vegetables and cook another 20 minutes. Add salt and pepper as needed. Serve the onion, cilantro, and chiles separately, so that each diner may add condiments as desired.

Asado de Boda

This is more common in San Luis Potosí and Zacatecas than in more northern states, although a similar dish is called *asado de puerco* (or *de cerdo*) in Coahuila and Nuevo León.

Ingredients:

2 lb. fairly lean pork loin, cut into small pieces
4 *ancho* chiles
3 cups water
4 cloves of garlic
$1/4$ tsp cumin
$1/2$ tsp oregano
$1/2$ tsp marjoram
$1/4$ tsp ground cloves
$1/2$ tsp ground cinnamon
$1/4$ cup cooking oil
$1/2$ cup finely chopped onion
2 bay leaves
2 tsp cider vinegar
2 tsp sugar
Salt to taste
$1/2$ tsp ground black pepper
1 tbsp well chopped bittersweet chocolate
2 tsp orange zest

Briefly roast the chiles, making sure they do not burn. When they have cooled, rinse them and clean out the centers, then cut them into small pieces and put them in a blender. Bring the water to boiling, add it to the chiles in the blender, leave them to soak for a good 20 minutes, then drain. Add the garlic, cumin, oregano, marjoram, cloves, cinnamon, and a little fresh water to the blender and blend for a minute. Then add a little more water and repeat. Brown the meat in oil in a heavy saucepan or Dutch oven, turning the meat over once or twice to make sure it gets browned all over. Set the meat aside and sauté the onions until brown, then return the meat to the pot; add the contents of the blender, plus the vinegar, bay leaves and salt; cover and simmer for 45 minutes. Remove the top of the pot and turn the heat up a little to reduce the liquid, stirring constantly. Add the chocolate after about 10 minutes, together with the orange zest. Continue cooking until the sauce is smooth and fairly thick. This dish is normally served with white rice and tortillas.

Glossary

Antiplano An elevated area of flatland, a plateau

Bolero A song genre (romantic ballad)

Bracero Mexican guest worker in the United States

Cacique Regional strongman (a word of pre-Hispanic derivation)

Caudillo Regional strongman

Charro Stereotypical, traditional Mexican cowboy

Chicle Chewing gum (latex)

Churrigueresque In the style of Churriguera, a Spanish architect of the baroque known for his busy and ornate decorative designs

Corrido Narrative song ballad telling of life in the northern region or exploits of the famous

Criollo Person of European descent born in the Americas

Ejido Smallholding or communal land

Encomienda A right to land and Indian labor granted to Spanish settlers by the Crown

Epazote An herb (*dysphania ambrosioides*)

Hacienda Large ranch or agricultural estate

Huipil A blouse or shirt commonly worn by Mayan women

Indendencia A Spanish colonial administrative entity concerned mainly with taxes

Latifundios Large ranches or estates

Maquiladora Assembly (and sometimes manufacturing) plant located close to the U.S. border

Matachines Dances involving masked performers (mummers) and representing stock figures, some of them from Mexican history

Mesa/meseta Plateau, tableland

Mestizo Person of mixed European and Indian descent

Mole A think and complex sauce, commonly served over poultry

Mudéjar An architectural style revealing the influence of the Muslims in Spain

Norteño Popular music associated with the northern part of the country, particularly the U.S. border region

Peninsular A person born in Spain

Peyote A small cactus with hallucinogenic properties

Pib An oven made by digging a hole in the ground

Plateresque A delicate, decorative style of stone- and ironwork, associated with the sixteenth century

Porfiriato The long period dominated by President Porfirio Díaz (1877–1911)

PRI The Partido Revolucionario Institucional (Institutionalized Revolutionary Party), which held power for some seventy consecutive years during the twentieth century

Pulque An alcoholic beverage made from cactus

Retablo An altarpiece, often ornate, gold-painted, and including effigies of saints

Señoríos Principalities or kingdoms ruled by indigenous leaders

Selected Bibliography

This bibliography offers sources in English.

Barry, Tom, ed. *Mexico: A Country Guide*. Albuquerque, NM: Inter-Hemispheric Education Resource Center, 1992.

Bauer, K. J. *The Mexican War, 1846–1848*. New York: Macmillan, 1974.

Bazant, J. *A Concise History of Mexico: From Hidalgo to Cárdenas, 1805–1940*. Cambridge: Cambridge University Press, 1977.

Beezley, William H., Cheryl English Martin, and William E. French. *Rituals of Rule, Rituals of Resistance: Public Celebrations and Popular Culture in Mexico*. Wilmington, DE: SR Books, 1994.

Benjamin, Thomas. *A Rich Land, a Poor People: Politics and Society in Modern Chiapas*. Albuquerque: University of New Mexico Press, 1996.

Bethell, Leslie, ed. *Mexico since Independence*. Cambridge: Cambridge University Press, 1991.

Bierhorst, John. *Cantares Mexicanos: The Songs of the Aztecs*. Stanford, CA: Stanford University Press, 1985.

Bonfil Batalla, Guillermo. *México Profundo: Reclaiming a Civilization*. Translated by P. A. Dennis. Austin: University of Texas Press, 1996.

Brading, David A. *Prophecy and Myth in Mexican History*. Cambridge: Cambridge University Press, 1986.

Brandenburg, Frank. *The Making of Modern Mexico*. Englewood Cliffs, NJ: Prentice-Hall, 1964.

Brenner, Anita, and George R. Leighton. *The Wind That Swept Mexico: The History of the Mexican Revolution of 1910–1942*. Austin: University of Texas Press, 1984.

Caistor, Nick. *Mexico City: A Literary and Cultural Companion*. New York: Interlink Books, 2000.

Calderón de la Barca, Fanny. *Life in Mexico*. Edited by Howard T. Fisher and Marion Hall Fisher. New York: Doubleday, 1966.

Camp, Roderic Ai. *Crossing Swords: Religion and Politics in Mexico*. New York: Oxford University Press, 1997.

———. *Politics in Mexico*. New York: Oxford University Press, 1989.

Cline, Howard F., ed. *Handbook of Middle American Indians*. Austin: University of Texas Press, 1972. Several volumes.

———. *Mexico: Revolution to Evolution, 1940–1960*. Oxford: Oxford University Press, 1963.

Cockcroft, James D. *Mexico: Class Formation, Capital Accumulation, and the State*. New York: Monthly Review Press, 1990.

Coe, Michael D. *The Maya*. London: Thames & Hudson, 1999.

———. *Mexico: From the Olmecs to the Aztecs*. London: Thames & Hudson, 1994.

Cook, Sherburne F., and W. W. Borah. *The Indian Population of Central Mexico, 1531–1610*. Berkeley: University of California Press, 1960.

Cooper Alarcón, Daniel. *The Aztec Palimpsest: Mexico in the Modern Imagination*. Tempe: University of Arizona Press, 1997.

Davies, Nigel. *The Aztecs: A History*. London: Macmillan, 1973.

———. *The Toltec Heritage*. Norman: University of Oklahoma Press, 1980.

Dwyer, Augusta. *On the Line: Life on the U.S.-Mexican Border*. London: Latin American Bureau, 1994.

Everton, MacDuff. *The Modern Maya: A Culture in Transition*. Albuquerque: University of New Mexico Press, 1991.

Fuentes, Carlos. *The Buried Mirror*. Boston: Houghton Mifflin, 1992.

Fuentes, Patricia de. *The Conquistadors: First-Person Accounts of the Conquest of Mexico*. Norman: University of Oklahoma Press, 1993.

García Canclini, Néstor. *Hybrid Cultures: Strategies far Entering and Leaving Modernity*. Translated by C. L. Chiappari and S. L. López. Minneapolis: University of Minnesota Press, 1995.

———. *Transforming Modernity: Popular Culture in Mexico*. Translated by L. Lozano. Austin: University of Texas Press, 1993.

Gerhard, Peter. *A Guide to the Historical Geography of New Spain*. Norman: University of Oklahoma Press, 1993.

———. *The Northern Frontier of New Spain*. Princeton, NJ: Princeton University Press, 1982.

Gómez-Peña, Guillermo. *The New World Border*. San Francisco: City Lights, 1996.

Gutmann, Matthew C. *The Meanings of Macho: Being a Man in Mexico City*. Berkeley: University of California Press, 1996.

Hamnett, Brian. *A History of Mexico*. New York: Cambridge University Press, 1999.

Handelman, Howard. *Mexican Politics: The Dynamics of Change*. New York: St. Martin's Press, 1996.

Hanke, Lewis. *The Spanish Struggle for Justice in the Conquest of America*. Boston: Little, Brown, 1965.

Harvey, Neil. *The Chiapas Rebellion: The Struggle for Land and Democracy*. Durham, NC: Duke University Press, 1998.

Hayes, Joy Elizabeth. *Radio Nation: Communication, Popular Culture, and Nationalism in Mexico, 1920–1950*. Tucson: University of Arizona Press, 2000.

Hoyt-Goldsmith, Diane. *Day of the Dead*. New York: Holiday House, 1994.

Ingham, J. M. *Mary, Michael, and Lucifer: Folk Catholicism in Central Mexico*. Austin: University of Texas Press, 1986.

Israel, J. I. *Race, Class, and Politics in Colonial Mexico*. London: Oxford University Press, 1975.

Johnson, H. L. "The Virgin of Guadalupe in Mexican Culture." In *Religion in Latin American Life and Literature*, edited by L. C. Brown and W. F. Cooper. Waco, TX: Markham, 1980.

Joseph, Gilbert M., and Timothy J. Henderson. *The Mexico Reader*. Durham, NC: Duke University Press, 2002.

Kandell, Jonathan. *La Capital: Biography of Mexico City*. New York: Random House, 1988.

Katz, Friedrich. *The Life and Times of Pancho Villa*. Stanford, CA: Stanford University Press, 1998.

Kennedy, Diana. *The Art of Mexican Cooking*. New York: Clarkson Potter, 2008

Kissam, Edward, and Michael Schmidt. *Flower and Song: Poems of the Aztec Peoples*. London: Anvil Press, 1977.

Knight, Alan. *Mexico*. Cambridge: Cambridge University Press, 2002.

Krause, Enrique. *Mexico: Biography of Power*. New York: HarperCollins, 1998.

La Botz, Dan. *Democracy in Mexico: Peasant Rebellion and Political Reform*. Boston: South End Press, 1995.

Ladd, Doris M. *Mexican Women in Anahuac and New Spain*. Austin: University of Texas Press, 1978.

Lafaye, Jacques. *Quetzalcóatl and Guadalupe: The Formation of Mexican National Consciousness, 1531–1813*. Translated by Benjamin Keen. Chicago: University of Chicago Press, 1976.

Leonard, Irving A. *Baroque Times in Old Mexico*. Ann Arbor: University of Michigan Press, 1966.

León-Portilla, Miguel. *Aztec Thought and Culture*. Norman: University of Oklahoma Press, 1963.

———. *Broken Spears*. Boston: Beacon Press, 1992.

———. *Pre-Columbian Literatures of Mexico*. Norman: University of Oklahoma Press, 1969.

Lewis, Oscar. *Life in a Mexican Village*. Champaign: University of Illinois Press, 1951.

Livermore, H. A. *The War with Mexico*. New York: Arno, 1969.

Lockhart, J. *The Nahuas after the Conquest: A Social and Cultural History of the Indians of Central Mexico, Sixteenth through Eighteenth Centuries*. Stanford, CA: Stanford University Press, 1992.

Lomnitz, Claudio. *Deep Mexico, Silent Mexico: An Anthropology of Nationalism*. Minneapolis: University of Minnesota Press, 2001.

Lowry, Malcolm. *Under the Volcano*. New York: Signet, 1965.

Maciel, David R., and Marfa Herera-Sobek, eds. *Culture across Borders: Mexican Immigration and Popular Culture*. Tucson: University of Arizona Press, 1998.

Martínez, Oscar J. *Border People: Life and Society in the U.S.-Mexico Borderlands*. Tucson: University of Arizona Press, 1994.

Merrell, Floyd. *A Sense of Culture: The Mexicans*. Boulder, CO: Westview Press, 2003.

Merrill, Tim L., and Ramón Miró. *Mexico: A Country Study*. Washington, DC: Library of Congress, 1997.

Meyer, Michael C., and William H. Beezley. *The Oxford History of Mexico*. Oxford: Oxford University Press, 2000.

Meyer, Michael C., William L. Sherman, and Susan M. Deeds. *The Course of Mexican History*. New York: Oxford University Press, 2002.

Miller, Mary Ellen. *The Art of Mesoamerica: From Olmec to Aztec*. London: Thames & Hudson, 2001.

Miller, Robert Ryal. *Mexico: A History*. Norman: University of Oklahoma Press, 1985.

Monsiváis, Carlos. *Mexican Postcards*. London: Verso, 1997.

Nelson, Cynthia. *The Waiting Village: Social Change in Rural Mexico*. Boston: Little, Brown, 1971.

Noriega, Luis Antonio de, and Frances Leach. *Broadcasting in Mexico*. London: Routledge & Kegan Paul, 1979.

Oppenheimer, Andrés. *Bordering on Chaos: Mexico's Roller-Coaster Journey to Prosperity*. Boston: Little, Brown, 1998.

Orme, William A., Jr., ed. *A Culture of Collusion: An Inside Look at the Mexican Press*. Miami: North-South Center Press, 1997.

Oster, Patrick. *The Mexicans: A Personal Portrait of a People*. New York: William Morrow, 1989.

Pasztory, Esther. *Aztec Art*. Norman: University of Oklahoma Press, 1998.

———. *Teotihuacan*. Norman: University of Oklahoma Press, 1997.

Paxton, Meredith. *The Cosmos of the Yucatec Maya*. Albuquerque: University of New Mexico Press, 2001.

Paz, Octavio. *Children of the Mire*. Cambridge, MA: Harvard University Press, 1970.

———. *The Labyrinth of Solitude: Life and Thought in Mexico*. Translated by L. Kemp. New York: Grove, 1961.

———. *The Other Mexico: Critique of the Pyramid*. Translated by L. Kemp. New York: Grove, 1970.

Peña, Devon Gerardo. *The Terror of the Machine: Technology, Work, Gender and Ecology on the U.S.-Mexico Border*. Austin: University of Texas Press, 1997.

Poole, Stafford. *Our Lady of Guadalupe: The Origins and Sources of a Mexican National Symbol, 1531–1797*. Tucson: University of Arizona Press, 1995.

Press, Irwin. *Tradition and Adaptation: Life in a Modern Yucatan Maya Village*. Westport, CT: Greenwood Press, 1975.

Price, John A. *Tijuana: Urbanization in a Border Culture*. Notre Dame, IN: University of Notre Dame Press, 1973.

Rama, Angel. *The Lettered City*. Durham, NC: Duke University Press, 1996.

Ramos, Samuel. *Profile of Man and Culture in Mexico*. Translated by P. G. Earle. Austin: University of Texas Press, 1962.

Reed, John. *Insurgent Mexico*. New York: International, 1969.

Ricard, R. *The Spiritual Conquest of Mexico*. Berkeley: University of California Press, 1966.

Riding, Alan. *Distant Neighbors: A Portrait of the Mexicans*. New York: Vintage, 2000.

Rodríguez O., Jaime E., ed. *Mexican and Mexican American Experience in the 19th Century*. Tempe: Bilingual Press/Editorial Bilingüe, 1989.

Rodríguez O., Jaime E., and Kathryn Vincent, eds. *Common Border, Uncommon Paths: Race, Culture, and National Identity in U.S.-Mexican Relations*. Wilmington, DE: Scholarly Resources, 1997.

Rodríguez, Jeanette. *Our Lady of Guadalupe*. Austin: University of Texas Press, 1994.

Rodríguez, Victoria Elizabeth. *Women's Participation in Mexican Political Life*. Boulder, CO: Westview Press, 1998.

Rotella, Sebastian. *Twilight on the Line: Underworlds and Politics at the U.S.-Mexican Border.* New York: Norton, 1998.

Ruiz, Ramón Eduardo. *On the Rim of Mexico: Encounters of the Rich and Poor.* Boulder, CO: Westview Press, 1998.

Ruiz, Vicki L., and Susan Tiano. *Women on the U.S.-Mexico Border: Responses to Change.* Boston: Allen & Unwin, 1987.

Ryan, Alan, ed. *A Reader's Companion to Mexico.* San Diego: Harcourt Brace, 1995.

Sanderson, Susan R. Walsh. *Land Reform in Mexico, 1910–1980.* New York: Academic Press, 1984.

Scarborough, Vernon L., and David R. Wilcox, eds. *The Mesoamerican Ballgame.* Tucson: University of Arizona Press, 1991.

Schmidt, Henry C. *The Roots of Lo Mexicano: Self and Society in Mexican Thought, 1900–1934.* College Station: Texas A&M University Press, 1978

Schroeder, Susan, ed. *Indian Women in Early Mexico.* Norman: University of Oklahoma Press, 1997.

Sharer, Robert J. *The Ancient Maya.* Stanford, CA: Stanford University Press, 1994.

Sheehy, Daniel. *Mariachi Music in America.* New York: Oxford University Press, 2005.

Simpson, Lesley Byrd. *Many Mexicos.* Berkeley: University of California Press, 1967.

Smith, Bradley. *Mexico: A History of Art.* New York: Harper & Row, 1968.

Smith, J. B. *The Image of Guadalupe: Myth or Miracle?* New York: Doubleday, 1983.

Smith, Michael E. *The Aztecs.* Oxford, England: Blackwell, 2003.

Soustelle, Jacques. *Daily Life of the Aztecs.* Stanford, CA: Stanford University Press, 1961.

Standish, Peter. *A Companion to Mexican Studies.* Woodbridge, England: Tamesis, 2006.

Standish, Peter, and Steven M. Bell. *Culture and Customs of Mexico.* Westport, CT: Greenwood Press, 2004.

Stevenson, Robert. *Music in México: A Historical Survey.* New York: Thomas Crowell, 1952.

Suchlicki, Jaime. *Mexico: From Montezuma to NAFTA, Chiapas, and Beyond.* New York: Brassey's, 1996.

Szanto, George. *Inside the Statues of Saints: Mexico Writers on Culture and Corruption, Politics and Daily Life.* New York: Vehicle, 1997.

Tangeman, Michael. *Mexico at the Crossroads: Politics, the Church, and the Poor.* Maryknoll, NY: Orbis, 1995.

Taylor, W. B. "The Virgin of Guadalupe in New Spain: An Inquiry into the Social History of Marian Devotion." *American Ethnologist* 14, no. 1 (1987): 9–33.

Thomas, Hugh. *Conquest: Moctezuma, Cortés, and the Fall of Old Mexico.* New York: Touchstone, 1995.

Toor, Frances. *A Treasury of Mexican Folkways.* New York: Crown, 1947.

Toussaint, Manuel. *Colonial Art in Mexico.* Translated and edited by E. Wilder Weismann. Austin: University of Texas Press, 1967.

Van Young, Eric, ed. *Mexico's Regions: Comparative History and Development.* San Diego: UCSD Center for U.S.-Mexican Studies, 1992.

Wilkie, James W., and Albert I. Michaels. *Revolution in Mexico: Years of Upheaval, 1910–1940.* Tucson: University of Arizona Press, 1984.

Wolf, Eric. *Sons of the Shaking Earth.* Chicago: University of Chicago Press, 1959.

Index

ABOUT THE AUTHOR

Peter Standish is Professor of Hispanic Studies at East Carolina University and the author of numerous works on Latin America. On Mexico, he has published *Culture and Customs of Mexico* (Greenwood, 2004; co-authored with Steven Bell) and *A Companion to Mexican Studies* (Tamesis, 2006). He serves as academic editor of Greenwood's series Culture and Customs of Latin America and the Caribbean.